FRENCH RIVIERA

S. Sauvignier/ MICHELIN

Executive Editorial Director   David Brabis

Chief Editor   Cynthia Clayton Ochterbeck

THE GREEN GUIDE FRENCH RIVIERA – CÔTE D'AZUR

Editor   Gwen Cannon

Principal Writer   Heather Stimmler-Hall

Production Coordinator   Allison Michelle Simpson

Cartography   Alain Baldet, Michèle Cana, Peter Wrenn

Photo Editor   Brigitta L. House

Proofreader   Meg Moss

Layout & Design   Allison Michelle Simpson, Nicole D. Jordan
Agence Rampazzo

Cover Design   Laurent Muller

Interior Design   Agence Rampazzo

Production   Pierre Ballochard, Renaud Leblanc

Contact Us :

The Green Guide
Michelin Travel Publications
One Parkway South
Greenville, SC 29615
USA

☎ 1-800-423-0485

www.michelintravel.com

michelin.guides@us.michelin.com

Special Sales :

For information regarding bulk sales, customized editions
and premium sales, please contact our Customer
Service Departments:

USA	1-800-423-0485
UK	(01923) 205 240
Canada	1-800-361-8236

One Team...
A Commitment to Quality

There's just one reason our team is dedicated to producing quality travel publications—you, our reader. We want you to get the maximum benefit from your trip—and from your money. In today's multiple-choice world of travel, the options are many, perhaps overwhelming.

In our guidebooks, we try to minimize the guesswork involved with travel. We scout out the attractions, prioritize them with star ratings, and describe what you'll discover when you visit them.

To help you orient yourself, we provide colorful and detailed, but easy-to-follow maps. Floor plans of some of the cathedrals and museums help you plan your tour.

Throughout the guides, we offer practical information, touring tips and suggestions for finding the best views, good places for a break and the most interesting shops.

Lodging and dining are always a big part of travel, so we compile a selection of hotels and restaurants that we think convey the feel of the destination, and organize them by geographic area and price. We also highlight shopping, recreational and entertainment venues, especially the popular spots.

If you're short on time, driving tours are included so you can hit the highlights and quickly absorb the best of the region.

For those who love to experience a destination on foot, we add walking tours, complete with a map. And we list other companies who offer boat, bus or guided walking tours of the area, some with culinary, historical or other themes.

In short, we test and retest, check and recheck to make sure that our guidebooks are truly just that: a personalized guide to help you make the most of your visit. After all, we want you to enjoy traveling as much as we do.

The Michelin Green Guide Team
michelin.guides@us.michelin.com

PLANNING YOUR TRIP

INTRODUCTION TO THE FRENCH RIVIERA

SYMBOLS

🄰	**Tips to help improve your experience**
🄰	**Details to consider**
🕮	**Entry fees**
👣	**Walking tours**
🔑	**Closed to the public**
🕐	**Hours of operation**
🕐	**Periods of closure**

CONTENTS

DISCOVERING THE FRENCH RIVIERA

How to Use this Guide

Orientation

To help you grasp the "lay of the land" quickly and easily, so you'll feel confident and comfortable finding your way around the region, we offer the following tools in this guide:

- Detailed table of contents for an overview of what you'll find in the guide, and how it is organized.
- Map of the French Riviera at the front of the guide, with the Principal Sights highlighted for easy reference.
- Detailed maps for major cities and villages, including driving tour maps and larger-scale maps for walking tours.
- Map of seven Regional Driving Tours, each one numbered and color coded.
- Map showing the local specialities and vineyards for each area and town.

Practicalities

At the front of the guide, you'll see a section called "Planning Your Trip" that contains information about planning your trip, the best time to go, different ways of getting to the region and getting around, basic facts and tips for making the most of your visit. You'll find driving and themed tours, and suggestions for outdoor fun. There's also a calendar of popular annual events on the French Riviera. Information on shopping, sightseeing, kids' activities and sports and recreational opportunities is also included.

LODGINGS

We've made a selection of hotels and arranged them within the cities, categorized by price category to fit all budgets *(see the Legend at the back of the guide for an explanation of the price categories)*. For the most part, we selected accommodations based on their unique regional quality, their French Riviera feel, as it were. So, unless the individual hotel or bed & breakfast embodies local ambience, it's rare that we include chain properties, which typically have their own imprint. If you want a more comprehensive selection of French Riviera accommodations, see the red-cover *Michelin Guide France*.

RESTAURANTS

We thought you'd like to know the popular eating spots on the French Riviera. So we selected restaurants that capture the Côte d'Azur experience—those that have a unique regional flavor and local atmosphere. We're not rating the quality of the food per se. As we did with the hotels, we selected restaurants for many towns and villages, categorized by price to appeal to all wallets. If you want a more comprehensive selection of dining recommendations in the region, see the red-cover *Michelin Guide France*.

Attractions

The French Riviera, also known as the Côte d'Azur, is part of the larger Provence-Alpes-Côte d'Azur region of France. This guide covers two of the departments in the region, the Var and the Alpes-Maritimes, including the Principality of Monaco.

Principal Sights are arranged alphabetically. Within each Principal Sight, attractions for each town, village, or geographical area (such as the Massif de l'Esterel or Îles d'Hyères) are divided into local Sights or Walking Tours, nearby Excursions to sights outside the town, or detailed Driving Tours—suggested itineraries for seeing several attractions around a major town. Contact information, admission charges and hours of operation are given for the majority of attractions. Unless otherwise noted, admission prices shown are for a single adult only. Discounts for seniors, students, teachers, etc. may be available; be sure to ask. If no admission charge is shown, entrance to the attraction is free.

If you're pressed for time, we recommend you visit the three- and two-star sights first: the stars are your guide.

STAR RATINGS

Michelin has used stars as a rating tool for more than 100 years:

★★★	Highly recommended
★★	Recommended
★	Interesting

SYMBOLS IN THE TEXT

Besides the stars, other symbols in the text indicate tourist information ⓘ; wheelchair access ♿; on-site eating facilities ✕; camping facilities ⛺; on-site parking ⓟ; sights of interest to children 👶; and beaches ⚓.

See the box appearing on the Contents page for other symbols used in the text.

See the Maps explanation below for symbols appearing on the maps.

Throughout the guide you will find peach-coloured text boxes or sidebars containing anecdotal or background information. Green-coloured boxes contain information to help you save time or money.

Maps

All maps in this guide are oriented north, unless otherwise indicated by a directional arrow.

See the map Legend at the back of the guide for an explanation of other map symbols.

A complete list of the maps found in the guide appears at the back of this book.

Addresses, phone numbers, opening hours and prices published in this guide are accurate at press time. We welcome corrections and suggestions that may assist us in preparing the next edition. Please send your comments to:

Michelin Travel Publications
Editorial Department
P.O. Box 19001
Greenville, SC 29602-9001
Email: michelin.guides@us.michelin.com
Web site: www.michelintravel.com

Principal sights

MONACO	★★★	Highly recommended
Antibes	★★	Recommended
Biot	★	Interesting
Cogolin		Sight described in this guide

Seaside resorts ⚓ are classified according
to the quality and range of facilities offered.

Itinerary described in this guide: look up one
of the sites in the index at the back of the guide
to find the page where the tour is described.

0   20 km

BRIANÇON

D 900

GAP

Digne-les-Bains

N 85

Bléone

N 85

Asse

D 907

D 953

Manosque

Durance

D 41

Verdon

VAUCLUSE

D 11

Lac de Ste-Croix

A 51

D 13

D 30

Montmeyan

Aups

Tourtour

D 554

Haut

Villecroze

Varages

Cascade de Sillans

Barjols

Var

BOUCHES-

Cotignac

Entrecasteaux

N 7

Argens

D 554

† le Thoronet

A 8

Arc

D 560

le Val

Pays brignolais

Cabasse

A 52

St-Maximin-la-Ste-Baume

A 8

Brignoles

le Luc

DU-

RHÔNE

N 560

N 7

Montagne de la Loube

VAR

Gapeau

A 50

A 520

N.-D. des Anges

A 501

A 52

Aubagne

A 57

Col de Babaou

N 8   Circuit du Castellet
Paul-Ricard

le Castellet

*Baou de
4 Oures*

Mont Caume

Solliès-Ville

MASSIF

St-Cyr-s-Mer

A 50

le Gros Cerveau

MONT FARON

N 98

le Fenouillet

⚓ **Bandol**

⚓ Île de Bendor

TOULON

le Pradet

Hyères

⚓ Sanary-s-Mer

le Mourillon ⚓

⚓ Six-Fours-les-Plages

Hyères-Plage ⚓

Musée
de la Mine

⚓ Île des Embiez

Presqu'île de St-Mandrier

Giens

Presqu'île du Cap Sicié

N.-D. du Mai

Presqu'île de Giens

Î. DE PORQUEROLLES

ÎLES

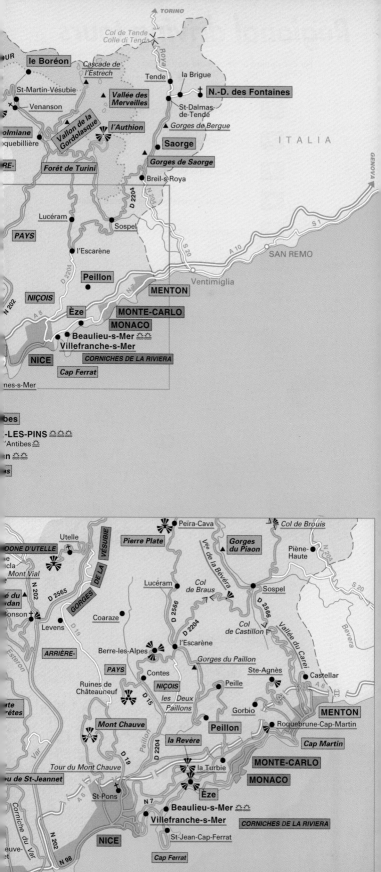

Regional driving tours

For descriptions of these tours, turn to the
Planning Your Trip section following.

1 Varois coast and the Golden Islands

2 Le Haut-Var

3 Le Massif des Maures

4 Massif de L'Esterel and the Fayence region

5 Fragrances and colours of the Pre-Alps

6 L'arrière-pays Niçois

7 The corniches of the Riviera

Hotel Négresco, Nice

D. Pazery/ MICHELIN

WHEN AND WHERE TO GO

Driving Tours

For an overall impression of these various driving tours, consult the map on pp 11-13.

1 VAR COASTLINE AND THE GOLDEN ISLANDS

Round tour of 235km/146mi starting from Toulon

The city of Toulon should be visited in the local tradition, in other words at a leisurely pace, taking time to explore the intricate streets shaded by century-old plane trees. After dropping by the lively marché Lafayette and choosing a few fresh vegetables and mouthwatering local treats, set out to discover "the most beautiful harbour" on the Riviera, passing by Pointe du Fort Balaguier and Cap Sicié. Nestled between land and sea, Sanary and Bandol, and their islands of Bendor and Embiez, will seduce you by their heavenly setting. Further on, the perched villages of Le Castellet, Beausset and Evenos compose the perfect picture of Provençal bliss. Then admire the harbour from atop Mont Faron. Continue to the bird sanctuary at La Londe for an escape to the tropics. Treat yourself to a stay on the gorgeous islands of Port-Cros and Porquerolles, and the underwater sightseeing trail offers incomparable views of the sea's fauna and flora for divers and snorkelers. A tour of the Mine de Cap-Garonne at Le Pradet is the perfect way to round off your outing.

2 LE HAUT-VAR

Round tour of 245km/153mi starting from Draguignan

This itinerary will take you across the upper stretches of the Var Valley, characterised by rolling wooded countryside dotted with old abbeys and remarkable sites: Tourtour nestling on the crest of a hill overlooking olive groves; Cotignac precariously perched on a cliff; Villecroze and Seillans enhanced by hardened volcanic ash rock formations; Entrecasteaux, whose château is graced by gardens attributed to Le Nôtre. You may be surprised by the diversity of the villages and towns you will encounter. Some clearly enjoy perpetuating local tradition while others promote a more dynamic artisan culture. Don't miss the colourful markets offering truffles, goat's cheese or olives, depending on the season, and the restaurants, where you will be served tasty regional cuisine pleasantly seasoned with aromatic herbs.

3 LE MASSIF DES MAURES

Round tour of 275km/171mi starting from Fréjus

Far away from the coast and its bustling crowd, this tour will take you through refreshingly cool forests of cork oak and the pretty Gratteloup arboretum, where eucalyptus, chestnut, maple, cedar and juniper trees exude their intoxicating aroma. Visit the superb Domaine du Rayol, designed at the turn of the century and rediscover regional arts and crafts: the cork industry in Gonfaron, *marrons glacés* in Collobrières, pipe-making and carpet weaving in Cogolin. The hill villages of Ramatuelle, Grimaud and Gassin command panoramic views of the coast, as do the Moulins de Paillas. Before having a swim in one of the many sheltered inlets, you may want to settle on the terrace of the Sénéquier in St-Tropez alongside the rich and famous or you may prefer to browse among the market stalls in the old port in the hope of chancing upon a fake Picasso...

4 MASSIF DE L'ESTEREL AND THE FAYENCE REGION

Round tour of 285km/177mi starting from Cannes

Whatever the season, this itinerary will prove an enchanting experience on many counts: the rich, luxuriant vegetation, the chirping of the cicadas, the delicately fragrant mimosa blossoms, the warm embrace of the sun and the red rock of the Esterel heights. Running between La Napoule and Agay, the Corniche d'Or offers stunning views of the sea. You will succumb to the charms of St-Raphaël, a lively seaside resort, and Fréjus with its prestigious military past, not to mention Fréjus-Plage, which boasts the longest sandy beach on the

Riviera. Further inland, the Fayence area will introduce you to a host of perched villages huddled on mountain slopes, dominated by vestiges of their medieval citadels: Caillan, Fayence, Tourrettes, Seillan, Tanneron and Auribeau-sur-Siagne.

5 FRAGRANCES AND COLOURS OF THE PRE-ALPS

Round tour of 215km/134mi starting from Grasse

The Pre-Alps of Provence, extending to the foot of the Alpine range and cut across by steep ravines, offer a delightful combination of colours and fragrances, where the heady smells of olive and cypress tree vie with the more subtle scent of rose, jasmin, oleander and violet. Flowers have given Grasse its reputation, so your first stop in this city must be the International Museum of Perfume and the different *parfumeries* explaining the secrets of the trade. The entrance to the Gorges du Loup is the perfect place to stop and admire the hill village of Gourdon, jealously guarding its abyss, and the Caussols Plateau, a curiously barren stretch of land riddled with chasms. After observing the geological formations in the caves of St-Vallier and St-Cézaire, continue to St-Paul-de-Vence, a typical medieval village known for its arts and crafts, and to the delightful hamlet of Tourrettes-sur-Loup, where terraced violet fields have been cultivated from generation to generation. The Baou of St-Jeannet dominating the Var River is a sheer rocky cliff popular among seasoned climbers. Lastly, the coastal road stretching between Cagnes-sur-Mer and Antibes offers pretty views of the Baie des Anges and access to a number of contemporary art museums.

6 L'ARRIÈRE-PAYS NIÇOIS

Round tour of 270km/168mi starting from Nice

This driving tour will provide you with a fascinating selection of natural sites and architectural riches: quaint perched villages, chapels decorated by famous painters or unknown artists from the Middle Ages, steep cliffs overlooking gorges echoing with the swirling of crystal clear waters, and lush forests rustling with the sounds of local fauna. Running alongside the lower Var Valley, bordered to the west by the Baou of St Jeannet, you will

start to approach the heights beyond Nice, dominated by Mont Chauve. After driving through Aspremont, Levens and Duranus, you will reach the breathtaking Vésubie Gorges. From there, brace yourself for the long series of steep hairpin bends leading up to the Madone d'Utelle sanctuary, a popular place of pilgrimage, and the nearby belvedere commanding a splendid panorama of the Alpes-Maritimes and Mediterranean Sea. Proceeding upstream along the Vésubie River in the direction of Col de Turini, you will come to Bollène-Vésubie, precariously nestling on the mountain slope. On reaching L'Authion, go round to Pointe des Trois-Communes to feast your eyes on the sweeping landscape. Continue towards the Gorges of Piaon. After the curious Notre-Dame-de-la-Menour Chapel with its two-storey Renaissance façade, you will come to Sospel, springing from its verdant setting, where tasty regional dishes can be sampled. Drive through several passes before rejoining Lucéram Valley, famed for its Christmas festivities attended by local shepherds. Finally, three belvederes, each home to a small village, Berre, Falicon and Tourrettes, will complete this charming tour of the Nice hinterland.

7 THE CORNICHES OF THE RIVIERA

Round tour of 250km/155.5mi starting from Nice

If you have seen Hitchcock's thriller *To Catch a Thief,* then you will know that it is advisable to hug the road winding its way between Nice and Monte-Carlo as closely as possible. This route, which features a series of vertiginous viewpoints, goes past some of the prettiest spots on the Côte d'Azur. Set

Blue, the sea and sky at St-Jean-Cap-Ferrat

S. Sauvignier/ MICHELIN

out from Villefranche, famous not only for its Chapelle St-Pierre decorated by Jean Cocteau, but also for its pretty harbour and succulent seafood dishes. Follow the Grande Corniche up to Roquebrune, with forays downhill to Beaulieu (Villa Kérylos), St-Jean-Cap-Ferrat (Villa Rothschild) and Èze, clinging to its rocky spur, where a tour of artists' workshops can be pleasantly rounded off by a visit to the Jardin Exotique. Enjoy the view from the Vistaero before descending towards Roquebrune with its medieval castle and venerable olive tree believed to be over 1,000 years old. After Menton, the road will take you through the perched villages of Ste-Agnès, Peille and Peillon, where the steep alleyways (calades) lead to chapels adorned with fine frescoes.

Themed Tours

FOREST PARKS

All along the Alpes-Maritimes coast there are islands of greenery (parcs forestiers départementaux) provided for walkers of all ages

- **Parc de la Grande-Corniche** in Èze (access from Col d'Èze on the Grande Corniche)
- **Parc de Vaugrenier** (access by N 7 between Antibes and Marina Baie des Anges)
- **Parc de la Vallée de la Brague** (at the eastern end of Biot village)
- **Parc du San Peyre** (from La Napoule towards A 8 motorway and a left turn onto Route du Cimetière), a former look-out post (alt 131m/430ft) which offers a superb panorama of Cannes Bay
- **Parc de la Pointe de l'Aiguille** (car park on N 98 at the edge of Théoule)
- **Route Historique des Hauts-Lieux de Provence** – A circuit from St-Maximin-la-Ste-Baume via Draguignan and Les Arcs to Fréjus returning along the coast to Toulon, organised by an association at the Office de Tourisme, 83460 Les Arcs-sur-Argens ☎ 04 94 73 37 30.
- **Route des Côtes de Provence** – *see pp 80-81.*

SCENIC VIEWS

Riviera Caves

The limestone region of the Pays Grassois (especially the Caussols Plateau) features many interesting geological features dating from different periods – the caves (grottes) at St-Cézaire (*see GRASSE*), the gigantic limestone crevices such as the Grotte des Audides (*see CABRIS*) or the original caves consisting of a succession of natural dams (gours) such as the Grotte de Baume Obscure (*see ST-VALLIER-DE-THIEY*). The **Grottes de Villecroze** near Draguignan (*see VILLECROZE*) are formed of tufa (hardened volcanic ash). Other caves, which are accessible with adequate equipment and some technical knowledge, belong in the caving category (*see p 38*). People with no caving experience can get an idea of the activity in the first section (about 12m/39ft) of the **Embut de Caussols** (embut is the Provençal word for "swallowhole").

Military Fortifications of the Alpes-Maritimes

The strategic significance of the frontier zone in the southeast was developed in 1880 by Sérés de Rivières. The project was completed and improved in 1929 by its integration into the Maginot Line which defended the eastern frontier from Dunkirk to Menton. The whole construction gives an interesting view of military architecture in the 19C and 20C. Some of the buildings have been disarmed, restored, and are accessible to visitors:

- Fort de Ste-Agnès (*see MENTON*)
- Fort du Barbonnet (*see Forêt de TURINI*)
- Fort Suchet (19C), the only one that can be visited (*see Forêt de TURINI*)
- Fort St-Roch (*see SOSPEL*).

Other less interesting forts make pleasant destinations for walks with fine views.

☞ *Visitors should bear in mind that, although the buildings of the Maginot Line appear to be in good condition, they may conceal indoor wells or dangerous passages. Some properties are private as they have been acquired by individuals.*

In the highly strategic sector of L'Authion, near Col de Turini (*see Forêt de TURINI*), several structures designed by Sérés de Rivières have survived and can be reached by the loop road encircling the massif:

- Fort des Mille-Fourches
- La Forca
- Redoute des 3 Communes (1897), the first building constructed of reinforced concrete.

From Mont Chauve d'Aspremont (♦ see NICE) there is a brilliant view of the whole coast under clear skies. On the summit (854m/2 802ft) is a Sérés de Rivières fort with a monumental south façade typical of the period; it is occupied by the Service des Télécommunications. Mont Chauve de Tourette is visible further north capped by a fort of similar period.

The section near Col de Tende, which was Italian from 1860 to 1947, is an impressive example of the Italian system of defence. The remarkable central fort is set on top of the col and approached by the narrow road which branches off by the entrance to the road tunnel; each of its façades has a different architectural style. The interior (☺ difficult access) resembles a small town, self-sufficient in supplies.

On the Track of Macaron

The old rail bed of one of the dismantled sections of the pinecone train (train des pignes), which linked Toulon to St-Raphaël from early in the 20C to 1950, is open to walkers. Although the track and stations have mostly disappeared owing to the effects of time and events, such as the Allied landings at the end of the Second World War, works of art and some stations (Carqueiranne) have survived. The tunnels are often used by walkers as short cuts, providing unusual and surprising glimpses of the Maures coast.

Seasons

CLIMATE

The **tourist season** on the French Riviera lasts virtually all year round. The **winter months** are characterised by a mild, sunny climate and are ideal for those who seek to avoid the peak influx of tourists. However some hotels, restaurants and attractions are closed between November and February.

Spring and **autumn** can sometimes bring heavy rainfalls and the infamous mistral wind, but neither overshadows the magnificent display of flora in full bloom at these times.

Summer is of course the best season for bathing and working up a suntan, not to mention taking part in the energetic nightlife. Traffic on the coast is, however, always very congested during this period; it can also be difficult to find accommodation so it is advisable to book well in advance, particularly in August.

WEATHER FORECASTS

Recorded report
(€0.34/minute)

- for the Alpes-Maritimes – ☎ 08 92 68 02 06
- for the Var – ☎ 08 92 68 02 83
- for conditions at sea – ☎ 08 92 68 08 77
- for the region – ☎ 08 92 68 00 00
- for the mountains – ☎ 08 92 68 04 04

Online weather reports

- www.meteo.fr
- www.meteo123.com

Road conditions

- www.ViaMichelin.com (itineraries and updates)
- snow and avalanche reports – ☎ 08 92 68 10 20

WHAT TO PACK

As little as possible! Cleaning and laundry services are available everywhere. Most personal items can be replaced at reasonable cost. Try to pack everything into one suitcase and a tote bag. Porter help may be in short supply, and new purchases will add to the original weight. Take an extra tote bag for packing new purchases, shopping at the market, carrying a picnic, etc. Be sure luggage is clearly labelled and old travel tags removed. Do not pack medication in checked luggage, but keep it in your carry-on.

KNOW BEFORE YOU GO

Useful Web Sites

www.ambafrance-us.org

The French Embassy in the USA has a Web site providing basic information (geography, demographics, history), a news digest and business-related information. It offers special pages for children, and pages devoted to culture, language study and travel, and you can reach other selected French sites (regions, cities, ministries) with a hypertext link.

www.franceguide.com

The French Government Tourist Office / Maison de la France site is packed with practical information and tips for those travelling to France. The home page has a number of links to more specific guidance, for American or Canadian travellers for example, or to the FGTO's London pages.

www.FranceKeys.com

This sight has plenty of practical information for visiting France. It covers all regions, with links to tourist offices and related sites. Very useful for planning the details of your tour across France!

www.fr-holidaystore.co.uk

The French Travel Centre in London has gone on-line with this service, providing information on all French regions, including updated special travel offers and details on available accommodation.

www.visiteurope.com

The European Travel Commission provides useful information on travelling to and around 27 European countries, and includes links to some commercial booking services (ie vehicle hire), rail schedules, weather reports and more.

VIRTUAL RIVIERA

Here are a few selected Web sites devoted to Cote d'Azur

www.beyond.fr

"Beyond the French Riviera" is a site in English with lots of links, information on places, sports, history, accommodation and more; practical and comprehensive.

www.provenceweb.fr

"Provence on the Web" includes an on-line magazine with featured villages, upcoming events, recipes, and touring suggestions (thematic tours, bike tours and others) for surfers.

www.rivieratimes.com

The online edition for the monthly English newspaper *The Riviera Times* includes the latest news, classified ads, and a link to the sister newspaper, "The Monaco Times".

www.angloinfo.com

"AngloINFO Riviera" is a popular Web site for the English-speaking expatriate community along the Côte d'Azur. It includes a directory of local businesses and organizations, particularly those run by or catering to English speakers, and lively community Forums .

www.riviera-reporter.com

This is the Web site for the monthly printed English magazine, *Riviera Reporter*. It has archived articles that are helpful for both visitors and English-speaking locals on the Riviera.

D. Pazery / MICHELIN

Tourist Offices

Information can also be requested from **France on Call**, ☎ (514) 288-1904.

AUSTRALIA – NEW ZEALAND

Sydney
Level 13, 25 Bligh Street,
Sydney, New South Wales 2000
☎ (02) 9231 5244
Fax: (02) 9221 8682.

CANADA

Montreal
1981 Avenue McGill College,
Suite 490,
Montreal PQ H3A 2W9
☎ (514) 288-2026
Fax: (514) 845 4868.

EIRE

info.ie@franceguide.com
☎ (15) 60 235 235

SOUTH AFRICA

P.O. Box 41022, Craig Hall 2024
☎ (011) 880 8062
Fax: (011) 770 1666.

UNITED KINGDOM

London
178 Piccadilly, London WIJ 9AL
☎ (09068) 244 123
Fax: (020)7493 6594.

UNITED STATES

East Coast – New York
444 Madison Avenue,
16th Floor, NY 10022-6903,
☎ (212) 838-7800
Fax: (212) 838-7855.

Mid West – Chicago
676 North Michigan Avenue,
Suite 3360, Chicago, IL 60611-2819
☎ (312) 751-7800
Fax: (312) 337-6339.

West Coast – Los Angeles
9454 Wilshire Boulevard,
Suite 715,
Beverly Hills, CA 90212-2967.
☎ (310) 271-6665
Fax: (310) 276-2835.

Local/Regional Tourist Offices

Visitors may also contact local tourist offices for more detailed information, to receive brochures and maps. The addresses and telephone numbers of tourist offices for individual towns in this guide are located in that town's listing after the symbol 🛈. Below, the addresses are given for local tourist offices of the *départements* and *régions* covered in this guide.

Comité Régional du Tourisme de Provence-Alpes-Côte d'Azur
Espace Colbert,
14 Rue Sainte-Barbe 13001
Marseille
☎ 04 91 39 38 00.
www.crt-paca.fr.

Comité Régional du Tourisme Riviera-Côte d'Azur
55 Promenade des Anglais, BP 602,
06011 Nice Cedex 1
☎ 04 93 37 78 78.
www.guideriviera.com.

Comité Départemental du Tourisme du Var
1 Boulevard Foch, BP 99, 83003
Draguignan Cedex
☎ 04 94 68 58 33

5 Avenue Vauban, BP 5147,
83000 Toulon
☎ 04 94 09 00 69.
www.tourismevar.com.

Office de Tourisme et des Congrès de la Principauté de Monaco
2A Boulevard des Moulins,
98000 Monaco
☎ 04 93 50 60 88.
www.monaco-tourisme.com.

Parc Naturel National du Mercantour
23 Rue d'Italie, 06000 Nice
☎ 04 93 87 86 10.
www.parc-mercantour.com.

Parc Naturel National de Port-Cros
Castel Ste-Claire, Rue Ste-Claire,
83400 Hyères
☎ 04 94 65 32 98.
www.portcrosparcnational.fr.

Fédération Nationale des Comités Départementaux de Tourisme
2 Rue Linois, 75015 Paris
☎ 01 45 75 62 16.
www.fncdt.net.

Tourist Information Centres – The **Michelin Guide France** gives the addresses and telephone numbers of the Tourist Information Centres (*Syndicats d'Initiative*) to be found in most large towns and many tourist resorts. They can supply large-scale town plans, timetables and information on local entertainment, accommodation, sports and sightseeing.

International Visitors

EMBASSIES AND CONSULATES

Australia   **Embassy**
4 Rue Jean-Rey, 75015 Paris
☎ 01 40 59 33 00
Fax: 01 40 59 33 10.
www.france.embassy.gov.au.

Canada   **Embassy**
35 Avenue Montaigne, 75008 Paris
☎ 01 44 43 29 00
Fax: 01 44 43 29 99.
www.amb-canada.fr.

Eire   **Consulate**
4 Rue Rude, 75016 Paris
☎ 01 44 17 67 00
Fax: 01 44 17 67 60.
www.embassyofirelandparis.com.

New Zealand   **Embassy**
7 ter Rue Léonard-de-Vinci, 75016 Paris
☎ 01 45 01 43 43
Fax: 01 45 01 43 44.

South Africa   **Embassy**
59 Quai d'Orsay, 75007 Paris
☎ 01 53 59 23 23
Fax: 01 53 59 23 33.
www.afriquesud.net.

UK   **Embassy**
35 Rue du Faubourg St-Honoré, 75008 Paris
☎ 01 44 51 31 00
Fax: 01 44 51 31 27.
www.amb-grandebretagne.fr.

UK   **Consulate**
24 Avenue du Prado
13006 Marseille
☎ 04 91 15 72 10.

USA   **Embassy**
2 Avenue Gabriel, 75008 Paris
☎ 01 43 12 22 22
Fax: 01 42 66 97 83.
www.amb-usa.fr.

USA   **Consulate**
7 Avenue Gustave V,
3rd floor, 06000 Nice
☎ 04 93 88 89 55
Fax: 04 93 87 07 38.

DOCUMENTS

Passport

Nationals of countries within the European Union entering France need only a national identity card. Nationals of other countries must be in possession of a valid national **passport**. In case of loss or theft, report to your embassy or consulate and the local police.

Visa

No **entry visa** is required for Canadian, US or Australian citizens travelling as tourists and staying less than 90 days, except for students planning to study in France. If you think you may need a visa, apply to your local French Consulate.

US citizens should obtain the booklet *Safe Trip Abroad*, which provides useful information on visa requirements, customs regulations, medical care, etc for international travellers. Published by the Government Printing Office, it can be ordered by phone – ☎ (202) 512 1800 – or consulted on-line (www.access.gpo.gov). General passport information is available by phone toll-free from the Federal Information Center (item 5 on the automated menu), ☎ 800-688-9889. US passport application forms can be downloaded from http://travel.state.gov.

CUSTOMS

Contact the Customs Office (UK) for a leaflet on customs regulations and the full range of duty-free allowances; available from HM Customs and Excise, Eldon Court, 75 London Road, Reading RG1 5BS, ☎ 0845 010 9000, www.hmce.gov.uk. The US Customs Service offers a publication *Know Before You Go* for US citizens: for the office nearest you, consult the phone book,

Duty-Free Allowances	
Spirits (whisky, gin, vodka etc)	10 litres
Fortified wines (vermouth, port etc)	20 litres
Wine (not more than 60 sparkling)	90 litres
Beer	110 litres
Cigarettes	800
Cigarillos	400
Cigars	200
Smoking tobacco	1 kg

Federal Government, US Treasury (www.customs.ustreas.gov). Canadian citizens should check the website of the Canada Customs and Revenue Agency, www.ccra-adrc.gc.ca.

There are no customs formalities for holidaymakers bringing their caravans into France for a stay of less than six months. No customs document is necessary for pleasure boats and outboard motors for a stay of less than six months but the registration certificate should be kept on board.

Americans can bring home, tax-free, up to US$ 800 worth of goods (limited quantities of alcohol and tobacco products); Canadians up to CND$ 750; Australians up to AUS$ 400 and New Zealanders up to NZ$ 700.

Persons living in a member-state of the European Union are not restricted with regard to purchasing goods for private use, but there are recommended allowances for alcoholic beverages and tobacco.

HEALTH

First aid, medical advice and chemist/pharmacy night service are available from pharmacies identified by a neon sign in the shape of a green cross.

It is advisable to obtain comprehensive insurance coverage, as the recipient of medical treatment in French hospitals or clinics must pay the bill. **Nationals of non-EU countries** should check with their insurance companies about policy limitations. Reimbursement can then be negotiated with the insurance company according to the policy held. All prescription drugs should be clearly labelled; it is recommended that you carry a copy of the prescription.

✚ **British and Irish citizens** should apply to the Department of Health and Social Security for Form E 111, which entitles the holder to urgent treatment for accident or unexpected illness in EU countries. A refund of part of the costs of treatment can be obtained on application in person or by post to the local Social Security Offices (*Caisse Primaire d'Assurance Maladie*).

✚ **The American Hospital of Paris** is open 24hr for emergencies as well as consultations, with English-speaking staff, in the southwest Paris suburbs at 63 Boulevard Victor-Hugo, 92200 Neuilly sur Seine, ☎ 01 46 41 25 25. Accredited by major insurance companies.

✚ **The British Hospital** is located just outside Paris in Levallois-Perret, at 3 Rue Barbès, ☎ 01 46 39 22 22.

ACCESSIBILITY

The sights described in this guide which are easily accessible to people of reduced mobility are indicated by the symbol ♿.

Useful information on transportation, holidaymaking and sporting associations for the disabled is available from the *Comité National Français de Liaison pour la Réadaptation des Handicapés* (CNRH), 236 bis Rue de Tolbiac, 75013 Paris. Call their international information number ☎ 01 53 80 66 44, or write to request a catalogue of publications. Web-surfers can find information for slow walkers, mature travellers and others with special needs at www.access-able.com. For information on museum access for the disabled contact La Direction, Les Musées de France, Service Accueil des Publics Spécifiques, 6 Rue des Pyramides, 75041 Paris Cedex 1, ☎ 01 40 15 35 88.

The **Michelin Guide France** and the **Michelin Camping Caravaning France** publications indicate hotels and camp sites with facilities suitable for the disabled.

GETTING THERE

By Air

The French domestic network operates frequent services from Paris (Charles de Gaulle and Orly), covering the whole country. The main holiday destinations in the south of France are Nice, Marseille, Toulon and Monaco. Air France is the leading airline for domestic flights but there are also flights available on the European carrier, EasyJet. Direct flights from England can be booked on board EasyJet, British Airways, British Midland, and Ryan Air.

There are transfer buses to town terminals and to rail stations. **Roissy-Rail** and **Orly-Rail** operate fast rail links to the centre of Paris. There are also package tour flights with a rail or coach link-up. Air France sells tickets including a boat shuttle service that will take you directly to St-Tropez or St-Raphaël. Information, brochures and timetables are available from airlines and travel agents.

EasyJet
☎ 08 25 08 25 08 *within France*
www.easyjet.com

British Airways
☎ 0870 8509 850 *from England*
☎ 0825 825 040 *from France*
www.britishairways.com

British Midland
☎ 0870 6070 222 *from England*
☎ 01 55 69 83 06 *from France*
www.flybmi.com

Air France
☎ 0 820 820 820 *within France*
www.airfrance.com

Ryan Air
☎ 08 92 55 56 66 *within France*
www.ryanair.com

BMI Baby
☎ 08 90 71 00 81 *within France*
www.bmibaby.com

Aéroports de Paris
☎ 0 836 681 515
www.adp.fr

Aéroport de Nice-Côte d'Azur
☎ 04 89 88 98 28
www.nice.aeroport.fr

Aéroport international de Toulon-Hyères
☎ 0825 01 83 87
www.var.cci.fr

By Sea

From the UK or Ireland

There are numerous **cross-Channel services** (passenger and car ferries, hovercraft) from the United Kingdom and Ireland, as well as the Shuttle rail service through the Channel Tunnel (**Le Shuttle-Eurotunnel**, ☎ *0990 353-535. www.ferries.fr/eurotunnel. htm*). To choose the most suitable route between your port of arrival and your destination use the **Michelin Tourist and Motoring Atlas France**, **Michelin map 726** (which gives travel times and mileages) or **Michelin 300-series Local Maps**.

P & O Stena Line Ferries
Channel House,
Channel View Road,
Dover CT17 9JT
☎ 0990 980 980 *or*
☎ 01304 863 000 *(switchboard)*
www.poferries.com

Hoverspeed
International Hoverport,
Marine Parade,
Dover, Kent CT17 9TG
☎ 0870 460 7157
www.hoverspeed.co.uk

Brittany Ferries
Millbay Docks,
Plymouth, Devon PL1 3EW
☎ 0990 360 360
www.brittany-ferries.com

Portsmouth Commercial Port *(and ferry information)*
George Byng Way, Portsmouth,
Hampshire PO2 8SP
☎ 01705 297391
Fax 01705 861165

Irish Ferries
50 West Norland Street,
Dublin 2
☎ (353) 16 610 511
www.irishferries.com

Seafrance
Eastern Docks, Dover,
Kent, CT16 1JA
☎ 0870 5711 711
www.seafrance.fr

By Rail

Eurostar runs via the Channel Tunnel between London (Waterloo) and Paris (Gare du Nord) in 3hr *(bookings and information ☎ 0345 303 030 in the UK; ☎ 1-888-EUROSTAR in the US; www.eurostar.co.uk)*. In Paris it links to the high-speed rail network **(TGV)** which covers most of the country and which has recently been extended to the South of France *(☝ see box below – for details call ☎ 0 836 676 869)*. The main towns served by the new TGV network are Lyon, Avignon, Valence, Montpellier, Aix-en-Provence, and Marseille. As far as the Riviera is concerned, there are 6-8 trains leaving daily from Paris-Gare de Lyon for Nice station, running roughly between 8am and 10.30pm (night train). The fastest schedule takes 5hr.

Eurailpass, Flexipass and **Saverpass** are three of the travel passes which may be purchased by residents of countries outside the European Union. In the US, contact your travel agent or Rail Europe 2100 Central Avenue, Boulder, CO, 80301 ☎ 1-800-4-EURAIL or **Europrail International** ☎ 1 888 667 9731, www.europrail.net. If you are a European resident, you can buy an individual country pass, if you are not a resident of the country you are buying it for. In the UK, contact Europrail at 179 Piccadilly London W1V 0BA ☎ 0990 848 848. Information on schedules can be obtained on websites for these agencies and the **SNCF**, respectively: **www.raileurop. com.us, www.eurail.on.ca, www. sncf.fr.** At the SNCF site, you can book ahead, pay with a credit card, and receive your ticket in the mail at home free of charge (7 days minimum before leaving in the case of foreign countries, 4 days for France).

Practical Information

The French railway company SNCF operates a telephone information, reservation and prepayment service in English from 7am to 10pm (French time). In France call ☎ 08 36 35 35 39 *(when calling from outside France, drop the initial 0)*.

There are numerous **discounts** available when you purchase your tickets in France, from 25-50% below the regular rate. These apply to passengers over 60 years of age **(Carte Senior)**, young people aged between 12 and 26 **(Carte 12-25)** and passengers travelling with a child under 12 (Kids **Carte Enfant +**). Cheaper tickets may also be purchased last minute (three days before) or at least 20 days in advance **(Prem's)** There are a limited number of discount seats available during peak travelling times, and the best discounts are available for travel during off-peak periods.
Tickets bought in France must be validated *(composter)* by using the orange automatic date-stamping machines at the platform entrance (failure to do so may result in a fine).

Local rail service is provided by the Le **TER**, ☎ 0892 35 35 35. *www.ter-sncf. com.*

Line no 2:
Marseille, Toulon, Les Arcs-Draguignan

Line no 3:
Les Arcs, Draguignan, Fréjus, St-Raphaël, Cannes, Nice

Line no 4:
Mandelieu, Cannes, Nice, Ventimiglia

Line no 5A:
Nice, Breil-sur-Roya, Cueno, Torino

TGV Méditerranée

In June 2001, the President of the Republic, Jacques Chirac, officially inaugurated France's southern high-speed rail link, bringing Provence within three hours of Paris and six of London. The smart, streamlined blue and silver train will now reach Marseille after a mere 177 minutes, leaving from Paris. The 12-year campaign to complete the route followed by the TGV Méditerranée was fraught with difficulties. Besides the opposition shown by local residents, there were a number of geographical, architectural and ecological constraints. Considerable care was taken to preserve the natural environment and to avoid disturbing protected species. Moreover, new bridges and viaducts had to be built with local stone in order to blend in with the surrounding landscape.
The new trains provide a far better service to passengers: more legroom, a central luggage rack, an area set aside for bicycles, facilities for changing babies and heating up bottles, telephone booths, electric plugs for laptop computers *(1st class)*, a wide range of light snacks or meals and even a free newspaper with your breakfast!

▦ **Line no 6:**
Marseille, Toulon, Nice, Ventimiglia

▦ **Line Grasse-Cannes:**
Grasse, Le Bosquet, Cannes, Nice

From 1 July to 30 September the **"Carte Isabelle"** (⌖ 11€) is an unlimited day-pass between Fréjus and Vintimille, and Nice and Tende.

By Coach

Regular coach services between London and Paris, connection for Nice:

◆ **Eurolines (London)**
52 Grosvenor Gardens, Victoria, London SW1W 0AU, ☎ 0870 580 8080.

◆ **Eurolines (Paris)**
28 Avenue du Général-de-Gaulle, 93541 Bagnolet, ☎ 08 92 89 90 91. www.eurolines.co.uk.

Driving in France 🚗

The area covered in this guide is easily reached by main motorways and national routes. **Michelin map 726** indicates the main itineraries as well as alternative routes for avoiding heavy traffic during busy holiday periods, and gives estimated travel times. The latest Michelin route-planning service is available on Internet, **www.ViaMichelin.com**. Travellers can calculate a precise route using such options as shortest route, route avoiding toll roads, Michelin-recommended route and gain access to tourist information (hotels, restaurants, attractions). The service is available on a pay-per-route basis or by subscription.

The roads are very busy during the holiday period (particularly weekends in July and August) to avoid traffic congestion it is advisable to follow the recommended secondary routes (signposted as *Bison Futé – itinéraires bis*). The motorway network includes rest areas (*aires d'autoroute*) and petrol/gas stations, usually with restaurant and shopping malls attached, about every 40km/25mi, so that long-distance drivers have no excuse not to stop for a rest every now and then.

DOCUMENTS

Travellers from other European Union countries and North America can drive in France with a valid national or home-state **driving licence**. An **international driving licence** is useful because the information on it appears in nine languages (bear in mind that traffic officers are allowed to fine motorists). A permit is available from the National Automobile Club, 1151 East Hillsdale Boulevard, Foster City, CA 94404 ☎ 650-294-7000 or nationalautoclub.com; or contact your local branch of the American Automobile Association. For the vehicle, it is necessary to have the registration papers (logbook) and a nationality plate of the approved size. Certain motoring organisations (AAA, AA, RAC) offer accident **insurance** and **breakdown** services for members. Check with your current insurance company with regard to coverage while abroad. If you plan to rent a car using your credit card, check with the company, which may provide liability insurance automatically (and thus save you having to pay the cost for optimum coverage).

ROAD REGULATIONS

The minimum driving age is 18. Traffic drives on the right. All passengers must wear **seat belts.** Children under the age of 10 must ride in the back seat. Headlights must be switched on in poor visibility and at night; use side-lights only when the vehicle is parked. In the case of a **breakdown**, a red warning triangle or hazard warning lights are obligatory. In the absence of stop signs at intersections, cars must **yield to the right**. Traffic on main roads outside built-up areas (priority indicated by a yellow diamond sign) and on roundabouts has right of way. Vehicles must stop when the lights turn red at road junctions and may filter to the right only when indicated by an amber/yellow arrow.

The regulations on **drinking and driving** (limited to 0.50g/l) and **speeding** are strictly enforced – usually by an on-the-spot fine and/or confiscation of the vehicle.

Speed Limits

Although liable to modification, these are as follows:

◆ **toll motorways (autoroutes):**
130kph/80mph (110kph/68mph when raining);

◆ **dual carriageways and motorways without tolls:**
110kph/68mph (100kph/62mph when raining);

- **other roads:** 90kph/56mph (80kph/50mph when raining) and in towns 50kph/31mph;
- **outside lane on motorways during daylight, on level ground and with good visibility:** minimum speed limit of 80kph/50mph.

Parking Regulations

In town there are zones where parking is either restricted or subject to a fee; tickets should be obtained from the ticket machines (*horodateurs*) and displayed inside the windscreen on the driver's side; failure to display may result in a fine, or towing and impoundment.

Tolls

In France, most motorway sections are subject to a toll (*péage*). You can pay in cash or with a credit card (Visa, Mastercard).

CAR RENTAL

There are car rental agencies at airports, railway stations and in all large towns throughout France. European cars have manual transmission; automatic cars are available in larger cities only if an advance reservation is made. Drivers must be over 21; between ages 21-25, drivers are required to pay an extra daily fee; some companies allow drivers under 23 only if the reservation has been made through a travel agent. It is relatively expensive to hire a car in France; Americans in particular will notice the difference and should make arrangements before leaving, take advantage of fly-drive offers, or seek advice from a travel agent, specifying requirements.

Rental Cars – Central Reservation in France	
Avis:	☎ 08 20 05 05 05
Europcar:	☎ 08 25 358 358
Budget France:	☎ 08 25 00 35 64
Hertz France:	☎ 01 41 91 95 25
Century:	☎ 01 53 70 68 48
Rent A Car:	☎ 01 55 43 29 99
Prestige Limousines:	☎ 01 40 43 92 92
Executive Car:	☎ 01 42 65 54 20

MOTORHOME RENTAL

Worldwide Motorhome Rentals

Offers fully equipped camper vans for rent. You can view them on the company's web page.

☎ 888- 519-8969 *US toll-free*
☎ 530-389-8316 *outside the US*
Fax 530-389-8316.
www.mhrww.com

Overseas Motorhome Tours Inc.

Organises escorted tours and individual rental of recreational vehicles.

☎ 800-322-2127 *US*
☎ 1-310-543-2590 *outside the US*
www.omtinc.com.

GASOLINE

French service stations dispense:

- *sans plomb 98* (super unleaded 98)
- *sans plomb 95* (super unleaded 95)
- *diesel/gazole* (diesel)
- *GPL* (LPG).

Petrol, or gasoline, is considerably more expensive in France than in the USA. Prices are listed on signboards on the motorways; it is usually cheaper to fill up after leaving the motorway; check the large hypermarkets on the outskirts of town.

WHERE TO STAY AND EAT

Finding a Hotel

Hotel and Restaurant listings fall within the description of each region. See the Legend at the back of the guide for a key to the price categories.

THE GREEN GUIDE is pleased to offer a new feature: lists of selected hotels and restaurants for this region. Turn to the pages bordered in blue for descriptions and prices of typical places to stay and eat with local flair. The key on page 9 explains the symbols and abbreviations used in these sections. Use the **Map of Places to Stay** *(below)* to identify recommended places for overnight stops. For an even greater selection, use the **Michelin Guide France**, with its famously reliable star-rating system and hundreds of establishments all over France. Book ahead! The French Riviera is a very popular holiday destination.

For further assistance, **Loisirs Accueil** is a booking service that has offices in some French *départements* – contact tourism offices for further information. A guide to good-value, family-run hotels, **Logis et Auberges de France,** is available from the French tourist office, as are lists of other kinds of accommodation such as hotel-châteaux, bed-and-breakfasts, etc.

Relais et Châteaux provides information on booking in luxury hotels with character: 15 Rue Galvani, 75017 Paris, ☎ 08 25 323 232.

Economy Chain Hotels

If you need a place to stop en route, these can be useful, as they are inexpensive (45-75€ for a double room) and generally located near the main road. While breakfast is available, there may not be a restaurant; rooms are small, with a television and bathroom. Central reservation numbers:

🛏 **Akena**	☎ 01 69 84 85 17
🛏 **B&B**	☎ 0 803 00 29 29
🛏 **Etap Hôtel**	☎ 08 36 68 89 00
🛏 **Mister Bed**	☎ 01 46 14 38 00
🛏 **Villages Hôtel**	☎ 03 80 60 92 70

The hotels listed below are slightly more expensive (from 75€), and offer a few more amenities and services. Central reservation numbers:

🛏 **Campanile**	☎ 01 64 62 46 46
🛏 **Kyriad**	☎ 0 825 003 003
🛏 **Ibis**	☎ 0 825 88 22 22

Cottages, Bed & Breakfasts

The **Maison des Gîtes de France** is an information service on self-catering accommodation on the French Riviera (and the rest of France). *Gîtes* usually take the form of a cottage or apartment decorated in the local style where visitors can make themselves at home, or bed and breakfast accommodation *(chambres d'hôtes)* which consists of a room and breakfast at a reasonable price.

Contact the Gîtes de France office in Paris: 59 Rue St-Lazare, 75439 Paris Cedex 09, ☎ 01 49 70 75 75, www.gites-de-france.com, or their representative in the UK, **Brittany Ferries**. You can also contact the local tourist offices which may have lists of available properties and local bed and breakfast establishments.

Hostels, Camping

To obtain an International Youth Hostel Federation card (there is no age requirement, "senior cards" are available too), you should contact the IYHF in your own country for information and membership applications (US ☎ 202 783 6161; UK ☎ 1727 855215; Canada ☎ 613-273 7884; Australia ☎ 61-2-9565-1669). There is a new booking service on the internet (www.iyhf.org), which you may use to reserve rooms as far as six months in advance.

There are two main youth hostel associations *(Auberges de Jeunesse)* in France, the **Ligue Française pour les Auberges de la Jeunesse** (38 Boulevard Raspail, 75007 Paris, ☎ 01 45 48 69 84, Fax 01 45 44 57 47, www.auberges-de-jeunesse.com) and the Fédération Unie des Auberges de Jeunesse (27 Rue Pajol, 75018 Paris, ☎ 08 36 688 698).

There are numerous officially graded **camping sites** with varying standards of facilities on the French Riviera. The **Michelin Camping Caravaning France** guide lists a selection of camp sites. The area is very popular with campers in the summer months, so it is wise to reserve in advance.

MENU READER

La Carte...The Menu

ENTRÉES ....STARTERS

Crudités ....Raw vegetable salad

Terrine de lapin ....Rabbit terrine (pâté)

Frisée aux lardons ....Curly lettuce with bacon bits

Escargots ....Snails

Cuisses de grenouille ....Frog's legs

Salade au crottin ....Goat cheese on a bed of lettuce

PLATS (VIANDES) ....MAIN COURSES (MEAT)

Bavette à l'échalote....................................Sirloin with shallots

Faux filet au poivre ....Sirloin with pepper sauce

Côtes d'agneau..Lamb chops

Filet mignon de porc ....Pork filet

Blanquette de veau...................................Veal in cream sauce

Nos viandes sont garnies....... Our meat dishes are served with vegetables

PLATS (POISSONS, VOILAILLE) .... MAIN COURSES (FISH, FOWL)

Filets de sole ....Sole fillets

Dorade aux herbes ....Sea bream with herbs

Saumon grillé ....Grilled salmon

Coq au vin ....Chicken in red wine sauce

Poulet de Bresse rôti.............Free-range roast chicken from the Bresse

Omelette aux morilles ....Wild-mushroom omelette

PLATEAU DE FROMAGES.....................SELECTION OF CHEESES

DESSERTS ....DESSERTS

Tarte aux pommes... Apple pie

Crème caramel .... Cooled baked custard with caramel sauce

Sorbet: trois parfums ....Sherbet: choose 3 flavours

BOISSONS... BEVERAGES

Bière... Beer

Eau minérale (gazeuse) ....(Sparkling) mineral water

Une carafe d'eau ....Tap water (no charge)

Vin rouge, vin blanc, rosé ....Red wine, white wine, rosé

Jus de fruit..Fruit juice

MENU ENFANT.....................................CHILDREN'S MENU

Jambon..Ham

Steak haché .... Ground beef

Frites ....French fried potatoes

Places to stay

- Seaside resort

  Seaside resorts ⚲ are classified according to the quality and range of facilities offered.

- Spa resort

- Winter sports resort

▲ Mountain resort

• Popular holiday destination

▭ Weekend destination

— Overnight stop

⛵ Marina

Terrace of restaurant looking onto an old street of Cannes

Finding a Restaurant

Turn to the pages bordered in blue for descriptions and prices of selected restaurants in the different locations covered in this guide. The key on page-9 explains the symbols and abbreviations used in these sections. Use the **Michelin Guide France,** with its famously reliable star-rating system and hundreds of establishments all over France, for an even greater choice. If you would like to experience a meal in a highly rated restaurant from the Michelin Guide, be sure to book ahead! In the countryside, restaurants usually serve lunch between noon and 2pm and dinner between 7.30pm and 10pm. It is not always easy to find an establishment open between lunch and dinner, as "round-the-clock" restaurants are still scarce in the provinces. However, a hungry traveller can usually get a sandwich in a café, and ordinary hot dishes may be available in a brasserie.

For information on local specialities, see Understanding the Region.

In French restaurants and cafés, a service charge is included. Tipping is not necessary, but French people often leave the small change from their bill on their table, or about 5% for the waiter in a nice restaurant.

WHAT TO DO AND SEE

Outdoor Fun

BOAT TRIPS

There are regular ferries to the Île de Bendor, Île des Embiez, Île d'Hyères and Île de Lérins, and also boat trips from the following resorts.

Bandol

- Les Embiez – Toulon via Cap Sicié, Gare Maritime (☎ 04 94 32 51 41), Cassis and the Calanque d'En-Vau via Lla Ciotat – Whole day to the Château d'If and Le Frioul – Underwater exploration with l'Aquascope (Cie Atlantide)

Sanary

- Îles des Embiez – Toulon Anchorage and Cap Sicié – Calanques de Cassis

Le Lavandou

- Île du Levant

Cavalaire

- Îles d'Hyères

St-Tropez

- Îles d'Hyères.

Ste-Maxime

- Les Issambres, Port-Grimaud (navettes), Baie des Cannebiers.

Ste-Maxime

- St-Tropez (shuttle) – Îles d'Hyères

Cannes

- Îles de Lérins – excursion to St-Tropez and Monaco on a catamaran

Juan les Pins

(departure from Ponton Courbet)

- Underwater viewing cruise off Cap d'Antibes

Nice

- La Riviera

Menton

- The Riviera – Monaco (with and without stopping)

Toulon

- La Seyne-sur-Mer, Les Sablettes, Tamaris, St-Mandrier (navettes). Harbors of Toulon.

St-Raphaël

- St-Tropez
- Îles de Lérins.

SAILING

Most of the seaside resorts on the French Riviera, from Lecques to Menton, have well-equipped marinas, making this coast the best in France for sailing. Although nearly every port has moorings with good facilities, the enthusiasm for sailing is such that enormous marinas have been constructed with extensive services to satisfy even the most exacting yachtsman. Ports providing over 1 000 berths are Bandol, Toulon, Hyères (Port-St-Pierre), La Londe (Port Miramar), Le Lavandou, St-Raphaël (Ste-Lucia), Cannes (Pierre Canto and the Vieux Port), St-Laurent-du-Var and Antibes (Port-Vauban), which is the largest to date.

Sailing into the blue

S. Sauvignier-MICHELIN

The marinas open to visiting crafts are marked on the Places to Stay map on pp 30-31.

There are sailing clubs which provide lessons in most resorts; during the summer it is possible to hire craft with or without a crew.

The services available in each port are listed in the Guide du Plaisancier en Méditerranée, published by Editions France Yachting Service.

Further information is available from each port authority and from the **Fédération Française de Voile** (*55 Avenue Kléber, 75084 Paris Cedex 16* ☎ *01 44 05 81 00. www.ffvoile.org*).

SCUBA DIVING

There are many clubs providing scuba diving lessons accompanied by instructors. The main centres are Bendor (Centre Padi is one of the largest in Europe), Le Pradet (Garonne beach), Giens (La Tour Fondue), Sanary, Cavalaire, Ramatuelle (L'Escalet), St-Tropez, Ste-Maxime, St-Raphaël, La Napoule, Cannes and Villefranche. A brochure listing all the local clubs is available from **La Maison du Tourisme du Golfe de St-Tropez** in Gassin (☎ 04 94 43 42 10).

Excursions to explore the Mediterranean flora and fauna are provided by the Centre du Rayol-Canadel and the Parc National de Port-Cros.

The **Fédération Française d'Études et de Sports Sous-Marins** (24 Quai de Rive-Neuve, 13007 Marseille ☎ 04 91 33 99 31. www.ffessm.fr) is an umbrella organisation, comprising 100 local clubs, which publishes a comprehensive yearbook covering all underwater activities in France. Information also available from the **Comité Régional Côte d'Azur des Sports Sous-Marins** (Cap Blanc, Port de Bormes, 83230 Bormes-les-Mimosas, ☎ 04 94 71 63 43. www. ffessmcotedazur.com).

Finest Underwater Landscapes

The coves of the Maures and the Esterel on the Var coast and the clear water around the Îles d'Hyères are invitations to discover the charm of the Mediterranean (La Grande Bleue) and of the silent underwater world. The volume of marine traffic over the centuries has turned the seabed into a museum of shipwrecks – about 100 ships and upwards of 20 aircraft have sunk along this coast.

Most of them are lying in more than 20m/65ft of water, accessible only to experienced divers who are members of specialist clubs. Other wrecks, lying in shallower waters, can easily be visited by amateurs. Information about underwater centers near such wrecks is available from the Fédération des Sports Sous-marins in Marseille.

The wrecks of the Provençal coast and their history are described in *Naufrages en Provence* by J-P Joncheray.

UNDERWATER FISHING

The abundance of creeks along the coast should satisfy all demands. The sport is strictly regulated; the essential regional regulations are given below.

Underwater fishing is forbidden in certain areas of the coastline from early November to the beginning of March. It is essential to check with the local maritime authority – Toulon, 244 Avenue de l'Infanterie-de-Marine ☎ 04 94 46 92 00 and Nice, 22 Quai Lunel ☎ 04 92 00 41 50.

Some areas are out of bounds to fishing all the year round – south coast of St-Mandrier Peninsula, part of Porquerolles Island, Port-Cros Island and its neighbouring islets.

There are underwater nature reserves, marked by buoys, near Golfe-Juan, Beaulieu and Roquebrune-Cap-Martin. Villefranche harbour is a protected area. Underwater anglers must comply with general fishing regulations and bear in mind that in the Mediterranean Sea:

- it is illegal to catch or fish for grouper and oysters (for mother-of-pearl)
- it is illegal to fish for sea urchins from 1 May to 30 September
- it is illegal to pursue or catch marine mammals (dolphins, porpoises), even without intending to kill them
- the minimum size of catch is 12cm/4.72in (except for sardines, anchovies), 18cm/7.09in for crayfish.
- Whatever the circumstances, it is illegal to be in possession of both diving equipment and an underwater gun.

Underwater safety

Enthusiasm for exploring the superb underwater landscape of the Riviera should not blind the occasional diver to the need to observe certain regulations

- never go diving alone, nor after eating a heavy meal, nor after drinking alcohol or fizzy drinks, nor when tired
- avoid shipping lanes and areas used by wind-surfers
- when signalling for help, make it known that it is a diving accident so that the rescuers can prepare a decompression chamber, which is the only effective aid in the case of diving accidents, even minor ones.

SEA FISHING

In Sanary, in the Cogolin Marina and in Ste-Maxime there are organisations through which visitors may hire out boats and professional fishermen for sea fishing or join a sea fishing party (usually in summer from 6am to 10am). Contact these local tourism offices for more information.

OTHER SEASIDE ACTIVITIES

The long stretches of the Var coast, consisting of beaches where the *mistral* blows, have become some of the most popular locations in the Mediterranean for those who enjoy riding the waves on a **sail-board** (wind-surfing) or a **funboard**; the shorter board used for the latter makes acrobatics possible. Almanarre beach on the west side of the Giens peninsula has become a mecca for funboarders and played host to the World Championships. More technical skill is required on other beaches such as Six-Fours-les-Plages and the two sides of Cap Nègre.

For a different view of their favourite beaches, holidaymakers can fearlessly indulge in the joys of **parascending**: flying over the water below a parachute towed by a motorboat. The aim is to stay in the air for as long as possible and as high as possible. Instruction in this sport is available on nearly all the organised beaches, where there is enough wind.

Jet-skiing is practised on certain stretches of coast, which have been carefully chosen and are not accessible from the land. The sport provides a superb experience of moving along at speed. It is, however, strictly regulated

- machines must be 150m/164yd apart;
- machines may operate only during the day;
- machines may operate between 300m/328yd outside the channels and up to 1 nautical mile
- in future pilots must hold a proficiency certificate.

Most of the large resorts offer jet-ski rentals by the hour or the half day. It is also possible to hire sea canoes in Salins d'Hyères and certain resorts on the Var coast.

Motor vessels are forbidden within 300m/328yd of the shore (except in the access channels) and must not exceed 5 knots in certain restricted areas (Îles d'Hyères, Îles de Lérins and Villefranche harbour). Elsewhere the top speed is 10 knots.

Lac du Basto

B. Kauffmann/ MICHELIN

B. Kaufmann/ MICHELIN

COASTAL WALKS

Before the recent building boom the famous Customs Path ran all along the Riviera coast; some particularly picturesque sections still survive and have been developed by the Coast Conservancy *(Conservatoire du Littoral)*. There are several signed country footpaths along the Var coast, of which about 10, from Bandol to St-Aygulph, are described in a topo-guide published by the **Fédération Française de la Randonnée Pédestre.**

HIKING

A network of waymarked paths covers the region described in this guide. **GR (Grande Randonnée) paths,** which are fully open only from the end of June to early October, are for experienced hikers accustomed to mountain conditions.

- **GR 5,** the oldest and most majestic, which terminates in Nice after crossing Europe; the last section from Nice to St-Dalmas-Valdeblore passes through Aspremont, Levens, the Vésubie gorge and Madone d'Utelle.

- **GR 52,** from St-Dalmas-Valdeblore to Menton via Le Boréon, La Vallée des Merveilles, Turini Forest, Sospel and Val Rameh Tropical Garden.

- **GR52A,** among the peaks in the eastern part of the Parc National du Mercantour beyond the Col de Tende.

Other paths, open all year, for walkers of all levels of competence:

- **GR 4,** from Grasse via Gréolières and Entrevaux to the Verdon Gorge.

- **GR 51**, nicknamed "the Mediterranean balcony", from Castellar (east of Menton) to Col de la Cadière (Estérel) providing panoramic views of the coast from the first ridge.

- **GR 510**, entirely in the Alpes-Maritimes region, from Breil-sur-Roya via Sospel, Villars-sur-Var, Puget-Rostand, Roquestéron, St-Auban and Escragnolles to St-Cézaire-sur-Siagne, discovering another valley dotted with hill villages at each stage of the 10-day hike.

- **GR 9**, from Signes through the Massif des Maures to St-Pons-les-Mûres.

- **GR 99**, from Toulon through the Brignolais country to the Verdon Gorge.

- **GR 90**, the shortest, from Le Lavandou through the Massif des Maures to Notre-Dame-des-Anges, where it meets the GR 9.

Topo-guides for the **Grandes Randonnées** and **Petites Randonnées** are published by the Fédération Française de la Randonnée Pédestre – Comité National des Sentiers de Grande Randonnée, and are obtainable from the Centre d'Information, 64 Rue de Gergovie, 75014 Paris ☎ 01 45 45 31 02 (or order the catalogue of 170 publications by internet at the association's site - in French - www.ffrf.asso.fr).

NATURE PARKS

Wildlife – Parc National du Mercantour

Mercantour National Park, the last of the French National State Parks, was created in 1979 and covers an area of 68 500ha/169 267 acres in the Alpes-Maritimes and Alpes-de-Haute-Provence *départements* (encompassing 22 and 6 *communes* from each respectively).

The park, which was once the French part of Italian royal hunting grounds and extended over both sides of the Alps prior to 1861, has been twinned since 1987 with the Italian Argentera Nature Park with which it shares a border along 33km/20.5mi. These two organisations are in charge of introducing and monitoring animal species in the whole of this protected region. In this way, ibexes which have wintered in the Argentera arrive to spend the summer months in the Mercantour, while wild sheep (moufflons) do the opposite.

The Mercantour is a high, mountainous park, with terraces from 500-3 143m/1 640-10 312ft in altitude, offering breathtaking views of natural amphitheatres, glacial valleys and deep gorges.

It contains a rich variety of flora; over 2 000 species have been counted there, including **Saxifraga florulenta** which was for a time the park's emblem. All levels of vegetation are present, from olive trees to rhododendrons and the gentians which make such a splendid display of colour in the spring.

Fauna includes some 6 300 chamois, nearly 300 ibixes and 1 250 moufflons which are well adapted to the Mediterranean climate. The wooded slopes at medium altitude are home to various deer and smaller mammals such as hares, ermines and marmots. Feathered members of this community include black grouse, ptarmigans and splendid examples of birds of prey such as the short-toed eagle (circaëtus) and the golden eagle.

The reintroduction of the bearded vulture was achieved successfully in the summer of 1993. There are now five birds in the park. For the first time in France since 1942, wolves have returned of their own accord to live in the park. They come from Italy where this protected species is now spreading. The 600km/373mi of footpaths laid out within the park's boundaries enable tourists to discover the park on foot. These include the GR5 and the GR52A 🚴, or the Mercantour panoramic footpath which crosses the Vallée des Merveilles, as well as footpaths at L'Authion, Le Boréon and Madone de Fenestre.

This guide describes the regions of the Vésubie and Merveilles valleys, the Authion Massif and Turini Forest. *Mountain bikes are not allowed in the central area of the park.*

OTHER PARKS

The old royal hunting ground of the Sardinian monarchy extended until the Second World War over the two slopes of the Mercantour and the Marguareis. Since then the Italian section has been administered as a nature reserve with an active policy for the conservation of species and habitats. Two large natural parks have been created – **Parco dell'Argentera**, the largest, and Alta Valle Pesio, further east. Together with the Parc du Mercantour they have conducted a campaign for the reintroduction of endangered species – the bearded vulture and the ibex. In the Parco dell'Argentera there are many "royal" botanical paths easily accessible to hikers from the French side of the border by the frontier passes – Col de la Lombarde and Col de Tende. From the latter pass two paths (each about 3hr) follow the peaks towards Rocca dell'Abisso (2 755m/ 9 039ft – west) and Cima di Pepino (2 335m/7 661ft – east).

The **Alta Valle Pesio** park, in the Marguareis, is the wildest and least easy to reach from France. Hikers should branch into the northeast route from Limone-Piemonte or go up the valley from Savone.

The Vermenagna Valley which extends from Col de Tende to the Cuneo Plain is still within the range of the Provençal culture; Provençal spectacles (Roumiage de Provenço) are held in the Grana Valley in July. Among the specialities of the district is a famous cheese, Castelmagno, and handmade cutlery, such as the Vernantino pocket knife.

Parco Naturale Regionale dell'Argentera

Corso Dante Livio Bianco 5 – 12010 Valdieri (CN) ☎ 39 171 97 397

Parco Naturale Regionale Alta Valle Pesio e Tanaro

Via Sta Anne 34 – 12013 Chiusa Pesia (CN) ☎ 39 171 73 40 21

Tourist office in Limone-Piemonte

Via Roma (CN) ☎ 39 171 92 101.

HORSEBACK RIDING

Ligue Provence

🐎 Côte d'Azur de Tourisme Équestre – 19 Boulevard Victor-Hugo, 06130 Grasse ☎ 04 93 42 62 98

Comité national de tourisme équestre

🐎 9 Boulevard Mac-Donald, 75019 Paris, ☎ 01 53 26 15 50. www. tourisme-equestre.fr. They produce an annual guide (in French) called "Tourisme et loisirs équestres en France".

Comité régional de tourisme équestre Provence-Côte d'Azur

🐎 33 chemin du Collet, 06650 Opio, ☎ 04 93 77 39 36 or 04 93 77 38 75. www.find-your-horse.com.

Association Varoise de Développement du Tourisme de Randonnée (AVDTR)

🐎 1 Boulevard Foch, 83000 Draguignan ☎ 04 94 68 97 66 – which publishes the brochure *Guide Annuaire de Cavalier Varois*.

Exploring the Border on Horseback

This is an unusual way of exploring the Massif du Mercantour. There is a waymarked route on the **Franco Italian Natural Spaces Equestrian Itinerary** *(Itinéraire Équestre des Espaces Naturels Franco-Italiens – Itinerario Equestre degli Soazi Naturali Franco-Italiani)* from St-Martin-Vésubie through the Italian parks – Argentera and Alta Valle Pesio – to Certosa di Pesio; there are 10 staging posts with facilities for riders and their mounts. Practical information is available from the Parc du Mercantour and the Parco dell'Argentera information offices (🕭 *see Hiking*).

The Parc du Mercantour publishes a brochure containing various bridle routes and staging posts in the Argentera and Mercantour highlands.

WINTER SPORTS

It is only a short distance (less than 2hr by car) from the coast to a range of winter sports stations:

- ⛷ La Colmiane-Valdeblore
- ⛷ La Gordolasque-Belvédère
- ⛷ Boréon-St-Martin-Vésubie
- ⛷ Turini-Camp d'Argent
- ⛷ Peïra-Cava
- ⛷ Gréolières-les-Neiges
- ⛷ L'Audibergue

There are off-trail runs near La Haute-Roya – La Brigue (alt 900m/2 953ft) and Tende-Val Casterino (alt 1 500m/4 921ft).

The proximity of the Italian ski resort, Limone-Piemonte, which can be reached by rail, means that many types of snow sport are available.

MOUNTAINEERING

There is a large variety of climbing in the highlands from the Pre-Alps of Nice via the steep faces of the *baous* in the Var Valley and the Rock in Roquebrune-sur-Argens to the rock faces of the Verdon Gorge. Guided excursions in rock-climbing, mountaineering, rambling, downhill skiing and overland skiing are organised by:

- ◆ the **Club Alpin Français** 3 Place de la Poissonnerie, 83000 Toulon ☎ 04 94 62 19 16 http://clubalpin-toulon.online.fr.

- ◆ the **Club Alpin Français** 14 Avenue Mirabeau, 06000 Nice ☎ 04 93 62 59 99 www-cafnice-org

- ◆ the **Association des Guides et Accompagnateurs des Alpes Méridionales** Roquebillière ☎ 04 93 03 44 30 St-Martin-Vésubie ☎ 04 93 03 26 60 Tende ☎ 04 93 04 69 22 or 04 93 04 68 72

- ◆ **Bureau des Guides de la Côte d'Azur** 3 Rue de la Suisse, 06000 Nice ☎ 04 93 39 64 77. 06450 St-Martin-Vésubie ☎ 04 93 03 26 60 www.perso.wanadoo.fr/altitude

- ◆ **Compagnie des Guides du Mercantour** Place du Marché, 06450 St-Martin-Vésubie Tende ☎ 04 93 04 77 85

CAVING

The Var has many sites of original configuration; the Siou Blanc Plateau is a catalogue of variants of chasms and potholes which the amateur can explore. Among these is the deepest pothole in the region (350m/1 148ft). The Grotte de Mouret, near Draguignan, is useful for practice. In the Alpes-Maritimes, both the Pays Grassois and the Caussols Plateau offer many opportunities for seasoned cavers. The legendary Massif du Marguareis (northeast of Tende), the site of the exploits of the potholer Michel Siffre in the 1960s, is still a paradise for the experienced caver. This immense chalky plateau is peppered with sinkholes, with vertiginous rock faces overhanging the Italian slopes, and contains deep chasms (more than 900m/2 953ft). Information available from:

- ◆ **Comité Départemental de Spéléologie du Var** l'Hélianthe, Rue Émile-Olivier, 83000 Toulon ☎ 04 94 31 29 43

- **Comité Départemental de Spéléologie des Alpes-Maritimes**
  Boulevard Paul-Montal, bâtiment 5, l'Alsace, 06200 Nice
  ☎ 04 93 62 09 54
- Speleology divisions of the Club Alpin Français in Nice or Toulon.

WATER SPORTS

Canoeing

Some of the rivers in the Alpes-Maritimes can be explored by canoe throughout the year but the best time is in spring. In any season beware of sudden floods caused by heavy rain upstream.

The most attractive stretches of river are to be found just inside the boundaries of the Mercantour or near St-Martin-Vésubie. Shooting rapids excursions through gorges accompanied by experts are organised by the Toulon division of the Club Alpin Français. Those offering the best services are awarded the title **Point-Canoë-Nature** by the **Fédération Française de Canoë-Kayak** *(87 Quai de la Marne, 94340 Joinville-le-Pont ☎ 02 48 89 39 89. www.ffcanoe.asso.fr).*

Canyoning

The most attractive stretches of water provided by the Alpes-Maritimes for this activity, which combines rock-climbing, potholing and swimming in running water, are to be found within the Parc du Mercantour and in St-Martin-Vésubie. There are also two exceptional sites in the valley of the Haute-Roya near Saorge – La Maglia (through caves) and La Bendola (two days in the water). Canyoning is strictly forbidden in the central part of the Parc du Mercantour.

Between St-Martin-Vésubie and its confluence with the Var, the River Vésubie offers a variety of canyons – Duranus, the agreeable site at L'Imberguet, La Bollène and Gourgas, which is technically demanding.

The Estéron, an eastern tributary of the Var, provides classic stretches in exceptional settings between Roquestéron and St-Auban.

The network of rivers in the Var provides many opportunities for canyoning, with 11 authorised sites of varying difficulty suitable to all levels of competence. The Destel Gorge, between Caramy and Carcès, the lower stretches of the Jabron (downstream of Trigance) and the Pennafort Gorge are suitable for beginners. Seillans-la-Cascade, the Nartuby and the Destéou in the Maures demand greater skill.

At all times of the year there is a risk of sudden increases in the volume of water following a storm upstream and the sudden release of retained water. Canyoning trips with guides are organised by the Toulon branch of the Club Alpin Français.

Information is also available from the **Comité Départemental de Spéléologie du Var** (☎ 04 94 87 42 72) and a guide called "Clues et Canyons" by the Conseil Général des Alpes-Maritimes (**DEDD**, *service des randonnées, BP 3007, 06201 Nice Cedex 3. www.cg06.fr*) available in Tourism Offices throughout the Alpes-Maritimes.

Lakes

The largest lake in the Estérel, **Lac de St-Cassien** (430ha/1 062 acres), not only supplies electricity and water to the eastern Var and provides water for the fire-fighting aircraft but also has a nature reserve at the west end with a reed-bed where more than 150 species of over-wintering migrating seabirds have been recorded. There are facilities for wind-surfing and pedalo – tuition from the base and equipment for hire from the open-air cafés along the sometimes steep banks; motorised vessels are forbidden.

Centre Régional d'Entraînement et de Formation à l'Aviron
Lac de St-Cassien
83440 Montaurous
☎ 04 94 76 43 08

The **Lac de Carcès** (100ha/247 acres) is a reservoir formed by a dam and fed by the River Argens. There is a pleasant wooded road along the eastern bank; the opposite bank, more rural, is much used by fishermen. Canoeing in kayaks is permitted.

Game Fishing

Local and national fishing regulations apply to fishing in lakes (Carcès and St Cassien) and in rivers (Gapeau, Réal Martin, Argens, Roya, Bévéra etc). It is also advisable to join the Association de Pêche et de Pisciculture in the area in question by paying the annual fees appropriate to the form of fishing practised and then by buying a daily permit from an authorised vendor. Trout fishing is permitted from the 2nd Saturday in March to the 3rd Sunday in September; pike fishing is allowed only between 31 January and 15 April.

Fishing for common grayling in the Siagne is banned through the year. Up-to-date information available from

- **Fédération Départementale du Var**
  ☎ 04 94 69 05 66

- **Fédération Départementale des Alpes-Maritimes**
  ☎ 04 93 72 06 04

- **Conseil Supérieur de la Pêche**
  134 Avenue Malakoff, 75016 Paris
  ☎ 01 45 01 20 20, which provides a leaflet *Pêche en France*.

CYCLING AND MOUNTAIN BIKING

The diversity of terrain inland and the network of cycle tracks along the coast and in the massifs of the Estérel and the Maures are very popular with mountain bike enthusiasts. Many organisations, hotels and clubs in the region hire out this kind of bicycle and provide details of local cycle tracks. Lists of suppliers are also available from local tourist offices.

Main Railway Stations

Antibes, Bandol, Cagnes-sur-Mer, Cannes, Hyères, Juan-les-Pins, and St-Raphaël hire out various types of bicycles, which can be returned to a different station.

The regulations concerning admission to the Parc du Mercantour apply also to cyclists; details available from the Maisons du Parc and the headquarters (23 Rue d'Italie, Nice).

The **Comité Départemental du Tourisme du Var** distributes a leaflet describing more than 20 signed routes for cyclists; among the principal ones are:

- 🚲 Roof of the Var *(Toit du Var)* (70km/43mi)
- 🚲 Bauxite Road *(Route de la Bauxite)* (80km/50mi)
- 🚲 North face of the Maures *(l'Ubac des Maures)* (80km/50mi)
- 🚲 Maures chestnut woods *(Châtaigne-raies des Maures)* (90km/56mi)

One of the most famous mountain biking events in Europe is the Roc d'Azur at Ramatuelle with a height difference of nearly 200m/656ft (50km/31mi long) (🕭 *see Calendar of events*).

Comité Départemental de Cyclotourisme des Alpes-Maritimes, 22bis Rue Trachel, 06000 Nice ☎ 04 93 82 16 39 (Mr Rény Bernage)

Pushing Pedals from Sea to Sea

EuroVelo is a venture funded by the European Union and about 60 local organisations in 22 countries. Access the Web site **www.EuroVelo.org** to find out about the 12 cycling routes that will eventually trace more than 60,000km throughout Europe. Routes include Moscow to Galway, Ireland and another from northern Norway to the tip of Sicily. The Mediterranean route will trace the coastline from Cadiz, Spain to Athens, via the Rench Riviera and Monaco.

Comité Départemental de Cyclotourisme du Var, L'Hélianthe, Rue Émile-Ollivier, 83000 Toulon, ☎ 04 94 36 04 09. http://perso.wanadoo. fr/codep.var

Fédération Française de Cyclotourisme, 12 Rue Louis-Bertrand, 94207 Ivry-sur-Seine Cedex, ☎ 01 56 20 88 87. www.ffct.org

AERIAL SPORTS

Hang-gliding, parachuting and ultra-light craft

There are about 20 suitable sites for parachuting, hang-gliding *(vol libre)* and ultra-light craft *(planeur ultra léger motorisé)*.

- **Comité Départemental de Vol Libre Varois,** Domaine de la Limatte, 83870 Signes ☎ 04 94 90 86 13

- **Fédération Française de Vol Libre,** 4 Rue de Suisse, 06000 Nice ☎ 04 93 88 62 89. www.ffvl.fr

- **Fédération Française de Planeur Ultra-Léger Motorisé,** 96bis Rue Marc-Sangnier, 94700 Maisons-Alfort ☎ 05 49 81 74 43. www. ffplum.com

Gliding

The main gliding centre, which is run by the **Association Aéronautique Provence-Côte d'Azur,** is near Fayence where aerological conditions are exceptional. It has become the leading gliding centre in Europe and has contributed to the rapid development of glider aerobatics. Each year champions from all over the world demonstrate their skill at the *Open de France de Planeur*.

- **Association aéronautique Provence-Côte d'Azur**
  83440 Fayence ☎ 04 94 76 00 68. www.aapca.net

Air trips

It is possible to fly over part of the Riviera such as St-Tropez Bay, the Estérel, the Îles de Lérins, Monaco and the Verdon Gorge.
 For details of timetables and fares contact the following companies, all based at the international airport of Cannes-Mandelieu, 06150 Cannes-la-Bocca

◆ **Compagnie Air Nice**
☏ 04 93 90 40 26
Cannes-Mandelieu Airport, 06150 Cannes la Bocca

◆ **Toulon-Hyères Airport**
☏ 04 94 22 81 60.

Short trips over the Riviera by **helicopter** are available from

◆ **Héli-Air-Monaco**
Monaco-Fontvieille heliport
☏ 00 377 92 05 00 50.

Family Fun

For a change from the beach, on cloudy days or when the *mistral* is blowing, there are many attractions all along the Riviera – leisure pools, animal parks and miniature collections.

LEISURE POOLS

▧ **Parc Nautique Niagara**
Route du Canadel, 83310 La Môle
☏ 04 94 49 58 87.
www.parcniagara.com

▧ **Aquasplash**
RN7, 06600 Antibes
☏ 04 93 33 49 49
www.marineland.fr

▧ **Aquatica**
RN98, 83600 Fréjus
☏ 04 53 58 58
www.parc-aquatica.com

▧ **Aqualand**
559 Chemin Départemental, 83270 St-Cyr-sur-Mer
☏ 04 94 32 09 09

ANIMAL PARKS

◆ **Sanary-Bandol** – Zoo

◆ **Toulon** – Zoo du Mont-Faron

◆ **La Londe-les-Maures** – Jardin d'Oiseaux Tropicaux (◔ *HYÈRES*)

◆ **Gonfaron** – Village des Tortues (◔ *Massif des MAURES*)

◆ **Fréjus** – Zoo

◆ **Antibes** – La Jungle des Papillons, La Petite Ferme, le Golf Adventureland and Marineland

◆ **St-Jean-Cap-Ferrat** – Chimpanzee shows at the Zoo

◆ **Monaco** – Jardin Animalier

Calendar of Events

FÊTES, FESTIVALS & SPORTING EVENTS

January

Barjols — Festival of St Marcel

Valbonne — Grape and Olive Festival (last weekend).

Monaco — International Circus Festival

Monaco and hinterlands — Monte-Carlo Rally (end of the month)

27 JANUARY

Monaco (La Condamine) — Festival of St Devota

FEBRUARY

Menton — Lemon Festival

Villefranche-sur-Mer — Flowered Naval Parade

Bormes-les-Mimosas — Mimosa Procession/Croso (third Sunday)

TWO WEEKS AROUND SHROVE TUESDAY (MARDI GRAS)

Nice — Carnival and Flower Festival *(Batailles de Fleurs). www. nicecarnaval.com.*

EVENING OF GOOD FRIDAY

Roquebrune-Cap-Martin — Procession of the Entombment of Christ

S. Sauvignier/ MICHELIN

EASTER SUNDAY AND MONDAY

Vence — Provençal Folklore Festival

THIRD SUNDAY AFTER EASTER

Fréjus — St Francis' Procession
(*Bravade St-François*)

MARCH

Golfe-Juan — Reenactment of Napoléon's landing (first weekend)

Nice (Cimiez) — Feast of the Gourds (with dried and painted gourds) (end of the month)

Nice — Arrival of the Paris-Nice Cycling Race

APRIL

Mouans-Sartoux — Honey Festival (last Sunday)

Monaco — Printemps des arts. ☎ (00377) 93 15 85 15. (through May)

Monaco, Nice — International Tennis Tournament (one week)

MID-APRIL TO MID-MAY

Monaco — Spring Arts Festival

MAY

Cannes — International Film Festival ☎ 05 45 61 66 00 (reserved for professionals)

Nice (Cimiez) — May Folk Festival (weekends)

Grasse — Rose Festival (penultimate weekend)

Monaco — Formula One Grand Prix

LATE MAY TO MID-JULY

Toulon — Music Festival and International Music Competition (wind instruments)

JUNE

St-Tropez — Spanish Procession (Bravades) (15th)

St-Tropez — Votive Fishermen's Festival (29th)

LATE JUNE TO LATE SEPTEMBER

Peille — Musical Evenings ☎ 04 93 79 90 32

Cagnes-sur-Mer — International Art Festival

EARLY JULY TO LATE SEPTEMBER (EVEN YEARS)

Vallauris — Biennial International Festival of Ceramic Art

JULY

Cannes (Le Suquet) — Musical evenings

Cap d'Antibes (La Garoupe) — Seamen's Festival

Hyères — Festival of Jazz and Lyrical Song

Vence — Classical Music Festival: ☎ 04 93 58 78 75

Villefranche-sur-Mer — Feast of St Peter, fishermen's festival (first weekend)

Villeneuve-Loubet — Shingle Castle Competition (thirdSunday)

Tende — Feast of St Eligius, patron saint of muleteers (second Sunday)

FIRST FORTNIGHT IN JULY

Vallées de la Roya et de la Bévéra — Les Baroquiales festival of baroque art, ☎ 04 93 04 12 55. www.lesbaroquiales.org

SECOND FORTNIGHT IN JULY

Juan-les-Pins-Antibes — World Jazz Festival

Ramatuelle — Classical Music Festival ☎ 04 98 12 64 00

Toulon — Jazz Festival ☎ 04 94 09 71 00.

Nice (Cimiez: Amphitheatre) — Jazz in Nice: ☎ 04 93 87 16 28

Îles des Embiez — Les Voix du Gaou: salsa, rock, soul, reggae, raï, etc.

Abbaye du Thoronet — Medievalmusic festival ☎ 04 93 52 26 38.

JULY AND AUGUST

Cannes — American Festival Sea Theatre: Jazz concerts, variety shows and theatre

St-Tropez — Music Festival (evenings)

Cotignac — La Falaise Theatre Festival

AUGUST

Vallauris — Pottery Festival (13th)

Entrecasteaux — Chamber Music Festival: ☎ 04 94 04 44 83

Grimaud — Wool Festival (Ascension Day)

Menton — Chamber Music Festival about 13 concerts are held in front of the Church of St-Michel)

Grasse — Jasmine Festival (first weekend)

Fréjus — Grape Festival (first Sunday) ☎ 04 94 51 83 83.

Roquebrune-Cap-Martin — Passion Procession through the old village streets (5th)

Bendor — Fishermen's Festival (15th)

Barjols — Leatherwork Fair (17-18th)

FIRST FORTNIGHT IN AUGUST

Abbaye du Thoronet — Poetry Festival

Ramatuelle — Theatre Festival ☎ 04 94 79 20 50

SEPTEMBER

Cannes — Royal Regattas (last week)

Peille — Folk Festival *Festin des Baguettes* in honour of a young dowser-shepherd, who during a drought found water with a divining rod made from an olive branch (first weekend)

Monaco — Vintage Car Rally (third weekend)

Fayence — Aïoli Festival (beginning of the month). ☎ 04 94 76 20 08.

Many villages — Michaelmas Celebrations (29th)

Throughout France — Heritage Days (third weekend)

OCTOBER

Gonfaron — Chestnut Festival ☎ 04 94 78 30 05.

Ollioules — Olive Festival (first weekend)

Collobrières — Chestnut Festival (last three Sundays) ☎ 04 94 48 08 00.

Roquebrune-sur-Argens — Honey Festival (first weekend)

La Garde-Freinet — Chestnut Festival (last two Sundays)

Vence — Folk festival of music, dancing (beginning of the month)

NOVEMBER

Monaco — Monaco's National Day (19th)

Taradeau — New wine festival (third Sunday)

DECEMBER

Bandol — Wine Festival (first Sunday) ☎ 04 94 90 29 59.

Lucéram — The Shepherds' Christmas Offering and Provençal Mass ☎ 04 93 79 46 50

Vallée de la Roya — Santon Festival (Nativity Scenes) ☎ 04 93 04 92 05.

Cannes — International Dance Festival

Shopping

Most of the larger shops are open Mondays to Saturdays from 9am to 6.30 or 7.30pm. Smaller, individual shops may close during the lunch hour. Food shops – grocers, wine merchants and bakeries – are generally open from 7am to 6.30 or 7.30pm; some open on Sunday mornings. Many food shops close between noon and 2pm and on Mondays. Bakery and pastry shops sometimes close on Wednesdays. Hypermarkets usually open until 9pm or later.

Provencal Markets	
Aups	Wednesdays, Saturdays
Bargemon	Thursdays
Le Beausset	Fridays (fair)
Bormes-les-Mimosas	Wednesdays
Brignoles	Saturdays
Callas	Tuesdays, Saturdays
Cogolin	Wednesdays, Saturdays (fair)
La Croix-Valmer	Sundays
Draguignan	Wednesdays, Saturdays
Fayence	Tuesdays, Thursdays (fair)
Fréjus	Wednesdays, Saturdays (fair)
La Garde	Tuesdays, Saturdays (fair)
Grimaud	Thursdays (fair)
Hyères	Tuesdays, Thursdays (fair)
Le Lavandou	Thursdays
Lorgues	Tuesdays
Le Luc	Fridays
Ramatuelle	Thursdays, Sundays (fair)
St-Tropez	Tuesdays, Saturdays (fair)
Ste-Maxime	Thursdays (fair)
Toulon	daily
Tourtour	Tuesdays, Saturdays
Trans-en-Provence	Sundays
Villecroze	Thursdays (fair)

A list of traditional craft markets, where the products of the Var region are sold, is published annually by the **Chambre des Métiers**, BP 69 – 83402 Hyères Cedex ☎ 04 94 21 00 57.

Santon Fairs in the Var

Clay figurines *(santons)* became popular in Provence at the time of the French Revolution, when many churches were officially closed. A craftsman in Marseille decided to market these figurines so that people could set up nativity scenes at home. The term derives from the Provençal word *santoun*, meaning "little saint". Originally, these statuettes were confined to religious or biblical themes but over the years they came to represent traditional aspects of the region (arts and crafts, folklore, animals).

People travelling to the USA cannot import plant products or fresh food, including fruit, cheeses and nuts. It is acceptable to carry tinned products or preserves.

RECOVERING THE VALUE ADDED TAX

There is a Value Added Tax in France (TVA) of 19.6% on almost every purchase (some foods and books are subject to a lower rate). However, non-European visitors who spend more than 175€ in any one participating store can get the VAT amount refunded. Usually, you fill out a form at the store, showing your passport. Upon leaving the country, you submit all forms to customs for approval (they may want to see the goods, so if possible don't pack them in checked luggage). The refund is usually paid directly into your bank or credit card account, or it can be sent by mail. Big department stores that cater to tourists provide special services to help you; be sure to mention that you plan to seek a refund before you pay for goods (no refund is possible for tax on services). If you are visiting two or more countries within the European Union, you submit the forms only on departure from the last EU country. The refund is worthwhile for those visitors who would like to buy fashion wear, furniture or other fairly expensive items, but remember, the minimum amount must be spent in a single shop (though not necessarily on a single day).

CRAFTS AND SOUVENIRS

In high season many villages and resorts organise courses focusing on local arts and crafts – painting on porcelain in Le Cannet, weaving and woodwork in the Cannes district and regional cuisine in St-Martin-Vésubie. Certain villages are designated "Ville et Métiers d'Art" such as Biot, Cagnes-sur-Mer, Fréjus, Ollioules, and Vallauris. For more information on these call ☎ 01 48 88 26 56 or www.vma.asso.fr.

PROVENCAL MARKETS

Provençal markets, fragrant with thyme, tarragon, lavender and garlic, are part of the traditional image of the South of France.

As a rule, during the summer season, stalls selling fruit and vegetables and craftwork can be found under the plane trees of even the smallest village.

They typically open at about 8am or 9am, and finish at lunch or about 1pm. The most picturesque and lively markets of the Var and the days on which they are held are listed below.

REGIONAL SPECIALITIES

The main areas where craftwork and local produce can be bought by visitors from the producers are shown on the map – Spécialités et Vignobles (see p 84).

Further information on specialist products:

Sweets

Confiserie des Gorges du Loup, Le Pont-du-Loup, 06140 Tourrettes-sur-Loup ☎ 04 93 59 32 91. Also find nougat in Roquebrune-sur-Argens and honey in Bandol, Cotignac, or the Massif du Tanneron.

Marrons glacés and preserved chestnuts

Nouvelle Confiserie Azuréenne, Boulevard Koenig, Collobrières ☎ 04 94 48 07 20.

Crystallised fruit

J.L. Gallo/ MICHELIN

Glassware

Verrerie de Biot in Biot where it is possible to watch master glassblowers at work.

Perfume

Scents for the home or body are made in Grasse, Eze and Gourdon.

Ceramics

Biot, Vallauris, and Salernes (& *see AUPS*) specialize in pottery and ceramics.

Liqueur de Lérina

This is made on the Îles de Lérins, by the monks of the Abbaye St-Honorat.

Leather

The *sandale tropézienne* is the same model that has been made by the same company since 1927 (& *see SAINT-TROPEZ*).

WINE TASTING

Wine Cooperative Cellars

The **Côte de Provence wine road** winds its way through the vineyards; the wine cellars which are open for tasting are advertised on the roadside signs (look for "dégustation"). To organise tours and tastings of particular wines, contact these organisations:

Vins de Bandol
La Maison des Vins du Bandol, 22 allée Alfred-Vivien, 83150 Bandol, ☎ *04 94 29 45 03. www.vins-de-bandol.com.*

Coteaux varois
La Maison des Vins Coteaux Varois, inside the Abbaye Royale de la Celle. 83170 La Celle, ☎ *04 94 69 33 18.*
The Coteaux Varois AOC is spread out over 28 communes around Brignoles, and Sainte-Baume to Bessillons.

Côtes-de-Provence
La Maison des vins des Côtes de Provence, RN 7, 83460 Les Arcs-sur-Argens, ☎ *04 94 99 50 20. www.cotes-de-provence.com.*
This is the most popular wine of the Provence-Alpes-Côte d'Azur region. There are three vineyards on Île de Porquerolles producing an AOC (*Appellation d'Origine Contrôlée*) Côte de Provence wine. All offer wine tasting sessions:

Domaine de l'Île, the oldest

Domaine Perzinsky

Domaine Courtade

Summer Aïoli Festivals in the Var (& see p 83)	
8-11 July	Châteauvieux
8 August	Mazaugues
9 August	Entrecasteaux (one of the largest)
12 to 15 August	La Motte-du-Var
12 to 15 August	La Celle
12 to 16 August	Collobrières
14 to 16 August	Ampus
20 to 22 August	Solliès-Ville
26 to 28 August	Fayence

(Reserve and pay entrance fees at the local tourist office.)

Other Côte de Provence wines are made in Les Arcs, Draguignan (organic wine), Fréjus, Gassin (& *see RAMATUELLE*), Le Luc (organic wine), and Lorgues. This Maison des Vins also give classes on wine tasting.

Vins de Bellet
Syndicat des vignerons de Bellet, 06200 St-Roman-de-Bellet, ☎ *04 93 37 81 57. www.vinsdebellet.com.*
Vin de Bellet is produced on the hillsides behind Nice around St-Romain-de-Bellet; it is on sale in the cellars which are open to the public; further information from the Nice tourist office.

Domaine de Lauzade
Route de Toulon, 83340 Le Luc, ☎ *04 94 60 72 51. www.lauzade.com.*
Tastings of Provençal wines every day except Saturday afternoon and Sunday.

La Cave du Moulin
50 avenue Mallet, 06250 Mougins, ☎ *04 92 92 06 88.*
Oenologie courses and wine tasting.

COOKING CLASSES

The Comité Régional du Tourisme Provence-Côte d'Azur (*www.crt-paca.fr*) provides information on cooking classes throughout the region, and publishes an annual brochure on local gastronomy, "Terre de saveurs". Some examples:

École de Cuisine du Moulin de Mougins
Restaurant l'Amandier, place du Cdt-Lamy, Mougins, ☎ *04 93 75 35 70.*
Classes of 2.5hr for beginners.

Demonstration of two dishes followed by a tasting.

🍲 **La Route des Saveurs**
N 202, La Manda, 06670 Colomars,
☎ *04 93 08 76 31.*
www.canton-de-levens.com.

L'Association touristique du Canton de Levens invites you to visit their "Canton aux 10 sourires" (Canton of Ten Smiles) through its themed tours of olive mills, Bellet vineyards, chocolate makers, as well as cooking classes based on traditional Niçois cuisine.

Sightseeing

The single-track main railway line between Nice and Cuneo in Italy crosses the old County of Nice passing through Peille, L'Escarène, Sospel, Breil-sur-Roya, Fontan-Saorge, St-Dalmas-de-Tende, Tende, Vievola and finally Limone in Italy. The track was built from 1920 onwards and incorporates some spectacular engineering feats as it twists and turns through the tortuous mountain landscapes, sometimes even spiralling to change level. The train affords wonderful views that are not always visible from the road, particularly between L'Escarène and Sospel and between Breil and Tende along the rugged gorges of the River Roya. The line is 119km/74mi long; over a stretch of 85km/53mi it rises from sea-level to 1 279m/4 196ft at the entrance to the tunnel bored through Col de Tende. The French section of the line suffered extensive damage during the Second World War and repair work was not completed until 1980. On the Italian side of the border, the line descends less steeply down to Cuneo through the charming Vermegnagna Valley.

Scarassoui Viaduct, Nice-Cuneo railway

M. Braun

The frequent service enables skiers to reach the Massif du Mercantour and spend the day skiing in the Italian winter sports resort of Limone-Piemonte.

There are at least four daily return services to and from Nice-Ville station. In Breil-sur-Roya the line rejoins the main line running between Ventimiglia and Cuneo, which has better interconnections with the Italian train network; for timetable information ☎ 04 93 87 50 50.

PROVENÇAL RAILWAY

The famous pine-cone train *(Train des Pignes)* is named after the pine cones which were used as fuel to stoke the engines. It runs between Nice and Digne-les-Bains (150km/93mi) passing through Puget-Théniers, Entrevaux, Annot, St-André-les-Alpes. The single track was constructed from 1890 to 1911 and comprises 60 remarkable feats of engineering – metal bridges, viaducts, tunnels (one of which is 3.5km/2.3mi long). It is a relic of a vast regional network which early in the 20C served the whole inland area from Toulon to Draguignan. The journey, 2hr by train, 3hr by omnibus, passes through five valleys, offering fine views of the landscape and perched villages which are often difficult to reach by car. All year round it is possible to take the train to Lac de Castillon, the Verdon Gorges and the winter sports stations in the Alpes-Maritimes département. From Plan-du-Var there is a service to the walking country in the Vésubie Valley. In summer the Alpazur service runs from Nice as far as Grenoble and there is a tourist steam train on the Puget-Théniers section. There are wayside halts at which walkers can leave or rejoin the train at the beginning and end of a day's hike. Chemins de Fer de Provence, Gare du Sud, 4 Rue Alfred-Binet, 06000 Nice ☎ 04 97 03 80 80. www.trainprovence.com. Other addresse : Station/Gare, Avenue P.-Sémard, 04000 Digne-les-Bains, ☎ 04 92 31 01 58.

Books and Films

BOOKS

Voices in the Garden, by Dirk Bogarde (first published by Chatto & Windus in 1981, reprinted by Triad Paperbacks in 1982). The British actor, who resided in Grasse for many years during the latter part of his life, wrote this fascinating novel about a middle-aged couple living on the Riviera, whose life is irrevocably changed after meeting a young English tourist and his girlfriend and offering them hospitality in their sumptuous villa. The book was brilliantly adapted to the screen with Anouk Aimée starring in the lead role.

Tender is the Night, by F Scott Fitzgerald (first published in 1934, reprinted by Scribner, NY, in 1995) is a classic story of Americans adrift on the French Riviera. Inspired by the Boston art collectors Gerald and Sara Murphy, as well as by his own wife, Zelda, Fitzgerald's book describes the slow demise of Dick Diver, a psychiatrist who marries his patient Nicole. The wealthy couple pay a steep emotional price to support many friends and hangers-on, revealing the human frailties of both privileged and ordinary people.

The Garden of Eden, by Fitzgerald's contemporary, Ernest Hemingway, was unfinished by the author when he died, and first published in 1986 (Scribner). Some readers find the novel disturbingly unlike his other works, and others find it richer for its "imperfections". The story unfolds on the Riviera and involves a young writer, his glamorous wife, and the pressures of a destructive love triangle.

The Rock Pool, by Cyril Connolly (reprinted in 1996 by Persea Books) is the author's only novel. The Englishman examined the decadent side of the expatriate community in Juan-les-Pins and Antibes; it was published in Paris in 1936 after British publishers rejected it on grounds of obscenity.

Maigret on the Riviera (Harcourt, Brace 1988) may be the perfect beach book, by Georges Simenon and starring, of course, Inspector Jules Maigret. Only mildly distracted by the balmy weather and lush vegetation, the famous, pipe-smoking detective must discover how an inoffensive, down-at-the-heels Australian came to be murdered in this idyllic setting.

Bonjour Tristesse (Hello Sadness), by Françoise Sagan, has become a classic of French literature. The French version is suitable for readers with an intermediate language level and high school students. First published in 1954, it has been read and loved by many young people in France since then. The heroine, Cécile, is a precocious 17-year-old (the author's age when she wrote the story), who grapples with her widowed father's second marriage and her own coming-of-age on the Esterel Coast.

Once Upon a Time: The Story of Princess Grace, Prince Rainier and Their Family (J. Randy Taraborrelli) is a recent (2003) biography of the Monégasque Royal family, which starts with the history of the principality to the life of Grace Kelly and, finally, Monaco today. A great introduction into the lives of this tragedy-ridden royal family.

Artists and their Museums on the Riviera (Barbara Freed, Alan Halpern; Harry Abrams, 1998) is a useful paperback guide for exploring the art museums in the region. It places the artists and their work in context.

Art-Sites France: Contemporary Art & Architecture Handbook (Sidra Stich; Artsites Press, San Fransisco, 1999). This new series is invaluable for those interested in contemporary artwork. The book covers the whole of France with detailed descriptions of galleries, museums, film and video centres, specialised bookstores, sculpture parks and many architectural sites. This well-organised, well-written book includes useful maps.

France in the New Century is by an expert on things continental, John Ardagh (Viking, 1999). The author has chronicled events and cultural changes in France for more than 20 years. The book offers excellent explanations of how the country's regions, cities and départements are run, and paints a portrait of the nation from the Mitterand years up to the present.

The French, by Theodore Zeldin (Kodansha International, reprinted 1996) was first published in 1984. Readers continue to admire its jocular (yet thoughtful) portrayal of the present-day Gauls, packed with funny advice on how to laugh at their jokes, love their grandmothers and more; it includes cartoons, interviews, charts and footnotes.

FILMS

Because of the high number and diversity of its natural sites and the quality of the light, the whole of the Riviera seems to have been predestined to become a backdrop for all the varied scenarios of film-makers. Here are the main locations which have featured in the history of the cinema.

The steep inlets of the south coast of the Île de Porquerolles enabled Jean-Paul Belmondo to demonstrate his skills in *Pierrot le Fou*. Several districts of Hyères can be spotted in *Le Passager de la Pluie* by René Clément, starring Marlène Jobert, as well as in *Vivement Dimanche!* by François Truffaut.

Roger Vadim launched both Brigitte Bardot and **St-Tropez** with his provocative *And God Created Woman* (1956). The resort is renowned in the world of the cinema and has provided the setting for many location shots – *The Collector* (1967) by Eric Rohmer, *La Cage aux Folles* (1978) by Édouard Molinaro and, of course, the celebrated comic series *Le Gendarme de St-Tropez* by Jean Girault with Louis de Funès, six episodes of which were filmed between 1964 and 1982.

The old port in Cannes still contains the galleon *Neptune* on which Roman Polanski's *Pirates* was set in 1986; admirers of *Mélodie en Sous-Sol* by Henri Verneuil will be nostalgic at the sight of the Palm Beach Casino.

The **Studios de la Victorine** in **Nice** have been closely involved in the development of cinema on the Riviera (& *see NICE)*. In 1929 *À Propos de Nice* by **Jean Vigo** focused on the contrast between holidaymakers loafing around on the beach and the working-class districts.

La Nuit Àméricaine directed by François Truffaut, partly filmed at the Studios de la Victorine, used several locations on the coast – the Atlantic Hotel in Nice, the Vésubie Valley and the Nice hinterland.

The location shots for *Les Visiteurs du Soir* were filmed in Tourrettes-sur-Loup by Marcel Carné in 1942. Villefranche-sur-Mer and its picturesque *Rue Obscure* were used by Jean Cocteau in *The Testament of Orpheus* (1960). The medieval setting of Sospel was ideal for cloak-and-dagger scenes in *The Man in the Iron Mask* (1962) by Henri

Decoin with Jean Marais and, more recently, in *Un sac de Billes* by Jacques Doillon.

Beginning with the 1913 silent comedy, *Max in Monaco*, featuring Max Linder, the Principality has been popular with film-makers looking for exotic locations. The jet set clientele of the Monte-Carlo Casino has inspired several directors, namely Ernst Lubitsch who made *Monte-Carlo* with Jeanette MacDonald in 1930.

The impressive drops of the Grande Corniche provided a marvellous backdrop for *To Catch a Thief* (1955), a thriller by Alfred Hitchcock with Cary Grant and Grace Kelly; this film also provides an unintended record of the urban development of the Principality. The comic adventures of the *Love Bug* throughout the world had to include an episode in Monaco – *Herbie Goes to Monte Carlo* (1977) by Vincent McEveety, with Dean Jones.

The film *Le Fils Préféré* by Nicole Garcia (1994) with Gerard Lanvin makes use of the natural setting of Nice, Menton and Grasse.

Provençal Cinema

Local writers – Jean Aicard, Marcel Pagnol, etc – and famous southern comedians are among those involved in the cinema who have drawn on local tradition. The location shots for *La Femme du Boulanger* (1938) by Pagnol were filmed in Le Castellet.

Together with Pagnol, film-maker André Hugon, who made the first French talking film, and who was fond of the Mediterranean coast, portrayed typical Provençal characters – *Maurin des Maures* (1932), *L'Illustre Maurin* and *Gaspard de Besse*.

The colorful pre-war setting of **Toulon** has made a contribution to Provençal cinema – *César* (1936) by Marcel Pagnol with the local film actor **Raimu** (& *see COGOLIN*), *L'Étrange Monsieur Victor* (1937) by Jean Grémillon, also with Raimu, and *Fleur d'Amour* (1927) by Maurice Vandal, which portrays the formerly "hot" district of "Chicago". Other works made in the Var – *Les Démons de l'Aube* (1945) by Yves Allégret about the Provençal landings and *En Haut des Marches* (1982) by Paul Vecchiali with Danielle Darrieux, the behind-the-scenes story of historical events in Toulon.

BASIC INFORMATION

Electricity

The electric current is 220 volts. Circular two-pin plugs are the rule. Adapters should be bought before you leave home; they are on sale in most airports.

Public Holidays

Museums and other monuments may be closed or may vary their hours of admission on the following public holidays:
National museums and art galleries are closed on Tuesdays; municipal museums are generally closed on Mondays. In addition to the usual school holidays at Christmas and in the spring and summer, there are long mid-term breaks (10 days to a fortnight) in February and early November.

1 January	New Year's Day (Jour de l'An)
	Easter Day and Easter Monday (Pâques)
1 May	May Day (Fête du Travail)
8 May	VE Day (Fête de la Libération)
Thurs 40 days after Easter	Ascension Day (Ascension)
7th Sun-Mon after Easter	Whit Sunday and Monday (Pentecôte)
14 July	France's National Day (Fête de la Bastille)
15 August	Assumption (Assomption)
1 November	All Saint's Day (Toussaint)
11 November	Armistice Day (Fête de la Victoire)
25 December	Christmas Day (Noël)

Mail

Main post offices open Monday to Friday 8am to 7pm, Saturday 8am to noon. Smaller branch post offices generally close at lunchtime between noon and 2pm and at 4pm.
Postage via air mail:

✉ UK: letter (20g) 0.55€

✉ North America: letter (20g) 0.90€

✉ Australia and NZ: letter (20g) 0.90€

Stamps are also available from newsagents and bureaux de tabac. Stamp collectors should ask for timbres de collection in any post office.

Metric System

France operates on the metric system. Some equivalents:

    1 gram = 0.04 ounces
    1 metre = 1.09 yards
    1 kilogram = 2.20 pounds
    1 kilometre = 0.62 miles
    1 litre = 1.06 quarts

Money

CURRENCY

There are no restrictions on the amount of currency visitors can take into France. Visitors carrying a lot of cash are advised to complete a currency declaration form on arrival, because there are restrictions on currency export.

Notes and coins

Since January 2002, the **euro** is the official currency of France and other participating EU Member Sates. One euro is divided into 100 cents, or *centimes*. Franc notes can be exchanged only at the Banque de France (until 2012).

Banks

Banks are open from 9am to noon and 2pm to 4pm and branches are closed either on Monday or Saturday. Banks close early on the day before a bank holiday. A passport is necessary as identification when cashing travellers' cheques in banks. Commission charges vary and hotels usually charge more than banks for cashing cheques. One of the most economical ways to use your money in France is by using **ATM/cash machines** to get cash directly from your bank account or to use your credit cards to get cash advances. Be sure to remember your 4-digit PIN, you will need it to use cash dispensers and to pay with your card in most shops, restaurants, etc. ATM code pads are numeric; use a telephone pad to translate a letter code into numbers. Visa is the most widely accepted credit card, followed by MasterCard; other cards (Diners Club, Plus, Cirrus) are also accepted in most cash machines. American Express is more often accepted in premium establishments. Most places post signs indicating the cards they accept; if you don't see such a sign, and want to pay with a card, ask before ordering or making a selection.

Conversion Tables

Weights and measures

1 kilogram (kg)	2.2 pounds (lb)	2.2 pounds	
1 metric ton (tn)	1.1 tons	1.1 tons	

to convert kilograms to pounds, multiply by 2.2

1 litre (l)	2.1 pints (pt)	1.8 pints
1 litre	0.3 gallon (gal)	0.2 gallon

to convert litres to gallons, multiply by 0.26 (US) or 0.22 (UK)

1 hectare (ha)	2.5 acres	2.5 acres
1 square kilometre (km²)	0.4 square miles (sq mi)	0.4 square miles

to convert hectares to acres, multiply by 2.4

1 centimetre (cm)	0.4 inches (in)	0.4 inches
1 metre (m)	3.3 feet (ft) - 39.4 inches - 1.1 yards (yd)	
1 kilometre (km)	0.6 miles (mi)	0.6 miles

to convert metres to feet, multiply by 3.28, kilometres to miles, multiply by 0.6

Clothing

Women								Men
	35	4	2½		40	7½	7	
	36	5	3½		41	8½	8	
	37	6	4½		42	9½	9	
Shoes	38	7	5½		43	10½	10	**Shoes**
	39	8	6½		44	11½	11	
	40	9	7½		45	12½	12	
	41	10	8½		46	13½	13	
	36	6	8		46	36	36	
	38	8	10		48	38	38	
Dresses &	40	10	12		50	40	40	**Suits**
suits	42	12	14		52	42	42	
	44	14	16		54	44	44	
	46	16	18		56	46	46	
	36	30	8		37	14½	14½	
	38	32	10		38	15	15	
Blouses &	40	34	12		39	15½	15½	**Shirts**
sweaters	42	36	14		40	15¾	15¾	
	44	38	16		41	16	16	
	46	40	18		42	16½	16½	

Sizes often vary depending on the designer. These equivalents are given for guidance only.

Speed

kph	10	30	50	70	80	90	100	110	120	130
mph	6	19	31	43	50	56	62	68	75	81

Temperature

Celsius (°C)	0°	5°	10°	15°	20°	25°	30°	40°	60°	80°	100°
Fahrenheit (°F)	32°	41°	50°	59°	68°	77°	86°	104°	140°	176°	212°

To convert Celsius into Fahrenheit, multiply °C by 9, divide by 5, and add 32.
To convert Fahrenheit into Celsius, subtract 32 from °F, multiply by 5, and divide by 9.

Cards are widely accepted in shops, hypermarkets, hotels and restaurants, at tollbooths and in petrol stations. If your card is lost or stolen in France, call one of the following 24-hour hotlines:

American Express ☎ 01 47 77 70 00
Visa ☎ 08 36 69 08 80
MasterCard/Eurocard ☎ 01 45 67 84 84
Diners Club ☎ 01 49 06 17 50

You must report any loss or theft of credit cards or travellers' cheques to the local police who will issue you with a certificate (useful proof to show the issuing company).

Tipping

Since a service charge is automatically included in the price of meals and accommodation in France, any additional tipping is up to the visitor, generally small change, and generally not more than 5%. Taxi drivers and hairdressers are usually tipped 10-15%. As a rule, prices for hotels and restaurants as well as for other goods and services are significantly less expensive in the French regions than in Paris.

Here are a few indicative prices (in euros; one euro = 6.55 French francs), based on surveys conducted by French authorities between 1999 and 2000.

Restaurants usually charge for meals in two ways: a *forfait* or *menu*, that is a fixed price menu with two to three courses, sometimes a small pitcher of wine, all for a set price, or *à la carte*, the more expensive way, with each course ordered separately.

Cafés have very different prices, depending on where they are located. The price of a drink or a coffee is cheaper if you stand at the counter (*comptoir*) than if you sit down (*salle*) and sometimes it is even more expensive if you sit outdoors (*terrace*). In some big cities, prices go up after 10pm in the evening.

DISCOUNTS

Significant discounts are available for senior citizens, students, under 25-year-olds, teachers, and groups for public transportation, museums and monuments and some leisure activities such as movies (at certain times of day). Bring student or senior cards with you, and bring along some extra passport-size photos for discount travel cards.

The **International Student Travel Conference** (www.istc.org), global administrator of the International Student and Teacher Identity Cards, is an association of student travel organisations around the world. ISTC members collectively negotiate benefits with airlines, governments and providers of other goods and services for the student and teacher community, both in their own country and around the world. The non-profit association sells international ID cards for students, youngsters under the age of 25 and teachers (who may get discounts on museum entrances, for example). The ISTC is also active in a network of international education and work exchange programes. The coorporate headquarters address is Herengracht 479, 1017 BS Amsterdam, The Netherlands ☎ 31 20 421 28 00; Fax 31 20 421 28 10.

🕭 *See the section below on travelling by rail in France for discounts on transportation.*

> ### 🖼 Museum Passes 🖼
>
> The Comité Régional du Tourisme Riviera Côte d'Azur has three different museum passes available: City of Nice Pass (municipal museums), Museums of Menton pass (eight sights in and around Menton), and the French Riviera Museum Pass, which offers unlimited free priority access to museums, monuments, gardens on the Riviera from Fréjus to Menton. For more information contact any of the Tourism Offices within the region, or visit **www.guideriviera.com**.

Telephone

Public Telephones

Most public phones in France use pre-paid phone cards *(télécartes)*, rather than coins. Some telephone booths accept credit cards (Visa, Mastercard/Eurocard). Phone cards (50 or 120 units) can be bought in post offices, branches of France Télécom, *bureaux de tabac* (cafés that sell cigarettes) and newsagents and can be used to make calls in France and abroad. Calls can be received at phone boxes where the blue bell sign is shown; the phone will not ring, so keep your eye on the little message screen.

National Calls

French telephone numbers have 10 digits. Paris and Paris region numbers begin with 01; 02 in northwest France; 03 in northeast France; 04 in southeast France and Corsica; 05 in southwest France.

International Calls

To call France from abroad, dial the country code (33) + 9-digit number (omit the initial 0). When calling abroad from France dial 00, then dial the country code followed by the area code and number of your correspondent.

International Dialling Codes (00 + code)			
Australia	☎ 61	New Zealand	☎ 64
Canada	☎ 1	United Kingdom	☎ 44
Eire	☎ 353	United States	☎ 1

International Information:
US/Canada: ☎ 00 33 12 11
International operator:
☎ 00 33 12 + country code
Local directory assistance: 12

Cellular Phones

To use your personal calling card	
AT&T	☎ 0-800 99 00 11
Sprint	☎ 0-800 99 00 87
MCI	☎ 0-800 99 00 19
Canada Direct	☎ 0-800 99 00 16

Cellular phone numbers in France begin with 06. French networks include SFR, Bouygues, and Orange. *Mobicartes* are pre-paid phone cards that fit into mobile units. Cell phone rentals (delivery or airport pickup provided):

The Cell Phone Cie
☎ 0 800 747 100
E-mail: info@thecellphonecie.com

Emergency numbers	
Police:	17
SAMU (Paramedics):	15
Fire (Pompiers):	18

Rentacell Monaco
E-mail: info@rentacell.mc

Time

France is 1hr ahead of Greenwich Mean Time (GMT).

When it is **noon in France**, it is	
3am	in Los Angeles
6am	in New York
11am	in Dublin
11am	in London
7pm	in Perth
9pm	in Sydney
11pm	in Auckland

In France "am" and "pm" are not used but the 24-hour clock is widely applied.

Riviera Radio

Feeling pangs for your native language? Desperately seeking an English-speaking doctor or nanny? Looking for rented accommodation? Riviera Radio is the answer to all your problems. The only 100% English-speaking radio in the area, it broadcasts on FM *(106.5 in the Alpes-Maritimes, 106.3 in Monte-Carlo – ☎ 00 377 97 97 94 94 from France)* and covers the stretch of coastline running between St-Tropez and the Italian resort of San Remo. This Monaco-based radio station provides useful tips for tourists and residents alike and presents a great many regular programmes: business and financial news, local traffic and weather reports, guide to English-speaking films in VO (Version Originale), job offers, updated news bulletins in conjunction with the BBC World Service, calendar of major fairs and conferences, etc. One of Riviera Radio's most popular features is their Saturday morning Community Chest *(10-11am)*, when listeners call in to buy or sell miscellaneous items.

Villefranche-sur-Mer

NATURE

This guide describes the Riviera from Bandol to Menton and the mountainous inland region which comprises the Provençal Tableland, the Pre-Alps of Grasse and the high country north of Nice. Located within the larger administrative region known as Provence-Alpes-Côte d'Azur (PACA), the *départements* within the guide's boundaries are Alpes-Maritimes (06) and Var (83). There are 22 Régions in France, which encompass 96 *départements* (exclusive of overseas territories). The smallest administrative unit in France is the *commune* (they number 36 394), which is governed by the elected members of the municipal counsel and the mayor, or *maire*, who carries out the town's business in the town hall *(mairie)*. The town offices are generally centrally located, and play an important role in daily life; these offices often handle tourist affairs as well.

Monaco is a small principality on the Riviera, surrounded by the Alpes-Maritimes.

Adjacent regions described in the Michelin Green Guides are *Provence* and *French Alps*, both available in English.

Topography

CONTRASTS

This is a country of contrasts:

...in coastline

The Riviera extends from Bandol to Menton and is extremely varied (💧 see 'The Coast' below). The little sheltered inlets between the red rock promontories of the Esterel differ markedly from the great sweeping bays with flat shores which gently punctuate the coastline; while elsewhere on the coast, mountains plunge steeply into the sea, sheer as a wall, as at Cap Sicié.

...in relief

A countryside just as varied lies inland. The fertile plains and foothills of Provence are typically Mediterranean in their vegetation but among them are barren, rugged heights like those to the north of Toulon.

Then follow the mountain masses of the Maures and the Esterel which rise to no more than 800m/2 600ft: the first is criss-crossed by many valleys and ravines and covered with fine forests of cork oak and chestnut; the second massif is dominated by the outline of Mont Vinaigre and the peaks of Pic de l'Ours and Pic du Cap Roux. The country behind Cannes and Nice is one of undulating hills stretching to the Pre-Alps of Grasse, where gorges have been cut into the plateaux and the mountain chains are split by rifts *(clues)*, particularly in Haute-Provence.

Lastly, behind the Riviera the peaks of the Pre-Alps of Nice rise to more than 2 000m/6 560ft, while further to the north and northeast the true Alpine heights tower on the Italian border.

...in climate

There is a winter warmth on the Nice coast (the average temperatures for January in Nice are max 13°C/55°F; min 4°C/39°F) and, less than two hours away by car, the icy air of the ski slopes; the summer heat of the coast and the exhilarating coolness of the mountain resorts; the cold *mistral* wind and the burning *sirocco*; long days of drought, dried-up rivers and, suddenly, tremendous downpours and overflowing torrents.

...in vegetation

The forest of Turini, with its centuries-old beeches and firs, is like that of a northern land; the woods of the Maures and the Esterel are typically southern with their cork oaks and pines, periodically ravaged by forest fires. The wild scrub and underbrush of the *maquis* is far from the orderly rows of the orange and lemon groves; the lavender and thyme growing wild from the vast cultivated fields of flowers; the palm trees, agaves and cacti of the coast from the firs and larches of the highlands.

...in activity

The coast attracts all the activity of the area: the busiest roads, the most important towns and the varied and the best equipped resorts are concentrated there. Inland, however, there is peace and quiet, even complete solitude; sleepy little towns and old villages, perched like eagles' nests high up on the hillsides but now almost deserted (💧 see HILL VILLAGES).

...in economy

Nice is the coast's tourist capital; Monte-Carlo, a great gambling city. The busy flower trade and the production of

S. Sauvignier/ MICHELIN

The Pines of Porquerolles

perfume exist side by side with the new research centres dealing with oceanography and data processing.

Land of the Sun

Such a multiplicity of impressions has one common factor – the Mediterranean climate. In the Land of the Sun, the sun shines continually (2 725 hours annually in Nice compared with 1 465 hours in London).

Except in high summer, outlines are sharpened and natural features acquire an architectural aspect in the clear air. The shining blue of the sea and sky blends with the green of the forest, the silver-grey of the olive trees, the red porphyry rock and the white limestone.

TERRAIN

Provence was formed from two mountain systems: one very old – the Maures and the Esterel – the other much younger – the Provençal ranges of Pyrenean and the Pre-Alps of Alpine origin.

The Maures

This crystalline mountain mass spreads from the River Gapeau in the west to the Argens Valley in the east, from the sea in the south to a long depression in the north, beyond which are the limestone Pre-Alps. Long low parallel ranges, covered with fine forests which have not escaped the forest fires, make up the Maures Massif; the highest point is La Sauvette (779m/ 556ft).

The Esterel

The Esterel, separated from the Maures by the lower Argens Valley, has also been eroded by time, and is therefore of low altitude. Its highest peak is Mont Vinaigre at 618m/2 027ft. The deep ravines cut into its sides and its jagged crests dispel any impression of mere hills.

The Esterel, like the Maures, was once entirely covered with forests of pine and cork oak but these have been ravaged periodically by forest fires.

Quantities of shrubs and bushes grow beneath the trees: tree heathers, arbutus, lentisks and lavender, while scrub *(maquis)* covers the open ground. In spring the red and white flowers of the cistus, yellow mimosa and broom and white heather and myrtle form a brilliant floral patchwork.

Provençal Ranges

These short limestone chains, arid and rugged, rise to heights of 400-1 150m/1 200-3 500ft. Of Pyrenean origin with a highly complex structure, they do not have the continuity of those of Alpine origin such as the Southern Pre-Alps. The most southerly peaks, just north of Toulon, are the Gros Cerveau (429m/1 407ft), which is bisected by the Ollioules gorges, Mont Faron (542m/1 778ft), which dominates the town; and Le Coudon; Montagne de la Loube rises 28km/17mi to the north. Between the ranges are fertile valleys where the traditional crops of cereals, vines and olives are cultivated.

Maritime Alps and Mercantour

Away to the northeast the horizon is dominated by a vast mountainous mass (altitude: 1 500-2 900m/4 922-9 515ft), which is dissected by the upper valleys of the Var, Tinée, Vésubie and Roya. On the Italian border these mountains meet the great crystalline massif, Le Mercantour, the peaks of which exceed 3 000m/9 843ft.

Pre-Alps

This region contains a large part of the Southern Pre-Alps. Between the River Verdon and River Var the **Pre-Alps of Grasse** are formed by a series of parallel east-west chains, with altitudes varying between 1 100-1 600m/3 609-5 249ft which are frequently indented by wild and narrow rifts (clues).

The **Nice Pre-Alps** rise from the coast in tiers to a height of 1 000m/3 281ft, affording a wide variety of scenery inland from Nice and Menton. These ranges, which are Alpine in origin, run north-south before changing direction abruptly to finish up parallel with the coast.

Provençal Tableland

From Canjuers plateau to the Vence pass, the Pre-Alps are rimmed with a table-land of undulating limestone plateaux, similar to the *causses*, into which water infiltrates, penetrating through rifts to feed resurgent streams like the Siagne. The River Loup has carved out a very picturesque gorge.

Below lies a **depression** or "lowland" where the towns of Vence, Grasse and Draguignan are situated. Beyond the River Argens, the depression extends east down the river to Fréjus and west towards Brignoles; the main axis, however, is southwest to Toulon to the northern slopes of the Maures and Le Luc basin.

RIVERS

Mediterranean rivers are really torrents and their volume, which varies considerably from a mere trickle to a gushing flood, is governed by melting snow, rainfall and evaporation, depending on the season.

The lack of rain and the intense evaporation of the summer months reduce the rivers to little dribbles of water along their stony beds.

In spring and autumn the rains fall suddenly and violently and even the smallest streams are immediately filled with rushing water; little brooks, trickling through the undergrowth, soon turn into torrents and their raging waters advance at the frightening speed of a galloping horse.

The flow of the Argens varies from 3-600m3/60-132 000gal a second and that of the Var from 17-5 000m3/3 790 to over a million gallons. At the height of its spate the Var is more than half a mile wide and the stain of its muddy waters can be seen in the sea as far away as Villefranche on the far side of Nice.

The water level in rivers in limestone regions is always very uneven. The rains seep into the ground through numerous fissures to reappear often a considerable distance away as large springs gushing out from the sides of valleys. Some of the springs rise in riverbeds, such as the gushers (foux), which cause the River Argens to flood. Most of the rivers with torrential rates of flow transport material but the River Argens is the only one to have built up an alluvial plain comparable to those of the Languedoc coast. All the torrential rivers have created beautiful valleys, deep gorges (the Loup and the Siagne gorges) or rifts (clues – the Clue de Gréolières), which are among the attractions of inland Provence.

CAVES AND CHASMS

In contrast to the deeply dissected green valleys, such as the gorges of the Loup and the Siagne, the Caussols plateau (◖ *see ST-VALLIER-DE-THIEY*) rolls away to the far horizon, stony and deserted, a typical karst relief. The dryness of the soil is due to the calcareous nature of the rock which absorbs rain like a sponge.

Water Infiltration

Rainwater, charged with carbonic acid, dissolves the carbonate of lime to be found in the limestone. Depressions, which are usually circular in shape and small in size and are known as **cloups** or **sotchs**, are then formed. The dissolution of the limestone rocks, containing especially salt or gypsum, produces a rich soil particularly suitable for growing crops; when the *cloups* increase in size they form large, closed depressions know as **dolines**. Where rainwater infiltrates deeply through the countless fissures in the plateau, the hollowing out and dissolution of the calcareous layer produces wells or

Development of a resurgent spring

natural chasms which are called **avens**. Little by little the chasms grow, lengthen and branch off, communicating with each other and enlarging into caves.

Underground rivers

The infiltrating waters finally produce underground galleries and collect to form a more or less swiftly-flowing river. The river widens its course and often changes level, to fall in cascades. Where the rivers run slowly they form lakes, above natural dams, known as **gours**, which are raised layer by layer by deposits of carbonate of lime. The dissolution of the limestone also continues above the water-level in these subterranean galleries: blocks of stone fall from the roof and domes form, the upper parts pointing towards the surface of the earth. When the roof of the dome wears thin it may cave in, disclosing the cavity from above and opening the chasm.

Monaco – The Riviera Proper

Allison M. Simpson/ MICHELIN

THE COAST

The mainly rocky coastline reflects the different types of mountain and plateau to be found inland emerging as cliffs and rocks where they meet the sea.

The Toulon Coast

This highly indented section of the coast provides well-sheltered harbors; Bandol and Sanary bays and the outstanding Toulon port. The stretches of almost vertical cliffs are interrupted by some fine beaches.

The Maures Coast

Between Hyères and St-Raphaël, the Maures Massif meets the sea and the coastal scenery offers charming sites and enchanting views.

The Giens peninsula, formerly an island, is now joined to the mainland by two sandy isthmuses. Nearby are the Hyères islands, densely covered with vegetation, and the Fréjus plain, once a wide bay but now filled by alluvial deposits brought down by the Argens. Characteristic also of this particular section of the coast are great promontories such as Cap Bénat and the St-Tropez peninsula, narrow tongues of land such as Cap Nègre and Cap des Sardinaux and wide bays like the Bormes harbor and the gulf of St-Tropez.

The Esterel Coast

The red porphyry rocks of the Esterel Massif, steep and rugged, make a striking contrast with the blue of the sea. Along this stretch of coast the mountains thrust great promontories into the sea,

between inlets *(calanques)* and small bays. Offshore, the surface of the sea is scattered with thousands of rocks and small, green moss-covered islets, while submerged reefs can be seen beneath the clear water. The Corniche d'Or (← *see Massif de l'ESTEREL*) is reputed internationally for its breathtaking scenery, superb viewpoints and various resorts.

The Antibes Coast

The vista changes once again between Cannes and Nice. The shore is no longer eaten away by the sea; it is flat and opens into wide bays. It is a smooth, unbroken coast on which the Cap d'Antibes peninsula is the sole promontory.

The Riviera Proper

From Nice to Menton the Alps plunge abruptly into the sea. Here the coastline forms a natural terrace, facing the Mediterranean but isolated from its hinterland. Cap Ferrat and Cap Martin are the two main promontories along this stretch of coast. The term Riviera, which has already passed into the language of geography, is applied to this type of coast line. A triple roadway has been cut over the steep slopes, lined with villas and terraced gardens.

THE MEDITERRANEAN SEA

The Mediterranean is Europe's bluest sea. The shade – cobalt blue to artists – comes from the clarity of the water. Visitors soon realise that the colour often changes depending on the nature of the sky, the light, the seabed and the depth of water so that at times the "blue Mediterranean" is opal or a warm grey.

The water

The temperature of the water, governed on the surface by the sun's heat, is constant (13°C/55.4°F) from 200-4 000m/650-13 000ft downwards, whereas in the Atlantic it drops from 14-2°C/57.2-35°F. This is an important factor in the climate, for the sea cools the air in summer and warms it in winter. Rapid evaporation makes the water noticeably more salty than that of the Atlantic. The waves are small, short and choppy; storms come and go quickly.

The Tides

Tides are almost non-existent (about 25cm/10in). Sometimes when the wind is very strong the tide may reach as much as 1m/3ft. These figures are markedly different from the tides of the Atlantic or from the tides of 13-15m/40-50ft round Mont-St-Michel off the Normandy coast. This relative tidal stability has resulted in the Mediterranean being chosen as the base level for all French altitudes.

The Provençal coastline drops sharply into water that becomes relatively deep a short distance from the shore. Between Nice and Cap Ferrat soundings indicate a depth of 1 000m/3 280ft about half a mile out.

THE SEASONS

A superb climate

Crowds come flocking in summer and the tourist season lasts almost the whole year.

The Côte d'Azur is one of the most inviting names in the world! Properly speaking, the name Riviera applies to the French coast between Nice and Menton and to the Italian coast between Ventimiglia and Genoa. English visitors, at first for the sake of health but later more and more in search of pleasure, were attracted to the Riviera (especially Nice) in the 18C. The Côte d'Azur (Bandol to Menton) has become widely known as the French Riviera.

Winter

The proverbial mildness of the French Riviera is due to a number of factors: a low latitude, the presence of the sea which moderates temperature variations, a wholly southern aspect, and the screen of hills and mountains which protects it from cold winds. The average temperature for January in Nice is 8°C/16°F. Icy winds blow from the east and from the southeast bringing rain. Fog and sea-mists appear only on the coast in the height of summer; harsh winters with ice and snow are rare.

The thermometer may rise to 22°C/72°F but at sunset and during the night the temperature drops suddenly and considerably. There is little rainfall: it is the dew that keeps the vegetation fresh. The hinterland is cold and often snow-covered but the air is limpid and the sun brilliant – an ideal climate for winter sports.

Spring

Short but violent showers are characteristic of springtime on the Riviera. This is when the flowers are at their best and a joy to look at. The only drawback is the *mistral*, which blows most frequently at this season, especially west of Toulon. The mountains, however, act as a buffer and the wind is never as intense as it can be in western Provence and the Rhône Valley.

The Romans made a dreaded god of this fearsome wind. It comes from the northwest in cold gusts; after several days this powerful blast of clean air has purified everything and the wind-swept sky is bluer than ever.

Summer

The coast offers an average temperature of 26°C/79°F throughout July and August. The heat, however, is bearable because it is tempered by the fresh breeze that blows during the daytime. This is not the season for flowers: overwhelmed by drought the vegetation seems to sleep. When the hot breath of the *sirocco* comes out of the south everyone grumbles.

The hinterland offers a wide variety of places to stay at varying altitudes up to 1 800m/5 905ft; the higher one climbs the more invigorating the air.

Autumn

Autumn is the season for violent storms after which the sun reappears, brilliant and warm. In the whole year, there is an average of only 86 days of rain in Nice (150 in London), but the quantity of water which falls is higher (863mm/34in in Nice against under 609mm/24in in London). There are plenty of perfect days during the Mediterranean autumn.

Flora and Fauna

Plants and trees do not grow in the same way on the Riviera as they do further north. New shoots appear, as they do elsewhere, in the spring but a second growth begins in the autumn and continues throughout most of the winter. The dormant period is during the summer when the hot, dry climate favours only those plants that are especially adapted to resist drought. These have long tap roots, glossy leaves which reduce transpiration, bulbs acting as reservoirs of moisture and perfumes which they release to form a kind of protective vapor.

Umbrella pine

TREES

Olive Trees

2 500 years ago, the Greeks brought olive trees to Provence where they grow equally well in limestone or sandy soils. The olive has been called the immortal tree for, grafted or wild, it will always grow from the same stock. Those grown from cuttings die relatively young, at about 300 years old. Along the coast, the trees reach gigantic dimensions, attaining 20m/65ft in height, their domes of silver foliage 20m/65ft in circumference and trunks 4m/13ft round the base. The olive tree, which has more than 60 varieties, is found up to an altitude of 600m/2 000ft and marks the limit of the Mediterranean climate. It grows mainly on valley floors and on hillsides. The trees begin to bear fruit between their sixth and twelfth year and are in full yield at 20 or 25. The olives are harvested every two years. Olive groves are numerous in the areas around Draguignan, Sospel and at Breil, in the Roya Valley.

Oak Trees

The oaks native to the Mediterranean region are evergreen. The durmast and holm oaks grow in chalky soil at altitudes below 800m/2 500ft. As scrub-oaks, they are a characteristic feature of the *garrigue* (rocky, limestone moors). In its fully developed state the holm oak is a tree with a short thick-set trunk covered in grey-black bark and with a dense, rounded crown. The cork oak is distinguished by its large dark-colored acorns and its rough bark. Every eight to twelve years the thick cork bark is stripped off, exposing a reddish brown trunk.

Pine Trees

The three types of pine to be found in the Mediterranean region have unmistakable silhouettes.

The **maritime pine,** which grows only on limestone soil, has dark, blue-tinged green needles and deep red bark.

The **umbrella pine** is typically Mediterranean and owes its name to its easily recognizable outline. It is often found growing alone.

The **Aleppo pine** is a Mediterranean species that thrives on chalky soil along the coast; it has a twisted, grey trunk and lighter, less dense, foliage.

Other Provençal Trees – The smooth-trunked **plane tree** and the **lotus tree** shade the courtyards, streets and squares and also line the roads.

The dark silhouette of the coniferous, evergreen **cypress** is a common feature of the countryside; planted in rows, the pyramidal cypress forms an effective windbreak.

The common **almond tree**, a member of the Rosaceae, is widespread in Provence and blossoms early. The robust **chestnut** flourishes in the Maures Massif. Certain mountain species of **fir** and **larch** are to be found in the Alps; the forest of Turini is a fine fir-growing region.

Exotic Trees

In parks and gardens and along the roads stand magnificent **eucalyptus trees**. This hardy specimen is particularly suited to the climate. In winter another Australian import, **mimosa**, covers the slopes of the Tanneron Massif with a yellow mantle.

Olive tree

Almond tree

Lavandin

Lavandin is a hybrid plant resulting from the cross of true lavender with spike lavender. Its flowers may be blue, like true lavender or grey, like aspic. The plants are used for landscaping but they also produce oil of an excellent quality. In France, lavandin has been grown in Provence on a large scale for many years. Thanks to its camphoraceous smell with strong eucalyptus overtones, it is often used to scent soaps and detergents.

The greatest concentration of **palm trees** is to be found in the Hyères district. The two types most common to the Riviera are the date palm with its smooth, tall trunk sweeping upwards and the Canary palm which is much shorter and has a rough, scaly trunk.

Orange and **lemon groves** flourish on the coastal stretches between Cannes and Antibes, and Monaco and Menton.

BUSHES AND SHRUBS

The **kermes oak** is a bushy evergreen shrub, which rarely grows more than 1m/3ft in height. Its name comes from the kermes, an insect half-way between a cochineal fly and a flea, which lives throughout its existence attached to the stems of the oak.

The **lentisk** is an evergreen shrub with paired leaves on either side of the main stem and no terminal leaf. The fruit is a small globular berry, which turns from red to black when it is mature.

The **pistachio** is a deciduous shrub which can grow to a height of 4-5m/ 13-16ft. The leaves grow in groups of five to eleven, one of which is terminal. The fruit is a very small berry, red at first, ripening to brown.

The Mediterranean **thistle** is a perennial, which attains a height of 1m/3ft. The irregular pointed leaves are bright green on top and covered with white down on the underside.

The Garrigue

Some of the limestone areas are so stony (Vence pass road and D 955 from Draguignan to Montferrat) that even thorns (kermes oak, gorse and thistle) and aromatic plants (thyme, lavender and rosemary) can survive only here and there in between the bare rocks; this is the *garrigue*.

The Maquis

Scrub *(maquis)* thrives on sandy soil and forms a thick carpet of greenery, which is often impenetrable. In May and June when the cistus is in flower it is a marvellous spectacle, especially in the coverts of the Esterel.

SUCCULENTS

Some varieties of succulents are African in character: Barbary figs, agaves, cacti and aloes grow in open ground. Ficoids with large pink and white flowers cling to old walls.

The **aloe** has thick and fleshy leaves, from which a bitter juice is extracted for medicinal use.

The **Barbary fig** is an unusual plant from Central America, which grows in arid soil in hot climates; its broad, thick, fleshy leaves bristle with spines. The Moroccans call it the Christian fig; it is also known as the "prickly pear".

For a wider knowledge of exotic flora, take a stroll in:

- *Jardin Exotique in Monaco*
- *Jardin de la Villa Thuret in Cap d'Antibes (🍃 see ANTIBES)*
- *Several botanic gardens in Menton*
- *Domaine du Rayol (including Val Rameh) (🍃 see CAVALAIRE)*
- *Jardin Olbius Riquier in Hyères*

FOREST FIRES

From time immemorial the scourge of the Provençal woodland, especially in the Maures and the Esterel, has been the forest fire, which causes more damage than deforestation by man, now carefully monitored, and destruction by goats which live on the tender young shoots. During the summer the dried-up plants of the underbrush, pine needles, resins exuded by leaves and twigs are highly combustible and sometimes catch fire spontaneously. Once started, a fire may spread to the pines with disastrous results in a strong wind. Great walls of flame, sometimes 10km/6mi in length and 30m/100ft high, spread at speeds of 5-6km/2-3mi per hour. When the fire has passed, nothing remains standing except the blackened skeletons of trees while a thick layer of white ash covers the ground.

The Riviera still bears the scars of the particularly severe forest fires that raged during the summer of 2003, fueled by the worst drought and heatwave in

15 years, and it will be many years before regeneration of its natural habitat is complete.

Preventive measures include the removal of undergrowth near residential areas, creation of fire-breaks and the appointment of fire-watchers and patrols. Active intervention is provided by the fire brigade and the airborne water carriers based in Marignane. In the event of a major fire risk, the ALARME plan enables access roads to private homes to be cleared for firefighters and limits the movements of walkers. For information on the closures in forests, there is a recorded message service (☎ 04 94 47 35 45) for the use of hikers.

MEDITERRANEAN MARINE LIFE

Life in the Mediterranean Sea resembles a house full of animal tenants with astonishing characteristics living one above the other. During an underwater dive, the following species may be observed.

Brown Grouper

Depending on its age and size, the grouper is first female, then male. It changes sex at about nine years old when it weighs 10kg/22lb. Since the fish can live for about 50 years, it spends most of its life as a male. The young female grouper lives on rocky seabeds in shallow water (less than 10m/33ft deep) which makes it an easy prey for underwater hunters and other predators. As it reaches adulthood it makes its home in holes in the rocks at a depth of at least 50m/164ft where it lives as a formidable carnivore at the extremity of the marine food chain. It may eventually reach a length of 1.20m/4ft and weigh 30-40kg/66-88lb. This fish, which had become very rare in the Mediterranean, has benefited from a 5-year moratorium prohibiting the catching of groupers.

A project currently under way, led by the Parc Naturel de Port-Cros, is designed to protect the grouper within an area around the island.

Jellyfish

Jellyfish, which appear seasonally in coastal waters, sometimes cause problems for holidaymakers. The most common species, **pelagia**, can sting with its mouth, tentacles and umbrella. The poison, which is intended to immobilise prey, is powerful enough to cause redness and burning of the skin. The population of pelagia follows a 12-year cycle, depending on climatic conditions, and their arrival is usually preceded by a very dry spring. Another species of jellyfish, the Portuguese Man-of-Wa,r has long tentacles (up to 10m/33ft), which are invisible to swimmers and have a very powerful sting. They are fortunately rare in the Mediterranean.

Posidonia

This flowering plant, which has bunches of long dark-green leaves, plays an essential role in the Mediterranean environment. Its rhizomes grow slowly, thus allowing it to fix the sediments from the coast and create a habitat rich in oxygen and favorable to many animal species. When the posidonia dies, these animal species either die out or migrate.

A dive into the colorful world of the posidonia provides the possibility of seeing many amazing species. The **sea cucumber**, also known as holothurian, is the dustbin of the sandy seabed and lives only in the posidonia. The **sea-slug,** found all over the Mediterranean, is a white mollusc with brown spots which contrasts with the red sponges. The **striped weever fish** lives on the seabed near the posidonia, buried in the sand with just its head visible. It has a very poisonous dorsal fin, the sting of which can be serious. The **sea-horse** likes to hide near its relative, the **pipefish**, whose amazing threadlike form, with trumpet-shaped mouth, mimics the leaves of the posidonia among which it lives.

In the last few decades harbor works and construction along the coast have caused much sedimentation and the

The Three Musketeers of the "Silent World"

In August 1937, two young divers with homemade equipment based on recycled tubes, attempted to beat a harpooning record. In the absence of any substantial booty, J-Y Cousteau and P Taillez found that their dive in the midst of shoals of grouper and bass revealed the potential of underwater exploration. A third leading harpoonist, J Dumas, soon joined them and the hunt for pictures superseded the hunt for sea-bass. In the autumn of 1943, Dumas, experimenting with an aqualung, dived to a depth of 62m/203ft and was affected by nitrogen narcosis (rapture of the deep). After the Second World War the underwater explorers' odyssey was immortalised on film and their craft, *Calypso*, was seen all round the world.

resultant pollution is endangering the fragile habitat. Since 1989, a genetically altered strain of algae, the non-toxic **taxifolia**, has spread rapidly along the French Riviera. It is feared that the spread of this alga, originally created to decorate aquariums, may be harmful to the posidonia as well as other marine life in the Mediterranean, although experts still haven't agreed on the best way to eradicate the alien species.

HISTORY

Events in italics indicate milestones in history.

BC

1000 — The Ligurians occupy the Mediterranean seaboard.

600 — Foundation of Massalia (Marseille) by the Phocaeans. They bring olive, fig, nut, cherry trees, the cultivated vine; they substitute money for barter.

5-4C — The Greek settlers in Marseille introduce trading posts: Hyères, St-Tropez, Antibes, Nice and Monaco. The Celts invade Provence, mingling with the Ligurians.

Gallo-Roman Provence

122 — The Romans defeat the Celts.

102 — Marius defeats the Teutons from Germania near Aix.

58-51 — *Conquest of Gaul by Julius Caesar.*

49 — Julius Caesar founds Fréjus.

6 — Building of the Alpine Trophy at La Turbie.

AD

1, 2 and 3C — Roman civilization in evidence in some coastal towns (Fréjus, Cimiez, Antibes); the Via Aurelia (Ventimiglia-Brignoles-Nice) is the country's main highway.

313 — *Constantine grants Christians freedom of worship by the Edict of Milan.*

4, 5C — Christianity takes root in the coastal towns, then inland.

5, 6C — Vandals, Visigoths, Burgundians, Ostrogoths and Franks invade Provence in turn.

496 — *Clovis, King of the Franks, defeats the Alemanni from Germania at Tolbiac.*

8C — The Saracens sack the seaboard in the first half of the century.

800 — *Charlemagne is crowned Emperor of the West.*

Provence up to the "Reunion"

843 — *Treaty of Verdun regulates the division of Charlemagne's Empire between the three sons of Louis the Debonair. Provence is restored to Lothair (one of Charlemagne's grandsons) at the same time as Burgundy and Lorraine.*

855 — Provence is made a kingdom by Lothair for his son, Charles.

884 — The Saracens capture the Maures and for a century terrorize the land.

962 — *Restoration of the Western Empire as the Holy Roman Empire under Otto I.*

10, 11C — Provence, after passing from hand to hand, is finally made part of the Holy Roman Empire. Despite this, the counts of Provence enjoy effective independence. The towns are freed and proclaim their autonomy.

12C — The County of Provence passes to the counts of Toulouse, then to the counts of Barcelona. The counts maintain an elaborate court at Aix.

1226 — *Accession of St Louis.*

1246 — Charles of Anjou, brother of St Louis, marries the daughter of the Count of Barcelona and becomes Count of Provence.

1254 — Landing of St Louis at Hyères on return from the seventh Crusade.

1308 — Overlordship of Monaco is bought from the Genoese by a member of the Grimaldi family.

1343-82 — Queen Jeanne becomes Countess of Provence. Plague decimates the population.

1388 — Nice hands itself over to the Count of Savoy.

1419 — Nice is officially ceded to the Duke of Savoy.

1434 — René of Anjou, "Good King René", becomes Count of Provence.

1481 — Charles of Maine, nephew of René of Anjou, bequeaths

Provence (except Nice, which belongs to Savoy) to Louis XI.

1486 — Reunion of Provence with France ratified by the "Estates" of Provence (assembly of representatives of the three orders); Provence attached to the Kingdom "as one principal to another".

Provence after the "Reunion"

1501 — Establishment of Parliament at Aix (Parliament of Provence), sovereign court of justice, which later claims certain political prerogatives.

1515 — *Accession of François I.*

1524 — Provence is invaded by the Imperialists, commanded by the High Constable of Bourbon.

1536 — Invasion of Provence by Emperor Charles V.

1539 — Edict of Villers-Cotterêts decrees French as the language for all administrative laws in Provence.

1543 — Nice besieged by French and Turkish troops. Catherine Ségurane instrumental in causing the Turks to withdraw.

1562-98 — *Wars of Religion.* Promulgation of the Edict of Nantes.

1622 — Louis XIII visits Provence.

1643-1715 — *Reign of Louis XIV.*

1691 — Nice taken by the French.

1696 — France returns Nice to Savoy.

1707 — Invasion of Provence by Prince Eugene of Savoy.

1718 — County of Nice becomes part of the newly created Kingdom of Sardinia.

1720 — The great plague decimates the population of Provence.

1746 — Austro-Sardinian offensive is broken at Antibes. Austrian War of Succession.

1787 — Reunion of the "Estates" of Provence.

1789 — *The French Revolution.*

Revolution-Empire

1790 — Provence divided into three *départements*: Bouches-du-Rhône, Var, Basses-Alpes.

1793 — Siege of Toulon, in which Bonaparte distinguishes himself. Nice is reunited with France.

1799 — On 9 October, Bonaparte lands at St-Raphaël on his return from Egypt.

1804 — *Coronation of Napoleon.*

1814 — *Abdication of Napoleon at Fontainebleau, 6 April.* Embarkation of Napoleon at St-Raphaël, 28 April, for the Island of Elba. The County of Nice is restored to the King of Sardinia.

1815 — Landing of Napoleon at Golfe-Juan, 1 March. *Battle of Waterloo, 18 June.*

19th Century

1830 — *Accession of Louis-Philippe.*

1832 — The Duchess of Berry lands at Marseille, hoping to raise Provence in favour of a legitimist restoration.

1852-1870 — *Reign of Napoleon III.*

1860 — County of Nice restored to France.

1878 — Opening of the Monte-Carlo Casino. Development of the winter tourist season of the Riviera.

late 19C — St-Tropez School of Painting.

20th Century

1914-18 — Many village populations depleted by First World War.

1940 — The Italians occupy Menton.

1942 — The Germans invade the Free Zone. The scuttling of the French Fleet in Toulon harbour.

1944 — Liberation of Provence.

1946 — First International Film Festival in Cannes.

Since 1946 — Development of summer tourist trade on the Riviera. Harnessing of the River Durance and River Verdon.

1947 — Upper valley of the Roya incorporated into France.

1970 — International technology park opened at Sophia Antipolis near Valbonne reflects increasing emphasis on development of the region into a hi-tech industrial belt.

1980 — The Provençal Motorway (A8) links the Rhône and Italian networks.

1989 — Law passed to strengthen measures against forest fires which pose an increasing threat to the region.

1989 — The **TGV** (train à grande vitesse – high speed train) arrives on the Riviera.

August 1994 — Celebration of the 50th anniversary of the Liberation of Provence.

1996 — A high speed boat service (NGV) between Nice and Corsica.

June 2001 — The TGV Méditerranée is inaugurated, bringing down the Paris-Marseille trip to three hours.

2003 — Construction begins on the new tramway in Nice, due to open December 2006

April 2005 — Prince Albert succeeds his father, Prince Ranier III, who died after ruling the Principality of Monaco for 57 years.

ALLIED LANDING IN PROVENCE (1944)

Operation "Dragon" – This was the aftermath of operation "Overlord" which had liberated Normandy three months earlier. At a critical moment in the battle of Normandy the Allies landed on the coast of Provence fortified by the Germans under the name "Südwall" with the American 7th Army under **General Patch,** of which the French Ist Army (composed mostly of African soldiers) formed the principal part.

"Nancy a le torticolis" (Nancy has a stiff neck) – This laconic message, broadcast on the BBC in the evening of 14 August announcing the landings in Provence, raised the hopes of the Resistance groups which had been on alert since the projected landings reported on 6 June 1944. Between June and August, the dropping of arms by parachute was stepped up, notably in the *pouvadous*

(dry and stony moors); these arms were destined for the Maquis (Resistance) in the Maures, the Alps, Bessillon and Ste-Baume. In the early hours of 15 August, airborne Anglo-American troops were dropped around Le Muy to take control of the strategic communications route, RN 7. The village of **La Motte** became the first Provençal village to be liberated. At the same time, French commandos from Africa landed at Cap Nègre, and Esquillon Point, while American Special Forces attacked the Îles d'Hyères. Thus protected, the main army, assembled on the 2 000 ships, including 250 battleships, landed at 8am on the beaches of Cavalaire, St-Tropez, Le Dramont and the Esterel. Despite a rapid advance, the two sectors were still separated at the end of the day by pockets of German resistance at St-Raphaël and Fréjus which fell only the following day. On 16 August the B Army under General De Lattre landed at Cavalaire Bay and in the gulf of St-Tropez and, having relieved the Americans, attacked the defences of Toulon. General Montsabert outflanked the town to the north to fall on Marseille. After the fall of Hyères and Solliès, Toulon was reached on 23 August but fighting continued until 28 August with the surrender of the St-Mandrier peninsula. On the same day, after five days of fighting, Marseille was liberated.

To the east, the Americans of the First Special Force advanced to the Alpes-Maritimes to back up the Resistance forces and drive the Germans back into the Italian Alps: Nice fell on 30 August and Menton on 6 September. In the hinterland, the Massif de l'Authion, transformed into an entrenched camp by the Germans, was the site of hard fighting for 8 months. L'Authion was overcome on 13 April 1945, Saorge on 18 April but Tende was liberated only on 5 May, three days before the general armistice!

Provence had been liberated in less than 15 days. The Allies pursued the Germans, who retreated up the Rhône Valley; the 1st French Army under De Lattre de Tassigny effected a link-up with the 2nd Amoured Division under Leclerc in Côte d'Or south of Châtillon-sur-Seine.

Architecture and art

ABC OF ARCHITECTURE

Roman Era

LA TURBIE – The Alpine Trophy (1stC BC)

This monument was erected in homage to Augustus' victory in the Alps. Damaged and despoiled over the years, it was finally restored by the architect Formigé in the 1930s.

Frieze in the Doric order: alternating metopes (plain panels) and triglyphs (slightly raised blocks of 3 vertical bands, separated by V-shaped grooves)

Peristyle

Commemorative inscription

Plinth: visible projecting base of the wall.

Blind arcading

Circular tower built in the feudal period

Column shaft

Pedestal: base of a column or a statue

Trophy: sculpted composition of arms and armour

Early Christian Era

FRÉJUS – Interior of the baptistery (5C)

This is one of the few edifices from the Early Christian Era visible in the region. Some parts date from the Roman Era. An early 20C restoration restored the building to its former appearance.

Semicircular arch

Masonry course alternating brick and stone

Corinthian capital

Wrought iron gate (18C)

Baptismal font

Cupola (partly reconstructed during restoration works)

Embrasure: enlargement of the opening for the bay at the inside face of the wall

Arcading: series of small arcades

Springer: stone block supporting the curve of the arch

Monolithic column

Base: foot of the column

Terra cotta basin for washing the feet of the faithful

R. Corbel

Religious architecture

LE THORONET – Ground plan of the abbey church (11C)

Because it did not serve a parish, the church in Thoronet does not have a central doorway. The rounded east end is typical of the region of Provence, in contrast to the flat chevet usually preferred by the Cistercian order.

Bay: transverse section of the nave between two pillars

Transept chapel

Side aisles

Apse: the eastern end of a church behind the main altar (interior). Compare to **chevet** (exterior)

Nave — Transept

Chancel, generally facing east

Pilaster

Transept crossing or arm of the transept

Cross-section of a Romanesque Provençal church

The right and left-hand sides of the drawing show two main variations of this type of church.

Transverse arch: placed under the vault to reinforce it

Broken barrel arch

Rampant arch: the impost on one side is higher than that on the other

High window

Half-barrel arch

Grooved **colonnette**

Side aisle

Nave

Impost: The a moulding on which an arch without capitals rests

Pilaster

GRASSE – Doorway of the Chapelle de l'Oratoire (14C)

The Gothic doorway and windows of this chapel were recovered from the old Franciscan church. In 1851, they were moved to this chapel, set on a hill in the old town centre.

Broken barrel arch

Arch: a curved construction which spans an opening; a series of arches forms the archivolt

Quatrefoil

Open-work tympanum

Flamboyant ornamentation: the flame-like shapes give this style its name

Coussinet: this overhanging stone reduces the load of the lintel on the jamb shaft

Trefoil arch decorative motif

Lintel

Upright post or bearing shaft

Jamb shaft with a capital and base, bearing the arch above

R. Corbel

NICE – Cathédrale Sainte-Réparate (17C)

Sainte-Réparate was originally a chapel, built in the 13C. The current Baroque façade and ground plan are the work of the local architect Jean-André Guilbert.

Crown

Candelabrum: an ornamental torch-shaped spike on top of a tower, chimney, etc

Curved pediment

Pilaster or attached pier: rectangular support projecting partially from a wall

Composite capital: with details from both Ionic and Corinthian Orders

Scroll

Triangular pediment

Moulding

Statue in a niche

Table: a vertical slab

Entablature: the projecting crown is made up of the architrave (lowest member), frieze and cornice

Modillions: horizontal bracket or console supporting the corona under the cornice

LES ARCS – Altar screen of the Sainte-Roseline chapel (early 16C)

Baroque altar screens in Nice and the surrounding region are mostly made of coloured marbles and stucco; gilded wood is more common on the other side of the Var.

Attic: a small story built above the wall cornice and crowning the building

Rinceau: an ornamental band of undulant and recurving plant motifs

Twisted column with a flower garland

Altar table

Console with scrolling

Angel

Shell-shaped niche

High-relief sculpture

Predella: the bottom tier of the altarpiece

Cherub: an angel represented by a child's head with wings

Antependium: a decorative panel suspended over the front of the altar

R. Corbel

Traditional architecture

SAINT-TROPEZ – Houses on the harbour

The houses typically found in a village on the Riviera, known in France as the Côte d'Azur, are narrow and high, packed together along the waterfront or the winding streets of a hillside town; they are enlivened by colourful façades.

Louvered shutters: the slats filter out the sun and let in the air

Curved tiles

Chimney cap: crowning termination

Dormer cheek: the side of a dormer

Modern **dormer window**

Shade

Roof with **two slopes**

Canvas awning

Tile creasing: two courses of tiles project beyond both faces of the wall to throw off rainwater

Balcony

LE VIEUX-CANNET – Campanile

Campaniles appeared in the 16C, atop bell towers or belfries. Of various sizes, some are quite elaborate.

Metal frame withstands wind

Masonry course: the height of the regular rows is variable

Ressaut (projecting part)

Weather vane

Cross atop the **gable**

LORGUES – Fontaine de la Noix (1771)

Each town or village has one or more fountains, whether a simple spigot or a sculpted, dated monument.

Pin-and-ball

Blazon or **coat of arms**

Fish

Console: supporting bracket

Basin

R. Cortel

Seaside architecture

HYÈRES – Villa Tunisienne (1884)

Seaside architecture of the 19C was inspired by Moorish culture. Chapoulart, the architect who designed the Villa Mauresque in Hyères, built this variation on the theme for himself, with a patio. Previously, it was also known as the "Algerian Villa".

Crenellations: made of crenels (notches) and merlons

Rosette: round pattern with a floral motif

Projecting pointed arch

Denticulated merlons

Interlace

Ceramic ornamentation

Multifoil arch

Meshrebeeya: lattice screen

Fore part of the building, projecting from the façade and as high as the main building

Balustrade: railing with balusters

MONTE-CARLO – Game room in the casino (late 19C)

Monte-Carlo grew up around the casino, which typifies the eclectic style of seaside architecture at the end of the 19C. The luxurious decoration inside echoes the elaborate ornamentation on the outside.

Sun

Winged cartouche: framing a decorative embellishment

Framework: a set of iron stays to support and protect the glass roof

Pine cone ornament

Rocaille ornamentation combining forms based on water-worn rocks, plants and shells, made in **stucco** (a fine plaster mixed with marble dust)

Shell

Grooved Ionic column

Bull's eye

Cabling: embellishing the grooves on the lower third of the column

Basket-handle arch

Gaming tables

Chandelier

R. Corbel

Military architecture

ANTIBES – Fort Carré (16C)

The ramparts of Antibes were demolished in 1895. All that remains is this fort, completed in 1585; the bastion design is a precursor of the star bastion defensive system developed by Vauban in the century following.

Straight stair: a steep stairway built against a fortification

Old St-Laurent tower (first fort)

Governor's lodge

Bastion: pentagonal projection from the fortified wall

Chapel

Second fortified wall

Sentry box

Watchpath

Curtain wall between two bastions

Cavalier: raised portion of the fortress for commanding adjacent defences or for the placement of weapons

Cannon carriage fitting

Batter slope: the inclined plane on the outer surface of the wall

Contemporary architecture

SOPHIA ANTIPOLIS – Commercial building (1978)

The buildings in the Valbonne business park were constructed beginning in 1970. They have been designed to fit into the natural shape of the landscape. Some are equipped to use solar energy.

Roof terrace

Glass wall

Pole

Balcony terrace

Open-work railing

Solid railing or parapet

French window

Band of windows

Terrace garden

R. Corbel

History of Architecture

Compared with Provence, which is rich in monuments of all sorts, the Riviera has less to offer. Here, however, the visitor will discover art in its earliest forms side by side with its most modern expressions. Right up until the 19C the art of the region remained highly conservative. When the Romanesque and Gothic styles were flourishing elsewhere in France, the Riviera remained untouched.

E. Baret/MICHELIN

GALLO-ROMAN ANTIQUITIES

Provence and particularly the Riviera have been thriving areas since Roman times. As later generations took the materials used by the Romans for the construction of their own new buildings, only a few fragments of the ancient civilization have survived. In the districts of Fayence, Fréjus and St-Raphaël, Roman canals are still being used to carry water.

The Roman ruins at Cimiez (👁 see NICE) are extensive. At Fréjus (👁 see FRÉJUS), as well as the arena, there are traces of the harbour installations. The Alpine Trophy at La Turbie (👁 see LA TURBIE) is of special interest; it is one of the few such Roman trophies still in existence. Buildings from the Merovingian and Carolingian periods include the baptistry at Fréjus and the chapels of Notre-Dame-de-Pépiole and La Trinité at St-Honorat de Lérins

ROMANESQUE PERIOD

In the 12C an architectural renaissance in Provence blossomed in the building of numerous churches. The Romanesque style here is more eclectic than innovative, resulting not in large buildings, such as those in Burgundy, but rather in unpretentious churches, remarkable for the bonding of their evenly cut stones with fine mortar work.

The churches are plain outside, their façades being often poor in style; the only break in the flatness of the sides comes from powerful buttresses. The square belfry and the east end are sometimes decorated with applied blind arcades, known as **Lombard bands**, evidence of northern Italian influence.

On entering, the visitor is struck by the simplicity and austerity of the interior which often consists of a single nave and a shallow transept. If aisles form part of the plan, the apse ends in a semicircle flanked by two apsidal chapels.

The interesting abbey of Le Thoronet (👁 See Le THORONET) contains a church of the Cistercian Order with the wide transept and bare appearance characteristic of the churches built by the Benedictines. In contrast, however, the roof of broken barrel vaulting and the semicircular apse show the influence of local craftsmen.

J.L. Gallo/ MICHELIN

Russian Orthodox Cathedral, Nice

P. Ricou

Baroque house (1890), Nice

GOTHIC TO BAROQUE

There are few Gothic buildings in the region. Provençal Gothic is a transitional style which depends heavily on Romanesque traditions. The style is represented in the powerful groined vaulting at Fréjus and Grasse. The cloisters at Fréjus are remarkable.

In the 15C, Good King René brought numerous Italian craftsmen to Provence, but, though Provençal painting was influenced by the Renaissance, architecture remained unaffected.

Classical buildings, however, abound (17C and 18C). Design lost its original style and became more severe and majestic. In the towns the wealthier citizens built town houses. The development of Baroque is to be seen in ecclesiastical buildings in the County of Nice at Sospel, Menton, Monaco, La Turbie and Nice. Façades are adorned with pediments, niches and statues; inside, the architectural lines are often concealed by highly ornate altarpieces, panelling and baldaquins.

Ste-Jeanne d'Arc, (1934), Nice

The Romanesque-Byzantine style was employed in the church of Notre-Dame-de-la-Victoire-de-Lépante, St-Raphaël, the neo-Gothic on the west front of the church at Cimiez and neo-Romanesque for Monaco's cathedral. Slightly later, the Casino in Monte-Carlo and the Hôtel Negresco in Nice were designed in an ostentatious style borrowed from Belle Epoque (c 1900).

Examples of 20C works include the church of Ste-Jeanne-d'Arc in Nice, the country church of St-Martin-de-Peille and the Chapelle Matisse at Vence. The Fondation Maeght in St-Paul, the Musée Marc-Chagall in Nice, and the striking property development at the Baie des Anges Marina in Villeneuve-Loubet or Port-Grimaud are other fine examples of modern architecture.

MODERN PERIOD

The 19C showed little originality and Baroque continued to be favoured for new constructions and restorations.

Amphorae

From ancient times, the Provençal coasts have been visited by numerous merchants ships often of imposing size (more than 30m/98ft long) and heavily laden (up to 8 000 amphorae, or two-handled jars). The problems of manœuvring these heavy boats with oar, sail and a lack of knowledge of the reefs led to innumerable shipwrecks. The wrecks salvaged with their cargoes of amphorae bear witness to the busy commercial exchanges between areas of production and the consumers in urban centres. Navigation took place between April and September when the weather conditions were most favourable. Foodstuffs such as wine, oil and fish were also transported. The cargo on these boats was arranged at right angles to the keel; the pointed ends of the amphorae were wedged in place by the branches of trees, and the empty spaces between their necks were filled with the next row, thus assuring that the whole cargo was stable. Some holds contained up to four levels of amphorae.

☻ Regulations concerning underwater ☻ archeological finds:

☻ All cultural goods from the sea (amphorae etc) found on public property belong to the State. Therefore anyone diving who finds any archeological remains must leave them in place and untouched.

☻ In the event of objects being brought up by chance (in nets, for example), it is forbidden to dispose of them and the find should be reported to the nearest Affaires Maritimes within 48 hours. Offenders are dealt with in the High Courts.

☻ Lastly, a small consolation, divers who have declared a find of a wreck or archeological remains could benefit from a reward fixed by the government.

Art

PAINTING

Primitives

From the middle of the 15C to the middle of the 16C a school of painting, at first purely Gothic then influenced by the Italian Renaissance, flourished in the County of Nice. It is best-known through the works of **Louis Bréa** and **Durandi**. It is said of Bréa that he was a "Provençal Fra Angelico", praise justified by the sincerity and sobriety of his brushwork and his gift

Pierre Puget (1620-94)

This native of Marseille was one of the greatest French sculptors of the 17C. He began by carving the prows of ships and later developed huge carved poops. During a journey in Italy, he developed his many talents by working as a pupil of Pietro da Cortona.
After the fall of Fouquet, his patron, he established himself away from Versailles and was appointed director of Toulon harbour by Colbert, who thought well of him. Jealousy and conspiracy soon brought him into disgrace, so he threw himself into the embellishment of Toulon. His best-known works are the atlantes supporting the balcony of Toulon Town Hall and the *Milo of Croton*, which is exhibited in the Louvre in Paris. His Baroque style could express power, movement and pathos.

for stressing the humanity of his subjects. However, his simplicity is a far cry from the mysticism of Fra Angelico, and his colors and dull tones lack the sparkle of the great Italian genius. These Provençal artists worked mainly for the Penitent brotherhoods, which explains why their paintings are scattered in many churches and pilgrim chapels. They can be seen in Nice (where Brea's brother Antoine and nephew François are represented), Gréolières, Antibes, Fréjus, Grasse and Monaco.

During the same period, the humblest churches of the County of Nice were decorated with the most striking mural paintings. These are to be seen at Coaraze, Venanson, Lucéram, Saorge and Notre-Dame-des-Fontaines where Renaissance Primitive **Giovanni Canavesio**, working beside **Jean Baleison**, created Gothic-inspired works of exceptional quality.

The Classical Period

The 17C and 18C were marked by the fine pictures of the Parrocles, the Van Loos, Joseph Vernet and Hubert Robert. It is **Fragonard**, however, who is the pride of Provence. Rakish scenes were his favorites; he painted them with great enthusiasm and exquisite style. He often used as background to his jubilant party scenes, the landscapes flooded with light and the gardens full of flowers seen round his native town of Grasse.

Modern Painting

At the end of the 19C numerous artists, representing the main trends in modern painting, were fascinated by the radiant light of the Mediterranean South of France.

Impressionism

The Impressionists sought to portray the subtle effects of light on Mediterranean landscapes. **Berthe Morisot** lived in Nice, **Monet** in Antibes and **Renoir** in Cagnes where he spent his last years, painting flowers and fruits, landscapes and people of the South.

Impressionism gave birth to a new school, **Pointillism**, a method of painting created by **Seurat**, which consisted of dividing shades into tiny dots of pure color distributed so as to intensify the effect of light.

Paul Signac, Seurat's disciple, established himself in St-Tropez in 1898 and many of his friends followed him, namely Manguin, Bonnard and Matisse.

Fauvism

Matisse and Dufy, who had settled in Nice, reacted against Impressionism and, through the use of pure and brilliant colors, juxtaposed in simplified forms and perspectives, tried to express not just the fleeting sensation evoked by the spectacle of nature but the very thoughts and emotions of the artist.

Contemporary Movements

Picasso, co-founder with Braque of Cubism – an art concerned above all with form – was in his turn seduced by the Riviera, and lived in Vallauris in 1946, then in Cannes and finally in Mougins.

Braque spent his last years painting in Le Cannet while **Fernand Léger**, another Cubist painter, lived in Biot.

Dunoyer de Segonzac was untiring in his portrayal of St-Tropez.

Chagall found the light and flowers of Vence a marvellous stimulus to his multicolored dreams.

Other artists, such as **Kandinsky** in La Napoule, **Cocteau** in Menton, **Van Dongen** in Cannes, **Magnelli** in Grasse and **Nicolas de Staël** in Antibes, although not spending much time in the region, nevertheless marked their stay in an unforgettable manner.

At the same time in Nice in the 1960s a group of artists including **Arman, César,** Dufrêne, Hains, **Klein**, Raysse, Rotella, Spoerri, Tinguely and Villeglé formed the **Nouveau Réalisme** joined later by Niki de Saint Phalle, Deschamps and Christo. They were reacting against Abstraction, which was the prevailing artistic trend after the war, and experimented with new approaches to reality making use of objects found in the modern industrial and consumer world. Alongside these innovators were the members of the **Nice School,** who each sought his own vision (**Ben**, Bernar Venet, Sacha Sosno); and **Bernard Pagès** and **Claude Viallat,** who, closely linked to the theories of Conceptual Art, led to the creation of the Support-Surface in the 1970s *(for more on contemporary movements see NICE Musée d'Art Moderne et d'Art Contemporain).*

THE REGION TODAY

Agriculture and Crafts

FLOWERS AND EARLY VEGETABLES

Cut Flowers – Alphonse Karr (⚓ *see ST-RAPHAËL*), a political refugee living in Nice before the annexation, is generally credited with having founded the flower trade. With the help of an associate, Karr began large-scale cultivation and had the idea of sending bunches of fresh violets and small packets of mixed seeds to Paris. From this modest start the trade in cut flowers and mimosa has developed considerably owing to irrigation and hothouses.

Flowers and Scented Plants of the Grasse Region – The two main flower crops of this area are roses and jasmine. The May tea-rose is the same as that grown in the east but the Mediterranean variety has a fine scent. Jasmine is of the large flowering variety which has been grafted on to jasmine officinalis. It is a particularly costly and delicate plant which flowers from the end of July to the first winter frosts.

The orange blossom used for perfume is obtained from the bitter fruit tree, known as the Seville orange (*bigaradier*). Orange-flower water is made from direct distillation. The cherry laurel, eucalyptus and cypress are distilled both for essence and for *eau de toilette*. Mimosa is used for the production of essence by extraction. Sweet basil, clary (sage), tarragon, melissa or balm mint, verbena, mignonette, peppermint and geranium all yield products used in perfumery, confectionery and pharmaceuticals. Scented plants include wild lavender, aspic, thyme, rosemary, sage etc.

Le Bar-sur-Loup, Golfe-Juan, Le Cannet and Vallauris as well as Seillans (Var *département*), are major centres for the production of natural aromatic raw materials, although Grasse is number one in this domain.

This luxury industry, which caters mostly to the export market, is supplemented by the synthetic perfume industry. The French perfume industry's exports exceed €5.9 billion, the most important customers being the United States, Japan, Germany and the United Kingdom.

First Vegetables – After North Africa, Spain and Italy, the region of Toulon and Hyères provides the first seasonal vegetables and fruit. The Var is noted for the cherries of Solliès-Pont and the peaches from around Fréjus.

Olive Trees and Oils – Traditionally, the northernmost place where olive trees (symbol of Southern agriculture) are grown, is also the limit of the Midi or South of France.

Production of olive oil in the region accounts for more than two-thirds of that of the whole country, and is spread throughout the Var, around Draguignan and Brignoles, and in the Bévéra and Roya valleys. Following the frosts of 1956, when nearly a quarter of the olive trees died, the olive groves have been replanted progressively with two more hardy species: the **aglandau** and the **verdale**. There are many other varieties, with flavours which vary according to the soil and the date of harvest. Traditionally, several varieties are grown in one olive grove. Harvest is from the end of August, depending on the area; table olives are picked by hand, while those destined for miling are shaken off the tree and collected in nets. Around Nice, shaking (*gaulage*) is always used. Olives from Nyons (*tanches*) are the only ones to be designated AOC (*Appellation d'origine contrôlée* – of guaranteed quality). The **belgentiéroise** olive, harvested at the end of August, can be eaten within the month; the **grossane** is a fleshy black, salted olive; the **salonenque** is a green variety also known as *olive des Baux*. The **cailletier**, or little Nice olive, is stored in brine for six months before being eaten. All of these can be eaten as an apéritif or made into oil.

CRAFT WORKSHOPS

Numbers of craftsmen have moved into the old inland villages, which they have often restored with care, and are producing traditional objects made by the old methods or highly original creations.

Biot – The production of large earthenware jars in Biot goes back to the days of the Phoenicians. In the Middle Ages Biot was an important centre for ceramics and it was not until the 19C that it was eclipsed by Vallauris. There are several modern workshops specializing in traditional earthenware jars, pottery, ornamental stoneware and metalwork.

Since the 1960s Biot has owed its growing international reputation to its glass craftsmen. By visiting a glass workshop one can see how the various pieces are made using early techniques. Exhibits include carafes, bottles, glasses, small oil lamps and traditional Provençal jugs with long spouts *(calères, ponons)* for drinking without touching the vessel with one's lips.

Vallauris – Ceramics from Vallauris enjoy a worldwide reputation. In 1947 Picasso came to work in a studio in the town and attracted a crowd of followers. Nowadays it is difficult to distinguish between the mass-produced pot and the hand-made article in the shop windows.

Many of the potters – whether they use old methods (wood firing) or new techniques – produce attractive work: glazed kitchenware (tureens, bowls, jugs), handsome stoneware, various glazed or unglazed articles and clay pipes.

Besides pottery, many other interesting activities have been introduced, including the production of hand-crafted puppets, handsome furniture and decorative sculpture made from olive wood, colorful painted chests and cupboards, fine hand-woven linen and furnishings.

Tourrettes-sur-Loup – Tourrettes has been revived by its craftsmen. It was an important weaving town in the Middle Ages and renewed its connection with this craft after the Second World War.

It has become a centre for hand-woven fabrics. The weavers produce very high quality goods in small quantities.

Several of the workshops in the winding streets offer a very varied range of cloth: reproductions of old Provençal fabrics, shot material for the high fashion market or furnishings, and hand-woven ties. Tourrettes also houses potters (making earthenware sheep using a Mexican process, engraving in vivid enamels), painters and sculptors in olive wood.

Life on the Riviera

ON THE COAST

The Riviera has attracted man since the earliest times and strongholds have been built on isolated hills; the curious village of Èze is the best example.

Since the great expansion of the tourist trade, life on the Riviera has been dominated by a beach and holiday atmosphere nearly all year round. Local life is gradually being overshadowed by the great influx of visitors.

A Holiday Destination – Visitors seeking fashionable and elegant resorts can choose between the bustle of Cannes and Monte-Carlo or the quieter and more discreet setting of Hyères, Beaulieu, Menton, Cap Ferrat or Cap Martin. Those longing for the appeal of a big city with all its amusements will undoubtedly turn to Nice. Lively St-Tropez will attract a large number of summer visitors; the seeker of solitude will find isolated inlets and localities; and a full range of hotels will cater to every budget.

The region features charming country houses, built in Provençal rustic style, with pink or ochre-colored façades, overhanging red-tiled roofs and arbors covered with wisteria and climbing plants. There are also beautiful gardens in which great earthenware jars, which once contained olive oil or wine, are now purely decorative. Magnificent parks offer fine views from their terraces, and everyone can enjoy the light and color in a charming and relaxed atmosphere.

Numerous constructions are invading the coast and one can see here and there towns built over water, such as the lake town of Port-Grimaud, the Cogolin Marina and the marine city of Port-la-Galère.

Ambitious building projects, some of which are totally out of proportion, have sprung up on all sides; a great number of private properties have appeared at the water's edge, although the public has right of access all along the coast.

Ports and Fishing – The naval port of Toulon is in a league of its own on the popular recreational coast. Cannes, Monaco and Antibes are long-established pleasure boat ports: beautiful yachts with gleaming steelwork lie at anchor in the bay or are moored to the quays.

Fishing on the Riviera is confined to the coast and, as the catch is insufficient for the area, it has to be supplemented by shipments from the Atlantic.

There are no large fishing ports but numerous little harbours along the coast: Bandol, St-Tropez, St-Raphaël, Villefranche-sur-Mer, for example, are adapting to the demands of tourists and equipping themselves with moorings for pleasure boats.

For some years now the Nice region has made efforts to modernise the fishing industry and increase the number of boats in use. This has been achieved through the use of very large running nets known as *lamparos* and *seinches* and the construction of fish canneries.

The Markets – Most of the coastal towns have their own flower and fish markets where, to the colorful banks of flowers and stalls of gleaming fish, are added the

SPECIALITIES AND VINEYARDS

Olive trees

Cork, Sweet Chestnut

Citrus fruits

Other fruits, Vegetables

Flowers

Recognised vintages :

Bellet

Bandol

Côtes de Provence

Coteaux Varois

Olive oil production, famous localities

Perfume distillery

Wine cellars open to the public

Especially picturesque markets

Crafts, Specialities

Castellane

Verdon

DURANCE

Verdon

Aups

Bargemon

Varages

Salernes

Entrecasteaux

Callas

Barjols

Draguignan

Cotignac

la Motte

Arc

Argens

le Thoronet

Vidauban

Brignoles

MAURES

Aubagne

Signes

Cuers

Cogolin

le Castellet

Collobrières

Ollioules

Pierrefeu-du-Var

Anthemis (camomile), mimosa

St-Cyr-sur-Mer

le Lavandou

Bandol

TOULON

Hyères

Stocks, roses, violets, bulbs

Carnations, bulbs

Îles d'Hyères

0   10   20 km

ITALIA

Tende

St-Martin-Vésubie

Breil-sur-Roya

Sospel

Castillon

Menton

Tourrettes-sur-Loup

le Bar-sur-Loup

Vence

MONTE-CARLO
MONACO

Biot

NICE

Carnations, roses, anthemis
(camomile), exotic flowers

Grasse

Opio

Flowers for perfume :
Jasmin, roses, violets, orange blossom

Mougins

Fayence

Antibes

Vallauris

CANNES

Nursery

Mandelieu-la-Napoule

Roquebrune-
sur-Argens

Fréjus

Mimosa

Roses

les Issambres

Ste-Maxime

St-Tropez

Ramatuelle

MÉDITERRANÉE

MER

Barjols	Leather
Biot	Glass
Castillon (A.-M.)	Crafts, specialities
Cogolin	Pottery, pipes, carpets, cork
Collobrières	Sweets (chestnuts)
Fayence	Pottery
Mandelieu-la-Napoule	Glass
Roquebrune-sur-Argens	Sweets (nougat), Santons
Salernes	Pottery, floor tiles
Signes	Sweets (nougat)
St-Cyr-sur-Mer	Santons
Ste-Maxime	Wood carvings
Tourrettes-sur-Loup	Sweets (candied fruit)
Vallauris	Ceramics
Varages	Ceramics

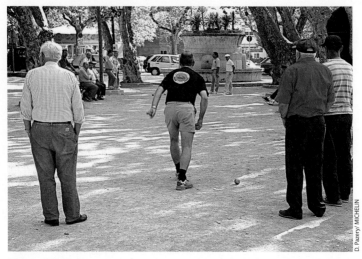

Pétanque in St-Tropez

noisy bustle and the warmth of the local accents of buyers and sellers, creating a true Côte d'Azur scene.

INLAND

The interior reveals the last vestiges of what was once a rough and precarious way of life: valley sides and hill slopes terraced with stone walls retaining small strips of soil for growing cereals or two or three rows of vines and a few olive and almond trees. The *garrigue*, where small flocks of sheep and goats were put to graze, formed a sharp contrast with the fertile valleys and irrigated plains of the lowlands and the coast, where cereals, early vegetables and flowers were harvested and vines and fruit trees flourished. The lonely villages clinging to solitary ridges *(details below)* and small farms lying abandoned among their terraced walls bore no resemblance to the market towns of the plains, spread along the main roads, or to the farms *(mas)* scattered in the midst of large cultivated areas.

The centre of the village is the little square *(cours)* shaded by plane trees round a small fountain. This is where the cafés are to be found, always full in this region where people love social life, conversation and politics and where much of the day is spent away from the houses, which are left with the shutters closed to keep out the heat and insects.

THE GAME OF BOULES

This, the most popular game of the region, is played with ironclad balls. Matches are between teams of three players *(triplettes)* or four *(quadrettes)*. The *pointeurs* (attackers) must roll their balls as close as possible to a small ball *(cochonnet)*, acting as a jack, which is set at the limit of the pitch. The *tireurs* (defenders) must knock away the balls of their opponents by striking them with their own, and the best players can do this so that their ball takes the exact place of the one knocked away. Over short distances, in which it is forbidden to move the feet, the play is *à la pétanque*. Over long distances (10m/30ft or more), where the players throw their balls after making three hopping steps, the play is *à la longue*. The intense concentration of the players, often mirrored in their facial expressions, and the passionate disputes which break out when judging the distance between balls make this a fascinating game to watch.

Perched Villages

Many old villages may be seen perched like an eagle's nest on a hilltop or set on the flank of a hill; some are practically deserted, while others have been restored. For centuries the peasants built their villages in this way, at a distance from their lands and water supplies, and surrounded them with ramparts.

This was a wise precaution in the days of the great Germanic invasions, the Moslem pirates, and the attacks by the mercenaries of the Middle Ages and the Renaissance. The coming of security, better communications and the development of farming techniques in the 19C ended this isolation. Villages began to expand in the plains, sometimes doubling in size, and country dwellers were able to live on the land they cultivated and build their houses there. Gourdon, Èze, Utelle, Peille and many other villages (👁 *see map below*) still bear witness to the ancient Provençal way of life.

These secluded villages are picturesque to visit. Built with stones from the hillsides, they seem to blend in with the countryside. The winding streets and alleyways *(calades)*, which are steeply sloped and only to be traversed on foot, are paved with flagstones or cobbles, intersected by tortuous stairways and crossed overhead by vaults and arches. Sometimes arcades follow one another at ground level, affording the passerby shelter from the sun and rain.

The houses, roofed with curved clay tiles, have high narrow fronts, worn by the centuries. They buttress each other and surround the church or château, which dominates the village. Old nail-studded doors, wrought-iron hinges and bronze knockers still adorn the more prosperous residences.

Sometimes the little townships, which have attracted many craftsmen, are still enclosed by ramparts and one enters by a fortified gate.

Food and Wine

The main features of Provençal cooking are garlic and frying in oil (preferably olive oil). Garlic has inspired many poets who have written of the "Provençal truffle", the "divine condiment", "man's friend". Olive oil is used wherever butter would be used further north. "A fish lives in water and dies in oil" according to a local proverb.

Bouillabaisse – Here we salute the most celebrated of Provençal dishes. The classic *bouillabaisse* must consist of the "three fishes": scorpion fish *(rascasse)*, red gurnet and conger eel. Several other kinds of fish and shellfish are usually added – it is essential that the fish be freshly caught and cooked in good quality olive oil. The seasoning is just as important: salt, pepper, onion, tomato, saffron, garlic, thyme, bay leaves, sage, fennel and orange peel. Sometimes a glass of white wine or brandy gives the final flavour to the broth, which is poured onto thick slices of bread.

Aïoli – *Aïoli* is another Provençal speciality and is a mayonnaise made with olive oil, strongly flavoured with crushed garlic. Comparing the northern variety of mayonnaise with *aïoli*, Mistral dismissed it as insipid "jam". *Aïoli* is served with *hors-d'œuvres*, or with *bourride* (a soup of angler fish, bass and whiting etc), or many other dishes.

Fish – One of the Mediterranean's tastiest fish is the red mullet *(rouget)*, which the famous chef, Brillat-Savarin, called the "woodcock of the sea" probably

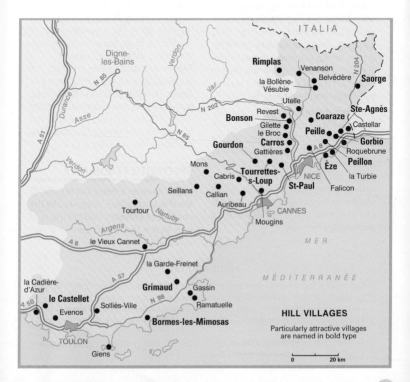

HILL VILLAGES

Particularly attractive villages are named in bold type

0   20 km

How to Recognise a Good Olive Oil

The essential characteristic of virgin olive oil is its extraction by a mechanical process from the first cold pressing without being refined. Six further operations are necessary before the oil is ready to be marketed: grading *(calibrage)* and washing in cold water *(lavage)*, crushing *(broyage)* in a traditional mill, after which the resulting paste is pressed on fibre mats *(scourtins)*. The oil thus obtained is purified by centrifuge (by natural settling and decanting if the traditional process is followed throughout).

Regulations define several categories of oil which must be mentioned on the label:
– Extra-virgin oil *(huile vierge extra)* which is easily digested, has most flavour and very low acidity (less than 1%)
– Virgin oil *(huile vierge)* which also has a very good flavour but can have double the acidity of extra-virgin oil
– Olive oil *(huile d'olive)* which has an acceptable taste for local cooking but fairly high acidity (about 3%)
– Refined oil *(huile d'olive lampante)* which is mixed with virgin oil as its acidity (nearly 4%) makes it unfit for consumption.

because gourmets cook it without first scaling or cleaning it. The *loup* (local name for bass) grilled with fennel or vine shoots is another delicious dish. *Brandade de morue* is a purée of pounded cod mixed with olive oil, some garlic cloves and truffle slices.

Aromatic herbs – Considered with garlic and olive oil to be one of the basics of Southern cooking, aromatic herbs, cultivated or growing naturally on sunny hillsides, perfume gardens and markets and enhance local cuisine. Known as *herbes de Provence,* the mixture includes **savory** *(sarriette)*, used to flavour goats' and ewes' milk cheeses; **thyme** *(thym)* cooked with most vegetables and also grilled meat; **basil** *(basilic);* **sage** *(sauge),* **wild thyme** *(serpolet);* **rosemary** *(romarin)* which is good for the digestion; **tarragon** *(estragon);* **juniper** *(genièvre),* used to flavour game; **marjoram** *(marjolaine);* and **fennel** *(fenouil)*. It is used in many dishes and can, according to taste, be a main constituent or just a trace.

Thirteen desserts – Provençal tradition presents diners at Christmas with 13 desserts (representing Christ and the 12 Apostles): raisins, dried figs, walnuts, hazelnuts, almonds, grapes on the vine, apples, pears, black nougat (made with honey), *fougasse* (sort of brioche), prunes stuffed with almond paste, melons stored in straw and dry cakes flavoured with orange blossom.

At Epiphany, a **galette des rois** is served in the form of a brioche filled with almond paste and topped with a paper crown which goes to whoever finds the china figure in their slice.

Wines – Vines have been cultivated in Provence since Antiquity.

The **rosé wines**, their glowing color achieved by a special process from black grapes, are gaining increasingly widespread popularity; pleasant and fruity to the palate, they go well with any dish.

The **white wines** are generally dry in character but have a good bouquet and are an excellent accompaniment to shellfish and Mediterranean fish.

There is a wide variety of full-flavoured **red wines**: full-bodied or subtle and delicate depending on whether they come from Bandol or the southern slopes of the Maures or, on the other hand, from the Argens Valley or St-Tropez.

The most popular wines are from the region of Bandol, Ollioules, Pierrefeu, Cuers, Taradeau and La Croix-Valmer, from the Niçois area and particularly the wines of Bellet, La Gaude, St-Jeannet and Menton (👓 *see Planning Your Trip: Wine tasting and Regional Produce*).

SPECIALITIES FROM NICE

Niçois cuisine, a lively expression of the character of Nice, is inspired by the cooking of Provence and of Liguria in Italy as it is the meeting point of the

Pan Bagnat

Cut a round loaf of wholemeal bread in half horizontally. Moisten the dough with a generous measure of olive oil and rub vigorously with a clove of garlic.
On the lower half lay some slices of tomato, a few lettuce leaves, rings of white onion, black Niçois olives and cover with anchovy fillets. Garnish with salt, pepper and chopped basil leaves.
Cover with the upper half, wrap in a cloth and leave for a good hour for the flavours to mingle – the perfect choice for a picnic.

two traditions. The narrow streets of Old Nice, clustered at the foot of the castle hill, overflow with opportunities to try the best-known specialities as well as seasonal variations.

Two well-known examples of the cooking of Nice are an **onion tart** *(pissaladière)*, garnished with a thick anchovy sauce *(pissala)* and black Nice olives, and **salade niçoise,** a tasty combination of local tomatoes, cut into four, lettuce leaves, beans, radishes, peppers, onions, hard-boiled eggs and Nice olives, garnished with anchovy fillets and basil leaves and moistened with olive oil.

For a snack to be eaten in the street there is a large chickpea flour pancake *(socca)*, divided into portions and accompanied by a small glass of local wine *(pointu)*; it is sold in and around place St-François.

At lunchtime recharge the batteries for more sightseeing with a round sandwich *(pan bagnat* – soaked bread*)* containing tomatoes, lettuce, onions, anchovies and olives, moistened with olive oil and flavoured with garlic.

Teatime hunger *(merenda)* can be appeased with fried slices of a thick chickpea pancake *(panisses)*.

Salad or soup or omelette may accompany a marinade of young fish *(poutina)* which are caught with the permission of the local authorities between Antibes and Menton in February. During the rest of the year gourmets may console themselves with a **fish soup** *(soupe aux poissons de roche)* made with little crabs *(favouilles)*.

The evening menu may be enlivened by a slice of **suckling pig** *(porchetta)* stuffed with herbs and its own offal, served with a mixed salad *(salade de mesclun* in the local dialect*)* composed of 14 types of young salad plants picked in the area.

The dishes on offer in the tiny restaurants in the villages inland include stuffed squash blossoms *(fleurs de courgette farcies)*; a vegetable stew *(ratatouille)* made of tomatoes, eggplant *(aubergines)*, peppers and zucchinis gently cooked in oil; shell-shaped pasta *(gnocchi)* made of wheat and potato flour and served with a thick sauce *(daube)*; deep-fried pastry parcels *(barbajouan* – Uncle John*)* filled with rice, squash, garlic, onion and cheese; a stockfish dish known as **estocaficada** (✎ *see below*).

Market, Nice

The convivial family dish, known as **pistou**, is a vegetable soup to which is added an unctuous concoction of basil, garlic, tomatoes and unstinted olive oil.

For dessert there is a sweet tart *(tourte de blea)* garnished with chopped chard leaves, pine kernels and currants.

Halfway through Lent the pastry cooks' windows display small sweet pastry cushions known as **ganses**. A cake flavoured with orange flower water *(fougasse)* is sold all year round; in Monaco it is decorated with aniseed in the national colors of red and white.

One may resist the torpor of midday by sitting in the shade with a glass of crushed ice flavoured with mint *(gratta queca)*.

Estocaficada – This is the local version of the stockfish of Marseille, known for short by old hands as "estocafic". As it takes a whole day to prepare, it has become a dish for special occasions. To fillets of stockfish (dried cod), flaked with a fork and lightly browned, are added peeled and de-seeded tomatoes, the tripes of the stockfish cut into strips, chopped olives and bouquets of herbs including fennel, marjoram, parsley, thyme, bay and savory. The dish is braised for three to four hours, generously laced with brandy *(la brande)*. When the liquor has reduced to a level which only the vigilance of the cook can determine, a good measure of stock is added to the pot.

At a family gathering this imposing dish is accompanied by a full-bodied wine from Le Bellet.

Peillon

ANTIBES★★

POPULATION 72 412

MICHELIN MAP 341 D6

The highly popular port town of Antibes, hugging the coastline halfway between Nice and Cannes, has long been one of the most inspirational settings for artists on the Côte d'Azur. Home to the largest pleasure port on the Riviera, Antibes also features a scenic old town that's lively year-round, and stunning natural scenery surrounding the mansions of the Cap d'Antibes (👣 *see CAP d'ANTIBES below*), making this one of the must-see towns of the region.

▶ **Orient Yourself:** Antibes can be divided into four major areas of interest: the Port Vauban at the foot of the Fort Carré to the north, the Old Town (*Vieil Antibes*) within the ancient ramparts, the sandy beaches of La Salis, and the Cap d'Antibes to the south, with the Garoupe lighthouse crowning its highest point. The narrow streets of the Old Town should be explored on foot, but there is also a sightseeing train and the public buses for getting around more easily (👣 *see Address Book*).

🅿 **Parking:** While there are a few underground parking garages in the Old Town, it's to park in one of the vast lots along the Port Vauban *(fee in high season)*. In summer there's a free navette that shuttles pedestrians between the parking areas and the Old Town gate. Parking places along La Salis beach are almost impossible to find in summer.

🕏 **Don't Miss:** The Picasso Museum in the Château Grimaldi, the covered market at the Cours Masséna, the immense yachts on the Quai de la Grande Plaisance, the panoramic views of the coastline from La Garoupe lighthouse, and the scenic beach and walking trail at the Plage de la Garoupe.

🕓 **Organizing Your Time:** Antibes deserves a full day if you have the time. The sights of the Old Town and port should be visited first. Plan on about three hours, or a half day if you plan on visiting any museums or the Fort Carré. Then after lunch drive around the Cap d'Antibes, planning on at least two hours if you want to hike along the coastal path (*sentier*) or the sandy beaches at La Salis.

🚸 **Especially for Kids:** At the northeast end of Antibes just off the RN7 is the popular Marineland waterpark, Antibesland amusement park, a mini-golf course and Wild West adventureland for children of all ages.

Old town, Antibes

A Flowering Trade

The Antibes area is one of Europe's main centers for the commercial production of flowers. About 800 firms keep some 300ha/50 acres under glass frames or greenhouses. Roses take first place, followed by carnations, anemones and tulips. Evergreen plants and spring vegetables are also cultivated.

A Bit of History

Greek Antipolis – From the 4C BC the Greeks of Massalia set up a chain of trading posts with the Ligurian tribes along the coast. A new city sprang up opposite Nice; Antipolis, the Greek name for Antibes, may have meant "the town opposite" although this derivation is disputed. Antipolis was contained between the present Cours Masséna and the sea, the Greeks holding only the area commanded by their ships, their warehouses and their ramparts. The prevailing atmosphere was one of mutual mistrust; the Ligurians never actually entered the town, which featured only one gate opposite the present town hall; all transactions took place outside the city walls.

The Greeks were succeeded by the Romans, and subsequently by pirates and Barbarians, whose invasions gradually undermined the city's prosperity.

Antibes, frontier outpost – The kings of France realised the key military role that Antibes could play, above all from the end of the 14C when the town stood on the Franco-Savoyard frontier. It became the property of the Grimaldis in 1386 and was later purchased by Henri IV (1589-1610).

Each reign brought improvements or enlargements to its fortifications until the work was completed by Vauban in the 17C. Only the Fort Carré and the seafront ramparts remain.

Bonaparte at Antibes – In 1794 Bonaparte, charged with defending the coast, settled his family in Antibes. He was a general but his pay seldom arrived on the appointed day. Times were hard. Mme Lætitia, his mother, did the household laundry herself in a nearby stream. His sisters made furtive expeditions to the artichoke and fig plantations and were chased away by the landowner. Bonaparte was imprisoned for some time in Fort Carré after the fall of Robespierre during the French Revolution.

Notable inhabitants – Born in Valence, **General Championnet** died in Antibes in 1800 from the cholera that was ravaging his army. This selfless leader, who performed admirably in the German and Italian campaigns, was barely 38. He asked to be buried in the moat of Fort Carré. His bust stands in Cours Masséna. **Nikos Kazantzakis** (1885-1957) wrote *Zorba the Greek* and the *Last Temptation of Christ* while living in Antibes. **Nicolas de Staël** (1914-55) painted his last canvases in Antibes, before taking his own life. A young glamorous American couple, **Sara** and **Gerald Murphy,** fell in love with Antibes in the mid-1920s, and their villa became a favoured holiday haunt for their many American friends, including the **Fitzgeralds** and **Hemingways**.

Walking Tour

OLD ANTIBES★ *Allow 2hrs* (📱 *see town map*)

▶ *Begin at Avenue de Verdun.*

Port Vauban

Avenue de Verdun commands a good view of the marina and the 16C **Fort Carré** (📱 *see Sights*) perched on its rock, with Cagnes and the heights of Nice in the background. The **Port Vauban**, one of the largest in the Mediterranean, is predominantly used by luxury cruise yachts, the largest that can be found along the Quai de la Grande Plaisance (also known as *Quai des Millionaires)*. The famous French novelist Maupassant had his yacht Bel Ami moored here in the 19C.

▶ *Enter the old town by the old sea gate and follow Rampe des Saleurs on the left as far as the Promenade Amiral-de-Grasse.*

Promenade Amiral-de-Grasse

This road, once the seafront promenade, runs along the vestiges of 17C ramparts facing the sea, below the old cathedral and Grimaldi Château (*Musée Picasso*, 📱 *see Sights*). It gives a fine **view**★ of the coastline stretching towards Nice with the Alps rising in the background, snow-covered for most of the year.

ANTIBES

> *Make a left onto the Rue du Haut Castelet and follow it around to the right to the Place du Safranier.*

Place du Safranier

This square is the heart of the free commune known as "Le Safranier", set up in the wake of the Second World War. The writer Nikos Kazantzakis lived at 8 Rue du Bas-Castellet. The plaque adorning the front door encapsulates his philosophy: "I fear nothing. I expect nothing. I am a free man".

> *Double back and take a left onto the Rue de la Touraque.*

Old streets

To the left and right are picturesque side streets, bright with flowers in season and barely a stone's throw from the sea.

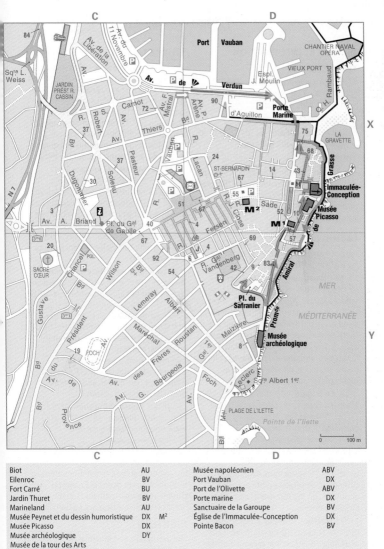

▶ *You'll arrive at the Cours Masséna, which serves as the market place; turn right on Rue de l'Orme, then on Rue du Bateau.*

Église de l'Immaculée-Conception

Of the original Romanesque church, which served as a cathedral in the Middle Ages, only the east end remains. The belfry is a converted 12C watchtower. The west front (carved **door panels** – 1710) is in the 17C Classical style. The art treasures feature a wooden Crucifix (1447) in the choir, a former pagan stone altar in the south apsidal chapel, a 1515 **altarpiece** by Louis Bréa in the south transept – the centre panel has been touched up but the 13 surrounding panels and the predella are treated like miniatures – and a 16C **Recumbent Christ** carved in lime wood.

▶ *Take Rue de l'Horloge (right), Rue du Revely (left) and Rue Aubernon (right) for a picturesque route heading back to the port.*

Sights

Château Grimaldi (Musée Picasso)

🕐 *Open daily (except Mon) 10am-noon, 2-6pm; Jun-Sep 10am-6pm; Jul-Aug Wed, Fri open late until 8pm.* 🕐 *Closed 1 Jan, 1 May, 1 Nov and 25 Dec.* 🎟 *6€ (child 3€), 5€ from 15 Sep-15 Jun.* ☎ *04 92 90 54 20.*

Address Book

PRACTICAL INFORMATION

TOURISM OFFICE

11 Place du Général-de-Gaulle – 06200 – ☎ 04 92 90 53 00 – www.antibes-juanlespins.com.

HÔTEL DE VILLE (TOWN HALL)

Cours Masséna – 06200 – ☎ 04 92 90 50 00 – www.antibes-juanlespins.com.

TOURS

The Tourism Office provides a fold-out map with four walking itineraries called "Balades au Coeur d'Azur". They can also help arrange mini-bus excursions for the surrounding region.

EATING OUT

For coin categories, see the Legend at the back of the guide.

La Croustille – *4 Cours Masséna – ☎ 04 93 34 84 83 – ⏰ Closed during Nov school holidays, 20-26 Dec and Tue.* Settle on the charming terrace of this creperie-salad bar in old Antibes and soak up the lively, colourful atmosphere of the local market. The cosy interior is decorated with family photographs and models of sailing boats. Warm, hospitable welcome at highly reasonable prices.

Le Troppo – *2 Boulevard du Maréchal-Leclerc – ☎ 04 93 34 00 21 – ⏰ Closed 15 Nov-15 Dec, Mon evening and Tue off season.* A stone's throw from the Archeological Museum, this restaurant is a kaleidoscope of warm, earthy hues that harmonise well with its Provençal backdrop. Crêpes or more elaborate cuisine can be served in the cool interior or outside, on the sun-drenched terrace. Excellent service.

L'Oursin – *16 Rue de la République – ☎ 04 93 34 13 46 – ⏰ Closed 18 Feb-1 Mar, 17-31 May, 18-29 Nov, Sun evening and Mon.* The tempting displays of oysters laid out on the terrace of this quaint, old-fashioned restaurant are the perfect excuse to enter and sample their deliciously fresh fish and seafood dishes. A great favourite among locals.

Le Sucrier – *6 Rue des Bains – ☎ 04 93 34 85 40 – 🍽 – ⏰ Open nightly for dinner and lunch on Sun – ⏰ Closed 11-19 Nov, 8 Jan-4 Feb.* Tucked down a tiny side street, this cozy restaurant features contemporary French cooking based on the fresh market produce of the season. Exposed stone walls and wooden beams give the dining room an authentic Provençal feel.

La Jarre – *14 Rue St-Esprit – ☎ 04 93 34 50 12 – ⏰ Closed Wed (except in Jul-Aug).* Located in an old monastary between the Cours Masséna and the sea, this restaurant specializes in regional cuisine. The patio courtyard is shaded under the canopy of a giant fig tree.

WHERE TO STAY

Hotel La Jabotte – *13 Avenue Max-Maurey – Cap d'Antibes – ☎ 04 93 61 45 89 – www.jabotte.com – 10 rooms – �︎ 🅿 – Restaurant (🍽).* On a street perpendicular to La Salis beach, this charming little hotel features individually decorated rooms overlooking a sunny patio. The owner's decorative calligraphy work is on display throughout the hotel.

Le Ponteil – *11 Impasse Jean-Mensier – ☎ 04 93 34 67 92 – http://leponteil.savati.net – ⏰ Closed 14 Nov-26 Dec – �︎ 🅿 – 14 rooms.* Unassuming bed and breakfast with a homey atmosphere within walking distance of the beaches. Quiet, welcoming rooms. Leafy garden bursting with colour. Restaurant open to residents only.

Chambre d'Hôte La Bastide du Bosquet – *14 Chemin des Sables, (Domaine des Mûriers) – 06160 Cap-Antibes – ☎ 04 93 67 32 29 – www.lebosquet06.com – ⏰ Closed mid-Nov-20 Dec – 🚭 – 3 rooms.* Attractive 18C country house at the heart of a residential area that will guarantee you a peaceful stay (three nights minimum). Cool, pleasing rooms of different sizes with colourful Provençal furnishings. The garden and terrace are great assets in high season.

Impérial Garoupe – *770 Chemin de la Garoupe – ☎ 04 92 93 31 61 – www.hotelimperialgaroupe.com – ⏰ Closed Nov-16 Apr – 🍽 🅿 �︎ 30 rooms – Restaurant (🍽).* This Mediterranean-style hotel is hidden within lush gardens of the Cap d'Antibes. L'Anse restaurant serves gourmet Provençal cuisine, and a small path leads to the hotel's own private beach at La Garoupe.

NIGHTLIFE

The trendy bars and British-style pubs of Antibes are concentrated around the **Cours Masséna**, **Rue Aubernon**, and along the ramparts of the **Boulevard d'Aguillon** to the **Rue Lacan.** The ever-present population of young, international "yachties" (crew) stationed in Antibes gives the town a more lively nightlife in the off-season than its neighbor, JUAN-LES-PINS.

TOURS AND PUBLIC TRANSPORTATION

BUSES

EnviBus – Gare Routière, Place Guynemer – ☎ 04 93 34 37 60 – www.envibus.fr – 🚌 1€ (1hr), 3€ (day pass). There are 15 bus lines. The most convenient ones are 1A and 3A (going towards Juan-les-Pins), 2A (going towards Cap d'Antibes), 10A (going towards Biot), 2VB (going towards Sophia-Antipolis and Valbonne) and 5V (going towards Vallauris). Look for the "Noctantibes" bus in Jul-Aug, between Antibes and Juan-les-Pins 8pm-midnight.

TAXI

The main **taxi** stand is located at the Gare SNCF (train station), or call ☎ 04 93 67 67 67 or ☎ 04 92 93 07 07.

TOURIST TRAIN

Le Petit Train – *Rue République, in front of the Carrousel* – ☎ 06 03 35 61 35 🕐 *Daily 10am-7pm (11pm Jul-Aug)*. 🚃 *7€ (4€ children)*. This small tourist train departs hourly for a 50-minute sightseeing tour between Antibes and Juan-les-Pins. Commentary in English.

BOAT TRIPS

Small **power boats** can be rented by the hour from Port Vauban's Quai des Pêcheurs, just outside the Porte Marine (🚶 *see JUAN-LES-PINS for glass-bottom boat tours of the CAP d'ANTIBES*).

SHOPPING

Marché Provençal – *Cours Masséna* – 🕐 *every morning (except Mon in low season)*. This colorful covered market features regional produce and specialty items such as honey, lavender, cheeses, jams, spices, olive oil, and dried meats.

Marchés des Pêcheurs – *Place des Martyrs-de-la-Résistance (near the main Post Office)* – 🕐 *every morning Jul-Aug (Tue and Sun in low season)*. A relatively new market displaying the fresh catch of the day from local fishers.

Rue Sade – This picturesque street stretching from the Cours Masséna to the Place Nationale is full of charming boutiques and gourmet food shops.

HAVING A DIP

Swimming pool – The fabulous pool belonging to the Cap Eden Rock Hotel is also open to non-residents. 🚃 Admission: 70€ (includes the poolside mattress).

Beaches – The long pebble beach of Antibes extends way beyond Fort Carré. Four other public beaches are covered in fine sand: La Gravette (south of the old port), the Îlette, La Salis and La Garoupe.

Water Sports – Antibes is a "station nautique", with a wide variety of water sports on offer from water skiing and scuba diving to sailing and windsurfing. Contact the Tourism Office for more information, or visit the website: www.france-nautisme.com.

The original castle was built in the 12C on a terrace overlooking the sea on the foundations of a Roman camp situated on the Antipolis acropolis. It was reconstructed in the 16C but the square Roman tower, the battlement walk and pairs of windows remain from the original structure. The castle, which was the bishops' residence in the Middle Ages, was home to the Grimaldi family until the 17C.

Donation Picasso★

▶ *On the first floor of the museum.*

Soon after his arrival on the Riviera in the autumn of 1946, **Pablo Picasso** (1881-1973), who had part of the castle at his disposal, started work on some large-scale paintings. His output was remarkable; the majority of the paintings, lithographs and drawings on view in the castle were the result of one season's work. The original supports used by the artist, consisting of fibro-cement and plywood, testify to the shortages of the post war period.

La Joie de Vivre, a huge work in fibro-cement, is a smiling pastoral composition of a plant-woman dancing among exuberant goats and satyrs. Preliminary sketches and drawings are also on show.

His other **paintings** are mainly joyful works bursting with imagination, inspired by the marine and mythological life of the Mediterranean (fish, sea urchins, fishermen, centaurs...): *Ulysses and the Sirens*, *The Oak Tree* and an imposing triptych – *Satyr*, *Faun* and *Centaur with Trident*. Two still-life paintings of exceptional quality – *Fish* and *Watermelon* – illustrate strict geometrical design.

The showcases hold an impressive collection of Picasso's **ceramics**. His great powers of imagination and ingenuity are revealed in the variety of decoration and the beauty and originality of form, often quite humorous. In the case of some pieces, decoration and form combine to suggest a silhouette: woman, owl, bull, goat... These were created at Vallauris between 1948 and 1949.

The prints and drawings of the Vollard Collection, which are grouped around monumental statues, date from the 1930s.

On the second floor, works by Nicolas de Staël are on display in Picasso's old studio. Note in particular *Still Life with Chandelier, Fort Carré* and the gigantic canvas entitled *Grand Concert*. The pieces by Nicolas de Staël are the result of a winter which he spent in Antibes.

Around the Museum

The **stairwell** presents a display taken from the museum's collection of modern art: works by Arp, Magnelli, Ernst. In the **courtyard** there is a composition by the sculptor Arman depicting guitars, reminiscent of a painting by Picasso, *À ma Jolie*. In the **terrace** garden, fragrant

First View of Antibes

In the chapel hangs the **Deposition from the Cross**★ (1539) by Antoine Aundi, which contains the earliest known view of Antibes.

with aromatic plants, are displayed seven statues by Germaine Richier and works by Miró, Pagès, Amado Spoerri and Poirier. The Musée Picasso boasts an **Archeological Collection** of Roman pottery, friezes, funerary urns and stelae, many of which carry inscriptions, displayed both inside the museum and outside on the terrace.

Musée Peynet et de la Caricature★

♿ ◷ *Open daily (except Mon) 10am-noon, 2-6pm; Jul-Aug open Wed, Fri open late until 8pm.* ◷ *Closed 1 Jan, 1 May, 1 Nov, 25 Dec.* ⊜ *3€ (kids under 18 free).* ☎ *04 92 90 54 30.*

Located in an old 19C school are several hundred works (lithographs, stage sets, ink drawings, watercolors, sculptures, greeting cards, dolls...) by **Raymond Peynet** (1908-1999). The famous cartoonist, who moved to Antibes in 1950, is known for his two young lovers, Les Amoureux, whose adventures were published in magazines such as *Paris Match, Marie-Claire, Elle* and others.

Fort Carré

◷ *Open daily (except Mon) 10am-6pm, Jun-Sep; 10am-6.30pm Oct-May. Guided tours (45 mins) every half hour.* ◷ *Closed 1 Jan, 1 May, 1 Nov, 25 Dec.* ⊜ *3€.* ☎ *06 14 89 17 45. www.antibes-juanlespins.com.*

Built atop an isolated outcrop in 1550, the central St-Laurent tower was consolidated by four surrounding citadels 15 years later, named respectively, "Antibes", "Nice", "France" and "Corse". Thanks to the fortification work carried out by Vauban, this stronghold braved many an assault during its existence, yielding only to the Duke of Epernay and Napoleon's enemies.

Musée Archéologique

♿ ◷ *Open daily (except Mon) 10am-noon, 2-6pm; 15 Jun-15 Sep open daily (except Mon) 10am-6pm; Wed, Fri in Jul-Aug open late until 8pm .* ◷ *Closed 1 Jan, 1 May, 1 Nov, 25 Dec.* ⊜ *3€.* ☎ *04 92 90 54 35. www.antibes-juanlespins.com.*

The Bastion St-André, part of Vauban's fortifications, presents a **collection of archeological artefacts** illustrating 4 000 years of history. The back of a large vaulted room, built on a reservoir, houses a bread oven and, to the right, the reconstruction of a Roman ship used for transporting amphorae.

Some of the particularly interesting exhibits include a copy of the Mask of Silenus in bronze (the original is in the Musée Archéologique in Nice) and an ornamented lead sarcophagus. Local excavations are continually adding to the exhibits of pottery (Massaliote, Greek and Roman amphorae) as well as objects salvaged from shipwrecks from the Middle Ages to the 18C.

Excursions

MARINELAND★

4km/2.5mi north towards Nice. 🧒 ♿ ◷ *Open Jul-Aug daily10am-midnight; spring 10am-7pm; autumn and winter 10am-5pm.* ◷ *Closed Jan.* ⊜ *28€ (adult), 19€ (children 3-12 years).* ☎ *04 93 33 49 49. www.marineland.fr.*

This marine zoo, the first in Europe, consists of many large pools containing **killer whales**, dolphins, elephant seals, seals and sea lions. The dolphins and killer whales give regular acrobatic displays. In a penguin enclosure *(manchotière)*, about 20 king penguins have been reared. The spectacular show **"Sharks"** takes visitors down a 30m/98ft tunnel with a view of a dozen grey sharks and tiger sharks swimming in a vast tank. The zoo has been successful in breeding from many species which rarely reproduce in captivity: killer whales, maned sea lions and king penguins. Among other activities intended to protect the marine environment, specialists from Marineland offer a veterinary service to marine mammals in the Mediterranean.

Marineland also houses a small museum containing a fine collection of models, marine instruments and other items, including a reconstitution of the 1944 allied landings in Provence.

EDEN-ROC, an Edwardian Paradise

This majestic palace surrounded by an estate (8ha/20 acres) is set on a promontory of Cap d'Antibes. Famous for its quaint huts *(cabanes)* and its private beach, it has become an essential port of call for film stars visiting the Riviera. For a century it was also a favoured holiday destination among crowned heads from all over the world. A wonderful party given by Russian princes in spring 1870 launched the Grand Hôtel du Cap. After a slack period, during which Stephen Liégeard compared the hotel to Sleeping Beauty's castle, the Grand Hôtel was resuscitated at the instigation of the American Gordon Bennett. In 1914 an annexe, the Eden Roc together with its private beach, was built, foreshadowing the popularity of the Riviera as a summer resort. Since then, it has known unflagging success, with a varied and cosmopolitain clientele featuring celebrities such as General Eisenhower, who used it as his winter quarters, the painters Picasso and Chagall, who worked here, and a number of rich eccentrics like the oil magnate Gulbenkian *(Mister 5%)*. The swimming pool is open to non-residents.

Parc Aqua-Splash

Entrance via Marineland. 📷 ⏲ *Open mid-Jun to early Sep daily 10am-7pm.* ⏲ *Closed mid-Sep to mid-June.* 🎟 *18€ (13€ children 3-12 years).* ☎ *04 93 33 49 49. www.marineland.fr.*

This water leisure park offers an impressive range of water games: a swimming pool with waves, water slides, giant pool, and kiddie pool.

La Petite Ferme du Far West

Entrance via the Marineland car park. 📷 ♿ ⏲ *Open 10am to dusk.* ⏲ *Closed Jan.* 🎟 *12€ (10€ children 3-12 years).* ☎ *04 93 33 49 49. www.marineland.fr.*

Kids have fun in this Wild West town that re-creates the spirit of the frontier with a fort, Mississippi riverboats, friendly horses and cattle.

Adventure Golf

Entrance via the Marineland car park. 📷 ♿ ⏲ *Open 10am to dusk.* ⏲ *Closed Jan.* 🎟 *10€ (7€ children 3-12 years).* ☎ *04 93 33 49 49. www.marineland.fr.*

Miniature golf featuring three different 18-hole courses with a Jules Verne theme.

DRIVING TOUR OF CAP D'ANTIBES 🚗 *10km/6mi – allow 2hrs*

Strictly speaking the name Cap d'Antibes refers only to the southernmost tip of land ,but it has come to mean the whole peninsula, which is an enchanting garden dotted with sumptuous hotels and villas catering for both summer and winter visitors.

▶ *Begin at the Pointe Bacon, just past La Salis beach on the Boulevard de Bacon.*

Pointe Bacon

This point gives a **view**★ of Antibes and Fort Carré, sweeping across the Baie des Anges opposite Nice and the surrounding countryside to Cap Ferrat and even Cap Martin near the Italian frontier.

▶ *Continue on Boulevard de La Garoupe, turn right onto Boulevard Francis Meilland and follow signs to the Phare de La Garoupe.*

Sanctuaire de la Garoupe

♿ ⏲ *9.30am-noon, 2.30-7pm (winter 10am-noon, 2.30-5pm).* ☎ *04 93 67 36 01.*

Outside this church are two 17C wrought-iron grilles. Inside, two adjoining chapels, communicating by wide arches, form two aisles.

The widest aisle is ornamented with a fresco by J Clergues. It also contains an interesting **collection of votive offerings**; the oldest dates back to 1779.

On either side of the altarpiece over the high altar are: on the left the **Sebastopol icon**, a magnificent Russo-Byzantine work, believed to date from the 14C, and on the right the *plachzanitza* of the Woronzoffs, a splendid painted silk, also brought back at the time of the siege of Sebastopol.

In the second aisle, decorated with frescoes by Édouard Colin, are some 60 naval votive offerings and maritime souvenirs as well as a gilded wood statue of **Notre-Dame-de-Bon-Port** (Our Lady of Safe Homecoming), patron saint of sailors. Every year on the first or second Sunday in July the statue of Our Lady, taken to the old cathedral in Antibes on the previous Thursday, is brought back in procession to La Garoupe by the seamen. Beside the sanctuary stands the curious Oratoire de Ste-Hélène, first patron of Antibes, who has been worshipped here since the 5C AD in what was originally a pagan shrine.

Phare de la Garoupe

🕐 *Guided tours (30min) 3-6pm (Oct-Apr 3-5pm).* ☎ *04 93 61 57 63.*

The **lighthouse**, one of the most powerful on the Mediterranean coast, with a luminous intensity of 2 300 000 candelas, has a beam which nominally carries 52km/32mi out to sea and 100km/33 000ft up to aircraft. The radio beam has a range of 185km/100 nautical miles.

▶ *Double back and turn right on the Boulevard Meilland, following the Boulevard du Cap to the INRA - VIlla Thuret.*

Jardin Thuret★

🕐 *Open Jun-Oct, Mon-Fri 8am-6pm; Nov-May, Mon-Fri 8.30am-5.30pm.* 🕐 *Closed public holidays.* 🆓 *Free entry.* ☎ *04 93 67 88 66. http://jardin-thuret.antibes.inra.fr.*

These **botanical gardens** covering 4ha/10 acres carry the name of the scientist Gustave Thuret, who created them in 1857. He sought to acclimatise plants and trees from hot countries, successfully spreading the different species throughout the region: the first eucalyptuses, from Australia, were planted here. Bequeathed to the state, these gardens are currently administered by the National Institute of Agronomic Research.

They contain a magnificent collection of 3 000 rare plant and tree species: palm trees, mimosas, eucalyptuses, and cypresses. Villa Thuret, the gardens' botanical center, contains offices and research laboratories.

▶ *Return to Boulevard Meilland and continue along the Avenue Mrs. L.D. Beaumont.*

Villa Eilenroc

🕐 *Open Sep-Jun, Wed 9am-noon, 1.30-5pm. Gardens Tue-Wed 9am-5pm.* 🕐 *Closed Jul-Aug, public holidays.* 🆓 *Free entry.* ☎ *04 93 67 74 33.*

This beautiful seaside estate, built for a Dutchman between 1860-1867, was designed by Charles Garnier, architect of the Paris Opera. It was left to the city of Antibes, which uses it for receptions and the annual "Musiques au Cœur d'Antibes" lyrical arts festival (*early July; contact the Tourism Office for more information*). The interior retains its 1930s decor. The villa grounds include a rose garden and olive tree conservatory.

🚶 *1hr.* Follow the street around the back of the gardens to join the "Sentier Littoral" walking path that leads back to La Garoupe beach.

▶ *Return to the Avenue Beaumont and turn left onto Boulevard John F. Kennedy.*

Musée Napoléonien

Kids 🕐 *Open daily (except Sun-Mon) 10am-6pm (until 4.30pm mid-Sep to mid-Jun).* 🕐 *Closed public holidays.* 🆓 *3€.* ☎ *04 93 61 45 32.*

The former Le Grillon battery has been converted into a museum devoted to Napoleon's reign. At the entrance stand two replicas of a magnificent Louis XIV bronze cannon. Also on display are **Napoleon's bust** sculpted by Canova in 1810, model soldiers and officers of the Great Army, Napoleon's autograph and imperial proclamations. From the roof, there is a fine **view**★ over the wooded headland to the Îles de Lérins and to the distant Alps.

Les **ARCS**

POPULATION 5 334

MICHELIN MAP 340 N5

The town, nestling in the heart of vineyards that produce excellent wines, vies with Brignoles (*see BRIGNOLES*) for the title of capital of the Côtes de Provence area. It is dominated by the ruins of Château Villeneuve, where St Roseline was born, and which is the starting point for the Provence wine circuit.

Les ARCS is also known as Arcs-sur-Argens, after the Latin word for the arch of a bridge (*arcus*), most likely referring to a Roman bridge at the neighboring village, Pont-sur-Argens.

▶ **Orient Yourself:** The town is located in the Var, 25km/15.5mi west of FREJUS on the RN7 and D57. The modern part of Les Arcs is at the foot of the old town, separated by the Tour d'Horloge (clocktower). *Place du Général-de-Gaulle – 83460 – ☎ 04 94 73 37 30.*

◔ **See Also:** the neighboring towns of *LORGUES (17km/10.5mi northwest on the D57 and D10) and DRAGUIGNAN (13km/8mi north on the D555 and N555).*

Walking Tour

▶ *From Place de l'Église take Rue de la Paix leading up to the dungeon keep.*

Le Parage

Around the ruins of the medieval castle are the stepped streets and alleys of the old town winding between and beneath the houses. In the Middle Ages, from the keep, a watch was kept to ward off Saracen invasions.

Church

It attracts many visitors to its **automated nativity scene** *(left on entering)*; the backdrop is the old village of Les Arcs. The side chapels are painted with frescoes: *(left)* the miracle of St Roseline's roses by Baboulaine; *(right)* a **polyptych**★ in 16 sections by Louis Bréa (1501) of the Virgin and Child surrounded by Provençal saints.

Address Book

WHERE TO STAY AND EAT

▭▭ **Aurélia** – *Route nationale 7, Le Pont-d'Argens* - ☎ *04 94 47 49 69* - *hotel. aurelia@wanadoo.fr* - ◔ *Closed Jan ; Restaurant closed off-season Sun night, Mon and holidays* - ▣ ▭- *20 rooms* – *restaurant (▭▭).* Located on the outskirts of the village, this hotel is protected from the noise of the nearby RN7, and many rooms have their own balcony. The traditional restaurant has a fireplace and terrace overlooking the Argens River.

▭▭▭ **Logis du Guetteur** – *Medieval village* - ☎ *04 94 99 51 10* – *www. logisduguetteur.com* - ◔ *Closed 15 Jan-8 Mar* – *12 rooms*– ▭ ▣▤ – *Restaurant (▭▭▭).* In an 11C fort at the heart of the village, this hotel-restaurant has used its superb vaulted stone cellars as a setting for its lounges and dining rooms. Outdoor pool.

SHOPPING

Maison des Vins côtes-de-Provence – *Route nationale 7* - ☎ *04 94 99 50 20* - *www.caveaucp.fr* - ◔ *Open daily Apr-Sep.* ◔ *Closed Sun Oct-Mar.* This country mansion and grounds along the Argens River make up the headquarters of the Côtes-de-Provence appellation wines, bringing together 700 different winemakers in one place. There's a modern tasting area, with 16 different wines available for "dégustation" each week *(free)*. There's a gourmet restaurant on the upper floor.

Château Ste-Roseline – *Quai Sauteirane (next to the Chapelle Ste-Roseline)* – ☎ *04 94 99 50 30* – *www.sainte-roseline.com* – ◔ *Open 9am-12.30pm, 2-6.30pm; weekends 10am-noon, 2-6pm.* This vineyard is set within the grounds of an 11C abbey, home to the St-Roseline chapel. Tasting sessions and wine sales for visitors, tours available for groups of 15 (fee).

The Legend of Sainte Roseline

Ste Roseline (1263-1329) was born in the Château de Villeneuve, daughter of the Lord Arnaud de Villeneuve and Sybille de Sabran. As a young child she would hide food in her apron and distribute it to the poor. One day someone in the palace stopped her and asked what she was carrying. "Roses," she replied, and when she opened her apron the roses miraculously appeared. On the right of the church nave lies the shrine of St Roseline, whose body is amazingly well-preserved. Pilgrimages take place five times a year, the most popular being on Trinity Sunday and the first Sunday in August.

Excursion

Chapelle Ste-Roseline★

4km/2.5mi east of Les Arcs by the D91. ◷ *Open 3-7pm; Mar-May 2-6pm; Oct-Feb open 2-5pm.* ◷ *Closed Mon.* ☞ *Free entry.* ☎ *04 94 73 330 13.*

In the quiet countryside and vineyards around Les Arcs stands the chapel of Ste-Roseline, part of the old abbey of La Celle-Roubaud, founded in the 11C. In the 13C it became a charter house and flourished during the priorate of **Roseline de Villeneuve** from 1300 to 1328. The 12C cloisters and the Provençal-style Romanesque chapel are all that remain.

Interior★

A Renaissance chancel grille surmounted by a polychrome statue of St Catherine of Alexandria divides the nave; on the high altar stands a superb early 16C Baroque altarpiece depicting the Descent from the Cross; the delicately carved choir stalls date from the 17C. The altar at the far end of the nave bears a Renaissance altarpiece showing the Nativity; on the left of the chancel hangs a precious 15C predella. Contemporary works of art include a large mosaic by Chagall (south aisle) inspired by the legend of Ste Roseline; a bronze low relief illustrating Ste Roseline and the miracle of the roses and a lectern in the shape of a bush by Alberto Giacometti's brother, a stained-glass window in iridescent colours (rose petals) by Bazaine and others by Ubac.

AUPS

POPULATION 1 903

MICHELIN MAP 340 M4

With its soothing stone fountains, picturesque old streets and squares shaded by magnificent plane trees, Aups is a charmig place to stroll. The old city ramparts and a ruined castle evoke the past, while the scents and sounds of the open Provençal market add a festive atmosphere. The real draw of Aups, however, is its famous truffle market, attracting professionals from all over France each winter.

▸ **Orient Yourself:** Aups sits at the foot of the Espiguières hills in the Var, bordered to the northwest by the steep highlands of Haute-Provence with the Massif des Maures dominating the horizon to the south.
🛈 *Place F.-Mistral – 83630 –* ☎ *04 94 84 00 69.*

🅿 **Parking:** Parking can be found just off the Avenue Verdun, near the Tourism Office.

Visit

Collégiale St-Pancrace

Place Frédéric Mistral. ☎ *04 94 70 00 80.* ◷ *Open daily 9am-noon, 3-7pm (Jul-Aug 7am-7pm).* ☞ *Free entry.* The collegiate church of St Pancras is 15C Provençal Gothic with a Renaissance doorway; the simple nave ends in a square apse. The church treasury houses some interesting 15C-18C gold- and silver-plate tableware.

Musée Simon-Ségal

Avenue Albert I. ◷ *Open Jul-Aug 10am-noon, 4-7pm.* ◷ *Closed Tue.* ☞ *2.50€.* ☎ *04 94 70 01 95.* This museum of modern art contains 280 pictures, of which 175 are attributed to the Paris School, on display in the former Ursuline Convent's chapel.

Address Book

SHOPPING

Specialities – Here the famous truffle reigns supreme and can be found in many dishes, notably salads, omelettes and spinach. The area is also known for its production of honey and especially the delicious goat's cheese made in the Upper Var Valley.

Moulin à Huile Gervasoni – *Montée des Moulins* – ☎ *04 94 70 04 66* – ◷ *Open Jul-Aug 9.30am-12.30pm, 2-7pm; Apr-Sep 10am-noon, 2.30-7pm.* This 18C olive mill still manufactures and sells olive oil alongside other regional specialities such as tapenade, Provençal fabrics, old fashioned soap and carved olive wood items.

Atelier "La Grange" – *2 Rue Gourguette-Salernes* – ☎ *04 94 70 62 94.* A friendly boutique with pottery, colorful ceramic tiles, and paintings by Lucien Vernet.

Markets – Wednesdays and Saturdays on Place Frédéric-Mistral. Truffle market on Thursday *(Nov to mid-Mar)*. Artisan market evenings *(Jul-Aug)*.

SPORTS IN SILLANS-LA-CASCADE

Office du tourisme de Sillans – ☎ *04 94 04 78 05* – *www.tourisme83.com/sillans. htm.* Canoeing along the waterfalls, hiking and riding in the lush countryside around Sillans.

Musée de Faykod

3.5km/2mi on the Route de Tourtour (D 77). Look for arrows on the right and follow the long driveway. ◷ *Open Jul-Aug 10am-noon, 3-7pm; Sep-May 2-6pm (7pm in Jun).* ◷ *Closed Tue.* ⚲ *6€ (kids 2€).* ☎ *04 94 70 03 94.* Collection of white marble sculptures by Maria de Faykod in a park set within the *garrrigue* scrubland.

Driving Tour

Le Haut Var★ *53km/33mi – about 5hr.*

▷ *From Aups take D 77 east.*

The scenic road winds along the steep slopes of the Espiguières hills and then into the forest. Soon after Château de la Beaume bear left on D 51 through **Tourtour**★ (ⓖ *see TOURTOUR*) , passing the olive trees, pines, oaks and vineyards on the way to **Villecroze** (ⓖ *see VILLECROZE*).

▷ *From Villecroze continue along the D 51, then turn right at the D 560.*

Salernes

An agricultural and industrial centre, Salernes is known for the manufacture of floor tiles and pottery. The distinctive russet-coloured Provençal tiles known as *tomettes* can be seen adorning a great many local houses. Traditionally of hexagonal shape, they are made with local clay, featuring a high iron content, and their warm hues blend in harmoniously with the earthy landscape, echoing the reddish-pink roofs that characterise most Mediterranean *mas*.

The **church**, set among 17C houses, boasts a belfry at both ends. Fountains abound and trees shade the main square where a market takes place every Wednesday and Sunday.

🚶 A fold-out map detailing six walking and mountain biking trails is available from the Tourism Office in Salernes. 🛈 *Place Gabriel-Péri* ☎ *04 94 70 69 02. www.ville-salernes.fr.*

Black Gold of the Haut-Var

The truffle (called *rabasse* in Provence) is a fungus which grows on the secretions which seep out of diseased oak trees. There are two categories of truffle: the white, which are not particularly tasty, and the black, which ripen in the autumn and are recognisable by their distinctive smell. They are harvested from November to February by dogs or by sows that take two years to train. The largest truffle market in the Var takes place in Aups every Thursday during the gathering season. The uninitiated may be surprised by the unusual air of excitement which pervades transactions. Traditionally, the town of Aups hosts a large truffle fair on the fourth Sunday in January. In this truffle-producing region many restaurants offer dishes cooked with truffles – spinach or salad or eggs for example.

▶ *Take D 31 south to follow the Bresque Valley.*

Entrecasteaux (👣 *see ENTRECASTEAUX*)

▶ *From Entrecasteaux take D 31 south; turn right onto D 50.*

Cotignac (👣 *see COTIGNAC*)

▶ *Take D 22 north.*

On your way back towards Aups on the D 22 is a good view back over the site of Cotignac. Farther on to the right the Cascade de Sillans can be glimpsed through the trees.

Cascade de Sillans★

▶ *Before entering the village turn right onto a path (sign; car park).*

🚶 *30min on foot there and back.* In an enchanting setting the Bresque cascades over a 42m/138ft drop. Water sports enthusiasts can go canyoning on the waterfalls and there are also hiking and riding facilities in the lush countryside around Sillans (👣 *see the Address Book for more information*).

Sillans-la-Cascade

Surrounded by forests on the edge of the Bresque, this attractive village has ancient ramparts and picturesque streets around the post office, which boasts a pinnacle turret. The 18C château hosts regular art and artisan expositions (🕐 *Apr-Dec, except Mon-Tue;* 🎟 *Free entry.*)

▶ *Continue on D 22 to return to Aups.*

BANDOL ⛅

POPULATION 7 905

MICHELIN MAP 340 J7

Bandol is a pleasant resort lying inside a pretty bay, sheltered from the north winds by high wooded slopes. It has always been a popular holiday destination among artists and literary celebrities such as Katherine Mansfield, Thomas Mann, or the great French actors Raimu and Fernandel.

▶ **Orient Yourself:** Accessible by the A 50, Bandol lies 18km/11mi west of Toulon. The bay is protected from the harsh northern winds that characterize the region by the steep, forested hills surrounding it. 🅸 *Allée Alfred-Vivien – 83150 – ☏ 04 94 29 41 35 www.bandol.fr.*

Resort Life

The Marina

Enjoy the bracing sea air by following the **Allée Jean-Moulin**★ and Allée Alfred-Vivien along the port, both charmingly bordered with pine trees, palms and brightly colored flower beds.

🚶 **Chemin de la Corniche** skirts the little peninsula with Bendor Island lying off shore, affording a fine view of the coast from Cap de l'Aigle to Cap Sicié.

The Beaches

This seaside resort has four sandy beaches: the east-facing Lido, the well-sheltered Rènecros facing west and the Centrale and Casino beaches facing due south. The rest of the coast (👣 *towards ST-CYR-SUR-MER*) offers smaller beaches alternating with rocky areas.

Bandol AOC

Beyond the villas scattered in groves of pine and mimosa behind the seafront are fields of flowers and vineyards which produce Bandol, the best-known of the Côtes-de-Provence wines. Ask at the Tourism Office for the brochure detailing Bandol vineyard tours.

Côtes-de-Provence Wine

Wines from Provence have always been a great favourite in France, relished by both locals and foreign visitors. These vineyards cover five different *appellation d'origine contrôlée* (AOC) areas and therefore feature a variety of soils and micro-climates. The dry, aromatic white wines from the coastal region and the lively rosés are best enjoyed young. However, the full-bodied reds, in particular those produced on the sun-blessed terraces around Bandol, are definitely for laying down: made with the *mourvèdre* grape, they are high in tannin and their subtle flavour combining pepper, cinnamon, vanilla and black cherries are the perfect complement to venison or red meat. Provençal dialect is still spoken on some of the estates and it has given rise to some curious descriptions of the bunches of grapes: *ginou d'agasso* (magpie's knee) or *pecoui-touar* (twisted tail)!

Sights

Jardin Exotique et Zoo de Sanary-Bandol
3km/2mi north; 500m/550yd after passing over the motorway (A50), turn right (sign "Zoo-Jardin Exotique"). &. 🧒 🕐 *Open Jun-Sep 9am-noon, 2-7pm (from 10am Sun and holidays; open Oct-May 9am-noon, 2-6pm (afternoon only Sun and holidays).* 👓 *8.50€ (child 6€).* ☎ *04 94 29 40 38. http://zoosanary.com.*

In these shaded gardens cacti and tropical plants are grown to remarkable sizes. Among hundreds of rare plants, animals from all over the world can be seen – monkeys (marmosets, Capuchin monkeys, gibbons and their offspring) and also coatis, lemurs, fennecs, kinkajous, peccaries, deer, ponies, miniature goats and llamas. Our feathered friends have not been forgotten either as you can observe the noisy, colorful world of parrots, peacocks, pink flamingoes and cranes.

Île de Bendor ⚓

The **boat trip** (🕐*Departures every 30min leaving from Bandol, 7min).* 👓 *7€ round-trip.* ☎ *04 94 29 44 34)* to the island makes a pleasant summer excursion. The island is an attractive tourist center offering fine beaches, a harbor, as well as a Provençal village with craft shops. Named after the famous *pastis* maker, the **Espace Culturel Paul-Ricard** features a curious **Exposition des Vins et Spiritueux** (🕐 *Open daily Jul-Aug 10am-12.30pm, 3-7pm.* 🕐 *Closed Wed, Sat morning.* 👓 *Free entry.* ☎ *04 94*

Address Book

BOAT TRANSPORTATION

Atlantide 1 – *Quai d'honneur,* ☎ *04 94 32 51 41. www.atlantide.com* ⏰ *Open from Easter through mid-Sep.* Boat excursions and links to the calanques of Cassis, Îles des Embiez and the Porquerolles.

WHERE TO EAT

For coin categories, see the Legend at the back of the guide.

⊖ **Snack Bar Le Souco** – *1 Rue de la Poste – Le Castellet –* ☎ *04 94 32 67 94 –* ⊼. This café-restaurant frequented by the locals is open year-round. Terraces at the front and back allow you to follow the sun.

⊖⊖ **L'Oasis** – *15 Rue des Écoles –* ☎ *04 94 29 41 69 –* ⏰ *Closed Dec and Sun evening off season.* Delightful dining room painted in warm Mediterranean tones. In summer, enjoy the charming terrace looking out onto the garden. Smallish but impeccably kept rooms are being renovated one by one for overnight stays.

⊖⊖ **Le Clocher** – *1 Rue Paroisse –* ☎ *04 94 32 47 65 –* ⏰ *Closed 10-24 Jan, 10-30 Nov, Wed and lunch Jun-Sep.* In an ancient stone house at the foot of the church belltower in Vieux Bandol, this tiny restaurant serves typical regional dishes of the Midi. Small terrace on the street.

⊖⊖ **Restaurant La Farigoule** – *2 Place du Jeu-de-Paume – 83330 Le Castellet –* ☎ *04 94 32 64 58 –* ⏰ *Closed three weeks in Nov, Tue and Wed off season. – Reservation required in summer.* Nestling in the heart of the village, this restaurant boasts a fine dining room with a colourful Provençal decor and a host of mementos surrounding the open fireplace where tasty grilled meat is prepared. Shaded terrace graced by a century-old plane tree.

⊖⊖⊖ **Castel Lumière** – *1 Rue Portail – Le Castellet –* ☎ *04 94 32 62 20 –* ⏰ *Closed 7 Jan-9 Feb, Sun evening and Mon except public holidays.* This restaurant is set up in the house where the Frères Lumière once lived, right in the medieval quarter. The long dining hall affords a panoramic view of the surrounding vineyards. The upstairs rooms are light and cool.

WHERE TO STAY

⊖⊖ **Golf Hôtel** – *10 Corniche Bonaparte, on Rénecros Beach by Boulevard Louis-Lumière –* ☎ *04 94 29 45 83 –* ⏰ *Closed 4-29 Jan, 1-23 Dec – 23 rooms –* 🔲 📶 – *Restaurant (⊖⊖).* A seaside hotel, complete with deckchairs and beach restaurant during the summer season. Most of the homey rooms give onto the sea; some are fronted by a small balcony. Dinner is served only in July and August (special menus for children).

⊖⊖ **Chambre d'Hôte Les Cancades** – *1195 Chemin de la Fontaine de Cinq-Sous – Le Beausset – 3km/2mi E of Le Castellet, take Chemin de la Fontaine de Cinq-Sous which is* just across from the Casino supermarket – ☎ *04 94 98 76 93 – charlotte.zerbib@wanadoo.fr –* ⊓ *– 4 rooms.* A steep, narrow path leads to the wooded, residential area where the owner of this hotel, a retired architect, has set up his charming Provençal mas. The fine, handsomely furnished rooms, the suite, the park, the swimming pool and the summer kitchen are all blissfully quiet and relaxing.

⊖⊖⊖ **Hôtel La Ker-Mocotte** – *103 Rue Raimu –* ☎ *04 94 29 46 53 – www.kermocotte.com –* ⏰ *Closed 15 Nov to Mar –* 🅿 *– 20 rooms – Restaurant (⊖⊖⊖).* This imposing villa, once the property of the actor Raimu, overlooks Rénecros Bay and provides direct access to the beach. A selection of early film posters pay homage to the French entertainer. The quiet rooms are decorated strictly in Provençal style and the dining room opens onto the Mediterranean.

⊖⊖⊖⊖ **Hôtel Delos** – *Île de Bendor – Access by boat –* ☎ *04 94 29 11 60 – www.hoteldelos.com –* ⏰ *Closed Nov-Apr – 55 rooms –* 🅿 ⊠ *– Restaurant (⊖⊖⊖).* Attractive location on the Île de Bendor, half-way between sea and port. Pretty views overlooking the sea can be had from all the comfortable rooms arranged in two stone cottages. Lovely pool.

ON THE TOWN

Tchin Tchin – *11 Allée Jean-Moulin –* ☎ *04 94 29 41 04 –* ⏰ *Daily 8am-3am.* This prestigious bar saw its golden age in the 1970s, when it attracted many celebrities from the entertainment world, namely Jacques Brel and Richard Antony, who coined the title of the club. A good selection of cocktails and cigars, and regular jazz music.

Casino de Bandol – *2 Place Lucien-Artaud –* ☎ *04 94 29 31 31 –* ⏰ *Daily 10am-4am.* Not only does this casino have 120 slot machines, a traditional gaming room and a piano bar, it's also a popular place in the region for its nightclub and special events.

SHOPPING

Beausset Market – Friday and Sunday in the center of town: fresh produce, gourmet specialities, local crafts and clothing.

Le Tonneau de Bacchus – *296 Avenue du 11-Novembre –* ☎ *04 94 29 01 01 – www.letonneaubacchus.com –* ⏰ *Open Tue, Sun 9.30am-12.30am, 4-8pm ; open daily Jul-Aug.* ⏰ *Closed 15 Nov-Dec.* This cellar offers a wide selection of wines from France and especially the Bandol area. The cellarman is extremely knowledgeable about wine and he will be delighted to introduce you to his vintage bottles. All year round, Le Tonneau de Bacchus organises oenology courses and

Bandol port

thematic evenings. Fine gastronomic specialities from Provence are also on sale.

Domaine de Souviou – *83330 Le Beausset – ☎ 04 94 90 57 63 – ○ Open daily Easter-Sep 9.30am-noon, 3-7pm (until 6pm off season). ○ Closed weekends in winter.* Producer and seller of both wine and olive oil. Tastings and tours of the ancient farm available.

OUTDOOR ACTIVITIES

Bandol is classified as a "station nautique", with a diverse offering of water sports and a renowned diving center on the Ile de Bandol. ⓘ *Ask for more information at the Tourism Office or visit www.france-nautisme.com.*

Aquascope – *Tours (30min) leaving from the landing-stage on Quai d'Honneur – ☎ 06 03 44 59 63 (high season).* 🚸 *○ 10am-noon, 2-7pm. ○ Closed Oct-Apr, Mon. ⊕ 11€ (child 6€).* Boat with transparent hull for underwater observation of marine flora and fauna.

Var Voltige – *3250 Route des Hauts-du-Camp – 83330 Le Castellet – ☎ 04 94 90 62 44 – ○ Wed-Sun from 9am (during the day).* This club organises maiden ("baptisme") flights specialised in hair-raising aerobatics. Several other clubs nearby also organise "baptism" flights in planes or helicopters.

29 44 34). Set up in a large hall decorated with frescoes, it covers the production of wine, aperitifs and liqueurs in 51 different countries; 8 000 bottles are on display as well as a collection of glasses and decanters.

Driving Tours

Perched Villages★   *Round-trip of 55km/29mi – allow a half day.*

▸ *From Bandol take D 559 northeast; turn left on D 559B towards Le Beausset and pass under the railway bridge.*

Just after Le Beausset (where you should stop on market days; ⓘ *see the Address Book*), turn right on N 8 towards Toulon. The narrow road winds its way through olive groves, orchards and vineyards dotted with clumps of broom and cypress trees.

Chapelle Notre-Dame-du-Beausset-Vieux

Leave the car below the chapel. ○ Open Tue, Wed, Sun 10am-5pm (until 6pm in summer), rest of the week from 2-5pm (6pm in summer). ☎ 04 94 98 61 53.

The **chapel** has been restored by volunteer workers. It is a stark Provençal Romanesque structure with barrel vaulting in the nave and oven vaulting in the apse. The Virgin and Child in the choir comes from Pierre Puget's studio. In the left niche a group of 400-year-old **santons** illustrates the Flight to Egypt. Some of the votive offerings *(side aisle)* date back to the 18C.

From the terrace above the chapel a **sweeping panorama**★ takes in Le Castellet, Ste-Baume, Gros Cerveau and the coast from Bandol westwards to La Ciotat.

▸ *Return to N 8 and continue north towards Aubagne.*

Circuit du Castellet Paul-Ricard

▶ *8km/5mi north of Beausset by N 8.*

This track, built in 1970 on 1 000ha/2 471 acres of desolate scrubland, has become an essential feature in the lives of Formula 1 and Formula 3 racing drivers. The track (5.8km/3.5mi long) was officially opened on the occasion of the first Grand Prix de France, won by Jacky Stewart. Since then, many international drivers, such as Alain Prost in 1976, have attended the driving school on the circuit. Developments to comply with new regulations and the building of an airfield at Le Castellet have permitted a far greater variety of track events as well as air shows. Meetings popular among the general public include the **Grand Prix Historique de Provence** and the **Deux Tours d'Horloge** (shows and races for vintage cars in April). Every year in May a colourful truck show, the **Grand Prix International de Camions** provides an opportunity to see stunts, early models and a *concours d'élégance* – a competition where first prize goes to the most creatively decorated juggernaut!

▶ *On leaving the circuit, turn left on RN 8 towards Aubagne. At the Camp-du-Castellet crossroads, turn left and left again on D 26 towards Le Beausset. 3km/2mi before the hill to Le Beausset, turn right on D 226 towards Le Castellet.*

Le Castellet★

Nestled on a woody hill dominating the vineyards, this remarkable stronghold, formerly owned by the lords of Les Baux and subsequently by King René, has well-preserved ramparts, a carefully restored 12C church and a castle, parts of which date back to the 11C. From beyond the gate on Place de la Mairie there is an attractive **view** inland towards Ste-Baume. Many houses were originally built in the 17C and 18C. There are art and craft workshops – painting, pottery, weaving and leatherwork. Because of its charm, this perched village has often been used as a setting for films.

▶ *Leave Le Castellet going downhill towards D 66.*

La Cadière-d'Azur

This very old hill town, which had 4 000 citizens at the Revolution, produces Bandol wine. Some of its former defences are still standing. The 13C Peï Gate, in front of the town hall leads to a maze of picturesque old streets. From the eastern end of the village there is a fine **view** ★ inland over Le Castellet to Ste-Baume.

▶ *Follow D 66 to St-Cyr-sur-Mer.*

St-Cyr-sur-Mer – 👁 *see St-CYR-SUR-MER.*

▶ *Return to the D 66 to Les Lecques.*

Les Lecques – 👁 *see Les LECQUES.*

From Les Lecques the road south via La Madrague affords fine **views** of the coast and hinterland before joining D 559 which returns to Bandol.

BARJOLS

POPULATION 2 414

MICHELIN MAP 340 L4

The small town lies in a natural amphitheatre in lush countryside fed by springs and streams. Known for its many fountains and the unusual St-Marcel Festival, Barjols also contributes to traditional Provençal life by making tambourines and flutes *(galoubets)*.

▷ **Orient Yourself:** The town of Barjols is in the Var, 22km/13.6mi north of Brignoles (*see BRIGNOLES*) off the D 554. *Boulevard Grisolle, 83670 Barjols,* ☎ *04 94 77 20 01. www.ville-barjols.fr.*

P **Parking:** Parking can be found to the west of the village, near the Tourism Office.

Walking Tour

The Old Town

Maps detailing the circuit of 30 fountains are available from the Tourism Office.

Old Barjols contains 12 wash-houses and 30 **fountains**. The most remarkable fountain, near the town hall, is a limestone-encrusted mushroom-shaped one, known locally as the "Champignon". A magnificent **plane tree** (circumference 12m/39ft), said to be the largest in Provence, dominates the town hall square.

In the lower town, the **Pontevès House**, named after an old Provençal family from a nearby village, is enhanced by a Renaissance doorway.

Clinging to the hillside, north of the church, lies **Réal**★, the town's oldest quarter. Inhabited since the 12C, it has been occupied for the most part by tanners as water is an essential tool of their trade; 3 levels of partial troglodyte (16C-17C) soaking and rinsing basins were uncovered in the 1980s. Nearby, beneath a vault, the entire text of the Déclaration des Droits de l'Homme et du Citoyen, has been carved on glazed stelae.

Church

The original Romanesque structure was rebuilt in the 16C with a fine Gothic nave. The organ loft, choir panelling and carved misericords are 17C. To the right of the entrance, behind a beautiful 12C font, is the original carved tympanum depicting Christ the King with angels and the symbols of the Evangelists.

Maison Régionale de l'Eau

Kids ◷ *Open 9am-noon, 2-6pm.* ◷ *Closed Sun, holidays, and school breaks.* ⊜ *Free entry.* ☎ *04 94 77 15 83.*

Built within an 18C hospice, this Regional House of Water is both an educational center and an aquarium with fish found in local rivers.

Address Book

WHERE TO STAY

⊜ **L'Auberge de l'Eau Salée** – 606 Chemin de l'Eau Salée – ☎ 04 94 77 26 30 – ◷ Closed Mon evening and Tue off season – Kids ✕. This newly opened motel-style inn at the entrance to the village is a big favorite among families because of its fun, fully equipped playing area for children. The dining hall, decorated in soft, low-key hues, features large bay windows.

EATING OUT

⊜ **Le Val d'Argens** – 83570 Correns – 13km/8mi SE of Barjols – ☎ 04 94 59 57 02 – www.argens83club-internet.fr – ◷ Closed Nov to Feb and Wed off season. This friendly restaurant is named after the Argens, a lively stream running at the foot of the terrace, pleasantly shaded by plane trees. Unusual ornamentation consisting of posters, street plaques, bells and other curiosities. Tasty homemade cuisine with a Provençal flavor.

SHOPPING

Market – Saturday is the largest market day, with a smaller flower market on Thursday, at the Place de la Mairie. The Leather Market takes place every weekend in August.

CALENDAR

Fête de la St-Marcel second weekend in January.

Hunting Dog festival in La Verdière fourth weekend in July.

Festival of St Marcel

Since time immemorial the people of Barjols have slaughtered an ox every year to celebrate their survival during a siege. In 1350 a group of pious citizens, rescuing the relics of St Marcel (a 5C bishop) from the abandoned abbey near Montmeyan, fell in with the other celebrants and religious and secular festivities were thus combined. St Marcel was adopted as the patron saint of Barjols and each year in January his bust is dutifully carried in procession throughout the town. Sometimes the ox is adorned with trappings and blessed by the priest in front of St Marcel's statue. While it is being led round the town on its way to the abattoir, the people sing compline and light bonfires. On the following day, after High Mass, the statue, escorted by the clergy and the band, joins the float bearing the ox on a spit and proceeds to the main square where the ox is roasted whole, while people celebrate in true Provençal style with flutes, tambourines, music and dancing. On the third day the roast ox is distributed to the crowd (*see Calendar of Events*).

Excursions

Source d'Argens *15km/10mi to the southwest.*
▷ *From Barjols take D 560.*

Vallon de Font-Taillade

The road plunges into a green valley of fields and meadows and follows a winding stream. On the slopes vineyards alternate with pines and holm oaks.

▷ *500m/547yd after Brue-Auriac a narrow path to the left leads to a chapel.*

Chapelle Notre-Dame

Next to a graveyard stands an abandoned Romanesque chapel built from the local red stone. Its pleasant façade, pierced by an oculus and a bay and topped by a wall-belfry with twin windows, is obscured by undergrowth.

▷ *Return to D 560 and turn left. Park the car after 3km/2mi, in front of the bridge.*

Source d'Argens

On the right of the road a path leads through the bushes straight to the spring which is one of the sources of the River Argens.

Driving Tour

Plateaux du Haut-Var *52km/32mi – half a day.*

▷ *Leave Barjols just before the public pool, following a small street northwest towards Varages.*

Varages

This pleasant village shaded by plane trees once vied with Moustiers in the production of faience. The decorative patterns here are often similar to those found in Moustiers – the craftsmen would sometimes work in several ceramicist centers – and the production of faience continues today in two factories in Varages, which export much of their production. A fair dedicated to faience, Terre et Feu (earth and fire), takes place each summer alongside an exhibition of works.

Church

Guided tours by appointment through the Tourism Office ☎ 04 94 72 85 14. Built in the 17C in the Provençal Gothic style, the church has a fine bell-tower covered in glazed multicoloured tiles. Inside, the altar of St Claude, patron saint of faience-makers, is decorated with medallions and crosses made locally.

Provençal Bell-Towers in the Var

Les Arcs	Tour de l'Horloge (18C)
Aups	Tour de l'Horloge (Clock tower)
Carces	Bell-tower crowning a fortified gateway (17C)
Carmoules	Belfry (17C)
Cotignac	Bell-tower (16C)
Flassans	Bell-tower (18C)
Salernes	Steeple (18C)
Tavernes	Finely carved bell-tower (18C)

Musée des Faïences

On Place de la Libération. 🕐 *Open Jul-Aug 10am-noon, 3-7pm (Mon 3-7pm); Sep-Jun Wed-Sun 2-6pm.* 🕐 *Closed 15 Dec-Jan.* 📷 *2.50€.* ☎ *04 94 77 60 39.* This museum, housed in the Maison Gassendi, contains a complete retrospective of the history of faience in Varages from the end of the 17C, displayed on two levels. In the many glass cases the different techniques used by local dynasties such as the Armand, Clerissy and Niel families, are explained: hand decoration, decoration with stamps and enamelling techniques. On the first floor, there is a remarkable 19C faience fountain attributed to Mazières.

The **Faïencerie Belle Epoque** (🕐 *Open daily Jun-Sep 9.30am-7.30pm.* 🕐 *Closed Tue Oct-May.* 📷 *Free entry.* ☎ *04 94 77 64 95*) has perpetuated these traditions and produces many Provençal items. It's also possible to watch the artisans at work.
To the north of Varages, D 554 runs between hills planted with vines and olive groves interspersed with holm oaks and pines.

▶ *Take D 554 north from Varages, through the hills and terraces of grape vines and olive trees, to La Verdière.*

La Verdière

This village, on the slopes of a hill, is dominated by its church and castle. The fortress, built in the 10C by the Castellane family, was acquired in the 17C through a marriage by the rich Forbin d'Oppède family. The castle today, in a dilapidated condition, shows the results of efforts by Louis-Roch de Forbin to make the building more comfortable in the 18C.

▶ *East of La Verdière take D 30 towards Montmeyan.*

The road crosses a barren limestone plateau covered with sparse vegetation typical of such an area. Juniper, holm oaks and hawthorn bushes thrive here, as do Scots pine trees, indicating that you have reached the northern edge of the region. This forest of stunted trees is scattered with piles of stones, the remains of attempts to clear and acclimatise the land during the rural expansion of the 19C.

Montmeyan

This medieval village, perched on a hill, dominates the mouth of the Verdon Gorge. There is a fine **view** ★ from the southern entrance to the village over the rocky ridge of the Castellane Pre-Alps to the east. After passing the Tour Charlemagne, vestiges of the 14C castle, there is a panoramic viewpoint overlooking the *causse*, a barren limestone plateau with occasional bursts of color provided by holm oaks alongside clumps of broom and hawthorn blossom.

▶ *Take D 13 south from Montmeyan, then D 71 to Tavernes.*

Tavernes

This is a pleasant village, set in the midst of olive groves and vineyards, in an attractive dip surrounded by hills: there is a square belfry with an 18C wrought-iron campanile on top, and the remains of medieval walls.

🚶 *2hrs.* At the top of the village sits Notre-Dame-de-Bellevue, a chapel dedicated to Our Lady of Bellevue.

▶ *D 554, which takes you back to Barjols, crosses then runs along a charming brook called the Ruisseau des Écrevisses.*

Le BAR-SUR-LOUP ⋆

POPULATION 2 465

MICHELIN MAP 341 C5

Nestled between the River Loup and its tributaries, Le Bar enjoys a privileged site⋆ on a hillside surrounded by terraces planted with orange trees and beds of jasmine and violets. From the church square (Place de l'Église) is a spectacular view⋆ up the Gorges du Loup and eastwards over the hills to Vence. The tranquil medieval village features a well-preserved castle dungeon and significant religious artworks.

▶ **Orient Yourself:** Le Bar is in the Alpes-Maritimes, inland from Antibes. The town is located on the right bank of the Loup River, just at the exit of the lower Loup Valley. It is best visited on foot. *Place F.-Paulet – 06600 – ☎ 04 93 42 72 21. www.bar-sur-loup.com.*

P **Parking:** Park your car at the Place des Carteyrades, a short walk from the Tourism Office.

Visit

The narrow streets of the old town wind round the massive 16C castle with its four corner towers and ruined keep.

Église St-Jacques

🕐 *Open Mon-Sat 9am-noon, 2-5pm, Sun 9am-noon (until 6pm in summer).* ☎ *04 93 42 72 21.*

Embedded in the stonework at the foot of the church's bell-tower is a Roman tombstone. The magnificently carved panels of the Gothic door are attributed to the sculptor Jacques Bellot, who was responsible for the choir stalls in Vence. A fine **altarpiece**⋆ by Louis Bréa consisting of 14 scenes in three tiers painted on a gold background (high altar) depicts the Apostle James the Greater (St Jacques le Majeur) and the Virgin and Child surrounded by 12 saints; the pediment above is adorned with the Trinity and the symbols of the Evangelists.

Under the gallery there's a curious 15C painting on wood titled the **Dance of Death**⋆, naive in technique; it includes a poem in Provençal. The composition illustrates a legend: the Count of Le Bar gave a ball during Lent and his guests were struck dead in the middle of the revels. The Dance of Death was painted to record the divine punishment. Death, in the guise of an archer, strikes down the dancers with his arrows, and their souls, escaping from their bodies through the mouths as tiny naked figures, are weighed in the balance by St Michael, at the feet of Christ, and are flung headlong into the gaping jaws of a monster representing the entrance to Hell.

Practical Information

EATING OUT

⊖⊖ **La Jarrerie** – *8 Avenue Amiral-de-Grasse* – ☎ *04 93 42 92 92* – 🕐 *Closed 2-31 Jan, Wed for lunch, and Tue.* Housed in a wing of a former 17C monastery, this restaurant provides first-rate cuisine in a majestic setting: visible beams, huge fireplace, stone masonry... Large reception hall. The pleasantly shaded terrace is a delight in summer.

CALENDAR

Fête de l'Oranger – Every Easter Monday the villagers celebrate the annual orange blossom harvest, with plenty of *vin d'orange*.

BEAULIEU-SUR-MER ⌂ ⌂

POPULATION 3 675

MICHELIN MAP 341 F5

LOCAL MAP & SEE CORNICHES DE LA RIVIERA

This fashionable resort is protected by a ring of hills against the north winds, making it one of the warmest spots on the Riviera, an asset especially in winter. The town is also an oasis of peace and quiet. For the tourist, the charm of Beaulieu is centred chiefly round the **Baie des Fourmis**★ and Boulevard Alsace-Lorraine, lined with attractive exotic gardens giving it the nickname "Petite Afrique."

▶ **Orient Yourself:** Hugging the coastline between Nice and Monaco, Beaulieu sits right next to Villefranche The best way to get there is by the Basse Corniche (& see Corniches de la RIVIERA). ▯ Place Georges-Clemenceau, ☎ 04 93 01 02 21. www.ot-beaulieu-sur-mer.fr

▯ **Parking:** It's easiest to park around the port, behind the Hôtel de Ville. For walking along the Promenade Maurice-Rouvier, it's best to leave the car along the Avenue Blundell-Maple.

& **Also See:** see VILLEFRANCHE-SUR-MER.

A Love Story

In 1891 this small harbour was discovered by the American press tycoon **Gordon Bennett,** who immediately fell in love with it. He offered to finance the building of a pier but the proud local fishermen declined his offer. However, the winding corniche road linking Beaulieu to Villefranche was his doing and it still bears his name.

Walking Tours

Sentier du Plateau St-Michel★★ 2hrs on foot round-trip – stiff climb.

▮ Starting north of Boulevard Édouard-VII. The path leads up the Riviera escarpment to the plateau (viewing-table), affording wonderful views from Cap d'Ail to the Esterel.

Promenade Maurice-Rouvier★ 1hr on foot there and back.

▮ This remarkable promenade runs parallel to the shore from Beaulieu to St-Jean-Cap-Ferrat. On one side are fine white villas in beautiful gardens and on the other the sea with distant views of the Riviera and peninsular point of St-Hospice.

Address Book

For coin ranges see the Legend at the back of this guide.

EATING OUT

⌒ **Le Petit Paris** – *Boulevard Marinoni* – ☎ 04 93 01 69 91. Rattan chairs, white tablecloths and advertising posters are the main features of this brasserie-type restaurant. Simple, traditional fare served in the dining room or on the mezzanine.

⌒⌒ **Le Marco Polo** – *On the marina* – ☎ 04 93 01 06 50 – ⏲ Closed Tue-Wed Oct-May, and Wed-Thu morning Jun-Sep. Whether they are served on the radiant veranda or the terrace facing the marina and its luxury yachts, the dishes here all pay tribute to the Mediterranean, centering on fish, seafood and pasta. Attractive, reasonably priced menus.

WHERE TO STAY

⌒ **Le Havre Bleu** – *Boulevard Maréchal-Joffre* – ☎ 04 93 01 01 40 – 22 rooms – ⌷.

A blue and white house off the main road provides simple accommodation at affordable prices. The bedrooms, which are gradually being refurbished, are quieter when they give onto the back of the building.

⌒⌒ **Le Sélect** – *1 Rue André-Cane and Place Général-de-Gaulle* – ☎ 04 93 01 05 42 – ⏲ Closed 15 Nov-15 Dec – ⊟ – 19 rooms – ⌷. Housed in a handsome residence, this hotel with Provençal decor offers recently renovated rooms with large, comfortable beds and fully equipped bathrooms. In summer, visitors can settle on the square opposite to have breakfast.

STONES, SEA AND SUN

Small stony beaches are well sheltered from the northerly winds, enjoying a southern exposure. They are located on either side of the marina: Baie des Fourmis beach and Petite Afrique au Nord beach.

Sight

Villa Grecque Kérylos★★

Audio tour. ◷ *Open Feb-Jun and Sep-Oct 10am-6pm; Jul-Aug 10am-7pm; Nov-Jan 2-6pm, Sat-Sun, public holidays, school holidays 10am-6pm.* ⊛ *7.80€ (5.50€ child).* ☏ *04 93 01 61 70. www.villa-kerylos.com.*

This faithful reconstruction of a sumptuous Greek villa of ancient times was conceived by the archeologist Théodore Reinach, and built in 1902 by the architect Pontremoli. It was bequeathed to the Institut de France in 1928. On a **site**★ reminiscent of the Aegean, the villa stands in a pleasant garden above the sea looking out over the Baie des Fourmis, Cap Ferrat, Èze and Cap d'Ail.

Precious materials such as Carrara marble, alabaster and rare and exotic woods were used on the interior. The frescoes are reproductions or variations on originals. The furniture, made of wood inlaid with ivory, bronze and leather, is modeled on examples seen on vases and in mosaics. Some of the pieces are originals: mosaics, amphorae, vases, lamps, statuettes. Although the villa is well-equipped with modern conveniences, these are all extremely well concealed.

BIOT★

POPULATION 7 385

MICHELIN MAP 341 D6

Biot (the final "t" is voiced) is a picturesque hillside village where cut flowers particularly roses, carnations, mimosas and anemones, are cultivated for the market. In ancient times the village was known for its pottery, but today it's more famous for its blown glass and, since 1960, the artist and former *Biotois,* **Fernand Léger.**

▶ **Orient Yourself:** Biot lies 4km/2.5mi inland, about 7.5km/4.6mi from Antibes on the N 7 then the D 4. ▯ *46 r.St-Sébastien,* ☏ *04 93 65 78 00. www.biot-coteazur. com.*

▯ **Parking:** Only residents can drive into the village, but there are several free parking areas with regular shuttles to the village center.

Sights

Old Village

The evening is the best time to appreciate the authentic charm of the picturesque streets, starting from the Tourist Office *(syndicat d'initiative)* and following the arrows, through the town gates, Porte des Migraniers (Grenadiers) and Porte des Tines (both 16C), and emerging into the beautiful **Place des Arcades** with its rounded and pointed arches.

Church

Set back from the Place des Arcades with a mosaic stone pavement, the church is actually below street level, with stairs leading down from the entrance. Rebuilt in the 15C it was decorated with murals which the bishop of Grasse considered crude and had painted over.

On the west wall is the **altarpiece**★ of the Virgin of the Rosary in red and gold attributed to Louis Bréa: on the central panel a Virgin of Pity covers the Child Jesus, clerics and laymen with her cloak and stands against a blue-green sky, holding a

---

2 500 Years of History

There is evidence of settlement by the Celto-Ligurians, Greeks and Romans from finds made in the area and in the La Brague plain. In 1209 the Templars took over from the local lords and unified the village. In 1312 the deeds passed to the Hospitallers of St John of Jerusalem and order reigned. In the 14C Biot suffered from the Black Death and warring factions; the decline was reversed only following an edict in 1470 by Good King René allowing 40 families from Oneglia and Porto Maurizio (now Imperia on the Ligurian coast) to settle in the village.

A Story of Success

The architect Andreï Svetchine was the son of a Russian general; he was born in Nice, where he grew up and attended the Academy of Decorative Arts. He soon demonstrated remarkable skills as an architect and was to design some of the most prestigious private residences and museums on the Riviera, notably the Fernand Léger Museum in Biot. In early 1960s, the painter Marc Chagall asked him to build a house and adjoining studio. The result, "La Colline", was a splendid construction in white Provençal stone arranged in rectangular shapes. He also undertook to refurbish La Colombe d'Or, the famous hotel in St-Paul-de-Vence that caters to an exclusive international clientele. In 1984, towards the end of his life, he supervised the challenging task of restoring St-Nicolas, the superb Russian Orthodox Cathedral in Nice.

rosary in her hands. A graceful Mary Magdalene is depicted twisting a strand of golden hair between her fingers.

On the right at the far end of the church there is another altarpiece attributed to Canavesio who married a local girl: an **Ecce Homo** with two cherubs and the instruments of the Passion; above the Flagellation, Christ Reviled and the Resurrection.

Musée National Fernand-Léger★★

Southeast of the village, just off D 4 (signposted).   *Open 10am-12.30pm, 2-5.30pm (Jul-Sep open 10.30am-6pm). Closed Tue, 1 Jan, 1 May and 25 Dec.* 4€. *Free entry 1st Sun of each month, or for children under 18.* 04 92 91 50 30. www.musee-fernandleger.fr.

Built in 1960 by **Andreï Svetchine,** a local architect, the museum, which contains 348 works by Léger (1881-1955), and the gardens were given to the French nation by Mme Nadia Léger and Georges Bauquier.

The façade is decorated by a vast **mosaic** (500m2/5 382sq ft) celebrating sports, designed for the Hanover Stadium. On the left is a monumental ceramic *Children's Playground* and two large bronzes *Women with Parrot and Walking Flower.* Displayed in the entrance hall, lit by a stained-glass window, is a large tapestry in beige and grey: *The Bathers.*

The ground-floor gallery presents original ceramics produced between 1950 and 1955 in the Brice workshop in Biot and **paintings** reflecting the artist's evolution from 1905 to his death. *Portrait of the Uncle* (1905) and *My Mother's Garden* are Impressionist in

Address Book

TOURS

Several themed self-guide maps to the village are available at the Tourism Office, including the "Chemin des Verrieres." For exploring the area, purchase a copy of their Vallée de la Brague hiking map with 11 trails along the Brague River (*see VALBONNE*).

EATING OUT

Le Café de la Poste – *24 Rue St-Sébastien* – 04 93 65 19 32 – *Closed 11 Nov-11 Dec.* One of the oldest cafés on the Riviera, the decor of this bistro-type restaurant features a pretty wooden counter, a huge fresco on painted ceramics and a collection of humorous paintings. Good service. Traditional cuisine.

SHOPPING

Verrerie de Biot – *Chemin des Combes, at the foot of the village, along D 4* – 04 93 65 03 00 - www.verreriebiot.com - Apr-Oct 9.30am-7pm (Jul-Aug 9.30am-8pm), Sun and public holidays 10am-1pm, 3-7pm;

S. Sauvignier/ MICHELIN

Nov-Mar 9.30am-6pm, Sun and public holidays 10.30am-1pm, 2.30-6.30pm. This small factory founded in Biot in 1956 features several workshops that demonstrate the successive stages of the art of glass blowing, characterised by a bubbly texture peculiar to the Biot production. The different shops sell all kinds of glassware: vases, glasses, bottles, small oil lamps, jugs etc.

style while Cézanne's influence is evident in *Study of a Woman in Blue* (1912) and *14 July*. Between the two World Wars the artist experimented with contrasting primary colors (unusual *Gioconda with Keys* – 1930) and geometrical compositions (*The Great Tug* – 1923). In *Study of Adam and Eve* (c 1934), the artist shows a total disregard for facial features – which was to become the rule – and the characters become secondary to the general composition.

At a later stage (1942) Léger gave equal importance to color and line *(Divers)* used at random within a strict composition. After 1945 the artist painted large canvases praising the virtues of hard work and industrial civilization – *Builders*, 1950, marks a significant achievement in style and inspiration – relaxation and *joie de vivre (Campers)*. *The Great Parade* (1954) pays homage to the fabulous world of the circus. A staircase lit through a stained-glass window leads to the graphic arts room on the ground floor, in which drawings and gouaches reflecting the artist's various phases of development are on display.

Outside, this wing features huge mosaic works (including one of 300m2/3 230sq ft) executed in 1990 after original designs by the artist. On the west front is a design planned for the Triennale de Milan; another version of *Les Oiseaux sur Fond Jaune* adorns the east façade.

Musée d'Histoire Locale et des Céramiques Biotoises

Entrance from the Tourist Information Center. ⏱ *Apr and Jul-Sep open daily (except Mon and Tue) 10am-6pm; Oct-Jun open daily (except Mon and Tue) 2-6pm.* ⏱ *Closed public holidays.* ⊷ *2€. Free entry 1st Sun of each month.* ☎ *04 93 65 54 54.*

This museum of local history and ceramics is situated in the ruined Chapelle des Pénitents-Blancs, topped by a three-sided pinnacle, and retraces the main events in Biot's history. It was under the Phoceans that the production of ceramic jars originated in Biot. They were made with local clay extracted from nearby quarries. In the Middle Ages the town was famed for its large jars used for keeping and carrying oil. Today a few workshops have maintained the tradition, branching out into pottery, ornamental stoneware and silver plate. A collection of 19C domestic water cisterns in yellow enamel streaked with green and brown, jars bearing the stamps of former craftsmen and a reconstructed local kitchen are of great interest.

Bonsaï Arboretum

Chemin du Val de Pôme, 100m/109yd south of the Musée Fernand Léger. ⏱ *Open daily (except Tue) 10am-noon, 2-6pm.* ⏱ *Closed 1 Jan, 1 May.* ⊷ *4€.* ☎ *04 93 65 63 99. www. museedubonsai.free.fr.*

This sloping garden (53 000m2/32 300sq ft), displays a large collection of bonsai trees against the backdrop of a reconstructed Japanese garden, as well as other tropical plants in nearby greenhouses.

For those interested in modern art

Antibes: Musée Picasso
Biot: Musée Fernand-Léger
Cagnes-sur-Mer: Musée Renoir and Musée d'Art Moderne Méditerranéen
Menton: Musée du Palais Canolès, the Salle des Mariages in the town hall and the Musée Jean-Cocteau
Nice: Musée Marc-Chagall, Musée des Beaux-Arts, Musée Matisse and the Musée d'Art Moderne et Contemporain
St-Paul: Fondation Maeght
St-Tropez: Musée de l'Annonciade
Vallauris: Musée National "La Guerre et la Paix" and the donation Magnelli
Vence: Chapelle du Rosaire (Chapelle Matisse)
Villefranche: Chapelle St-Pierre (Chapelle Jean-Cocteau)

Where to see the works of the great masters

Chagall: Musée National du Message Biblique in Nice
Cocteau: Chapelle St-Pierre in Villefranche-sur-Mer, Musée Jean-Cocteau and the Salle des Mariages in the Menton town hall, Chapelle Notre-Dame-de-Jérusalem in Fréjus
Dufy: Musée des Beaux-Arts in Nice
Léger: Musée National Fernand-Léger in Biot
Matisse: Musée Matisse in Nice and the Chapelle du Rosaire in Vence
Picasso: Musée Picasso in Antibes and Musée National "La Guerre et la Paix" in Vallauris
Renoir: Musée Renoir in Cagnes-sur-Mer

BORMES-LES-MIMOSAS ★

POPULATION 6 324

MICHELIN MAP 340 N7 - LOCAL MAP SEE MASSIF DES MAURES

Bormes-les-Mimosas stands in an enchanting **setting**★ near the sea, on a steep slope at the entrance to the Forêt du Dom. It's an attractive place, with a colorful profusion of oleander, camomile, eucalyptus, and mimosa that scent the winding streets of the old village, and a marina and beaches which attract the sun seekers.

▶ **Orient Yourself:** The beaches of this Var village stretch 17km/10.5mi from Le Lavandou to the bay of Brégançon: La Favière with its pleasure port, the Bay of Gaou, Cap Bénat *(private)*, Cabasson, Léoube, and the coves to be discovered along the seaside walking trails. Hikers will particularly enjoy exploring the Massif des Maures, which flank the village. 🚹 *Place Gambetta* , ☎ *04 94 01 38 38. www. bormeslesmimosas.com.*

♿ **Also See:** *LAVANDOU, Massif des MAURES)*

Address Book

TOURS

Guided Tour – 🕐 Apr-Sep, Thu 5pm. ⊕ Tickets 5€. A 90-minute walking tour of the old town architecture and flora. SIgn up at the Tourism Office.

Brochures – The Tourism Office has a map of the old village designating all of the main sights. They also sell a guide to the local flora, "Guide des Fleurs," for 5€.

Wine – Ask at the tourism Office for the brochure "Route des Vins de Bormes-les-Mimosas" for information on visiting the 12 local Côtes-de-Provence vineyards.

EATING OUT

For coin ranges see the Legend at the back of the guide.

⊖⊖ **La Ferme des Janets** – *378 Chemin des Janets – Route d'Hyères* – ☎ *04 94 71 4511* – 🕐 *Closed 2 Jan-11 Feb, Mon evening, Tue evening, Thu evening and Wed Nov to late Mar.* A footpath wending its way past vineyards, cork oak trees, cypresses and oleanders leads to a charming mas where chickens and ducks are raised. After a hearty meal of traditional country food, relax on the leafy terrace or indulge in a game of boules with the owner.

⊖⊖ **Lou Portaou** – *Rue Cubert-des-Poètes* – ☎ *04 94 64 86 37* – 🕐 *Closed 15 Nov-20 Dec, Mon night and Tue off season, lunch in season – Reservation required* . Set up in a 12C watchtower overlooking the village, this restaurant exudes an unpretentious atmosphere, enhanced by stone walls and antique furniture. Local cuisine is served in the dining room or on the terrace.

WHERE TO STAY

⊖ **Le Grand Hôtel** – *167 Route du Baguier – Exit N of Bormes, towards Collobrières –* ☎ *04 94 71 23 72 – www.augrandhotel.com –* 🕐 *Closed Nov-Feb –* 🅿 *– 50 rooms –* ⊠ *– Restaurant (⊖).* For a whiff of Victoriana, check in at this grand hotel built in 1903 on the slope of the hill, dominating the town center. Large, soundproofed rooms, most of which have a balcony overlooking the sea.

⊖⊖ **Hôtel Les Palmiers** – *Chemin du Petit-Fort – 8km/5mi S of Bormes –* ☎ *04 94 64 81 94 – les.palmiers@wanadoo.fr –* 🕐 *Closed 15 Nov-31 Jan –* 17 *rooms –* ⊠ *– Restaurant (⊖⊖).* Lying in a residential district half-way between the beach and Brégançon Fort, this hotel is a haven of peace. Most of the rooms boast a large balcony. The dining room opens out onto a flowered terrace where meals are served in high season. Half-board only in summer.

SHOPPING

Markets – Wednesdays in the old village, Saturdays at La Favière (in summer), and Marché Provençal at Pin-de-Bormes (last weekend in September).

CALENDAR

Mimosalia – *Last weekend in January* Open market for show plants.

Corso – *Third weekend in February* Bormes celebrates Mardi Gras with a Corso parade and floats throughout the village streets.

Foire aux Santons – *First weekend in December* Display and sale of the Provençal dolls called Santons.

Latin American Ties

Two inhabitants of Bormes played an important part in the wars of independence in Latin America in the 19C. **Hippolyte Mourdeille** (1758-1807) lost his life chasing the Spaniards out of Montevideo and **Hippolyte Bouchard** (1780-1837) organised the Argentinian navy. Bormes honours their achievements by celebrating Argentina's National Independence Day on 9 July.

Walking Tour

Old Streets★

Below the church the streets of old Bormes are typical of a Provençal village. Several covered passageways run between the lanes, providing shade for passers-by. Many steep alleyways tumble down from the castle: the steepest of these, known as "neck-breaker" *(Rompi-Cuo)*, is laid with smooth paving stones separated by a central drain.

Place St-François

A statue commemorating Francesco di Paola, who is said to have saved Bormes from the plague in 1481, stands in front of the massive 16C **Chapelle St-François** surrounded by dark cypress trees. Among the exotic plants in the neighbouring graveyard with its 18C tombs is a monument to the painter Jean-Charles Cazin, who was particularly attached to the place.

Terrace

Fronting the chapel, it affords a good **view** of Bormes port and Cap Bénat. The round tower to be seen in the distance is the base of an old mill.

Église St-Trophyme

▶ *200meters/218 yards from the Hôtel de Ville*

The robust three-aisled church near the town hall was built in the 18C in the Romanesque style. The façade bears a sundial with the Latin inscription: *Ab Hora Diei ad Horam Dei* (from daily time to divine time). The interior is decorated with 14 oil paintings by Alain Nonn (1980) depicting the Way of the Cross. Six reliquary-busts crowning the pillars date from the 18C.

Château

The signs *"Parcours Fleuri"* near the church lead to a flower-lined walk round the castle, which has been partially restored as a dwelling. Beyond the castle the terrace provides a fine **view**★ over Bormes, the port, Cap Bénat and the islands of Port-Cros and Le Levant.

Sights

Musée Arts et Histoire

65 Rue Carnot. ⏱ *Open 10am-noon, 2.30-5pm, Sun 10am-noon. (Jul-Aug 10am-noon, 3-6pm, Sun and public holidays 10am-noon).* ⏱ *Closed Mon, 1 Jan, 1 May, 25 Dec, 31 Dec.* ▧ *free entry.* ☎ *04 94 71 56 60.*

This museum presents the history of Bormes, Fort Brégançon and the Chartreuse de la Verne. It also retraces the lives of Bouchard and Mourdeille (⌚ *see above*). A century of regional painting, including the works of **Jean-Charles Cazin** (1841-1901), a landscape painter and decorator, are also on show.

Excursion

Cap de Brégançon

On the eastern edge of Hyères harbor a fortress sits on a rocky promontory. The **Fort de Brégançon** (⊶ *Not open to the public*) is built on a small island linked to the shore of Cap Bénat by a footbridge. It was neglected from the beginning of the 18C but the young General Bonaparte began its restoration, which was completed between the two World Wars. The oldest parts of the building date from the 16C. The drawbridge and the two crenellated towers can be seen from the beach beside the walls. In 1968 it officially became the summer retreat of the French President of the Republic. Georges Pompidou was said to be particularly fond of the place and Jacques Chirac can sometimes be seen relaxing among the mimosa trees.

BREIL-SUR-ROYA

POPULATION 2 058

MICHELIN MAP 341 G4 - LOCAL MAP SEE NICE

Breil-sur-Roya

Breil lies below the summit of l'Arpette (1 610m/5 282ft), astride the Roya River, a few miles from the Italian border, giving the town an Italian look and feel. Several small industries, such as leather, olives, dairy farming, sustain Breil, which is also a popular location for fishing and river water sports.

Address Book

TOURS

Self-Guided Tours – The Tourism Office provides a detailed map for exploring the village as well as three hiking intineraries promising "fascinating and panoramic views" starting from Breil.

EATING OUT

Le Roya – *Place Brancion –* ☎ *04 93 04 47 38 –* Ⓒ *Closed Mon –* ⌿. Has visiting the chapel made you hungry? Sit down in the vaulted dining room of this rustic restaurant adorned with early presses. Traditional French cuisine in a convivial setting.

WHERE TO STAY

⊖⊖ **Le Roya** – *Place Biancheri –* ☎ *04 93 04 48 10 – 13 rooms –* ⌶ *– Restaurant* *(*⊖⊖*).* This hotel erected on the left bank of the Roya stands out because of its brightly coloured façade. Simple, unadorned rooms and roomy bathrooms await you here. We recommend the rooms overlooking the mountain or the river.

⊖⊖ **Castel du Roy** – *Route de Tende, 1km/0.6mi –* ☎ *04 93 04 43 66 – www. castelduroy.com –* Ⓒ *Closed 24 Oct-3 Apr – 18 rooms –* ⌶ Ⓟ *– Restaurant (*⊖⊖*).* Set in a carefully tended park running along the banks of the Roya, this homey hotel is

beautifully quiet. It is the perfect starting-point for many excursions: to the nearby mountains, the Vallée des Merveilles or the Parc du Mercantour. Have a dip in the swimming pool to recover from the day's exertions.

TRANSPORT

Access by train – The Italian and French rail links from Nice and Vintimille towards Cuneo and Turin pass by the stations of Breil (Roya-Bévéra), Sospel and Tende. A particularly scenic trip.

In summer take the "Train des Merveilles," which has live commentary of the route (Ⓒ *see Planning Your Trip*).

LEISURE ACTIVITIES

A.E.T. Nature – *392 Chemin du Foussa –* ☎ *04 93 04 47 64 - www.aetcanyonnig.com –* Ⓒ *Open daily by reservation.* This company organizes hikes, via ferrata, rafting, and a camping refuge for up to 20 *(reservations required).*

Roya Évasion – *1 Rue Pasteur –* ☎ *04 93 04 91 46 – www.royaevasion.com –* Ⓒ *Open Wed-Fri 9am-noon, 2-7pm; daily Jul-Aug –* Ⓒ *Closed Nov.* Roya Évasion organises a great many sporting activities: canoeing, rafting, hiking, mountain biking etc. Equipment for hire.

▶ **Orient Yourself:** Breil is situated on the main road from Ventimiglia to Turin, via the Col de Tende (pass), between Sospel (*23km/14mi away*) and Saorge (*11.5km/7mi away*). The town straddles both banks of the Roya, whose waters are controlled by a small dam. The old town is found on the left bank. ⓘ *Place Bianchéri,* ☎ *04 93 04 99 76. www.breil-sur-roya.fr.* ⓘ *Office du tourisme de la Vallée de la Roya,* ☎ *04 93 04 92 05. www.royabevera.com.*

⚲ **Also See:** *SAORGE, SOSPEL.*

Visit

Situated on the east bank, the old village consists of picturesque streets where traces of the ramparts and gateways can be seen among the old buildings. The Renaissance **Chapelle Ste-Catherine** (which hosts regular art exhibitions) with its doorway flanked by two Corinthian pillars stands south of the parish church.

Santa-Maria-in-Albis
🕐 *Open daily 9am-noon, 2-6pm.*

The vast 18C church with its carved doors (1719) and Baroque interior on a Greek cross plan, is adorned with an ornate 17C **organ loft** of carved and gilded wood (gallery) and an early **altarpiece** (1500) to the left of the chancel: St Peter as Pope with the triple crown between St Paul and St Jerome and above St Catherine and St Bartholomew on either side of the Transfiguration.

BRIGNOLES

POPULATION 12 487

MICHELIN MAP 340 L5 - LOCAL MAP SEE EXCURSIONS BELOW

The narrow twisting streets of old Brignoles form a dense hillside labyrinth below the venerable crenellated castle once home to the counts of Provence. All around, green rolling countryside stretches over the broad Carami Valley. This rich market town produces peaches, honey, olives and oil, but its modern prosperity is due to the marble quarries situated at Candelon (*southeast of the town, closed in 1980*) **and the annual wine exhibition-fair held in the first fortnight in April which has made the town the wine capital of the Var and of Provence.**

▶ **Orient Yourself:** Brignoles is in the lower Carami Valley, with the old town clinging to the north side of a hill and the new town in the plain below. Coming from the south (*50km/31mi from Toulon;* or from the north (*22km/13.6mi from Barjols*), all roads lead to the town's large parking area at the Place des Augustins. ⓘ *Syndicat d'Initiative, 10 Rue Palais,* ☎ *04 94 69 27 51.* ⓘ *Office intercommunal de tourisme de la Provence Verte, carrefour de l'Europe,* ☎ *04 94 72 04 21. www.la-provence-verte.org.*

⚲ **Also See:** *TOULON, BARJOLS.*

Visit

A map of the medieval city is available from the Tourist Office (⚲ see Syndicat d'Initiative above).

South of Place Carami, picturesque old streets lead to the church of St-Sauveur and to the castle of the counts of Provence. Walk along the covered Rue du Grand-Escalier, Rue du St-Esprit and Rue des Lanciers, in which there is a **Romanesque house** with twin windows.

Église St-Sauveur
🕐 *Open Sunday morning.*

This church boasts a fine exterior Romanesque doorway (12C) framed by Ionic columns. The simple interior consists

Brignoles Church (detail)

E. Barey/MICHELIN

Address Book

For coin ranges see the Legend at the back of the guide.

EATING OUT

La Remise – *4 Avenue de la Libération – Besse-sur-Issole – 15km/9mi –SE of Brignoles on N 7 towards Le Luc and right on D 13 –* ☎ *04 94 59 66 93 –* 🕐 *Closed Mon in Jul-Aug.* Small, unpretentious establishment discreetly located at the entrance to the village. The white walled decor has a simple, minimalist feel with a few paintings and photographs. Outside is a shaded courtyard. The kitchen, which can be glimpsed from the dining room, serves simple fare with a Mediterranean touch.

Le Resto – *Place de la Mairie –* ☎ *04 94 77 29 87 –* 🕐 *Closed Wed in winter and Thu.* The small dining room is rustic and intimate, with reproduction Gauguin paintings decorating the walls and a flowered terrace under the Plane trees. The cuisine is traditional French with a Provençal touch, all home-made on the premises.

WHERE TO STAY

La Cordeline – *14 Rue des Cordeliers –* ☎ *04 94 59 18 66 – Reservations a must – 5 rooms – Meal (*😋😋*).* Handsome 17C mansion providing accommodation in tastefully furnished rooms, complete with fully equipped bathroom and small salon. Delightful terrace with arbour for basking in the sun. A haven of tranquillity at the heart of the town.

Chambre d'Hôte Château de Vins – *Vins-sur-Caramy – 9.5km/5.5mi from Brignoles on D 24, Route du Thoronet –* ☎ *04 94 72 50 40 –* 🕐 *Closed Nov to Apr –* 🛏 *– 5 rooms.* Listed 16C building with four turrets whose austere yet imposing rooms carry the names of famous musicians. Cultural events, concerts, music lessons and exhibitions will liven up your stay in this hotel, carefully renovated by its dedicated and impassioned landlord.

SHOPPING

Specialities – Brignoles delicacies are jams and sweets made with plums, to be found in many local stores, such as the tarte Brinonia at **Lafitau Bakery** *(31 Avenue Dréo –* ☎ *04 94 69 22 83 –* 🕐 *Open Tue-Sun 6am-8pm).*

Open-Air Markets – Every Wednesday at the Place Carami and Saturday at the Place Général du Gaulle and Place du 8 Mai.

Agricultural Fair – This fair-exhibition launched in 1921 is dedicated to wines from Provence and the Var region, as well as honey, olives, olive oil and other typical produce. It is held for ten days during the month of April.

Maison des Vins Coteaux Varois – *Abbaye de la Celle - La Celle -* ☎ *04 94 69 33 18 -* 🕐 *Open winter Mon-Sat 10am-noon and 2-6pm; summer Mon-Sat 10am-noon, 3-7pm, Sun 10am-noon.* This boutique is in a 12C abbey, part of which has been renovated to present local regional products, including 80 different wine producers. There's also a small vineyard on the premises open to visits.

Atelier Debuisson-Cetani – *Rte du Lac - Carcès -* 🕐 *Open daily 9am-7pm.* Jean Debuisson, one of the last pewter tableware makers, has passed along his craft to Valérie, his daughter. She offers free demonstrations of the two different traditional methods used, and all of the items in the boutique can be custom engraved.

---

of a nave in Provençal Gothic style. The 15C low-relief sculptures in gilded wood, depicting the sacrifice of Abraham and the distribution of manna, frame the high altar. The south chapel contains a **Descent from the Cross** by Barthélemy Parrocel, who died at Brignoles in 1660 and whose descendants were also painters. The door to the sacristy is 16C.

Musée du Pays Brignolais

🕐 *Open Apr-Sep 9am-noon, 2.30-6pm, Sun 9am-noon, 3-6pm; Oct-Mar 10am-noon, 2.30-5pm, Sun 10am-noon, 3-5pm.* 🕐 *Closed Mon and Tue and public holidays.* 😋 *4€.* ☎ *04 94 69 45 18.*

This regional museum is housed in a building which dates in part from the 12C, formerly the castle of the counts of Provence. The chief exhibit is the **La Gayole tombstone**★ (late 2C-early 3C) illustrating the transition from pagan to Christian iconography (bust of Apollo, the Sun God on the left).

Brignoles Plums

Brignoles plums were famous throughout the kingdom until the 16C. As sugar-plums, they were a delicious addition to the sweetmeat dishes of the time: the Duke of Guise was nibbling one a few minutes before he was assassinated at Blois. All the plum trees used to belong to a local lord but during the League in the 16C, the people of Brignoles ransacked his lands and destroyed 180 000 trees. Since then "Brignoles plums" have actually been grown around Digne.

BRIGNOLES	
8 Mai 1945 R. du	38
Carami Pl.	3
Cavaillon Traverse	4
Comtes-de-Provence Pl. des	6
Dr-Barbaroux R. du	8
Dréo Av.	9
Ferry R. Jules	12
Foch Av. Mar.	14
Grand-Escalier R. du	15
Lanciers R. des	19
Liberté Cours de la	21
Mistral Av. Frédéric	22
Ottaviani R. Louis	25
Palais R. du	2
Parrocel Pl.	26
République R. de la	28
St-Esprit R.	30
St-Louis Bd	32
St-Pierre Pl.	34

Maison romane	E
Musée du Pays brignolais	M

Also on the ground floor is a reproduction of an 18C Provençal kitchen and an exhibition on the local mining of bauxite, with a reconstruction of a mine gallery. On display is a cement boat by Joseph Lambot, who invented reinforced concrete. There is some fine 17C woodwork in the castle chapel, as well as a beautiful 11C black **Virgin and Child** in carved wood.

Barthélemy and Joseph Parrocel and Montenard (1849-1926) are represented in the gallery of religious and pagan art upstairs. An exhibition on local customs includes a **Nativity scene**, created in 1952 in the Provençal tradition.

Excursion

Abbaye de la Celle

Leave Brignoles by the D 554 going south and turn right on the D 405. ◔ *Guided tours (45min) Apr-Sep daily 9.30am-noon, 2-6pm, Sat-Sun and public holidays 9am-noon, 2-5pm; Oct-Mar daily 9am-noon, 2-5pm, weekends 9am-noon, 2-5pm (from 10am Sun).* ◔ *Closed 1 Jan, 1 May, 1 and 11 Nov, 25 Dec.* ◷ *2.30€.* ☎ *04 94 59 19 05. www.la-celle.fr.*

In the 13C the Benedictine convent attracted the daughters of the Provençal nobility, but by the 16C standards had fallen so low that the nuns were distinguished from other women only by their dress and the number of their lovers. Efforts at reform failed and the convent was closed in 1660 on the orders of Mazarin.

The 17C Prioress' house has been converted into a country hotel. The cloisters, chapterhouse and refectory can be visited. The austere Romanesque abbey church is now the parish church, containing a 15C Crucifixion executed with striking realism.

Driving Tours

1️⃣ **Brignoles Country★** *56km/35mi – allow 3hr – see local map below.*

▶ *Leave Brignoles to the north on D 554.*

The dark green of the pines in this undulating countryside contrasts with the varied colors of farmlands, dominated by vineyards, and red-stained earth (from the bauxite mines).

Le Val

The village lies beside the Roman Via Aurelia and was once enclosed by ramparts. Its narrow houses cluster around an elaborate, 18C wrought-iron campanile. Skilled development of the site has preserved its Provençal character.

On the way into the village stands the **Hôtel des Vins,** whose façade proudly bears a fresco painted by one of Dali's pupils. The Romanesque church still has some beautiful 18C frescoes as well as some 16C polychrome statues.

Musée du Santon

🧒 ♿ ◔ *Open 9am-noon, 2-6pm.* ◔ *Closed 1 Jan, 25 Dec.* ◷ *2€.* ☎ *04 94 37 02 22.*

Housed in the old communal oven (12C) the museum features glass cases in the long vaulted bakehouse with a miscellaneous collection of Provençal santons as well as Nativity scenes from Venice, Israel, Latin America and Africa. The oven contains a large Nativity of Neapolitan origin.

"A Stacada"

This unusual and highly colourful event takes place every four years (*the last time was in 2005*) to commemorate the abolition of the *droit du seigneur* brought about by the rebellion of the Breil inhabitants who had been subjugated by a local tyrant. Some of the villagers, adorned in rich medieval costumes, parade through town, stopping along the way to re-enact scenes from this historical event. The unexpected arrival of the lord allows the inhabitants to demand reparation. After many races between the lord's Turkish guard and the nobles, the latter are finally captured and put in chains (*a stacada*).

Musée d'Art Sacré
North of the village. 🔈 🕓 *Same times and charges as for the Musée du Santon.*

Located in a former Penitents' Chapel (16C) is a sizeable religious art collection of commemorative plaques dating from the 17C onwards, statues and richly embroidered pastoral robes.

Musée de la Figurine Historique
Southeast of the village. 🔈 🕓 *Same times and charges as for the Musée du Santon.*

Near a picturesque old wash-house framed by lovely columns, this museum features antique toys, some dating from 1850, while old figurines and some antique military uniforms are displayed on the first floor. Remarkable dioramas of the Napoleonic period can be seen alongside old sheets of paper soldiers.

▶ *Go to Carcès on D 562, 17km/10.5mi northeast.*

Carcès

Tall narrow houses crowned by flat roofs cover the hillside below the Gros Bessillon. The town produces oil and honey and has extensive wine cellars. The colorful glazed tiles adorning the roofs of Carcès afford protection against the strong *mistral* winds in winter.

▶ *2km/1mi south of Carcès, heading towards Cabasse on the D 13 to the Pont Carami*

Carami Falls

🚶 *2.5hrs* Park at the bridge and follow the marked trail 8km/5mi to a waterfall where the river drops 7m/22ft in several tiers.

▶ *Continue along the D 13.*

Lac de Carcès

The pine-clad shores of this lake are a favorite haunt of fishermen (*swimming not allowed*). The reservoir, retained by the beaten earth dam, supplies Toulon and other coastal towns. There is a fine **view** from the southern end of the lake.

▶ *Continue on D 13. Leaving behind the lake, turn left onto D 79 for the Abbaye du Thoronet.*

Abbaye du Thoronet★★ – 🕙 *see Abbaye du THORONET.*

▶ *Return to D 13 and turn left towards Cabasse along the Issole Valley.*

Cabasse

The village on the Côtes de Provence wine road has a shady square around a mossy fountain. The lush valley has seen many generations of human habitation as the nearby dolmens, standing stones and Gallo-Roman ruins prove. The 16C **Église St-Pons** (🕙 *Open during services only*) has two aisles and a 16C doorway although the tympanum was carved in 1900. In the fifth bay an altarpiece of the Rosary is made up of several small paintings. Most noteworthy is the **high altar**★ of carved and gilded wood in Spanish Renaissance style (1543). The altarpiece depicting the Virgin and Child with St Michael and St Pontius is crowned by an elegant canopy. In the side aisle the ribbed vaulting is supported on pendants representing faces with grotesque or gentle expressions. There are also Gallo-Roman remains. Milestones stand near a 2C funerary inscription set in the outside wall.

▶ *Proceed along D 13 then turn right onto N 7, which leads back to Brignoles.*

② Vallon Sourn

Round-trip 39km/25mi – about 1hr – 🕙 see local map

▶ *From Brignoles take D 554 north. In Le Val turn right onto D 562 and then left onto D 22.*

Montfort-sur-Argens

The ramparts and ruins of a forbidding feudal castle mark this former Templar commandery, which now produces excellent grapes and peaches. Two square towers remain, with mullioned windows, as well as a fine 15C spiral staircase.

▶ *Return to the crossroads and turn right onto D 45, following the Argens upstream.*

Correns

This riverside village with its fountains beneath the towering Gros Bessillon is known for its white wine. The castle keep has interesting gargoyles.

Vallon Sourn

In Provençal *sourn* means somber, used here to describe the upper valley of the River Argens, which is enclosed between steep cliffs riddled with caves where people sought refuge during the Wars of Religion.

▶ *In Châteauvert turn left onto D 554 to return to Brignoles.*

③ Montagne de La Loube★ *14km/10mi southwest – about 3hr, including*
hike – 🕙 *see local map.*

▶ *From Brignoles take D 554 south. Turn right onto D 405; turn left onto D 5. 1km/0.6mi before La Roquebrussanne, turn left onto a narrow road closed to traffic where there is room to park.*

Montagne de la Loube★ *2hr on foot round-trip.*

🚶 The narrow road up this mountain (*closed to vehicles*) bordered by flowers in springtime, passes strangely shaped rocks resembling animals and human beings.

▶ *The final stage of the ascent is a rock climb (not dangerous) near the telecommunications mast.*

From the summit (830m/2 723ft), there is an interesting **panorama**★. In the valleys the farmland is hemmed in by barren ridges and on the hillsides the bauxite mines cast red gashes in the green covering of pine and holm oak. Beyond the Carami Valley to the north are the hills of Haute Provence; to the east are the Alps; to the south the mountains round Toulon, and to the west the long ridge of Ste-Baume.

▶ *Return to Brignoles by D 5 and N 7.*

La **BRIGUE**

POPULATION 595

MICHELIN MAP 341 G3 - LOCAL MAP SEE NICE

La Brigue is a charming mountain village located inland from Nice. It sits among the vineyards in the beautiful Levense Valley, with views of Mont Bégo in the distance. Known as a center of Primitive Niçois artworks, the village has also preserved the ruins of the castle and tower of the Lascaris Lords, local rulers from the 14C to the 18C. Until 1947, La Brigue was part of Italy.

🛈 *Place Saint-Martin,* ☎ *04 93 04 60 04. www.labrigue-tourisme.com.* 🛈 *Vallées Roya-Bévéra,* ☎ *04 93 04 92 05. www.royabevera.com.*

Walking Tour

Old Village

At the foot of the 14C chateau ruins are a number of medieval houses with green schist rooftops. Some of the houses are built over arcades; on some of the others the lintels are carved, often with a heraldic device (*particularly Rue de la République*). The Place Vieille commands a fine **view** of Mont Bégo.

To the right of the parish church stand two Penitents' Chapels: the 18C **Chapelle de l'Assomption** (🕒 *Guided tours only, available on request. Ask at the Tourist Office),* with its Baroque façade and graceful Genoese bell-tower; and to the left the **Chapelle de l'Annonciation** (🕒 *Guided tours available on request. Ask at the Tourist Office),* also Baroque on a hexagonal plan. The latter houses the church treasure and a collection of ecclesiastical ornaments.

> **HIKERS' REFUGE**
>
> 🛏 **Le Pra-Réound** – *On D 43 outside the village after the Maison Adapeï –* ☎ *04 93 04 65 67 –* 🕒 *Closed 20 Nov-1 Mar –* 🚫 *– 6 rooms –* 🍴*.* Hikers will appreciate this small refuge located at the entrance to a picturesque mountain village. Motel-style rooms with terraces face the snowcapped peaks. Fully equipped kitchens are available for a quick meal or snack.

Collégiale St-Martin★

🕒 *Guided tours available on request. Ask at the Tourism Office.*

This parish church has a fine late-15C square Romanesque bell-tower; Lombard bands decorate the gable end and the side aisles. The doorway, framed in the Antique style (1576) with an older (1501) green schist lintel, opens onto a sumptuously decorated gilded nave in the Italian tradition. The 17C organ in the gallery was repaired in the 19C by the same Italians who worked at Saorge. The white marble font is crowned by a painted and gilded conical baldaquin.

Jesus questioned by Pilate by J Canavesio

E. Baret/ MICHELIN

Painted Chapels of the Nice Hinterland

Scattered in the valleys of the Roya, the Paillon and the Basse-Tinée, many medieval chapels contain superb frescoes designed to teach the Scriptures:
– Coaraze, St-Sébastien;
– Lucéram, Notre-Dame-de-Bon-Cœur and St-Grat;
– Peillon, Pénitent Chapel;
– St-Dalmas-Valdeblore Church;
– Saorge, Notre-Dame del Poggio (private chapel);
– Venanson, St-Sébastien.
As well as these remarkable Gothic paintings, there are several modern successors worthy of note: Matisse in Vence, Cocteau in Villefranche and Tobiasse in Le Cannet. The frescoes of the chapels and parish churches of the Tinée Valley north of the Alpes-Maritimes are described in the Michelin Green Guide *French Alps*.

The church contains a remarkable collection of **Primitive paintings from the Nice School**★. Chapels along the south aisle contain a Crucifixion with saints and donors comparable to Louis Bréa's in Cimiez; an altarpiece of St Martha recounting on the predella the local legend of her arrival at Marseille on a boat, here pictured as a sailing ship; the Sufferings of St Elmo, revealing a cruel realism unusual in the gentle Bréa; also by Bréa the fine altarpiece of the **Adoration of the Child;** and, finally, by the same school, the central panel of a triptych representing the Assumption.
On the north side, the first chapel contains a triptych of the Italian Fuzeri of **Our Lady of the Snows** (1507) with its 18C Baroque frame.

Local Trails 🥾

Ask for the maps from the Tourism Office.
The "Chemin des Oratoires" from la Brigue to St-Dalmas-de-Tende *1hr*
Nature Interpretation Trail between La Brigue and Notre-Dame-des-Fontaines*1.5hr*

Excursion

Chapelle Notre-Dame-des-Fontaines★★ *4km/2.5mi. Travel east on D 43.*
🕐 *Guided tours 3-5pm. Ask at the Tourism Office in La Brigue.*

Set alone in the Mont Noir Valley, not far from the fascinating Mont Bégo, and overlooking one of the region's many mountain streams, the chapel of Notre-Dame-des-Fontaines is a pilgrimage center on the site of a former sanctuary dedicated to water.
It was built at two different periods: the chancel is 12C and the nave 14C; the latter was raised in the 18C in order to add seven clerestory windows. Although the exterior is plain and simple, the interior turns out to be unexpectedly ornate as the walls are covered with delightful **frescoes**★★★.
These are undoubtedly the most striking feature of the church. The chancel panels (badly damaged) were discovered in c 1950 under a coat of wash. They were painted in c 1451 by **Jean Baleison**, master of the Gothic style in this region of the Alps. These frescoes, peopled with delicate dancing figures, depict the Four Evangelists (on the vault), the Resurrection of Christ and the Virgin's Assumption (on the walls).
The nave, however, was decorated by the Renaissance Primitive **Giovanni Canavesio** (1420-early 16C), whose exuberant artistic style, always Gothic-inspired, asserts itself with a more lively brush and a better sense of perspective.
According to the theme and nature of the frescoes, it would seem that Canavesio painted those on the triumphal arch (scenes of the life of the Virgin and Jesus' Childhood) at the same time as Baleison painted those in the chancel.
The frescoes behind the façade and on the sides are dated 12 October 1492 (Latin inscription). They illustrate the Last Judgement and the Passion (🕐 *see plan above*). The compositions, often somewhat elaborate, seem by specific details to want to reveal different levels of interpretation as well as the theories expounded at that time. For example Simon Peter is depicted brandishing a dagger during the Last Supper and a sword during the Arrest of Christ; in the Garden of Gethsemane he sleeps lying down and not seated and is found warming his feet during the Denial; in the Washing of the Feet, his feet float on top of the water before Jesus washes them. These irregularities may, perhaps, reveal the first hints of the Pre-Reformation, criticising the Papacy as avid of political and temporal (the dagger) power, attached to physical comfort and unconcerned with purity (symbolised by water).

Yet in this same scene (Washing of the Feet) Judas is the only one to remove his sandals, as if desirous to have his sins washed away; moreover, he is shown barefoot when overcome with remorse. His depiction hanged and disembowelled – the same scene uniting both versions of his death – with double internal organs (two hearts, two livers, two intestines), may perhaps symbolise his dual destiny of traitor, essential to the message discussed in the Scriptures, and the Repentant Sinner.

CABRIS★

POPULATION 1 472

MICHELIN MAP 341 C6

This charming village occupies a magnificent site★ on the edge of the Provençal plateau, looking out over the Grasse countryside to Lac de St-Cassien and the sea (20km/12mi). The village and its neighborhood have long been a favorite haunt of writers and artists. The cool air of the Grotte des Audides makes it a refreshing place to visit in summer.

🛈 *9 Rue Frédéric-Mistral, ☎ 04 93 60 55 63.*

Visit

Church

The 17C church contains a painted wooden pulpit and a fine rustic altarpiece under the gallery. Behind the altar hangs a copy of a Murillo painting.

Castle Ruins

From the defensive wall and terrace, there is a superb **view**★★: southeast to Mougins and the hills running down to Le Cannet, out to sea over La Napoule Bay to the Îles de Lérins, south beyond Peymeinade and over the brow of the Tanneron to the Esterel, swinging westwards to the Lac de St-Cassien with the Massif des Maures in the distance. *See the orientation table.*

Excursion

Grotte des Audides

Kids ⏱ *Guided tours (45min) Apr-Jun Wed-Sun 2-5pm; Jul-Aug 11am-noon, 12.30-6pm; Mon 12.30-6pm; Nov to mid-Feb on request only.* ⏱ *Closed 1 and 8 May, Ascension.* ⊙ *5€ (child 3€).* ☎ *04 93 42 64 15. www.grottesdesaudides.free.fr.*

▶ *On leaving Cabris, take D 4 towards St-Vallier-de-Thiey for 4km/2.5mi. The entrance to the cave is located below the level of the road to the left coming from Cabris. It is advisable to wear waterproof shoes.*

This cave, discovered in 1988 and explored to a depth of 186m/610ft, is a chasm in which formation is still taking place, which has given rise to a small underground river. Visitors take a narrow staircase *(275 steps)* down to a depth of 60m/197ft, where a permanent flow of air keeps the air fresh. All the way down there are beautiful formations to be admired: "giant medusas" and stalagmites.

The site encompasses six caves of the chasm type, many of which were inhabited during prehistoric times. Outside in a park are reconstructed scenes of life in prehistoric times, as well as exhibits dug up during the excavation and exploration of the caves: carved tools, fossils and various bone fragments, testifying to these early settlements. Other geological exhibits include strange limestone shapes, some containing giant grooves eroded by water.

CAGNES-SUR-MER★

POPULATION 43 942

MICHELIN MAP 341 D6

Cagnes-sur-Mer is set in a landscape of hills covered with olive and orange trees and cultivated flowers (carnations, roses, mimosas). The picturesque upper town has become home to many painters who come each year in great numbers, attracted by the beautiful setting and the incomparable light.

▶ **Orient Yourself:** Cagnes is located on the coast between Nice and Antibes. The town comprises: Haut-de-Cagnes, crowned by a medieval castle, Cagnes-Ville, the modern residential and commercial quarter and Cros-de-Cagnes, an unusual fishing village and beach. From June through September a free shuttle bus (ST2N #44) operates between the central bus station (*gare routière*) and Haut-de-Cagnes.

🅿 **Parking:** The largest car park *(fee)* is at the Place St-Luce (🛈 *see map*) in Cagnes-Ville near the bus station. There are also some spaces at the train and bus stations, and in Haut-de-Cagnes at the Parking "Boule de Château".

👁 **Don't Miss:** The ancient streets of Haut-de-Cagnes, the panoramic views from the Château Museum, and the wakeboarding or jet skiing at the beach.

🕐 **Organizing Your Time:** Allow a half day for visiting Haut-de-Cagnes, the château and Renoir Museum. If you have time, check out the events at the hippodrome, shop in Cagnes-Ville, explore the marina or spend a few hours at the beach.

A Bit of History

The Grimaldis of Cagnes – The history of Cagnes is that of its castle. This was originally a fortress built by Rainier Grimaldi, Lord of Monaco and Admiral of France, after he became Lord of Cagnes in 1309. A branch of the Grimaldi family (🛈 *see MONACO*) remained in possession of Cagnes up to the French Revolution.

Cagnes-sur-Mer

Address Book

PRACTICAL INFORMATION

Tourism Office – *6, Boulevard Maréchal-Juin* – ☎ *04 93 20 61 64. or 20 Avenue des Oliviers* – ☎ *04 93 07 67 08. www.cagnes-tourisme.com*

Guided Tours of the City –The Tourism Office organises tours of the small fishing village in Cros-de-Cagnes *(Thu at 9am by appointment two days in advance)* and the picturesque cobbled district of Haut-de-Cagnes *(Sat at 11am, Sun at 4pm)*. Contact the Tourism Office for rates.

EATING OUT

For coin ranges, see Legend at the back of the guide.

⊜ **Le Vertigo** – *12 Place du Château – Le Haut-de-Cagnes* – ☎ *04 92 02 00 00* – ⊙ *Closed Nov to Jan.* On a square pleasantly shaded by acacia trees, this pub offers a wide choice of beers from all over the world, alongside freshly prepared salads and delicious homemade ice cream. Pretty setting in ochre hues.

⊜ **La Goutte d'Eau** – *108 Montée de la Bourgade, Le Haut-de-Cagnes* – ☎ *04 93 20 81 23* – ⊙ *Closed Mon and 10 days in Oct.* After climbing the steep, cobbled alleys, you will reach this small restaurant serving simple fare, where the owner-chef also waits on customers. The sun-blessed terrace welcomes you in the holiday season.

⊜⊜ **La Villa du Cros** – *Port du Cros - Cros-de-Cagnes* - ☎ *04 93 07 57 83* - ⊙ *Closed Dec-Jan, Sun and Mon night off-season, Sun lunch in season.* A friendly welcome at this restaurant on the port, elegantly decorated with fine furnishings and paintings. Typical Provençal dishes and specialities based on the local catch of the day.

WHERE TO STAY

⊜ **Hôtel Le Mas d'Azur** – *42 Avenue de Nice* – ☎ *04 93 20 19 19* – ⊙ *Closed 15 Nov-15 Dec* – 🅿 – *15 rooms* – ⊠. Just off a main road, in a building believed to be 18C, this hotel has small, tidy rooms with excellent soundproofing. Lush, flowery setting and lovely terrace for enjoying breakfast in the shade of pine trees.

⊜⊜ **Hôtel Chantilly** – *31 Rue Minoterie* – ☎ *04 93 20 25 50* – *hotel.chantilly.cagnes@wanadoo.fr* – *20 rooms* – 🅿 – ⊠. This hotel housed in a villa located behind the famous racecourse offers a modicum of comfort at extremely reasonable prices. Clean rooms in a verdant setting and a relaxed, family atmosphere are the key words at the Hôtel Chantilly, which succeeds in attracting a regular clientele throughout the year.

⊜⊜ **Les Jardins Fragonard** – *12 Rue Fragonard* – ☎ *04 93 20 97 12* – ⊠ – *3 rooms – Restaurant (⊜⊜).* A peaceful park planted with Mediterranean species forms the heavenly backdrop to this 1925 villa. The large rooms, renovated in the Provençal spirit with rattan furniture, all have new bathrooms. Start the day with a scrumptious breakfast out on the terrace.

⊜⊜⊜ **Villa Estelle** – *5 Montée de la Bourgade* – ☎ *04 92 02 89 83* – *7 rooms* – ⊠ – ⊙ *Closed 23-27 Dec.* Villa Estelle is fit for royalty. The splendid terrace with its red clay tiling overlooks the town and, in the background, the sweeping coastline. The luxurious interior and tasteful ornamentation, including many paintings and works of art, ensure that your stay here will be a resounding success.

LEISURE ACTIVITIES

Tampa Beach – *On the seafront between Madrague and Neptune restaurants.* ⊙ Open Jun-Sep. ☎ *04 93 20 17 46.* Learn how to water ski or wake board. Jet ski (no permit needed) and parasailing also possible.

Hippodrome de la Côte d'Azur – ☎ *04 92 02 44 44. www.hippodrome-cotedazur.com.* This famous racecourse is the backdrop to many equestrian events between December and March, as well as in July and August.

Rainier's castle was converted in 1620 by Henri Grimaldi into a finely decorated château. Entirely loyal to the king of France, he persuaded his cousin, Honoré II of Monaco, to renounce Spanish protection and to place himself under French protection, invoking the *Treaty of Péronne* (1641). Heaped with honors and riches by Louis XIII and Richelieu, Henri led a life of luxury at Cagnes. This was the zenith of the family's power. When the Revolution broke out, the reigning Grimaldi was driven out by the inhabitants and sought refuge in Nice.

The Village

Haut-de-Cagnes★

▶ *It is advisable to take the free shuttle from the central bus station or walk up to Haut-de-Cagnes along Montée de la Bourgade.*

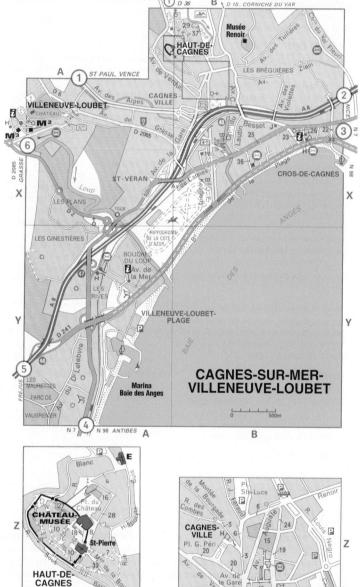

This quaint old town circled by ramparts and dominated by its medieval castle is a joy to visit. Its steep paved streets and vaulted passageways feature many 15C and 17C houses (look for the Renaissance houses with arcades near the castle). The **Porte de Nice** near the church tower dates back to the 13C.

Église St-Pierre

🕐 *Open daily 2-7pm.* 🕐 *Closed on rainy days.* ☎ *04 93 20 67 14.*

The entrance to the church, unpredictably, is through the gallery. Inside, the early Gothic nave contains the Grimaldi tombs, while a larger nave added in the 18C houses an 18C statue of the Virgin and Child (south side of chancel) and an altarpiece of the 18C Spanish School portraying St Peter receiving the keys to Paradise. Residents of the village posed for the 15 images at the stations of the Cross for the Catholic church's 2000 Jubilee.

Sights

Château-Musée★

🕐 *Open 10am-noon, 2-5pm (May-Sep until 6pm).* 🕐 *Closed Tue, Nov, 1 Jan, 1 May, 25 Dec.* 👛 *3€ (free first Sun of the month).* ☎ *04 92 02 47 30.*

A double staircase and a Louis XIII doorway give access to this imposing castle crowned with machicolations.

Ground floor

The Renaissance **patio**★★ has an agreeable freshness and elegance in sharp contrast to the feudal castle's austere façades. Two storeys of marble-columned galleries decorated with arabesques surround the courtyard where thick foliage adds a note of greenery. Eight low-vaulted medieval rooms open onto the patio galleries: Rooms 1 and 2 (fine Renaissance fireplace) present medieval history; Room 6 contains Roman sculpture dating from the 2C discovered in Cagnes. Rooms 3, 4 and 5 contain an **Olive Tree Museum**: its history and cultivation, the use of its wood, pressing and olive oil.

Suzy Solidor Bequest★ *First floor*

The former boudoir of the Marquise of Grimaldi houses 40 paintings donated by the famous singer: portraits of her attributed to famous contemporary artists. The ceiling of the adjoining oratory is decorated with Louis XIII style plasterwork *(gypseries)*. An antiphonary dates from 1757. Receptions were once held in these 17C rooms. The ceiling of the banqueting hall represents the **Fall of Phaeton**★; this *trompe-l'œil* was painted between 1621 and 1624 by the Genoese, Carlone, and conveys an extraordinary illusion of perspective. Once he had finished, the artist could not bring himself to leave it: "My beautiful Fall," he sighed, "I shall never see you again." As it happened, he died only six weeks after he left Cagnes.

Musée d'Art Moderne Méditerranéen *Second floor*

The museum, which pays tribute to contemporary Mediterranean art, is housed in the banqueting hall on the first floor and in the apartments on the second floor. The rich collection of works by 20C painters who were either born on the shores of the Mediterranean or came to live there, such as Dufy and Vasarely, is shown in rotation or in temporary exhibitions.

Tower

From the top of the tower there is a fine **view**★ over the roofs of Old Cagnes to the sea, from Cap Ferrat to Cap d'Antibes and the Alps.

Musée Renoir

🕐 *Open 10am-noon, 2-5pm (May-Sep until 6pm).* 🕐 *Closed Tue, 12-30 Nov, 1 Jan, 1 May, 25 Dec.* 👛 *3€ (free the first Sun of the month).* 🅿 *Free parking.* ☎ *04 93 20 87 29.*

This memorial museum is located at Les Collettes, where Pierre-Auguste Renoir (1841-1919) spent the last 12 years of his life. The artist's house and two studios *(first floor)* have been preserved just as they were.

Ten of his **canvases** are exhibited on the ground floor; they belong to his last, especially sensual period; a shimmering palette expressing the beauty of nature with lovely rounded female forms (second version of his *Bathers*, 1901-02). It is also at Cagnes that he attempted sculpture and a few masterpieces are on display. Right in front of the house stands **Venus Victrix**★; the large bronze statue overlooks the lovely garden, landscaped with olive, orange and lemon trees.

Renoir at Les Collettes

Pierre-Auguste Renoir, the painter, was born in Limoges but, as a young man, he went to Paris where his talents soon developed under the influence of the Impressionists and the world of art. From 1882 he made several visits to Provence, particularly in the company of Cézanne, and learned to appreciate the Mediterranean light and landscape. In 1900, as he was suffering from rhumatism, his doctor advised him to try a change of climate and he spent some time near Grasse with his wife and younger son Jean, who later became a film director.

Once his reputation was universally established, he settled permanently in the South of France and in 1907 he bought the property of Les Collettes in Cagnes-sur-Mer, attracted by the view of the sea and the old village. Four of his paintings were inspired by the surrounding countryside. In 1913, at the suggestion of his friend Vollard, he took up sculpture with a pupil of Maillol called Guino and built a studio in the garden of Les Collettes where he worked. Under his directions, Guino created a little Venus and then the famous *Venus Victrix*, which is displayed in the garden of the museum.

Renoir's last years were saddened by the death of his wife, his sons being wounded in the First World War, and the inexorable progress of his illness, which confined him to a wheelchair; he managed to paint despite the arthritis which paralysed his right hand. As his physical capacity diminished, he stated that "he was beginning to know how to paint". In August 1919, in addition to having received many honors and having his work hung in the major museums of the world, he was officially accepted by the Louvre where several of his works are displayed. On 2 December 1919, just before his death, he was still at work, painting a bouquet of anemones.

Chapelle Notre-Dame-de-Protection

Access on foot up Montée du Château. ◷ *Open Sat, Sun 3-5pm.* ☞ *Can be visited Sunday 4.15pm as part of the "Medieval Village" tour, departure from the Maison des Artistes.* ◷ *Closed 1 Jan, 1 May, 25 Dec.* ✆ *Free entry (tour 6€).* ☎ *04 93 20 61 64.*

The Italianate porch and bell-tower of this chapel inspired Renoir. The apse is decorated with rather stilted 16C frescoes: on the dome the Evangelists, Isaiah, the Sibyl; on the walls, scenes from the childhood of Christ and from the life of the Virgin; in the center Our Lady of Protection as a Virgin of Mercy. A 17C altarpiece of the Virgin of the Rosary is in the north chapel.

Driving Tours

The Baous and the Corniche du Var ★

Round-trip of 32km/20mi – about 1hr 15min (excluding the ascent of the Baou of St-Jeannet).

▶ *From Cagnes take Avenue Auguste-Renoir and D 18 north to La Gaude.*

The road runs past elegant residential properties, olive groves, market gardens and flower fields, with **views** of Vence, the hills and La Gaude.

La Gaude

From the ridge above the River Cagne, La Gaude, which owes its prosperity to vineyards and flower cultivation, now houses research centers in the fields of data processing, agronomy and horticulture. The 14C castle in the St-Jeannet district is thought to have been built by the Templars.

▶ *At the crossroads in Peyron continue north on D 18 through orchards and vineyards.*

St-Jeannet

The charming village occupies a remarkable **position**★ on a scree terrace at the foot of the Baou of St-Jeannet, among orange groves, flower fields and vineyards producing good quality wine. Behind the church on the left a sign "Panorama" points to a terrace offering a **view**★ of the peaks *(baous)*, the coast and the Var Valley.

Baou de St-Jeannet★★ *2hr on foot round-trip.*

▶ *The signposted path starts from Place Ste-Barbe by Auberge St-Jeannet.*

⬚ Also known as the Baou des Blancs, this sheer cliff 400m/1 312ft high dominates the village. From the top *(orientation table)* a huge **panorama** ★★ extends from the Esterel to the French and Italian Alps.

▶ *Return to D 18 towards La Gaude. Turn left onto D 118.*

Centre d'Études et de Recherches IBM

The huge buildings on the left of this IBM Research and Study Center, consisting of two opposing Y-shapes raised on concrete pillars to accommodate the uneven ground, were designed by Breuer and are a good example of architecture harmonising with its natural surroundings.

Corniche du Var★

This scenic road follows the ridge or clings to the hillside on the west bank of the Var with a clear view of the river valley and the Nice hinterland. The steep slopes of the valley are covered with the flower fields and olive groves.

St-Laurent-du-Var

Until the County of Nice passed to France in 1860, the Var formed the frontier with the Kingdom of Sardinia. Locals usually forded the river, often on another man's back. The first permanent bridge was built downstream in 1864.

Near the mouth of the River Var, a vast lake, protected by a dyke, has been developed into a yachting harbor (over 1 000 moorings).

▶ *Return to Cagnes by N 7.*

CANNES �288

POPULATION 67 304

MICHELIN MAP 341 D6 -

LOCAL MAP SEE MASSIF DE L'ESTEREL

Star of the Côte d'Azur, Cannes became known as early as 1834 for its mild climate, making it the preferred winter salon of the world's aristocracy. Framed to the west by the red rocks of the Esterel and across the bay by the forested Îles de Lérins, the beauty of its setting★★ forms the perfect backdrop to the palm-lined beaches of La Croisette, where cinema stars from around the world gather each year for the annual Cannes Film Festival. More than just a summer resort, the town's busy port and important conference schedule make it a lively place to visit year-round.

▶ **Orient Yourself:** You'll find the most interesting areas of Cannes between the RN 7 and the sea. The center of the action is at the Old Port, where the Palais des Festivals and the Tourism Office can be found. The old town extends from the port up the hillside known as Le Suquet, while the upscale shops and hotels extend east along the Boulevard de la Croisette, where the best sandy beaches are found. A small tourist train covers all of the main sights (& *see Address Book*).

🅿 **Parking:** Parking on the street is metered and only allowed for two hours maximum. Large parking garages *(fee)* can be found around the port, near the market, at the Noga Hilton, and next to the train station.

🕾 **Don't Miss:** The colorful Marché Forville, the fortified monastery ruins on the Île Saint-Honorat, the spectacular yachts in the Old Port, shopping along the Rue d'Antibes, or the sandy beaches along La Croisette.

🕐 **Organizing Your Time:** You'll need a full day to enjoy the sights of Cannes. Begin in the morning with a visit to the covered Marché Forville, followed by a stroll though the winding up to the top of Le Suquet. Then window shop along La Croisette, or shop where the locals do on the parallel Rue d'Antibes. After lunch at one of the beach restaurants (or across from the port off-season), take the 10-minute boat shuttle to the Île St-Honorat or Île Ste-Marguerite. If you have time to stay the evening, Cannes has a large selection of entertainment from the casinos and palace hotel bars to nightclubs and local pubs.

🄺🄸🄳🅂 **Especially for Kids:** The car-free Île Ste-Marguerite is the perfect place to let the kids run loose under the pines and rocky coves. Visit the Fort Vauban where soldiers kept a lookout for pirate ships from the ramparts and the Man in the Iron Mask was imprisoned below. Next to the Palais des Festivals are the handprints in cement of the stars from the annual film festival.

A Bit of History

Cannes, the coastal watchtower – By the 10C, following the earlier Ligurian and Roman settlements (42BC), a small cluster of dwellings, constructed by Genoese families, stood at the foot of the rock known today as Mont Chevalier or Le Suquet. The place was called Canoïs, cane harbour, after the reeds *(cannes)* that thrived in the surrounding marshes.

In 1131, the Count of Provence, Raymond Bérenger II, gave the settlement to the abbots of Lérins. They built a tower and fortifications to protect the fishermen against possible attacks by the Saracens. As soon as the first enemy ships loomed

Carlton Hotel terrace

D. Parzey/ MICHELIN

Croisette, Cannes

on the horizon, the Lérins watchers gave the alarm. The defences were directed by the religious orders – first the Templars, then the Knights of Malta. The Fathers of Mercy dealt with the ransoming of prisoners.

Lord Brougham and the birth of the resort (1834) – Cannes' riches and renown are due to the misfortunes of a Lord Chancellor of England (1830-34), Lord Brougham (politician, famous orator; he designed the four-wheeled one-horse carriage, which bears his name, the brougham), who was on his way to Nice in 1834. Cholera in Provence prevented the wealthy traveller from crossing the *cordon sanitaire* to Nice; he returned to Cannes. The place, then a small fishing village, pleased him so much that he built himself a house there. For the next 34 years, right up to the time of his death (d 1868), Lord Brougham exchanged the winter fogs of London for the Mediterranean sunshine. His example was soon followed by the English aristocracy of the time and the town's population of 4 000 grew rapidly.

Two famous French writers dearly loved Cannes: Prosper Mérimée died there in 1870; Guy de Maupassant anchored his yacht in the bay between 1884 and 1888 and wrote his enthusiastic impressions of the town in his story *Sur l'Eau (On the Water)*. **Frédéric Mistral,** the Provençal poet, celebrated Cannes, and there is scarcely a famous person in art or literature who has not visited the town.

Cannes Festivals – The festivals hosted by the city of Cannes are world famous. **The International Film Festival** is the most glittering artistic gathering on the Riviera (*see box*). Other popular events include the prestigious regattas, the International Record and Music Market (MIDEM), which takes place in January, and the International Market for Television Programmes held in April and May.

Exploring Cannes

[1] **SEAFRONT**★★ *by car: 30min*

Boulevard de la Croisette★★

Local residents enjoy strolling here in winter. This elegant promenade, bordered by palm trees and gardens, overlooks a fine sandy beach.

Luxury hotels and elegant boutiques line the front and the side streets as far as Rue d'Antibes. The chic crowd meets here, in the galleries and antique shops, the cinemas, nightclubs, cafés and bars.

At the top end of La Croisette, east of the port, stands the ultramodern **Palais des Festivals et des Congrès** *(Esplanade Georges-Pompidou – La Croisette – ☎ 04 93 39 01 01 – www.festival-cannes.org – ⏱ Guided tours Wed, Sun (except during events) ⏱ 2€. Contact the Tourism Office. ☎ 04 92 99 84 22)* and casino. Known as "The Bunker," the building comprises a 2 400-seat auditorium, Debussy Theatre (1 000 seats), broadcasting studios and the Office of Tourism.

The Stuff of Dreams

A number of exceptional residences have contributed to the history of Cannes.
Avenue Roi Albert 1: **Villa Kazbeck,** known for the lavish parties thrown by the Grand Duc de Russie and **Villa Champfleuri,** famous for its exotic gardens which can be seen in the film *Macao, Enfer du Jeu* by J Delannoy.
Avenue Jean-de-Noailles: **Villa Marie-Therèse** and **Villa Béatrice** (1881), formerly Rothschild properties, built in the Classical style, which now house the Médiathèque de Cannes.
Avenue Maréchal-Juin (eastern edge of town): **Château Scott**, an amazing combination of styles, dominated by Flamboyant Gothic; *Le Mystere de la Chambre Jaune* by M L'Herbier was filmed here in 1930.
Avenue Victoria (in Cannet): **Villa Yakimour** (👆 see LE CANNET).

Between the conference center and the gardens lies the **Allée des Stars,** an avenue consisting of 200 tiles where handprints of the great movie stars who attended the Film Festival have been set in the concrete.

Farther east on the opposite side of the road, beyond the sumptuous Majestic Hotel, stands a private 19C mansion, **La Malmaison** (🕐 *Open Jul-Sep 11am-8pm (until 10pm mid-Jul to mid-Sep); Apr-Jun 10am-1pm, 2.30-6.30pm; Oct-Mar 10am-12.30pm, 2.30-6pm.* 🕐 *Closed Mon, 1 Jan, 1, 11 Nov, 25 Dec.* 👁 *3€.* ☎ *04 93 38 55 26).* Once part of the Grand Hotel, it now houses the municipal cultural service and art exhibitions. Nearby stands the Hôtel Noga-Hilton, incorporating the façade of the former Palais des Festivals, which was pulled down in 1988 after serving as the venue for the Cannes Film Festival for 40 years.

Further on is the Belle Epoch Carlton Hotel, the Art Déco Martinez Hotel, and beyond the rose gardens the modern Port-Canto.

▷ *Proceed east along Boulevard de la Croisette to Pointe de la Croisette.*

Pointe de la Croisette★

This point owes its name to a small cross which used to stand there. It offers splendid views of Cannes, the Iles de Lérins, and the Esterel, particularly at sunset. In addition to the beautiful gardens, modern tourist developments include artificial beaches, the Palm Beach Casino complex, and Mouré Rouge port. Beyond Palm Beach at the point is a splendid **view**★ of Golfe-Juan and Cap d'Antibes.

▷ *Follow the Avenue Maréchal-Juin, continued by the Rue d'Antibes, back into town.*

Quartier de la Californie

This district to the east of the old town consists of luxurious villas, the majority dating from the 19C, set in magnificent gardens. There are stunning examples of extravagant architecture with exotic, quirky features: pagodas and Moorish minarets, façades surmounted by turrets and colonial villas, bow-windows and moucharaby etc. All are private residences and the outside view is often obscured by thick foliage.

② OLD CANNES AND THE PORT – *1hr 30min*

The Harbor

Between the Palais des Festivals and Le Suquet lies the Old Port with its rows of fishing boats and luxury yachts. Larger cruise liners and merchant ships anchor farther out. The west side of the harbor is lined with shops, restaurants and the embarkment quay for trips to the Îles de Lérins (👆 *see Address Book).* In the northeast corner is the **shipping terminal** (note the large frieze running along the top).

Allées de la Liberté

Beneath the plane trees, overlooking the port, is a large square where an early morning flower market takes place and locals play pétanque.

▷ *Take Rue Félix-Faure and Rue Rouguière to Rue Meynadier.*

Rue Meynadier

Formerly the main street linking the new town to Le Suquet, it is bordered by a variety of local specialty shops and some fine 18C doorways.

▷ *Go to Le Suquet via Rue Louis-Blanc, Rue Félix-Faure and Rue Mont-Chevalier.*

Le Suquet

The old town, built on the site of the former Canoïs castrum on the slopes of Mont Chevalier, is known locally as Le Suquet. Rue Perrissol leads to Place de la Castre

surrounded by a defensive wall and dominated by the church of Notre-Dame-d'Espérance, built in the 16C and 17C in the Provençal Gothic style.
The old bell-tower leads to a long tree-lined terrace offering a fine **view** of the town and port and Île Ste-Marguerite.

Sights

Musée de la Castre★★

🕐 *Open 10am-1pm, 2-6pm (Jul-Aug 10am-1pm, 3-7pm; Oct-Mar 10am-1pm, 2-5pm).*
🕐 *Closed Mon, Nov and public holidays.* 👓 *3€, free the first Sun of the month.* ☎ *04 93 38 55 26. www.cannes.fr*

The old Cannes Castle, built in the 11C and 12C by the Lérins monks to watch over the harbor, houses substantial collections of archeology and ethnography brought back from the five continents and bequeathed by two learned travelers in the 19C.
The small Cistercian Chapelle Ste-Anne at the entrance holds temporary exhibits. The rooms that follow are concerned with religion and mythology (works from the Fontainebleau School) as well as paintings of Provence and Cannes by 19C and 20C artists.
Room 4 looks out onto the 12C square watchtower (22m/72ft), **Tour du Suquet,** where temporary photographic exhibitions are held. From the top there's a panoramic **view** ★ of La Croisette, La Napoule Bay, the Îles de Lérins, the Esterel heights and the hills to the north of Cannes.
The extensive archeological collection displays objects from the Mediterranean Basin and the Middle East (Iran, Lebanon, Syria, Cyprus, Egypt, Etruria, Rome...) as well as Primitive art from Africa, Oceania, the Americas and Asia. Contemporary works of art are also on display.

▷ *Follow Rue J.-Hibert and Rue J-Dollfus to reach Square Frédéric-Mistral where a statue of the "immortal bard of Provence" was erected in 1930 to commemorate the centenary of his birth.*

Chapelle Bellini

From the Cannes-Nice motorway, take the first exit to the left towards Vallauris, turn right onto Avenue de Vallauris. At no 67, turn right onto Avenue Poralto, then left onto Allée de la Villa-Fiorentina. ♿ 🕐 *Open 2-5pm, Sat-Sun on request.* 🕐 *Closed public holidays.* 👓 *Free entry.* ☎ *04 93 38 61 80.*

This chapel was included in the grounds of the sumptuous Tuscan palace "Villa Fiorentina" built at the end of the 19C for the Balkan nobility.
This religious building, in elaborate Baroque style, proudly sports the coat of arms of Count Vitali on its west face. The interior retains several works by the last owner, the Cannes painter Bellini (1904-1989), who had his studio here.

Cannes Film Festival

In 1939, Jean Zay, the French Minister of Fine Arts, founded the International Film Festival at Cannes, whose location was chosen on account of its sunny climate. The inauguration, planned for 1 September, was cancelled when the declaration of war broke out two days later. The real launch of the festival took place on 20 September 1946 in the former Casino Municipal near the Old Port; the festival returned to this site 40 years later at the time of the inauguration of the Nouveau Palais des Festivals in 1983.
In 1949 the festival moved to the Palais de la Croisette (demolished in 1988). In spite of its suspension in 1948 and 1950 for financial reasons and an interruption in May 1968, the fame of the festival has grown over the years, with a star-studded jury presided over by celebrities such as Jules Romains, Marcel Pagnol, Jean Cocteau, and, more recently, David Lynch and Emir Kusturica. As it became a forum for international cinema, the Festival brought together an impressive number of participants and works. In 2005, 30 000 professionals (buyers and sellers) were present for screenings.
During the 10 days of the event, several competitions take place: the *Selection Officielle* (competing for the prestigious **Palme d'Or**); *Hors-Compétition* (not in competition); *Semaine de la Critique* (critics' picks); *Quinzaine des Réalisateurs* (film directors' programme); *Caméra d'Or* (first films); *Un Certain Regard* (independent productions). The great media interest in the various ceremonies of the festival offers a unique springboard to all films, whether mainstream or fringe, and confirms its role in uncovering talent in the so-called seventh art.

CANNES

PORT (CANNES I)

ÎLES DE LÉRINS

Chapelle Bellini	X	B
Chapelle St-Sauveur (Musée Tobiasse)	V	B[1]
Château: musée national "La Guerre et la Paix", musée Magnelli et musée de la Céramique	V	D
Croix des Gardes		X
Gare maritime		BZ
Malmaison		CZ
Musée de l'Automobiliste		V

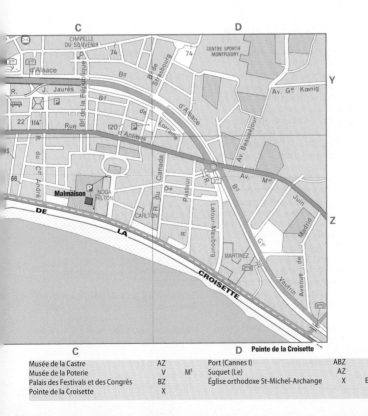

Musée de la Castre	AZ		Port (Cannes I)	ABZ	
Musée de la Poterie	V	M^1	Suquet (Le)	AZ	
Palais des Festivals et des Congrès	BZ		Église orthodoxe St-Michel-Archange	X	E
Pointe de la Croisette	X				

Address Book

PRACTICAL INFORMATION

TOURISM OFFICES

Cannes – *Palais des Festivals, 1, La Croisette – 06400 –* ☎ *04 93 39 24 53* (**Train Station Branch** – *Aile Est of the Gare SNCF –* ☎ *04 93 99 19 77). www.cannes.fr*

Le Cannet – *Avenue du Campon – Le Cannet –* ☎ *04 93 45 34 27. www.lecannet. com.*

EATING OUT

For coin ranges, see the Legend in the back of the guide.

☞ **Côte d'Azur** – *3 Rue Jean-Daumos –* ☎ *04 93 38 60 02 –* ⏰ *Closed evenings and Sun.* Modest restaurant with a friendly ambience and cosy setting with period furnishings. The traditional cooking attracts a great many locals. Low prices guaranteed.

☞ **Aux Bons Enfants** – *80 Rue Meynadier –* ⏰ *Closed Aug, 24 Dec-2 Jan, Sat evening Oct to Apr, and Sun –* 🍴 *– reservations highly recommended.* Simplicity, generosity and congeniality are the hallmarks of this informal establishment where there's no telephone and customers are required to pay in cash. A true locals' hangout since 1935, with tasty Mediterranean dishes.

☞☞ **Le Comptoir des Vins** – *13 Boulevard de la République –* ☎ *04 93 68 13 26 – www.comptoirdesvins.com –* ⏰ *Closed Feb, evenings Mon-Wed, Sun and public holidays.* This handsomely stocked wine boutique leads to a colorful dining area where light snacks can be served, washed down with a glass of wine.

☞☞ **Le Caveau 30** – *45 Rue F.-Faure –* ☎ *04 93 39 06 33.* Large restaurant comprising two dining rooms done up in the style of a 1930 brasserie. The terrace overlooks a shaded square popular among boules players. Fish and seafood are the specialities of the house.

☞☞ **Au Poisson Grillé** – *8 Quai St-Pierre – Vieux Port –* ☎ *04 93 39 44 68.* Appropriately located in the old port, this fish restaurant was opened back in 1949. It serves grilled fish alongside many other Mediterranean dishes, in a warm setting of varnished wood evoking the interior of a luxury cabin. Attentive service at affordable prices.

☞☞☞ **Fred L'Écailler** – *7 Place de l'Étang –* ☎ *04 93 43 15 85 – http://fredlecailler. com.* A large neon sign marks the entrance to this rustic-style restaurant whose walls are draped with fishing nets. The tiny square affords a glimpse of village life with its bustling activity and daily games of pétanque. Fine selection of freshly caught fish and seafood.

☞☞☞ **Côté Jardin** – *12 Avenue St-Louis –* ☎ *04 93 38 60 28 –* ⏰ *Closed 1-11 Jan and Sun –* 🍽. Just off the Boulevard Carnot,

this Provençal-style restaurant attracts the locals with its covered terrace and courtyard seating.

WHERE TO STAY

☞ **Le Chanteclair** – *12 Rue Forville –* ☎ *04 93 39 68 88 –* ⏰ *Closed 15 Oct-3 Jan –* 🍴 *– 15 rooms –* 🛏. After walking through a building, you will discover this friendly hotel laid out on several floors, offering a selection of variously priced rooms depending on the level of comfort. Pleasant inner courtyard where breakfast is served in summer.

☞ **Hôtel National** – *9 Rue du Maréchal-Joffre –* ☎ *04 93 39 91 92 – hotelnationalcanneswanadoo.fr – 17 rooms –* 🖥 🛏. The main advantage of this hotel is its location near the Palais des Festivals and the sea. The bedrooms designed in white and grey with tiled bathrooms are on the small side but they are clean and carefully maintained.

☞☞ **Hôtel Albert 1** – *68 Avenue de Grasse –* ☎ *04 93 39 24 04 –* ⏰ *Closed 1-15 Dec –* 🅿 *– 11 rooms –* 🛏. In a quiet, residential area tucked away from the town center, this villa houses a small, family-run business that will give you a warm welcome. Have breakfast on the shaded terrace enhanced by the intoxicating aroma of pink oleander.

☞☞ **Hôtel Appia** – *6 Rue Marceau –* ☎ *04 93 06 59 59 – www.appia-hotel.com –* ⏰ *Closed 21 Nov-27 Dec – 31 rooms –* 🖥 🛏. Practicality takes precedence over comfort in this downtown hotel where the well-kept, smallish rooms are both air-conditioned and soundproofed. Pristine bathrooms.

☞☞ **Villa L'Églantier** – *14 Rue Campestra –* ☎ *04 93 68 22 43 –* 🍴 *– 4 rooms.* Impressive white villa dating from 1920, surrounded by palm trees and other exotic species, dominating the city of Cannes. The large, peaceful rooms are all extended by a terrace or a balcony.

☞☞☞ **Le Cavendish** – *11 Boulevard Carnot –* ☎ *04 97 06 26 00 – www. cavendish-cannes.com – 34 rooms –* 🖥 🅿 🛏. A beautiful Belle Epoch era building with a 1920s elevator and a stylish, contemporary decor, this family-run hotel is a comforting retreat in the center of Cannes. Breakfast includes homemade jams and cakes, and every evening is a free open bar Happy Hour in the lounge.

☞☞☞ **Le 3.14 Hôtel** – *5 Rue François Einesy –* ☎ *04 92 99 72 00 – www.3-14hotel. com –* 🖥 🅿 🛏 *– 80 rooms – Restaurant (*☞☞☞☞*).* As one of the only design boutique hotels in Cannes, this exotic and trendy establishment around the corner from the Carlton is a breath of fresh air. In the lobby live love birds and a Murano glass fountain welcome you, while each of the five floors is decorated according to a different continent theme: America, Europe, Africa, Asia and Oceania. The rooftop spa, swimming pool and jacuzzi, private beach, and a stunning Mahatma bar and restaurant make it hard to leave this pampering cocoon of a hotel.

ON THE TOWN

The best way to get to know this glamorous city is to frequent its luxury hotel bars: order a cocktail on the terrace of the Ritz-Carlton hotel, on the beach of the Majestic or in the piano-bar of the Martinez.

L'Amiral – *73 Boulevard de la Croisette –* ☎ *04 92 98 73 00 – www.hotel.martinez. com –* ⏱ *Daily 10am-2am.* Attached to the Martinez Hotel, this bar is by far the most popular meeting place along the coast. It owes its reputation to the head barman and to Jimmy, the American piano player. Live music every evening from 8pm.

Le Bâoli – *Port Pierre Canto, Boulevard de la Croisette –* ☎ *04 93 43 03 43–* ⏱ *Wed-Sat from 8pm (off-season Fri-Sat from 8pm).* The hottest night spot in Cannes with beachfront views over the bay, this luxurious bar-restaurant-nightclub with the exotic decor can host up to 1500 partygoers in high season. Popular with the international jet-set crowd and beautiful locals.

SHOPPING

Market – *Marché de Forville: daily 7am-1pm except Mondays in low season;* fine stalls displaying fresh regional produce.

Allées de la Liberté – Flower market every morning. Popular flea market on Saturdays.

Shopping streets – Rue Meynadier: tempting window displays of food and craftwork in a lively pedestrian area. Rue d'Antibes: luxury clothes and luggage.

Cannolive – *16 Rue Vénizelos –* ☎ *04 93 39 08 19 –* ⏱ *Open 8am-noon, 2.15-7pm. – Closed Sun, Mon morning, and two weeks in Dec.* This shop boasts an incredible choice of Provençal products to take back home: household linen, tapenades, crockery, santons, soap, and even Lérina liqueur from the nearby islands for those who get seasick!

Vilfeu Père et Fils – *19 Rue des Etats-Unis –* ☎ *04 93 39 26 87 –* ⏱ *Open Thurs-Mon 11am-7pm (Jul-Aug daily 10am-midnight). –* ⏱ *Closed 15 Oct-Apr.* For 30 years this family has perfected their home-made ice cream with the freshest ingredients. Some of the startling flavors include saffron, thyme, rosemary and olive oil.

La Ferme Savoyarde – *22 Rue Meynadier –* ☎ *04 93 39 63 68 –* ⏱ *Open Tue-Sat 7am-12.30pm, 4-7.30pm (open Sun morning Jul-Aug)* . Not only is this the preferred cheese boutique of the local Cannois, but they also ship their Chèvre de Provence, Camembert de Calvados and Brie with Truffles to four-star hotels around the world. Ask for your cheeses "sous-vide" if you plan on traveling with them.

LEISURE ACTIVITIES

For sailing, deep-sea diving or water-skiing, contact the Tourism Office or visit www.france-nautisme.com.

Beaches – Not all the beaches on La Croisette charge a fee (details of prices are listed at the top of the steps), or belong to a hotel (located opposite). There are also three free beaches, one of which is located behind the Palais du Festival. The other public beaches lie west of the old port, on Boulevard Jean-Hibert and Boulevard du Midi, at Port Canto and on Boulevard Gazagnaire beyond La Pointe.

Ponton Majestic Ski Nautique – *Boulevard de la Croisette –* ☎ *04 92 98 77 47/ 06 11 50 77 53 –* ⏱ *Apr-Oct daily 8am until dusk.* If you want to get away from the bustling crowds, why not try your hand at water-skiing or parascending?

TOURS AND TRANSPORTATION

TAM – *Gare routière, Place de l'Hôtel-de-Ville –* ☎ *04 93 39 11 39 – www.rca.tm.fr.* These buses operate between Cannes and Nice, including direct service to the airport.

Train Station – *SNCF Gare de Cannes –* ☎ *0 892 35 35 35 – www.ter-sncf.com/paca.* This train station is served by SNCF trains, the TGV, and the local TER trains (service between Mandelieu-La-Napoule and Vintimille).

Les Trains Touristiques – *Cannois de Loisirs, La Croisette –* ☎ *06 14 09 49 39 –* ⏱ *10am-11pm (in summer; until dusk off-season). –* ⏱ *Closed Nov –* ☜ *8€ (child under 10 years, 5€).* This tiny train does tours of La Croisette and Le Suquet with commentary in English. Departs from in front of Majestic Plage.

Trans Côte d'Azur – *3 Quai des Îles –* ☎ *04 92 98 71 30 –* ⏱ *Feb-Oct daily 8.30am-noon, 1.30-6pm (Jul-Aug 8am-7pm).* ☜ *10€ (child 5€). www.trans-cote-azur.com.* Regular service to the Île Ste-Marguerite (15 minutes), plus seasonal tours to l'Île de Porquerolles, Monaco, Saint-Tropez, San Remo, la Corniche d'Or, etc.

Planaria– *Quai des Îles –* ☎ *04 92 98 71 38 –* ⏱ *May-Sep hourly 8am-12.30pm, 2-6pm (Oct-Apr until 5pm, fewer departures).* ☜ *10€ (child 5€). www.abbayedelerins.com.* Regular service to Île St-Honorat *(15 min).*

CALENDAR OF EVENTS

International Film Festival – 10 days in May; free open-air cinema retrospectives on the beach (official screenings open to accredited professionals only). *www.festival-cannes.org.*

Nuits Misicales du Suquet – End of July; classical concerts on the esplanade in front of the Église du Suquet. ☎ *04 92 99 33 83.*

Église Orthodoxe St-Michel-Archange

30 Boulevard Alexandre-III. ⏲ *Guided tours on request. Contact Mr. Wsevolojsky.* ☏ *04 93 43 35 35.*

Since Empress Maria Alexandrovna, wife of Czar Alexandre III, had taken to spending the winter months in Cannes, it was necessary to build a church large enough to accommodate her court. The construction of the church was supervised by the Cannes architect Nouveau and its inauguration took place in November 1894. The richly ornamented interior contains some remarkable icons (one of which represents **St Michael the great captain**) and banners received from the Russian imperial family. The spire with its onion-shaped dome is of a later date than the main building.

The church's choral group is particularly renowned for its interpretations of the liturgy. The crypt (⦿ *closed to the public*) contains the bodies of members of the imperial family who died in exile and of the white Russian general Youdenitch who took part in the siege of Petrograd in 1919.

Opposite the church, and slightly to its right, in Alexandra Square, is the **Chapelle Tripet-Skryptine,** a neo-Byzantine building which was the first Russian Orthodox church in Cannes.

Driving Tours

③ LE CANNET ⛄ *see map of Cannes.*

▸ *Leave Cannes by Boulevard Carnot (there is no break between Cannes and Le Cannet).*

Admirably sheltered from the wind by a circle of wooded hills, Le Cannet, at an altitude of 110m/361ft, complements the climate of Cannes. This bustling resort has been popular with many artists: the actress Rachel, the painter Renoir and the playwright Victorien Sardou. The artist **Pierre Bonnard** (1867-1947) stayed here and spent the last years of his life painting views of Le Cannet from Villa Le Bosquet (Avenue Victoria).

Le Vieux Cannet

The old town is reached by Rue St-Sauveur *(mostly pedestrian)* which features 18C houses with unusual façades as well as pleasant small squares shaded by plane trees and linked by alleyways. At no 19, where a side road goes up to the left, a blank façade has been covered with a mural by Peynet representing *Les Amoureux (The Lovers)*. Farther on the left is the little 15C **Chapelle St-Sauveur** (⛄ ⏲ *Guided tours on request through the Office of Tourism.* ⬚ *No charge.* ☏ *04 93 46 74 00 or* ☏ *04 93 45 34 27)* sheltering behind a large lime tree, with a pediment decorated with polychrome mosaics. The **Musée Tobiasse** inside the chapel is a museum exhibiting mosaics, wooden panels adorned with figures (to be read from right to left) and objects made by the artist. The interior is lit thanks to five stained-glass windows of vivid design by Tobiasse.

Place Bellevue overlooks the square tower of Ste-Philomène Church and offers a superb view of Cannes and the Îles de Lérins. The old **Calvys Tower** (12C) still stands nearby, as well as the taller **Danys Tower** (14C). Both towers have fine façades topped with machicolations. There is an amusing fresco dedicated to the founding families of Le Cannet on one wall. The Jardins de Tivoli can be reached from the Hôtel de Ville via the pedestrian Rue Cavasse, passing some luxurious 1900 villas.

Chemin des Collines★

This is a particularly attractive, if dizzying, road along the flanks of the hills above Cannes, with many fine views over the Gulf of La Napoule and the Îles de Lérins.

▸ *Continue to the east, to the Col de St-Antoine.*

On the left in Avenue Victoria, at the top of a magnificent avenue of populars, sits the **Villa Yakimour** *(private property, no visiting)*. This Oriental residence was given by the Aga Khan to his wife Yvette Labrousse (Yakimour is derived from their initials and "amour").

▸ *To continue to Vallauris, over the Col de St-Antoine, turn left onto D 803. To return to Cannes follow the Avenue Victoria.*

Vallauris – ⛄ *see VALLAURIS*

Golfe-Juan ⬚⬚ *2km/1.2mi southeast of Vallauris by D 135.* ⛄ *see GOLFE-JUAN.*

On returning towards Cannes on N 7, the road skirts round the hills of Super-Cannes while on the horizon can be seen the Îles de Lérins and the red barrier of the Massif de l'Esterel; the **view**★ is at its best at sunset.

Russia on the Riviera

The attraction of the French Riviera for the Russian aristocracy gave rise to a large number of Russian Orthodox churches:

- In Cannes – St-Michel-Archange (1894)
- In Menton – the Russian sanatorium chapel (1908)
- In Nice – the church in Rue Longchamp (1858), which is the oldest, and St-Nicholas (1912), the most recent and most magnificent.

▶ *Return to Cannes along the seafront (Bord du Mer).*

4 **LA CROIX DES GARDES**★ *Round-trip of 8km/5mi (steep climb).*

▶ *Leave Cannes on Avenue Dr-Picaud. At the traffic lights near the Sol-Hôtel turn right on Boulevard Leader. 100m/110yd beyond the entrance to the Pavillon de la Croix des Gardes, turn right onto Avenue J-de-Noailles and leave the car 100m/110yd further on in the car park provided.*

Take a footpath on the right which leads to the top of the hill (alt 164m/538ft), where there is a large cross 12m/39ft high. This strategically placed feature, which has given its name to the hill, has been a permanent lookout post since the 16C. From the foot of the cross there is a marvellous **panorama**★ over Cannes and its setting, the Îles de Lérins, the Esterel and, in clear weather, the St-Tropez peninsula.

▶ *Continue along Avenue J.-de-Noailles to return to Cannes.*

Îles de Lérins★★ *see Îles de LÉRINS. Allow half a day's walk.*

CAP FERRAT★★

POPULATION 1 895

MICHELIN MAP 341 E5

LOCAL MAP SEE CORNICHES DE LA RIVIERA

Tucked between Villefranche and Beaulieu, the dense vegetation and dramatic cliffs of the prestigious Cap Ferrat peninsula hide some of the most luxurious villas on the Riviera, including the spectacular Villa Ephrussi. Some of the best views of the coastline can be seen from the Sentier Littoral, the streets of St-Jean, and St-Hospice Point. Also known as St-Jean-Cap-Ferrat (St-Jean being the name of the actual town), the peninsula is accessible by the narrow Bas Corniche, which hugs the coastline. The tourist office is located in the center of the cap, to the west of the Nouveau Port.

🛈 *59 av. Denis-Semeria, St-Jean-Cap-Ferrat, ☎ 04 93 76 08 90. www.ville-saint-jean-cap-ferrat.fr.*

Sights

Villa Ephrussi-de-Rothschild★★
🕐 *Open 10am-6pm; Nov-Jan 2-6pm, Sat-Sun and public holidays 10am-6pm; Jul-Aug 10am-7pm. ⊜ 9€ (child 6.50€). ☎ 04 93 01 33 09. www.villa-ephrussi.com.*

The foundation, which was bequeathed to the Institut de France on behalf of the Academy of Fine Arts in 1934 by the Baroness Ephrussi de Rothschild, boasts an incomparable **setting**★★★ in magnificent gardens on the narrow neck of the peninsula and enjoys a fine view of the Villefranche and Beaulieu ports. Inside is a museum exhibiting more than 5 000 works of art.

Musée Île-de-France★★
🕐 *Open only for guided tours. ⊜ Supplement of 2€.*

The villa that houses this museum was built in the Italianate style soon after 1900 to hold the furniture and works of art that the Baroness collected throughout her life. Her favorite period was the 18C. Pink marble columns from a palace in Verona surround a covered patio in which pieces of medieval and Renaissance furniture stand on an 18C Savonnerie carpet and a mosaic floor; the walls are hung with 16C and

Villa Île-de-France, St-Jean-Cap-Ferrat

17C Flemish tapestries. It is decorated with a collection of medieval and Renaissance works of art: a late-15C altarpiece depicting St Bridget of Ireland; a Carpaccio painting depicting a Venetian condottiere.

The adjoining rooms and galleries display works of art from various periods: 18C furniture (some items belonged to Marie-Antoinette), Savonnerie carpets, Beauvais, Aubusson and Gobelins tapestries, canvases by Boucher, Coypel, Fragonard, Lancret, Hubert Robert, terracottas by Clodion and candelabra by Thomire. The private apartments of Madame Ephrussi, which can be visited, include her bedroom, bathroom, boudoir and the Sèvres dining room.

On the first floor, the outstanding presentation of porcelain from Vincennes, Sèvres and Dresden adds to the dazzling effect of the whole collection. The curious monkey room ("Salon des Singes") evokes the theme of animals which was so dear to

Albert-1er Av.	2
Centrale Av.	3
États-Unis Av. des	5
Gaulle Bd Gén.-de	6
Grasseuil Av.	7
Libération Bd	9
Mermoz Av. J.	12
Passable Ch. de	13
Phare Av. du	14
Puncia Av. de la	15
St-Jean Pont	16
Sauvan Bd H.	17
Semeria Av. D.	18
Verdun Av. de	20
Vignon Av. C.	21

Villa Ephrussi-de-Rotschild	M

Address Book

For coin ranges see the Legend at the back of the guide.

EATING OUT

🍴 **Capitaine Cook** – *Avenue Jean-Mermoz* – ☎ *04 93 76 02 66* – 🕐 *Closed 8 Nov-26 Dec, Thu for lunch and Wed.* Lying half-way between Paloma beach and the marina, this family-style restaurant serves traditional cuisine with a strong emphasis on fish and seafood. Clients sit side-by-side together at long tables.

🍴 **Plage de Passable** – *Chemin de Passable* – ☎ *04 93 76 06 17* – 🕐 *Closed mid-Oct to Mar.* Beach restaurant located in Villefranche port on the way to St-Jean-Cap-Ferrat Peninsula serves salads, pizzas, pasta and seafood. Enchanting spot sheltered by umbrella pines and palm trees.

WHERE TO STAY

🛏 **Hôtel Frégate** – *Avenue Denis-Séméria* – ☎ *04 93 76 04 51* – 🕐 *Closed 15 Dec-5 Jan – 10 rooms – Restaurant (🍴).* An unpretentious establishment in a lively shopping street, recently renovated by its current owners. Some of the small but well-kept rooms have a balcony. Conveniently located 100yards from the beach and the town center.

🛏 **Hôtel La Bastide** – *3 Avenue Albert-1* – ☎ *04 93 76 06 78* – 🅿 *– 14 rooms – 🍽 – Restaurant (🍴).* Although this small hotel may not have all the latest comforts, its rooms command pretty views of the bay and, in the far distance, Cap d'Ail; one has a private terrace. Home cooking in the restaurant.

🛏 **Hôtel Brise Marine** – *Avenue Jean-Mermoz* – ☎ *04 93 76 04 36* – *www.hotel-brisemarine.com* – 🕐 *Closed Nov to Jan – 18 rooms – 🍽.* Located in a quiet street, this charming house with a welcoming façade is reached through lush, blossoming grounds. Superb views of the bay and Cap Ferrat. It is advisable to book the rooms in the villa, more comfortable than those in the annexe.

BEACHES ON THE CAP

There are several "galet" (smooth stone) beaches in Cap Ferrat. To the west is **Plage de Passable** facing Villefranche. To the east **Plage Paloma** facing Beaulieu, **Plage du Cro des Pins** near the port, and a beach at the **Pointe St-Hospice.**

Baroness Ephrussi; note the unusual monkey orchestra in Meissen porcelain. Two Chinese lacquer panels open into the gallery of Far Eastern art, arranged in Gothic decor and including lacquerwork from Coromandel, Chinese vases and carpets and a series of Mandarin costumes. The Impressionists' Gallery contains landscapes by Monet, Renoir and Sisley.

Gardens★★

Magnificent grounds (7ha/17 acres) surround the villa. The French garden abounds in Mediterranean flora and terminates in a stepped cascade spilling into a rockery by a Temple of Love copied from Versailles. Broad steps lead down among the arums, papyrus, pomegranates and daturas of the Spanish garden, which is followed by the Florentine garden with its graceful marble statue. Fountains, columns, gargoyles and sculptures, both medieval and Renaissance, ornament the Stone Garden. A delightful Japanese garden contrasts with the unusual plants in the tropical garden. The Baroness Ephrussi was very partial to roses, many varieties of which can be seen in the rose garden.

Driving Tour★★

Cap-Ferrat Peninsula – *10km/6mi – about 3hr*

Plage de Passable

This gently sloping shingle beach faces Villefranche port.

Zoo

🧒 ♿ 🕐 *Open summer 9.30am-7pm; winter 9.30am-5pm* – ☎ *04 93 76 07 60* – 👛 *11€ (child 7€)* – *www.zoocapferrat.com*

A drained lake on grounds that once belonged to Leopold II of Belgium has been converted into a **tropical garden** in which a 3ha/7-acre zoo has been set up. It contains 350 species of animals and exotic birds. Several times a day a troop of chimpanzees performs in front of an enthusiastic audience.

Phare

The beam of this **lighthouse** is visible from a distance of 46km/30mi. The top *(164 steps)* commands a **panorama**★★ from Bordighera Point in Italy to the Esterel heights including the Alps and Pre-Alps. The Sun Beach swimming pool has been hollowed out of the rocks nearby.

St-Jean-Cap-Ferrat★

Once a fishing village, St-Jean is now a quiet resort, its old houses looking down on the harbor of pleasure yachts.

The stepped street to the south of Boulevard de la Libération leads to a **viewpoint**★ from which Èze, the Tête de Chien, Mont Agel and the Alps on the Italian border can be seen.

Pointe St-Hospice

A pleasant stroll up between the private houses, past an 18C prison tower, leads to a 19C chapel, which replaces an old oratory dedicated to St Hospice, a hermit from Nice. From the chapel there is a good **view**★ of the coast and inland from Beaulieu to Cap Martin.

Walking Tours

From St-Jean, visitors can take pleasant walks, mostly in the shade.

Promenade Maurice-Rouvier★

🚶 *1hr round-trip on foot, leaving from the port of St-Jean.*

Starting at the northern end of Plage de St-Jean, the walk follows the coast towards Beaulieu, offering pretty views of Èze and the Tête de Chien.

Sentier Touristique de la Pointe St-Hospice★

🚶 *1hr round-trip on foot. Take Avenue Jean-Mermoz to the Paloma-Beach restaurant and go down the steps on the left.*

The path winds along the shore past Paloma Beach with a view of Èze, Monaco and Cap Martin. Once round the Pointe St-Hospice, it skirts the Pointe du Colombier and leads along the shoreline of the Baie des Fossettes before leading back to Avenue Jean-Mermoz.

Sentier Littoral

🚶 *2hrs on foot, leaving from the port of St-Jean, arriving at the Tourism Office.*

Starting at the Port St-Jean, this footpath along the steep cliffs of the peninsula offers a tranquil escape from the summer crowds. Sturdy footwear required *(path closed when the sea is rough).*

COARAZE★

POPULATION 654

MICHELIN MAP 341 E4 -LOCAL MAP SEE NICE

The impeccably restored medieval village of Coaraze is situated at an altitude of 640m/2 100ft on the **Col St-Roch** road (altitude of pass: 990m/3 248ft), also called the Route du Soleil ("Sunshine Road"). The villagers, of a naturally lively disposition, make a point of celebrating several festivals every year, such as the Fête de St-Jean *(end of June)*, the Fête de Ste-Catherine *(end of August)*, the Olive Festival *(15 August)* and the Chestnut Festival *(end of October)*. 🛈 *Place Ste-Catherine – ☎ 04 93 79 37 47.*

Visit

To reach Coaraze from Nice, take the D 2204, passing through the Férion mountain range and the Vallée du Paillon de Contes on the D 15.

Craftsmen have taken up residence in this nicely restored village with its picturesque **old streets**★, long vaulted passageways and pretty little squares adorned with fountains.

From the terraced gardens, flanked by cypress trees, there is a lovely view down into the valley and north to the upper slopes of Rocca Seira.

The square is decorated with sundials designed by Cocteau, Goetz and Ponce de Léon.

▶ *Access the church through the old cemetery.*

The Church

In the old cemetery around the church, the graves are above-ground, because it's impossible to dig into the hard bed-rock. The church interior is Baroque. At the far end hangs an early painting of St Sebastian pierced by arrows.

▶ *Take D 15 north and turn left almost immediately onto a narrow road.*

Chapelle Notre-Dame-de-la-Pitié

The "blue chapel" was decorated in 1962 with blue monochrome scenes illustrating the life of Christ. Behind the altar a glass panel enhances a metal Pietà. The terrace affords a lovely view of the village.

▶ *Take D 15 heading south and after 2km/1mi turn right towards La Gardiola.*

Chapelle St-Sébastien

Nestled in the lush countryside, this chapel is dedicated to St Sebastian, who protected his disciples by warding off epidemics of the plague. It is decorated with elegant 1530 frescoes (restored in the 19C) depicting the saint pierced by arrows and surrounded by his archers, in a style reminiscent of Il Perugino. The soft hues and delicate contours are inspired by the Renaissance period.

▣ *Hikers will find a brochure of local footpaths at the Tourism Office.*

COGOLIN

POPULATION 9 079

MICHELIN MAP 340 O6 - LOCAL MAP SEE MASSIF DES MAURES

This typical Provençal village in the Gulf of St-Tropez lies at the foot of an ancient tower and a ruined mill. Cogolin is a well-known wine-growing center, but the town also has many artisans producing woven carpets, pipes and bottle corks. Reeds and canes collected from the local marshes are used for clarinets, fishing rods and furniture. ▯ *Place de la République,* ☎ *04 94 55 01 10. www.cogolin-provence. com.*

Walking Tour

At the top of the village, behind the Hôtel de Ville, the many alleyways joined by vaulted passages have retained their medieval character.

▶ *From the Tourism Office, go past the Hôtel de Ville, turning left on the Rue du 11-Novembre 1918.*

Église St-Sauveur

Parts of the church date from the 11C and a fine Renaissance serpentine gateway remains. Inside, a side chapel houses a fine altarpiece by Hurlupin (1540) depicting St-Antony accompanied by St-Eligius and St-Pons, alongside a beautiful 17C Baroque bust.

▶ *On leaving the church, don't miss the ancient fountain on Place Abbé-Toti.*

Rue Nationale

Along this street are many fine Renaissance doorways in green serpentine stone, some

Pipes from Cogolin

D. Pazery/ MICHELIN

Address Book

For coin ranges, see the Legend at the back of the guide.

WHERE TO EAT

▱▱ **Côté Jardin** – *Rue Pasteur, facing the Place du Marché, aka Place des Boules - Accessible also by the passage at 1 Rue Gambetta* – ☎ 04 94 56 80 40 - ◷ *Open for lunch and dinner in summer except during rain.* This open-air restaurant in the heart of Cogolin serves grilled meats, sandwiches, snacks, ice cream and beverages in a leafy, shaded garden.

WHERE TO STAY

▱▱ **Le Coq'Hôtel** – *Place de la Mairie* – ☎ 04 94 54 63 14 – ◷ *Closed 1-15 Jan* – 🅿 – *25 rooms* – ▱ – *Restaurant (▱▱).* The hotel's mascot is the rooster, whose emblem can be found on the pretty façade, decorated with blue shutters, or perched inside the lounge. Gay, lively colors adorn the rooms, with an eclectic selection of furnishings. Double-paned windows overlook the square, while other rooms face the quiet inner courtyard where breakfast is served in summer.

SHOPPING

Provençal Market – There is a lively market every Wednesday and Saturday.

Fabrique de M. Rigotti – *Zone Industrielle – 5 Rue François-Arago* – ☎ 04 94 54 62 05 –

◷ *Open daily 8am-noon, 1.30-5.30pm.* ◷ *Closed Aug.* This workshop *(guided tours available)* manufactures and sells reeds and parts for musical instruments.

Cogolin Pipes – *Maison Courrieu – 42/58 Avenue Georges-Clémenceau* – ♿ – ◷ *Workshop open 9-11.30am, 2-6pm; Sun and public holidays by appointment. Boutique open 9am-noon, 2-5.30pm (until 7pm in summer)* – ☎ 04 94 54 63 82 – *www. courrieupipes.fr.* Briar roots from the nearby Maures Forest provide the raw material for the manufacture of pipes along the Avenue Clémenceau, including the Maison Courrieu, more than 200 years old. Visitors can see the manufacturing techniques as well as beautiful collections of the finished product.

Manufacture de Tapis de Cogolin – *10 Boulevard Louis-Blanc (off Avenue Georges-Clemenceau* – ◷ *The exhibition gallery is open daily except Sat-Sun 8.30am-noon, 2-5.30pm (Fri 5pm)* – ◷ *Closed 15 days in Aug and 24 Dec to 2 Jan* – ☎ 04 94 55 70 65. In the early 1920s, some Armenian refugee weavers settled in Cogolin, and the carpet factory was established in 1928, with the transfer of some high warp looms from Aubusson. A tour shows the two techniques currently used: hand weaving on request (using low warp looms – *la basse lisse*), and hand tufting.

of which date back to the 12C; the bourgeois building at no 46 is know as Château Sellier (♿ *see Sights*).

▶ *Follow Rue Nationale to Place Bellevue.*

The **Chapelle St-Roch** is decorated with contemporary art, while further up on the summit of the hill, via Montée Aloes, is the **clock tower** (14C), all that remains of the fortified castle *(access at the end of Rue Nationale, via Montée de l'Horloge).*

Sights

Demeure-Musée Sellier

◷ *Open Jun-Sep 10am-1pm, 3-6pm; Oct-May 10am-12.30pm, 2.30-5.30pm.* ◷ *Closed Sun, Mon.* ▱ *2.30€.* ☎ 04 94 54 63 28.

In addition to temporary arts expositions, this château houses the Musée de Coq (or Rooster Museum, the town's emblematic symbol), with roosters in wood, iron, ceramic, glass, and even a stuffed one with four feet!
There's also the **Medieval Templars Museum**, with documents and uniforms that illustrate the history of the religious order of knights from the 11-14C (Cogolin was the seat of the Templars in Provence).

Espace Raimu

Avenue Georges-Clemenceau. ♿ ◷ *Open Jul to mid-Sep 10am-noon, 4-7pm, Sun 4-7pm; mid-Sep to end of Jun 10am-noon, 3-6pm, Sun 3-6pm.* ◷ *Closed Tue, 1 Jan, 15-30 Nov, 25 Dec.* ▱ *3.5€.* ☎ 04 94 54 18 00. *www.musee-raimu.com.*

Located on the ground floor of the local cinema, this center pays homage (posters, photographs, memorabilia) to the French actor Jules Auguste César Muraire (1883-1946), better known as Raimu. Raimu is best-known to English-speaking audiences for his performance as César in Marcel Pagnol's trilogy *Marius, Fanny, César* and for his role in *La Femme du Boulanger*, also by Pagnol.

Marines de Cogolin

▶ *5km/3mi northeast by N 98 and D 98A*

Near Cogolin lies a fine sandy beach and a marina (22ha/54 acres) with more than 1 500 moorings. The four basins are surrounded by a residential complex built in a striking architectural style. There are regular boat shuttle services to the ports nearby, including the more intimate Port Cogolin, with just 150 moorings.

COTIGNAC ★

POPULATION 2 026

MICHELIN MAP 340 L4

This peaceful Provençal village seems to flow down from a cliff (80m/262ft high) of varying colors, shaped by the course of the Cassole River and riddled with caves and chasms, some more than 50m/164ft deep. On top of the cliff sit two 14C towers, the remains of Castellane Castle. Famed for its wine, olive oil and honey, Cotignac is also known for its croissants made with pignon nuts.

▶ **Oriented Yourself:** Cotignac is in the Var *département*, 15km/9.3mi south of Aups (& *see AUPS*) on the D 22. *Rue Bonnaventure,* ☎ *04 94 04 61 87.*

P **Parking:** Parking is available near the main square and at the exit of the village (in the direction of Carcès).

Visit

The Old Village

A detailed walking tour map is available at the Tourism Office.

Shaded by the plane trees, the **cours centrale** (main square) has beautiful 16C-18C façades and an ancient fountain.

The 13C church has been rebuilt many times and now has an 18C-façade. On the Grande-Rue, look up to see the three caryatids at no 7. Follow the street to the Place de la Mairie to see the 18C Hôtel de Ville with its 15C belfry. Across from the square stands the **Théâtre de Verdure**, home to the annual summer music and theatre festival.

Address Book

WHERE TO EAT

⊜⊜⊜ **Restaurant Le Clos des Vignes** – *Route de Montfort – 5km/3mi S of Cotignac heading towards Brignoles –* ☎ *04 94 04 72 19 –* ◷ *Closed Mon, and Oct-Jun Sun evening and Tue – Reservation recommended.* This former sheep barn surrounded by vineyards has been restored with a dining room-verandah and a pretty terrace for summer days. The strong personality of the owner and the succulent cuisine made with fresh regional produce all make for an unforgettable meal. A popular address among locals.

WHERE TO STAY

⊜⊜ **Chambre d'Hôte Domaine de Nestuby** – *5km/3mi S of Cotignac towards Brignoles –* ☎ *04 94 04 60 02 – www.sejour-en-provence.com –* ◷ *Closed 15 Nov-1 Mar –* ⊟ *– 5 rooms – Restaurant (*⊜⊜*).* Lying at the heart of a vineyard, this welcoming cottage contains fine, comfortable rooms furnished with antiques unearthed in second-hand markets. The owner will be happy to introduce you to the wine made on the estate at his table d'hôte, set up in the former stables.

SHOPPING

Local Specialities – The village is known for its wine, oil, and honey making. In the bakeries you'll find the delicious *croissants aux pignons*.

Markets – *Cours Gambetta* – Provençal market on Tuesday, and agricultural market on Fridays (mid-June through mid-September).

Les Ruchers du Bessillon – *5 Rue de la Victoire –* ☎ *04 94 04 60 39 – www.sejour-en-provence.com –* ◷ *Open summer 10am-12.30pm, 3.30-7pm; winter daily except Mon 10am-noon.* This boutique sells organic honey made with pollen from acacia, chestnut, pine and linden trees, as well as from heather, rosemary and lavender.

> ## Nuts about them!
>
> Pine nuts, also called pignons, are delicately flavoured seeds taken from the cones of the stone pine. Their presence in Provençal cooking is by no means recent as the Romans are believed to have used them to make wine and mustard. Today pine nuts are a common feature of Mediterranean cuisine. In savoury dishes, they add texture to green vegetables and lend a crunchy consistency to stuffings. They are also used in pastries, preferably toasted, notably in the delicious almond tarts known as *amandines*.

Follow the path up to the clifftop overlooking the countryside, where a two-storey **grotto** (Ⓖ *Guided tours: Jul-Aug 10am-noon, 2-6pm; 15 Apr-Sep 2-5pm.* ⮾ *2€*) where the village inhabitants used to hide their provisions from pillagers during invasions. The view is worth the effort (although not recommended for those who suffer from vertigo). Return via the Place de la Mairie, passing by the ancient olive oil mill on your way.

Chapelle Notre-Dame-des-Grâces
1km/0.6mi south on D 13 via a side road to the right. Ⓖ *Open 8-11am, 12.30-6pm ,* ☎ *04 94 69 64 85 or 04 94 69 64 97.*

The chapel, surmounting Mont Verdaille, is associated with an appearance of the Virgin in the 16C, which is depicted in a painting above the altar. In 1660 young Louis XIV came here on a pilgrimage with his mother Anne of Austria, an event commemorated by a black marble tablet on a pillar.
From the esplanade around the church, there is a pleasant **panorama** of Carcès, the Argens Valley and the Brignoles region to the south.

🚶 *45min on foot round-trip.*

A wooded path from the chapel leads to **St-Joseph Monastery**. Only the church is open to the public.

DRAGUIGNAN

POPULATION 32 829

MICHELIN MAP 340 N4

Situated between the Haut-Var and the Haute-Provence plateau, the town of Draguignan developed from a Roman fort built on an isolated knoll where the 17C Tour d'Horloge (clock tower) now stands. Known for its colorful festivals and popular Provençal markets, the town is at the center of the Var's wine-growing region, making it an ideal hub for visiting the surrounding villages and towns.

▸ **Orient Yourself:** The town is in the Var off the N 555, 30km/18.6mi northwest of Fréjus (Ⓖ *see FREJUS).* ⓘ *Avenue Carnot,* ☎ *04 98 10 51 05.* www.ot-draguignan.fr Ⓖ *Guided tours of the city available through the Tourism Office, departure at 9am.* ⮾ *5€. Call for more information.*

🅿 **Parking:** The most convenient place to park between the Tourism Office and the Old Town is at the Allées d'Azémar *(fee; first hour free).*

A Bit of History

From the Middle Ages to the present – In the 13C the town grew at the foot of the hill, where a defensive wall with three gates, two of which remain (Porte des Portaiguières and Porte Romaine), and a keep (on the bluff) were built. Louis XIV ordered the keep to be razed in retribution for the conflict between local factions in 1649.
In 1797 the town became the administrative centre *(préfecture)* of the Var by order of Napoleon; in 1974 Toulon took over. In the 19C barons Azémar and Haussmann, both prefects of the Var, laid out tree-lined walks and straight boulevards to the west and south of the town.
An American Cemetery, to the east of the town, and a memorial to the Liberation on the corner of Avenue Lazare-Carnot and Avenue Patrick-Rosso, recall the fierce fighting that took place in the region in August 1944, notably around Le Muy, where 9 000 British and American soldiers were parachuted or landed from gliders on the morning of 15 August. The town has been home to an artillery school since 1976.

St Hermentaire and the dragon
– The name Draguignan is derived from Draconio, from the Latin *draco* meaning dragon.

Legend has it that, in the 5C, pilgrims on their way from Ampus to the renowned Lérins Abbey via Lentier encountered a dragon roaming the marshes, now meadows watered by the Nartuby. The terrified pilgrims appealed for the help of the hermit Hermentaire, who lived in the area. He slayed the dragon and built a chapel dedicated to St Michael the Archangel.

The existing church of **St-Michel**, north of Place du Marché, contains an 18C statue of St Hermentaire in gilded wood.

Clock tower, Draguignan

Visit

The Old Town

▶ *Begin at the Place du Marché.*

The tip of the Rue des Marchands opens onto Old Draguignan (pedestrian precinct), where the 14C gates, **Porte Romaine** and **Porte des Portaiguières**, frame an intricate maze of charming streets lined with ornate doorways and houses at odd angles. The marketplace is set with fountains and shaded by plane trees.

▶ *Follow the Rue de l'Observance and turn left on the Montée de l'Horloge.*

Tour de l'Horloge

🕐 *Guided tours (1 hr) Jul-Aug 3-6.30pm; the rest of the year, contact the Tourism Office.* 🎟 *3€.* ☎ *04 98 10 51 05.*

The clock tower replaced the keep, which was pulled down in 1660. It has four flanking turrets and an ornate wrought-iron campanile. The **view** from the top encompasses the town and the Nartuby Valley; on the horizon stretch the Maures mountains.

▶ *Double back to the Rue des Tanneurs, to the Porte de Portaiguières, which pierces a 15C square tower.*

The vast façade of an old 13C **synagogue** in Rue de la Juiverie and the old mansion at no 42 are worthy of interest.

▶ *At the end of the street turn right to reach the church and return to the Place du Marché.*

Sights

Musée Municipal

♿ 🕐 *Open 9am-noon, 2-6pm.* 🕐 *Closed Sun and public holidays.* 🎟 *Free entry.* ☎ *04 94 47 28 80.*

The museum, an old Ursuline convent built in the 17C and remodelled in the 18C by the Bishop of Fréjus for use as his summer residence, displays some interesting and rare items, as well as antique furniture, sculpture, ceramics from France (Vallauris, Moustiers, Sèvres) and the Far East.

One gallery presents three paintings by Ziem (1821-1911), including two of Venice, *The Deliverance of St Peter* by J-B Van Loo, a suit of parade armour made between 1570 and 1575 for François de Montmorency, and a graceful composition sculpted by Camille Claudel (1903).

The next room, devoted to 17C French and Dutch painting, displays a Rembrandt *(Child Blowing Bubbles)*, a small Frans Hals *(Kitchen Interior)* and a *Head of Christ* by P de Champaigne.

Also on display are a bust of the Count of Valbelle, Marquis of Tourves, by Houdon and 17C-18C paintings: pastels by the Boucher School, two canvases by Teniers the Younger, a charming *Portrait of a Young Girl* by Greuze and *St Peter's Basilica* by Panini.

The final room is devoted to archeology and displays items discovered during the excavation of Gallo-Roman sites of St-Hermentaire and medieval sites of the town.

Address Book

TRANSPORTATION

Buses – The city is served by the bus network Draguibus *(4 lines)*. Single tickets available from bus drivers, books of tickets from the bus station on Rue des Martyrs-de-la-Résistance *(Mon-Fri 8am-noon, 2-6pm; Sat 8am-noon)*. Coaches will take you to St-Raphaël *(60 min)*, Toulon *(120 min)*, and to the SNCF train station of Les Arcs-Draguignan *(25 min)*. ☎ 04 94 68 15 34.

EATING OUT

For coin ranges, see the Legend at the back of the guide.

⊜⊜ **L'Accomedia** – *13 Rue des Endronnes* – ☎ *04 94 50 72 72* – ⏱ *Closed Sun-Tue night; 4-25 Jul, 20 Dec-2 Jan.* This Italian restaurant is situated right opposite the local theatre and is embellished with a fresco evoking the Carnival. In a light, modern setting, typical Mediterranean specialities are prepared and attractively served by friendly, smiling staff.

⊜⊜ **Restaurant du Parc** – *21 Boulevard de la Liberté* – ☎ *04 94 50 66 44* – ⏱ *Closed Sun-Mon in winter; Sat-Mon lunch in summer.* At the height of summer, the sturdy boughs of a century-old plane tree provide a welcome patch of shade to diners seated on the terrace of this restaurant specialising in Provençal cooking made with choice ingredients. The dining room features a simple decor with rustic-style furnishings.

WHERE TO STAY

⊜⊜ **Hôtel Les Oliviers** – *4km/2.5mi West of Draguignan by D 557 (Route de Flayosc)* – ☎ *04 94 68 25 74* – *hotel-les-oliviers@club-internet.fr* – ⏱ *Closed 5-25 Jan* – 🅿 – *12 rooms* – 🍽. Roadside hotel conveniently situated on the way to Flayosc. Fortunately, there is very little traffic at night. The rooms, all on the ground floor, are light and neatly arranged.

⊜⊜ **Chambre d'Hôte St-Amour** – *986 Route de la Motte – Trans-en-Provence – 5km/3mi S of Draguignan, Route du Muy* – ☎ *04 94 70 88 92* – *saint.amour83@wanadoo.fr* – 🚫 – *3 rooms.* A large, rambling park and a curious swimming pool are the backdrop to this old stone house offering a self-contained flat and several rooms, each decorated in a distinctive style (Africa, Provence). The nearby house also provides lodging in the form of a pretty studio.

SHOPPING

Markets – Place du Marché hosts a lively, colorful market on Wednesday and Saturday mornings.

Moulin Traditionnel "Lou Calen" – *1 Rue de l'Observance* – ⏱ *Open Sat 9am-12.30pm.* This early 20C mill situated on the hills above Draguignan presses olives grown by small local producers on a traditional stone wheel. There's no boutique, but it's possible to purchase the olive oil direct on-site.

Moulin du Flayosquet – *Rte d'Ampus - Le Bastidon - Flayosc* – ☎ *04 94 70 41 45* – *Open Tue-Sat 9am-noon, 2-6.30pm; Jun-Aug Mon-Sat 9am-12.30pm, 2-7pm.* ⏱ *Closed two weeks in Mar and Nov.* This superb 13C mill has preserved its original equipment and still uses its traditional blades for some of the pressing. The olive oil is produced in the traditional way, which is evident in the taste. The boutique sells a selection of regional products in addition to the different olive oils.

Domaine Rabiega – *Route de Lorgues* – ☎ *04 94 68 44 22* – *www.rabiega.com* – ⏱ *Open Mon-Sat 9am-noon, 2-5pm.* A beautiful property situated amongst the olive trees and vineyards, Domaine Rabiega has been operated since 1986 by Swedish owners who make about 20,000 bottles per year of organic wines (mostly reds). There's a wine boutique and tastings are available.

Ornetti – *30 Boulevard Georges-Clémenceau* – ☎ *04 94 67 00 28* – ⏱ *Open 6am-8pm.* Run by the same family for three generations, this bakery is a much-loved establishment among the locals, who regularly greet the owner with a familiar kiss on the cheek instead of a handshake. All of the products are made with old-fashioned methods, including the speciality Draçenoise, and breads with olives, figs, plums, chestnuts and walnuts.

Musée des Arts et Traditions Populaires de Moyenne Provence★

⏱ *Open 9am-noon, 2-6pm, Sun and public holidays 2-6pm.* ⏱ *Closed Mon, 1 Jan, 1 May, Easter and 25 Dec.* ⊛ *3.50€. Guided tours (1.5 hr) on request.* ☎ *04 94 47 05 72.*

This museum highlights the traditional activities of the region encompassing the Provençal tableland, the Haut-Pays Varois, the Maures and the Esterel. It was essentially an agricultural region where cereals (primary crop), vineyards (in Provence since Antiquity), olive trees and cork were cultivated. Other activities included bee-keeping, sheep-raising, hunting, arts and crafts (floor tiles from Salernes, glassworks from the area around Fayence to Fréjus) and the raising of silkworms. Everyday life is evoked with displays of religious objects, domestic furnishings and crockery, costumes...

DRAGUIGNAN		Gay Pl. C.	Y 6	Martyrs-de-la-Résistance	
		Grasse Av. de	Y 8	Bd des	Z 17
Cisson R.	YZ 3	Joffre Bd. Mar.	Z 9	Marx-Dormoy Bd	Z 18
Clemenceau Bd	Z	Juiverie R. de la	Y 12	Mireur R. F.	Y 19
Clément R. P.	Z 4	Kennedy Bd J.	Z 13	Observance R. de l'	Y 20
Droits-de-l'Homme		Leclerc Bd Gén.	Z 14	République R. de la	Z 23
Parvis des	Z 5	Marchands R. des	Y 15	Rosso Av. P.	Z 24
		Marché Pl. du	Y 16		

Façade d'une ancienne synagogue	Y	B	Musée municipal	Z	M¹
Musée des Arts et Traditions populaires de moyenne Provence	Z	M²			

At the junction of Allées d'Azémar, shaded by six lines of hundred-year-old plane trees, and Boulevard Clemenceau stands a bronze bust of Clemenceau by Rodin.

Musée de l'Artillerie
3km/2mi east of Draguignan by Boulevard J.-Kennedy and D 59; at the artillery school's main entrance, in a military zone. ◷ *Open Sun-Wed 9am-noon, 1.30-5.30pm.* ◷ *Closed mid-Dec to mid-Jan and public holidays.* ⌨ *Free entry.* ☏ *04 98 10 83 86.*

The artillery school (founded in 1791) was transferred to Draguignan in 1976; it merged in 1983 with the anti-aircraft school from Nîmes.

The museum, which the school uses for military instruction, presents the evolution of weaponry and military strategy from ancient times up to the contemporary period.

The ground floor contains displays of heavy arms. Old-fashioned small arms are represented by various types of guns: coastal guns, naval guns, drill guns, siege guns, field guns – and rockets. The display of modern artillery comprises field weapons, trench equipment, fortifications, mountain weapons, anti-tank weapons and anti-aircraft defence equipment. A life-size diorama illustrates the use of French 75mm guns during the First World War and the crucial role played by the artillery in the Battle of Garigliano during the 1944 Italian campaign.

The mezzanine has been laid out as a military camp at the time of the Second Empire. A series of tents house a display on the evolution of small arms, running from the invention of the cannon up to the Gulf War.

Cimetière Américain et Mémorial du Rhône
Leave Draguignan by Boulevard J-Kennedy. ♿ ◷ *9am-5pm.* ⌨ *Free entry.* ☏ *04 94 68 03 62.*

In the landscaped cemetery (5ha/12 acres) are the graves of 861 American soldiers belonging to General Patch's 7th Army who fell in Provence during the campaign launched on 15 August 1944 in support of the Normandy landings. At the foot of the memorial a bronze relief map traces the troop movements. The names of the fallen are inscribed on the supporting wall. The chapel is decorated inside with mosaics by the American Austin Purves.

Chapelle Notre-Dame-du-Peuple
Southwest of the Old Town; see map.

This chapel was originally built in the 16C in Flamboyant Gothic style and subsequently enlarged (west front in 19C). It is dedicated to the Virgin who saved the town from the plague *(pilgrimage, 8 September),* and contains many votive offerings. On the north wall is the central panel of a 16C altarpiece of the Nice School representing the Virgin saying her rosary.

Excursions

Pays Dracénois

Malmont Viewpoint (Table d'Orientation du Malmont)★ *6km/4mi – about 45min.*
From Draguignan take Boulevard Joseph-Collomp north. After 6km/4mi, the road reaches a pass. Turn left onto a narrow road which leads to a viewing table 300m/330yd away.

An extensive **view**★ covers Mont Vinaigre in the Esterel range, Agay port, the Argens Valley, the Maures heights and Toulon.

Trans-en-Provence
5km/3mi. Leave Draguignan by the south on the map and then take N 555.

Up to the Second World War, this lively village was renowned for its silk spinning, an industry fuelled by the two dozen mills spanning the River Nartuby.
The town hall, built in 1779, with its lovely Louis XV **façade**★ decorated in *trompe-l'œil,* is a rare example of 18C civic architecture.
There is a fine reredos in **St-Victor** (14C church).

Gorges and Waterfalls of the Nartuby

A path leads from Place de la Mairie in front of the town hall to the bridges. This outstanding **site**★ is best viewed from between Pont Vieux and Pont Bertrand.

Puit Aérien

▶ *Chemin du Cassivet (look for the signs on the left when entering the village; path passes under the D 555).*

This "aerial well" was an original design by the Belgian engineer Knapper, who built it in 1930. The well, which has never been used locally, works by recovering moisture during the night in order to water crops. It was originally intended for the African continent.

Flayosc – *7km/4.5mi – about 45min.*

▶ *From Draguignan take D 557, T on the map, going west.*

This typical Var village, overlooking a countryside of vineyards, meadows and orchards, has retained its 14C fortified gates. The typically Provençal **Place de la Reinesse** has plane trees, a mossy fountain and a small wash-house; the Romanesque **church** has a massive square bell-tower. The terrace commands a sweeping **view** of the countryside and the Massif des Maures.

Chapelle Ste-Roseline★
10km/7mi. Leave Draguignan to the south on N 555 and turn right onto D 91. ♿ See Les ARCS.

Driving Tour

Gorges de Châteaudouble★ *41km/26mi – about 1hr.*

▶ *Leave Draguignan on the Avenue de Montferrat and follow D 955, U on the map.*

Pierre de la Fée

This "fairy's stone" is a fine dolmen of which the table, 6m/19.5ft long, 4.50m/14.5ft wide and weighing 40t, rests on three raised stones more than 2m/6ft high.

Gorges de Châteaudouble★

The deep, green, serpentine gorge was hollowed out by the Nartuby, a tributary of the River Argens.

▸ *Before reaching Montferrat, return to Le Plan and turn right onto D 51 to the village of Châteaudouble.*

Châteaudouble

This village occupies an exceptional site on the top of a cliff overhanging the gorges of the Nartuby by 100m/330ft. Its medieval charm can be seen by following the many passages interspersed with little squares adorned with fountains. Notre-Dame-de-l'Assomption, a 16C church flanked by a Romanesque bell-tower, boasts a fine studded portal. The Saracen Tower offers a superb **view**★ over the whole village and the rough outlines of the gorges.

Several steep paths lead from the gorges to the prehistoric caves of Mouret, Chèvres and Chauves-Souris.

▸ *From Châteaudouble drive north towards Ampus. D 51 crosses a plateau through the Bois des Prannes.*

Ampus

The village church is a well-restored Romanesque building. At the back of the church, a path marked by modern Stations of the Cross (1968) leads to a rocky outcrop.

▸ *Return to Draguignan on D 49 for a good view of the town.*

ÎLES DES **EMBIEZ**★

MICHELIN MAP 340 J7

LOCAL MAP SEE SANARY-SUR-MER EXCURSIONS

Separated from the Port du Brusc by a lagoon, the five islands making up the Embiez archipelago are surrounded by rich fishing banks that are the delight of amateur anglers and divers. With its kitsch statues, Provençal houses, pleasant beaches and oceanographic museum, the Îles des Embiez makes for an enjoyable day.

The biggest of the five islands (95ha/235 acres), officially called **Île de la Tour Fondue** is commonly known as **Les Embiez**. The second largest one, **Grand Gaou,** with its public park, is linked to the mainland by a footbridge. The **Île du Grand Rouveau** has an automatically-manned lighthouse. **Petit Rouveau** is a bird sanctuary devoted to the reproduction of several species, namely gulls. The smallest isle, **Petit Gaou,** serves as a car park 🅿 on the road from Le Brusc. 🄸 *Société Paul Ricard,* ☎ *04 94 10 65 20 or 0 890 711 183. www.paul-ricard.com.*

Visit

Île des Embiez

🖱 *see Address Book for access information.*

This island boasts a remarkable variety of natural features: fine gravel beaches, rugged coastline with many coves, salt marshes, umbrella pine woods and vineyards yielding a popular rosé wine.

A Maritime Vocation

The French Institute for Research and Exploitation of the Sea (IFREMER) was founded by the French State in June 1984. Its purpose is to ensure better knowledge and assessment of maritime resources, to protect and restore the marine environment, to encourage scientific or economic research in this field and to disseminate international oceanographic information. To do so, it has considerable means at its disposal: a substantial budget, several teams of engineers, seamen and researchers, and 72 laboratories located both in France and overseas. Lastly, it contributes to implementing agreements and conventions for worldwide cooperation on all matters relating to the sea.

Address Book

TRANSPORTATION

Access to the Island – *Société Paul Ricard – ☎ 04 94 10 65 20 or 0 890 711 183 – www. paul-ricard.com –* ✉ *9€ Round-trip, (6€ children 3-12 years).* This company operates 13 to 24 crossings per day *(8 mins)* from the embarkment Brusc at Six-Fours.

ON THE WATER

Beaches – The beaches are located to the east side of the island, around the port. To the west are many small coves.

Aquascope – ☐ ☐ ☐ *Île des Embiez - Le Brusc - Six-Fours-les-Plages -* ☐ *Open Jul-Aug 9am-6pm; Apr-Jun and Sep 2.30-5pm.* ☐ *Closed Nov-Mar and public holidays. Tours (30min).* ✉ *16€ (child 8€).* ☎ *04 94 34 17 85.* An unusual way to observe underwater life through the transparent hull of a boat.

Centre de Plongée des Embiez – *Île des Embiez - Le Brusc - Six-Fours-les-Plages -* ☎ *04 94 34 12 78 or 06 07 58 65 96.* This diving centre will introduce you to the intricacies of marine fauna and flora thanks to its many courses and many outings.

There is a busy modern **marina** overlooked by the ruins of the medieval Château de Sabran, with houses built in the Provençal style. Those keen on diving will enjoy the waters teeming with an exceptional variety of fauna. For the less adventurous there is the small **tourist train** *(b 06 88 69 76 78)*, which tours the island, as well as an opportunity to view the underwater world from on board the *Aquascope* (☐ *see Address Book*).

Institut Océanographique Paul-Ricard★

☐ ☐ *Guided tours (30min) Jul-Aug 9.30am-5.30pm; Apr-Jun and Sep 2-5.30pm.* ☐ *Closed Oct-Mar.* ✉ *16€ (child 9€).* ☎ *04 94 34 02 49. www.institut-paul-ricard.org.*

The old naval gun site on St-Pierre promontory houses an oceanographic institute devoted to the Mediterranean Sea. The **Observatoire** is fitted with high-tech laboratories where research is carried out on marine biology, fish farming and sea pollution in conjuction with Elf-Aquitaine and the state body **IFREMER** (☐ *see box*).

A **museum** on the ground floor displays the main Mediterranean types of environment and the species which thrive on them, including an extensive collection of molluscs, stuffed fish and fossils.

About 30 large sea-water **aquariums** *(first floor)* provide a natural setting for some 100 species of Mediterranean aquatic animals, some in gorgeous colours: gorgonias, hermit crabs, grouper, blue lobsters, spider crabs, octopi, sting rays, scorpion fish, little eels.

ENTRECASTEAUX

POPULATION 863

MICHELIN MAP 340 M4

Built on the slopes of a hill overlooking the banks of the River Bresque, this village prides itself on its public gardens designed by Le Nôtre. It is a pleasure to wander through the old Provençal streets and the lively main avenue, shaded by hundred-year-old plane trees.

▶ **Orient Yourself**: The town sits 24km/15mi south of Aups (☐ *see AUPS*) on D 31. There's a map on the square next to the garden that highlights all of the places of interest in the village. ☐ *Cours Gabriel-Péri,* ☎ *04 94 04 40 50.*

Visit

The town's narrow streets wind their way around an old fortified church, which has a buttress spanning the road.

From the church esplanade, head down to the Pont St-Pierre and the wash house *(lavoir)*, where you'll see the château's round ice house. Go around the back through the narrowest section and the ancient entance gate.

Cross the gardens and exit by the pretty horse-shoe shaped staircase, to the **Chapelle des Pénitents** (now home to the Town Hall). Finally, follow the pleasant path up to the **Chapelle Ste-Anne** where you'll find a fine view of the city.

Address Book

For coin ranges, see the Legend at the back of the guide.

WHERE TO EAT

☺☺ **Lou Picatéou** – *Place du Souvenir* – ☎ 04 94 04 47 97 – ◷ *Closed Oct–Mar.* Lying the foot of the castle, this small restaurant with colorful walls, wooden beams and strong Provençal overtones proposes two menus to customers. Summer terrace shaded by the trees growing on the square.

☺☺ **La Fourchette** – *Le Courtil, near the château* - ☎ 04 94 04 42 78 – ◷ *Closed mid-Dec to mid-Feb, Sun eve-Tue.* Light and refined cuisine made from fresh market products and served on a pretty terrace with panoramc views over the valley. In winter, the tiny dining room with the old tile flooring and fresco of the village on the walls provides an intimate place to enjoy a meal.

OUTDOOR ACTIVITIES

Provence Canoë - *New Évasion – On the D 562 between Lorgues and Carcès* – ☎ 06 72 15 29 14 - *contact@provence-canœ.com* - ◷ *Open daily Apr-Nov.* Discover the Argens River by canoe or kayak. *Half-day excursions from 18P.*

SHOPPING

There's a market on Friday mornings.

CALENDAR

Local patron saints – Ste-Anne is celebrated on 26 July and St-Sauveur during the first weekend in August.

Flea market – The third Sunday in July (until midnight).

Pesto soup banquet – Mid-August.

Floralies – Plant and flower fair, second weekend in May.

Chamber Music Festival – Early September.

OUTDOOR ACTIVITIES

Les Trois Fers – *6001 Domaine des Lacs du Dramont – St-Raphaël* – ☎ 06 85 42 51 50 – *www.les3fers.com* – ◷ *Open all year, book in advance.* Horse lovers will appreciate the riding excursions that will take them through some of the prettiest spots in the Esterel Massif. Lovely views of the sea and Île d'Or can be seen from the Cap Dramont.

L'Esterel à Cheval – *St-Raphaël* - ☎ 06 15 16 49 48. Horseback riding initiation.

Ranch de l'Esterel – *St-Raphaël* – ☎ 04 94 82 89 47. Half-day horseback excursions.

Sport Loisirs Découverte – *St-Raphaël* - ☎ 06 86 38 00 69. Hiking and climbing courses.

JDC Loisirs et Découverte de l'Esterel – *281 Rue du 11-Novembre-1943 - Agay* - ☎ 06 09 09 73 90 - *www.decouverte delesterel.com* - ◷ *Open Feb-Dec every day on request (call to reserve).* Joseph, who works with the ONF, proposes a fun and original excursion into the Esterel forests in an open-top vehicle. The visit ends with a sampling of regional specialities.

Evolution 2 – *Cap Esterel, Route des Calanques - Agay* - ☎ 04 94 82 79 02. Archery, climbing, and orientation excursions are organized by this company.

Esterel Pêche – *St-Raphaël* - ☎ 06 07 14 51 14. Initiations in sport fishing and fishing outings.

Château

◷ *Guided tours: the times are displayed at the entrance to the château.* ☞ 6€. ☎ 04 94 04 43 95.

This austere 17C building dominates the valley of the Bresque, a tributary of the Argens. Its high façade is topped by a double row of tiles and wrought-iron balustrades. The château was the stronghold of the Castellane, followed by the Grignan (who received the Countess de Sévigné) before passing to the Bruni family. This family included **Admiral Bruni d'Entrecasteaux** who died at sea in 1793 during an expedition to find the explorer La Pérouse who had disappeared five years earlier. A group of islands in New Guinea has been named after him.

After a long period of neglect, the château was restored by the British painter Ian McGarvie-Munn who turned part of it into a museum before his death in 1981. The tour now includes the former castle kitchen and outbuildings in the basement, the guard-rooms and the salons on the ground floor.

MASSIF DE L'ESTEREL★★★

MICHELIN MAP 340 P/Q5

The Esterel between St-Raphaël and La Napoule is an area of breathtaking natural beauty. One of the loveliest parts of Provence, it was opened to large-scale tourism by the Touring Club's creation in 1903 of the scenic tourist road known as the Corniche d'Or (Golden Scenic Route). The fiery red of the rocks forms a strong contrast with the deep blue of the sea, while the bustling life along the coast contrasts with the seclusion of the inland roads. The latter will appeal to tourists who prefer to stray from the beaten track for the pleasure of exploring on their own.

▶ **Orient Yourself:** The Esterel stretches from along the coastline of the Var between Cannes and Fréjus, and encompasses several small villages and beachside resorts such as Théoule-sur-Mer, Le Trayas, and St-Raphaël. The Esterel is more developed along the coastline, and more secluded inland, where it's possible to hike all day without seeing anyone else.

🅿 **Parking:** Except in high season around the major towns, parking is relatively easy to find *(and free)* near hiking trailheads. It is advisable, even in official parking areas, to remove all valuables from your car when hiking.

😊 **Don't Miss:** The panoramic view from the Pointe de l'Esquillon, the scenic port in Agay, and for the robust hikers, the views from the peak known as Pic de l'Ours. 👋 *See "Visiting the Massif" (box) for helpful touring tips.*

🕐 **Organizing Your Time:** You could easily drive through the Esterel along N 98 coastal road from Cannes to Fréjus in less than an hour (depending on summer traffic and how seasick the winding roads make you), with a pause for a short hike at Dramont or the Point d'Esquillon. But for the longer hikes it's best to plan for at least a half day, and to be prepared with enough drinking water, food, and appropriate walking shoes. A full day could include a morning hike inland, lunch at one of the resorts, then a shorter hike along the coast and a bit of swimming.

👋 **Also See:** See specific chapters for more detailed information on ST-RAPHAËL, FRÉJUS, MANDELIEU-LA-NAPOULE and CANNES .

A Bit of History

The Massif – The Esterel, which is as old as its neighbour the Maures from which it is separated by the Argens Valley, has been worn down by erosion so that its highest point, Mont Vinaigre, is now a mere 618m/2 027ft. However, in this mountain mass, the deep ravines and broken skyline dispel any impression of this being mere hills. The Esterel is made up of volcanic rocks (porphyry), which were forced up during the Hercynian foldings, thus distinguishing it from the Maures. These hard porphyry rocks,

Mediterranean Pine Trees

Maritime Pine – This is the original species of the Mediterranean coast, and once covered much of the region in dense forests. In spite of its highly combustible nature, it had the advantage of being able to regenerate speedily after fires. However, in the past 25 years, it has been attacked by another enemy. A parasite, the Matsucocus feytaudi, has brought about its downfall by preventing it from reaching maturity, explaining its often bare appearance. It still accounts for 60% of the species in coastal forests.

Umbrella Pine – On account of its attractive appearance, which blends in wonderfully with the Mediterranean setting, this tree is a great favorite for replanting the *maquis* scrubland. The mushroom-shaped foliage casts a welcome ring of shade.

Aleppo Pine – More common inland, this tree is known to grow on dry soil up to an altitude of 500m/1 640ft. The tree, which can be seen on land left fallow or on isolated south-facing slopes, is easily identifiable thanks to its red-brown bark and the curve of its trunk.

Scots Pine – This variety thrives on the plateaux of the Haut-Var and the north of the Alpes-Maritimes. Together with the fir it forms magnificent forests.

Address Book

PRACTICAL INFORMATION

Guided Tours of the Massif – The tourism offices of St-Raphaël-Agay, Fréjus, Mandelieu and Le Muy work with the National Office of Forestry to organize tours of the forests in the Massif de l'Esterel. See these tourism offices for more information. ▣ *www.saint-raphael. com, www.agay.fr, www.ville-frejus.fr, www. lemuy-tourisme.com, www.onf.fr,* ☎ *04 94 19 52 52 (St-Raphaël Tourism Office).*

For coin ranges, see the Legend at the back of the guide.

EATING OUT

⊜⊜ **Le Marco Polo** – *Avenue de Lérins – Théoule-sur-Mer –* ☎ *04 93 49 96 59 –* ◷ *Closed mid-Nov to mid-Dec closed for lunch 1-15 Nov and mid-Dec to mid-Apr.* Ideally located at the water's edge, this restaurant boasts a giant aquarium. The dining room, furnished with rattan tables and chairs, serves salads for lunch and more elaborate dishes in the evening. The terrace commands a nice panorama of Cannes Bay. Informal service.

which give the range its characteristic profile, its harsh relief and vivid coloring, appear in full beauty in the red tints of the Cap Roux range. Agay is where the blue porphyry is found from which the Romans made the column shafts for their monuments in Provence; elsewhere the colors are green, yellow, purple or grey.

Via Aurelia – The Esterel was bordered to the north by the Via Aurelia (Aurelian Way) constructed during the reign of Aurelius. It ran from Rome to Arles, via Genoa, Cimiez, Antibes, Fréjus and Aix, and was one of the most important roads under the Empire. Paved, cambered, and more than 2.5m/8ft wide, the road was laid upon a cement base, like the N 7, which follows much the same route. In the local dialect it is still called *lou camin aurélian*. Taking the shortest route, it made use of many bridges and other civil engineering works.

At the end of each Roman mile (1 478m/1 617yd) distances would be indicated by a tall milestone – one of these can be seen in the museum at St-Raphaël (Musée Archéologique). As the road approached the towns, it had raised sidewalks for pedestrians, which also served as mounting blocks. Stage posts, equipped with hostelries, horses and workshops, minimised delays to the imperial post.

Esterel Gap – The road skirting the north side of the Esterel, which for many years was the only land route to Italy, was rife with highwaymen; "to survive the Esterel Gap" became a local saying. The most dangerous spot was to the west of Mont Vinaigre; in those days the coach road left the N 7 at the Carrefour du Logis-de-Paris and ran closer to the foothills past the forester's lodge (Maison Forestière du Malpey) at Le Malpey (Evil Mountain).

In 1787 the naturalist Saussure showed real courage in exploring the region on foot. Until the end of the 19C the massif remained the refuge of convicts escaping from Toulon.

M. Ajuria/ Sunset

Agay Viaduct

☺ Touring Tip ☺
Visiting the Massif

- Roads marked as "RF" on the map are open to traffic under certain conditions: speed limited to 40kph/25m, no vehicles weighing over 3.5t and no traffic between 9pm and 6am. The roads marked in a red dotted line are closed to public traffic and offenders may be liable to heavy fines. Pedestrian access is however possible.

- During periods of high fire risk, the ALARME plan is put into action and some public roads may be closed to vehicles. Hikers are strongly advised to avoid such areas for safety reasons.

- Camping is prohibited throughout the massif and within 200m/656ft of any of the forests.

- When walking in the massif, respect plants and wild animals, do not litter the grounds, stay on the paths and keep dogs under control. Mountain bikers must not stray from the signposted paths and tracks laid out in the forests.

- For up-to-date information concerning the massif, call ☎ 04 98 10 55 41.

Resorts

Stretching more than 30km/18.6mi between St-Raphaël and La Napoule, the striking landscape of the Corniche de l'Esterel is punctuated by several pleasant seaside resorts.

Boulouris ⌂

This small resort, where villas are dotted among pines in beautiful gardens, has several little beaches and a pleasure boat harbor (& *see ST-RAPHAËL*).

Agay ⌂

The resort borders a deep port, the best in the Esterel, used in earlier times by the Ligurians, the Greeks and the Romans. Roman *amphorae*, believed to have come from a ship that sunk some 2 000 years ago, have been found in these waters. The French aviator and novelist **Antoine de Saint-Exupéry** spent many a summer in Agay. In 1932 he married a local girl whose brother, Pierre d'Agay, was a well-known figure in the area

The bay, at the foot of the red rock slopes of the **Rastel d'Agay,** is lined by a large, sunny beach, which extends eastwards as far as the small jetty, and beyond by a more popular shady beach (& *see ST-RAPHAËL*).

Anthéor ⌂

The resort of Anthéor is dominated by the three peaks of the Cap Roux range. Just before the Pointe de l'Observatoire, there is a **view** inland of the red rocks of St-Barthélemy and Cap Roux. The road to the summit of Cap Roux is described under ④ below (& *see ST-RAPHAËL*).

Le Trayas★

The resort is divided into two parts: one terraced on wooded slopes, the other by the seashore. The creeks and inlets which mark the coast include many small beaches, the largest of which lies at the end of Figueirette Bay. This bay was once a thriving center for fishing in the 17C, when nets were cast offshore and left floating for four months. To watch the nets, a tower was built on the shore (& *see ST-RAPHAËL*).

Antoine de St-Exupéry

Born in Lyon in 1900, Antoine de St-Exupéry attended the Jesuits College and completed his education in Fribourg, Switzerland. Interested in flying from an early age, he joined the French Army Air Force in 1921 but resigned five years later to become a civilian pilot. He soon turned to literature and began writing in 1928. His second novel *Vol de Nuit* was awarded a prize by the French Academy in 1931. However, the book for which he will always be fondly remembered is *Le Petit Prince* (1943), a charming fable for children. In the Second World War, he served as an instructor and would carry out reconnaissance flights over the South of France. On 31 July 1944, he set out for the Alps on one of these assignments and never returned. A few days later, he was officially reported missing. His body was never recovered from the ocean waters, but the remains of his Lockheed Lightning P-38 were discovered off the coast of Marseille in 2004.

The Kingdom of Auguste I

Off Dramont beach is a small island of red porphyry, l'Île d'Or, marked by a strange tower which appears to grow out of the rock. This rock, less than 1ha/2.5 acres in area, has an unusual history which has contributed to the many myths associated with the Riviera. When it was put up for auction by the Domaines in 1897, a Parisian doctor bid for it. Doctor Auguste Lutaud transformed the island into the realm of the operetta and built a four-storey tower in medieval style out of the red stone of the Esterel. Thus the building merged both with its foundations and with the backdrop of the Esterel.

The eccentric proprietor proclaimed himself King Auguste I of the Île d'Or. He became the darling of fashionable society on the coast and organised lavish receptions. Many celebrities of the Belle Époque attended these parties, namely General Galliéni and Jean Aicard, a member of the French Academy. The monarch died in 1925 and is buried in his kingdom. Since then the island, which has remained private property, has changed hands several times.

The cartoonist Hergé, who created Tintin, used the island as a backdrop to his album L'Île Noire.

Miramar

This elegant resort, with its private harbor, lies in Figueirette Bay.

La Galère

The resort is built on wooded terraces on the slopes of the Esterel where it forms the western limit of La Napoule Bay. Below the road, the seaside development of **Port-la-Galère** (private port), an astonishing design by the architect Jacques Couelle, seems to merge into its rocky environment. The fronts of the houses are strangely hollowed to give the effect of a honeycomb.

Théoule-sur-Mer⌂

This resort, which is sheltered by the Théoule promontory, has three small beaches. The crenellated building on the shore, now a château, used to be a soap factory in the 18C.

Excursions

1 CORNICHE DE L'ESTEREL★★★

40km/25mi – about 5hr – see local map

St-Raphaël★ See ST-RAPHAËL.

▶ *From St-Raphaël take N 98, R on the map.*

The road skirts the marina. On the seafront stands a memorial to the campaigns of the French Army in Africa.

▶ *After driving through Boulouris, proceed along N 98.*

Plage du Dramont See ST-RAPHAËL.

A stele erected to the right of the road commemorates the landing of the US Army, 36th Division, on 15 August 1944. The beach is bordered by Dramont Forest which covers the headland.

Running alongside the lovely Camp-Long beach, the road leads to the resorts of Agay and Anthéor, situated on either side of the Rade d'Agay. Shortly before reaching the Pointe de l'Observatoire, enjoy the **view** to the left, encompassing the red rocks of St-Barthélemy and Cap Roux.

Pointe de l'Observatoire★

The ruins of a blockhouse command a stunning **view**★ of blood-red porphyry rocks standing out against the cobalt blue of the sea. From this point can be seen the Anthéor, Cap Roux and Esquillon Points and La Napoule Bay further north along the coast.

▶ *Drive through Le Trayas. On a bend near the Hôtel Tour de L'Esquillon, pull off the road into the car park. A path (sign) leads up to Pointe de l'Esquillon.*

Pointe de l'Esquillon★★

15min there and back on foot.

A beautiful **panorama**★★ (viewing table) of the Esterel heights, the coast, Cap Roux, the Îles de Lérins and Cap d'Antibes.

B. Kaufmann/ MICHELIN

After La Galère, the road skirts Pointe de l'Aiguille, opening up a **view**★ of La Napoule Bay, Cannes, the Îles de Lérins and Cap d'Antibes. On reaching La Napoule (♥ *see La NAPOULE)*, N 98 crosses the River Siagne and then follows the curve of the bay up to Cannes (♥ *see CANNES).*

② VIA AURELIA★
46km/29mi – about 6hr – ♥ see local map

Cannes♔♔♔ *– ♥ see CANNES.*

▷ *From Cannes take the N 7, T on the town map.*

For most of the way this route runs through Esterel Forest. After passing through the industrial zone of La Bocca, the road crosses the alluvial plain of the River Siagne.

▷ *Turn left onto the road leading to Cannes-Mandelieu airport, then right.*

Ermitage de St-Cassien
The 14C chapel set on a low rise in an oak plantation with a few cypress trees standing guard makes a charming picture. Tradition says it was once the site of a Roman temple; it is now a place of pilgrimage.

▷ *Return to N 7.*

Mandelieu-la-Napoule ♥ *see MANDELIEU-LA-NAPOULE.*
N 7 runs along the valley hollowed out between the Esterel and Tanneron Massifs.

Auberge des Adrets
This inn was the favourite haunt of the highwayman **Gaspard de Besse** whose exploits in the 18C have remained legendary (♥ *see box).* At the crossroads, Carrefour du Logis-de-Paris, the road skirts the foot of Mont Vinaigre, the highest peak in the Esterel (618m/2 027ft).

▷ *At the Carrefour du Testannier, turn left onto a road marked "Forêt Domaniale de l'Esterel". At the Le Malpey forester's lodge, follow signs to Mont Vinaigre.*

Mont Vinaigre★★
🚶 *30min round-trip on foot.*

A path leads to the top which offers a splendid **panorama**★★★ on all sides: on the coast Cap d'Antibes, Pointe de la Croisette, Cannes and La Napoule Bay, Pic de l'Ours with its tower and TV mast, Pic du Cap Roux and Fréjus Bay, inland the Massif des Maures and the Argens Valley, and the limestone hills of Provence. On a clear day you can see as far as the Alps and Ste-Baume.

▷ *Return to the N 7.*

At the bend, there is a **view** on the right towards Fayence; then the road follows the the Moure Valley. The original Via Aurelia, however, followed the line of the forest road on the opposite bank.

Fréjus★ 👁 *see FRÉJUS.*

▷ *Return to St-Raphaël by Boulevard S.-Decuers.*

St-Raphaël★ 👁 *see ST-RAPHAËL.*

③ PIC DE L'OURS★★

57km/35.5mi along steep, narrow roads that are not always surfaced – allow one day.

▷ *From St-Raphaël take N 98 heading southeast. Leaving Agay, take the Valescure road and bear right towards Pic de l'Ours. After Gratadis forester's lodge (Maison Forestière du Gratadis), bear right and, having crossed the River Agay, leave the Plateau d'Anthéor on the right and bear left towards Pic de l'Ours (Moutrefrey crossroads).*

The road climbs to the summit past evergreen oaks, barren land and red rocks, with the Mal Infernet ravine in the distance. Winding round the north side of St-Pilon and Cap Roux, the road reaches Col de l'Évêque and then Col des Lentisques *(one-way traffic between the two passes: take the road to the east of the peak on the outward journey, and the interior road on the way back),* with frequent **glimpses** of the sea to the right.

Pic d'Aurelle★★

🚶 *1hr round-trip on foot by a marked path starting from Col des Lentisques.*

The Aurelle is one of the major peaks in the coastal chain of the Esterel. From the top (323m/1 060ft) a fine **panorama**★★ takes in the area running from Cap d'Antibes to the Pointe de l'Observatoire.

The stretch between Col des Lentisques and Col Notre-Dame is one of the most beautiful drives in the Esterel. Immediately overlooking the coast, the road offers breathtaking **bird's-eye views**★ of the Corniche de l'Esterel cliff road and splendid perspectives of the shore facing Cap d'Antibes. From Col Notre-Dame (323m/1 060ft), a remarkable panorama extends over Cannes, the Îles de Lérins and La Napoule Bay.

Pic de l'Ours★★★

🚶 *1.5hr on foot round-trip. Car park at Col Notre-Dame.*

The series of hairpin bends by which the road *(private vehicles prohibited)* reaches the summit affords constantly changing views of the wooded ranges of the Esterel and the deeply indented coastline. The remarkable **panorama**★★★ from the summit (496m/1 627ft) where there is a television transmitting station, includes the coast – from the Maures to the Alps – the Esterel range, dominated by Mont Vinaigre and the Var countryside.

▷ *From Col Notre-Dame, drive to Col des Trois Termes.*

From Col Notre-Dame, the road *(surfaced for 5km/3mi)* clings to the peaks of the Petites Grues and the Grosses Grues before reaching Col de la Cadière where the **view**★ opens to the north towards La Napoule and the Massif du Tanneron. At Col des Trois Termes, take the track on the right (almost hairpin back on yourself) to join N 7.

▷ *Return to St-Raphaël on N 7 or by returning along the route described above.*

④ ROUTE DU PERTHUS★ *20km/12mi – 3 hr – see local map.*

▷ *Leave St-Raphaël by N 98 south, as far as the Gratadis Masion Forestière, then turn left towards the Belle-Barbe Pass. Parking at the pass. Beyond the parking area, no private cars are allowed.*

Ravin du Mal Infernet★

🚶 *2hr on foot round-trip.*

Follow the footpath which leads into the wooded ravine of Mal Infernet, a majestic setting overlooked by many jagged rocks. The path goes as far as the Lac de l'Écureuil. This lake contains a fine variety of fish: roach, tench, carp, perch and trout.

It is possible to continue on foot as far as Col Notre-Dame by skirting Pic de l'Ours and Dent de l'Ours to the north.

▷ *Return to Col de Belle-Barbe. Take the road heading northwest towards the Roussivau forester's lodge (Maison Forestière de Roussivau). Leave the car in the Col du Mistral car park and take the left-hand path.*

Ravin du Perthus ★

🚶 *1hr 30min on foot.*

The road skirts the Perthus summits to the south. At Pont du Perthus a marked footpath leads off into the pretty Perthus ravine. It offers a nice setting for some easy hikes before heading off towards the foothills of Mont Vinaigre. To the right stands **Pic du Perthus** (266m/887ft), with its scarlet porphyry rocks towering above the southern limit of Esterel Forest.

▶ *Return to the car park at Col du Mistral by the same path and head by car towards Valescure and St-Raphaël by the Col de Belle-Barbe on the D 100 and D 37.*

Hiking Tours

The following excursions offer wonderful opportunities to stretch your legs after a long ride in the car. You will be delighted to discover the magnificent views of the landscape.

5 Sémaphore du Dramont★★

🚶 *1hr round-trip on foot; the path is paved and signposted. Immediately after the Dramont camp site, turn right. 100m/110yd farther, leave the car and take a left-hand path leading up to the signal station.*

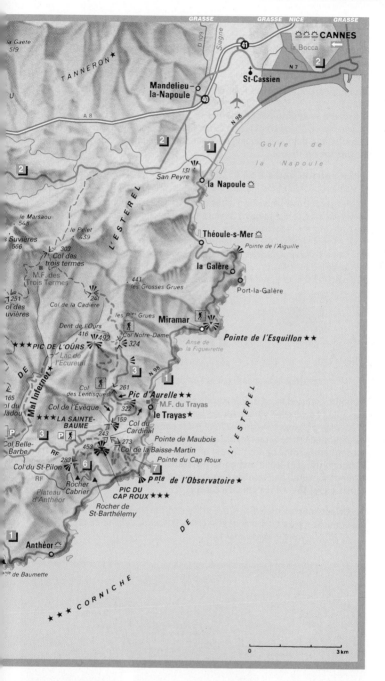

From below the signal station there is a **panorama**★★: to the southwest of the Maures, the two porphyry rocks guarding the entrance to the Gulf of Fréjus (the Sea Lion – *Lion de Mer* – and the Land Lion – *Lion de Terre*), and Île d'Or with its tower. On the horizon to the north lies Mont Vinaigre; behind the Rastel d'Agay peak in the foreground, can be seen the rocks of the Cap Roux range and lower down, on the right, the Agay anchorage. Walk back down along the signposted path leading to the little port; the attractive glimpses of clear water inlets will be a strong temptation for nature lovers.

6 Pic du Cap-Roux ★★★

🚶 *2hr on foot round-trip from the Ste-Baume parking area. You can reach the parking area from St-Raphaël by taking tour* 3 *by N 98 and the forest road.*

The footpath leads to the Cap-Roux pass. From the summit (452m/1 483ft), there is a superb **sweeping panorama**★★★ *(viewing table)*. If you continue on to the Col de l'Evêque, you can see as far as the Lérins Islands, before continuing on to the Sainte-Baume spring, where the waters are sure to refresh you!

7 La Sainte-Baume★★★

🚶 *5.5hr on foot round-trip from the Ste-Baume parking area.*

This longer and steeper version of the previous walk leads to the Col du Saint-Pilon (view over the Cap du Dramont). As you progress through meadows of wild rosemary, the view from the high road unfolds: to the right, Cabrier Rock, below, St Barthélemy's Rock. The path follows the coastline, partly on a paved road, and then on to a sloping trail that will get your muscles working. You come to a railway tunnel and then reach the Col de la Baisse-Martin, and then the Col du Cardinal. Then comes the reward: it's all downhill from here, and at the bottom is the heavenly spring.

> ## Hiking Map
>
> The ONF (National Office of Forestry) has a trail guide and hiking map available for sale at local Tourism Offices. 🏢 *www.onf.fr.*

ÈZE★★

POPULATION 2 509

MICHELIN MAP 341 F5 - LOCAL MAP SEE CORNICHES DE LA RIVIERA

A quaint, isolated hamlet dominating the Riviera coastline, Èze is the perfect example of a perched village (🕯 *see Introduction*). Like an eagle's nest, it clings to its rocky outcrop, towering 427m/1 410ft above the sea. Legend claims that it was founded by the Saracens, but in fact it was a Celto-Ligurian settlement that subsequently came under the rule of the Phœnicians, Romans and Saracens. Although the château is long gone, the stunning site★★ attracts visitors from around the world, and tourism now surpasses the cultivation of tangerines and carnations as the village's main industry.

▶ **Orient Yourself:** Between Nice and Monaco, Èze is accessible by RN 7 - Moyenne Corniche (🕯 *see Corniches de la RIVIERA*). 🏢 *Place du Général-de-Gaulle, ☎ 04 93 41 26 00, www.eze-riviera.com*

D. Pazery / MICHELIN

Exotic garden, Èze

P **Parking:** There are two parking areas (next to the Tourism Office) where you'll need to leave your car before climbing up to the village. The one at Place Fighiera is free, but often full. Parking is also available at the two perfume houses, for clients only though (& see *Address Book*).

ÈZE		Église Pl. de l'	6
		Paix R. de la	7
Brec R. du	2	Pise R. de la	8
Centenaire Pl. du	3	Planet Pl. du	9
Château R. du	4		
Colette Pl. de la	5	Chapelle des	
		Pénitents Blancs	B

Sights

A 14C double gateway with crenellations and a sentry walk leads into the steep, narrow streets of the **medieval village**★, in some places stepped and other places running beneath the tastefully restored houses converted into smart boutiques and artists' studios. At every corner there are flowers, shrubs, fountains and breathtaking views of the sea and mountains.

Church

🕐 *Summer 9am-7pm (winter 9.30am-6pm). Part of the Tourism Office's guided tour of the village.* ☎ *04 93 41 26 00.*

The church was rebuilt in the 18C with a Classical façade and a two-storey tower. The Baroque interior contains a fine statue of the Assumption (18C) attributed to Muerto and an emblazoned 15C font.

Chapelle des Pénitents-Blancs

🕐 *Summer 9am-7pm (winter 9.30am-6pm). Part of the Tourism Office's guided tour of the village.* ☎ *04 93 41 26 00.*

The simple 14C chapel is decorated with enameled panels illustrating the life and death of Christ and his mother.

To the left on entering is a Crucifixion, an early example of the Nice School; on the high altar an unusual Catalan crucifix, dating from 1258, in which Christ is pictured smiling; on the right a 16C hexagonal ciborium in mahogany; on the left a 14C statue, the Madonna of the Forest, so called because the child she is holding has a pine cone in his hand. A 16C wooden crucifix hangs on a pilaster in the gallery.

Jardin Exotique

🕐 *Apr-Sep 9am-7.30pm (Thur-Sat until 9pm Jun-Aug) Oct-Mar 9am-6pm.* ⊚ *3€ (children under 11 years free).* ☎ *04 93 41 26 00. www.eze-riviera.com.*

Tales of a Highwayman

After attacking and plundering the coaches and horsemen passing within their reach, Gaspard and his band would take refuge in a cave on the side of Mont Vinaigre. The brigand chief had a soft spot for sartorial elegance: he sported a splendid red costume studded with precious stones and fine silver buttons and buckles. For many years the mounted constabulary were at his heels. He was eventually arrested in an inn near Toulon and was broken on the wheel in 1781 at the age of 25. His head was nailed to a tree on the road which had been the scene of his many escapades.

Address Book

GUIDED TOURS

The Tourism Office conducts 90-minute walking tours of the medieval village and Jardin Exotique. ⬤ 6€. ☎ 04 93 41 26 00. www.eze-riviera.com.

WHERE TO EAT

For coin ranges, see the Legend at the back of the guide.

⬤⬤ **Bistrot Loumiri** – *Avenue du Jardin-Exotique* – ☎ 04 93 41 16 42 – ⏰ *Closed Feb school holiday, Wed evening and Mon – Reservation required.* At the bottom of Èze Village, this bistro-type restaurant is known for its simple but tasty Provençal food and its low prices. Try the chef's special, chalked up on a slate. Aimed at passing trade, and tourists who have come to admire the majestic setting.

⬤⬤ **L'Oliveto** – *Place du Général-de-Gaulle* – ☎ 04 92 41 50 40 . Housed in a building on the main square, this upstairs restaurant provides two venues: a large traditional dining hall and a smaller area whose light, fresh atmosphere recalls a winter garden. In either case, the menu is a vibrant homage to nearby Italy.

⬤⬤⬤ **Troubadour** – *4 Rue du Brec, Èze village (pedestrian access only)* – ☎ 04 93 41 19 03 – ⏰ *Closed 25 Jun-5 Jul, 19 Nov-20 Dec, 25 Feb-7 Mar, Mon lunch, and Sun – Reservation required.* A rustic, family-run restaurant in the village with an intimate dining room and classic French cuisine with a regional touch.

WHERE TO STAY

⬤⬤ **Hôtel Hermitage du Col d'Eze** – *2.5km/1.5mi by D 46 and Grande Corniche* – ☎ 04 93 41 00 68 – www.eze-riviera.com/hermitage – P – ⏰ *Closed 1 Dec-1 Feb* – 14 *rooms* – ⬤. Peace and quiet are guaranteed in this hotel with its splendid terraces and overflow pool. One side of the building faces the sea while the other affords nice views of the mountains. Try to book one of the more recent rooms; they are smaller but more attractive.

⬤⬤ **Auberge des Deux Corniches** – *Route du Col Èze – 1km/0.6mi on D 46* – ☎ 04 93 41 19 54 – ⏰ *Closed 10 Nov-1 Feb* – 7 *rooms* – ⬤. Modest inn on the road leading up to Èze, fronted by a large terrace and shaded by a cluster of trees. The renovated rooms are unsophisticated but carefully kept and some afford pretty views of the sea and the rocky outcrop serving as a backdrop to the village.

⬤⬤⬤ **Château de la Chèvre d'Or** – *Rue Barri, Èze Village (pedestrian access only)* – ⬤ P – ☎ 04 92 10 66 66 – ⏰ *Closed Nov- Feb –32 rooms* – ⬤. Restaurant (⬤⬤⬤⬤). A stunning hotel perched on the cliffs of the village, with its own hanging gardens and swimming pool. The interior, built into the rock of the village, is decorated with a mix of Provençal and medieval-style furnishings and antiques.

FRAGRANCES

Parfumerie Fragonard – ⬤ ⏰ *Guided tours (30min) Feb-Oct 8.30am-6.30pm; Nov-Jan 8.30am-noon, 2-6pm.* – ⬤ *Free entry* – ☎ 04 93 36 44 65 – www .fragonard. com. This annexe of the Grasse perfumery displays the various stages in the manufacturing process of essential oils, perfumes and soaps.

Parfumerie Galimard – *Place du Général-de-Gaulle* – ☎ 04 93 41 10 70 - www. galimard.com - ⏰ *Open daily 9am-6.30pm.* – ⬤ *Free entry.* Founded in 1747, this perfume house gives free tours of its manufacturing and small museum. Products are on sale in the boutique.

Many varieties of succulents and cacti flourish in the gardens crowned by the remains of a 14C château dismantled on the orders of Louis XIV in 1706. The terrace commands a splendid **panorama**★★★ of the Riviera and on a clear day one can even make out Corsica in the far distance!

Excursions

Astrorama

Take D 46 until you reach Col d'Èze (see map). ⏰ *Last admission 1hr before closing time. Fri, Sat 6-10pm; Jul-Aug open daily (except Sun) 6-11pm.* ⏰ *Closed 1 Jan and 25 Dec. 6€ (9€ including lecture).* ☎ 04 93 85 85 58. www.astrorama.net.

This observatory will allow you to gaze at shooting stars through a telescope on a fine summer's evening.

Sentier Frédéric-Nietzsche★

🚶 *About 2hr on foot round-trip.*

Nietzsche thought out the third part of his masterpiece *Thus Spoke Zarathustra* on the picturesque mule path which winds down towards the Corniche Inférieure. It leads through pine woods and olive groves to the seaside resort of Èze-Bord-de-Mer.

FAYENCE

POPULATION 4 253

MICHELIN MAP 340 P4

Fayence enjoys a privileged setting half-way between the mountains and the sea, surrounded by charming villages and only 10km/6mi from the Lac de St-Cassien. Potters, stone and wood carvers, weavers, painters and coppersmiths ply their trade in the narrow, picturesque streets, and a lively market is held on Place de l'Église Tuesdays, Thursdays and Saturdays.

▶ **Orient Yourself:** Fayence lies on the edge of the Provençal tableland in the Var, opposite its twin village, Tourrettes (see Driving Tours), on the road from Draguignan to Grasse. *Place Léon-Roux – 83440 – ☎ 04 94 76 20 08*.

Walking Tour

Old Town

Below the church, steep streets lined by handsome doorways of houses and a 17C gateway lead to the town gates. The Porte Sarrasine is still crowned by machicolations.

Church

This church was built in the mid-18C, replacing the smaller, older church unable to accommodate a growing congregation. The interior is very Classical with tall pillars supporting a gallery round the nave. The high altar, Baroque in style, is the work of the Provençal marble mason Dominique Fossatti (1757). In the nave's south aisle, a 16C gilded altarpiece represents scenes of the Passion and the Glorification of Christ; Christ in Agony is in the center with a giant St Christopher carrying the Infant Jesus below. From the terrace, to the right of the church, the **view** ★ extends beyond the hang-gliding field to the Maures and Esterel heights.

Panorama de l'Ancien Château

▶ *Follow the signs from the church.*

Address Book

LOCAL MARKETS

Marchés de Fayence – Place de l'Église, Tuesday, Thursday (fair) and Saturday.
Marché de Bargemon – Place St-Étienne: market on Thursday, flea-market first Sunday in May.
Marché de Callas – Large market Saturday mornings.
For coin ranges see the Legend at the back of the guide.

EATING OUT

◔◔◔ **Le Temp des Cerises** – *Place République – Fayence – ☎ 04 94 76 01 19 – ◷ Closed Tue, lunch on weekdays, 2-23 Nov, 18 Jan-8 Feb.* A typical Fayence restaurant serving regional specialities in an ochre and red dining room or the shady terrace.

WHERE TO STAY

◔◔ **La Sousto** – *Place du Paty– on the hill of the village; at the height of the hotel sign, take the stairs on the right and follow the signs – ☎ 04 94 76 02 16 – ◷ Closed one week in June – ⬚ – 6 rooms.* Not far from the Porte Sarrasinen in front of a fountain, this tiny, family-run hotel in a traditional country home is accessible by several different staircases. Rooms are basic, but equipped with a kitchenette (no breakfast service). The view from the terrace of room no. 5 is extraordinary.

◔◔◱ **Moulin de la Camandoule** – *Fayence – 2km/1.2mi west of Fayence by D 19 Route de Seillans and a country lane – ☎ 04 94 76 00 84 – moulin.camandoule@ wanadoo.fr – P – 11 rooms – ⬚ – Restaurant (◔◔◱).* An old olive mill at the foot of the village has been converted into a quaint Provençal stopping-place decorated in warm, southern colours. The grounds are home to a pool, a Gallo-Roman aqueduct and a terrace.

◔◔◱◱ **Four Seasons Provence at Terre Blanche** – *Tourrettes – 7km/4.3mi west of Fayence by the D 56 towards Bagnols en Forêt – ☎ 04 94 39 90 00 – www.fourseasons.com/provence – P Kids – 115 suites – ⬚ – Restaurant (◔◔◱◱).* A magnificent, Provençal-style resort with suites arranged in little villas throughout the property (guests are shuttled around by golf cart). There are two 18-hole golf courses, tennis, fitness center, heated outdoor pool and spa situated on grounds planted with lavender, rosemary, and mimosas. Suites have a contemporary classic decor, with terra-cotta tiled floors, neutral earth tones and private patios.

From the top of the hill, where the ancient chateau used to be, the view is to the north to the Provençal tableland, the Pre-Alps of Castellane and Grasse.

Driving Tours

COL DU BEL-HOMME 64km/40mi – about 4hr

▶ *From Fayence take D 563 south.*

Almost immediately on the right, then the left, is the turn *(signpost)* to Notre-Dame-des-Cyprès, nestled in the vineyards.

Notre-Dame-des-Cyprès

⊶ *Not open to the public.*

In a setting of tall cypress trees, this Romanesque chapel (12C) looks out over Fayence and Tourrettes.

▶ *Return to D 563 which skirts Fayence airport and turn right onto D 562 which crosses several streams as it winds among the trees.*

To the north the villages of Fayence, Tourrettes and Montauroux are perched along the ridge.

▶ *At Les 4 Chemins turn right onto D 25, heading towards Callas.*

Callas

Grouped round the castle ruins against a hillside of olive, oak and pine trees, Callas is still a typical village of the Haut-Var with its 17C belfry, its porches and its dovecote.

Church

🕐 Open 10-11.30am, 2.30-4.30pm. Guided tours possible any day but Sun, on request at the Tourism Office, ☎ 04 94 39 06 77

The Romanesque church, heavily restored in the 19C, displays a 17C altarpiece above nine hooded penitents on their knees.

From the terrace the **view** south takes in the Maures and Esterel heights.

▶ *Continue along D 25 which goes over Col de Boussague and winds up a pleasant valley to Bargemon.*

Bargemon

An old stronghold at the foot of the Provençal Tableland, Bargemon still recalls its past in its old streets, broken ramparts, ruined castle and 12C fortified gateways (in particular the so-called Roman gate, Place de la Mairie). Large shaded squares and many fountains add to its charm while the presence of mimosa and orange trees indicate a mild climate. The markets on Place St-Étienne (🕭 *see Address Book*) are a wonderful showcase for the delicious local produce.

Church

The 15C church near the town gateway was incorporated into the town's fortifications. Its square bell-tower is 17C. It has a fine flamboyant **doorway**. Pierre Puget is the putative artist of the angel heads on the high altar. Note the striking 16C triptych portraying St Antoine between St Raphaël and St Honorat.

Chapelle Notre-Dame-de-Montaigu

The village is dominated by the spire of this chapel, which houses three fine altarpieces resting on wreathed columns. It has been a place of pilgrimage since the 17C when a miraculous statue of the Virgin was brought here from Belgium by a monk who was a native of the village (the statuette, carved in olive wood, is shown only on Easter Monday).

Musée-Galerie Honoré Camos

🕐 Open summer 3-6pm, weekends 10.30am-noon; winter 2.30-5.30pm, weekends 10.30am-noon. 🕭 Free entry. ☎ 04 94 76 72 88.

Situated in the Chapelle St-Etienne, this museum highlights the local history and traditional activities. The life of the painter Honoré Camos (1906-91) and some of his canvases are presented in the apse. The museum also hosts temporary exhibitions.

> **ROWING**
> **Aviron St-Cassien-Club Intercommunal du Pays de Fayence** – In the locality called Biançon, by D 37 – Montauroux – ☎ 04 94 39 88 64 or 04 93 42 20 91 – 🕐 Open 9am-noon (closed Aug). Introductory courses on rowing are organised on the lake.

▶ *From Bargemon take D 25 west.*

The road climbs steeply offering fine views of Bargemon and its surroundings. This was once the path used by shepherds to lead their sheep and goats up to the summer pastures.

Col du Bel-Homme★

A path on the left leads to the top (*Alt 951m/3 210ft*). From the viewing table a **panorama** ★ extends south to the coast, northeast to Grasse, north to the Canjuers Plateau and the mountains around Castellane.

▶ *Return to Bargemon and take D 19 towards Fayence.*

The road climbs above the town before turning eastwards through pine trees, evergreen holm oaks and broom. On the southern horizon rise the Maures and Esterel heights.

Seillans ★ 🕭 *See SEILLANS.*

Notre-Dame-de-l'Ormeau – 🕭 *See SEILLANS.*

▶ *Return to Fayence on D 19 with open views of the countryside.*

Lac de St-Cassien *Round tour of 29km/18mi – allow 2hr.*

▶ *From Fayence take the road to Tourrettes.*

Tourrettes

This quiet village is lined with pretty houses decorated with flower boxes. The castle (⚷ *not open to the public*), modeled on the St Petersburg Cadet School, was built around 1830 by Alexandre Fabre, a native of Tourrettes. Its curious silhouette can be spotted from afar.

▶ *Turn left onto D 19, D 562 and D 56 to reach Callian.*

Callian

Streets lined with old houses wind round the castle in a delightful setting. A fountain plays under the trees of the main square, from where **views** look southwest over the local flower fields to the Lac de St-Cassien beneath the Tanneron heights. The Esterel and Maures Massifs dominate the horizon to the south.

▶ *North of the village take D 37 towards Montauroux.*

The road offers pleasant views of Callian and Montauroux.

Montauroux

Many craftsmen have settled in the village. There are 17C and 18C houses in Rue de la Rouguière, and the **view** from the square takes in the Lac de St-Cassien, the Tanneron heights, with a glimpse of the Maures and the Esterel. The **Chapelle St-Barthélemy,** built in the 17C by the Pénitents Blancs, features a great many painted panels depicting the Apostles, musical instruments, etc. It was recently restored at the instigation of the famous French designer Christian Dior. The local church presents paintings from the 17C.

▶ *Continue on D 37 crossing D 562.*

Lac de St-Cassien

Nestled at the foot of the Tanneron (🕭 *see Massif du TANNERON*), the scenic lake is set in lush countryside. From the Pré-Claou bridge, there is a view of the whole lake which mainly supplies water for irrigation purposes. Its wooded slopes and waters teeming with fish attract hunters and anglers alike. Water sports are allowed on the lake (*no motor boats*) and there are areas set aside for swimming.

▶ *Return to Fayence by D 37; turn left onto D 562 and right onto D 19.*

BAGNOLS-EN-FORÊT

▶ *14km/9mi south by the D 563 and then the D4.*

Beyond the Pic de la Gardette, this charming hilltop village appears before your eyes as you round a bend. The main square is shaded by plane trees, and the steep streets, some of them covered, give this town a special feeling of authenticity. Abandoned by the inhabitants in the 14C, it was empty until 1447 when a group of Italian immigrants from Liguria resettled it. Once the town was busy with the manufacture of millstones for making oil (*see some of the original ones in the* **Musée Archéologique** *set up within the Tourism Office on Place de la Mairie,* ☎ *04 94 40 64 68*).

Today the town is better knows as a departure point for discovering the **forêt domaniale de Saint-Paul** ★, where there are many inviting paths under the cork-oak trees.

FRÉJUS★

POPULATION 83 840

MICHELIN MAP 340 P5

LOCAL MAPS SEE MASSIF DE L'ESTEREL AND MASSIF DES MAURES

Known primarily as a popular beach resort, Fréjus still carries the vestiges of its colourful past as an important Roman settlement and a prosperous medieval town. Today its historic port vestiges, Roman ruins and ancient cathedral contrast with a unique military base, Buddhist pagoda and African mosque, giving Fréjus a rare cosmopolitan air. The town itself is built on a rocky plateau beween the Maures and the Esterel, with its hills descending gently towards the sea.

▶ **Orient Yourself:** The train tracks divide the town into two, with two large avenues connecting the North (center of town) with the South (port and beaches). Between the two, municipal housing projects and the farmer's market lie alongside the ancient port. The Tourism Office is in the center of the old town, near the cathedral known as Groupe Episcopal.

🅿 **Parking:** The town center has several car parks. You need to pay to get into the ones on Place Agricola and Place Paul-Vernet. However, there are free spots at Porte d'Orée (access via Avenue Aristide-Briant), Clos de la Tour (Rue Gustave Bret) and Aubenas (Rue Aubenas).

🕭 **Don't Miss:** The Groupe Episcopal and its 5C baptistry, the ruins of the Roman arena, the Mosque and the contemporary Port-Fréjus.

🕓 **Organising Your Time:** Much of Fréjus can be visited in a day. Start with the old town's medieval ramparts and Roman ruins, then perhaps one of the nearby excursions by car before settling onto the beach for the afternoon.

📷 **Especially for Kids:** Keep the kids busy at Park Aquatica, the largest water parkon the Côte d'Azur, or on the carnival rides at Luna Park. The Parc Zoologique, fifteen minutes to the north of Fréjus, is open year-round.

A Bit of History

Birth and Heyday (1C BC)

Fréjus takes its name from **Forum Julii,** a village founded by Julius Caesar in 49 BC, a trading and staging post on the great coastal road which was to become known as the **Via Aurelia.**

Octavian, the future Emperor Augustus, turned the market town into an important naval base (39 BC), where he built and trained the fast, maneuverable light galleys which were later to win the battle of Actium (31 BC) against the heavy ships of Cleopatra and Antony.

In the town then called Colonia Octavanorum, Augustus established a large colony of his veterans (soldiers who had finished their military duties and to whom a sum of money and some land were given, along with the full rights of a Roman citizen). The city expanded (construction of the Platform, or military headquarters, and the Butte St-Antoine) until it numbered 40 000 inhabitants. It was exceedingly prosperous.

Fréjus 2 000 Years Ago ⬡ See map p 168.

Ramparts surrounded the town, pierced by four gateways corresponding to the two broad streets, quartering the town in the tradition of Roman settlements. Soldiers, sailors and citizens enjoyed the arenas, amphitheatre and baths free of charge.

An aqueduct 40km/25mi long brought fresh water from the Siagnole near Mons (⬡ see MONS) as far as the water tower from which it was piped to the fountains and public buildings.

Among the naval bases of the Roman world only Fréjus and Ostia, in Italy, offer sufficient remains to be reconstructed: from the eastern end of the Esplanade Paul-Vernet (Roman forum), one can look down on the plain where the port lay 2 000 years ago and, with the aid of the vestiges still standing, one can easily conjure up its shape, size and facilities.

The port, originally created by dredging and deepening a lagoon, was reconstructed during the reign of Augustus. It measured 22ha/54 acres, a considerable area for those times, and included over 2km/1mi of quays, of which traces still remain. It was linked with the sea by means of a canal, protected from the mistral by a wall, and approximately 30m/98ft wide and 500m/1 640ft long – the shore line has receded since Roman times. The entrance was guarded by two large symmetrical towers, of which one, bearing Augustus' Lantern, still rises high above the plain at the end of the south quay. An iron chain, which lay on the bottom all day, was stretched between the towers at night.

A strong outward current, obtained by a secondary canal from the Argens, prevented the harbour from silting up.

A large tower, boatyards, baths and buildings – the harbor-master's office, a health control office and laundry – completed the installations, together with the palaestra (sports ground) and hospital, of which traces are to be found at the Villeneuve farm, southwest of the town.

Decline

During the long years of Roman peace, the military aspect of the port declined and in the late 2C AD the fleet was moved away but the port remained a lively commercial center until the 4C. Under Constantine an archbishopric was established. The harbor and canal, however, were neglected and began to silt up. At the beginning of the 10C the town was destroyed by the Saracens. In 990 under Bishop Riculphe, the city rose again on a much smaller scale; the medieval town walls (⬡ see map below) followed the line of Rue Jean-Jaurès and Rue Grisolle. Henri II turned Fréjus into a large naval base, and it wasn't until the French Revolution that the whole port was sold as a national estate and filled in by its new owner.

Walking Tour

AN EARLY ROMAN SETTLEMENT★

▶The Roman ruins are scattered over a large area; allow 1.5-2hr. Park at Place Agricola.

Porte des Gaules

The old gateway through the Roman ramparts is half-moon shaped. Of the two towers that once flanked it, only one remains. The Roman city covered about 40ha/99 acres.

▶ Go down the Rue H. Vadon.

Address Book

PRACTICAL INFORMATION

Tourism Office – *325 Rue Jean-Jaurès –* ☎ *04 94 51 83 83. Annex: 1 Boulevard de la Libération –* ☎ *04 94 51 48 42 – www.ville-frejus.fr.*

Guided tours – Anxious to share its precious cultural and architectural heritage, the Fréjus Tourism Office and Ministry of Culture organise **4 itineraries** (*2hr,* ⌐ *5€*) covering the old city and the Roman ruins, as well as a **special tour** of a different site or monument each month (*1hr*). In partnership with the ONF (National Office of Forestry), the Tourism Office also organises **forest hikes** in the Esterel. Contact the Tourism Office for information (*www.ville-frejus.fr*).

Small tourist train – ☎ *04 93 41 31 09 –* 🕐 *Jun-Sep 10am-noon, 2-8pm.* In summer, this charming little train will take you on a tour of the city, starting out from the Esplanade des Arènes.

Buses – *Information and tickets on Place Paul-Vernet –* ☎ *04 94 53 78 46.* The 12 lines of Esterel Bus serve the town of Fréjus and the surrounding area (St-Tropez, Roquebrune, St-Aygulf, etc.). *For coin ranges see the Legend at the back of this guide.*

EATING OUT

⌐ **Les Micocouliers** – *34 Place Paul-Albert Février –* ☎ *04 94 52 16 52 –* 🕐 *Closed Nov, 23 Dec-3 Jan.* This restaurant set up on the square opposite the Groupe Espiscopal (cloisters, cathedral, baptistry) has a most appealing summer terrace (covered and heated in winter). Inside, the brightly colored tablecloths and rustic-style decoration blend in well with the owner's Provençal cooking.

⌐⌐ **La Brasserie du Port** – *Port de Fréjus, Boulevard de la Libération –* ☎ *04 94 53 81 32 –* 🕐 *Closed Nov-Easter, Tue evening, Wed.* This Parisian-style brasserie is situated on the promenade overlooking the port. The menu includes traditional French cuisine with the specials of the day on the chalk board. Friendly, professional service.

⌐⌐ **Les Potiers** – *135 Rue des Potiers –* ☎ *04 94 51 33 74 –* 🕐 *Closed 1-20 Dec., lunch Jul-Aug, Wed lunch and Tue from Sep-Jun – Reservations required.* In a tiny street near the Église St-François and the Place Agricola, this friendly, family-run restaurant serves French classics and seafood dishes with a Mediterranean touch. The deco is rustic and cosy, but there are only a few tables, so reserve early!

⌐⌐ **Le Poivrier** – *52 Place Paul-Albert Février –* ☎ *04 94 52 28 50 –* 🕐 *Closed Nov, Mon Sep to May, and Sun.* The tasty homemade cuisine is a mix of Mediterranean tradition and a pinch of exotica, served in a small, vaulted cellar

going back to Roman times. In summer, have your meals out on the terrace on Place Paul-Albert Février or on the patio shaded by reed screening.

WHERE TO STAY

⌐ **Sable et Soleil** – *158 Rue P. Arène –* ☎ *04 94 51 08 70 – sableetsoleil@free.fr –* 🕐 *Closed 15 Nov-15 Dec –* 🅿 ▭ *– 20 rooms –* ⌐. Ten minutes' walk from the beaches and the Port-Fréjus, this family-run hotel has comfortable, spacious rooms with large bay windows. Upstairs is a terrasse-solarium.

⌐⌐ **L'Oasis** – *Impasse Charcot –* ☎ *04 94 51 50 44 – info@hotel-oasis.net –* 🕐 *Closed 11 Nov-31 Jan –* 🅿 *– 27 rooms –* ⌐. This peaceful hotel on a quiet residential street near the port is perfect for sun-worshippers. The rooms are lovingly decorated and breakfast is served on the terrace during nice weather.

⌐⌐⌐ **Hôtel L'Aréna** – *145 Boulevard du Général-de-Gaulle –* ☎ *04 94 17 09 40 – www.arena-hotel.com –* 🕐 *Closed 15 Dec-15 Jan – 36 rooms –* 🅿 ⌐ *– Restaurant (⌐⌐).* A former staging post with a colorful front provides pleasant accommodation in carefully kept rooms arranged in the Provençal style. Relax sipping your cocktail on the terrace or reclining by the pool.

ON THE TOWN

La Playa – *Boulevard de la Libération –* ☎ *04 94 52 22 98 –* 🕐 *Jul-Aug: nightly from 11pm; Sep-Jun: Thu-Sat from 11pm.* This nightclub is one of the most fashionable in the area and its tremendous success is continued throughout the year.

SHOPPING

Fréjus Markets – Wednesdays and Saturdays in the old quarter, Sundays on the Boulevard d'Alger and Boulevard de la Libération.

St-Aygulf Markets – Tuesdays and Fridays on Place de la Poste in St-Aygulf.

Cave Coopérative La Fréjusienne – *168 Rue Henri-Vadon –* ☎ *04 94 51 01 81 – www.frejusienne.com –* 🕐 *Closed Sun and holidays.* Tasting sessions and sale of Côtes-de-Provence and Pays du Var wines, as well as the sale of regional food products (tapenade, olive oil, etc.).

Cave des Cariatides – *53 Rue Sieyès –* ☎ *04 94 53 99 67 –* 🕐 *Open Jul-Aug Tue-Sat 8am-7.30pm, Sun 8am-noon, Mon 2-7pm; Sep-Jun Tue-Sun 8am-12.30pm, 2-7pm –* 🕐 *Closed Oct and holidays.* This wine cellar gets its name from the stone caryatids on the 17C doorway of the building, home to the Abbey of Sieyes, who instigated a coup d'état in 1799 (the building is a listed historic monument).

Forum Julii – *Place de la Mairie –* ☎ *04 94 17 03 00 –* 🕐 *Jul-Aug: Tue-Sat 9am-noon* and 3-7pm, Mon 3-7pm; Sep-Jun: closed Sun and Mon. A boutique selling the region's famous clay figurines (santons) offers a broad choice covering local arts and crafts, religious history and Mediterranean life: the Three Wise Kings, the Holy family, shepherds and their flock, the fishmonger, baker, farmer, etc.

LEISURE ACTIVITIES

CIP Port Fréjus – Aire de Carénage – Port Fréjus Est – ☎ 04 94 52 34 99 – www.cip-frejus.com – ⏱ Jun-Sep: daily 9am-noon, 2-7pm; Oct-May: daily 9am-noon, 2-5pm. A deep-sea diving center for both beginners and experienced swimmers will take you round the celebrated shipwrecks dotted along the Var coastline.

Parc Aquatica – 🧒 RN 98 – Le Capou – ☎ 04 94 51 82 51 – www.parc-aquatica.com – ⏱ Early Jun to mid-Sep: daily 10am-6pm; Jul-Aug: daily 10am-7pm. – ⏱ Closed Oct-May – ⏳ 23€ (kids under 12, 18€). Water sports enthusiasts will love this theme park, with its amazing waterslides "Twin-Twister" and "White Hole", its swimming pool with waves (the biggest in Europe) and its dodgem games with large rubber rings. Visitors in search of peace and quiet can play miniature golf or have a meal at the restaurant.

Marina – Capitainerie/Harbour Authority – ☎ 04 94 82 63 00 – www.portfrejus.fr. The 220m/722ft pier can accommodate more than 750 boats.

Base Nature – Boulevard de la Mer – ☎ 04 94 51 91 10 – ⏱ Mon-Fri 8.30am-10;30pm, 1.30-15.15pm; Sat-Sun 3-7pm (until 5pm off-season) . This nature park welcomes hikers, cyclists (80ha/198 acres) as well as swimmer and sun-bathers over a 2km/1.2 stretch of beach. Additional activities include sand-yachting, flying kites, playing boules and roller-skating.

Luna Park – RN 98 – 🧒 🅿 – ☎ 04 94 51 00 31 – ⏳ Free Entry. Treat your children to some of the 40 attractions in this amusement park. Free parking.

Arènes★

♿ ⏱ Open Apr-Oct 10am-1pm, 2.30-6.30pm; Nov-Mar 10am-noon, 1.30-5.30pm, Sat 9.30am-12.30, 1.30-5.30pm. ⏱ Closed Tue, Sun, 1-15 Jan, 1 May, 1 and 11 Nov, 25 Dec. ⏳ 5€ (kids under 12 free). ☎ 04 94 53 58 75. www.ville-frejus.fr.

Built outside the city in the 2C, the amphitheatre is 114m/124yd long by 82m/93yd wide, smaller than the ones in Nîmes (143yd by 109yd) and Arles (149yd by 117yd), and could accommodate approximately 10 000 spectators. Half the amphitheatre lies against the flank of the hill crowned by ramparts.

Destined primarily for the pleasure of soldiers and veterans, it was clearly built with an eye to austerity and economy. In this respect it differs from the amphitheatres erected in Arles and Nîmes, intended for a far more sophisticated audience. Bull-fights and other spectacles are held here in summer.

On the esplanade stands Le Gisant, a sculpture commemorating the Malpasset disaster, which claimed more than 400 lives (⏳ see Excursions). Two columns discovered on a Roman wreck in the gulf of St-Tropez, erected at the junction of N 7 and D 37, can be seen to the southwest from the lawn surrounding the arena.

In summer a little train (**Petit Train du Soleil,** ⏳ see Address Book) provides a tour of the site starting from the Esplanade.

▷ Take Rue Joseph-Aubenas, then Avenue du Théâtre Romain. A detour via Rue Gustave-Bret will lead you to the medieval ramparts.

Theatre

⏱ Open Apr-Oct (except Sun) 10am-1pm, 2.30-6.30pm; Nov-Mar weekdays 10am-noon, 1.30-5.30pm, Sat 9.30am-12.30, 1.30-5.30pm. ⏱ Closed Sun, 1 Jan, 15 Jan, 1 May, 1 and 25 Dec. ⏳ Free entry. ☎ 04 94 53 58 75. www.ville-frejus.fr.

This theatre is far smaller than the amphitheatre; it consists of only the radial walls on which the arches supporting the tiers of seats once rested. It measures 84m/92yd by 60m/66yd.

Inside, the orchestra pit is clearly visible, together with the stage foundations and the slot into which the curtain was lowered.

▷ Return to the top of the street, taking a right and then a left to the Aqueduct.

Aqueduct

Avenue du Quinzième-Corps-d'Armée.

Only pillars and ruined arcades remain of the aqueduct that reached the city level with the ramparts. The water was then channeled beneath the northern parapet as far as the water tower (castellum) from which the distribution conduits started. Some interesting remains can be seen in Avenue du Quinzième-Corps-d'Armée.

Platform

Still known as the eastern citadel, this area shows traces of a Roman platform which served as the military headquarters (*praetorium*): offices, storerooms, lodgings and baths. To the south lay the naval dockyard.

▶ *Go down the Avenue du Quinzième-Corps-d'Armée to the Place Paul-Vernet, which overlooks the site of the old port. At the end of the square take a right on Rue Raynaude, then a left to Place Castelli. Across the square take the vaulted passage of the Rue du Portalet to reach the Porte d'Orée, down the Rue des Moulins.*

The Old Port

The Porte d'Orée consists of a fine archway, most likely the remains of a chamber formerly attached to the harbor baths. The **Butte St-Antoine** formed a western citadel serving as a counterpart to the platform. A few towers remain on the southern front, one of which may have been a lighthouse.

Nearby stood the military laundry where the soldiers' uniforms were cleaned by a process using fuller's earth and sulphur vapor.

▶ *Follow the signed path skirting the south face of the Butte St-Antoine.*

Augustus' Lantern

Beside the base of a tower the path turns right onto the southern quay; part of the defence wall still has survived.

At the far end of the quay a tower marked the entrance to the port and the beginning of the canal leading out to sea. Although the tower was a ruin by the Middle Ages a construction known as **Augustus' Lantern** was erected on it to act as a landmark for sailors entering the port. The wall marking the line of the sea canal stretches away to the southeast.

A WALK THROUGH THE OLD CITY *45min on foot*

▶ *Start from Place Formigé.*

Walk down the Rue du Beausset to see the ancient Episcopal Palace (now housing the Town Hall), with its original 14C façade in pink sandstone from the Esterel.

▶ *Return to the Place Formigé, and go north on the Rue de Fleury.*

At no 58, the Maison du Prévôt (also called Capitou) has an interesting façade and a doorway pierced into a fortified tower. This is now the entrance to the Groupe Episcopal (⬡ *see Sights*). At the end of the street (*no 92 right*) there is a handsome doorway in green serpentine from the Maures.

▶ *Turn left onto Rue Jean-Jaurès, which follows the outline of the medieval ramparts.*

The old 18C town hall (*no 112*) features an unusual façade embellished with a curved balcony and a loggia supported on columns.

▶ *Take a right on the Rue Sleyès.*

At no. 53 is a doorway framed by two 17C stone atlantes is all that remains of the former mansion of Abbé Sieyès.

▶ *Continue past Place Liberté to Rue Grisolle.*

This street also follows the line of the medieval enclosure, with a handsome round tower (*no 71*) and a medieval façade (*no 84 right*).

The picturesque **Passage du Portalet** (*at the end of the street*) connects a string of scenic little squares.

▶ *From Place Paul-Vernet return to Place Formigé.*

Sights

GROUPE ÉPISCOPAL★★ *1hr.*

Entrance at Place Formigé. At the bottom of the steps the Basptistry is to the left, the cathedral to the right and the cloisters straight ahead (⬡ closed to the public). ♿ 🕐 *Open Jun-Sep daily 9am-6.30pm; Oct-May open daily (except Mon) 9am-noon, 2-5pm.* 🕐 *Closed 1 Jan, 1 May, 1 and 11 Nov, 25 Dec.* 🎟 *4.60€ (free first Sun of the month Oct-May).* ☎ *04 94 51 26 30.*

Portal

Guided visits only.

Under an ogee arch are two **panels**★ carved in the 16C to illustrate scenes from the life of the Virgin, St Peter and St Paul, portraits and military motifs.

Baptistry★★
Guided visits only.

This baptistry, one of the oldest buildings in France, is thought to date back to the 5C. Separated from the cathedral by the porch, it has a square external appearance with sides about 11m/36ft long. The octagonal-shaped interior features alternate curved and rectangular niches separated by black granite columns. These are topped by capitals of marble taken from Fréjus'

ancient forum. Excavations have uncovered the original white marble pavement and the piscina. A wrought-iron grille, given by Cardinal de Fleury, tutor and minister to Louis XV, who was at one time Bishop of Fréjus, leads to the baptistry.

Cathedral★

The cathedral is dedicated to Our Lady (south aisle) and to St Stephen (north aisle), and is an early example of Gothic art in Provence. Some parts of the building may date back to an earlier basilica.

The porch supporting the 16C belfry was erected 200 years later. Over the apse rises the battlemented tower which once defended the Episcopal Palace. In the 12C the north aisle was heavily restored and covered by a semicircular vault while in the 13C the nave was roofed with pointed vaulting resting on massive square pillars.

The lovely **choir stalls** date from the 15C and the high altar of white marble from the 18C. There are also two 14C tombs; the **altarpiece of St Margaret** above the sacristy door is attributed to the Nice artist **Jacques Durandi**, and at the end of the aisle, near the tombs of the bishops of Camelin (17C), is a remarkable Renaissance crucifix in wood.

Cloisters and garden

The Baptism

The two doors on either side of the grille were used: by the lower door the candidates for baptism entered and, after being baptised by the bishop, left by the upper, triumphal door as new Christians. Clad in a white tunic, they then went to the cathedral, attended full Mass for the first time and received their first Communion. Baptism was often administered to adults. It is believed that the bishop originally washed the feet of candidates in an earthenware basin *(dolium)* found in the ground. Then immersion took place in the octagonal font set up in the centre of the baptistry. A curtain, fixed to columns, surrounded the font. Unction was then administered on the head with holy oil.

Cloisters★★

The 12C-13C cloisters were intended for the chapter canons and comprised two storeys; only one upper gallery remains. The ground level clerestory is formed by a series of twin columns of white marble with varied capitals. The groined vaults which once covered the galleries were replaced by a pinewood ceiling with exposed beams, decorated in the 15C with curious little **painted panels**★ of animals, chimerae, grotesques and characters from the Apocalypse. On the first floor the columns are finer and the arches round; on the ground floor the arches are pointed – such variations are often found in the architecture of Provence. In the garth there is a well. The west gallery is flanked by a once fortified building, where the monks lodged.

Archeological Museum

First floor of the Cloisters. 🕐 *Open Apr-Oct 10am-1pm, 2.30-6.30pm; Nov-Mar 10am-noon, Sat 9.30am-12.30pm, 1.30-5.30pm.* 🕐 *Closed Sun and holidays.* 🆓 *Free entry.* ☎ *04 94 52 15 78.*

This museum presents a fine collection of Gallo-Roman antiquities recovered from the Fréjus excavations. Particularly outstanding are a rare Roman mosaic with floral motifs and geometrical designs found undamaged, a two-headed Hermes in marble (uncovered in 1970), a head of Jupiter (1C BC) and several statues in marble and bronze.

On the Water

Port-Fréjus

In 1989, after 10 years' work, Fréjus paid tribute to its long-standing maritime traditions by opening a yachting pleasure port. The complex, whose architecture was inspired by the work of the Italian architect Palladio, recalls the town's Roman origins and offers a full range of services and accommodation. The different areas are joined by gangways which are the scene in summer of much colourful and lively activity. In the shelter of a breakwater (220m/240yd long) there are berths for more than 750 boats.

Fréjus-Plage⌂

The magnificent beach of fine sand that extends this new area runs several miles from the Port-Fréjus to the Pont du Pédégal. Further west, the Plage d'Aviation is another fine sand beach. Beside the sea (at Boulevard de la Libération) stands a memorial recalling the sacrifice of Senegalese infantrymen (L'Armée Noire).

Military History

In 1910 Fréjus resumed an active military role with the creation of the first air and sea base in France. At the beginning of the First World War this became a centre for colonial troops from Africa and Asia, who established a rest and recreation base in the town as a gentle acclimation to the European climate. The different cultures represented in the armies at that time have left a legacy of exotic buildings.

Mosquée de Missiri

▶ *Leave Fréjus by Avenue de Verdun, then proceed towards Fayence on D 4. After 3km/2mi turn left. The mosque is currently undergoing restoration.*

In a pine wood *(left)* stands a large ochre Sudanese mosque, built in the 1920s by Senegalese soldiers from the naval camp. It is a concrete replica of the celebrated Missiri de Djenné mosque in Mali and consists of a central courtyard with a first-floor gallery around which one can walk, despite the rather dilapidated appearance of the building. Two false termite mounds have been raised nearby to create an impression of Africa.

Missiri Mosque, Fréjus

▶ *Continue in the same direction. 1km/0.6mi after D 4 joins motorway A 8, past the bridge, on the right.*

Musée des Troupes de Marine

🕐 *Open mid-Jun to mid-Sep 10am-noon, 3-7pm; mid-Sep to mid-Nov 2-6pm; mid-Nov to mid-Jun 2-5pm.* 🕐 *Closed Tue, Sat, 24 Dec - 2 Jan.* 🌐 *Free entry.* ☎ *04 94 17 86 55.*

This museum is attractively housed in a modern building and contains fine collections of objects and documents arranged in chronological order to retrace the history of the Marine Corps which, since 1622, has played a decisive role both overseas and in world wars. The expeditions during the great colonial period from the Second Empire (1852-70) to 1914 (Africa, Indochina, Madagascar) are re-created using a collection of pieces of equipment, arms, pennants and local crafts, as well as many illustrations (watercolours, drawings, photographs). There are many personal belongings of General Galliéni, including his study in Indochina and the car which he used in Madagascar from 1900 to 1905. On the first floor a table in rare wood inlaid with mother-of-pearl features a map of Hanoi in 1906 as well as the famous "zinc palm" from Djibouti.

In the crypt are buried unknown marines from the Infantry Division who fell when fighting the Bavarians at Bazeilles (Ardennes) in 1870.

▶ *Take Avenue du Quinzième-Corps and then Avenue du Général-Callies towards Nice. Turn right after the roundabout. Leave car in the car park midway between the two monuments and continue on foot.*

Mémorial des Guerres en Indochine

🕐 *Open daily (except Tue) 10am-5.30pm.* 🕐 *Closed Tue, 1 Jan, 1 May, 25 Dec.* 🌐 *Free entry.* ☎ *04 94 44 42 90.*

At the foot of a hill this imposing circular necropolis symbolically faces the sea. Since 1987, the remains of 24 000 soldiers and civilians who died in active service in former Indochina have been repatriated and gathered here. The bodies of soldiers are housed in a vast colombarium while unidentified casualties lie in an ossuary in the crypt. In the historical room, in front of the necropolis, the events and battles in the history of Indochina are displayed. Illuminated maps and models are used to describe the geographical locations of these events.

Pagode Bouddhique Hông Hiên

Near the Memorial. 🕐 *Open 9am-noon, 2-6pm; Apr-Oct until 7pm.* 🌐 *1.50€.* ☎ *04 94 53 25 29.*

This Buddhist pagoda stands in the center of an Asian garden. The pagoda was built in 1917 by Vietnamese soldiers who had come to fight for France, then restored and extended during the 1970s. Traditional Vietnamese architecture was the inspiration for the building and the statues in the park are arranged in accordance with Buddhist tradition. The grounds surrounding the pagoda are planted with exotic flowers, including some superb lotus, and contain impressive representations of sacred animals and guardian spirits (dragons, white elephants...).

Excursions

Chapelle Notre-Dame-de-Jérusalem★

▶5km/3mi north of Fréjus by the RN 7. Park, then 5 minutes on foot. ◷ Open Apr-Oct 2.30-6.30pm, Sat 10am-1pm, 2.30-6.30pm; Nov-Mar 1.30-5.30pm, Sat 9.30am-12.30pm, 1.30-5.30pm. ◷ Closed Tue, Sun, 1-15 Jan, 1 May, 21 Dec. ☎ 04 94 53 27 06.

This tiny chapel, situated in the Tour de Mare district, was the last building to be designed by Jean Cocteau. He had finalised the layout and the interior decor as early as 1961 but the chapel remained unfinished until after the poet's death in 1963. It was completed in 1965, thanks to Édouard Dermit.

Parc Zoologique★

▶In Capitou, 5km/3mi north from Fréjus on Avenue de Verdun (N 7) west. Turn right onto D 4. After 3km/2mi bear right onto a narrow road which crosses the motorway. 🅺 &. ◷ Open Mar-Oct 10am-5pm (until 6pm Jun-Aug); Nov-Feb 10.30am-4.30pm. ⌾ 10€ (child 3-10 years, 6€). ☎ 04 94 40 70 65. www.zoo-frejus.com.

The Zoological Park covers about 20ha/49 acres in the foothills of the Esterel Massif. Visitors may walk or drive beneath the umbrella pines, cork-oaks and olive trees to observe a great variety of birds (pink flamingoes, vultures and parrots) and many wild animals (African elephants, zebras and lemurs). Animal training shows.

Étangs de Villepey

▶ 5km/3mi. From Fréjus take N 98 west towards St-Tropez. Compulsory parking on the premises (fee charged at the entrance).

Fed by both sea water and by freshwater streams, these wetlands are one of the only nature reserves between Marseille and Nice. A great variety of vegetation is visible: reed-beds in the centre, umbrella pine groves in the south and brackish stretches along N 98. In this protected environment more than 200 species of birds, mostly migrants, are thriving. Spring is the best time to see pink flamingoes, grey herons and egrets. Among the nesting birds are several pairs of bee-eaters.

St-Aygulf⌂

▶ Just beyond the Étangs de Villepey.

The resort of St-Aygulf is shaded by pines, cork and holm oaks; from the beach of fine sand, ringed with rocks, there is an attractive view of Fréjus Bay and Les Issambres. Beyond St-Aygulf extends a beautiful **panorama** of the plain of the Lower Argens which separates the Maures from the Esterel. The magnificent rocks of Roquebrune Mountain stand out from the Maures Massif while in the Esterel chain, behind the Dramont semaphore, one can make out the summit of Cap Roux.
To the left the road runs alongside the **Aquatica** water park (⌂ see Address Book), before leading into Fréjus.

Remains of Malpasset Dam

▶ From Fréjus follow signs to "Nice par l'autoroute A 8". At the last roundabout before the motorway sliproad, take D 37 signposted "Barrage de Malpasset" for 5km/3mi. Park the car under the motorway viaduct; 1hr on foot there and back.

🚶 The dam was an arch dam, built in 1954 with a capacity of 49 million m³/1 730 million cu ft. It was intended to relieve the scarce water supplies in the Var coastal region during the summer months. On the evening of 2 December 1959 the torrential rains of previous weeks reached the danger limit of the dam and caused the abutments of the arch to collapse. Within 20 minutes, a 55m/180ft high wave had surged through Fréjus, claiming 400 victims.
The footpath leading off from the barrier goes up the Reyran Valley through sparse *garrigue* vegetation and huge scattered blocks of concrete, which were torn off the dam. Follow it down to the bottom of the valley, to the foot of the dam. From here, the size of the breach in the dam's arch makes a striking impression. The turbine is still in the middle of it.
Another viewpoint can be found by going up a footpath which forks to the left of the first one; a little lookout point reveals the remains of the dam and the west side of the valley.

La GARDE-FREINET

POPULATION 1 619

MICHELIN MAP 340 N6

LOCAL MAP SEE MASSIF DES MAURES

In the heart of the Maures Massif, between the Argens Valley and St-Tropez Bay, lies the quiet village of La Garde-Freinet. A flourishing crafts center, the town is also known for its scenic cork-oak and chestnut forests, perfect for a day of hiking, biking or horseback riding.

▶ **Orient Yourself:** La Garde-Freinet is 10km/6.2mi north of Grimaud (⟲ see GRI-MAUD) on the D 558. The Tourism Office has marked out a promenade through the steep, winding streets of the village (1hr) with arrows and an accompanying map. The Tourism Office also sells hiking guides to the surrounding forests. ▣ 1 Place Neuve – ☎ 04 94 43 67 41 – www.lagardefreinet-tourisme.com.

A Bit of History

Owing to its strategic location La Garde-Freinet suffered over a century of occupation by the Saracens. In local tradition the name Saracen is applied collectively to the Moors, Arabs, Turks and Berbers who harassed the country from the 8C to the 18C. After being defeated by Charles Martel at Poitiers in 732 the Arabs drifted down into Provence. Although driven back several times, they managed to hold on to the region around La Garde-Freinet. On the height which dominates the present village they built a fortress from which they used to descend to pillage inland Provence. It was only in 973 that Count William, the Liberator, managed to expel them.

In contrast to the damage they caused, the Saracens taught the Provençal people about medicine, how to use the bark of the cork oak and how to extract resin from pine trees. They also introduced the flat house tile and the tambourine.

Excursions

Ruins of Fort Freinet 1km/0.6mi – plus 45min on foot round-trip.

▶ Take GR 9 on the south side of the village. Leave the car in the parking area leveled out at a bend in the road and follow the signs painted on a rock. This rough trail is not recommended for small children or anyone with restricted mobility.

🔼 There is a good view of the Le Luc Plain and the first Alpine foothills. A path leads first to a mission cross (Croix des Maures) and then climbs quite steeply to the fortress ruins of the feudal castle attributed to the Saracens. It blended in for many years with the rocky site. Excavation work carried out has resulted in the discovery and uncovering of the foundations of a 15C fortified village. From the summit, the **panorama**★ extends out to sea and a long way inland.

▶ Take the path running along the moat, leading back to the village. Or go back to the car park and follow the forest track for 5km/3mi until you reach the sign for Roches Blanches.

Panorama des Roches Blanches★

At this spot, known as White Rocks (for access, walk round the barrier), there is a view in all directions: (left) Garde-Freinet Forest and the valley of the River Argens (right) over the slopes of the north Maures and (east) the bay of St-Tropez.

GOURDON★

POPULATION 379

MICHELIN MAP 341 C5

Gourdon "the Saracen" was built on the remarkable **site**★★ of a rocky spur more than 500m/1 640ft above the River Loup. The village's old houses have been restored and converted into boutiques and artists' workshops.

▶ **Orient Yourself:** The secluded Alpes-Maritimes village is found 14km/8mi north-east of Grasse on D 2085, then D 3. Gourdon can also be reached by a scenic, winding route through the Gorges du Loup (& see Vallée du LOUP) leaving from Vence. ⧉ Mairie, Place de l'Église – ☎ 04 93 09 68 25 – www.gourdon-france.com.

🅿 Parking: All roads lead to a parking area just below the village. The village is accessible only on foot.

Visit

Panorama★★

There is a magnificent panorama from the small church square with a 50km/30mi radius covering the coast from the mouth of the Var to Cap Roux and from the Esterel Massif inland to Pic de Courmettes, beneath which the Loup, a lively mountain stream, emerges from the upper gorge and winds its way to the coast.

Château

The fortress of Gourdon, built in the 13C on the foundations of an old Saracen fortress and restored in the 17C, contains architectural features of the Saracens (vaulted rooms), of the Tuscans of the 14C and of the Renaissance (doorway at the far end on the main courtyard).

Musée Historique

Ground floor of the chateau. ⧖ *Open Jun-Sep 11am-1pm, 2-7pm; Oct-May (except Tue) 2-6pm.* ⊚ *4€.* ☎ *04 93 09 68 02.*

The entrance hall contains a fine collection of arms and armour. The imposing fireplace in the dining room is 14C and the furniture 17C.

In the drawing room the furniture is 16C; there is an Aubusson tapestry, a secretaire which belonged to Marie-Antoinette, a *Self-Portrait* by Rembrandt and a fine 1500 painting from the Cologne School: **St Ursula.** The chapel contains a 16C triptych, a *Descent from the Cross* from Rubens' studio, a *Golgotha* by the Flemish School and a polychrome wood sculpture of St Sebastian by El Greco.

The guard-room contains a collection of 16C and 17C oriental arms. In Henry IV's Tower, the documents on show bear the Royal Seal; an opening in the floor reveals the former dungeon.

Gardens and park of the château

B. Kaufmann/ MICHELIN

Address Book

For coin ranges see the Legend at the back of this guide.

EATING OUT

Au Vieux Four – *Rue Basse (in the village)* – ☎ 04 93 09 68 60 – 🕐 *Closed Sat and weekday nights off-season* – 📇 – *Reservation recommended*. This is the perfect stopping-place to round off your visit of the village. The young couple who run the place prepare delicious Provençal food and grilled meat in an open fireplace before your eyes. Simple, refreshing decoration and reasonable prices.

Taverne Provençale – *Place de l'Église* – ☎ 04 93 09 68 22 – 🕐 *Closed 3-28 Jan, 12 Nov-17 Dec and Wed except Jul-Sep.* Settle on the terrace and admire the superb views of the heights beyond Nice, as well as those of the Mediterranean. This Provençal bistro serves French cuisine according to tradition: trout, coq au vin, guinea fowl with mushrooms...

SHOPPING

Sainte-Catherine – *Rue des Écoles* - ☎ 04 93 09 68 89 – *www.sainte-catherine.com* – 🕐 *Open daily 10am-7pm (9.30am-8pm in summer)*. Gourmet food lovers will find their happiness in this delicious-smelling boutique stocked full of herbs and spices, original jams, jellied fruits and plenty of regional mustards, vinaigres, honey and olive oil.

La Source Parfumée – *Rue Principale* – ☎ 04 93 09 20 00 – *www.galimard.com* – 🕐 *Open daily 9.30am-7pm.* 🚹
The old perfume distillery and flower fields may be visited by appointment.

Musée des Arts Décoratifs et de la Modernité

First and second floors. 🕐 *Guided tours (1hr) Jul-Aug 11am-1pm, 2-7pm; Sep-Jun on request.* 🎟 10€. ☎ 04 93 09 68 02.

This collection brings together some of the best examples of decorative arts and furniture design from the 1920s to the 1930s, including important examples from the Union des Artistes Modernes (UAM). The rooms are arranged to look like vintage apartments: from the Art Nouveau room to the Art Deco room, you'll see pieces by Eileen Gray, Mallet-Stevens, etc.

Gardens

🕐 *Guided visits (1hr) Jul-Aug at 3pm; Apr-Jun and Sep on request.* 🎟 4€. ☎ 04 93 09 68 02.

The terraced gardens were designed by Le Nôtre in the 17C, and laid out on three levels. They are now part of a botanical garden centre, preserving typical flora of the Pre-Alps.

Local Specialities

From the surrounding forests of cork-oaks and chestnut trees comes the raw material for the manufacture of bottle corks and the production of sweet chestnuts sold under the name *Marrons de Luc*. In the autumn, **chestnut festivals** are organised to celebrate the harvest. Local markets are held on Wednesdays and Sundays.

GRASSE★

POPULATION 43 874

MICHELIN MAP 341 C6

The perfume capital of France is nestled at the foot of a high plateau overlooking the fragrant plains, where the flowers that have made the town's fortune are cultivated. The blue sea off the coast of Cannes can be seen from the modern town and its terraced houses, while below, the narrow alleys of the old Provençal town are linked by steep ramps and steps that wind between hidden gardens and perfumeries which attract visitors with their heavenly scents.

▶ **Orient Yourself:** Grasse is located 17km/10.5mi northwest of Cannes on the N 85, which leads past the industrial and residential zones right into the heart of the old town (*vieille ville*). Most of what is interesting is found here, between the Cours Honoré-Cresp, Boulevard du Jeu-de-Ballon and the Place du 24 Août. Park as soon as possible, since most of the interesting sights are accessible only on foot. There are several city buses and a newly opened rail line between Grasse and Nice (with a stop in Cannes). In summer there is a tourist train that circulates through the town's main attractions (⏷ see *Address Book*).

🅿 **Parking:** There are five parking garages in the center (*from 1.10€ to 1.40€/hr, open 24hr*), including Place du Cours Honoré Cresp, Place de la Foux and at the Hôtel de Ville. ☎ *04 92 60 91 17.*

🕿 **Don't Miss:** The Musée International de la Parfumerie brings to light the town's main industry, while the narrow streets of the old town offer many charming views and souvenir boutiques.

🕐 **Organising Your Time:** Plan on a half day for the old town, starting off with a visit to the perfume museum before taking a free tour of one of the perfume makers. Then explore the streets of the old town, an ideal place for lunch or a snack. If you have time and a car, try one of the excursions or hikes around the surrounding countryside for some excellent panoramic views.

Kids **Especially for Kids:** The Grottes de St-Cézaire are popular with kids of all ages.

A Bit of History

A Small Republic (12C)

In the Middle Ages, Grasse was a tiny republic, administered by a council whose members called themselves "Consuls by the Grace of God". This regime was based on the Italian model and had diplomatic relations with Pisa and Genoa. By way of Cannes, it exported soap, oil and tanned skins to these cities; in exchange it received raw hides and arms. Raymond Bérenger, Count of Provence, put an end to this independent existence in 1227.

An 18C Winter Resort

During the winter of 1807-08 the gay and impetuous Princess Pauline Bonaparte, separated from her husband, Prince Borghese, and on bad terms with her brother, the Emperor, came to Grasse to seek relief from family worries and regain her strength in

---

The Great Artists of Grasse

Two children of Grasse excelled in the arts and letters. **Bellaud de la Bellaudière** (1532-88), a soldier-poet, was born and died in Grasse although he lived mainly in Aix, Marseille and Avignon. His work, inspired by Rabelais and Petrarch, is both tender and vigorous and briefly revived the Provençal language in literature between the troubadours (12C) and Mistral (19C). **Jean-Honoré Fragonard** (1732-1806), although the son of a tanner and glove-maker, was possessed by the urge to draw and left for Paris as a young man. He painted with Chardin and then Boucher. Winner of the Prix de Rome by the age of 20, he achieved great renown but the Revolution deprived him of his fashionable clientele and dictated a more severe style of painting.

Address Book

PRACTICAL INFORMATION

Tourism Office – *Palais des Congrès, 22, Cours H.-Cresp* – ☎ *04 93 36 66 66 – www.grasse-riviera.com.*

Guided Tours – There are several themed guided tours of the town, its history, its perfumeries and artists in English from July through September. ☐ *Inquire at the Tourism Office or visit www.vpah.culture.fr.*

For coin ranges see the Legend at the back of this guide.

EATING OUT

🍽 **Le Gazan** – *3 Rue Gazan* – ⏱ *Closed 15 Dec-5 Jan, Mon-Thu evening off season, and Sun* – ☎ *04 93 36 22 88.* Two delightful dining rooms with rustic furniture, linked by a spiral staircase, provide the setting for a succulent meal seasoned with local olive oil and aromatic herbs. Warm, friendly welcome and good service in this restaurant in the old quarter of Grasse.

🍽 **Arnaud** – *10 Place Foux* – ☎ *04 93 36 44 88* – ▤ – ⏱ *Closed Jun, Sat lunch, and Sun.* Treat yourself to the speciality of the house – the homemade ravioli and gnocchi lovingly prepared by the owner's mother. Meals are served in a small vaulted cellar, or on the mini-terrace, which can be noisy.

WHERE TO STAY

🍽 **Hôtel Ste-Thérèse** – *39 Avenue Y.-E.-Baudoin* – ☎ *04 93 36 10 29* – *hotelstetherese@wanadoo.fr* – ⏱ *Closed Nov* – ℗ – *Restaurant for hotel patrons only* (🍽) – *31 rooms* – 🚪. A humble establishment overlooking the city of Grasse. Peace and quiet are guaranteed in the lightly decorated rooms, which have pretty views of the coastline. Provençal fabric adds a lively touch to the dining room.

🍽 **Hôtel Victoria** – *7 Avenue Riou-Blanquet* – ☎ *04 93 40 30 30* – ⏱ *Closed 3 Jan-6 Feb* – ℗ – *49 rooms* – 🚪 – *Restaurant* (🍽🍽). Handsome turn-of-the-century residence commanding outstanding views of both Grasse and the sea beyond. Large comfortable rooms, pleasant lounges, a panoramic terrace, a brightly coloured dining hall and outdoor pool all make for an extremely pleasant stay. Themed evenings and other events can be organised.

🍽 **Chambre d'Hôte Mas de Clairefontaine** – *3196 Route de Draguignan – Val du Tignet – 10km/6mi SE of Grasse on Route de Draguignan/RD 562* – ☎ *04 93 66 39 69 – andre.lapostat@wanadoo.fr* – 🍴 – *3 rooms*. A stone cottage surrounded by a terraced garden dotted with umbrella pines and reeds is the charming backdrop to your stay at Mas de Clairefontaine. The rooms are tastefully appointed and the service of excellent standard. The terrace, shaded by a

century-old oak tree, is the perfect place to relax after a tiring excursion. Or take a dip in the pool!

SHOPPING

Maison Venturini – *1 Rue Marcel-Journet - Old Town* – ☎ *04 93 36 20 47* – ⏱ *Open Tue-Sat 9am-1pm, 3-6.30pm.* – ⏱ *Closed one week in Feb and Oct.* Although the facade of this bakery seems uninteresting, once inside you'll find some of the most wonderful traditional sweets, nougat noir, fougassettes, soft breads made with orange blossom, lemon sablés.

Le Moulin de la Brague – *2 Rue de Châteauneuf - Opio* – ☎ *04 93 77 23 03 – moulinopio@wanadoo.fr* – ⏱ *Open Mon-Sat 9am-12.30pm, 2-6.30pm.* – ⏱ *Closed 15-30 Oct.* For six generations the Michel Family has preserved this rare working olive mill (part of which dates back to the 15C). The pretty boutique sells olive oil, tapenades and regional specialities like honey, jams, pottery, soaps and fabrics.

PARFUMERIES

Usine Fragonard – *20 Boulevard Fragonard* – ☎ *04 93 36 44 65 – www.fragonard.com.* ⏱ *Feb-Oct guided tours (30min) 9am-6.30pm; Nov-Jan 9am-noon, 2-6pm.* 🎫 *Free entry.* Perfume has been made here since 1782. Introductory course on "The Essence of Aromas" (*Absolus Aromatiques*) on request.

Fragonard-La Fabrique des Fleurs – *Carrefour des Quatre-Chemins – Route de Cannes* – ☎ *04 93 77 94 30.* ⏱ *Same times as above.* A modern perfume factory on the edge of Grasse, with tours and a pretty aromatic flower and herb garden.

Parfumerie Molinard – *60 Boulevard Victor-Hugo* – ☎ *04 93 36 01 62 – www.molinard.com.* ⏱ *Guided tours May-Sep 9am-6pm; Oct-Apr 9am-12.30pm, 2-6pm.* 🎫 *Free entry.* Traditional Provençal perfume house founded in 1849. Visitors are explained the successive stages in the making of a perfume. There are also courses on how to create perfumes *(fee)*.

Usine Galimard – *73 Route de Cannes (going towards Mouans-Sartoux)* – ☎ *04 93 09 20 00 – www.galimard.com* – ⏱ *Guided tours Apr-Oct 9am-6.30pm; Nov-Mar 9am-noon, 2-6pm.* 🎫 *Free entry.* Created in 1747, the free tours include the perfume museum, labs, workshops and boutique.

Galimard-Studio des Fragrances – *5 Route de Pégomas, Rond Point des 4 Chemins* – ☎ *04 93 09 20 00 - www.galimard.com – Course (2hr) on perfume-making.* ⏱ *Daily by appointment (sessions at 10am, 2pm, 4pm)* – ⏱ *Closed Sun* – 🎫 *34€.* Make your own fragrance with the help of a real "nose" from Grasse (they keep your "formula" on file in case you want to order more).

TRANSPORTS

Buses – *Bus station at the Notre-Dame-des-Fleurs car park – Place de la Buanderie -* ☎ *04 93 36 37 37.* The city is served by 16 lines which also go to Nice and Cannes.

Small tourist train – 🏻 *Apr-Sep 10am-6pm* – 🕐 *Closed Sun and Oct-Mar* – 🎟 *5€.* Guided tours with commentary *(45min)* from Cours Honoré-Cresp to the heights of Grasse and ending at Parc de la Princesse-Pauline.

SNCF Train – There is newly reopened train service between Grasse and Nice via Cannes. 🗐 *www.regionpaca.fr or www. grasse-riviera.com.*

IT'S A GAMBLE

Casino – *Boulevard du Jeu-de-Ballon –* ☎ *04 93 36 91 00.* Come here to indulge in a spot of gambling (roulette, blackjack). The café is open from 8.30pm to 2am. There are musical evenings at weekends. Package formulas available (casino, dinner and transport).

CALENDAR

Rallaye de Grasse – April.

Exposition Internationale de la Rose – Over 30 000 cut roses on display in bouquets in mid-May.

Fête du Jasmin – First weekend in August.

a warm climate. Every day she was carried in a sedan chair to a grove of holm oaks, which she particularly liked and which is now known as her garden: "Jardin de la Princesse Pauline". Later, Queen Victoria spent several winters in Grasse at the Grand Hotel and at the Rothschild property.

Napoleon's Passage (2 March 1815)

After the cool welcome he received in Cannes after his escape from Elba Island, the Emperor decided to take the Alpine road (Route des Alpes) via Grenoble and advance on Grasse, but perhaps because he feared of a hostile demonstration from the populace, the Emperor skirted the town on what is now known as Boulevard du Jeu-de-Ballon. The "Plateau Napoléon" carries his name although he is believed to have camped there for barely an hour.

A Kaleidoscope of Fragrances

The Perfume Industry

Grasse had long specialised in leather work and glove making when perfumed gloves came into fashion in the 16C. This was the beginning of the perfume industry. The great *parfumeries* were born in the 18C and 19C and still enjoy an international reputation.

There are three manufacturing processes: distillation, *enfleurage* and extraction. **Distillation** is the oldest process. Flowers and water are brought to boiling point in a still. The water and essence are condensed in a "florentine" flask where they separate owing to the difference in density and to their insolubility.

B. Kaufmann/ MICHELIN

Old town

In the 18C **enfleurage** was invented. It uses the property that animal fats have of absorbing the scent of flowers. Fresh flowers are repeatedly laid on different layers of animal fat; washing with alcohol separates the perfume from the fats; a pomade is obtained. Today, few firms use this labor-intensive process.

The latest process is **extraction** by which the flowers yield their perfume in its most concentrated form. The flowers are brought into contact with a solvent which is then evaporated. A concretion *(concrète)* is thus obtained, consisting of perfume and wax. One tonne of Grasse jasmine blossoms yields 3kg/6.6lb of concretion. The wax is removed using alcohol and the 40% which remains is called absolute *(absolue de concrète)*.

The essences produced in Grasse, which are the base material of the perfume industry, are used locally or sent to Paris where the great perfume houses blend them according to secret formulas to produce the fascinating creations for which France is famous throughout the world.

The Grasse perfume industry has now diversified and has started the production of food flavourings.

Musée International de la Parfumerie★

⚬┳ *Closed for renovations until September 2006.* ☎ *04 93 36 80 20. www.musees-degrasse.com.*

This museum is devoted to one of the most famous activities in Grasse. It occupies three buildings of different periods: a mansion with a neo-Classical façade from the time of Napoleon III and two late-19C buildings. The exhibits cover more than 3 000 years in the history of perfumemaking throughout the world.

The ground floor, set up like a perfume factory, presents the different techniques used to make perfume from the extraction of the sweet-smelling raw materials to the end product, with machines and explanatory panels. On the mezzanine is the research laboratory. Exhibited on the first floor are different kinds of perfume vessels (flasks, scent bottles…), boxes, chests and posters which indicate human involvement with perfume, and other fragrance-related products (toiletries, cosmetics…) through the ages; famous names are evoked: Guerlain, Patou, Lanvin, Chanel… Note the travel accessories belonging to Marie-Antoinette.

A greenhouse on the terrace contains many different local and tropical plants used in the manufacture of perfume.

Parfumeries

🅿 *Visitor parking.* 👣 *See the Address Book for addresses and admission times.*

There are several perfume manufacturers in Grasse (also known as *parfumeries* or *usines*) which give free guided tours of their perfume-making process, such as Fragonard, Molinard and Galimard. Try to visit on weekdays when the workers can be seen making eau de toilette, scented soaps and creams that are on sale in the boutiques.

Flower Fields

ℹ *Information at the Office of Tourism and at the Reception of each perfume manufacturer.*

In spring and summer, Fragonard and Molinard will take you on tours of their lovely flower fields. The Domaine de Manon allows access to its rose garden *(May-June)* and jasmine fields *(July-November)*.

Walking Tour

THE OLD TOWN★ *allow 1hr*

The houses of old Grasse are the colour of the sunset: red ochre, orange, yellow, pink… and sometimes grey. Many of the villagers have abandoned the historic centre for more modern housing in the valley, giving parts of the old town a run down feel.

▶ *Leave the car in the car park on Cours Honoré-Cresp and take Rue Jean-Ossola, continued by Rue Marcel-Journet. Turn right into Rue Gazan and walk on until you reach Place du Puy.*

Cathedral Notre-Dame-du-Puy

🕐 *Open weekdays 9.30-11.30am, 3-6pm.*

The cathedral dates back to the late 10C-11C but was restored and remodeled in the 17C; the double staircase at the entrance, with its wide stone handrail, and the two crypts were added on in the 18C. Note the panels of the main door (1721) in the façade, adorned with horizontal bands and arcading. The high narrow nave, with heavy pointed rib-vaulting, marks the beginning of the Gothic style in Provence. Together with the robust round pillars it gives a grandiose air to the whole building.

The organ (1855) is by Junk of Toulouse. In the south aisle there are three **paintings**★ by Rubens (*The Crown of Thorns*, *Crucifixion* and *St Helen in Exaltation of the Holy Cross*) executed in Rome in 1601 and offered to the town in the 19C by a generous patron. There is a fine **triptych** attributed to Louis Bréa depicting St Honoratus between St Clement and St Lambert and a rare religious painting by Fragonard, *The Washing of the Feet*.

▸ *Have a look at the Tour de Guet at the 12C Town Hall before going to the Place du 24-Août.*

Place du 24-Août

From the far side of the square you can admire the chevet and bell-tower of the cathedral. There is also a fine **view** eastwards over the Grasse countryside. Close at hand is the Clock Tower (Tour de l'Horloge).

▸ *Turn left onto the Rue de l'Évêché.*

Place de l'Évêché

At the center stands an elegant three-tiered **fountain**. The old houses bordering the square are built over uneven arcades. At the tiny Place de la Poissonnerie, follow the street of the same name to the Place aux Herbes, where the colourful Grasse market takes place.

▶ *Go along the Rue Courte, turn left on Rue Droite, and then right onto Rue Amiral-de-Grasse to the Place aux Aires.*

Place aux Aires

This square used to be used by local tanners. At no 33 is the **Hôtel Isnard**, a town house built in 1781, with a fine door and an attractive wrought-iron balcony.

▶ *Leave the square on your left and exit the old town via Boulevard du Jeu-de-Ballon, and down to the Place du Cours.*

Place du Cours★

This fine terraced promenade offers a charming view★ over the cultivated and wooded countryside, which rolls gently towards the sea. The huge fountain dates from the Revolution, and a monument to Fragonard stands in the small square where Promenade and Boulevard du Jeu-de-Ballon meet.

GARDENS OF GRASSE

Jardin de la Princesse Pauline

▶ *Access via Avenue Thiers, Boulevard Alice-de-Rothschild and Boulevard de la Reine-Jeanne. Stay to the left and look for the signs.*

This grove of oaks that Napoléon's sister adored during her winter stay here is now a large ornamental garden with **panoramic views**★ of Grasse, the Massif du Tanneron, the Esterel and the coast *(viewing table).*

Parc Communal de la Corniche *30min on foot there and back.*

▶ *Access as above; then turn a sharp left on Boulevard Bellevue and then right on Boulevard du Président-Kennedy.*

🚶 At the bend, a path to the right *(sign)* leads to the edge of the steep Pre-Alps of Grasse. From the lookout point, the **view**★★ extends from the Baou of St-Jeannet and from the Tanneron mountains to the peaks of the Esterel. On the horizon you can see the bays of La Napoule, Golfe-Juan, and the Îles de Lérins.

Sights

Musée d'Art et d'Histoire de Provence★

🕐 *Open Jun-Sep 10am-6.30pm; Oct-May open daily (except Tue) 10am-12.30pm, 2-5.30pm.* 🕐 *Closed in Nov and public holidays.* ⊗ *3€ (free the first Sun of the month in winter).* ☎ *04 93 36 01 61. www.museesdegrasse.com.*

This museum provides a remarkable compendium of the art and history of eastern Provence. It's set in an 18C mansion erected by Louise de Mirabeau, sister of the tribune Mirabeau, when she married the Marquis de Cabris. The mansion, called "Petit Trianon", was planned and decorated by the Marquise with a view to entertaining on a grand scale, but all she ever experienced there were days troubled by court actions and family scenes.

Ground floor

Pottery (18C-19C) from Apt and Le Castellet is displayed in the entrance hall. Some rooms are decorated in the style of Louis XIV and Louis XV. There are two rooms devoted to paintings: one to 19C Provençal artists (Chabaud, Camoin) and the other to reconstructed scenes of life in Grasse in the 18C and 19C.

Basement

On view are the reconstructed kitchens of the Cabris Mansion, fine pieces of Moustiers faience and ceramics from Biot and Vallauris. One room contains Provençal nativity scenes and *santons*, and cherubs which once adorned altarpieces. Another features the Gallo-Roman period: pediment from a 4C funerary monument, lamps, flasks, jars. The archeological section evokes the daily life of local people from Prehistoric times to the late Middle Ages. The display includes objects used during burial rites and in peasant life from day to day, unearthed in local excavations.

A "nose" at work

B. Kaufmann/ MICHELIN

Villa-Musée Fragonard

🕐 *Same times and charges as for the Musée d'Art et d'Histoire de Provence.*

Fragonard took refuge during the Revolution in this elegant country house when it belonged to Maubert, a local glove-maker and perfumer. It now belongs to the municipality and serves as a cultural center and museum devoted to a whole family of artists.

One of the ground-floor rooms contains copies (originals in the Frick Collection in New York City) of the panels painted by Fragonard between 1771 and 1772 and originally commissioned by the Duchesse du Barry. The stairwell is decorated with Republican and Masonic allegories executed in *trompe-l'œil* and monochrome by the artist's son, **Alexandre-Évariste Fragonard** (1780-1850) at the age of 14.

Upstairs the **Fragonard Room**★ displays a broad spectrum of his works: original drawings and etchings, sketches, paintings – two self-portraits, *Landscape with Washerwomen*, *The White Bull* and *The Three Graces*. Another gallery is devoted to a grandson, **Théophile Fragonard** (1806-76): *Embarkation for Cythera* and *Visiting the Sick*. There are also canvases by Marguerite Gérard (1761-1837), Fragonard's pupil and sister-in-law *(Portrait of a Girl)*.

Musée de la Marine

🕐 *Open Jun-Sep 10am-7pm; Oct-May open daily (except Sun) 10am-5pm.* 🕐 *Closed in Nov and public holidays.* 🎫 *3€.* ☏ *04 93 40 11 11.*

Housed in five vaulted rooms in the Hôtel Pontevès-Morel, the Marine Museum retraces the distinguished career of **Admiral de Grasse**, who was born at Bar-sur-Loup (👆 *see BAR-SUR-LOUP*), and his involvement in the American War of Independence. Among the 29 models are 18C sailing ships, a Maltese galley, the flagship *La Ville de Paris* (Washington and Lafayette came on board on 17 September 1781) and the cruiser *De Grasse*, decommissioned in 1974.

Musée Provençal du Costume et du Bijou

🕐 *Open Feb-Oct 10am-6pm; Nov-Jan 10am-noon, 2-6pm.* 🎫 *Free entry.* ☏ *04 93 36 44 65. www.fragonard.com.*

These private collections housed in an annexe of the Fragonard perfumery focus on women's clothing during the 18C. Peasants' robes, weavers' skirts and middle-class finery are on show alongside a series of crosses and curious ornaments made out of sea fossils *(étoiles de Digne)*. A fine, interesting presentation in which all the exhibits are genuine, except for the aprons. A shop selling charming accessories rounds off the tour.

Driving Tours

Préalpes de Grasse★★ *Round-trip of 104km/65mi – about 5hr*

▶ *From Grasse take Boulevard Georges-Clémenceau and turn left onto D 11.*

After crossing the Plateau Napoléon, the road rises towards Cabris offering fine **views** of the Grasse countryside.

Cabris★ 👆 *see CABRIS.*

▶ *Towards St-Cézaire, a small twisting route (on the right) passes close to the "9 Puits de la Vierge" nine wells of Roman origin.*

Grottes de St-Cézaire★

Kids 🕐 *Guided visits (40min), Jul-Aug 10.30am-6.30pm, Jun and Sep 10.30-noon, 2.30-6pm, Feb-May and Oct 2.30-5pm, Nov and Jan and Sun 2.30-5pm.* 🕐 *Closed Dec.* 🎫 *5€.* ☏ *04 93 60 22 35. www.lesgrottesdesaintcezaire.fr.*

Discovered by accident in 1888, the caves are hollowed out of the limestone and remain at a constant temperature of 14°C/57°F. Both the stalactites, which have great musical resonance, and the stalagmites are remarkable for the variety of their shapes – toadstools, flowers, animals – and their reddish colour, which is ascribed to the presence of iron oxide in the rock.

The caves, which comprise several chambers with evocative names such as "Hall of Draperies", "Organ Chamber", "Fairies' Alcove" and "Great Hall", are connected by narrow passages, one of which arrives suddenly at the edge of an abyss, 40m/130ft below ground level.

St-Cézaire-sur-Siagne

From its site dominating the steep Siagne Valley, the walls and towers of this inter-esting village testify to its feudal past. Standing in its own churchyard is a pleasant

Romanesque chapel which shelters the Gallo-Roman tomb of Julia Sempronia. From the church a marked path leads to a **viewpoint** *(viewing table)*.

▶ *Leaving St-Cézaire, take a left onto the D 105, direction Mons. Be careful of the narrow road.*

Gorges de la Siagne

The road runs up through the rich vegetation in the deep gorge which the waters of the Siagne have worn in the limestone.

After crossing the Siagne (from the bridge, **view** up and down the gorge), turn right onto D 656, a very steep and narrow road.

After meandering steeply above the gorge, the road broadens out into a colourful rock circus before entering a wooded valley which brings it to the plateau. Turn left onto D 56 following the hillside. Fig and olive trees grow on terraces retained by low drystone walls.

▶ *At the crossroads, drive to Mons or turn left onto D 56. Cross the Siagnole.*

Sources de la Siagnole – *30min on foot there and back.*

On the right beyond the bridge a path leads to a very pleasant spot where several Vauclusian springs rise to form the River Siagnole.

Roche Taillée

There is a sign to indicate the remains of a Roman aqueduct (on the left of the road) which carried water from around the Mons area to Fréjus on the coast and is still in use. There is a lovely **view**★ eastwards towards Grasse.

▶ *Turn right onto D 37 and then right again onto D 563 to reach Mons.*

The road is cut into the hillside high above the Siagnole Gorges. Once over the Col d'Avaye, the road offers a magnificent **view**★★ reaching as far as the Esterel.

Mons★ 🕭 *see MONS.*

The mountainous and wooded environs of Mons give way to a barren landscape with outcrops of white rock. Follow the D 563 towards Castellane to Col de Valferrière (alt 1 169m/3 835ft), then turn right onto N 85, the Route Napoléon.

PLATEAU DE GRASSE★★ *round-trip of 38km/24mi, allow 2hrs*

▶ *From Grasse take D 2085 going northeast.*

The northeastern suburb of Grasse comprises attractive villas scattered among olive, cypress and orange trees.

Magagnosc

▶ *900m/984yd after the town signpost and immediately past the restaurant "La Petite Auberge" turn right at the sign "Église St-Laurent".*

There are two churches here decorated with frescoes by the contemporary painter Robert Savary: the Tuscan-style **St-Laurent,** and **St-Michel**, the Romanesque chapel of the White Penitents. From the churchyard there is a **view** ★ of the sea near Cannes and the Esterel Massif.

▶ *Return to D 2085 and at Pré-du-Lac take the first road, D 203, to Châteauneuf-de-Grasse.*

Châteauneuf-de-Grasse

This elegant village perched on a promontory exudes a whiff of Provençal atmosphere with its lovely old houses grouped together on the overhang. The narrow stepped streets and the vaulted passageways are dominated by the wrought-iron campanile of the church. The interior features a lovely 18C altarpiece.

▶ *From the town head east towards Opio – a good view of the plain. At the crossroads turn left onto D 3 and continue as far as Pré-du-Lac, turning right onto D 2210. The picturesque site★ of Bar-sur-Loup (🕭 see BAR-SUR-LOUP) comes into view. Return to Grasse via Opio, where you'll find the Moulin de la Brague (🕭 see the Address Book), then onto the D 7.*

GRIMAUD ★

POPULATION 3 780

MICHELIN MAP 340 O6

Isolated from the summer crowds of the coast, the perched village of Grimaud has retained its Provençal character with its small shaded squares, fountains and winding alleyways enlivened by the many artisans. At the other end of the spectrum is the modern Port-Grimaud, built in the 1960s, a lively and bustling summer destination. Choose according to your whims!

▶ **Orient Yourself:** The old town is 10km/6mi west of St-Tropez on the N 98A, then D 61. 🄸 *Boulevard des Aliziers* ☎ *04 94 55 43 83. www. grimaud-provence.com*

🄿 **Parking:** In high season it's best to leave your car near the cemetery *(Parking du Château)* on the north side of the town, near the Pont des Fées and the ancient aqueduct.

The Ancient Grimaldi Feifdom

This large perched village owes its name to the **Gibelin de Grimaldi**, who received it as a gift in the 10C from the Count of Provence in recognition of his help in expelling the Saracens from Provence.

Walking Tour

OLD TOWN ★ *1hr*

▶ *Tour marked by arrows. Ask for the map with commentary at the Tourism Office.*

The Eglise St-Michel is a small Roman (11C) church in the form of a Latin cross, with restored 19C frescoes decorating the interior (the timed light switch is to the left of the entrance).

Château

The castle, built at the beginning of the 11C, originally consisted of three enclosures surrounded by four three-storey towers. The imposing ruins of this great building were left after the demolition ordered by Mazarin in 1655.

From the upper covered way there are fine **views** ★ of the Maures and the Golfe de St-Tropez. The castle hosts live performances on summer evenings.

On the hill in the graveyard beyond there is a charming windmill, and from there a fine **view** ★ of the gulf.

Go down to the **Chapelle des Pénitents** *(to the east)*, which houses the relics of St. Theodore, then join the Route Départementale *(county road)* where you'll find the **Musée d'Art et Traditions Populaires** *(🕐 Open Easter-Sep 2.30-6pm, Oct-Easter 2-5.30pm. 🕐 Closed Tue, Sun. ⊜ Free entry. ☎ 04 94 55 43 83)*, which retraces the history of the village in an ancient olive mill.

Port-Grimaud

Address Book

GUIDED TOURS

Coches d'Eau de Port-Grimaud – *12 Place du Marché* – ☎ *04 94 56 21 13* – ⏱ *Tours mid-Jun to mid-Sep 9am-10pm; mid-Sep to mid-Jun 10am-noon, 2-6pm (call to confirm)* – ⏱ *Closed mid-Nov to mid-Dec.* Boat tours on the canal of Port-Grimaud (20min). It's also possible to rent electric boats.

Petit Train Touristique – ☺ *Apr-Oct.* – ☎ *04 94 54 09 09*. This tourist train circles between Grimaud (Place Neuve) and Port-Grimaud (at the entry to Port-Grimaud Nord, near the tour bus parking lot).
For coin ranges see the Legend at the back of this guide.

EATING OUT

☺ **Lou Faitou** – *Camping la Pinède D 14* – ☎ *04 94 56 50 27* – ⏱ *Closed 15 days in early Nov, 15-31 Dec and evenings off season.* Lying at the entrance to La Pinède camp site, this restaurant decorated in the Provençal spirit offers regional fare at affordable prices. Settle on the cool terrace and sip a pastis before tasting the local dishes.

☺☺ **Jardin des Cabris** – *1km/0.6mi S – intersection of D 552 and D 14* – ☎ *04 94 43 26 48* – ⏱ *Closed Nov to Jan, Tue evening and Wed*. You will instantly feel at home in this friendly inn with its pretty flowered terrace beneath the trees, where generous helpings of tasty Mediterranean cuisine will be served to you in a simple yet attractive setting.

☺☺ **La Bretonnière** – *Place des Pénitents* – ☎ *04 94 43 25 26* – ⏱ *Closed 15 Nov-15 Mar, Sun evening and Mon*. This restaurant in the Medieval district is run by two Belgian chefs who use fresh Mediterranean products in classic dishes. Try the salmon paté with apple chutney, lamb with parsley and wild mushrooms, or steamed bass in a virgin olive oil dressing.

WHERE TO STAY

☺☺ **La Bastide de l'Avelan** – *Quartier Robert - 2 km from Grimaud-village by the D 94* - ☎ *04 94 43 25 79 - bastide.avelan@ wanadoo.fr* - 🍴 *- 4 rooms*. Simple but charming rooms in this typical Provençal house. All rooms face the ground floor garden, and under the plane trees and pines is a welcoming pool in summer. The friendly owner offers good advice on sightseeing in the region.

☺☺ **Chambre d'Hôte La Toscane** – *Route départemental, Villa la Toscane - 4km from Grimaud Village* - ☎ *04 94 43 24 11 - latoscane@free.fr* - 🍴 *- 4 rooms*. This villa with ochre-orange walls has a Tuscan feel. The rooms are cheerfully decorated with Provençal furnishings, hand-sewn linens and tiled floors. The garden terrace and pergola are surrounded by lush vegetation, and teak chaise lounges are the perfect place to relax after a swim in the pool.

SHOPPING

Markets – Thursdays on Place Vieille in Grimaud. Thursdays and Sundays in Port-Grimaud.

Themed Fairs in Grimaud – Foire de la Chandeleur (Candlemas Fair) in February. Foire de la Laine (Wool Fair) on Ascension Thursday.

CALENDAR

Fête du Moulin – June.

Les Grimaldines – Festival of World Music, every Tuesday night from mid-July to mid-August.

Fêtes de la St-Michel – September.

▶ *Pass by the Tourism Office and go up the street to the Place Neuve.*

A fountain here commemorates the installation of running water in Grimaud in 1886. On the Rue des Templiers (which leads back to the church), stop to admire the arcades and serpentine doorway on the Maison des Templiers.

Excursion

Port-Grimaud★

▶ *Follow the signs for Port-Grimaud (Nord) – and not Port-Grimaud (Sud) – 5km/3mi to the visitors' car park. Only residents are allowed to drive into town.*

Port-Grimaud, which was designed by the architect **François Spoerry**, has a unique charm but remains as controversial as Marina Baie des Anges (⏱ *see VILLENEUVE-LOUBET*). It looks like a Mediterranean fishing village on the north shore of St-Tropez Bay. in fact it is a modern complex of luxury housing with a fully equipped marina and a fine beach, and provides facilities for a wide range of leisure activities.

It's pleasant to stroll through this lively village, past the colored houses with their *trompe-l'œil* façades, covered with Roman tiles, linked by canals, narrow alleys, tiny shaded squares and neat little bridges. Public transport is available in passenger barges *(coches d'eau)* which ply the lagoon.

Église St-François-d'Assise

This is an ecumenical church dedicated to St Francis of Assisi; it was conceived as part of the overall plan and is resolutely modern although inspired by the Provençal Romanesque style. The interior is plain; no ceiling conceals the wooden roof beams. The stained glass is by Vasarély. The tower affords a pretty **view**★ of Port-Grimaud, St-Tropez Bay and the Maures Massif.

Chapelle Notre-Dame-de-la-Queste

▸ *3km/1.8mi towards Port-Grimaud.*

This chapel, built by the monks of the abbey of St-Victor in Marseille, houses a remarkable Baroque altarpiece (1677) in gilded wood illustrated with scenes from the life of the Virgin. There is a pilgrimage here on 15 August.

HYÈRES★

POPULATION 51 417

MICHELIN MAP 340 L7

LOCAL MAP SEE MASSIF DES MAURES

The palm trees and mild climate are a good indication of what has attracted winter visitors to Hyères (aka Hyères-les-Palmiers) for more than a century. And its magnificent villas and Belle Epoch palace hotels reveal the faded glory of the town once populated by wealthy aristocrats. Lying in a pleasantly sheltered site, Hyères is the southernmost Riviera resort. Today its old village, pleasure port and lush gardens continue to draw visitors looking for a sunny escape to paradise.

▸ **Orient Yourself:** The greater Hyères area is divided into two by the Voie Rapide (Olbia, or N 98), with the old quarters clinging to the slope of the Castéou hillside (204m/670ft) to the north, and the airport, beaches and the harbour enclosed by Cap Bénat and the Giens peninsula to the south. The new harbour is used by pleasure boats and the ferries commuting between the mainland and the Îles d'Hyères. (☞ *see Address Book*).

▣ **Parking:** No charge for parking in the harbor or on Place Louis-Versin. Underground car parks *(fee)* can be found outside the Casino, in the Olbia shopping mall and in the Denis gardens on Place du Maréchel-Joffre.

◉ **Don't Miss:** The best panoramic views can be found from the hilltop sites of ruined castles: Château des Pontevès on Giens peninsula and Château des Aires in the Old Town. Take a tour of the Belle Epoch villas and hotel palaces in summer through the Tourism Office. Over 20km/13mi of beaches and the sunny ports offer the chance to practise almost any water sport.

◉ **Organising Your Time:** An entire day should be reserved for Hyères. Start with walking the scenic streets of the old town *(vieille ville)*, shopping on the Rue Massillon and tours of the palm-lined streets and villas of the 19C town center.

A Touch of Exoticism

Hyères is famous for palm trees. The cultivation of palms began to expand in 1867 and reached its peak in the 1930s. There are no less than 10 varieties named Hyères palms. The renown of these trees has brought about their export as far as Saudi Arabia. In Hyères itself, strollers can enjoy the exotic charm of the palms in Avenue Godillot, one of the most attractive roads in France, and in three public gardens: the Casino gardens, Roy gardens and Denis gardens. In the fine Olbius-Risquier gardens there is a complete range of existing species.

Address Book

PRACTICAL INFORMATION

Tourism Office –*3 Avenue Ambroise - Thomas* – ☎ *04 94 01 84 50 – www.ot-hyeres.fr.*

Guided Tours – The Tourism Office organises many different themed tours of the town, as well as nature hikes and excursions.

For coin ranges see the Legend at the back of this guide.

EATING OUT

☺ **L'Abri-Côtier** – *Place Daviddi, Plage de l'Ayguade* – ☎ *04 94 66 42 58.* Located in a beach cabana on the Port de l'Ayguade and decorated in cheerful, bright colours, this restaurant offers up tasty Mediterranean dishes such as marinated sardines, roasted camembert with pesto and octopus stew. Sporty types can impress diners at the sand volleyball court.

☺☺ **Le P'tit Clos** – *27 Avenue Riondet -* ☎ *04 94 35 75 29* – ⏰ *Closed Wed, Mon lunch and Sun evening, and 15 Jul-15 Aug.* This tiny restaurant (with just seven tables) is located near the top of the old town. Chef Frédéric Chiron serves fresh market-inspired dishes such as asparagus with truffles and tomato-basil chutney, changing the entire menu every three months.

☺☺ **Les Santonniers** – *18 Rue Jean-Jaurès – Carqueiranne (town center)* – ☎ *04 94 58 62 33* – ⏰ *Closed Mon off-season.* Set up in a local building in the town centre, this homey restaurant decorated in Provençal tradition has two undeniable assets: a lovely terrace sheltered from the beating sun by a plane tree and a menu offering extremely attractive prices. Two reasons to give in to temptation.

☺☺ **La Colombe** – *663 Route de Toulon – 2.5km/1.5mi west of Hyères in La Bayorre* – ☎ *04 94 35 35 16* – ⏰ *Closed Sun evening Sep-Jun and Mon* – ☺ *22.11/29.73€.* Carefully prepared local cuisine is served in a traditional Provençal house. The spacious sun-drenched terrace and friendly service make it a popular establishment.

TRANSPORT

Buses – *Bus station on Place Joffre* – ☎ *0825 000 650.* Hyères and the Giens Peninsula are served by several bus lines, particularly going to the beaches (Almanarre, Ayguade), and links with boat trips headed for the Îles d'Or (☎ *04 94 57 44 07).*

SHOPPING

Shopping streets – Rue Massillon, walking up towards the old quarter. The Briand pedestrian district. Avenue du Général-de-Gaulle and Avenue des Îles-d'Or.

GOURMET

Claude Ré – *10 Rue de Limans (Old Hyères)* - ☎ *04 94 65 28 41* – ⏰ *Tues-Sun morning 8.15am-1pm, 3-7.15pm.* More than 15 types of cookies to go, made with butter and topped with toasted Provençal almonds, raisins or hazelnuts. They also sell artisanal sorbets and ice cream in flavours like dried fig, lavender, melon and nougat.

Dominique – *3 Avenue des Îles d'Or* – ☎ *04 94 65 18 56* – ⏰ *Open Tues-Sun morning 9am-12.30pm, 3-7.30pm.* This chocolate boutique is one of the oldest shops in Hyères, passed down from family to family while retaining the traditional methods of hand-making candies and chocolates. Specialities include macarons in different flavours, and the Princesse des Îles d'Or (orange chocolate covered in iced sugar).

Pastor – *86 Avenue Gambetta* - ☎ *04 94 01 46 46* - ⏰ *Open Tue-Sat 6.45am-1pm, 3-7.30pm.* One of the most popular bakery-pastry boutiques in Hyères, with olive or bacon fougasses, lavendar bread in summer, Christmas pastries with anisette, and sorbet sold by the half-litre in amazing flavors: try the hot wine of Provence!

Wine – Ask at the Tourism Office for the guide to the Hyères Wine Road, which covers 43 local vineyards and cellars.

MARKETS

Provençal – Tuesdays mornings on Place de la République and Saturday mornings in the center of town and along Avenue Gambetta.

Organic – Tuesday, Thursday and Saturday mornings Place Vicomtesse de Noailles.

Antiques – Every first Sunday of the month Place Clémenceau and République.

SPORTS AND LEISURE

Hyères is considered on of France's "stations nautiques", meaning there are endless opportunities for water sports of all kinds. Ask at the Tourism Office for more information.

Diving – There are many excellent underwater delights to explore with one of the many diving clubs in the area: in Hyères, La Londe; in the Porquerolles, Porquerolles Plongée; at Port-Cros, Sun Plongée; and in Levant, Levant-Plongée.

Var Voltige – *Aérodrome de Cuers-Pierrefeu – Cuers* – ☎ *06 61 30 78 97* – ⏰ *Open daily with reservations.* This club organises parachuting "baptisms" for beginners for 46€ per person. In the same air field it's possible to find flying and helicopter clubs as well.

Casino – *Casino des Palmiers – Avenue Ambroise-Thomas* – ☎ *04 94 12 80 80.* Slot machines, roulette, blackjack... Restaurant and nightclub.

Hippodrome – *Route de Giens*– ☎ *04 94 58 14 45.* There are 20 racing days per year in spring and fall, with trotting and flat-racing. Panoramic restaurant and snacks.

Karting – *Speedkart Hyères – 1714 Avenue de l'Aéroport* – ☎ 04 94 38 76 99.

Hyères-Port Saint-Pierre – ☎ 04 94 12 54 40 (Hyères), 04 94 58 02 30 (La Capte, 125 moorings), 04 94 66 33 98 (l'Ayguade, 500 moorings) – *www.ville-hyeres.fr.* Four basins able to accommodate 1 350 moorings, 120 of which are for temporary stays.

WHERE TO STAY

◎◎ **Hôtel Port Hélène** – *D 559 – At L'Almanarre* – ☎ 04 94 57 72 01 – *www. hotel-port-helene.fr* – 12 rooms – 🍴. A friendly atmosphere awaits you at this cute hotel fronted by a pink façade, lost among umbrella pines and palm trees. The rooms are extremely well kept and have balconies offering views of the sea. Good service and very reasonable prices for the area.

◎◎ **Chambre d'Hôte L'Aumônerie** – *620 Avenue de Fontbrun – Carqueiranne* – ☎ 04 94 58 53 56 – ⏱ *Closed 1-15 Aug* – ⚟ – *Reservation recommended* – 4 rooms. Away from the bustling crowd, this pink house, which once belonged to a navy chaplain, is set against a leafy backdrop of maritime pines. The simply appointed rooms are blissfully quiet. There is a private path leading directly to the beach.

◎◎ **Hôtel La Rose des Mers** – *3 Allée E.-Gérard – 5km/3mi southeast of Hyères* – ☎ 04 94 58 02 73 – *rosemer@club-internet. fr* – ⏱ *Closed 15 Nov-14 Mar* – 🅿 – 20 rooms – 🍴. This small, welcoming hotel at the water's edge has tidy rooms with white shutters that look out to sea and the Hyères Islands. Beach mattresses are supplied free of charge.

The afternoon can be spent exploring the Giens peninsula, or making the most of the mild climate with a few hours at one of the many beaches and ports.

🄺🄸🄳🅂 **Especially for Kids:** Young children will enjoy the zoo at the Jardins Olbius-Riquier, while older kids might prefer karting or watching a race at the hippodrome.

A Bit of History

Early History

Excavations on the coast at L'Almanarre reveal that Greeks from Marseille set up a trading station called **Olbia**, which was succeeded by a Roman town **Pomponiana,** and then a nunnery called **St-Pierre-d'Almanarre** during the medieval period. In the early Middle Ages the inhabitants moved further up the hill to where the lords of Fos had built a castle. Agriculture and particularly the salt marshes brought Hyères success. The port of L'Aygade (subsequently silted up) was a base for Crusaders; **St Louis** disembarked there in 1254 on returning from the Seventh Crusade. Soon afterwards the town passed to the Counts of Provence. In 1620 the castle was demolished by Louis XIII and Hyères declined in favour of Toulon.

Modern Revival

The town became a well-known resort in the 19C, particularly among the English, Irish and Americans. In the 20C tourism led to the development of the beaches, although Hyères is a lively town throughout the year and not solely dependent on tourism. The surrounding plain is extensively cultivated to produce early fruit (strawberries, peaches) and vegetables, and great vineyards thrive on rich soil. The town also exports potted palms and ornamental plants.

White Gold

The Conservatoire du Littoral acquired Les Pesquiers in 2001, but from 1848 to 1995, the laguna produced up to 30 000 tons of sea salt per year. How? In the salt tables, vast rectangles of 2-4ha/5-10 acres, the sea water deposits its salt. The constant dry wind speeds evaporation. The "harvest" or collection of the salt occurs in the last week of August (according to tradition between harvest and grape-picking). The operation involved first lifting the salt crust which had formed on the salt tables. This crust, or *sel gris* (grey salt) was set aside to be sprinkled on snow-covered roads. The white salt, washed and fit for consumption, was collected and piled into immense white mountains *(camelles)*, which signalled the presence of salt-marshes from afar. The area is now a nature preserve. 🖹 *www.conservatoire-du-littoral.fr*

View of the old town

Resort Living

BEACHES

Hyères has 20km/13mi of beaches, all under lifeguard watch in the summer, except for the wilder coastline along the Giens Peninsula.

L'Almanarre

Long sandy beach near the ancient site of the Greek town of Olbia (*see above*), where you'll find many surfing schools.

▶ *Take the salt road (Route du Sel; accessible only in summer) down the western side of the peninsula.*

This picturesque route passes a vast salt-marsh (400ha/988 acres) and then the Étang des Pesquiers, home of many aquatic birds.

Hyères-Plage⌂

A small forest of umbrella pines shelters this area, which includes the beaches of the Hippodrome, La Capte and La Bergerie up to Giens. The water is very shallow along much of the shoreline. Boats leave from the **port** for the Îles d'Hyères.

Ayguade-le Ceinturon

This is the old port of Hyères, where St Louis disembarked on his return from the Seventh Crusade. It is now a pleasant resort area with two sand beaches.

▶ *Continue via Berriau-Plage to Port-Pothuau, a picturesque little fishing port.*

Almanarre Funboard Festival

Almanarre beach stretches (6km/3.7mi) along the salt-marshes of the Étang des Pesquiers, facing the Golfe de Giens. On windless days it is popular with families on holiday but, when the *mistral* starts to blow, it becomes a mecca for "funboarding". The beach offers ideal conditions because it is protected by the slight tombolo to the east, the low-lying land to the west and by Cap de Carqueiranne from the heavy swell out at sea.

Almanarre is known as the top windsurfing location on the Riviera. In 1966 it was chosen as the venue for the European Championships for production boards and funboarding.

The beach also attracts many spectators who come to marvel at the spectacular acrobatics, particularly "jibes" – amazing somersaults in the air which have become the symbol of funboarding.

There are schools all along the beach offering windsurfing lessons for beginners and for more seasoned adepts.

GARDENS

Jardins Olbius-Riquier★

Avenue Ambroise-Thomas. Kids ○ *Open daily 8am-7pm.* ⊗ *Free entry.*

The gardens are very extensive (6.5ha/16 acres) and grow a rich variety of tropical plants, particularly palms and cacti, in the open air.

In the **greenhouse** the more fragile species of tropical and equatorial plants can be seen together with a few rare animals.

The gardens include a small **zoo** in a special enclosure, and the lake is home to aquatic birds.

Parc St-Bernard (Jardin de Noailles)

▶ *From Cours de Strasbourg drive north, take Avenue Paul-Long following the signs "Montée de Noailles" on the left.*

The park encloses the castle ruins and boasts a remarkably wide range of Mediterranean flora.

The terraces command a picturesque **view**★: from the old town and the Collégiale St-Paul, over Pic des Oiseaux and Costebelle Hill to the peninsula and the islands; to the east is the outline of the Massif des Maures.

Parc du Château Ste-Claire

Avenue Edith-Warton. ○ *Open in summer 8am-7pm; in winter 8am-5pm.* ⊗ *Free entry.*

A fine villa built in 1850 by Colonel Voutier, the man who discovered the *Venus de Milo*, sits in the middle of this park filled with exotic plants. The château currently houses the administrative offices of the Parc National de Port-Cros.

Visiting Hyères

A STROLL THROUGH THE OLD TOWN 1 *Allow 1.5hr*

▶ *Leave from Place Georges-Clémenceau.*

Porte Massillon

The gate leads onto Rue Massillon, a bustling shopping street, once the main street of the old town. Note the many Renaissance doorways.

Place Massillon

In the square, where the daily market is held, stands the 12C tower, **Tour St-Blaise,** last remnant of a Knights Templar commandery, which now houses temporary art exhibitions (○ *Open Apr-Oct Wed-Sun 10am-noon, 4-7pm; Nov-Mar Wed-Mon 10am-noon, 2-5.30pm.* ⊗ *Free entry.* ☎ *04 94 35 22 36).* To the left is Rue Rabaton where the great preacher, Massillon (1663-1742) was born (no 7).

▶ *From Place Massillon take the steps to the Rue Ste-Catherine and the Place St-Paul.*

Place St-Paul

From this terrace square, once the site of the cloisters of the **Collégiale St-Paul** (⌖ *see Sights*), there is a good **panorama**★ *(viewing table).*

Old Streets

Porte St-Paul (gateway) near the collegiate church is incorporated into a handsome **Renaissance house** with a turret at one corner. Pass beneath and follow Rue St-Paul to Rue Ste-Claire where Porte des Princes stands framing the chevet and bell-tower of the Collégiale St-Paul.

Retrace your steps to Rue de Paradis where there is a fine **Romanesque house** (no 6) which has been restored (twin windows with slender columns).

▶ *From the Rue St-Bernard, walk to the top of the old town until you reach the Villa Noailles (⌖ see Sights). A large path on the left leads to the ruins.*

Château des Aires Ruins

▶ *The ruins can also be reached by car along Montée de Noailles (car park).*

The Château d'Hyères passed from the Lords of Fos to the Counts of Provence, who rebuilt it in the 13C. The ruins are quite extensive, particularly the towers and crenellated keep which dominate the town. The wind is particularly strong at this height! From the top *(viewing table)* a vast **panorama**★ of the coast and the interior can be seen.

▶ *Return to Rue St-Bernard, taking a right onto Rue Barbuc (pass through the doorway), and go down Rue Bourgneuf. Just before the bottom of the street take a right to arrive at the Place Bourgneuf, then left onto Rue St-Louis.*

Église St-Louis

This former church of the Franciscan convent has three elegant doors beneath round arches, a rose window and a cornice. It brings to mind the Italian Romanesque style. The nave, with its thick-ribbed pointed vaulting, ends in a square apse, as do the side aisles. The whole ensemble is an example of the transition from Romanesque to Provençal Gothic.

THE 19C TOWN ②　*By car.*

The development of winter tourism in Hyères dates back to the mid-19C, with the mass visits of the English, including many celebrities: Queen Victoria, the novelist RL Stevenson, and some great French figures: Victor Hugo, Michelet and Maupassant. The resort is therefore endowed with the luxury hotels that needed to meet the requirements of these wealthy visitors.

The "Godillot" District

This is the official name of the western part of the town developed by **Alexis Godillot**, supplier to the armies of the Second Empire and owner of a quarter of the town.

▶ *Go down the Avenue Godillot and turn left on the Avenue de Beauregard.*

Across from the Anglican St Paul's Church is the Villa Tunisienne in Moorish style, once home to Godillot's architect, Chapoulart.

▶ *Go left here.*

On Rue Gallieni you'll find the ex-Hôtel des Palmiers (1884). On the Avenue des Îles-d'Or, the Hôtel des Ambassadeurs still displays a grand entrance decorated with caryatids.

▶ *At Place Georges Clemenceau, follow the Rue Dr-de-Seignoret.*

Quartier Chateaubriand

The Quartier d'Orient was developed from 1850. The most beautiful villas have a Classic style, with a touch of fantasy. On Boulevard Chateaubriand and Boulevard d'Orient, you can admire the Villa Léon-Antoinette, La Favorite and Villa Ker-André.

Sights

Villa de Noailles

🕐 *Guided tours possible on request. Open 10am-noon and 2-5.30pm (10am-noon , 1-4.30pm in summer).* 🕐 *Closed Mon and Tue in winter.* 🐷 *6€ (free for children).* ☎ *04 94 01 84 40. www.villanoailles-hyeres.com. Access by Rue St-Bernard or Montée de Noailles.*

In 1923 the Noailles, a rich couple of art patrons, commissioned a winter villa from the Belgian architect Mallet-Stevens, which was to be as open to the sunlight as possible. The villa (1 600 m2/1 914sq yd), which features a covered swimming pool and 60 or so rooms, was one of the first modern homes on the Riviera. All the famous artists of the 1920s (Picasso, Dali...) attended the extravagant parties given at the villa. The American photographer Man Ray shot some sequences of a Surrealist film here and Buñuel set *L'Âge d'or* in the villa.

After a long period of neglect, the first stage of restoration in 1986 has meant that temporary exhibitions can be held on the first floor. Note the curious Cubist garden designed by Gabriel Guévrékian.

Musée Municipal

Rotonde Jean Salusse. ♿ 🕐 *Open Apr-Oct Wed-Mon 10am-noon, 4-7pm; Nov-Mar Wed-Sun 10am-noon, 2-5.30pm, weekends 10am-noon, 4-7pm.* 🕐 *Closed public holidays.* 🐷 *Free entry.* ☎ *04 94 00 78 42.*

The Greek and Roman archeological specimens displayed in this museum come from excavations conducted at Olbia, including minerals, fossils, shells, fish and birds. There is also a gallery of local artists and furnishings from Louis XV and Louis XVI.

Ancienne Collégiale St-Paul

🕐 *Open Apr-Sep Wed-Mon 10am-noon, 4-7pm; Oct-Mar Wed-Sun 10am-noon, 2-5.30pm.* 🐷 *Free entry.* ☎ *04 94 00 55 50 (Église St Louis).*

The oldest parts of the former collegiate church go back to the 12C; the bell-tower is pure Romanesque. A fine Renaissance door and monumental stairway give access. The narthex, which is probably the nave of the original structure to which a ceiling has been added, is covered with votive offerings (some dating from the 17C).

To the left of the entrance is a large nativity scene of Provençal *santons* with the medieval town as a backdrop. The Gothic nave, set at right angles to the original church, has Flamboyant Gothic side chapels. Altarpieces adorned with wreathed columns, reliquaries and gilded wooden statues date from the 17C.

Olbia Archeological Site

Access from Hyères on the D 559, direction Carqueiranne. ○ *Open Apr-Sep, guided visits fom 9.30am-12.30pm, 3-7pm.* ○ *Closed when raining.* ⊚ *4.60€. www.monum.fr*

Defensive village and maritime market port, Olbia was founded in the 4C BC by the Phoenicians of Marseille as a stopping point along shipping routes. It's one of the only sites of its kind still existing on the Mediterranean coast.

Chapelle Notre-Dame-de-Consolation★

▶ *From Hyères take the D 559, direction Carqueiranne, to the summit of the Colline de Costebelle.*

There has been a sanctuary on the top of Costebelle hill since the 11C. The present chapel was built in 1955. There is a huge coloured sculpture of Our Lady against the cross which forms the bell-tower's vertical axis. A series of sculpted groups depicting the main events in the Virgin's life are portrayed in cement and stone on the principal front between the windows. The stark architecture of the interior is enhanced by the Apostle sculptures in the apse and the shimmering play of colors from the monumental blue and gold **stained-glass windows**★ designed by Gabriel Loire to illustrate the cult of Mary and the history of the sanctuary.

The neighbouring promenade *(viewing table)* gives a **view**★ of the Hyères *(left)* and Toulon *(right)* ports.

Touring the Coast

Giens Peninsula★★

Double Isthmus

The Gien peninsula is a rare natural phenomenon: the former island of Giens is linked to the mainland by two coastal bars (each 4km/2.5mi long). In similar cases, such as Quiberon, a single isthmus (tombolo, or sandbar) has formed, joining the island to the coast. At Giens, a curious combination of circumstances – the mouths of two rivers, the Gapeau and the Roubaud, one on each side of Giens, coupled with strong currents at sea – has given rise to a double isthmus on the rocky seabed.

The parallel bars enclose a lagoon, the **Étang des Pesquiers,** that provides an ideal habitat for birds. Pink flamingoes and avocets are common here. The best time to see flamingoes is in mid-September when up to 1 500 birds migrate here. The flora is interesting and unusual: glasswort, sea rocket, white mignonette and thorny rushes.

A project aimed at replanting posidonia is underway in the gulf of Giens to slow down the erosion of the sea-bed and encourage the revival of species which live in it.

For three decades the west isthmus has been eroded by wind and by storms which attack the sea walls, sweep away the beach and cover parts of the road with sand. A project by the Conservatoire du Littoral is currently in progress to preserve this site.

Giens

The village, in the middle of a former island, is a small seaside resort. The castle ruins form a mound from which there is a magnificent **panorama**★★ *(viewing table)*. The poet St-John Perse stayed here and lies at rest in the cemetery.

To the south is the little port of Niel, surrounded by a lovely pine wood.

▶ *Drive east from the village to the Tour Fondue.*

Restricted access

The western tombolo at Giens, under the protection of the Conservatoire du Littoral, is subject to strict regulations:

⊛ Road traffic is permitted from Easter to All Saints' Day on the tombolo road, with no parking en route; the road is closed the rest of the year.

⊛ Parking is allowed only in the two car parks at each end of the western tombolo.

⊛ To reach the beaches, use only the marked paths, without walking on the dunes or vegetation, and avoiding the marked protected zones.

⊛ Drying sails or any canvas on the vegetation is not allowed.

S. Sauvignier/ MICHELIN

Tour Foudue, Gien peninsula

Tour Fondue

Boats sail from here to the Île de Porquerolles. The name comes from the fort built under Richelieu to control the narrows of La Petite Passe, which was also protected by forts on the small islands of Grand and Petit Ribaud *(private property)*. There is a beautiful view of the islands and the Giens peninsula.

Tour of the peninsula on foot – *18km/11mi – allow 5hr.*

The route, which is partly signed, links the port of La Madrague to Badine beach. Take D 97 along the eastern side of the peninsula – fine views of the Hyères plain and the Maures. Continue to Hyères-Plage via La Bergerie and La Capte set in pine woods.

Excursions

Sommet du Fenouillet★ *4km/2.5mi – plus 30min on foot round-trip*

▸ *From Hyères take Avenue de Toulon then turn right onto a signed road to Le Fenouillet.*

From the neo-Gothic **chapel** there is a marked path to Le Fenouillet, the highest point of the Maurettes (291m/955ft) with a very good **panorama**★, particularly of the Hyères and Toulon harbors and the surrounding mountains.

Jardin d'Oiseaux Tropicaux

13km/8mi east on the N 98, to La Londe-les-Maures (see massif des MAURES).

A signposted trail through this **exotic bird sanctuary,** shaded by eucalyptus and pine trees, leads past large aviaries containing, one after another, many species of parrot, toucan and hornbill, large birds such as the hooded cassoway and emus all the way from Australia.

Îles d'HYÈRES ★★★

MICHELIN MAP 340 M/N7/8

LOCAL MAP SEE MASSIF DES MAURES

These popular Côte d'Azur islands off the Hyères harbour are just a short sea crossing from the coast, and offer many beautiful scenic walking trails, both along the sandy beaches and the rocky inland hills. They're also known as the Îles d'Or (Golden Islands), a name given to them during the Renaissance, no doubt due to the fact that in certain lights their mica shale rocks cast golden reflections. Whether you prefer Le Levant, Port-Cros or the Porquerolles, you'll find your visit a memorable one.

▶ **Orient Yourself:** There are three islands making up the Îles d'Hyères, accessible by ferry boats. The largest is the Île de Porquerolles to the west, closest to the Giens peninsula. The best way to get around here is by bike. The second island is Île de Port-Cros, slightly smaller and more mountainous. Because it's a nature preserve, bicycles are not allowed. To the east is the last island, Île du Levant, occupied primarily by a military base and private nudist beaches. No matter which island you visit, be sure to take along plenty of drinking water. ⓘ *Bureau d'Information at the port, Porquerolles.* ☎ *04 94 58 33 76. www.porquerolles.com.* ⓘ *Parc National de Port-Cros, Castel Ste-Claire.* ☎ *04 94 12 82 30. www.portcrosparcsnationaux.fr.*

A Bit of History

A Land of Asylum

In the 5C the monks of Lérins arrived, succeeding the Ligurians, the Greeks and the Romans as the islands' overlords. In the following centuries they were repeatedly attacked by pirates until François I put the islands of Port-Cros and Levant under the protection (and rule) of the Marquis of the Îles d'Or, provided that the Marquis kept them under cultivation. Despite exemption from taxes, the islands lacked manpower until a right of asylum was established under which criminals were granted immunity so long as they remained on the islands. This idea had unfortunate consequences. Jailbirds swarmed to the islands, where they turned to piracy, being so bold as to attempt the capture of one of the king's ships from Toulon. Only in the reign of Louis XIV did the last of these dubious characters leave the area.

A British Coup

In 1793, after the capture of Toulon by the Revolutionaries (⏺ *see TOULON),* British and Spanish squadrons anchored off the Îles d'Hyères. The commander of Fort Ste-Agathe at Porquerolles, forgotten on his island by the French authorities, had only

Address Book

ACCESS

The islands are accessible from several ports, with many companies offering half-day or full-day excursions or links. Be sure not to miss the last boat back to the mainland!

From La Tour Fondue (Giens Peninsula) – TLV (Transports Littoral Varois), Port de La Tour Fondue – ☎ 04 94 58 21 81 – www.tlv-tvm.com – ☎ 15€. Regular daily service to the Porquerolles. Circuits of the Porquerolles and Port-Cros available weekdays Jul-Aug.

From Hyères – TLV, Port Saint-Pierre – ☎ 04 94 57 44 07 – www.tlv-tvm.com – ⏱ 1 to 4 departures per day depending on the season – ☎ 22-25€. Trips to Port-Cros (1hr), Le Levant (1.5hr); circuit of Port-Cros and Levant available Jul-Aug.

From Le Lavandou, Cavalaire – Vedettes des Îles d'Or – ☎ 04 94 71 01 02 – ⏱ Port Cros: daily except Tue and weekends, 11am-6.55pm (3/4 hr); Porquerolles: 9.30am-5pm (1.5hr).

A FEW GUIDELINES

Fire – During periods of major fire risk, the ALARME plan comes into force (announced before embarkation); it means that access is limited to the beaches, the coastal path and the villages. A recorded message is available by phone from 7pm the evening before, ☎ 04 98 10 55 41.

Rules – At Porquerolles and Port-Cros, it is forbidden to smoke (outside the village), make fires, camp, pick the plants or flowers, leave the marked paths, litter or walk pets (outside the village); at Port-Cros it is forbidden to use bicycles, collect seashells, or fish.

Water– There are few or no places to find water on the island (but it can be purchased in the village boutiques), so bring plenty on your own and be sure to fill up before going on long hikes.

For coin ranges see the Legend at the back of this guide.

EATING OUT

PORQUEROLLES

Butcher/Deli – Place d'Armes. Cold meats, jams, olive oil.

Bakery – ⏱ 7.30am-12.30pm, 2-6pm in winter; 7am-1pm, 3-7.30pm Easter-Oct; open non-stop Jul-Aug.

Convenience Store – Place d'Armes – ⏱ Open 8am-8pm Jul-Aug, 8.30am-12.45pm and 4-7.30pm Easter-Oct. Mornings only off-season.

☎☎ **Villa Sainte Anne** – Place d'Armes - ☎ 04 98 04 63 00 - www.sainteanne.com - ⏱ Closed 1 Nov-25 Dec, 3 Jan-Feb. This restaurant near the church has a shady terrace and cuisine that makes the most of the fresh catch of the day. Real Provençal atmosphere and great people-watching on the square. Also 22 rooms available (☎☎☎).

PORT-CROS

Deli – Off the main quay (look for signs for epicerie) – ⏱ Open Apr-Nov 8am-8pm.

☎ **Sun Bistrot** – At the port - ☎ 04 94 05 90 16 - ⏱ Apr-Oct. Brasserie and snack bar frequented by students from the diving school, selling pizzas, salads, fish and patés.

☎ **La Trinquette** – At the port - ☎ 04 94 05 93 75 - Reserve off-season. The only restaurant-bar open all year, this is the preferred hangout of the tiny band of locals and regulars. Pizzas and family-style food overlooking the port.

☎ **Le Petit Café Tahitien** – Place d'Armes - ☎ 04 94 12 32 70 - ⏱ Open mid-Apr to mid-Oct. A hint of the tropics at this rare reasonably-priced restaurant. Hearty salads and an interesting cocktail list.

LE LEVANT

Outside the floating snack boats on the port, the only place to eat is in Héliopolis.

WHERE TO STAY

☎☎☎ **Hôtel Manoir** – Port-Cros - ☎ 04 94 05 90 52 - lemanoir-portcros@wanadoo.fr - ⏱ Closed 4 Oct-9 Apr. - 18 rooms - ☐ - Restaurant (☎☎☎). Charming 1830s hotel in an exceptional garden setting a few feet from the port. Minimalist rooms, swimming pool. Half-board only.

☎☎☎ **Mas du Langoustier** – West of the port - Porquerolles - ☎ 04 94 58 30 09 - langoustier@wanadoo.fr - ⏱ Closed Oct-Apr. - 44 rooms, half-board - ☐ - Restaurant (☎☎☎). The prices are usually high on the Porquerolles, but at least in this chic hôtel-restaurant the quality and service are worth it. The dining room overlooks the sea and the Fort du Langoustier. The cuisine is gourmet Mediterranean and French classics. A shuttle from the hotel takes guests to and from the port.

☎☎☎ **L'Auberge des Glycines** – 22 Place d'Armes - Porquerolles - ☎ 04 94 58 30 36 - ⏱ Closed at lunch- 11 room, half-board - ☐ - restaurant (☎☎☎). This adorable cottage with lavender-blue shutters has rooms that open onto a patio shaded by a fig tree or the village square. The restaurant serves Provençal cooking.

SPORTS AND LEISURE

Cycling – Bikes can be rented on Porquerolles near the port and around the Town Hall.

Diving – The great depths and the lack of strong currents around the islands and in the Baie de Carqueiranne provide ideal conditions for diving as well as for underwater photography of the many wrecks. There are several diving clubs in Hyères and La Londe; Sun Plongée in Port-Cros and Porquerolles Plongée in Porquerolles.

Aquascope – [Kids] – Port-Cros – ☎ 04 94 05 92 22 – ☜ 15€ (4-12 years, 10€). Guided tours *(30min)* in a boat specially designed to observe underwater life. Departures every 40min. Only 10 seats available (rest standing).

TMV – Port de la Tour-Fondue – 83400 Giens – ☎ 04 94 58 95 14 – www.tlv-tvm. com – Jun-Sep, 5 departures per day – ☜ 11.50€. Glass-bottom boat tours of the underwater flora and fauna *(35 min)*.

Tour of Porquerolles – A sailboat race takes place every Whit Sunday (Pentecost) around the island, starting from the port.

Le Levant –The accessible areas of the island are in the west and north; in the north a channel is reserved for water sports and an area is set aside for windsurfing. The main beaches, reached by the coast path on each side of the landing-stages, are for the exclusive use of nudists.

LOCAL WINES

Domaine de la Courtade – Porquerolles – ☎ 04 94 58 31 44. This reputable vineyard can be reached after a pleasant 15-minute walk. Call ahead if you would like to purchase wine at the domaine.

Domaine de l'Île – Place d'Armes – Porquerolles – ◷ Open 9am-8pm. Made on the island, but sold only in this boutique in the village.

Domaine Perzinsky – Porquerolles – ☎ 04 94 58 34 32. Created in 1989, this vineyard is the closest to the village *(welcome tour and tasting 9€ with a bottle of rosé).*

the vaguest idea of what was happening on the mainland. The British admiral invited him on board his flagship and the commander went unsuspectingly. While the whisky was circulating, British sailors landed, surprised the garrison and destroyed the fort (it was rebuilt in 1810). The ships then raised anchor taking with them, as prisoner, the crestfallen commander.

Allied Landing (August 1944)

During the night of 14 to 15 August 1944, American troops landed on the islands of Port-Cros and Levant to eradicate the German batteries that threatened the Allied landing.

Touring the Islands

ÎLE DE PORQUEROLLES★★★

Porquerolles measures 7km/4mi long by 3km/2mi wide, and was called Protè (First) by the Greek settlers who came to live along its shores. The best way to discover the island is by bicycle (rented in the village). The north coast is well supplied with sandy beaches bordered by pine trees, heather, arbutus and scented myrtle; the south coast is steep and rugged with one or two inlets that are easily accessible. There are few inhabitants inland, where you'll find vineyards, pine and eucalyptus woods and thick Mediterranean vegetation.

The Village

The small village of Porquerolles, which lies at the end of a minute port now used as a harbour for pleasure boats, has given its name to the whole island. The village was built by the military in the mid-19C and consists of a main square, a humble church containing an unusual Stations of the Cross carved by a soldier with his penknife and a few fishermen's cottages as well as more recently constructed hotels and private houses.

Mexico-sur-Mer

For 60 years this island was the private property of a single family. In 1911, a Belgian engineer, F-Joseph Fournier, having made his fortune in Mexico, decided to give Porquerolles as a wedding gift to his young bride. Once settled on the island with his family and an army of gardeners, he attempted to re-create the atmosphere of a south American hacienda by importing exotic plants. He began with the cultivation of several exotic fruits then unknown in France, pineapples and kumquats. Along the walks are South American plants such as the bellombra with its massive roots. Also witness to this replanting, the 180ha/445 acres of vines originally planted have been reduced to half the quantity but continue to produce a reputable rosé. This was the first vineyard to gain the AOC Côtes de Provence *appellation*.

Fort Ste-Agathe

🕐 *Open May-Sep 10am-noon, 2-5.30pm.* 🚌 *4€.* ☎ *04 94 12 30 40.*

This fort is the first building one sees before landing on the island. Dominating a mound that overlooks the port, it occupies an enviable strategic position. Its walls in the shape of a trapezium are surmounted by a massive corner tower, all that remains of the original structure built by François I in 1532. The English ruined and subsequently burnt the fort in 1793 and reconstruction began in 1810 with buildings adapted to meet new military requirements. The round tower is constructed on a massive scale: walls 4m/13ft thick, 20m/66ft in diameter and 15m/49ft high. The Parc de Port-Cros has organised exhibitions in the tower's various rooms on underwater archeology, artefacts, and on the history of the islands and Hyères harbour. The great circular room has a 6m/20ft-high ceiling and fine wooden beams. From the terrace on top of the tower, with its five embrasures for large-bore cannon, there is a magnificent **view**★ over most of the island: La Courtade beach, Notre-Dame beach, the Sémaphore peak (summit 142m/466ft) to the east and, to the west, wooded hills obscuring the beaches.

▶ *At the exit of the village of Porquerolles, follow the direction of the Route du Phare, then turn right at the Carrefour des Oliviers to the Hameau Agricole.*

Conservatoire Botanique National Méditerranéen

🕐 *Open May-Sep 9.30am-12.30pm, 1.30-5pm.* ☎ *04 94 12 30 32.* 🚌 *Free entry.*

Since 1985 the major part of the island has been managed by the National Park of Port-Cros, which owns the land. Created in 1979, the Conservatoire was set up to preserve the area and to protect the Mediterranean fauna and flora thriving in the basin.

Walks on the Porquerolles

Lighthouse Walk★★ *1.5hr on foot round-trip.*

🚶 This walk to the lighthouse *(phare)* is a "must" even for tourists with only a few hours to spend on the island. The **lighthouse** (🕐 *Guided tours 10am-noon, 2-4pm.* 🚌 *Free entry. The lighthouse may be closed for safety or technical reasons.)* stands on the most southerly point of the island some 96m/307ft up, and has a beam which carries 54km/34mi.

From the top a **panorama**★★ extends over most of the island: the Langoustier hills, Fort Ste-Agathe, the signal station and the cliffs on the south coast, the Hyères harbour and the Maures Massif.

Beach Walk★★ *2hr on foot round-trip.*

🚶 This pleasant walk along sandy paths, in the shade of the pine trees, starts from Fort Ste-Agathe *(bear left)* and skirts the Plage de la Courtade.

After Pointe du Lequin the path dips towards the sea, revealing the **Plage Notre-Dame,** a beautiful sandy beach bordered by pine trees.

The **signal station** *(sémaphore)*, Plage d'Argent, **Pointe du Grand Langoustier** and **Cap des Mèdes** all make excellent walks.

A **boat** with underwater viewing facilities makes cruises off shore (🧭*see Address Book).*

ÎLE-DE PORT-CROS★★★

Port-Cros Island is hillier and more rugged and rises higher above the sea than its neighbours. Its lush vegetation is unrivalled – it is a true Garden of Eden and a peaceful place in which to stay. The island is 4km/2.5mi long by 2.5km/1.5mi wide and its highest point, Mont Vinaigre, reaches 194m/679ft. A few fishermen's cottages, a bunch of shops and a small church adorn the area around the bay, which is commanded by Fort du Moulin (also known as the "Château").

Port-Cros, together with Île de Bagaud and the neighbouring islets, Rascas and La Gabinière, and an area extending 600m/656yd around the coastline, has been designated a **Parc National.** The park covers 700ha/2.69sq mi on land and 1 800ha/7sq mi at sea and forms a unique protected site for Mediterranean flora and fauna.

▶ *The principal walks are signed at the quayside; possible variations are shown by a broken line in red on the map.*

Plage de la Palud★ *1.5hr on foot round-trip (marked path).*

🚶 Climb up to the castle for a view of the neighbouring Île de Bagaud. A **botanical path** planted with Mediterranean specimens winds its way up along La Palud Bay before reaching the beach. It passes by the **Fort de l'Estissac** (🕐 *Open May-Sep.* 🚌 *Free entry.* ☎ *04 94 01 40 72)*, built under Richelieu, which houses exhibitions on the marine environment and the relation between humans and the sea.

La Palud Cove, Port-Cros Island

Underwater Trail★

🕐 *Open mid-Jun to end of Sep. Guided tours by one of the park attendants (except in the event of bad weather).* ⊚ *Free Entry.*

An underwater observation point, no deeper than 10m/33ft, is located in the section between the little island of Rascas and La Palud beach, marked by yellow buoys. Here anyone who can swim – diving is not necessary – can observe a great variety of typical Mediterranean species that live at this depth. Numbered buoys mark the best viewpoints: the highest numbered signposts indicate the best positions. Among other flora and fauna, the principal stages in the development of posidonia, and the types of animal that thrive on it, can be studied.

A preliminary visit to the park office in the port is strongly recommended. In the case of a solitary dive (bring along your own mask, breathing apparatus and flippers), a plastified aquaguide is provided which fastens onto the wrist to help you identify marine flora and fauna.

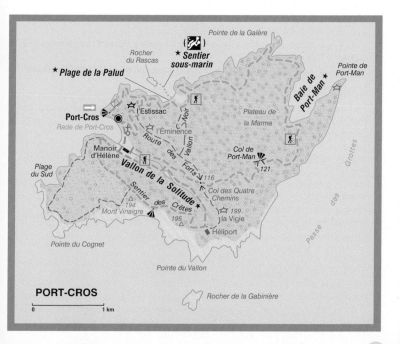

▶ *Return to the village passing between the forts of L'Éminence and L'Estissac.*

Vallon de la Solitude★ *2hr on foot round-trip (marked path).*

🚶 This is the ideal walk for visitors spending half a day on the island. At the beginning of the valley stands the Manoir d'Hélène – a manor house converted into a hotel – so called after the heroine in Melchior de Vogüé's novel *Jean d'Agrève* which is set on Port-Cros. The path is in deep shade for almost all its length.

Once within sight of Fort de la Vigie start back along the cliff walk (Route des Crêtes), which affords **views** of the sea.

▶ *At Mont Vinaigre bear right into the Vallon de la Fausse Monnaie (Valley of False Currency).*

Port-Man★ *Round tour of 10km/6mi – 4hr round-trip on foot (marked paths).*

🚶 This pleasant excursion is made along a shaded and nearly level path from which, at the end of the Col de Port-Man, there is a pretty **view** of the Île du Levant, the coast and the Maures. It ends in the **Baie de Port-Man**, a wonderful green amphitheatre or bay, which is well sheltered from the north winds.

▶ *Return via Pointe de la Galère, Plateau de la Marma and Plage de la Palud.*

Other Walks

Indicated by the dotted orange line on the map, these include the Plage du Sud (sand) and its impressive cliff, the Route des Forts, the Vallon Noir and the Col des Quatre Chemins.

ÎLE DU LEVANT *local map* 🧭 *see Massif des MAURES.*

The island consists of a rocky spine 8km/5mi long but only 1 200m/1 300yd wide rimmed by vertical cliffs inaccessible except at two points: the Avis and Estable *calanques*. The disembarkation point on the island is the Aiguade landing, from which a path leads up to Héliopolis.

When the Lérins monks inhabited the islands, the Île du Levant was the abbey's garden and granary. Today the majority of the island (90%) is occupied by the Marine Nationale *(access is forbidden)*.

Héliopolis

In the western part of the island, the village of Héliopolis and the Grottes area attract a considerable number of nudists each summer. This part of the island *(private property)* is one of the oldest nudist camps in Europe, opened in 1931. In season local clubs organise diving activities which are open to the general public (🧭 *see Planning Your Trip*).

JUAN-LES-PINS ☼☼☼

MICHELIN MAP 341 D6

Juan-les-Pins is one of the Riviera's most lively summer resorts, known for its jazz festival under the pines, numerous nightclubs and seemingly endless stretch of sandy beaches. Well protected by the luxurious Cap d'Antibes and Pointe de la Croisette, the bay enjoys a mild climate and easy access to both Cannes and Antibes.

▸ **Orient Yourself:** Technically part of the same municipality, Juan-les-Pins is connected to Antibes on the east by the Cap d'Antibes (see ANTIBES), and to the west by Golfe-Juan, all along the RN 7 or the coastal N 98. The train station is only a few blocks from the beaches. *51 Boulevard Charles-Guillaumont, Juan-les-Pins, ☎ 04 92 90 53 05. www.antibes-juanlespins.com.*

🅿 **Parking:** Parking spots are difficult to find in summer, but typically can be found by the station *(gare)* or along the beach *(fee)*.

A Bit of History

The "Swing" Era

The thriving musical nightlife of Juan-les-Pins began during the 1920s, with the arrival of the first American tourists. They revolutionised the atmosphere of the resort with their exuberance: they sunbathed on the beaches, they waterskied and they listened to strange music called jazz. A magnate named Frank Gould founded the first summer casino, and the young jet set whiled away the nights dancing to the lively music of Cole Porter, in the company of Douglas Fairbanks, Mary Pickford and Mistinguette.

> ### It Started Here
>
> Léo Ramon invented waterskiing in 1925 on the beaches of Juan-les-Pins, where it immediately became a popular water sport.

At the end of the Second World War, soon after the Liberation, the music started again thanks to a clientele from the US Navy based on the Riviera. In 1951 Sydney Bechet was married here in an atmosphere which recalled New Orleans carnivals. From then on each summer Juan-les-Pins was transformed into the European jazz capital by Sydney Bechet and Claude Luter. After Bechet's death in 1959 the first jazz festival was born. Its success was assured by the presence of Louis Armstrong, Count Basie, Duke Ellington, Dizzy Gillespie and Miles Davis. Jazz is now inseparable from the name of Juan-les-Pins.

Juan-les-Pins beach

D. Pazery / MICHELIN

Address Book

For coin ranges see the Legend at the back of this guide.

EATING OUT

Le Capitole – *26 Avenue Amiral-Courbet – ☎ 04 93 61 22 44 – alainfontfree. com – Closed 15 Nov-15 Dec, Mon evening and Tue off-season.* Of the former grocery shop, only the original shelves remain. The premises are now occupied by this smart restaurant serving traditional fare.

L'Amiral – *7 Avenue Amiral-Courbet – ☎ 04 93 67 34 61 – Closed 8-15 Mar, 1-19 Jul, 29 Nov-6 Dec and Mon.* Small family-run business providing tasty local cuisine on prettily decorated tables in a modern, friendly setting. If you like couscous, the day to go is Thursday but you must book first!

Bijou Plage – *Boulevard Guillaumont – ☎ 04 93 61 39 07 – bijou.plage@free.fr – Closed Tue night and Wed from Nov-Mar.* During the summer season, locals and tourists alike flock to this beach restaurant on the road to Golfe-Juan. The menu pays tribute to bouillabaisse and other fish dishes. Its low prices, private beach and water sports facilities are additional incentives.

Nounou – *On the beach – Golfe-Juan – ☎ 04 93 63 71 73 – Closed 12 Nov-25 Dec, Sun evening and Mon except Jul-Aug.* Settle on the terrace overlooking the beautiful sandy beach, or inside one of the dining rooms, and order a Provençal speciality or a fish dish. Choosing the menu is a better deal than eating à la carte.

WHERE TO STAY

Hôtel Les Charmettes – *25 Vieux Chemin de la Colle – ☎ 04 93 61 47 41 – Closed Nov school holidays – 17 rooms, half-board.* If you shy away from the throng and from loud, blaring night spots, this is definitely the place for you. The simple, narrow rooms are well kept and the pretty terrace ablaze with mimosa is sheltered by reed screening.

Hôtel La Marjolaine – *15 Avenue du Docteur-Fabre – ☎ 04 93 61 06 60 – Closed 15 days in Mar and Nov – 17 rooms.* This turn-of-the-century manor is charmingly set among flowers and provides quality accommodation: rooms with exposed beams decorated in warm, generous hues. The most appealing one is called "Manoir" with antique Provençal furniture.

Hôtel Cécil – *Rue Jonnard – ☎ 04 93 61 05 12 – Closed 3 Nov-30 Jan – 21 rooms, half-board.* A handsome residence built in accordance with local

tradition was converted into a hotel in 1920. The smallish, impeccably kept rooms are laid out over three floors. Dinner is served out on the terrace in high season. Conveniently situated in the town centre, yet not far from the beach.

Hôtel Ste-Valérie – *Rue de l'Oratoire – ☎ 04 93 61 07 15 – saintevalerie@juanlespins.net – Closed 16 Oct-8 Apr – P – 28 rooms – Restaurant ( ).* Just off a quiet street, this hotel has carefully kept rooms with terraces or balconies overlooking pretty gardens where breakfast is served on warm days. Outdoor pool. Peaceful ambience guaranteed.

ON THE TOWN

Pam Pam – *137 Boulevard du Président-Wilson – ☎ 04 93 61 11 05 – Apr to mid-Nov 2-5pm.* Diners come from afar to relish the famous *accras* (cod fritters served between 6pm and 9pm), to sip an exotic punch or to watch the Brazilian girls gyrate to the strains of a live orchestra in a Polynesian setting. One of Juan-les-Pins' hottest night spots.

Le Crystal – *Avenue Gallice – 06160 Juan-les-Pins – ☎ 04 93 61 02 51 – Open 8am-2am (until 4am Apr-Sep) – Closed 15 Nov-20 Dec and Mon off-season.* When it first opened in 1936, this family brasserie was housed in a small hut on a plot of land with palm trees where sheep would come to graze. The owner still remembers those early days. Today Le Crystal is hemmed in between the Casino and a host of other bars and discotheques. A must for any self-respecting night clubber...

LEISURE ACTIVITIES

Visiobulle – *Leaves from the Embarcadère Courbet, opposite the Maison du tourisme – ☎ 04 93 34 09 96 – www.visiobulle.com – Open Apr-Sep.* Booking recommended in Jul and Aug. This boat offering views of the fascinating sea depths takes its passengers right up to the tip of Cap d'Antibes, which cannot be reached by land.

Tourist Train – *(see ANTIBES Address Book)* A small tourist train has regular service between Juan-les-Pins and Antibes.

L'Île Ste-Marguerite – *67 Boulevard Charles-Guillaumont - Ponton-Courbet - across from the Tourism Office - ☎ 04 93 61 78 84 - www.ilesdelerins.com - Five departures per day Apr-Sep. (30mn) - 10€ (child 5€). (see Îles de LERINS).*

Resort Life

The exotic pine trees and the heavenly sand beaches make this resort one of the most attractive on the French Riviera. The Promenade au Soleil running between the landing-stage and the casino is strongly reminiscent of the star-studded Croisette in Cannes. In the evening, activity centers on the numerous restaurants, open-air cafés and nightclubs around the casino, where baccarat and roulette can be played. During the day you can admire the architecture of many hotels and private homes built in the 1920s and 1930s (*ask at the Tourism Office for the map*).

Beaches

The pines grow right down to the gently sloping beach of Juan-les-Pins, a superb stretch of fine sand some 2km/1.2mi long and sheltered from the winds. There are several private and public beaches all around, dotted between the ports of Golfe-Juan and Juan-les-Pins.

Parc Exflora

Off the N 7 in the direction of Golfe-Juan. ⏰ *Open spring 9.30am-7pm, summer 9.30am-9.30pm, winter 9.30am-5pm.* ☎ *04 92 90 53 05 (Tourism Office).* 🚗 *Free entry.*

Set within a vast olive tree orchard are the many different incarnations of Mediterranean gardens from antiquity to the 19C. The settings include a Roman garden, a palm tree garden, a labyrinth, a winter garden and an oasis overlooking the sea.

Excursions

Cap d'Antibes⌂ *10km/7.1mi. Allow 2hr.* 👣 *see ANTIBES: Driving tours.*

Massif de l'Esterel★★★ *96km/60mi. Allow half a day.* 👣 *see Massif de L'ESTEREL.*

Massif du Tanneron★ *56km/34.5mi. Allow 1.5hr.* 👣 *see Massif du TANNERON.*

Le **LAVANDOU** ☼☼

POPULATION 5 449

MICHELIN MAP 340 N7

LOCAL MAP SEE MASSIF DES MAURES

This charming family resort sheltered by the Cap Bénat has preserved its Provençal character. Its port, one of the most important fishing centers in the Var up to the 1930s, is now home to more pleasure yachts than trawlers. Le Lavandou is also a departure point for boat excursions to the scenic Îles d'Hyères (👣 *see Îles d'HYERES*).

Yachting harbour

B. Kaufmann/ MICHELIN

Address Book

For coin ranges see the Legend at the back of this guide.

EATING OUT

Chez Zète – *41 Avenue du Général-de-Gaulle* – ☎ *04 94 71 09 11* – ⏰ *Closed Dec, Mon, and Sun evening (except Jul-Aug).* In Le Lavandou's main shopping street, this family business has become a huge success and continues to draw large crowds all year round. Its main assets? Succulent Provençal cooking, an unpretentious setting and a shaded terrace behind the house.

Hélios Plage – *In Aiguebelle – Avenue du Général-Bouvet, then take the footbridge* – ☎ *04 94 71 49 79* – ⏰ *Closed mid-Nov-1 Apr and evenings*–. If you want to lounge around on the sand and enjoy views of Levant Island, sit down in this charming cabin with white wainscoting and choose between a salad, the chef's special or a tasty dish of pasta...before succumbing to a well-deserved siesta!

L'Auberge Provençale – *11 Rue Patron-Ravello* – ☎ *04 94 71 00 44* – *provençale.au bergewanadoo.fr* – ⏰ *Closed 10 Jan-1 Feb, 25 Nov-15 Dec.* A pedestrian street leads to this inn, entirely dedicated to Provence and its traditions: Mediterranean recipes and colourful tablecloths in a typical setting featuring a huge olive press screw.

Auberge de la Fossette – *16 Avenue Cap Thorel* – ☎ *04 94 71 08 76* – ⏰ *Closed 20 Sep-4 May and lunch (except Sun).* Located a few steps from the beach, this family-run restaurant specialises in grilled dishes and simple regional cuisine, with a terrace under a wisteria vine.

WHERE TO STAY

Roc Hôtel – *In St-Clair – 2km/1.2mi from Le Lavandou* – ☎ *04 94 01 33 66* – ⏰ *Closed 24 Oct-26 Mar – 25 rooms* – 🅿 – . An ochre building houses this hotel lying on a handsome sandy beach. Most of the light, modern rooms have balconies facing the sea. Breakfast is served on the terrace during the summer.

Hôtel Les Alcyons – *In Aiguebelle – 4.5km/3mi from Lavandou* – ☎ *04 94 05 84 18 – www.beausoleil-alcyons.com* – ⏰ *Closed 16 Oct-2 Apr – 24 rooms* – 🅿 – . At the foot of the Maures Massif, barely 20 minutes from the beach, this congenial establishment provides an opportunity to combine the pleasures of swimming with those of hiking across the countryside. Each of the rooms, decorated with rattan furniture, has a balcony and air-conditioning.

ON THE TOWN

Le Bora Bora – *Boulevard Maréchal de-Lattre-de-Tassigny* – ☎ *04 94 71 05 54* – ⏰ *Open Oct-Mar daily 7.30am-9pm; Apr-Sep daily 7.30-3am.* Bar lizards can choose among the 100 different cocktails prepared in this bar, served in coconut shells or large Thai seashells, which you can buy and take home to remember your trip. During the summer season, a live orchestra performs tunes from Latin America and the East Indies.

OUTDOOR THEATRE

Théâtre de Verdure-*Cinéma Plein Air – Avenue du Grand-Jardin* – ☎ *04 94 00 41 71* – ⏰ *Jul-Aug – See the programme for events.* This outdoor theatre puts on summer plays and organises concerts of classical music and contemporary pop.

SPORTS AND LEISURE

École de Voile de Cavalière – *Avenue du Cap-Nègre* – ☎ *04 94 05 86 78* – ⏰ *Apr-Oct daily 9am-6pm.* This club gives sailing lessons and rents various sailing boats (catamaran, dinghy, optimist) as well as windsurfing boards. On the same beach, bathers may try their hand at windsurfing, waterskiing, parascending or a sea version of dodgem cars in which contestants wear large rubber rings!

Hoëdic – *Port du Lavandou* – ☎ *04 94 71 69 89 or 06 09 37 30 62 – bateauhœdic@ clubinternet.fr* – ⏰ *Jun-Sep.* Give in to temptation and embark on a one-day cruise on the Hoëdic, a handsome sailing boat built 50 years ago. When you have finished swimming, diving and paddling around in a canoe, come back on board to tuck into the delicious cold buffet and soak up the sun on the deck.

Seascope – *Gare Maritime* – ☎ *04 94 71 01 02* – 🧒 – ⏰ *Open all year* – 🎫 *11.70€.* The Seascope's transparent hull affords wonderful views of the sea depths, marine flora and many Mediterranean fish species, notably mullet, bass and bream.

Vedettes Îles d'Or – *Gare Maritime* – ☎ *04 94 71 01 02 – www.vedettesilesdor. com* – 🎫 *22-28€* – ⏰ *Daily service.* This is the landing-stage for boats leaving for the islands of Levant and Port-Cros; Porquerolles from Apr-Sep. The first island, partly occupied by the French army, is a popular destination among nudists.

Small beach train – ☎ *04 94 12 55 12* – ⏰ *Jun-Sep.* Tour *(50min)* of Le Lavandou Port up to Pramousquier including access to the 12 beaches of the resort. *(1st departure at 9.40am, last departure at 7.30pm).* Nightly tours *(30min)* are also available.

CIP Lavandou – *Le Lavandou Port – Quai Gabriel-Péri* – ☎ *04 94 15 13 09.* Diving club.

Lavandou Scuba Diving School – *New Port – underneath the restaurant Le Barracuda* – ☎ *04 94 71 83 65 – www. lavandou-plongee.com.* Lessons for both beginners and experienced divers and various other services (equipment rental, tours of shipwrecks, exploring sites around Port-Cros, etc).

SHOPPING

Domaine de l'Anglade – *Avenue Vincent-Auriol –* ☎ *04 94 71 10 89 – dom.langlade@ wanadoo.fr –* 🕐 *Jul-Aug daily 9am-12.30pm, 4.30-7pm; Sep-Jun Tue-Sat 9am-noon, 5-7pm. This attractive vineyard,* located in the town of Le Lavandou, produces red, white and rosé wine, wine for apéritifs (orange and lemon-flavoured) and vinegar. Tasting sessions and shop on the premises.

Markets – Thursday morning *(all year)* at Avenue Vincent-Auriol, and Monday morning *(Jun-Sep)* in Cavalière.

▶ **Orient Yourself:** Le Lavandou sits on the Corniche des Maures (🕐 *see massif des MAURES*), east of Bormes-les-Mimosas (🕐 *see BORMES-LES-MIMOSAS*). The centre of town overlooks the port, while the hotels are mostly situated near the beaches and sports centre to the southwest. 🅱 *Quai Gabriel-Péri, Le Lavandou,* ☎ *04 94 00 40 50. At Cavalière : La Rotonde, Avenue du Golf,* ☎ *04 94 05 80 50. www.lelavandou. com.*

The Town

The main square, **Place Ernest-Reyer**, is laid out like a garden and commands a pretty **view** of the islands of Levant and Port-Cros. The **Boulevard de-Lattre-de-Tassigny** is a pleasant promenade running alongside the beach, with a **view** of the port and the coast eastwards to Cap Lardier.

There are lively, colourful **markets** on Place du Marché and along Avenue du Président-Vincent-Auriol on Thursdays and in Cavalière on Mondays *(Jun to Sep)*.

Beaches

All the beaches at Le Lavandou are sand, placed under constant surveillance and equipped with emergency signals. Standards of comfort, hygiene and sporting facilities vary from one beach to the other. Adventurous tourists can take up windsurfing in St-Clair and canoeing in La Fossette.

But for those who prefer to take it easy, there is nude sunbathing on Plage du Rossignol and a nudist beach in Le Layet.

Boat Trips

Îles d'Hyères★★★ *Allow one day. (For maps and description* 🕐 *see Îles d'HYÈRES.)*

The Song of Summer

The image of the Mediterranean is invariably associated with the song of the cicada, together with the game of boules *(pétanque)* and a siesta under the pine trees. The song of the cicada is stimulated by a combination of particular conditions – the temperature must be at least 25°C in the shade and there should not be too much noise. A tiny change – such as a cloud passing in front of the sun or the wind rustling in the trees – is enough to upset the insect. Only the male cicada sings, since the noise is a mating call to females. The dawn serenade is produced when the insect contracts two rigid plates, cymbals, on its abdomen which vibrate at 500 times a second. The sound is amplified by a ventral cavity full of air which acts as a resonance chambre. When the female has located the sound using ears on her abdomen, she joins her suitor in the tree. There are nearly 15 different varieties of cicada in France, of which the most common is the *cacau gris (cicada orni)*, an emblem of Provence.

Îles de LÉRINS★★

MICHELIN MAP 341 D6

The interest and attraction of an excursion to the Îles de Lérins lie in the enjoyment of the outing both at sea and on the islands themselves, in the fine panorama of the coast from Cap Roux to Cap d'Antibes and in the visits to the fortress on Ste-Marguerite and the keep of the old fortified monastery on St-Honorat.

▶**Orient Yourself:** The islands can be reached by Cannes (see Address Book) or Juan-les-Pins (see JUAN-LES-PINS), or on your own boat (just drop anchor in one of the coves). *Palais des Festivals, 1 Boulevard de la Croisette, Cannes, ☎ 04 93 39 24 53 - Annex GARE SNCF, Cannes, ☎ 04 93 99 19 77. www.cannes-on-line.com.*

A Bit of History

The Island in Antiquity

The Îles de Lérins were mentioned by the ancient historians. The Île Ste-Marguerite was called **Lero**, a name, according to Strabo, which commemorates a Ligurian hero to whom a temple was dedicated. Pliny, on the other hand, talks of a Roman port and town.

Recent excavations near Fort Royal have uncovered a number of houses, wall paintings, mosaics and ceramics dating from between the 3C BC and 1C AD. Various wrecks and port substructures found to the west of the island prove that Roman ships stopped at Lero.

Visiting the Islands

ÎLE STE-MARGUERITE★★ *2hr*

The higher and the larger of the two islands, Ste-Marguerite, is separated from the mainland by a shallow channel 1 100m/1 200yd wide. The island, which lies east-west and is 3km/2mi long and 900m/1 000yd wide, belongs to the State except for the Domaine du Grand Jardin in the south. Pleasant walks have been laid out in the pine and eucalyptus woods.

Botanical Nature Trail

Guided tours year-round of the island's flora, fauna and natural heritage. For details contact the Office National des Forêts, ☎ 04 93 43 49 24.

Many broad paths flanked by explanatory panels on Mediterranean flora cut through the forest to provide charming **walks**. Starting from the landing, follow the marked trail around the side of the fort. Then join the Eucalyptus Walk, which leads to the

---

The Riddle of the "Iron Mask"

In 1687 the fortress of Ste-Marguerite, a state prison, received the famous "Man in the Iron Mask", a character who, according to Voltaire, wore a mask with a chinpiece which had steel springs. His identity has never been established with certainty. He is said to have been an illegitimate brother of Louis XIV, a secretary of the Duke of Mantua who had tricked the "Sun King", a black sheep of the nobility, an accomplice of Madame La Brinvilliers the poisoner, etc.

According to another version, Anne of Austria's doctor, having performed an autopsy on Louis XIII, expressed misgivings about the king's ability to father a child. His son-in-law, who inherited the papers, is said to have let out this state secret and he, therefore, may have been the prisoner on Ste-Marguerite.

An even more interesting theory maintains that a lady companion to the Man in the Iron Mask gave birth to a son who was immediately taken away to Corsica. Entrusted (*remis de bonne part* in French – *di buona parte* in Italian) to reliable foster parents, this nameless child is said to have been called "Buonaparte" and to have been the great-grandfather of Napoleon.

The most recent theory is that the man was a black page given to Queen Maria Theresa by the Duke of Beaufort in 1661. The Queen allegedly had an affair with her page and gave birth to a daughter, Marie-Anne, who, like Sister Louis-Marie-Thérèse, became a nun in 1695, better known as the "Moresse de Moret".

M de Saint-Mars, charged with guarding the Man in the Iron Mask and bored to tears on Ste-Marguerite, managed to obtain the post of Governor of the Bastille in 1698. His prisoner went with him and died there in 1703.

Brotherly Love

When Honorat founded his monastery, women were banned from the island. His sister Marguerite wanted to stay close to him, so she set up a convent on the neighbouring island...but didn't ban men from visits so her brother could come see her regularly!

At the end of the 4C, St Honoratus settled on Lerina, the smaller of the two islands. Resigned to not living as a solitary, the saint founded a monastery which was to become one of the most famous and powerful in all Christendom. Pilgrims came in crowds to walk round the island barefoot – a Pope on a visit followed this ancient tradition in all humility. Many of the faithful from France and Italy were buried in the monastery. In 660 St Aigulf founded the Benedictine Order in the monastery.

Raids by Saracens and Genoese pirates, government by commendation, attacks by the Spaniards and the arrival of military garrisons were not favourable to monastic life so that by 1788 only four monks remained and the monastery was closed. During the Revolution it was confiscated and sold.

In 1859 the monastery once more became a place of worship and in 1869 it was taken over by Cistercians from Sénanque Abbey.

Domaine du Grand Jardin, cutting across the length of the island. The Allée Ste-Marguerite returns to the landing.

The cliffs are fairly steep making it difficult to reach the shore, but there is a path that skirts the edge of the entire island *(about 2hr walk)*.

Fort Royal

Open 10.30am-1.15pm, 2.15-4.45pm (Apr-Sep until 5.45pm). Closed Mon, Jan and public holidays. 3€ (free first Sun of the month). ☎ 04 93 38 55 26.

The fortress was built by Richelieu and reinforced by Vauban in 1712. Its main entrance on the west side is monumental. A small **aquarium** *(left)* contains Mediterranean specimens.

In the building beyond, Maréchal Bazaine was imprisoned from 1873 until August 1874 – when he escaped to Spain (official reports do not reveal how). From the terrace there is an extensive **view**★ of the nearby coast.

Pass behind Bazaine's quarters to reach the prisons and old castle; the latter currently houses a Marine Museum (Musée de la Mer).

Prisons

The entrance hall gives access to the museum *(right)* and the prisons *(left)*. Until the 19C the corridor leading to the cells used to open directly onto the courtyard.

On the right is the cell of the Man in the Iron Mask. The cells opposite were occupied by six Protestant pastors imprisoned after the Revocation of the Edict of Nantes (1685). There is now a Huguenot memorial with documents on the Protestants, the Wars of Religion, the Edict of Nantes and its Revocation.

Musée de la Mer

The castle's ground floor was built onto the original Roman vaulted rooms. The Marine Museum exhibits archeological finds excavated in the fort and offshore (1C BC Roman galley, 10C Saracen ship). There is an attractive display of artefacts salvaged from wrecked ships: a fine collection of Roman amphorae, glass and ceramics and Arab ceramics with elaborate decorative motifs. Other rooms are devoted to pleasure boating and regattas.

ÎLE ST-HONORAT★★

St-Honorat (1.5km/1mi long by 400m/437yd wide) has a less hospitable coastline than Ste-Marguerite, from which it is separated by a narrow strait known as the Plateau du Milieu. The island is the private property of the monastery but walking and bathing are permitted.

Some of the land is cultivated by the monks, who make a liqueur called Lérina, but the rest is covered by a fine forest of umbrella and sea pines, eucalyptus and a few cypress trees.

Island Tour★★ *2hr*

Starting from the landing, an attractive shaded path follows the coastline. Occasionally veering inland, it offers many different views of the island, its cultivated fields and forest paths, as well as Île Ste-Marguerite and the mainland.

Address Book

EATING OUT

▣▣ **L'Escale** – *Ste-Marguerite (Island)* – ☎ *04 93 43 49 25* – ◷ *Closed Dec and evenings Sep-Jun.* Cannes Bay, Cap d'Antibes and the Alpine range in the distance are the views glimpsed from this enchanting restaurant and its long terrace running alongside the beach. Choose between the buffet and seafood platter.

CISTERCIAN SOUVENIRS

Boutique de l'Abbaye de Lérins – *Île St-Honorat* – ☎ *04 92 99 54 00* – *www. abbayedelerins.com* – ◷ *Daily 10.10am-12.15pm, 2-5pm* – ◷ *Closed 8 Nov-8 Dec.* This shop attached to the Cistercian abbey sells wine, honey, lavandin (🕯 *see below*) and the famous liquor Lérina, whose ingredients include 45 different aromatic herbs.

TRANSPORT

To the Île Ste-Marguerite – *Compagnie Esterel Chanteclair* – ☎ *04 93 39 11 82* – ▣ *10€ (kids 5-10 years, 5€).* Regular shuttle service leaving from Cannes (Quai des Îles). Other excursions possible.

To the Île St-Honorat – *Société Planaria* – ☎ *04 92 98 71 38* – ▣ *9€ round trip (child 5€).* Shuttle service leaving from Cannes (Quai des Îles) every hour 8am-noon, 2-4.30pm *(6pm May-Sep).*

ON THE ISLANDS

On the Île Ste-Marguerite – No hotels, only restaurants and cafés. Visitors will find many watering places on the island but in high season they are nonetheless advised to bring food and water supplies with them for the day.

On the Île St-Honorat – The whole island is occupied by a Cistercian monastery and does therefore not have any restaurants *(sale of sandwiches at the landing between April and October).* There are few watering points but it may be rationed in summer. Bicycles are forbidden on the island. Tourists are expected to dress appropriately.

Ancien Monastère Fortifié★

◷ *Open Jul to mid-Sep 10.30am-12.30pm, 2.30-5pm, Sun 2.30-5pm; mid-Sep to end of Jun 9am-5pm.* ◷ *Closed Tue in Jul-Aug.* ▣ *2.50€ (free off-season).* ☎ *04 92 99 54 00. www.abbayedelerins.com.*

The remarkable high "keep" or "castle" of this old fortified monastery is set on a spit of land projecting into the sea from the southern coastline. It was built in 1073 by Aldebert, Abbot of Lérins, on Roman foundations, to protect the monks from Saracen pirates.

The gate is over 4m/13ft above ground level and access to it was by a ladder which has now been replaced by a stone stairway. Facing the entrance, a staircase leads to a barrel-vaulted storeroom. On the left, a few steps lead up to the first floor.

The **cloisters** with pointed arches and the 14C and 17C vaulting (one of the columns is a Roman milestone) enclose a square courtyard covering a rainwater tank paved with marble. The upper gallery, with small columns of white marble, goes to the chapel of the Ste-Croix (Holy Cross), a high room with Gothic arches still called the "Holy of Holies" owing to the many relics it contained.

From the platform with its 15C battlements and crenellations at the top of the old keep, the **view**★★ extends over the Îles de Lérins and the coastline from the Esterel to Cap d'Antibes, with the often snow-capped peaks of the Alps in the far distance.

Monastère Moderne

Only the church is open to the public. ◷ *Open daily 8.45-11.15am, 2-5.30pm, Sun 8.45-9.40am, 11.30am-12.25pm, 3-5.30pm.* ▣ *Free entry.* ☎ *04 92 99 54 00. www.abbaye-delerins.com.*

The early buildings occupied by the monks, parts of which date from the 11C and 12C, have been incorporated into the "new" 19C monastery.

The abbey **church** was built in the 19C in the neo-Romanesque style. In the north transept is an 11C Chapel of the Dead.

Seven **chapels** scattered about the island completed the monastery; they were intended for anchorites, monks who prayed in the privacy of their retreat. Two have retained their former appearance.

Tumbleweeds?

The balls of fibre which roll on the beaches and catch on the vegetation of the dunes are in fact the dry remains of posidonia. This marine plant forms "meadows" on the seabed and is an essential producer of oxygen.

La Trinité

Situated at the eastern tip of the island, it pre-dates the 11C. It is built on a trefoil plan with an oval cupola resting on pendentives. The Byzantine influence leads some experts to date it around the 5C.

St-Sauveur

The chapel located in the northwest corner of the island is as old as La Trinité but built to an octagonal plan. It was restored in the 17C and once again more recently.

LEVENS

POPULATION 3 700

MICHELIN MAP 341 E4

LOCAL MAP SEE NICE

Perched at an altitude of 600m/1 968ft, the medieval village streets of Levens are a pleasant place to stroll amongst the ancient houses and murmuring fountains.

▶ **Orient Yourself**: Levens is in the Alpes-Maritimes region, 19km/12mi north of Nice on the D 19. At the summit of the village, you'll find an open swimming pool! ▣ *3, Placette Paul-Olivier,* ☎ *04 93 79 71 00.*

🅿 To park, follow Levens-Centre, bearing left as you climb the hill, until you reach the municipal parking *(three levels)*. A staircase then leads to the center of town.

> ### Celebrating Liberty
>
> In 1621, the people of Levens were tired of paying taxes to their feudal Lord Grimaldi and destroyed the chateau. Ever since, on the Festival of St-Antonin, everyone in he village jumps off a symbolic stone in the Place de la Liberté to celebrate their escape from tyranny.

The Old Village

Place de la République opens onto an attractive public garden, its shaded terraces overlooking the valley, and the curved façade of the Baroque Chapelle des Pénitents-Blancs. In Rue du Docteur-Faraud, the Chapelle des Pénitents-Noirs presents a fine collection of works of art, many of which are displayed in the crypt.

▶ *Go up Rue Masséna.*

In Rue Masséna stands the house, dated 1722, of the Masséna family. At the end of the street, you walk past the surviving ramparts and the **Maison du Portal** (🕐 *Jul-Sep 10am-noon, 2.30-6.30pm; rest of the year open weekends 2.30-5.30pm.* ⊛ *Free entry.* ☎ *04 93 79 85 84),* which houses the sculptures of Jean-Pierre Augier and temporary exhibitions.

At the Place de la Liberté a vaulted passageway leads to the church, which was been heavily restored both inside and outside.

▶ *Take the path on the left and climb up towards the swimming pool.*

The **view**★ extends over the Var and the Vésubie, taking in the setting of high mountains from the Cheiron to Le Mercantour.

Outings

Duranus *8.5km/5mi – allow 30min.*

▶ *From Levens take D 19 north.*

The road overlooks the deep Gorges de la Vésubie (👣 *see Vallée de la VÉSUBIE)* from a great height, and affords a glimpse of the chapel of Madone d'Utelle *(left)* high up in the mountains.

Duranus, a pretty village set in the midst of orchards and vineyards, was founded in 17C by the people of Rocca-Sparviero, a ruined village at Col St-Michel.

> ### LOCAL SPECIALITIES
>
> ⊜⊜ **Les Santons** – *Levens Village –* ☎ *04 93 79 72 47 –* 🕐 *Closed 3 Jan-9 Feb, 25 Jun-4 Jul, 1-10 Oct, Wed and evenings except Sat – Reservation required.* Stop for a break on this pretty terrace in a restaurant ideally located in a perched village overlooking the Vésubie Gorges. The owner will be happy to introduce you to the gastronomic subtleties of local cuisine at reasonable prices.

Saut des Français★★

At the northern end of Duranus is Frenchmen's Leap, marked by a viewpoint. It commemorates Republican soldiers who were hurled over the edge in 1793 by bands of guerillas from the Vésubie Valley. The view is almost lost in the dizzy vertical drop to the bottom of the gorges with Utelle and its chapel dominating the scene.

LORGUES

POPULATION 7 319

MICHELIN MAP 340 N5

Lorgues is a small medieval town with a beautiful market square, graced with splendid plane trees originally planted in 1835. Beyond the village are wooded hilltops, where the ground is well suited to the cultivation of vines and olives. Oil, both from olives and grape seeds, is a local speciality.

▸ **Orient Yourself:** Lorgues is 13km/8mi southwest of Draguignan (⟨ *see DRAGUIGNAN*) on the D 557 and D 562. At the centre is the medieval city, which stretches along the main shopping street. The area to the south, around the collégiale, was built between the Renaissance and Revolution, and the more modern, 20C buildings lie to the west. ⓘ *Place d'Antrechaux,* ☎ *04 94 73 92 37.*

The Old Quarter

A Touch of Medieval Charm
The Tourism Office provides maps of the village walking tour.

The streets of the town, which radiate from a central square, are dotted with charming fountains and fortified 12C gateways. A stroll along any of them reveals many interesting old houses with their attractive façades, lintels, wrought-iron work and stairways.

Address Book

For coin ranges see the Legend at the back of this guide.

EATING OUT

⊖ **Sucrés-Salés** – *7 Avenue Allongue* – ☎ *04 94 67 63 80* – ⓒ *Closed Sun dinner and Mon* – ⌹ . Beyond the curious façade decorated with children's drawings lies a treasure trove of delicacies, both sweet and savoury. The owner is renowned for his delicious homemade chocolate (not in summer), honey and jam, along with olive oil, foie gras and rillettes available for sale. Besides the shop, there is also a small delicatessen where gastronomic specialities can be relished in the dining room or on the tiny terrace.

⊖⊖ **Le Chrissandier** – *18 Cours de la République* – ☎ *04 94 67 67 15* – ⓒ *Closed Tue dinner and Wed.* Nestled in the old medieval quarter, this recently decorated rustic-style restaurant attracts a regular clientele at lunchtime and caters for tourists in the evening. The menu changes every day as it is dictated by the availability of fresh market produce.

WHERE TO STAY

⊖ **Les Pins** – 🏨 - *3630 Route de St-Antonin* - ☎ *04 94 73 91 97* – ⓒ *Closed 15 Nov-15 Mar* - ⌹ *(at dinner) - 5 rooms – Restaurant (⊖⊖).* This grand villa under the pines is surrounded by vineyards. Three suites with a terrace next to the pool are in the annex. Two other rooms, in the main building, are decorated in the same Provençal style. Children get special attention.

SHOPPING

Marché – Tuesdays.

Wine – A dozen vineyards can be found around Lorgues, many offering tastings and direct sales of their Côtes-de-Provence and Vins de Pays du Var and d'Argens. Ask at the Tourism Office for a list.

Domaine de l'Estello – *Route de Carcès* – ☎ *04 94 73 22 22* – *www.lestello.com* – ⓒ *Open Mon-Sat 9am-12.30pm, 2-6pm (Sun in summer).* This small domaine, restarted in 1991 after years of abandonment, has won many national and European awards for its Côtes-de-Provence wines.

RIDING CLUBS

Appaloosa Ranch – *28 Hameau de Chateaurenard* – ☎ *04 94 73 74 92.* Pony-trekking and horseback riding.

Collégiale St-Martin

The 18C church was built by Bishop Fleury of Fréjus, who later became a cardinal and a minister to Louis XV. It is unusually large with a dressed stone façade. The high altar in multicoloured marble is decorated with angels' heads. The **Virgin and Child** is attributed to Pierre Puget. The church features a fine organ and a carved pulpit.

Excursions

Ermitage de St-Ferréol

▶ *1km/0.6mi. Follow the signs to the northeast of the town.*

The chapel stands on a low wooded hill with the traces of a Roman settlement.

Chapelle Notre-Dame-de-Benva

▶ *3km/2mi northwest (D 50) on the Entrecasteaux road.*
🕓 *Guided tours on request. Ask at the Tourism Office.* ☎ *04 94 73 92 37.*

The chapel of Our Lady of Benva (corruption of the Provençal *ben vai* "good journey") stands on a hillside. Its porch is built astride the old Entrecasteaux road so that passers-by will notice it. Both the porch and the interior are decorated with 15C frescoes in the Naïve tradition.

Monastère Orthodoxe St-Michel

▶ *8km/5mi north by D 10 or 10km/6mi by D 77.*
🕓 *Guided tours 9.30-11am, 2.30-5.30pm; Sun 2.30-5.30pm.* ☎ *04 94 73 75 75 or 04 94 67 64 64.*

These stone buildings of Byzantine inspiration were once home to an Orthodox community founded under the authority of the Patriarch of Antioch. The crypt, refectory and church are adorned with frescoes in the Romanesque and Byzantine styles. The only part open to the public is the wooden chapel, a miniature replica of Souzdal Cathedral in Russia.

Taradeau

▶ *9km/6mi – southeast on D 10.*

A "Saracen" tower and a ruined Romanesque chapel crown the bluff dominating the village of Tardeau, which produces reputable wines.

▶ *Take D 73 north uphill.*

Turn right into a stony path marked "Table d'Orientation 800m" *(viewing table)* and park the car. From the top there is a vast **panorama**★ over Lorgues, Les Arcs, the Provençal tableland and the Grasse Pre-Alps, the Esterel and the Maures.

Abbaye du Thoronet ★★

▶ *13km/8mi southwest. From Lorgues take D 562 towards Carcès. Bear left onto D 17 and turn right onto D 79.*

👣 *see Abbaye du THORONET.*

Vallée du **LOUP**★★

MICHELIN MAP 341 C/D5/6

The Loup begins at an altitude of 1 300m/4 250ft in the Pre-Alps of Grasse (north face of the Audibergue Mountain). For almost all of its short journey to the Mediterranean, the river has cut a valley gorge through the mountains, creating one of the most beautiful natural sights of Haute-Provence. The roads leading up to the gorges pass through a picturesque region where there are many perched villages.

▶ **Orient Yourself:** In following the Loup, you'll pass through countryside dominated by orchards of olive, then citrus trees, and finally even snow-capped peaks. These driving tours, starting from Vence (👣 *see VENCE*), lead you through both the high and low valleys of the scenic river.

Driving Tours

GORGES DU LOUP ★★ *56km/35mi – about 1 day leaving from Vence.*

Address Book

WHERE TO STAY

Auberge de Courmes – *3 Rue des Platanes – Courmes –* ☎ *04 93 77 64 70 –* 🕐 *Closed 5-29 Jan, Sun evening and Mon – 5 rooms – 🛏 – Restaurant (😋😋). This local inn on the square of a tiny hamlet dominating the Loup Gorges offers five small rooms and a welcoming dining area. Outstanding views of the mountains, facilities for hiking and rambling and a peaceful atmosphere will guarantee a most enjoyable stay.*

Chambre d'Hôte La Cascade – *635 Chemin de la Cascade – Courmes –* ☎ *04 93 09 65 85 – lacascade@wanadoo.fr – 6 rooms*

– Meal (😋). The sign marking this guest house illustrates the nearby waterfall of Courmes. The original building, now enlarged and restored, has six tidy rooms. Particularly suitable for nature lovers and overworked city executives.

SHOPPING

Confiserie des Gorges du Loup (Florian) – *Pont-du-Loup –* 🕐 *Guided visit of the candy manufacturing 9am-noon, 2-6.30pm.* Candied fruits, citrus jams, sugared flowers and preserves made with rose, jasmine, violet and chocolate, all made on-site.

Vence★ 👓 *See VENCE.*

▶ *From Vence take D 2210 northwest; after 2km/1.2mi bear right onto a road signposted "Galerie Beaubourg–Château-Notre-Dame-des-Fleurs".*

Château Notre-Dame-des-Fleurs 👓 *See VENCE: Excursions.*

The road is bordered by pleasant houses nestled among the olive trees. There is a view back over the hills towards Vence.

Tourrettes-sur-Loup★ 👓 *See TOURRETTES-SUR-LOUP.*

The road loops round the attractive village of Tourrettes-sur-Loup before passing the limestone fissures of the Loup Valley. The perched village of Bar-sur-Loup ★ (👓 *see BAR-SUR-LOUP*) comes into sight, followed by the tiny hamlet of Gourdon clinging to its promontory.

Pont-du-Loup

The Draguignan-Nice railway line, which crossed the entrance to the Gorges du Loup, was blown up by the Germans in 1944; the viaduct ruins are still visible.
The area has a good reputation for the fruit jellies *(pâte de fruits)* and delicately scented jams (roses, violets) it produces.

▶ *Outside the village turn right onto D 6.*

The road runs through the splendid **Gorges du Loup**★★, cut vertically through the Grasse mountains, with huge, gaping holes, smooth and round, hollowed out of their sides. Just before the second tunnel, in a semicircular hollow, the **Cascade de Courmes**★ spills down onto a mossy bed (40m/130ft).

▶ *Park your car at the exit of the third tunnel.*

Saut du Loup

🕐 *Open Jun-Sep, 9.30am-7.30pm.* 💰 *0.50€.* ☎ *04 93 09 68 88.*

Amid lush vegetation, a huge megalith marks the entrance to the Saut du Loup, an enormous cauldron shaped by marine and glacial erosion in the Tertiary and Quaternary eras, in which the waters of the Loup swirl furiously in spring. The waterfall known as **Cascades des Demoiselles** gushes down through a strange setting of mosses and vegetation petrified by the spray, which has a high lime carbonate content.

▶ *Just before the bridge, Pont de Bramafan, turn sharp left onto D 3.*

As the road rises to Caussols Plateau, the vegetation grows sparser but as far as Gourdon there are continual **views**★ down into the depths of the gorges with a particularly breathtaking **view**★★

The gorges of the Vallée des Loups

B. Kaufmann/ MICHELIN

where an overhang has been built out from a sharp right-hand turn *(signposted)*. Beyond the end of the gorges the view widens out southwards towards the coast.

Gourdon★ 👣 *see GOURDON.*

Interesting drive downhill from Caussols plateau along D 3.

▶ *In Le-Pré-du-Lac turn left onto D 2085.*

St-Pons

The small village lies on a slope where olives, vines and jasmine grow.

▶ *After Le Collet bear left onto D 7*

Drive down a wooded valley which becomes more and more enclosed until it joins the lower Loup Valley, where there is a good **view** of the river and of the precipitous Pre-Alps of Grasse in the background.

After a *corniche* section (cut into the rock face with good views), the road descends to the valley floor to cross the river.

La Colle-sur-Loup

The name comes from the Latin word *collis*, meaning hill or mound. A picturesque village in the plain where fruit and flowers are cultivated. The main street features a series of antique shops selling typical Provençal furniture. The church has a Renaissance door and a square bell-tower.

St-Paul-de-Vence★★ 👣 *see ST-PAUL.*

Beyond St-Paul the **view** extends to the foothills of the Pre-Alps of Grasse.

▶ *Return to Vence by D 2 and D 236.*

HAUTE VALLÉE DU LOUP *47km/29mi – about 1hr 30min leaving from Vence.*

▶ *Leave Vence by D 2 going northwest.*

The road descends a green valley and from the Pont de Bramafan, the D 3 suddenly emerges into the **upper Loup Valley★**, a beautiful stretch of country with superb views both before and after Gréolières.

Gréolières

This is a perched village at the southern foot of Mont Cheiron; to the north are the extensive ruins of Haut-Gréolières. To the south are the remains of an important stronghold.

The **church**, which has only one aisle, has a Romanesque façade and a squat bell-tower. On the left (on entering) stands a 15C silver-gilt processional cross and a fragment of a 16C retable of John the Baptist. Opposite stands a 14C wooden statue of the Virgin and Child. The finest work (high on the right) is the **retable of St Stephen ★** by an unknown artist with Christ and his Apostles on the predella (15C).

West of Gréolières the road climbs above the village and then snakes westward along the side of the gorge passing in and out of brief tunnels and beneath huge rock spurs of fantastic shapes and sizes. More than 400m/1 312ft below flows the River Loup.

Clue de Gréolières★

The rift was formed by a tributary of the Loup, its bare slopes pitted with giant holes and spiked with curious dolomitic rocks.

The road emerges from the rift onto a broad alluvial plateau, Plan-du-Peyron.

▶ *In Plan-du-Peyron turn right onto D 802.*

As the road climbs the south face of Mont Cheiron, there are interesting **views** to the west and north.

Gréolières-les-Neiges

Alt 1 450m/4 757ft

🄸 *Ski-lift, ☎ 04 93 59 70 02.*

The resort, which lies on the north face of Mont Cheiron, is the most southerly of the Alpine ski stations. It is well equipped (14 lifts, 25 runs, 30km/19mi of cross-country trails), easily accessible and attracts large crowds of local skiers.

▶ *Drive back via Col de Vence (👣 see VENCE: Excursions) or via the Gorges du Loup.*

Le **LUC**

POPULATION 7 282

MICHELIN MAP 340 M5

LOCAL MAP SEE MASSIF DES MAURES

Old Luc seems almost like a film set of an old Provençal village, with its romantic scruffiness, mossy fountains, impossibly narrow streets, uneven cobblestones and a cat sleeping in the sun of a flowered courtyard. Despite its sleepy atmosphere, Le Luc is an important farming center, serving as the collection point for the regional harvests of grapes and olives in the Var plain.

▶ **Orient Yourself:** Le Luc serves as an important Var crossroads, lying between the A 8 (the viaduct is high above the village) and the RN 7, and between Brignoles and Draguignan. *Château des Vintimille, Place de la Liberté,* ☎ *04 94 60 74 51.*

E. Baret/ MICHELIN

The Old Village

An Imposing Belfry

Le Luc lies in the shade of a 16C hexagonal bell tower (27m/89ft high) built in the style of Italian campaniles. An identification table on the main buildings provides a detailed description of the village.

View from the Oppidum de Fouirette

🚶 *1.5hr round-trip on foot. Walk towards the Vergeiras district, then follow a signposted path.*

From the top of the hill (300m/984ft high) is a wonderful **view**⋆ over the Maures plain, from Gonfaron to Rocher de Roquebrune.

Campaniles in the Var

Les Arcs	Clock Tower (18C)
Aups	Clock Tower
Carcès	Campanile atop a fortified gate (18C)
Carnoules	Belfry (17C)
Cotignac	Campanile (16C)
Draguignan	Tower (17C)
Flassans	Atop the belfry (18C)
Le Luc	Tower (16C)
St-Tropez	Campanile (19C)
Salernes	Belfry (18C)
Tavernes	Campanile (18C)
Toulon	Arsenal tower (18C)

Sights

Musée Historique du Centre-Var

♿ ◷ *Open 2-5pm (mid-Jul to mid-Sep 3-6pm).* ◷ *Closed Sun and public holidays.* Free entry. ☎ 04 94 60 70 12.

This museum about local history is housed in the 17C Chapelle Ste-Anne and displays collections of historical artefacts uncovered during excavations carried out in the area: fossils (dinosaur eggs), a carved Roman sarcophagus, medieval sculptures, minerals from the Maures Massif and ancient weapons. There is also a historical display on Le Luc and the life of the local marine engineer Jean-Baptiste Lebas (1797-1873), who was in charge of transporting the famous obelisk from Luxor to the Place de la Concorde in Paris.

Musée Régional du Timbre

♿ ◷ *Open Jul-Aug (except Mon and Tue) 2.30-6pm, Fri-Sun 10am-noon, 2.30-6pm (Oct-May 5.30pm).* ◷ *Closed Sep, 1 Jan, 1 May, 25 Dec* 1.5€. ☎ 04 94 47 96 16. www. lemuseedutimbre.com.

This regional museum devoted to the history of postage stamps and philately is housed in the Château de Vintimille, a striking 18C building. The clear and spacious display follows the different stages in the traditional (that is using copper-plate engraving) manufacture of postage stamps. A reconstruction of the studio of Albert Decaris, the designer and engraver of many stamps, both French and foreign, provides a fitting backdrop for these processes. Numerous examples of philatelic counterfeiting and non-French stamps round off the exhibition. A wide range of literature (documentation) on philately is available for visitors to consult.

LUCÉRAM★

POPULATION 1 035

MICHELIN MAP 341 F4

LOCAL MAP SEE NICE

Some 27km/16mi northeast from Nice, the pretty village of Lucéram, with its three ancient belltowers and colorful roof tiles, sits on a steep rock between two ravines in a wooded region beneath the mountain peak of Cime du Gros Braus. The town not only boasts a remarkable **setting**★★ but is exceptionally rich in works of religious art. ⬚ *Maison de Pays de Lucéram et du Haut-Paillon, Place Adrien-Barralis, ☎ 04 93 91 60 50.*

🅿 Parking is available at the two ends of the village. Coming from Nice, they're on the left after the fire department, or farther down on the right, just before the post office. Coming from Peïra-Cava, parking can be found on the right near the first intersection inside the village.

> **Noël des Bergers★**
>
> Each year shepherds from the neighbouring mountains make their offering of lambs and fruit to the church to the strains of fife and tambourine music.

Visit

Medieval Village★

▶ *On Place Adrien-Barralis, follow the arrows pointing to the church (église).*

A maze of stepped streets and vaulted alleyways make up the medieval town. Note the Ionic columns framing a 14C doorway to the right and the many Gothic houses all along the route. From the church terrace one can look down over Lucéram, its tower and crenellated walls, and beyond the hills behind Nice to the sea.

Église Ste-Marguerite

🕓 *Open daily (except Mon) 11am-noon, 2-6pm. For guided tours contact the Centre d'Interprétation du Patrimoine (Tourism Office) at ☎ 04 93 91 60 50.*

The interior of the simple 15C church was remodelled in the 18C with elaborate plasterwork.

The **altarpieces**★★ form the most complete group attributed to the Nice School and they are among the best presented in the County of Nice. In the south transept is the remarkable **altarpiece of St Antony** framed in Flamboyant Gothic panelling with decorative motifs.

Behind the high altar, the outstanding **altarpiece of Ste Margaret,** which is divided into 10 panels, is by Louis Bréa: around the central figure are Mary Magdalene *(bottom left)* and St Michael *(top left)*. Three fine altarpieces by the Bréa School are placed in the nave.

B. Kaufmann/ MICHELIN

Lucéram

The **treasury**★ comprises some remarkable pieces: a silver statuette of Ste Margaret (1500), a finely engraved 14C reliquary, a statue-reliquary of Ste Rosalie from Sicily, two candlesticks and an alabaster Virgin (16C).

Additional Works

On the left of the entrance stands an unusual Baroque Pietà in painted wood and to the left of the chancel another one in plaster on cloth dating from the 13C. Old processional lanterns in wrought iron are displayed.

▶ *When leaving, go down the stairs on the right and follow the Montée du Terron to the ramparts to see an ancient tower overlooking the valley.*

Chapels

Chapelle St-Grat

▶ *1km/0.6mi to the south on D 2566, on the left at the exit of the village, before the tunnel. Follow the path down on foot. If locked call ☎ 04 93 79 46 50.*

This chapel is decorated with frescoes attributed to Jean Baleison. Parts of the vaults show the four Evangelists writing. Beneath a triple Gothic canopy are the Virgin and Child who is holding a dove, St Grat bearing the head of John the Baptist and St Sebastian in elegant attire with an arrow in his hand.

Chapelle Notre-Dame-de-Bon-Cœur

▶ *2km/1.3mi northwest on D 2566, park on the left near a ruined house, then 15min on foot there and back. If locked call ☎ 04 93 79 46 50.*

The frescoes, attributed to Baleison, are interesting despite some unfortunate repainting. In the porch are *Good and Bad Prayer* and the martyred St Sebastian. In the chapel is the *Adoration of the Shepherds*, the *Adoration of the Magi* and scenes illustrating the life of the Virgin.

MANDELIEU-LA-NAPOULE ⚓

MICHELIN MAP 341 C6

LOCAL MAP SEE MASSIF DE L'ESTEREL

In the Middle Ages, Mandelieu was a small fishing harbour called Epulia, but today it is famed throughout the region for its lovely mimosa trees. The pretty bay and the River Siagne, bordered by lush plains and beaches further downstream, make this town a highly popular resort, both in summer and winter.

▶ **Orient Yourself:** Lying at the foot of the Esterel and Tanneron Massifs, Mandelieu extends right to the shores of the Mediterranean 8km/5mi west of Cannes on the N 98. 🈳 *340 Rue Jean-Monnet, ☎ 04 992 97 99 27. www.ot-mandelieu.fr.*

🅿 **Parking:** There are several free parking areas near the casino and along the coastline in La Napoule. .

The Seaside

Three heavenly beaches run along the bay, offering impressive views of the area. *(Victoria and Sweet are private beaches.)* The Port La Napoule can accommodate 1 140 pleasure craft, while the smaller Port de la Rague has 688 moorings. A coastal path (🈳 *1km/0.6mi*) connects the two.

Panoramic Tour

▶ *Leave from the post office by Rue des Hautes-Roches, then 45min on foot there and back along a signposted route.*

Address Book

For coin ranges see the Legend at the back of this guide.

EATING OUT

🍽️🍽️ **Le Marco Polo** – *Avenue de Lérins - Théoule-sur-Mer - 8km/5mi from Cannes towards St-Raphaël -* ☎ *04 93 49 96 59 -* 🕐 *Closed mid-Nov to mid-Dec.* Casual restaurant ideally situated on the beach, with rattan furniture and a terrace overlooking the Bay of Cannes. Salads at lunch and more hearty menus at dinner.

🍽️🍽️ **L'Armorial** – *Port La Napoule -* ☎ *06 18 46 73 73 - maryse.bottero@wanadoo.fr.* The pretty dining room has wicker furnishings and green plants for a cosy atmosphere. Regional dishes focus on the delights of the sea: bouillabaisse, bourride, grilled bass in sea salt, roasted farm pigeon with figs and dried tomatos, etc.

WHERE TO STAY

🛏️🛏️ **Corniche d'Or** – *Place de la Fontaine – La Napoule –* ☎ *04 93 49 92 51 – info@ cornichedor.com –* 🕐 *Closed 29 Nov-16 Dec – 12 rooms –* 🍴. On a tiny square near the station, this modest hotel has simple rooms, recently redecorated. Many have a small balcony, and two have a large terrace.

🛏️🛏️ **Hôtel Villa Parisiana** – *Rue Argentière –* ☎ *04 93 49 93 02 – villa. parisiana@wanadoo.fr –* 🕐 *Closed 19-27 Dec – 13 rooms –* 🍴. This Edwardian villa located in a residential area houses a congenial, family-style hotel with a treillised terrace, which makes for a pleasant stay despite the proximity of the noisy railway.

CASINO

Sofitel Royal Casino – *605 Avenue du Général-de-Gaulle –* ☎ *04 92 97 70 00 – rwww.sofitel.com –* 🕐 *Bar Blue-wave: 9am-2am. Piano bar: 7.30pm-10.30pm. Bar dancing: weekends 10.30pm-3am.* Luxury establishment with a terrace and pool overlooking Cannes Bay features a casino, two restaurants, a newly opened nightclub and a piano bar with live musical performances every evening.

SPORT AND LEISURE

Golf Club de Cannes Mandelieu – *Route du Golf.* ☎ *04 92 97 32 00.* This golf course founded by the Grand Duke of Russia in 1891 is one of the oldest in France. Located at the heart of town, its design is similar to that of St-Andrews, the prestigious golf course in Scotland.

Guy Durante Organisation – *Avenue du Général-de-Gaulle-Plage de Robinson –* ☎ *04 93 49 44 19 ou 06 80 64 03 50 - www. a-m-skinautique.com –* 🕐 *Open daily Mid-May to mid-Oct.* This is the landing used for water sports such as wake-board, waterskiing and parascending.

Sant'Estello Country Club – *3300 Avenue Paul-Ricard –* ☎ *04 93 49 44 00 –* 🕐 *8am-noon, 2-8pm (from 3-8pm Jul-Aug).* This tennis club set up on the handsome Sant'Estello estate is comprised of 10 courts, including four clay courts, which remain open all year round.

Domaine de Barbossi – 🧒 *3300 Avenue Paul-Ricard, San Estello –* ☎ *04 93 49 64 74 –* 🕐 *School holidays daily 10am-noon, 2-8.30pm; rest of the year Wed, Sat, Sun 10am-noon and 1.30pm-7pm.* A perfect outing for the whole family. Besides the tennis club, there are facilities for mountain biking, trampoline, miniature golf, pony rides, and several playing areas for children. Red and rosé wines, produced and bottled on the estate, are available for sale.

MARKETS

Mandelieu – Place du Mail, Wednesday and Friday mornings.

La Napoule – Place St-Fainéant Thursday morning, and Place Jeanne-d'Arc on Saturday morning.

CALENDAR

La Fête du Mimosa – Beginning of February. Ten-day festival and parade celebrating the mimosa blossoms.

🚶 This pleasant walk winding its way up Colline de San Peyré affords fantastic views ★ over the Tanneron, La Napoule Bay, Cannes and Cap d'Antibes (*orientatation table*).

Along the Siagne

🚶 A trail follows the River Siagne from the centre of Mandelieu (*behind the Salle Olympie*) all the way to the sea.

Sight

Château-Musée

In La Napoule. 🕐 *Guided tours (45min) Feb-Oct 10am-6pm; Nov-Jan 2-5pm, weekends and holidays 10am-5pm.* 💶 *6€.* ☎ *04 93 49 95 05. www.chateau-lanapoule.com.*

Only two towers remain of the original 14C stronghold converted by the American sculptor Henry Clews and his wife, who was an architect. Located in an outstanding **site** ★ at the foot of the Esterel corniche, the château offers a curious blend of Romanesque and Gothic styles enhanced by Oriental-like decoration. The public can visit the beautiful grounds, the salons, the cloisters and Henry Clews' studio. The walls are used as a backdrop for his extraordinary sculptures, combining grace, wit, realism and irony.

Les Nuits du Château

In July and August the Cour d'Honneur hosts a summer festival of dance, concerts, and theater.

Massif des **MAURES**★★★

MICHELIN MAP 340 M/P5/7

OR 528 FOLDS 47 TO 49

The emerald forests of the Massif des Maures stretch along the coastline from Hyères to St-Raphaël and up into the Gapeau and Argens river valleys. A drive through the Massif reveals glimpses of the colbalt blue sea against rocky inlets, contrasting with the wilder landscape of the inland hills and ravines. The view is particularly scenic from Le Lavandou to La Croix-Valmer, where the route is known as the **Corniche des Maures.** 🛈 *Maison du Tourisme Golfe de St-Tropez/Pays des Maures, Carrefour de la Foux, Gassin, ☎ 04 94 55 22 00. www.golfe-infos.com.*

The Maures is made up of four parallel chains of geographical relief. The Îles d'Hyères mark the southern chain, which is partially submerged. The second chain along the coast reaches its highest point at Les Pradels (528m/1 725ft). The two inland chains, La Verne and La Sauvette, are separated by the River Grimaud and the River Collobrières.

La Sauvette, the most northerly chain, includes the highest peaks, Notre-Dame-des-Anges (780m/2 559ft) and La Sauvette (779m/2 556ft), and ends in Roquebrune Mountain overlooking the lower Argens Valley.

The coastline juts out in the blunt promontories of Cap Bénat and St-Tropez peninsula, the pointed headlands of Cap Nègre and Cap des Sardinaux and retreats into the Bormes anchorage, and the bays of Cavalaire and St-Tropez.

A Bit Of History

Maouro, a Provençal word that refers to dark forests, has become *Maures* in French and is used to describe this densely wooded mountain range.

D. Pazery/MICHELIN

Gonfaron tortoises

Hermann's Tortoise

This tortoise, the only species native to France, appeared in Mediterranean Europe about one million years ago. It lives in the scrub *(maquis)* which provides all its food – oak leaves, fruit and molluscs. After hibernating in a tree stump until about June, the female lays her eggs in a nest which she immediately abandons. If they survive the first two months of life as well as predatory badgers, the baby tortoises can look forward to a life of 60 to 100 years.

Hermann's tortoise has already disappeared from mainland Spain, the Balearic Islands and part of the Balkans, because of natural predators as well as fire (which is the greatest threat). It is now falling victim to alterations in its habitat caused by man and unregulated collecting. The tortoises now survive only in Corsica and in the Massif des Maures, where a tortoise village has been established to protect the species.

les Arcs

le Muy

Missiri

36

37

★ FRÉJUS
St-Raphaël

Roquebrune-
s-Argens

Argens

Aquatica

Fréjus-
Plage

Étangs de Villepey

Golfe
de
Fréjus

Parc St-Donat

☖ St-Aygulf

M A U R E S ★★★

☖ les Issambres

les Calanques

Val d'Esquières

San-Peire-s-Mer

Préconil

la Nartelle

4

3

Cap des Sardinaux

la Garde-Freinet

Ste-Maxime

636

Beauvallon

Golfe de St-Tropez

Les Roches
Blanches ★

N.-D.-de-
la-Queste

★★ ST-TROPEZ

★ Grimaud

la Foux

Port
Grimaud ★

Cap de St-Tropez

2

Cogolin

les Marines
de Cogolin

4

★ Moulins
de Paillas

Plage de
Pampelonne

la Môle

Gassin

Ramatuelle ★

la Croix-Valmer

248

Col de Paillas

129

Phare de Camarat ★

les Pradels
528

Col de
Collebasse

Cap Taillat

372
Col de Barral

★★ Col du Canadel

269

Baie de Cavalaire

Cavalaire-s-Mer ☖

Cap Lardier ★★

1 2

Canadel-s-Mer

Rayol-Canadel-s-Mer

Domaine du Rayol ★★

Pramousquier

Cap Nègre

Cavalière ☖

D E S   M A U R E S

★★ C O R N I C H E

Île du Levant

MASSIF DES MAURES

0   5 km

225

Although traditionally the name is believed to be an allusion to the Moorish pirates from Spain, who ravaged the coast in the 8C and established themselves in the following century on the slopes around the Grimaud plain (although these pirates were really Saracens). Driven out in 973, they continued to raid the coast up to the 18C. To defend themselves, the inhabitants withdrew from the shore, going up into the hills from where they could watch the horizon.

The 20C vogue for sea-bathing, limited at first to an aristocratic clientele, brought this magnificent coast back to life and ended the economic isolation of the region. On 15 August 1944 the Allied and French armies landed on the Maures beaches to liberate the south of France.

Exploring

CORNICHE DES MAURES★★
From Le Lavandou to St-Tropez on the D 559

Le Lavandou ⚐ ⚐ ⚐ *see Le LAVANDOU.*

From Le Lavandou the road runs along the wooded coastline, which is bright and colourful with flowers in season.

St-Clair

The small resort of St-Clair, a short distance from the main road, has a large and beautiful beach.

Aiguebelle

A peaceful seaside resort at the back of a small bay.

Cavalière ⚐

Cavalière has a fine beach, sheltered from the *mistral*. The view extends over Cap Nègre and the Bormes anchorage as far as the Île du Levant and Port-Cros.

Pramousquier

A modest resort with a sheltered beach of fine sand.
The road leaves the shore and meanders up among pine trees and gardens.

Le Rayol-Canadel-sur-Mer ⚐

Canadel, lying at the base of the last foothills of the Pradels range and flanked by superb pine woods, possesses one of the most sheltered beaches on the Maures coast. A monument on the beaches commemorates the allied landings here on 14 August 1944.

Cavalaire-sur-Mer ⚐

A perfect holiday destination for the family, with a fine sandy beach 4km/2.5mi , scuba diving clubs, and a port with room for 1 200 moorings.

La Croix-Valmer

The village has been a winter retreat and spa for those in search of mild climate since the early 1900s. Today it's known for its reputable Côtes de Provence wines.

The site of La Croix village is said to be where Constantine had his vision while on his way to Rome to claim the Empire. According to legend he saw a cross in the sky with the words *In hoc signo vinces* "in this sign you will conquer", a prediction of his forthcoming victory. After the battle Constantine converted to Christianity. A stone cross erected on the pass commemorates this story and gives the village its name. It's worth noting that another version of the legend places Constantine at the Milvian Bridge outside Rome when he has this vision.

Col de Collebasse *Alt 129m/43ft.*

▶ *8km/5mi from La Croix-Valmer along the very winding D 93.*

Endangered Forests

The vegetation of the Massif des Maures consists primarily of pines along the coast, and cork oaks, holm oaks, arbutus, cistus and chestnuts inland. The massif's principal industry, the manufacture of bottle corks, derives from the cork oaks that are carefully cultivated. Unfortunately the region is constantly threatened by forest fires. In July 2003, two successive fires ravages 13,000ha/32,123 acres. This tragedy highlights the need for strict adherance to security regulations, both for residents and visitors (⚐ *see Address Book for details*).

Guided Nature Hikes

The 10 communes of the Massif des Maures organise hikes of 1-2.5hr with different themes (flora-fauna, the forest life, cultural heritage, night walks, etc.). The calendar of walks is available from the Comité Départemental du Tourisme du Var *(www.tour-ismevar.com or www.webvds.com/sorties)*. Information and registration at the following Offices of Tourism: Bormes-les-Mimosas ☎ 04 94 43 67 41; Hyères ☎ 04 94 01 84 50; La Londe-les-Maures ☎ 04 94 01 53 10; Le Muy ☎ 04 94 45 12 79; Le Pradet ☎ 04 94 21 71 69; Pierrefeu-du-Var ☎ 04 94 28 27 30; Ramatuelle ☎ 04 98 12 64 00; Roquebrune-sur-Argens ☎ 04 94 45 72 70.

There is a superb **view**★ of the Pampelonne Bay, Cavalaire Bay and the Îles d'Hyères.

▶ *Return to St-Tropez by the D 93.*

St-Tropez ★★ ♿ *See St-TROPEZ.*

ST-TROPEZ TO FRÉJUS ★★

On the opposite side of the peninsula, the Massif des Maures slopes gently down towards the Mediterranean. On the sunny coast running along N 98, these cheery seaside resorts boast fine beaches, with clusters of rocks breaking the clear surface (♿ *see Driving Tour* ③).

Beauvallon

Beauvallon is a beautifully located resort on the north shores of St-Tropez Bay shaded by pine and cork oak woods.

Ste-Maxime ⌂⌂ ♿ *see STE-MAXIME.*

The road, which skirts the coast closely as far as St-Aygulf, circles Cap Sardinaux.

La Nartelle

The beach of what is now the resort of La Nartelle was one of the landing points for the Allied forces in August 1944.

The coastline between La Nartelle and St-Aygulf is broken up into several inlets *(calanques)* with small beaches and rocks emerging from the sea.

Les Issambres ⌂

This pretty resort is associated with Val d'Esquières, San Peïre and Les Calanques and forms a rapidly expanding holiday centre. Houses of various sizes, some built in the Provençal style, are perched discreetly in the hills. Les Issambres probably takes its name from "Sinus Sambracitanus", the Roman name for St-Tropez Bay.

Driving Tours

① **In Maures Country** *70km/44mi leaving from Hyères – allow one day*

▶ *Leave Hyères to the northeast on N 98.*

After crossing the Gapeau, the road runs past the salt-marshes across the Hyères plain with views of Cap Bénat and the Île du Port-Cros.

Jardin d'Oiseaux Tropicaux

At La Londe-les-Maures. ⊱ *Strictly non-smoking.* ⏲ *Open Jun-Sep 9am-7pm, Feb-May and Oct 2-5pm, Nov weekends only 2-5pm.* ⊙ *8€ (child 5€).* ☎ *04 94 35 02 15. www.jotropico.com*

Kids In a large natural park full of palms and exotic plants from Australia, Mexico and Asia, are tropical birds of all sizes and colours, many in danger of extinction, from all corners of the world.

▶ *After the glassworks, turn right onto D 559. After Le Lavandou it follows the coast up to Canadel-sur-Mer. Turn left onto D 27.*

Col du Canadel★ *Alt 267m/876ft*

Suddenly the sea comes into view and there is a superb **panorama** ★★ of Canadel, Pramousquier beach, Cap Nègre, the Bormes harbour, Cap Bénat and, on the horizon, the Île de Porquerolles.

▶ *Park your car on the col. Take the forest track on the right to the Col de Caguo-Ven (closed to cars).*

Address Book

GENERAL ADVICE ABOUT VISITING THE MASSIFS

Cars – Roads belonging to the DFCI (Défense Forestière Contre l'Incendie – forest fire-fighters) are closed to public traffic. They count as private roads; an open barrier does not indicate that access is permitted. Parking in front of these barriers is prohibited and cars should be parked well to the side of narrow roads to allow the passage of emergency vehicles. Pedestrian access is always possible.

Fire Risk – Fires are prohibited at all times, and smoking is prohibited Mar-Oct. During periods of high fire risk, the ALARME plan is put into action and certain public roads (classed as major fire risks) may be closed to vehicles. Offenders are liable for heavy fines. Walkers are strongly advised to avoid such areas for reasons of safety. To check for closures call ☎ 04 98 10 55 41.

Camping – Camping is prohibited in the massif and within 200m/656ft of any of the forests.

Animals – Pets must be kept on a leash; do not disturb the wild animals.

Plants and chestnuts – Do not stray from marked paths or pick plants or fruit, in particular chestnuts, as you may be requested to pay a fine.

Litter – Use the trash cans or take any trash with you.

For coin ranges see the Legend at the back of this guide.

EATING OUT

○ **Maures** – *19 Boulevard Lazare-Carnot – Collobrières – ☎ 04 94 48 07 10.* This village inn enjoys a well-deserved reputation among its regular clientele on account of the excellent quality/price ratio and the warm welcome it extends. In summer meals are served on the terrace beneath the plane trees.

○○ **Alizés** – *Promenade de la Mer – 83240 Cavalaire-sur-Mer – ☎ 04 94 64 09 32.* A lively atmosphere and the undeniable charisma of the owners are the main assets of this modern-style hotel offering pretty views of the sea. Family cooking with an emphasis on fish and homemade desserts. Some of the recently refurbished rooms are extended by a balcony.

○○ **Chante-Mer** – *In the Village – Les Issambres – ☎ 04 94 96 93 23 – ⊙ Closed 15 Dec-31 Jan, Sun evening Sep to Easter, Tue for lunch Easter to Sep and Mon.* The running of this restaurant is, quite literally, a family business: the father busies himself in the kitchen while his wife and two daughters wait on customers. Settle on the terrace or inside the small, neat dining room and treat your tastebuds to a delicious experience… at no great expense.

WHERE TO STAY

○ **Chambre d'Hôte Le Mas des Oliviers** – *Chemin les Ferrières – Puget-Ville – 2.5km/1.5mi by N 97 Route de Cuers – ☎ 04 94 48 30 89 – sapori@club-internet.fr – ⌿ – 3 rooms – Meal (○○).* This charming Provençal *mas* seems lost among vineyards and olive groves. Large, carefully kept rooms are decorated in a Mediterranean style. Sauna and fitness room. Horse riding and cycling facilities available nearby.

○○ **Chambre d'Hôte L'Amandari** – *Vallat Emponse – Plan-de-la-Tour – ☎ 04 94 43 79 20 – ⌿ – 6 rooms – ⬚ – Meal (○○).* This former sheep barn tucked away by a river exudes a peaceful, friendly atmosphere. The small rooms, each with their own personal touch, overlook a patio. The swimming pool, terrace and leafy grounds make for the perfect escape.

○○○ **Golfe Bleu** – *Route de La Croix-Valmer – Cavalaire-sur-Mer – 1km/0.6mi from the wayside cross on D 559 Route de La Croix-Valmer – ☎ 04 94 64 07 56 – ⊙ Closed 2 Nov-31 Jan – ▥ – ℙ – 15 rooms – ⬚ – Restaurant (○).* Neat, homey establishment away from the town centre. The rooms are soundproofed and air-conditioned. The simply decorated restaurant opens out onto a small terrace.

SPORT AND RECREATION CENTRE

Smash Club – *Avenue du Golf – 83980 Cavalière – ☎ 04 95 05 84 31 – ⊙ Open daily Jul-Aug 8am-2am, Apr-Jun and Sep-Oct 9am-9pm, Nov-Mar 2.30-7pm.* A sports centre for all tastes, Smash Club has six tennis courts, golf links, a weight room, an archery gallery, a sauna, mountain bikes for rental… Tennis tournaments and badminton, beach-volley, football and boules competitions are organised during the summer season.

MARKET

Marché de la Croix Valmer every Sunday morning.

🚶 *1hr.* This is a picturesque route with magnificent **views**★ of the Maures Massif and, to the south, the coast and the Îles d'Hyères.

The forest track along a ridge, bordered with chestnuts and mimosas, is shared with GR 51 to Col de Barral. Vieux-Sauvaire is reached after one hour's walk *(restaurant open here in season)* after which the path goes back down to Col de Barral (372m/1 220ft). There are fine views from the ridge which the path follows for 5km/3mi to the Pierre d'Avenon.

▶ *Continue along D 27 then turn left onto N 98, heading towards La Môle. Proceed straight on until you reach Dom Forest.*

Forêt Domaniale du Dom★

This state forest, composed mainly of pines, cork oaks and chestnuts, spreads over the Les Pradels and La Verne ranges, which are separated by the steep-sided Môle Valley. **Jean Aicard** (1848-1921), poet and novelist, set his work *Maurin des Maures* in this area.

▶ *1km/0.5mi before the pass, stop by the Maison Forestière de Gratteloup.*

Arboretum de Gratteloup

Leave the car in the car park beside N 98. 🕐 *Open daily.* 🎫 *Free entry.* ☎ *04 97 71 06 07.*

This arboretum, created in 1935, consists of various areas covering almost 3ha/7 acres. The first, and oldest, part contains mostly Mediterranean species (cypress, pines, juniper, yoke elms and hop hornbeams). More varied species grow in other areas: red cedar, eucalyptus, maple, alder and birch. Lastly, an area is devoted specifically to the development of the chestnut tree.

▶ *At Col de Gratteloup, take D 41 heading for Bormes-les-Mimosas.*

Pierre d'Avenon★ *Alt 443m/1 450ft*

From the top of this mound of giant boulders the circular **view**★ encompasses the whole Maures coastline from Cap Lardier to Hyères with the port of Le Lavandou and Bormes in the foreground.

🚶 *From here it's a 45min walk to Col de Caguo-Ven.*

Col de Caguo-Ven *Alt 237m/778ft.*

From the pass, there is a **view** of the Hyères and Bormes ports and the Île de Porquerolles.

▶ *At the pass, take the forest lane heading east towards Col de Barral and Col du Canadel. Go back to Hyères via Le Pin, then take D 559.*

② **Pass Road**★★ *109km/67mi leaving from Le Lavandou – allow one day*

This beautiful circular tour, along very hilly but unfrequented roads, goes over at least seven passes *(cols)* and penetrates deep into the heart of the massif.

▶ *From Le Lavandou take D 559 west and when you reach Le Pin turn right onto D 41.*

The road winds uphill among cypresses, eucalyptus and mimosa alongside white, pink and red oleanders. Fine **view** ahead of Bormes and its castle.

Bormes-les-Mimosas★ 👶 *see BORMES-LES-MIMOSAS.*

▶ *Continue on D 41 to Col de Caguo-Ven. Continue downhill to Col de Gratteloup (alt 199m/656ft).*

The road passes over wooded slopes of cork oak and chestnut – deep valleys *(east)* and glimpses of the sea and the mountains around Toulon *(west).*

▶ *Continue along D 41.*

Col de Babaou★ *Alt 415m/1 362ft.*

There is an attractive **panorama**★ of the Hyères port, the Giens peninsula and the Îles d'Hyères.

Beyond the pass rise the tallest of the Maures summits, their slopes wooded by magnificent chestnuts and cork oaks. The road descends to the Réal Collobrier Valley which widens to form the Collobrières Basin.

▶ *Turn right onto D 14.*

Collobrières

The picturesque houses of this shaded town overlook the river swirling beneath an old humpback bridge. The local forests provide the raw material for bottle corks and the vineyards the grapes for rosé wine.

This is definitely a place to visit for those with a sweet tooth: the local specialities are *marrons glacés* (sugared chestnuts) and other delicacies made with chestnuts. The *confiserie* (confectionery) is open to the public.

▶ *Continue east on D 14. After 6km/4mi turn right.*

A narrow road leads to the ruins of the former Carthusian monastery of La Verne, in its majestic forest setting.

Monastère de la Verne

🕐 *Open 11am-5pm (Apr-Sep until 6pm).*
🕐 *Closed Jan, Tue, and holidays.* ⊜ *5€ (child 3€).* ☎ *04 94 43 48 28.*

The monastery was founded in 1170 on an isolated site★ of a wooded slope in the Maures, off the beaten track near a spring. It was rebuilt several times and survived until the Revolution, when the monks abandoned it. Since 1983 it has been occupied by the religious Order of Bethlehem. The buildings are of brown Maures schist but are distinguished by the use of serpentine (bluish-green polished stone) for the door frames, arcades, vaulting and additional ornamentation.

Porch

The huge doorway is built of serpentine stone. Two ringed columns flank the door, surmounted by a triangular pediment resting on two pilasters. A statue of the Virgin and Child stands in a recess.

Guesthouse

A path on the right of the porch leads to the guesthouse. Beyond the reception room is a large courtyard with a fountain at the centre, bordered by the buildings where guests were received. On the left is the bakery. Opposite is a Classical façade with a Regency panelled door. A porch on the left of this door opens into a passage which leads to the scullery and the 12C **kitchen** with rib vaulting.

▶ *Leave the building by the same route.*

A wooden staircase in the courtyard this side of the porch leads to the kitchen and the remains of the **little cloisters:** six barrel-vaulted serpentine bays. The ruins of the Romanesque chapel open off the little cloisters (handsome Renaissance door on the site of the chancel). The **great cloisters** have depressed vaulting and serpentine decoration.

▶ *Return to D 14 and proceed east.*

After Col de Taillude the road looks across La Verne Valley to the ruins of the charter house crowning the opposite slope and then, after passing high above the hamlet of Capelude, makes its way into the upper valley of the Le Périer stream. From the centre of the valley there is a **vista** of the Grimaud Plain and St-Tropez Bay.

Abruptly the road turns into the valley of the Giscle (or the Grimaud rivulet) from where Grimaud can be spotted in the distance.

A quiet retreat

Grimaud★ *see GRIMAUD.*

▶ *From Grimaud take D 558 south, crossing the Grimaud Plain.*

Cogolin *see COGOLIN.*

▶ *N 98 follows the Môle Valley upstream. 8km/5.1mi from Cogolin, just before La Môle, the winding D 27 strays from the valley to cut across the coastal range. Go back to Le Lavandou by the coast road.*

③ **From St-Tropez to St-Raphaël** *39km/24mi – half a day not including tours of St-Tropez and St-Raphaël*

St-Tropez ★★ *see ST-TROPEZ.*

▶ *Leave St-Tropez to the southwest on D 98A.*

The road skirts the southern shore of the bay looking across to the opposite coast.

▶ *After 4km/2.5mi turn right.*

Port-Grimaud ★ *see GRIMAUD.*

▶ *Return to N 98 which skirts the north shore of the bay, overlooking St-Tropez. Follow N 98 up to St-Aygulf.*

St-Aygulf *see FRÉJUS.*

On the left the road follows the nautical theme park **Aquatica** before entering the city of Fréjus. Beyond St-Aygulf the view sweeps over the lower Argens Plain. The splendid rocks of the Montagnes de Roquebrune stand out from the Maures Massif. Turning towards the Esterel range, you can see the Dramont Signal with the peak of Cap Roux looming in the background.

Fréjus ★ *see FRÉJUS.*

▶ *From Fréjus take Boulevard S.-Decuers south.*

Fréjus-Plage *See FRÉJUS: Port-Fréjus.*

▶ *Take N 98 by the sea to reach St-Raphaël.*

④ **The Summits Route★** *120km/74.5mi – allow one day*

Round tour starting from St-Tropez

This excursion passes through wooded countryside and affords some fine views. Quiet roads lead to the lower slopes of the twin peaks of Notre-Dame-des-Anges and La Sauvette.

▶ *Leave St-Tropez to the southwest on D 98A. The road skirts the southern shore of the bay of St-Tropez. At La Foux turn left onto N 98 heading for Cogolin.*

Cogolin *see COGOLIN*

▶ *Continue west on N 98 up the Môle Valley.*

Cork Oak

The cork oak is an evergreen that requires heat and humidity. It grows near the sea up to a height of 500m/1 640ft and has proved to be particularly resilient in the case of fire. It is easy to spot on account of its large blackish acorns and heavily textured bark. Gathering the bark (*démasclage*) takes place for the first time when the tree is 25 years old; this is known as the male bark. Subsequent harvests, which take place in July and August when the sap is rising, occur every 9 or 10 years, which is the time it takes for a new layer of cork to form; this is known as the female bark, which is highly prized by industry (manufacture of chipboard at Le Muy) and craftsmen (boards, ornamental objects and materials for ceramicists). The greater part of the production is exported, particularly to Sardinia.

By the mid-1960s the Maures area was producing 5 000t of cork every year, supplying 100 or so local firms. In 1994 the foresters of the Var *département* produced 500t of cork but the local firms had disappeared. The Cork Museum in Gonfaron pays homage to these regional traditions.

S. Sauvignier/ MICHELIN

Shortly before the village of La Môle stands a château *(right)* flanked by two round towers with pepper-pot roofs. It was here that **Antoine de Saint-Exupéry** (1900-44), aviator and writer, spent some of his childhood years (⏱ *see Massif de l'Esterel).* Vineyards give way to forest-covered slopes of **Dom Forest**★.

▷ *Continue along N 98. At Col de Gratteloup turn right onto D 41, proceeding up to Collobrières, then after La Rivière turn right onto D 14. 3km/2mi east of Collobrières turn left onto D 39.*

The road winds through wooded countryside overlooking a steep-sided stream and affords the occasional glimpse of La Sauvette peak to the right. Shortly before Col des Fourches the road to the left leads to the Notre-Dame-des-Anges Hermitage, pinpointed by the television relay mast.

Notre-Dame-des-Anges★

The priory near the summit (780m/2 559ft) stands in an attractive **setting**★ amid schist rocks where only trees such as the chestnut thrive. The Merovingian foundation may well have superseded an earlier pagan place of worship. Remodelled in the 19C, the buildings included accommodation for pilgrims and a chapel, the walls of which are covered with votive offerings.

Beyond the screen of trees surrounding the chapel there is a remarkable **view**★ *(north)* of the Argens depression backed by the Alps; *(west)* Ste-Baume; *(south)* over the Maures heights to the sea, the Hyères islands, the Giens Peninsula and Toulon; and even Corsica on a clear day.

▷ *Return to Col des Fourches and turn left towards Gonfaron.*

The road passes by La Sauvette (779m/2 556ft), the highest point in the Maures Massif, before descending to Le Luc Plain.

Gonfaron

This village, set against the backdrop of the Massif des Maures, is still an active center of cork manufacturing. At the north edge of the village rises an isolated hill, crowned by a chapel dedicated to St Quinis.

Écomusée du Liège

🕐 *Open on request for guided tours (1hr) Jan-Nov.* 👓 *4€. For information contact the Écomusée du Liège* ☎ *04 94 78 25 65.*

The traditions of the cork industry in the Maures region are preserved through these reconstructions and displays of tools.

Village de Tortues de Gonfaron

In Gonfaron turn right onto D 75. The best times to visit are during the morning (11am) and in the late afternoon (4pm). ♿ 🕐 *Open Mar to end of Nov 9am-7pm.* 👓 *8€ (child 6€).* ☎ *04 94 78 26 41. www.tortues.com.*

🔤 The village is a breeding centre for the Hermann tortoise species *(Testudo hermanni hermanni),* a one-million-year-old herbivore threatened with extinction. The village is also home to France's freshwater turtle and the common or European tortoise *(Testudo graeca).*

The visit includes the nesting house *(écloserie),* the nursery for the tortoises under five years, the terrarium for the hibernation of the young, the various enclosed areas set up according to age or species and the infirmary. Courtship occurs in April, May and September, egg-laying from mid-May to mid-June, and hatching in early September.

▷ *Continue on D 75; at the crossroads turn right onto D 558 towards La Garde-Freinet, which is dominated by the castle ruins.*

La Garde-Freinet ⏱ *see La GARDE-FREINET.*

▷ *Take D 558 south.*

Still descending, the road passes cork oak and chestnut-covered slopes and affords glimpses of the bay and peninsula of St-Tropez.

Grimaud★ ⏱ *see GRIMAUD.*

▷ *Return to St-Tropez by D 14 and D 98A at La Foux.*

The Legend of the Flying Donkey

In the 17C, during a procession in honour of St Quinis, a householder in Gonfaron refused to sweep the area in front of his house and suggested that the statue of the saint should fly over the rubbish. Some time later the same man and his donkey had reached the top of a hill when the animal slipped and they both tumbled into the ravine below.

The locals saw the saint's hand in this misfortune and the legend is told in respect to this hill which rises from the Luc Plain.

MENTON★★

POPULATION 28 812

MICHELIN MAP 341 F5

LOCAL MAPS SEE EXCURSIONS, NICE AND CORNICHES DE LA RIVIERA

Menton is a coastal resort famous for its annual lemon festival and mild climate, boasting the warmest winters on the Riviera. Winter, however, is hardly mentioned here where the sun reigns supreme, and long sandy beaches, two marinas and exotic vegetation welcome the summer visitor. The picturesque old town occupies a magnificent site★★ with a backdrop of steep mountain cliffs and terraced slopes planted with citrus fruits and olives.

▶ **Orient Yourself:** Menton is the last coastal town before the Italian border, about 30km/19mi east of Nice on the Corniches (⟨ see Corniches de la RIVIERA). For those interested in getting there faster on a less scenic route, take the A 8. Most of the sights are around the port. Getting around on foot is not difficult, however there is also a sightseeing train with commentary (⟨see Address Book).

🅿 **Parking:** Most of the public parking places are around the port; all require payment, whether they are parking garages or metered street parking.

🐾 **Don't Miss:** The colourful parades during the annual Lemon Festival (*Fête du Citron*) in February, the pictuesque streets of the old town (*vieille ville*), and the scenic views from the Cap Martin. Don't leave town without trying the famous Menton lemon pie (*tarte au citron*).

🕓 **Organizing Your Time:** Allow at least a half day to walk around the pedestrian shopping streets of the old town, enjoy the views of the Promenade du Soleil and visit one of the sights such as the Musée des Beaux-Arts. You could also make it a full day with an afternoon at the beach, a hike along the Cap Martin or a driving excursion inland to Gorbio or Castillon.

Kids **Especially for Kids:** Young children will enjoy the games, mini-golf and rides at the Koaland amusement park.

A Bit of History

Early history – Evidence of a human settlement in the Paleolithic Era from excavations near the Italian frontier is displayed in the Musée d'Anthropologie Préhistorique in Monaco and in the Musée de Préhistoire in Menton but little is known about the town's origins. The name Menton was first mentioned in 1261. In 1346 the town was bought

View of Menton by night

E. Baret/ MICHELIN

"Artium Civitas"

This inscription on the front of the town hall declared Menton's ambition to be a city of the arts. Art exhibitions are held throughout the year at the Palais de l'Europe. The **Chamber Music Festival** enjoys an international reputation with world-famous guest artists. There are flower carnivals throughout the summer, but the most famous festival is the **Fête du Citron**, held in the Biovès Gardens since 1929. The event calls for more than 100t of citrus fruit – oranges, grapefruit and kumquats as well as lemons – which are used to cover decorative metal frames erected in the gardens to illustrate a different theme each year (Brazilian Carnival in 2006). The festival closes with a procession of floats decorated with citrus fruit.

by the Grimaldis of Monaco although it remained under the Bishop of Ventimiglia. Together with Monaco it oscillated between the protection of France and Sardinia until it was permanently attached to France in 1860.

Modern town – In the late 19C and early 20C Menton benefitted from the popularity of the Riviera among the European aristocracy who came to nurse their health or simply enjoy the mild winters. Personalities from all over the world came to live here, including several writers – the New Zealander Katherine Mansfield (1888-1929), the Spaniard Blasco Ibáñez (1867-1928) and Ferdinand Bac (1859-1952), a French essayist and painter. 20C tourism brought new blood and light industry grew up in the Carei Valley, while the residential district spread west to Roquebrune-Cap-Martin and east to the Italian frontier. The old town and vast green spaces have been preserved.

Visiting the Old Town★★   *allow 2hr*

Rue St-Michel

This pedestrian street linking the old and new towns is bordered by boutiques interspersed with orange trees. Below on the left is the **Place aux Herbes**, with colored paving stones, a decorative colonnade and fountain framing a view of the sea. Nearby the covered market is a lively meeting-place offering delicious local produce. Note the splendid Belle Epoch façades: former Hôtel d'Orient (1 Rue de la République); Winter-Palace *(20 Avenue Riviera)*; Riviera-Palace *(28 Avenue Riviera)*; covered market *(Quai de Monléon)*.

▶   *At the Place du Cap, go up the Rue Logettes to the Rue Longue.*

Rue Longue

The steps up to St-Michel are cut across by Rue Longue, once the main street of the town and formerly called Via Julia Augusta.

Parvis St-Michel★★

▶   *Access by the Chanoine-Gouget ramps.*

At the top of the steps is a charming square in the Italian style, overlooking the sea and the coast, where the concerts of the Chamber Music Festival are held during August. The square is paved with a handsome mosaic depicting the Grimaldi arms in grey and white, framed by typical old houses and the façades of two churches.

Façade of the Chapelle de la Conception ★

On leaving the church climb a few steps on the left to admire this chapel of the White Penitents (1685, restored in the 19C), with its garlands of flowers and basket-handled pediment surmounted by statues of the three theological virtues.

Basilique St-Michel-Archange

🕐 *Open weekdays 10am-noon, 3-5pm.* ☎ *04 93 35 81 63.*

This is the largest and finest Baroque church in the region. Its two-tier **façade** in yellow and pale green reflects a variety of architectural motifs. The tower (15C) on the left, which belonged to an earlier building, was crowned with an octagonal campanile with a glazed tile roof in the 17C, and the great Genoese-style campanile (53m/174ft) on the right was added in the 18C. Above each of the three doors is a niche; the central one houses a statue of St Michael, with St Maurice on the left and St Roch on the right. Local artists such as Puppo and Vento contributed to the decoration of the side chapels, which commemorate various local celebrities.

In the first north side chapel is the fine Baroque **altarpiece** by Puppo, *Le Pape urbain VIII intercédant auprès de l'Enfant Jésus pour les âmes du purgatoire* (Pope Urban VIII interceding with the infant Jesus for the souls in Purgatory), framed by gilt columns wreathed with vine leaves. In front stands a marble altar under a crown-shaped canopy. Next door is a Crucifixion by Ferrari and an unusual 17C Virgin and Child. The third chapel contains an Assumption by Puppo embellished with angels, drapes and scrolls.

The choir contains the huge 17C **organ casing**. Above the handsome 18C choir stalls is the **altarpiece of St Michael** (1569) by Manchello: the saint is flanked by Peter bearing papal insignia and John the Baptist, while the upper sections show a fine Pietà. The exuberant Baroque high altar is crowned by St Michael slaying the Devil. The next side chapel is devoted to the Princes of Monaco: a late-17C painting shows St Devota, patron of the Principality, in front of the rock of Monaco. Prince Honoré III of Monaco was wedded in this church in 1757.

▷ *Climb the steps into the quaint Rue du Vieux-Château, which leads to the cemetery.*

Cimetière du Vieux-Château

This international cemetery, laid out in the last century on the site of the former medieval castle, consists of terraces one above the other which can be seen clearly from the port. Each level contains tombs associated with a different religion or nationality. The cemetery is the most striking souvenir of the time when Menton used to welcome rich summer residents from all over the world. Among the celebrities from this era whose fame still endures are several great Russian princes (Troubetzkoy, Volkonsky and Ouroussof), the uncle and aunt (Delano) of the American president Roosevelt, Webb Ellis who is credited with inventing the game of Rugby football and the Danish architect Georg Tersling, who designed many palaces and houses on the Riviera at the turn of the century.

From the southern corner of the English graveyard there is a beautiful view ★ of the old town, the sea and the coast from Mortola Point in Italy to Cap Martin.

▷ *Return to Parvis St-Michel by Montée du Souvenir, bordered by fragrant oleanders.*

The Seafront and Beaches★★

▷ *Start from the Casino Municipal.*

Promenade du Soleil★★

The promenade with its broad terraces facing out to sea follows the shore beneath the old town with the Alps in the background.

Old Port

The harbour is used by local fishermen and tourists alike. It is flanked by **Quai Napoléon-III**, which follows the jetty sheltering the harbour and ending in a lighthouse, and **Jetée Impératrice-Eugénie.** The far end of the port, home to Volti's sculpture of St Michael, commands nice **views** ★ of old Menton, fronted by a row of arcades. In the distance you can admire the mountains inland and the stretch between Cap Martin and Bordighera (Cap Mortola obscures Vintimiglia).

Plage des Sablettes

Jet skis and windsurfing boards forbidden.

This gravel beach is dominated by Promenade de la Mer and **Quai Bonaparte**. From the top, there is a nice view of the old quarter. A huge flight of steps leads up to the church of St-Michel between tall narrow houses.

Garavan

Once a cluster of elegant mansions set apart from Menton, Garavan has now become a luxurious residential suburb of the town, running between Promenade de la Mer and Boulevard de Garavan, where you'll find many examples of the eclectic architecture of the Belle Epoch (like the Fondation Barriquand-Alphand, d'Abel Gléna on Boulevard de Garavan). The marina can accommodate boats up to 40m/132ft. The pretty 17C Baroque **Chapelle St-Jacques** houses a municipal gallery displaying contemporary art exhibitions.

A Bit of Advice

Many pedestrian streets in Menton are decorated with traditional mosaics made with smooth *galets*, or river stones, which are colourful yet a bit uncomfortable to walk on. Be sure to have thick-soled shoes if you plan on doing a lot of walking.

Address Book

PRACTICAL INFORMATION

Tourism Office – *Palais de l'Europe, 8 Avenue Boyer* – ☎ *04 92 41 76 76 – www.villedementon.com.*

TOURS

Maison du Patrimoine – *5 Rue Ciapetta* ☎ *04 92 10 33 66 – www.vpah.culture.fr.* Guided walking tours of the old city, gardens, architecture, etc.

Small tourist train – Departures from Promenade du Soleil, near the citadel. Guided tours with commentary *(30min)* 10am-noon, 2.15-7pm (5pm Christmas to Easter). In high season there are nightly tours *(8.30-11pm)* to see the city of Menton illuminated.

Les Bateaux de la French Riviera – *Quai Napoléon III, Old Port*– ☎ *04 93 35 36 38* – ⏲ *Open Mid-Apr to mid-Oct (except Sat)* – ☞ *12-15€*. Boat trips with commentary in French going direct to Monaco, around the French Riviera *(1hr 45min)*, and to the Italian Riviera *(1hr 45min)*.

PUBLIC TRANSPORTATION

Buses – *Bus station on Avenue de Sospel* – ☎ *04 93 35 93 60*. The town of Menton and its outskirts are served by nine bus lines. Single tickets and one-day passes available from bus drivers. The "3 Villages Pass" will enable you to visit Gorbio, Ste-Agnès and Castellar at reduced rates within one month of purchase.

Train – ☎ *0892 35 35 35*– *www.ter-sncf.com/paca*. The TER line Nice/Vintimille has stops in Monaco and Menton.

For coin ranges see the Legend at the back of this guide.

EATING OUT

☞ **Au Pistou** – *9 Quai Gordon-Bennett* – ☎ *04 93 57 45 89* – ⏲ *Closed 15 Nov-15 Dec and Mon* – ☞ *13.42€*. A family business situated beneath the arcades at the far end of the port, with the senior member bringing in the day's catch every morning! An unusual summer terrace.

☞☞ **Au Petit Gourmand** – *11 Rue Trenca* – ☎ *04 93 35 79 27* – ⏲ *Closed 25 Jun-10 Jul, 10-25 Jan, Mon lunch and Wed*. The chef brings his considerable experience to the tasty Provençal dishes prepared in this tiny restaurant, popular with fans of gourmet dining. Small terrace.

☞☞ **Auberge Pierrot-Pierrette** – *Place de l'Église* – ⏲ *Closed 1 Dec-15 Jan and Mon* – ☎ *04 93 35 79 76* – *pierrotpierrette@aol.com*. In a tranquil hamlet perched on the hills above Menton, this family-run restaurant surrounded by gardens serves hearty Provençal meals to satisfy the biggest appetites.

A Braijade Méridiounale – *66 Rue Longue* – ☎ *04 93 35 65 65* – ⏲ *Closed 6-12 Jan, 15 Nov-5 Dec ,and Wed and lunch Sep-Jun.*

Discreetly located in an alley of the old quarter, this homey restaurant provides Provençal dishes and grilled meats at very reasonable rates. Pretty dining room with visible stonework, beams and a fireplace.

WHERE TO STAY

☞☞ **Le Globe** – *21 Avenue de Verdun* – ☎ *04 92 10 59 70* – ⏲ *Closed 15 Nov-15 Dec* – 🅿 *– 23 rooms – Restaurant* (☞☞☞). Homey establishment enjoying a privileged location on a luxuriant avenue just opposite the Palais de l'Europe and within walking distance of the casino. Cosy, tidy rooms. The terrace extending the bar has recently been refurbished.

☞☞ **Hôtel de Londres** – *15 Avenue Carnot* – ☎ *04 93 35 74 62* – ⏲ *Closed 20 Oct-27 Dec* – *27 rooms* – ▤ – *Restaurant* (☞☞☞). This recently renovated hotel near the coast features efficiently soundproofed rooms of varying sizes, appointed with either rustic or modern furniture. Pleasant terrace set back from the street.

☞☞ **Dauphin** – *28 Avenue du Général-de-Gaulle* – ☎ *04 93 35 76 37* – ⏲ *Closed 12 Nov-17 Dec* – *28 rooms* – ⊿ – *Restaurant* (☞). This hotel is a haven for musicians as it features two recording studios and air-conditioned, soundproofed rooms for the other residents! The rooms afford pretty views of the sea. Fitness room.

☞☞ **Orly** – *27 Porte de France* – ☎ *04 93 35 60 81* – *hotel.orly@wanadoo.fr*– ⏲ *Closed 15 Nov-27 Dec* – 🅿 *– 29 room* – ⊿ – *Restaurant* (☞). Seaside hotel facing the exclusive Garavan beach providing simple rooms; the ones facing the back are quieter. Traditional fare served on the terrace or inside the sober dining room fronted by huge bay windows.

THEATRE AND ARTS

Palais de l'Europe – *8 Avenue Boyer* – ☎ *04 92 41 76 50 – villedementon.com* – ⏲ *Gallery open daily except Tue 10am-noon, 2-6pm. Tickets at the tourist office: Mon-Fri 10am-noon, 2-5pm.* Handsome auditorium with a seating capacity of 730, where ballets, plays, operas, operettas and classical music concerts are organised. The premises is also home to a modern art gallery used as a venue for temporary exhibitions free of charge to the public.

SHOPPING

Lemons – Many shops in Menton pay tribute to this sunny fruit by selling a wide range of produce made or flavoured with lemons: tarts and pies, gingerbread, almond paste, boiled sweets, wine, vinegar, jam, soaps, candles, perfume...

Les Apéritifs du Soleil – *115 Route de Sospel* – ☎ *04 92 10 37 75* – ⏲ *Open Mon-Fri 8am-12.30pm, 3-7pm, Sat 18am-12.30pm.* This tiny boutique on the side of the road sellsits homemade liqueurs and apéritifs, as well as tapenades, olive oil, honey, local wines (including the hard to find Bellet from Nice's vineyards) and drinks made with wine and fruit (lemon, orange, grapefruit, etc).

Marchés – ⓒ *Daily in the morning.* Covered market on Quai de Monléon. Careï market at the top of the Biovès Gardens, beneath the railway bridge.

L'Arche des Confitures – *2 Rue du Vieux-Collège* – ☎ *04 93 57 20 29* – ⓒ *Open Mon-Sat 9.30am-noon, 3-7pm, Sun 10am-noon, 3-6pm.* Who could resist the impressive range of mouthwatering jams made on the premises of this family business? There's also different types of honey, vinegar, confit and mustard. It's possible to visit the kitchens.

TAKING IT EASY

Sports – La Promenade de la Mer is where most of the sports and recreation companies are found, including scuba, sailing, tennis and wind-surfing clubs.

Koaland – 🔲 *Avenue de la Madone* – ☎ *04 92 10 00 40.* ⓒ *Open daily except Tues 10am-noon, 3pm-midnight (2-7pm in winter).* Leisure park for children and the younger generation with a miniature golf course.

ULM Club – *Promenade de la Mer* – ☎ *04 93 14 00 12* – ⓒ *Open May-Sep 8am-9pm; Oct-Apr 9am-5pm (by appointment).* This club organises maiden flights and introductory courses for flying hydroplanes.

CALENDAR OF FESTIVITIES

Lemon Festival – Two weeks in February-March (*around Mardi Gras*). Book at least two months in advance for this popular event.

Chamber Music Festival – In August on the esplanade of the Église St-Michel. This prestigious event is attended by talented soloists and conductors from around the world.

Gardens of Menton★

The choice of tropical species and the unusual layout of these gardens reflect the fertile imagination of the foreign residents who have come here to stay over the past century. The best time of year to visit all these gardens is around June, when the trees, bushes and flower beds are ablaze with color.

Jardin Biovès

▶ *In the centre of town next to the Tourism Office.*

These beautiful gardens in the town centre are bordered by palms and lemon trees, planted with flowers and ornamented by fountains and statues (*Goddess of the Golden Fruit* by Volti). The grounds follow the loops of the River Careï and open up a view of the mountains rising beyond the town.

Jardin du Val Rameh★

From Promenade de la Mer take Chemin de St-Jacques. ⓒ *Open Apr-Sep 10am-12.30pm, 3-6pm; Oct-Mar 10am-noon, 2-5pm.* ⓒ *Closed Tue.* ⬅ *4€.* ☎ *04 93 35 86 72.*

These grounds were arranged around the Val Rameh Villa by the English in the 1930s and then taken over by the Musée d'Histoire Naturelle of Paris. The terraced garden features over 700 species of Mediterranean, tropical and sub-tropical flora. All these plants have grown accustomed to the Menton climate and flourish abundantly. Exotic species are dotted amid the citrus trees: passiflora, guava, avocado etc. The terraces afford a magnificent view of the old town and the sea.

Jardin Fontana Rosa

Avenue Blasco Ibañez. ⓒ *Guided tours only with the Maison du Patrimoine, (1.5hr) Fri at 2.30pm.* ⬅ *5€.* ☎ *04 92 10 97 10.*

This unusual residence, known as the Jardin des Romanciers, stands out because of its porch adorned with ceramics paying homage to leading names in Spanish literature. It was built in 1924 by the Spanish novelist **Blasco Ibañez.** Only the garden is open to visitors. It consists of a harmonious row of pergolas and structures, interspersed with ponds and embellished with ceramics of Spanish design. *Part of the gardens are undergoing restoration works.*

Jardin de Maria-Serena

Promenade Reine-Astrid. ⓒ *Guided tours only with the Maison du Patrimoine (2hr) Tue at 10am.* ⬅ *5€.* ☎ *04 92 10 97 10.*

This garden could be said to have the most temperate climate in France, since the temperature never falls below 5°C. Supposedly built by Charles Garnier (architect of the Paris Opera), it is known for its extensive collection of palm trees and views over Menton's old town.

MENTON		Guyau R.	Y	19	République R. de la	Z	33
Bosano R. Lt	Y 5	Herbes Pl. aux	Z	20	St-Michel R.	Z	
Boyer Av.	Z 6	Laurenti Av.	Y	21	St-Roch Pl. et R.	Z	35
Carnot Av.	Z 10	Logettes R. des	Z	22	Trenca R.	Z	37
Ciapetta R.	Z 12	Longue R.	Y	24	Verdun Av. de	Z	40
Félix-Faure Av.	Z	Monléon Quai de	Z	27	Vieux-Château R.	Y	42
Gallieni R. Gén.	Z 18	Partouneaux R.	Z	30	Villarey R.	Z	44

Basilique St-Michel-Archange	Y	B	Hôtel de Ville	Z	H	Sculpture de Volti	Y	V
Chapelle de la Conception	Y	D	Musée de Préhistoire					
Cimetière du Vieux-Château	Y	F	régionale	Y	M¹			

Serre de la Madone

74 route de Gorbio ⏲ *Open Apr-Oct 10am-6pm (call for winter hours). Guided tours (2hr) in English on request.* ⏲ *Closed Mon.* ⮑ *8€ (3.50€ children 7-13).* ☎ *04 93 57 73 90. www.serredelamadone.com.*

Once a private garden, the Serre de la Madone was purchased by the Conservatoire du Littoral in 1999 and is now open regularly to visitors. Its "palazzo" and restored gardens feature rare plants, a Moorish garden, a rock garden, a cool greenhouse and many antique garden statues.

Oliveraie du Pian

Boulevard de Garavan. Also accessible from a staircase in the Val Rameh gardens.

This olive grove is planted with more than 500 olive trees over 100 years old. It's a pleasant place for an afternoon stroll or picnic.

Sights

Musée des Beaux-Arts (Palais Carnolès)★

Access by Avenue Carnot. ⏲ *Open daily (except Tue) 10am-noon, 2-6pm.* ⏲ *Closed public holidays.* ⮑ *Free entry.* ☎ *04 93 35 49 71.*

This former summer residence of the princes of Monaco was built in the 17C in the spirit of the Grand Trianon of Versailles, according to plans by Robert de Cotte and Gabriel. After heavy remodelling in the 19C, it had the honour of welcoming celebrities such as Elisabeth-Louise, the last queen of Prussia, and Prince Metternich. It then fell into the hands of the American Allis, a celebrated ichthyologist, on whose instructions the building was restored by the Danish architect Georg Tersling and decorated with frescoes on antique themes by Matthiessen, a German artist. The original stuccowork and gilding have survived in the Grand Salon de Musique Antoine I and the Salon Bleu.

Upstairs

The first floor is dedicated to the collection of early religious art such as the beautiful 13C *Virgin and Child*, a Tuscan work by the Master of the Maddalena. There are works by French, Italian and Flemish masters, including Louis Bréa, Leonardo da Vinci, Bernardino Luini, Bernardino Orsi and Philippe de Champaigne. There are also modern works by Suzanne Valadon, Kisling and Camoin.

Ground Floor

A collection of contemporary and modern work is housed on the ground floor. The museum displays in rotation works from the Wakefield Mori Collection (Picabia, Forain, Dufy, etc), contributions from various Biennales de Peinture (up to 1980) and gifts from artists (Gleizes, Desnoyers, Delvaux, Sutherland).

Jardin d'agrumes

A vast **garden of citrus fruit trees** (grapefruit, mandarin, kumquat, orange and lemon) and avocado trees contains a number of modern sculptures.

Musée Jean-Cocteau

🕐 *Open 10am-noon, 2-6pm.* 🕐 *Closed Tue and public holidays.* 🖃 *3.05€.* ☎ *04 93 35 49 71.*

This museum is housed in a 17C bastion built by Honoré II of Monaco. Cocteau, the "Prince of the Poets", worked there from 1957 onwards. It was his initiative that led to the bastion being converted into a museum and it was he who oversaw the restoration. The remaining parts of the original building include a large vaulted salon and two small annexe rooms, one of which still contains an oven. The guard-rooms and the munitions store now contain the museum.

Outside, the artist has designed pebble mosaics in traditional Menton style on several themes – Orpheus, the Faun of youth, a lass of Menton and the fisherman. The floor of the entrance is decorated with the Mediterranean emblem, the lizard, made of small grey and white pebbles. On the wall hangs an Aubusson tapestry, *Judith and Holophernes*, which Matisse described as the "only truly contemporary tapestry". The wrought-iron display cases were designed by Cocteau especially for his museum; they contain zoomorphic ceramic vases. The tapestry hanging above the stairs, *l'Âge du Verseau,* was woven in the Gobelins workshops. The first floor gallery houses a series of pastels entitled *Gli Innamorati* (1961), and a large portrait of the poet by Marc Avoy depicting Cocteau leaving the body of a faun.

Hôtel de Ville

🕐 *The hall decorated by Jean Cocteau is open weekdays 8.30am-12.30pm, 1.30-5pm.* 🕐 *Closed public holidays.* 🖃 *1.50€.* ☎ *04 92 10 50 20. www.villedementon.com.*

The town hall is a handsome building inspired by the 17C Italian style. The **hall**★ where marriages are celebrated owes its decoration to Jean Cocteau. On the wall at the back, the angler, who has a fish as an eye, is wearing a typical Menton fisherman's hat; the girl opposite him is sporting a traditional hat from Nice. The walls depict Orpheus and Eurydice on one side and a fictitious marriage on the other. On the ceiling, Poetry is depicted astride Pegasus, Science is juggling with the planets, and Love is no longer blind.

In the entrance there are two Mariannes (the symbol of the French Republic, represented by a woman wearing the liberty cap) drawn by Cocteau, engraved onto two large mirrors. The furniture was chosen by Cocteau himself: candelabra in the form of palm trees, Spanish style chairs, and a panther skin leading to the marriage table.

Musée de Préhistoire Régionale

🕐 *Open 10am-noon, 2-6pm.* 🕐 *Closed Tue and public holidays.* 🖃 *Free entry.* ☎ *04 93 35 84 64.*

Katherine Mansfield (1888-1923)

This writer from New Zealand spent a year in Menton from spring 1920. Her delicate health caused her to choose Garavan and she moved into the Villa Isola-Bella *(now in Avenue Katherine-Mansfield)*. In this peaceful haven she wrote five of her best works including *The Stranger, The Chambermaid, The Girl*. Writing in her diary, she said: "The house faces the sea; on the right is the old town with its little port and pepper plants growing on a tiny quay... This old town... is the loveliest place I have ever set eyes on."

This museum was opened at the beginning of the century in a building specially designed by the architect Adrien Rey. It houses collections from local prehistoric sites, the oldest of which come from excavations carried out by Bonfils (a 19C naturalist from Menton) in the Grimaldi caves.

On the ground floor, reconstructions of everyday life illustrate the evolution of prehistoric man in the Alpes-Maritimes and Liguria from 1 000 000 BC to 1 500 BC. A film room and an interactive question-and-answer terminal enable visitors to test their knowledge.

The basement contains displays on the history of Menton and popular art and traditions. There are the reconstructions of the interiors of Menton houses during the last century. Two more rooms display traditional objects associated with the cultivation and harvesting of lemons and olives. A gallery of posters commemorates the golden age of Menton's popularity as a winter resort from 1870 to 1914.

Église Orthodoxe Russe

Rue Morillot, access by Avenue Carnot. ⏱ Guided tours 4th Sat of each month at 2.30pm from Jan-June and Sep-Oct. ⊙ 5€. ☎ 04 92 10 97 10.

The Russian Orthodox Church (1892) was designed by Georg Tersling, a Danish architect. Although its small size would be more appropriate to a chapel, the interior is lavishly decorated with murals by Prince Gagarin and many icons. In the 19C a sizeable Russian colony spent the winter months on the Riviera. In 1880 they founded a rest home, La Maison Russe, so that patients with tuberculosis could benefit from the mild climate of Menton. The home, which stands near the church, was particularly helpful to soldiers who had contracted tuberculosis in Manchuria during the Russo-Japanese War (1905).

Excursions

L'Annonciade★ *6km/4mi.*

▶ *From Menton take Avenue de Verdun then Avenue de Sospel, following the sign for l'Annonciade to the left up a steep, narrow road.*

The 17C **chapel** has been a center for pilgrimages to the Virgin since the 11C. From the terrace (225m/738ft) there is a panorama★ of the coast from Bordighera Point to Cap Martin and of the mountains ringing Menton.

Gorbio★ *9km/5.5mi.*

▶ *Leave Menton by the D 23 north to Gorbio, a narrow winding road where passing is often difficult.*

The Gorbio Valley, with its flowers, its olives and pines and its luxury residences, contrasts with the stark appearance of the village, perched on its wild and rocky **site** ★. Near the entrance to the narrow cobbled lanes stands the old Malaussène fountain. The elm tree in the square was planted in 1713. For the feast of Corpus Christi, the villagers organise a very attractive parade, known as the **Procession des Limaces,** in which everyone carries a snail shell filled with olive oil and lit by a little wick. Rue Garibaldi leads round the church to a fine **viewpoint** looking across to Bordighera Point.

Ste-Agnès★ *13km/8mi – about 45min.*

▶ *From Menton take Avenue Carnot north, turn right onto Cours René-Coty, Avenue des Alliés and Rue des Castagnins (D 22).*

The road is uphill all the way with views of the Gorbio Valley. Bear right at **Col St-Sébastien** (alt 600m/1 969ft) which has a particularly picturesque **view**★ of Ste-Agnès. Located barely 3km/2mi from the sea, yet at an altitude of 780m/2 559ft, the village (the highest on the coast) is perched like an eagle's nest at the foot of a grey limestone cliff which lights up in superb shades of pink at sunset.

The picturesque cobblestone streets of the village, lined with craft shops, include Rue Longue and the vaulted Rue des Comtes-Léotardi.

A rocky path leads from behind the graveyard to a viewing table in the ruins of the castle where you'll find a marvellous **panorama**★★.

Fort Maginot de Ste-Agnès

At the entrance to the village, turn towards the parking Sud, and park the car on the left near the entrance to the fort. Note: the interior is chilly, even in summer. ⏱ Guided tours (1hr) Jul-Sep 3-6pm; Oct-Jun Sat-Sun 2.30-5.30pm. ⊙ 3.05€. ☎ 04 93 35 84 58.

This imposing building, camouflaged by the overhanging rocks surrounding it, was built between 1931 and 1938 as part of the reinforcement of the Alpine Maginot Line.

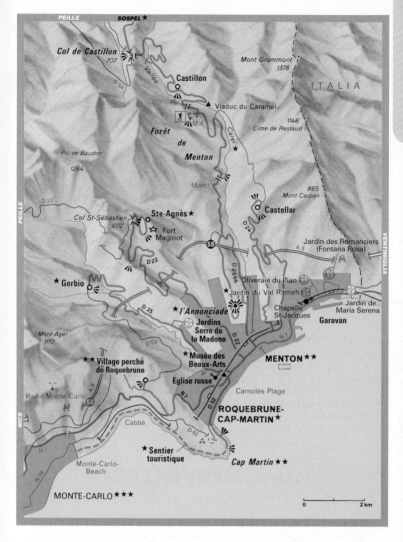

Its firing slots are equipped with 81mm mortars and 75/135mm guns faced southeast over Menton Bay to protect its approaches. The barracks, deep in the cliff, still house an electric generator, a neutralisation room and the kitchens. The tour of the fort gives an insight into life in such strongholds during the Second World War.

Outside, set slightly downhill, a platform overlooking the intricacies of the Provençal motorway affords a marvellous **view**★★ of the coast from Bordighera in Italy to Cap Martin and Mont Agel to the southwest.

Castellar – *13km/8mi – about 45min.*

▶ *From Menton take Route de Castellar, north on the map.*

Castellar is an attractive hilltop village and a popular place for hiking, as it lies at the crossroads of the GR 51 and 52 trails. Its parallel streets are linked by covered alleys. From the terrace on Place Clémenceau, there is a good **view** of the sea and the surrounding heights.

▶ *On the return drive, follow the same route for 2.5km/1.5mi, then turn right on the winding "Chemin du Mont-Gros". Admire the fine views.*

Roquebrune-Cap-Martin★ (♿see ROQUEBRUNE-CAP-MARTIN)

Driving Tours

Col de Castillon Road *21km/13mi – about 1hr 30min*

▶ *Leave Menton by Avenue de Verdun running into Avenue de Sospel.*

The road riding over Col de Castillon – also called Col de la Garde – makes its way through a break in the ridge of hills running parallel to the coast and dividing the Menton district from the Sospel Basin. From the pass the River Careï flows south to the Mediterranean, and the River Merlanson north to join the River Bévera.

After passing under the motorway, the D 2566 climbs, twisting and turning as it goes, up the beautiful **Vallée du Careï** ★ beneath the ridges of the Franco-Italian border to the east. The lemon groves eventuall give way to olive and pine trees. After leaving the hamlet of Monti, the road skirts Menton Forest, offering fine views.

Forêt de Menton

A variety of trees contributes to the beauty of the forest, perfect for a hike.

1hr on foot there and back. To the left of the forest refuge a path leads to a **view** ★ *(viewing table)* of the coast. The road soon passes the **Caramel Viaduct,** formerly used by the tramway running between Menton and Sospel.

Castillon

On the right lies the new village of Castillon, a model of rural planning, built halfway up the hillside in the Provençal style. The village was reconstructed twice: after the earthquake of 1887 and after the bombardments of 1944. Its main district overlooking the village is occupied by artisans, painters, sculptors, etc..

From the summit, the **view** opens out onto the Careï Valley and the Mediterranean Sea.

▶ *After the village, the road to the Sospel Valley leads off to the left, plunging in and out of tunnels following the tracks of the old tramway. The road leading off to the right soon brings you to the pass.*

Col de Castillon – *Alt 707m/2 320ft.*

The **view** to the north takes in the Bévera Valley with the Peïra-Cava and Aution peaks in the distance. To the left D 54 takes a picturesque route to Col St-Jean.

From here the road drops gradually down into the Merlanson Valley. The forest is gradually replaced by olive groves and terraced vineyards. First the stronghold on Mont Barbonnet looms into sight, followed by the town of Sospel and the surrounding heights.

Vallée des **MERVEILLES**★★

MICHELIN MAP 341 F3/4

To the west of Tende, around **Mont Bégo** (alt 2 872m/9 423ft), lies a region of glacial lakes and valleys, rocky cirques and moraines, formed during the Quaternary Era, cut off by the scarce roads and the harsh mountain climate. In this dramatic landscape is the Vallée des Merveilles, which is part of the **Parc National du Mercantour**. It's famous for the thousands of Pre-historic rock engravings discovered there, most of them dating back to the Bronze Age of 2800BC to 1300BC. These "marvels" are among the most impressive of their kind in Europe.

▶ **Orient Yourself:** The whole of the site known as the Vallée des Merveilles consists of five distinct regions around Mont Bégo:

- the Vallée des Merveilles itself, which is the largest area and contains more than half the carvings;

- the Vallée de Fontanalbe, which is narrower and contains about 40% of the carvings;

- the Valmasque, Valaurette and Sabion areas which contain only a few scattered carvings.

Access Routes

There are two different ways of getting to the Vallée des Merveilles, but all require a good hike:

▶ Take the N 204 up the Roya Valley to St-Dalmas-de-Tende, then D 91 to Casterino village and follow one of two footpaths:

3hr Lac des Meshes to the Arpette area and the Refuge des Merveilles

2.5hr Casterino refuge to the Fontanalbe refuge and the Fontanalbe district

▶ From Belvédère up the Gordalasque Valley to St-Grat (📖 *see Vallée de la VÉSUBIE*) and the footpath to Pas de l'Arpette.

Over 600km/373mi of marked trails cover the area, including sections of the GR 5 and GR 52A trails which circle the Mercantour National Park and cross through the Vallée des Merveilles. There are also trails which lead to Authion, Boréon and to the Madone de Fenestre (📖 *see Vallée de la VÉSUBI and Forêt de TURINI*).

The engravings can be visited from Jun through Sep (📖 *see Address Book for guided tour information*). 🛈 *Parc National du Mercantour, 23 Rue d'Italie, Nice,* ☎ *04 93 16 78 88. www.parc-mercantour.fr.* 🛈 *Maison du Parc National à Tende,* ☎ *04 93 04 67 00. www.tendemerveilles.com.*

Address Book

HIKING IN THE VALLÉE DES MERVEILLES

It is important to bear in mind that these sites are at high altitude (between 1 600-2 500m/5 429-8 202ft) and that certain preparations are advisable – good physical stamina, mountain boots or shoes and warm clothing providing protection from cold and rain. As storms are frequent and sometimes very violent, it is wise to listen to the weather forecast. To study the route in advance see Map 1/25 000 – Vallée de la Roya – published by the Conseil Général des Alpes-Maritimes.

REGULATIONS AT THE SITES

BASIC GUIDELINES

The main regulations are symbolised by the signs shown below (📖 *see box*). Violations of these regulations, detected by the official park guides, are punishable by heavy fines.

VISITING THE ENGRAVINGS

Although the Bronze Age rock engravings are protected for most of the year by a covering of snow *(from mid-October to late June)*, in recent years they have suffered considerable damage, inflicted intentionally or unintentionally by human visitors. To prevent such defacement the trustees and the officers of the Parc National du Mercantour have limited public access to the Arpette and Fontanalbe sectors only. Visitors may enter these two areas only if they are accompanied by seasoned guides who are on duty at these two sites daily throughout the summer season.

For the Vallée des Merveilles – 🕐 *Depart from the Refuge CAF des Merveilles. Jul- Aug 11am, 1pm and 3pm; Sep Mon, Fri, weekends 8am and 1pm; Jun weekends 8am and 1pm.*

For the Vallée de Fontanalbe – 🕐 *8am from the Refuge de Fontanalbe, 11am and 2pm from the Pont du Lac Vert; Jul- Aug daily; Sep Mon, Fri, weekends; Jun*

weekends. 8€ (child 4€). For information contact the Parc National à Castérino, ☎ 04 93 04 89 79 and in Tende, ☎ 04 93 04 67 00.

WITHIN THE NATIONAL PARK

The regulations appropriate to open-air sites apply within the boundaries of the Vallée des Merveilles: no domestic animals, no fires, no camping within an hour of the park boundaries and no disposing of waste within the boundaries.

Refreshments and accommodation are available from the two refuges. It is however wise to book in advance during the summer season by contacting the refuge directly.

OFFICIAL GUIDES

Merveilles, Gravures & Découvertes – *18 Rue Operto – Tende–* ☎ *06 86 03 90 13.* Registered mountain guides of the Mercantour National Park. Themed hikes and tours of the engravings.

Destination Merveilles – *10 Rue des Mesures – Villeneuve-Loubet –* ☎ *04 93 73 09 07 - www.destination-merveilles.com.* Organises various outings and hiking tours in the Vallée des Merveilles.

Association des Guides, Accompagnateurs et Amis des Alpes Méridionales – *Bureau de la Haute Vésubie – St-Martin-Vésubie –* ☎ *and fax 04 93 03 26 60.* This organisation stages events and supplies qualified guides for visits to the Vallée des Merveilles.

REFUGES

Refuge de Fontanalbe – ☎ *04 93 04 89 19.* 🕐 *Open by reservation from mid-Jun to mid-Sep.* Accommodation and snacks available on-site. Reserve well in advance in season.

Refuge des Merveilles – ☎ *04 93 04 64 64 or 04 93 04 69 22 (off-season).* 🕐 *Open Jun-Sep, call for off-season reservations* ☎ *04 93 62 59 99.* Accommodation and half-board available on-site. Reservations one night in advance necessary.

A Bit of History

The Engravings

The name Bégo is derived from an Indo-European root which means the sacred mountain *(Be)* inhabited by the bull-god (Go). The region of Mont Bégo is an **open-air museum** comprising over 40 000 engravings. Although they were discovered and identified at the end of the 17C, it was not until 1897 that they were studied systematically by the British scholar Clarence Bicknell. In 1947, when the region became part of France, more intensive research was carried out by a team working under Henry de Lumley, which spent 30 years recording every engraving within

The Wizard and the Mont des Merveilles

B. Kaufmann/ MICHELIN

a wide area (12ha/30 acres). The engravings are cut into the rock face worn smooth by glacial erosion 15 000 years ago. The linear engravings date from the Gallo-Roman period through the Middle Ages to the present. The engravings which are of most interest to the archeologists are even earlier – the majority date back to the early Bronze Age (c 2800 BC to 1500 BC). A stippling technique was used: the contours and surfaces were obtained by the juxtaposition of tiny dots (between 1 and 5mm/up to 0.2in across) punched in the rock face with flint or quartz tools.

The Mercantour National Park

Created in 1979, it covers 68 500ha/170 000acres in the Alpes-Maritimes and Haute-Provence. Once part of the hunting grounds of the kings of Italy (the area didn't become part of France until 1861), it's now twinned with the Parco Naturale delle Alpi Marittime across the border. These two organisations join to protect the flora and fauna of in the parks, as well as the cultural heritage of sites such as the Vallée des Merveilles.

Walking Tours

Vallée des Merveilles

▷   *10km/6mi north of St-Dalmas-de-Tende by D 91. Leave the car at Lac des Mesches.*
🚶 *8hr.* Take the signposted footpath *(3hr on foot)* to the Refuge des Merveilles and then to Lac Long, the starting point for a guided tour of the Arpette area *(2hrs there and back).*
It is possible to spend the night at the refuge (reservation necessary), and then the following morning, walk up the Vallée des Merveilles as far as the Baisse de Valmasque *(about 2.5hr).* Return by the same route to reach the car park in the late afternoon.

Fontanalbe

▷   *12km/8mi north of St-Dalmas-de-Tende by D 91. Park the car in Casterino. Allow one whole day.*

Magic Mountain

The engravings reveal the preoccupations of the Ligurian people who lived in the lower valleys. They made pilgrimages to Mont Bégo, which they believed had divine power – both protective, owing to the many streams which rise there, and awesome, owing to the sudden violent storms.

The engravings exhibit five themes – horns, arms or tools, anthropomorphs, geometric figures and other unidentified images. Here as elswhere, the mountain cult was linked to that of the bull; drawings of horns and bovine creatures feature in half the engravings. Ploughs and harrows harnessed to animals suggest that agriculture was practised. Some crisscross patterns may represent parcels of land. There are many representations of weapons that reflect those excavated on contemporary archeological sites. Human figures are, however, not very numerous; the best-known have been given names – Christ, the Wizard, the Chieftain, the Dancer. Others, of a more enigmatic nature, are open to interpretation such the Tree of Life at Fontanalbe (🔍 *guided tour only).*

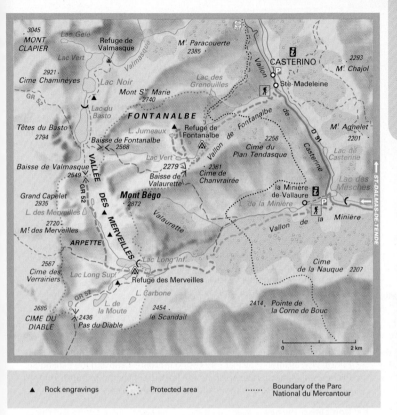

▲ Rock engravings   ⬚ Protected area   ······ Boundary of the Parc National du Mercantour

5hrs. *Easier walking than the first hike, ideal for families.* Start south of Casterino by the information panel *(sign: Fontanalbe),* taking the wooded path west and continuing to the refuge *(about 1hr).* Bear left of the refuge building and continue to Lac Vert *(about 45min),* the starting point for self-guided tours of the Sentier du Découverte *(1.5hr there and back).* For a guided tour of the engravings continue along the side of the lake to the guides' hut at **Lacs Jumeaux.**

By staying overnight at the Fontanalbe refuge *(reservation necessary)* it is possible to climb the foothills of Mont Bégo as far as the Baisse de Fontanalbe (alt 2 568m/8 423ft) – fine views of the three lakes in the Valmasque Valley. It is possible to continue towards the Valmasque Refuge or to return to Casterino by the outward route.

MONACO★★★

POPULATION 32 020

MICHELIN MAP 341 F5

LOCAL MAP SEE CORNICHES DE LA RIVIERA

The Principality of Monaco, a sovereign state overlooking the Mediterranean between Nice and the Italian border, perfectly captures the essence of the Côte d'Azur with its rococo palaces, lush gardens, world-famous casino and glamorous royal family. Luxury hotels, exclusive shopping boutiques, and the annual Formula 1 Grand Prix make this a favourite destination among the international jet-set.

▶ **Orient Yourself:** The 197ha/487 acres making up the Principality are divided into several different districts: Monaco-Ville, the old town on The Rock (*La Rocher*); Monte-Carlo, where luxury shops surround the historic casino and opera house; the busy port area linking them together, known as La Condamine; the new district of Font vieille to the east; and the beaches of Larvotto to the west. The Azur Express tourist train circles the major sights of Monaco between the Rock and Monte-Carlo, but the best way to get around the Principality is on the easy-to-navigate city bus (see *Address Book*).

> ### The Monégasques
>
> There are just over 6 000 native Monégasque citizens in the Principality, all exempt from taxes and military service. They are not, however, permitted to gamble in Monaco's casinos.

P **Parking:** Parking garages (free for the first hour) can be found throughout the Principality, including the Place du Casino in Monte-Carlo and the Parking des Pêcheurs in Monaco-Ville. Access to the Rock (Le Rocher) is permitted only to vehicles with Monaco or Alpes-Maritimes (06) licence plates.

Don't Miss: The newly restored interior of the Monte-Carlo Casino and Opéra, the winding streets of old Monaco-Ville leading to the Prince's Palace and the panoramic views of the coastline from the hillside Jardin Exotique.

Organizing Your Time: Count on at least a half day to see the best of Monaco, or a full day if you plan on visiting the museums, shopping or going to the beach. Start in Monaco-Ville, which has the most attractions and souvenir shops in one area. The casino tables don't open until 5pm.

Especially for Kids: There are several kid-friendly museums, such as the National Museum of Dolls and Automata, the Collection des Voitures Anciennes and the aquariums of the Musée Océanographique.

A Bit of History

The Grimaldi family – Monaco, which was inhabited in prehistoric times and later became a Greek settlement and a Roman port, first takes its real place in history with the Grimaldi dynasty. There are numerous branches of the family in France, at Cagnes and Beuil, and in Italy, at Genoa and Naples. During the conflict that broke out between the Guelphs and the Ghibellines, **François Grimaldi** was expelled from Genoa and, disguised as a monk together with his men, captured Monaco in 1297; hence the two armed monks on the Grimaldi coat of arms.

But François didn't hold it long, and it was only in 1308 that another Grimaldi bought the domain of Monaco from the Genoese. Since then, the name and the Grimaldi coat

> ### The Grimaldi Family Today
>
> In July 2005, the 47-year-old Prince Albert II of Monaco succeeded his father, Prince Rainier III, who died in April 2005 after ruling the Principality for 56 years. Albert and his sisters (Princesses Caroline and Stéphanie) lost their mother, the Hollywood actress Grace Kelly, in a tragic car accident in 1982. The new Prince's single status and his sisters' many rocky relationships are closely followed in the European tabloids.

of arms have always been carried by the heirs to the title, whether they come from the House of Goyon-Matignon (1731-1949) or, as in the case of the present Prince of Monaco, Albert II, from the House of Polignac.

A turbulent history – The history of Monaco has been fraught with family and political dramas. In the 16C Jean II was killed by his brother Lucien, who in turn was assassinated by his nephew; in 1604 Honoré I was thrown into the sea by his subjects. Monaco was subjected to foreign occupation: by the Spaniards from 1524 to 1641 (it was from the King of Spain that the Grimaldis received the title of Prince); by the French from 1641 to 1814; by the kingdom of Sardinia from 1815 to 1861. Menton and Roquebrune, which originally belonged to the Principality, were bought in 1861 by Napoleon III, at the time of the annexation of Nice.

Birth of Monte-Carlo – The first casino was an unremarkable establishment in Monaco-Ville itself, set up in 1856 by the Prince, who was short of funds. Only in 1862 did the casino move to its own premises in Monte-Carlo where it remained in humble isolation for several years. The arrival of **François Blanc**, director of the casino and spa in Bad Hamburg, brought success. Within a few years the casino became fashionable and the surrounding land was covered with luxurious houses, most of them the property of the casino company, La Société des Bains de Mer. The gaming tables in Monte-Carlo became the most famous and most popular in Europe.

A thriving economy – To accommodate the influx of visitors attracted by the gambling tables and tax concessions, Monaco began to put up buildings at a furious pace. Once all the available space had been occupied the shoreline was extended into the sea, providing 22% more land (the area known as Fontvieille).

Tourism remains the main activity. Without neglecting the traditional visitor, Monaco has sought to capture the business traveller and the conference trade. The hotel complex at Les Spélugues, built on pilons below the casino, includes a conference centre fitted with the latest equipment capable of seating 1 100 people. Monaco now has facilities rivalling those of Cannes and Nice. At Fontvieille light industry is being encouraged: clothing, printing, pharmaceutical products, plastics, precision engineering, perfumery, food processing. Around 40 international banking institutions count Monaco as a front-runner in the financial world. The media are represented by Radio Monte-Carlo and Télé Monte-Carlo. The Société des Bains de Mer, owner of the casino and the Hôtel de Paris, is the largest private employer in Monaco.

Original and revolutionary town-planning – The first large-scale town-planning projects that accompanied the economic explosion of the mid-1960s were hampered by the cramped nature of the territory.

During the first period, until the end of the 1970s, the solution favoured was to build upwards. A dozen high-rise buildings, more than 30 storeys high, were erected, adding an "American" touch to the landscape. Since the 1980s a new urban plan has been developed to satisfy the growing residential and service requirements: the future of property in Monaco would seem to lie underground. All the new access roads are now linked to the French network by deep tunnels. Connections between districts are facilitated by groups of automatic elevators or escalators. Behind the façade of some of Monaco's luxury hotels are access ramps to large public car parks hollowed out of the rock.

In the Fontvieille district, a bus station has been built 10m/33 ft below sea-level and a peninsula *(22ha/54 acres in area)* has been reclaimed from the sea. Around the town at the bottom of chasms between ancient buildings, minuscule excavators can be seen at work: every new building must be provided with a multilevel underground car park.

Projects completed in the new millennium include an underground railway station, the Grimaldi Forum conference and exhibition centre on the Larvotto shoreline, an extension of Port Hercule, and a new hotel and entertainment complex at the far eastern end of Larvotto Beach.

Allison M. Simpson/ MICHELIN

Address Book

PRACTICAL INFORMATION

TOURISM OFFICE

2a, Boulevard des Moulins – 98030 – ☎ *00 377 92 16 61 66. www.visitmonaco.com*

TOURS

Guided tours of Monaco and day-trips to the surrounding region can be booked at the Monaco Tourism Office.

TELEPHONE

To telephone Monaco from France, dial 00 followed by 377 (code for Monaco) and then the 8-digit telephone number.

CURRENCY AND POSTAGE

Monaco uses Euros just like France, but it has an independent postal system. All letters mailed from within the Principality must have Monégasque stamps.

For coin categories see the Legend at the back of this guide.

EATING OUT

☐☐ **Polpetta** – *2 Rue Paradis –* ☎ *00 377 93 50 67 84 –* ⏰ *Closed 10-30 Jun, Sat for lunch and Tue –*▥. A small Italian restaurant offering three different settings in which to enjoy a tasty tagliatelle alla carbonara or vitello al funghi: the verandah giving onto the street, the rustic-style dining hall or the cosy, intimate room at the back.

☐☐ **Richart** – *19 Boulevard des Moulins –* ☎ *00 377 93 30 15 06 – www.richart-monaco.com –* ⏰ *Closed Sun except in Dec .* The tiny squares of chocolate with their subtle aromas and intricate designs are a delight to behold... and savour! After buying a few boxes of chocolates to take back to friends, sit down in the elegant tea room decorated in white and grey and order one of the light snacks (salads, pastries, savoury tarts) while sipping a cup of delicately scented tea.

☐☐ **La Maison du Caviar** – *1 Avenue St-Charles –* ☎ *00 377 93 30 80 06 –* ⏰ *Closed 20 Jul-20 Aug, Sat for lunch and Sun.* This prestigious house has been serving choice caviar to Monaco residents for the past 50 years. In an unusual setting made up of bottle racks and wooden panelling, you can also purchase salmon, foie gras or bœuf strogonoff. Definitely worth a visit.

☐☐☐ **Zebra Square** – *Grimaldi Forum, 10 Avenue Princesse Grace –* ☎ *00 377 99 99 25 50 –* ⏰ *Closed 6 Feb - 2 Mar –*▥. This stylish restaurant has the same sleek decor as its Parisian namesake, featuring modern fusion cuisine and panoramic views over the sea from the terrace. At night the bar is packed with a young and trendy crowd.

☐☐☐ **Vistamar** – *Hôtel Hermitage, Place Beauarchais –* ☎ *00 377 92 16 40 00 –* ⏰ *Closed 24-26, 31 Dec, and lunch Jul-Aug –*▥. An elegant restaurant specialising in fresh seafood, with one of the best panoramic views of the Principality from its top-floor terrace.

WHERE TO STAY

☐ **Villa Bœri** – *29 Boulevard Général-Leclerc – 06240 Beausoleil –* ☎ *04 93 78 38 10 – 30 rooms –* ▭. A 1960s building on the French side of the border, fronted by a small garden planted with Mediterranean shrubs and flowers, offers a few rooms, some of which are lacking in modern comforts. Just cross the street and bingo... you are in Monte-Carlo!

☐☐ **Hôtel de France** – *6 Rue de la Turbie – Near the train station –* ☎ *00 377 93 30 24 64 -* ▭. *Recent renovation work on this hotel has graced it with charming, soundproofed rooms decorated in Provençal hues and a modern breakfast lounge enhanced with metal and wood furniture.*

☐☐☐☐ **Columbus Hôtel** – *23 Avenue Papalins – Fontvieille –* ☎ *00 377 92 05 90 00 – www.columbushotels.com –* ⇄🅿 *– 153 rooms –* ▭ *– Restaurant* (☐☐☐☐). Clean, contemporary lines and a soothing palette are combined with cozy fabrics and warm wood furnishings. A lounge bar and Italian-style brasserie with terrace seating attract fashionable locals. Access to a private pool; the heliport is just a block away.

☐☐☐☐ **Metropôle** – *4 Avenue Madone – Above the Metropôle Shopping Centre –* ☎ *00 377 93 15 15 15 – www.metropole. com –* ⇄ 🅿 SPA *– 131 rooms –* ▭ *– restaurant* (☐☐☐☐). This 1886 hotel got a complete facelift by the hot Parisian designer Jacques Garcia, with luxurious fabrics and timeless style. The outdoor pool and solarium have views overlooking the rooftops of the Place du Casino. The restaurant is managed by chef Joël Robuchon.

ON THE TOWN

Café de Paris – *Place du Casino –* ☎ *00 377 92 16 20 20 – www.sbm.mc –* ⏰ *Daily 7.30am-2am.* The terraces of this turn-of-the-century brasserie look out onto Place du Casino (for some excellent people-watching) and the Salon Bellevue upstairs commands a superb panorama of the Franco-Italian Riviera.

Casino de Monte-Carlo – *Place du Casino –* ☎ *00 377 92 16 20 00 – www.casino-monte-carlo.com –* ⏰ *Daily from noon until the last client leaves.* This is Europe's leading casino, with over a million euros in profits, attributed to gambling and not to slot machines as is the case in other casinos. The gambling salons and lavish dining hall Le Train Bleu, decorated in the style of the Orient-Express, are truly impressive. The terrace overlooking the sea is a haven of tranquillity, whether or not you have broken the bank!

La Terrasse (Bar du Vistamar) – *Square Beaumarchais* – ☎ *00 377 92 16 40 00* – *www.montecarloresort.com* – ◔ *Daily noon - 2.30pm and 7pm-1am.* ◕ *Closed Jul-Aug at lunch.* This famous bar has been patronised by many celebrities, such as Onassis and Maria Callas. Its superb terrace affords beautiful views of Monaco harbour. The specialities of the house are American cocktails, particularly those made with champagne!

Sass Café – *11 Avenue Princesse-Grace* – ☎ *00 377 93 25 52 00* – *www.sasscafe.com* – ◔ *Daily 8pm-2am (restaurant; until midnight in winter), 11pm to dawn (piano-bar).* Exclusive bar-restaurant with a cosy atmosphere where members of the local jet set drop in for a fancy vodka or champagne cocktail before meeting up at Jimmy'z.

Le Jimmy'z – *Quai Princesse-Grace* – ☎ *00 377 92 16 22 77* – ◔ *Daily 11pm to dawn. Reservations recommended.* It would be unthinkable to leave Monte-Carlo without having paid a visit to the legendary Jimmy'z. Formal evening wear is expected in this small but select club where the rich and wealthy love to congregate, whether they come from banking, advertising, fashion, film or the entertainment world... A unique, magic experience.

Stars'N'Bars – *6 Quai Antoine-1* – ☎ *00 377 93 50 95 95* – *www.starsnbars.com* – ◔ *Daily 11am-midnight; 4am for the dance hall.* This is the great American bar of the moment, where the ambience is slightly more relaxed than in the Principality's other establishments. Stars'N'Bars caters for a younger clientele eager to drink beer, eat a hamburger or two, play billiards, surf on the Internet and dance away the night. The decoration features the paraphernalia of stars. Rock concerts are organised on a regular basis. Terrace with a view of Monaco harbour.

The Living Room Club – *7 Avenue des Spélugues* – ☎ *00 377 93 50 80 31 ou 93 50 88 10* – *monte-carlo.mc/livingroom* – ◔ *Mon-Sat 11pm to dawn. Exceptionally open on Sun during the Formula 1 Grand Prix.* Select, high-class club where night owls meet up after leaving Jimmy'z. Try their special "Living Room cocktail" or one of their Champagnes. Piano bar music alternates with DJ evenings. Eclectic clientele.

Karé(ment) – *10 Avenue Princesse Grace, in the Grimaldi Forum* – ☎ *00 377 99 99 20 20* – *www.karement.mc* – ◔ *Thu-Sat 11pm to dawn.* The hottest night spot of the moment is this contemporary tapas bar and dance club located in the Grimaldi Forum. The trendy clientele tend to be younger than in the average Monégasque venues.

SHOWS

Salle des Etoiles, Le Sporting – *Avenue Princesse Grace* – ☎ *00 377 96 06 36 36* – *www.montecarloresort.com* . International stars perform regularly throughout the summer season at this Sporting Club venue with the retractible roof-top. *Jacket and tie required.*

Le Cabaret – *Place du Casino* – ☎ *00 377 92 16 36 36* – *www.montecarloresort.com* – ◔ *Shows Wed-Sat from 10.30pm; bar/restaurant open from 8.30pm.* This cabaret run by the Monte-Carlo Casino presents a Bellydance Superstars revue. Exceptionally, it also stages concerts of jazz and contemporary pop.

TOURS AND PUBLIC TRANSPORTATION

BUS

C.A.M. – ☎ *00 377 97 70 22 22* – *www.cam.mc* – ◔ *Service every 10 minutes from 7.30am-8.30pm* – ◉ *Tickets 1.45€ each or 3.50€ for an unlimited day pass.* Five regular bus lines that loop around the Principality. Maps available at the tourism office.

TAXI

Two main **taxi** stands are located near the casino and at the train station. ☎ *00 377 93 50 56 28 or 00 377 93 15 01 01.*

TOURIST TRAIN

Azur Express – *Avenue St-Martin, in front of the Musée Océanographique* – ☎ *00 377 92 05 64 38* – *www.visitmonaco.com* – ◔ *Operates 10.30-6pm (5pm in winter).* ◕ *Closed Jan and 15 Nov-26 Dec.* ◉ *6€.* This small tourist train in Monégasque colours makes 30-minute round-trip journeys around the Principality. Commentary in four languages.

BOAT TRIPS

Aquavision – *Compagnie de Navigation et de Tourisme de Monaco* – *Quai des Etats-Unis* – ☎ *00 377 92 16 15 15* – *www.aquavision-monaco.com* ◔ *Jul-Aug departures at 11am, 2.30pm, 4pm and 5.30pm; Jun and Sep daily except Mon departures at 11am, 2.30pm, 4pm; Apr, May, Oct daily except Mon departures at 2.30pm.* ◉ *11€ (child 8€).* Boat trips affording views of the sea depths, and marine fauna and flora, with commentary in four languages.

HELICOPTER

Héli Air Monaco – *Héliport de Monaco-Fontvieille* – ☎ *00 377 92 05 00 50.* Regular daily service (6min) every 15min between Monaco and the Aéroport de Nice-Côte d'Azur. Also 10-minute sightseeing tours of Monaco (◉ *50€ per person)* and daily flights between Monaco and Fréjus or St-Raphaël. For details call ☎ *04 94 51 83 83* (Fréjus tourist office).

SHOPPING

All the famous fashion brands have boutiques in Monte-Carlo.

Shops specialising in traditional goods are to be found in the narrow streets of the Rock (*Le Rocher*) opposite the palace.

The Boutique du Rocher in Avenue de la Madone is the official boutique for local arts and crafts.

CALENDAR OF EVENTS

Monte-Carlo Rally – *held every year since 1911 at the end of January.*

Feast of Ste-Dévote – *Monaco's Patron Saint feast, January 27.*

International Circus Festival – *January/ February in Fontvieille.*

Sciaratù Carnival – *Monégasque festival during the week of Mardi Gras.*

Rose Ball – *Held every March since 1954 to benefit the Princess Grace Foundation.*

Spring Arts Festival – *Art, music, theatre and dance festival throughout April .*

International Tennis Masters Series – *Held every April.*

Monaco Grand Prix – *every May in the streets of the Principality on a winding circuit (3.145km/2mi).*

Monte-Carlo Golf Open – *on the hills of Mont Agel every June.*

Fireworks Festival – *July and August.*

National Day of Monaco – *Picturesque procession on the Rocher and other cultural spectacles November 19th.*

Walking Tour

The Rock★★

Tour: allow 3hr. Park in Parking des Pêcheurs and take the elevator.

Monaco-Ville is picturesquely sited on a rock jutting 800m/875yd out to sea and overlooking the bay. Crowned by the old town's ramparts, the Rocher de Monaco, as it is known, is a lovely sight to behold, especially on a fine evening, when you can admire its floodlit outlines from the Grande Corniche road or the Belvédère de La Turbie. The town is so pretty that it resembles a studio set: neat little 18C houses with their salmon-pink façades, squeezed in along quaint alleyways. This is the medieval heart of the Principality, home to some of its most popular sights, including the **Musée Océanographique**★★ (✆ See *Discovering Local Flora and Fauna*) and Prince's Palace★. On the car park terraces, near the Musée Océanographique, is **Monte-Carlo Story.** (✆ ☺ *Open Jul-Aug 2-6pm; Sept-June 2-5pm.* ☺ *Closed Nov-Dec 25.* ☺ *6.50€ (child 3€).* ☎ *00 377 93 25 32 33)* In a large hall a multiscreen production retraces the history of the Grimaldi dynasty and the development of the Principality.

Fountain on the Rock

Allison M. Simpson/ MICHELIN

▶ *Above ground you'll find yourself in front of the Musée Océanographic. Take Avenue St-Martin on the left, through the Jardins St-Martin★, to the cathedral.*

Cathedral

The neo-Romanesque cathedral was built with white stone from La Turbie on the ruins of the church of St-Nicolas between 1875 and 1903. The high altar, the organ loft and the Bishop's chair, its canopy supported by granite columns, are of white marble inlaid with mosaic and copper motifs. In the south transept chapel stands a fine Spanish Renaissance style altar in red and gold. The Princes' tombs are located in the ambulatory.

The cathedral has a collection of **early paintings from the Nice School**★★. At the entrance to the ambulatory *(left)* is the **altarpiece of St Nicholas** by Louis Bréa: 18 sections in glowing colours surrounded by Renaissance carving of leaves and dolphins. In the centre St Nicholas is seated on a green throne; on most panels the names of the characters appear against a gold background: St Devota, patron of Monaco, in a small painting *(bottom left)*; a remarkable Mary Magdalene *(right)*; St Anne curiously cradling both the Virgin as a child and the Infant Jesus in her arms *(top* *right)*. Three panels – St Roch, St Anthony and the Rosary – decorate the ambulatory. In the south transept above the sacristy door is another altarpiece by Bréa: a **Pietà** set against a Monaco landscape.

▶ *Follow the Rue de l'Eglise to Rue Emile de Loth, then left at the Place de la Mairie to Rue Princesse-Marie-de-Lorraine.*

Chapelle de la Miséricorde

This chapel's classic pink and white façade was built in 1646 by the Black Penitents. In a niche on the south side is a **recumbent Christ**★ by the Monégasque sculptor Bosio; on Good Friday this statue is carried through the streets of the old town.

▶ *On leaving turn right onto picturesque Rue Basse.*

Historial des Princes de Monaco

♿ ⏱ *Open Oct-Feb 11am-5pm; Mar-Sept 10am-6pm.* ⚐ *3.80€ (child 2€).* ☏ *00 377 93 30 39 05.*

In a suite of handsome vaulted rooms the history of the Grimaldi family is set out in 24 scenes with 40 life-size wax figures.

▶ *Continue along Rue Basse to the Place du Palais.*

Place du Palais★

This vast square, ornamented with cannons given to the Prince of Monaco by Louis XIV, is bordered to the northeast by a crenellated parapet from which there is a **view** of the harbour, Monte-Carlo and the coast as far as the Bordighera headland. To the southwest is the **Promenade Ste-Barbe** with a view of Fontvieille and Cap d'Ail.

> ### Changing of the Guard
>
> The tightly choreographed changing of the guard takes place daily on the Place du Palais at precisely 11.55am.

Palais du Prince★

⏱ *Guided visits Jun-Sep 9.30am-6.30pm; Oct 10am-5pm.* ⏱ *Closed Nov-May.* ⚐ *6€ (child 3€).* ☏ *00 377 93 25 18 31. www.palais.mc.*

The palatial home of the Grimaldi family was built in the 17th century in place of the original 13C Genoese fortress. The buildings on the south side, in Italian Renaissance style, are 15C and 16C. The formidable perimeter is built into the vertical rock. Some battlemented towers remain standing. A monumental doorway with the Grimaldi arms adorns this robust-looking ensemble.

The audio tour leads first to the Hercules Gallery which overlooks the lovely main courtyard featuring a double staircase in white marble. The whole gallery is decorated with 16C and 17C frescoes – particularly by Ferrari. The Throne Room and the state apartments where official receptions are held are decorated with carpets and precious furniture and hung with portraits signed by Rigaud, Philippe de Champaigne and Van Loo.

▶ *Follow the Rampe Major through 16C, 17C and 18C gates down to Place d'Armes, where a lively market is held every morning.*

B. Kaufmann/ MICHELIN

Monte-Carlo Opera House

La Condamine
30min

In the Middle Ages this term applied to cultivable land at the foot of a village or a castle. Nowadays La Condamine is the commercial district stretching between the Rock and Monte-Carlo.

Port Hercule

Prince Albert I commissioned the building of the harbour skirted by a broad terraced promenade and crowded with luxury yachts. The Olympic swimming pool was added by Rainier III. In season, **boat trips** in a glass-bottomed catamaran leave from Quai des États-Unis (see *Address Book*).

From the northwest corner of the harbour a valley separating La Condamine from Monte-Carlo runs up under a viaduct to the church of Ste-Dévote.

▶ *Follow the Blvd Albert I to the passage leading to Place Ste-Dévote.*

Église Ste-Dévote

Built in 1870 on the ruins of an old church, it contains a fine 18C marble altar.

St Devota was martyred in Corsica in the 3C when, according to tradition, the skiff carrying her body to Africa was caught in a terrific storm and was guided by a dove towards the French coast, eventually landing at Monaco.

In the Middle Ages relics of the saint were stolen and taken away by ship. But the thieves were caught and their ship razed – a legend which has given rise to the ceremony which takes place every 26 January when a ship is burned on the square in front of the church; the next day there is a procession.

▶ *Turn right when exiting the church onto the Rue Grimaldi, a popular shopping street, taking a detour along the pedestrian-only Rue Princesse Caroline to finish at the Place d'Armes.*

Monte-Carlo★★★ *1hr 30min*

Monte-Carlo is a name famous throughout the world. It brings to mind high-stakes gambling as well as the majestic setting of its palaces, casinos, sumptuous villas, luxurious shops and exotic gardens. Monte-Carlo is also home to the National Museum and modern beachfront facilities at Larvotto Plage.

Place du Casino

The Place du Casino is the centre of the action, where the Café de Paris and the Hôtel de Paris flank the **casino** (see *Sights*), surrounded by beautiful gardens. Around the back of the casino is a fine **terrace**★★ overlooking the sea, with views stretching from Monaco to Italy. The terrace is extended by the roof-top promenades of the Spélugues complex, adorned by a composition in enamelled pumice stone by Vasarely entitled *Hexa Grace*.

▶ *Follow the Avenue des Spélugues down the hill to the Avenue Princesse Grace.*

Avenue Princesse Grace

The reclaimed seafront along the Avenue Princesse Grace features a tranquil **Jardin Japonais**★ (see *Discovering Local Flora and Fauna*) at the foot of the ultra-sleek Grimaldi Forum entertainment complex opened in 2000. Across the street is the elegant **Musée National** (see *Sights*).

Beyond the Grimaldi Forum are the luxurious beaches of **Larvotto Plage** ☺. Here you'll find boutiques, cafés and restaurants overlooking the pebble beach. Swimmers will find two anchored diving platforms past the jetty, and many colourful fish inhabiting Larvotto's underwater nature reserve. To the east of the beaches is the Monte-Carlo Sporting Club and famous Jimmy'z nightclub (see *Address Book*).

Sights

Le Casino de Monte-Carlo

🧸 *Forbidden to anyone under 18 years of age.* 🕐 *Slots and European gaming rooms open from 2pm (noon on weekends); blackjack tables open from 5pm.* 🕐 *Closed when the last person leaves.* ⊚*10€ Public rooms, 20€ private rooms. ID/Passport required.* ☎ *00 377 92 16 20 00. www.casinomontecarlo.com.*

This impressive building comprises several sections built between 1878 and 1910. The oldest sections, designed by **Charles Garnier,** architect of the Paris Opera House, make up the seafront façade and the recently renovated Opera-Theatre, once home to Diaghilev's famous Ballet Russe.

Before Laying a Bet

Stroking the knee of the equestrian statue of Louis XV in the entrance of the Hôtel de Paris before heading into the casino is said to bring the gambler good luck. Admission is free to the slot machine rooms in the casino, in the Café de Paris (also on the Place du Casino), and at the Sun Casino (in the Fairmont Hotel, 12 avenue des Spélugues). During the summer season *(Jul to mid-Sep)* gambling takes place in the Salles des Palmiers of the Sporting-Club de Monte-Carlo. Gaming tables usually require a fee of 10€-20€ to play.

As you enter the huge central hall, modern slot machines are on the right, the Opera-Theatre straight ahead and the sumptuously decorated gambling rooms on the left. First are the public rooms: the Renaissance Room, the European Grand Salon, the America Room and the Room of the Graces. A small gallery separates the America Room from the rooms of the Cercle Privé's two Touzet rooms and the vast and ornate François Médecin Room.

Musée Napoléonien et des Archives du Palais★

🕐 *Open daily (except Mon) Jun-Sep 9.30am-6.30pm; Oct to 11 Nov 10am-5pm; mid-Dec to end of May 10.30am-noon and 2-4.30pm.* 🕐 *Closed mid-Nov to mid-Dec, 1 Jan, 25 Dec.* ⊕ *4€ (2€ kids).* ☎ *00 377 93 25 18 31. www.palais.mc.*

The ground floor of a wing of the palace is devoted to a museum on Napoleon, including geneological charts showing how the Bonapartes are related to the Grimaldi princes. There are many of the Emperor's souvenirs and documents, such as his watch, tobacco pouch, tricolour scarf and hat belonging to the "little corporal". There are also coins, medals, uniforms, flags belonging to the grenadiers on Elba and busts of Napoleon by Canova and Houdon.

Apart from a portrait of Napoleon by Gérard, the upper floor is devoted to the history of Monaco, with the charter granted by Louis XII recognising the Principality's independence on display.

Musée National de Monaco★

Kids 🕐 *Open Easter to Sep 10am-6.30pm (last admission 1hr before closing time); Oct to Easter 10am-12.15pm, 2.30-6.30pm.* 🕐 *Closed 1 Jan, 1 May, 19 Nov, 25 Dec and during the 4 days of the Grand Prix Automobile de Monaco.* ⊕ *6€ (child 3.50€).* ☎ *00 377 93 30 91 26.*

The National Museum of Dolls and Automata, housed in a charming villa built by Charles Garnier and fronted by a rose garden dotted with sculptures – note the *Young Faun* by Carpeaux – contains a collection of 19C automata and some 400 dolls dating from the 18C to the present. The intricate internal workings are open to view; they are set in motion several times a day. Of note is an 18C Neapolitan Nativity scene including 250 figures.

Pierrot and Dogs by Vichy (1865), Musée National de Monaco

A. Soriano

Collection des Voitures Anciennes★

Kids ♿ 🕐 *Open 10am-6pm.* 🕐 *Closed 25 Dec* ⊕ *6€ (child 3€).* ☎ *00 377 92 05 28 56. www.palais.mc.*

About 100 old vehicles and carriages from the royal collection are on display on the five levels of this exhibition hall. On the first level are the barouches used by Prince Charles III. Next is the De Dion Bouton (1903), the first car owned by Prince Albert I, and other famous models: a Lincoln Torpedo convertible (1928), a Packard cabriolet (1935) and the Buick Skylark (1966). The Rolls Royce Silver Cloud given by Monégasque tradesmen to Prince Rainier on his wedding day in 1956, and a 1952 Austin London taxi converted for Princess Grace bring a personal touch to this collection. The milestones of the contemporary history of the motor car are represented by a tracked vehicle, Citroën de la Croisière Jaune, a fine selection of front-wheel drives, American military equipment, a Trabant and a 1986 Lamborghini built along futuristic lines.

Princess Grace

Grace Kelly was born in Philadelphia on 12 November 1929, the third of four children. After studying at the New York Academy of Dramatic Arts, she began working as an actress for television and the theatre. Her first breakthrough in the cinema was the movie *High Noon* (1952), in which she played a young bride married to Gary Cooper. Many films were to follow but her name has remained closely associated with that of the British director Alfred Hitchcock, for whom she starred in *Dial M for Murder* (1954), *Rear Window* (1954) and *To Catch a Thief* (1955), shot entirely on location in the South of France. Grace Kelly was introduced to Prince Rainier of Monaco at the Cannes Film Festival and they were married in April 1956. She gave birth to three children, Caroline, Albert and Stéphanie.

The new princess soon won the affections of the Principality's residents. She was a model mother and spent much of her time supporting charitable causes such as the Red Cross and AMADE, an organisation set up to help developing countries. Her life was to end tragically in 1982 when her car veered off the Grande Corniche and crashed into the cliff face.

The 1929 Bugatti (winner of the 1st Grand Prix) and a 1989 Ferrari F1 (600hp) have pride of place in the hall dedicated to Formula 1. On the left, on a pedestal surrounded by flowers, is a helmet worn by the racing driver Ayrton Senna, who died during the 1994 Italian Grand Prix, a permanent reminder of the dangers of this sport.

Musée Naval

   Open 10am-6pm. *Closed 1 Jan, 25 Dec.* *4€ (child 2.50€).* 00 377 92 05 28 48. www.musee-naval.mc.

The hundred exhibits in this museum are the cream of the royal collection of model ships covering a period from ancient times to the present day. The oldest models were built by Prince Albert I in 1874. Among the most remarkable are the **gondole impériale** made in 15 days for the inspection of Napoleon I at Anvers, and the *Missouri*, depicted in the state she was in on 2 September 1945 when the armistice was signed with Japan.

Musée des Timbres et des Monnaies

   Open 10am-5pm (Jul-Sep 6pm). *3€.* 00 377 93 15 41 50.

Housed in a very modern setting, this museum contains all the stamps produced in the Principality together with a fine retrospective of the Princes' collections. The first stamp bearing the head of a Monégasque sovereign was issued in 1885 during the reign of Charles III. Prior to that date, after the introduction of postmarks, Sardinian stamps were used for franking, and from 1860, overprinted "Monaco".

In the large gallery there is a line-engraving rotary press which was used for half a century to print Monaco's stamps. The rare stamps gallery contains several unique exhibits: letters sent from Fort Hercule (as Monaco was called under the Revolution), and the first stamps from Sardinia and Monaco printed in colour.

A set of current Monégasque stamps can be bought at the reception alongside boxes of coins, both those currently in use and collectors' items.

Musée de la Chapelle de la Visitation

   Open daily (except Mon) 10am-6pm. *Closed Mon, 1 Jan, 1 May, 1-4 Jun, 19 Nov, 25 Dec.* *3€.* 00 377 93 500 700.

This 17C Baroque chapel houses the rich Barbara Piasecka-Johnson collection of sacred works of art. Of particular interest are works by Zurbarán, Rubens and the Italian Baroque masters.

Local Fauna and Flora

Musée Océanographique★★

   Open Jul-Aug 9.30am-7.30pm; Apr-Jun and Sep 9.30am-7pm; Oct-Mar 10am-6pm. *Closed Sun during Grand Prix Automobile de Monaco.* *11€ (child 6-18 years 6€).* 00 377 93 15 36 00. www.oceano.mc.

Occupying an exceptional site on the south face of the Rock, the imposing freestone building housing the Oceanographic Museum and research institute overlooks the Mediterranean from an impressive cliff (80m/262ft).

It was founded in 1910 by marine research enthusiast Prince Albert I to house his scientific collections dating back to 1885. Located in the basement, the **aquarium**★★ is one of the finest in Europe. More than 4, 500 fish representing 400 different species swim

Musée Océanographique

Coral reef with its fauna

in 90 pools that recreate their natural habitat. The tropical species exhibit the most astounding colours. Among the most strange, magnificent or rare specimens are the flying scorpion fish, the orange clownfish, the surgeon fish and the sunfish. In a huge pool (25 000l/5 500gal of water) a nurse shark lives happily with large green turtles and hawksbill turtles. The live coral reef from the Red Sea is an outstanding exhibit.

The **Salle d'Océanographie Zoologique**★, also known as Salle de la Baleine, contains the skeletons of large marine mammals: a whale (20m/66ft), washed up on the Italian coast, a killer whale, a sperm whale, a sea-cow, a narwhal as well as stuffed specimens: giant Japanese crabs (2m/6ft wide), a giant turtle (200kg/441lb) and casts of coelacanths.

On the right of the **atrium** is a cinema showing films made by the legendary underwater filmmaker Jacques-Yves Cousteau, who was director of the museum from 1957-88. The central oceanographic hall presents the scientific journeys of Prince Albert: models of his four research vessels, notably *Princesse Alice II*. It was on board this ship that, in 1901, the Prince collected fish from a record depth of 6 000m/19 681ft and on an expedition to Spitzberg reached a latitude of 80°N. Nearby is the reconstruction of the laboratory installed on his last vessel, *Hirondelle II*, as well as his whaling boat from which he was able to recover animals living at great depths from the stomachs of the whales he hunted.

Next is the exhibition *Découverte de l'Océan* which explains the main marine phenomena: waves, salinity of the water, the effect of the ocean on the atmosphere and more complex questions such as the rise of deep water along certain coasts (upwelling). Among the remarkable animations are a reconstruction of the sinking of the *Titanic*, a gigantic model of the Marianus trench, the deepest in the world, and one of the first submarines, *Bushnell's Turtle*.

Terrace – From the second floor terrace *(lift)*, overhanging the sea, there is a magnificent **view**★★ of the coast from the Esterel range to the Italian Riviera and of the Tête de Chien and Mont Agel inland.

Jardin Exotique★★

🕐 *Open mid-May to mid-Sep 9am-7pm; mid-Sep to mid-May 9am-6pm or dusk depending on the season.* 🕐 *Closed 19 Nov and 25 Dec.* ⊷ *6.80€ (combined ticket with Grotte de l'Observatoire and Musée d'Anthropologie Préhistorique).* ☎ *00 377 93 15 29 80. www. monte-carlo.mc/jardinexotique.*

This exceptional collection of cacti, some more than a century old, clings dramatically to the cliffs above Monaco. The tropical gardens cascade down a steep rock face which has its own microclimate favourable to cacti and other succulents, particularly arborescents: huge candelabra-like euphorbia, giant aloes, "mother-in-law cushions", Barbary figs. There are 6 000 varieties of semi-desertic flora; many of the unusual shapes and vivid colours are native to Mexico and southern Africa. The garden offers many magnificent **views**★ of the Rock of Monaco, the harbour, Monte-Carlo, Cap Martin and the Italian Riviera *(viewing table)*.

After descending 279 steps, you will reach the **Grotte de l'Observatoire**★ *(*🕐 *Same times and charges as for the Jardin Exotique.)* The tour passes through a number of chambers at different levels, adorned with stalactites, stalagmites and other delicate and varied geological formations of dolomitic limestone.

Excavations at the cave mouth have revealed signs of human habitation some 200 000 years ago; tools and Prehistoric animal bones are on display in the **Musée d'Anthropologie Préhistorique**★ *(access through the Jardin Exotique).*

The presentation and extreme diversity of the exhibits make this museum of interest even to the non-specialist. The Rainier III Gallery contains regional collections (animal bones and Stone Age tools), including animals which once roamed the Riviera before the climate changed, such as reindeer, mammoths and cave bears and even hippos. The Albert-I Gallery contains a retrospective exhibition on the principal milestones of the evolution of mankind.

Jardin Japonais★

Access from Avenue Princesse Grace. ♿ 🕐 *Open 9am to dusk. Free entry.* ☎ *00 377 93 15 22 77.*

In the contemporary surroundings of the Larvotto district this garden provides a calm green oasis beside the sea. The garden (7ha/17 acres), which is designed according to Shintoist principles by a great Japanese landscape gardener, is a highly structured miniaturisation of the world of nature. The three key elements of a Japanese garden are illustrated: the line (path), the point (pool) and the surface (waterfall). The mineral constituents come from the Auvergne (granite), from Corsica (porphyry) and from the Tinée Valley (shingle in the pool).

The **Pont Cintré "Taïko"** is a scarlet bridge (the colour of happiness) illustrating the difficult journey towards the gods, represented by the central islands: the one with two pine trees has the shape of a turtle, symbol of longevity: the small island planted with a single pine depicts a nesting crane.

Near the tea room, the **Jardin Zen** invites contemplation of the barren countryside outlined by the seven stones of Cap Corse. The ellipses traced on the gravel symbolise the perpetual movement of the universe.

The tea rooms with their spartan decoration add another oriental note to this unusual display.

Jardin Animalier

Kids ♿ 🕐 *Open Jun-Sep 9am-noon, 2-7pm; Mar-May 10am-noon, 2-6pm; Oct-Feb 10am-noon, 2-5pm.* 👝 *4€ (child 2€).* ☎ *00 377 93 25 18 31. www.palais.mc.*

The zoo terraces, on the southwest face of the Rock, present a large and varied collection of mammals, reptiles, exotic birds and numerous monkeys. Fine view of the sea and Cap d'Ail.

Parc Paysager

Take city bus #5 or #6, or leave your car in the car park Stade Louis II.

In this park plant species from all over the world are clustered around a charming lake. Nearby lies the **Princesse Grace Rose Garden** boasting more than 4 000 bushes belonging to 150 different rose varieties, some of which were created by celebrated gardeners. The statue of the princess was erected in 1983, the year after her death, by Kees Verkade.

Hiking Tours

Coastal Path to Cap Martin★★

3hr on foot there and back leaving from Monte-Carlo, preferably in the afternoon – local maps 👣 *see MENTON and Corniches de la RIVIERA.*

🚶 Tourists wishing to take a shorter route can drive to the train station of Roquebrune-Cap-Martin and join up with the path running below.

On the left of the Monte-Carlo Beach Hotel, follow the steps down between two villas.

For a description of the walk in the opposite direction 👣 *see ROQUEBRUNE-CAP-MARTIN: COASTAL PATH.*

Coastal Path to Cap d'Ail★

1hr on foot there and back – local map 👣 *see Corniches de la RIVIERA. Park the car near Plage Marquet, the beach to the west of Fontvieille.*

From the beach there is a path along the shore. Monaco Rock soon disappears from sight as the path rounds the headland where the sea throws up a fine spray as it crashes on the rocks. Slowly Cap Ferrat and Beaulieu come into view. On the left of La Pinède Restaurant, steps lead up to the road and Cap-d'Ail station. The path can be followed as far as the Plage Mala, then a steep flight of steps leads to the road back into the conurbation.

Beausoleil; Mont des Mules★

3km/2mi then 15min on foot there and back – local map and description ⓒ *see Corniches de la RIVIERA.*

MONS★

POPULATION 671

MICHELIN MAP 340 P3

This old village is perched between earth and sky on a wild and sunny mountain plateau★ flourishing with every single type of sub-Alpine Provençal plant. Mons was repopulated after several plagues in the Middle Ages by Genoan families who skillfully rebuilt the village and cultivated the land with olives and wheat. The picturesque narrow streets and the tiny squares with their dry stone houses and carved fountains make for a pleasant walk.

▸ **Orient Yourself:** At an altitude of 800m/2625ft, Mons is located 13.5km/8mi north of Fayence (ⓒ *see FAYENCE*) and 16.5km/10mi northwest of St-Cézaire-sur-Siagne (ⓒ *see GRASSE*). 🛈 *Place St-Sébastien* ☏ *04 94 76 39 54.*

Visit

Place St-Sébastien

Set off by an 18C fountain, the square has a terrace that looks out over the Siagne and Siagnole Valleys and provides an exceptional **view**★★, which on a clear day, extends from Le Coudon (north of Toulon) via the Lérins islands and Corsica to the Alps on the Italian frontier *(viewing table)*.

A hike along Chemin de la Cha-pelle St-Pierre (in the village) will take you to three curious dolmens: **Riens** (400m/400yd), **La Colle** (3.5km/2mi) and **La Brainée** (7.5km/4.7mi).

Church

🕐 *Guided tours 2-6pm on request. Apply to the tourist office.* ☏ *04 94 76 39 54.*

The building, which was started in the Upper Provençal Romanesque style, was greatly altered in the 15C and 17C. It is fitted with unusually uniform furnishings: five Baroque altarpieces including a huge triptych dating from 1680 on the high altar dedicated to the Assumption of the Virgin and St Peter and St Paul. To the right of the high altar stands a beautiful 15C silver processional cross. The bell in the square belfry was cast in 1438.

MOUGINS

POPULATION 16 051

MICHELIN MAP 341 C6

The old village of Mougins dominates the summit of an extraordinary hilltop site ★. Its ancient ramparts and a 12C fortified entrance (known as the "Saracen Gate") contain the restored houses and narrow cobblestone streets which corkscrew up the hill amidst lush greenery and flowers.

▶ Orient Yourself: Mougins is in the Alpes-Maritimes department between Cannes (6km/3.7mi) and Grasse (11km/6.8mi) on the N 85. The vestiges of the old ramparts, which date back to the town's fiefdom under the Lérins Abbots, mark the limits of the pedestrian-only Old Town. 🗓 *15 Avenue Ch-Malet ☎ 04 93 75 87 67. www.mougins-coteazur. org*

🅿 Several parking areas can be found at the foot of the Old Town *(follow signs)*.

The Minotaur's Lair

As early as 1935 **Pablo Picasso** discovered Mougins in the company of Dora Marr and the photographer Man Ray. He and his wife Jacqueline settled in Mougins in 1961 and remained there until his death in 1973. They lived in the Notre-Dame-de-Vie district in the mas called L'Antre du Minotaure (The Minotaur's Lair), which became a creative workshop for artists.

Sights

Begin at the **Place du Commandant-Lamy** *(map with commentary available at the Tourism Office)*, which you'll easily find as it's a festive square where restaurants and an ancient fountain are shaded by a giant elm. Finish your walk at the **Place des Patriotes** which has a beautiful panoramic view★ over the coast *(orientation table)*.

Espace Culturel

🕐 *Open weekdays 9am-5pm.* 🕐 *Closed in Nov and public holidays.* 🎟 *Free entry.* ☎ *04 92 92 50 42.*

This former Chapel St-Bernardin of the White Peninents now houses the town hall, the Salle des Mariages, and the Musée Maurice Gotlobb (1885-1970), an artist who lived in Mougins from 1924-60. The museum displays his paintings, ceramics and music hall statuettes, as well as temporary exhibitions. There is also an interesting retrospective of the history of Mougins, including a section on **Commandant Lamy,** born in Mougins in 1858, who explored Africa and founded the capital of Chad (once called Fort-Lamy).

Address Book

For coin ranges see the Legend at the back of this guide.

EATING OUT

🍽 **La Broche de Fer** – *427 Avenue St-Basile, Route de Valbonne* – ☎ *04 92 92 08 08* – 🕐 *Closed 14-29 Feb, 22 Oct-6 Nov and Wed.* Tucked away from Mougins, this roomy restaurant laid out on four levels has been charmingly decorated in the true Provençal spirit. The main speciality is meat, either grilled or cooked on a spit.

🍽🍽 **L'Amandier de Mougins** – *In the village* – ☎ *04 93 90 00 91* – 🕐 *Closed 15-26 Nov.* A 14C press has been converted into a ravishing inn with a vaulted dining area and a tiny terrace that is invariably booked for both lunch and dinner. It has earned a well-deserved reputation thanks to its attractive setting, its homey cooking and its warm, congenial welcome.

🍽🍽 **Brasserie de la Méditerranée** – *In the village* – ☎ *04 93 90 03 47* – 🕐 *Closed 4-20 Jan and Tue Nov-Mar.* This bistro on the village square has a fine terrace overlooking the main street. Inside, the ambience is warm and intimate despite the popularity of the place. The menu presents Provençal specialities made with fresh local produce.

WHERE TO STAY

🛏🛏 **Hôtel du Val de Mougins** – *95 Avenue du Marechal-Juin* – ☎ *04 92 28 37 77* – *23 rooms* – 🍴. This family-run establishment on the Route Napoléon, at the foot of Old Mougins, has rooms decorated with pretty linens, many with balconies. The quietest rooms face the mountain flank at the back of the hotel.

Musée de la Photographie

🕐 *Open Jul-Sep 10am-8pm; Oct-Jun daily (except Mon and Tue) 10am-noon, 2-6pm (Sun and public holidays 2-6pm).* 🕐 *Closed in Nov.* 👓 *2€.* ☎ *04 93 75 85 67.*

The Photography Museum is to be found behind the church bell-tower, beside the Saracen Gate. The display occupies three floors and includes a lovely collection of old cameras, such as the **cidoscope**, an ancestor of animated cartoons, and numerous photographs of Picasso and his family by his friend André Villers. There are also works by famous photographers such as Clergue, Doisneau, Duncan, Lartigue, Roth, Otero, Denise Colomb and the press photographer Ralph Gatti.

Some rooms are given over to temporary exhibitions displaying the work of contemporary photographers.

Excursions

Ermitage Notre-Dame-de-Vie – *6km/3.5mi – about 45min*

▷ *East of Mougins by D 235 going northwest and D 35 east; after 2km/1mi turn right.*
🕐 *Open during Mass Sun mornings, 9am.*

The **site** ★ is strikingly beautiful: the **hermitage** of Notre-Dame-de-Vie stands at the top of a long meadow bordered by two rows of giant cypresses (on the right beneath the trees stands a 15C stone cross). The **view**★ towards Mougins is reminiscent of a Tuscan landscape. It is here that Picasso chose to spend his last years. His house, well screened by trees and bushes, is just opposite.

The 17C **chapel** has a bell-tower roofed in colourful tiles. There are three Gallo-Roman funeral inscriptions, a fine altarpiece of the Assumption in blue and gold, and on the left-hand wall a collection of votive offerings.

Notre-Dame-de-Vie (Our Lady of Life) was known throughout the area as a "Sanctuary of Grace". Stillborn babies were brought here, sometimes from great distances, where it was believed they resuscitated during Mass long enough to be christened.

▷ *A track suitable for motor vehicles leads to D 3, which takes you back to Mougins.*

Étang de Fontmerle

▷ *3km by D 35 towards the golf course, then at the round-about take avenue de Grasse, and then turn right on the Promenade de l'Étang.*

This large pond was neglected for many years until it became a protected site for the cultivation of the lotus flower. It is now the largest group of lotus plants in Europe. The pond is popular with both migrating birds and those who come to watch them from the observation tower. The best time to see the flowers in bloom is July through mid-September.

Musée de l'Automobiliste★ *5km/3mi southeast*

▷ *From Mougins take D 234 northwest; turn right onto D 3 towards Cannes. Just before the motorway turn left onto Chemin du Belvédère, which becomes Chemin des Collines. At the second junction turn left onto Chemin de Ferrandou, then left again to cross over the motorway. Turn right onto Chemin de Font-de-Currault, which leads to the museum car park. The Car Museum is located next to the Aire Nord des Bréguières (service area on the north side) of motorway A 8; it can also be reached via the footbridge from the service area on the south side.*

🕐 *Open Jun-Sep 10am-7pm; Oct-May 10am-1pm, 2-6pm.* 🕐 *Closed Mon, Jan and holidays.* 👓 *7€ (children under 12 free).* ☎ *04 93 69 27 80. www.musauto.fr.st.*

The façade of the futuristic building beside the motorway consists of concrete and glass to resemble a radiator. Two motoring enthusiasts, Adrien Maeght and Antoine Raffaelli, assisted by ESCOTA, the company running the French Riviera's motorways, have gathered a collection of vintage cars and more recent models, which are shown in rotation (about 90 at a time). Each vehicle in the gleaming display is in perfect working order; all the famous makes are represented: Benz (first serial model 1894), Bugatti (57, 1938), Ferrari, Hispano-Suiza, Delage, and Rolls Royce. The section devoted to racing cars, some of which have won Grand Prix competitions, contains a series of Matras from the years 1967 to 1974. Every year two thematic exhibitions are held, focusing on one particular aspect of motoring. The museum cinema shows films on the history of the automobile and the part played in it by each make.

Various activities and competitions held throughout the year in the entrance court include an exchange market, public auction, and best turned-out vehicle.

Mouans-Sartoux

▷ *3km/2mi northwest of Mougins on the N 2085.*

This town is made up of the medieval village of Sartoux, ruined by the Saracens, and Mouans and ancient fortress that once protected the Route de Grasse. In 1588, Suzanne de Villeneuve, widow of a Huguenot , defended her village against the troops of the Duke of Savoy. After he razed the château despite a pact signed between then, Suzanne had him chased down all the way to Cagnes, where he was forced to pay heavy reparations.

Espace de l'Art Concreta

🕐 Open Jul-Aug 11am-7pm, Sep-Jun (except Mon) 11am-6pm.👝 3€. ☎ 04 93 75 71 50.

In a pretty park, the Château de Mouans (19C ,on a 16C foundation) hosts temporary contemporary art expositions. as well as the Albers-Honegger Collection in a green-yellow concrete cube building on the premises. An exceptional collection of Abstract, Cubist, Minimalist and design arts.

Route **NAPOLÉON**

MICHELIN MAPS 341 B/D5/6

The Route Napoléon – Napoleon's Road – follows the route taken by the Emperor on his return from exile in Elba, from the point where he landed in Golfe-Juan to his arrival in Grenoble. The new road was opened in 1932. Commemorative plaques and monuments bear the flying eagle symbol inspired by Napoleon's remark: "The eagle, bearing the national colours, will fly from steeple to steeple until he reaches the towers of Notre-Dame." 🖥 www.route-napoleon.com.

🐾 The route as far as Col de Valferrière is described here. The continuation north of the route is described in the *Michelin Green Guide to the French Alps*.

A Bit of History

After landing at Golfe-Juan on 1 March 1815, Napoleon and 700 loyal troops, preceded by an advance guard, made a brief overnight stop at Cannes. Wishing to avoid the Rhône area, which he knew to be hostile, Napoleon headed towards Grasse in order to reach the Durance Valley by way of the Alps. Beyond Grasse the small column had a difficult time proceeding along the mule tracks. They halted at St-Vallier, Escragnolles and Séranon, from which, after a night's rest, they reached Castellane on 3 March. By the afternoon they had arrived in Barrême. The next day (4 March) the party lunched at Digne. Napoleon halted that evening at Château de Malijai, impatiently awaiting news from Sisteron, where the fort commanded the narrow passage of the Durance.

Sisteron was not guarded, so Napoleon lunched there (5 March) and left the town in an atmosphere of growing support for his cause. Once more on a coach road he arrived that night at Gap, where he was given an enthusiastic welcome. The next day (6 March) he slept at Corps. On 7 March he reached La Mure, only to find troops from Grenoble facing him at Laffrey. This was the site of the famous episode – commemorated today by a monument to Napoleon – which turned events in his favor. That same evening he entered Grenoble to shouts of: "Long live the Emperor!"

Driving Tour   57km/35mi – allow a whole day.

▶ *Leave from Golfe-Juan (👋 See VALLAURIS) on the N 7.*

The road winds round the west face of Super-Cannes hill, facing the Lérins Islands and the Esterel Massif. The view is best at sunset.

The Ascent of the Alps by Napoleon

"He disembarked at Golfe-Juan, several hours before nightfall, and established a bivouac. As the moon rose, between one and two o'clock in the morning, the bivouac was struck and they went on to Grasse. There the Emperor expected to find the road spanning the Alps that he had commissioned under the Empire but sadly it had never been built. He was therefore compelled to negotiate difficult passes in deep snow, which meant leaving his coach and two cannons in Grasse with the town guard.

... The Emperor moved like lightning. He felt that victory depended on his strength of will and that France would rally to him if he reached Grenoble. There were 100 leagues to go and we made it in five days, from 2 to 7 March, but on such roads and in such weather..."

Las Cases *(Mémorial)*

Re-enactment of Napoleon landing at Golfe-Juan on his return from Elba

Cannes ⌂⌂⌂ (see CANNES)

▶ *From Cannes take N 85 to the north, heading for Mougins.*

The road rises above the town and the sea past the perched village of **Mougins**★ (*see MOUGINS*).

Mouans-Sartoux (see MOUGINS)

On leaving Mouans-Sartoux, the road reveals Grasse spread out across the mountain slope ahead.

Grasse★ (see GRASSE)

▶ *From Grasse take N 85, going northwest.*

The road skirts "Napoleon's Plateau" where he halted on 2 March outside the town. Pass through the Provence Plateau and then the Pre-Alps of Grasse, Provence's limestone mountains. The route crosses three passes in succession: **Col du Pilon** (782m/2 566ft), **Pas de la Faye** (981m/3 218ft) and **Col de Valferrière** (1 169m/3 805ft), where the view south is magnificent.

Col du Pilon

From the southern slope there is a **view**★★ of La Napoule Bay with the Lérins Islands, Grasse, the Lac de St-Cassien, the Esterel and the Maures.

St-Vallier-de-Thiey (See ST-VALLIER-DE-THIEY)

As the road climbs to Pas de la Faye there are some very fine **views**★, particularly from the double bend.

Pas de la Faye ★★

Similar **view**★★ to that seen from Col du Pilon. Those travelling south over the pass suddenly discover the Mediterranean and the Riviera coastline spread out before them.

▶ *1km/0.5mi before Escragnolles, by a gasoline station, a road to the Belvédère de Baou Mourine branches off to the left.*

Belvédère de Baou Mourine★ *1km/0.6mi plus 30min on foot there and back.*

▪ *Path marked with red arrows.* Here you'll arrive at a terrace **viewpoint**★ over the Siagne Valley, La Napoule Bay, the Esterel and Maures Massifs.

After Escragnolles, where Napoleon made a brief halt, there are fine views to the south.

▶ *For an alternative route to Cannes via Grasse described in reverse order see GRASSE: Driving Tours.*

NICE ★★★

POPULATION 342 738

MICHELIN MAP 341 E5

LOCAL MAPS HEREIN AND CORNICHES DE LA RIVIERA

Sheltered in the Baie des Anges by an amphitheatre of hills, this popular Riviera resort has artistic treasures, countless attractions, a wonderful climate and a magnificent **setting**★★ that attract visitors all year-round. The Italian charm of Nice, capital of the Côte d'Azur, is immediately apparent in the colorful baroque buildings of the Old Town and the flavorful Niçois cuisine. Nothing epitomizes the French Riviera more than a stroll along the Promenade des Anglais, where the fresh sea air and shining sun are as inevitable as, alas, the traffic jams and exhaust fumes.

▶ **Orient Yourself:** Facing the vast Baie des Anges, Nice's wide seaside boulevard known as the Promenade des Anglais stretches all the way from the airport on the west side to the Château hilltop on the east, where it becomes the Quai des Etats-Unis. On the otherside of the hilltop lies the old port and the primarily residential Cap de Nice. The Old Town is wedged in the small area between the Château Hill, the Quai des Etats-Unis and the Promenade du Paillon green belt, bordered by busy Boulevard Jean Jaurès and Avenue Felix Faure. The western end of this promenade is called the Place Masséna, a large intersection surrounded by modern shopping streets to the north and pedestrian shopping streets to the west. Farther north, up a gradually rising hill, sits the Cimiez district, site of the former Roman settlement, with several museums and public gardens.

Getting around on foot is not difficult, but to visit Cimiez, the port, or the far western shores of the bay, consider using the city's vast bus network, or taking a sightseeing tour with commentary on a double-decker tour bus (🕭 see *Address Book*).

🅿 **Parking:** Avoid using a car to get around Nice, since work on the tramway *(the first section is scheduled to open spring 2007)* has caused several road closures. Instead, park your car in one of the many public car parks in the Old Town, the port, the casino, or the Promenade du Paillon for the day and walk or use public transportation. There is no free parking; even if you find open places on the street, you will need to pay the meter.

◉ **Don't Miss:** The winding streets and market of the Old Town , where you should try the local specialities of *socca* or *pan bagnat*; the views from the top of the Château Hill at sunset; the seaside along the palm-lined Promenade des Anglais; the Gallo-Roman ruins of Cimiez; and at least one of the city's many excellent museums.

J.-CH. Gérard/ PHOTONONSTOP

Nice Carnival

🕐 **Organizing Your Time:** You could easily spend a week in Nice and find plenty to do, but if you have just one full day, start in the morning on the seafront and in the Old Town, then in the afternoon visit Cimiez and one or two of the major museums such as the Musée des Beaux-Arts, the Musée d'Art Moderne et d'Art Contemporain and the Musée des Arts Asiatiques.

Kids **Especially for Kids:** Children will particularly enjoy the merry-go-round at the Jardin du Albert I or the playground in the park at the top of the Château Hill.

A Bit of History

From the Greeks to the House of Savoy – Excavations at Terra Amata (🕐 see SIGHTS in this chapter) reveal evidence of a human settlement in Nice 400 000 years ago. The Ligurian stronghold and trading-post of Nikaia was founded about the 4C BC by the Greeks of Marseille near what is now Quai des États-Unis. Later the Romans concentrated their colonisation efforts on Cimiez (Cemenelum), whose splendor eventually overshadowed the little Nikaia.

Barbarian and Saracen invasions, however, reduced Cimiez to nothing, and Nikaia, (now called Nice) returned to prominence under the Counts of Provence in the 10C.

In the 14C, the history of Nice was marked by an important event: Louis of Anjou and his cousin, Charles of Durazzo, Prince of Naples, both advanced their claims on Provence on the death of **Queen Jeanne,** Queen of Sicily and Countess of Provence, who had adopted them. Beautiful and beloved by the people of Provence, this princess was smothered to death on the orders of Durazzo (1382). They turned instead to **Amadeus VII,** Count of Savoy, who seized an opportune moment during the civil conflict dividing the country and moved to Provence. In 1388, after many secret negotiations, the govenor Jean Grimaldi announced the secession of Nice and its hinterland from Provence, and joined Savoy. Amadeus VII entered the city amid great rejoicing. Except for a few short interruptions, Nice belonged to the House of Savoy until its restoration to France in 1860.

Catherine Ségurane – In the 16C Nice began to feel the effects of the rivalry between the Houses of France and Austria. François I and his Turkish allies launched military operations in 1543 against the County of Nice, which belonged to the House of Savoy, under the redoubtable leader Barbarossa.

It was then that, according to local tradition, Catherine Ségurane, a woman of the people, earned her fame. As she was bringing food to a soldier on the ramparts, the order for the assault was given, and some Turks appeared at the top of the wall. Catherine flung herself forward, knife in hand, hurled several attackers into the

King of the Carnival!

The **Nice Carnival**★★★ is one of the biggest celebrations in the region, with two weeks of parades, confetti battles, fireworks and masked balls *(veglioni)*. The **floral parades**, or *batailles de fleurs,* offer a picturesque spectacle and attract huge and excited crowds, drawn by the colorful fruit and flowers.

The tradition dates back a long way in Nice, with references as long ago as 1294, on the occasion of the visit of the Count of Provence, Charles II. Nice Carnival has always been a welcome diversion from social tensions and conflicts which were constantly breaking out as a result of Nice's geographical location and disputed ownership. Until the end of the 18C, the carnival took place after the Lenten fast in the form of local festivities in the old part of the city.

After a break of several years, caused by the wars of the Revolution and the Empire, the first parade of carnival floats took place in 1830 in honour of the royal visit of King Charles Félix to Nice and the return to Sardinian sovereignty. The modern form of carnival dates back to 1873, with the establishment of the various stages of the festivities and the setting of a different official theme every year.

Carnival-going families from Nice belong to long lines of tradition verging on outright dynasties! Each "stable" of carnival floats has its own characteristics. On average, about one tonne of papier-mâché is used in the making of each float. Famous painters from this area have also played their part in enriching the carnival decorations.

The festivities begin with the triumphal entry of "Sa Majesté Carnaval" about three weeks before Shrove Tuesday, or Mardi Gras. An effigy of the King of the Carnival is later ceremonially burned to mark the end of the carnival season. During the intervening period celebrations are in full swing, with parades of carnival floats accompanied by people in costumes sporting huge comical heads made of papier-mâché.

moat below, seized a flag and put fresh courage into the men of Nice. The attack was contained. From the ramparts, as a gesture of contempt, Catherine turned her back on the Turks and lifted up her skirts. Although the town fell after more than 20 days of siege, the defenders took refuge in the castle and their resistance finally forced the besiegers to withdraw. A statue was erected to Catherine by her fellow citizens.

Bonaparte in Nice – The County of Nice, which under the Convention became the Département of Alpes-Maritimes, had been occupied by French troops in 1792 and was re-attached to France the following year. In 1794 Bonaparte, then General of Artillery in the army fighting against the Sardinians and the Austrians in the County of Nice, lived at no 6 in the street which now bears his name, and proposed to the daughter of his landlord. It was in this house that he was arrested after the fall of Robespierre. But his detention was short as he put forward a skillful defence.

In 1796 he was in Nice again on his way to take over the post of commander-in-chief of the army in Italy. The house where he lived is in Rue St-François-de-Paule, in front of the opera. He had married Josephine only a few days earlier and it was from Nice that he wrote the well-known letter: "My darling, anguish at our parting runs through my veins as swiftly as the waters flow down the Rhône... my emotion thunders in my ears like a volcano... I would like to tear out my heart with my teeth...."

At the fall of the Empire in 1814, Nice and its hinterland was handed back to the House of Savoy under the Treaty of Paris.

Two local heroes: Masséna and Garibaldi – **Maréchal Masséna** (1758-1817), son of a wine merchant, became, under Napoléon, a Maréchal de France, Duke of Rivoli and Prince of Essling. His military genius was coupled with a ruthless ambition that sometimes caused scandal. During his career he is said to have shouted successively: "Long live the Nation! Long live the Emperor! Long live the King!" After Napoleon, he was the general most esteemed by Wellington.

Giuseppe Garibaldi (1807-82), one of the principal authors of the Italian Revolution in 1860, had an extraordinarily turbulent political and military life in Europe and South America. A great friend of France, he served in the ranks of the French Army in 1870 with his two sons, and commanded a brigade in the Vosges. In the First World War other members of the Garibaldi family fought in the Argonne at the head of Italian volunteers.

Plebiscite – As a result of the 1858 alliance between France and Sardinia (House of Savoy), Napoleon III undertook to help the Sardinians drive the Austrians out of the provinces of northern Italy, for which he would receive Nice and Savoy in return. But the Peace of Villafranca, signed prematurely by the Emperor, left Venice to the Austrians, thus not fully meeting the objectives of the alliance. In 1860 the Treaty of Turin between Napoleon III and the King of Sardinia, Victor Emmanuel II, stipulated that Nice be returned to France "without any constraint on the will of the people". The plebiscite was an overwhelming victory for France: 25 743 in favour, 260 against. The entry of French troops and the ceremony of annexation took place on 14 June 1860. On 12 September the Emperor and the Empress Eugénie received the silver-gilt keys to the city from the mayor of Nice in what is today Place Garibaldi. These keys are displayed in the Masséna Museum.

The regions of Tende and La Brigue were to remain Italian territory for 87 years until the treaty of 10 February 1947 allowed France, once more, to extend its natural frontiers to the Alps.

"L'École de Nice" – At the beginning of the 1960s Nice became one of the most lively artistic centers in Western Europe. Futuristic exhibitions and other surprising events began to take place. Unlike the painters who, during the first half of the century, worked in total seclusion, the new wave combined life and art. At the instigation of **Yves Klein** who repositioned painting within a purifying process (vacuum, monochrome paintings symbolising the sky, fire etc) and **Arman** who elevated everyday accessories to the level of art, the "New Realists" gave a distinctive impulse to modern art in Nice. Other artists then joined the Nice School:

Baie des Anges, Nice

S. Sauvignier/ MICHELIN

Address Book

PRACTICAL INFORMATION

Tourism Offices – *5 Promenade des Anglais* – ☎ *0 892 707 707 (0.34€/minute) – and at Train Station , Av. Thiers – www. nicetourisme.com.*

SIGHTSEEING AND TOURS

Guided tours – Tours of the Old Town *(1.5hr)* Tue and Sun at 3pm. 3€. ▣ *Palais Lascaris, 15 Rue Droite*, ☎ *04 93 62 72 40.* Tours of the Old Town *(2.5hrs)* from the Tourism Office every Saturday at 9.30am, 12€. ▣ *5 Promenade des Anglais*, ☎ *0 892 707 707 (0.34€/minute).*

Carte Passe -Musées – A 7-day museum pass with free entry to all municipal museums of Nice, 6€. Available at all participating museums or the Tourism Office.

Petits Trains Touristiques – ⏰ *Tours 10am-6pm* – ⏰ *Closed mid-Nov to mid-Dec and 1-15 Jan* – ⏰ *6€ (3€ kids under 9)* – ☎ *04 50 60 05 55 – www. petittrainnice.com.* Departures from the seafront at the Jardins Albert 1re. Tours of the Old Town, port, Château Hill with commentary in English (30min).

Nice le Grand Tour – ⏰ *Tours 10am-5.30pm, hourly departures Jul-Oct, departures every two hours Nov-Jun.* – ⏰ *17€ (children 9€)* – ☎ *04 92 29 17 00.* Double-decker, open top bus tours with commentary in English (90 min), departing from the Jardins Albert 1re. Hop on-hop off the 11 different stops from Promenade des Anglais, Cimiez, Mont Boron, and the Port.

Trans Côte d'Azur – *Quai Lunel* – ☎ *04 92 00 42 30 – www.trans-cote-azur.com* – ⏰ *Operates Feb-Nov Tue, Wed, Fri and Sun at 3pm; Sun-Fri from 15 Jun-15 Sep.* Guided tours *(1hr)* of the coast of Nice, panorama of the Bay of Villefranche and Baie des Anges.

PUBLIC TRANSPORT

Aéroport Nice-Côte d'Azur – ☎ *08 20 42 33 33 (0.12€/min) – www.nice.aeroport.fr* Set up on the left bank of the Var estuary, this is France's second busiest airport.

Buses – The Sunbus network (*10 Avenue Félix-Faure;* ☎ *04 93 16 52 10; www.sunbus. com*) covers the city of Nice and its suburbs. Tickets 1.30€ each, or 4€ for an unlimited one-day pass *(includes airport buses 23, 98, and 99)*. The TAM network (*Gare routière, Promenade du Paillon;* ☎ *04 93 85 61 81; www.rca.tm.fr*) has service to other cities such as Antibes, Cannes and Grasse.

TER Train – *SNCF Gare, Avenue Thiers* – ☎ *0 892 35 35 35 – www.ter-sncf.com/paca.* Local train service to Draguignan, Fréjus, St-Raphaël, Cannes, Antibes, Menton Vintimille, Monaco. The Nice-Cuneo line crosses the Bévéra and Roya valleys.

EATING OUT

Salade niçoise, socca, pan-bagnat, poutine, tourte aux blettes, beignets de fleurs de courgettes…to experience the best in local cuisine, look for the restaurants displaying the label "Cuisine Nissarde". A guide to these restaurants is available for free at the Tourism Office. *For coin ranges, see Legend at back of the guide.*

⊝ **Le Pain Quotidien** – *3 Rue St-François-de-Paul (Cours Saleya)* – ☎ *04 93 62 94 32.* This country-style restaurant specializing in brunch has long wooden tables where guests sit side-by-side, an original formula conducive to a friendly, convivial atmosphere. In addition to the bread baskets and tatsy spreads of jam, honey and hazelnut, there is a wide selection of salads and open sandwiches.

⊝ **Nissa Socca** – *7 Rue Ste-Réparate* – ☎ *04 93 80 18 35* – ⏰ *Closed Jan, 10 days in Jun, Mon for lunch and Sun* – ⊘. Pasta, pizza and Mediterranean dishes are served here in two cosy dining areas with a Provençal touch. Simplicity and low prices guaranteed. Old-fashioned bread oven at the entrance.

⊝ **La Tapenade** – *6 Rue Ste-Réparate* – ☎ *04 93 80 65 63* – ⊘. Curious decor re-creating a typical street from the south of France, with its shutters, terra-cotta flower pots and strings of garlic. Do not miss the surprising fresco painted on the ceiling. The warm, friendly owners will serve you a pizza, a tapenade or any other local speciality.

⊝⊝ **Grand Café de Turin** – *5 Place Garibaldi* – ☎ *04 93 62 29 52.* This brasserie, which is over 200 years old, has become an institution in Nice. It serves seafood dishes à la carte at reasonable prices throughout the day. Pleasant, welcoming setting, although a bit noisy on the terrace.

⊝⊝ **L'Escalinada** – *22 Rue Pairolière* – ☎ *04 93 62 11 71 – restaurant-lescalinada@ wanadoo.fr* – ⊘ – ⏰ *Closed 15 Nov-15 Dec.* Nestling in the old quarter, this charming restaurant offers attractively presented regional cuisine in a spruce dining room with rustic overtones. Friendly service.

⊝⊝ **Lou Balico** – *22 Avenue St-Jean-Baptiste* – ☎ *04 93 85 93 71* – ⏰ *Closed lunch in Jul-Aug.* Three generations of the same family have been serving classic Niçois dishes in this cosy dining room adorned with a piano and guest book with signatures from around the world.

⊝⊝ **La Table d'Alziari** – *4 Rue François-Zannin* – ☎ *04 93 80 34 03* – ⏰ *Closed 11-22 Jan, 9-20 Aug, 6-17 Dec, Sun and Mon.* Unpretentious family restaurant set up in a small alley of the old district. Typical dishes from Nice and the Provence area, chalked up on a slate, are served in a homey decor, together with wine recommended by the owner.

Capeline – *Gilette – 9km/5.5mi from Gilette by D 17 Route de Roquesteron* – ☎ 04 93 08 58 06 – ⏱ *Open Mar-Oct, weekends only Nov-Feb* – ⏱ *Closed Wed – Reservation required.* Roadside inn whose charm owes much to the lady of the house, clad in a white apron, who officiates in the kitchen and lovingly prepares tasty delicacies exuding Provençal fragrances.

WHERE TO STAY

Star Hôtel – *14 Rue Biscarra* – ☎ 04 93 85 19 03 – *star-hotel@wanadoo.fr* – ⏱ *Closed Nov – 24 rooms* – ▱ – ▦. Small hotel away from the bustling town center offering simple accommodations, some with a balcony. Close to the Etoile Shopping Center.

Villa St-Hubert – *26 Rue Michel-Ange* – ☎ 04 93 84 66 51 – *hotel-villa-st-hubert@wanadoo.fr* – ⏱ *Closed 15 Nov-15 Dec – 13 rooms* – ▱ ▦. Turn-of-the-century villa near the university campus overlooking a quiet, secluded street. Smallish but well equipped rooms. Flowery patio where breakfast is served in summer.

Claire Hotel – *23 Boulevard Carnot, Impasse Terra Amata* – ☎ 04 93 89 69 89 – *10 rooms* – ▱. This converted schoolhouse near the archeological museum has rooms all on one floor (in the old classrooms) and a Mediterranean garden terrace where breakfast is served in the summer. Quiet neighborhood, friendly, family-run atmosphere.

Mercure Marché aux Fleurs – *91 Quai des Etats-Unis* – ☎ 04 93 85 74 19 – *www.accor-hotels.com – 49 rooms* – ▱ ▦ ⬚. Centrally located in the Old Town a block from the seafront and the Cour Saleya market. Rooms are simple and colorful, six with balconies facing the sea (and the traffic).

Château des Ollières – *39 Avenue des Baumettes* – ☎ 04 92 15 77 99 – ▣ – *8 rooms* – ▱ ▦ – *Restaurant (⬚⬚⬚)*. This princely manor surrounded by a small park behind the Museum of Fine Arts bears witness to the presence of Russian residents in Nice during the last century. Its devastating charm derives from the luxuriously appointed salons, the precious works of art and the large, comfortable suites exuding a hushed, cosy ambience.

La Pérouse – *11 Quai Rauba-Capéu* – ☎ 04 93 62 34 63 – ▣ – *58 rooms* – ▱ ▦ – *restaurant (⬚⬚⬚)*. A prime seaside location overlooking the Baie des Anges from the foot of the Château Hill, this cosy Provençal-style hotel features a heated swimming pool and grill restaurant set within a garden against the rocky hill. The top floor terrace has panoramic views over the sea, a hot tub and fitness room.

ON THE TOWN

Casino Ruhl – *1 Promenade des Anglais* – ☎ 04 97 03 12 22 – ⏱ *Daily 10am to dawn.* The casino boasts 300 slot machines and has facilities for French and English roulette, blackjack, stud poker, etc. American bar. Dinner is coupled with live performances on Fridays. Themed evenings on Thursdays.

Le Mélisande – *Hôtel Palais Maeterlinck, 30 Boulevard Maurice-Maeterlinck, Cap de Nice* – ☎ 04 92 00 72 00 – *www.palais-maeterlinck.com* – ⏱ *Daily 11am-midnight.* This bar attached to the luxury hotel whose terrace dominates the sea and offers splendid views of the Baie des Anges. Champagne cocktails, cigars. The Belgian writer Maurice Maeterlinck, 1911 Nobel Prize for Literature, once lived on the premises.

Le Relais – *Hôtel Negresco, 37 Promenade des Anglais* – ☎ 04 93 16 64 00 – ⏱ *Daily 11.30am-1am, until midnight in winter.* The sumptuous decoration of this bar belonging to the legendary Negresco Hotel has remained the same since 1913: Brussels tapestry (1683), 18C paintings, replicas of the wall lamps adorning the Ballroom in Fontainebleau Château and a rug similar to that chosen by Napoleon I for the King's Bedchamber in Rome. Piano bar every evening.

Ghost House – *3 Rue Barillerie* – ☎ 04 93 92 93 37 – ⏱ *Wed-Sat 7.30pm-2am.* A sleek and trendy nightclub (dinner and dancing) in the Old Town, with live DJs playing mostly dance and lounge electronic music. Expensive cocktails.

La Trappa – *Rue de la Préfecture and Rue Gilly* – ☎ 04 93 80 33 69 – ⏱ *Daily 5pm-2am.* A lively tapas bar with deep, comfortable settees and red walls awaits you at La Trappa, open since 1886. Sip a Cuban cocktail while you listen to Latin American music (DJ weekends). Friendly atmosphere and local wine list.

Les Trois Diables – *2 Cours Saleya* – ☎ 04 93 62 47 00 – ⏱ *Daily 4pm-2.30am.* Cours Saleya is at the heart of Nice and its bustling activity. This broad square is taken over by the terraces of cafés, pubs and restaurants, and notably that of Les Trois Diables. This is undoubtedly most popular among the student nightlife crowd. Regular rock concerts, karaoke evenings, and other themed nights.

Wayne's Pub – *15 Rue de la Préfecture* – ☎ 04 93 13 46 99 – *www.waynes.fr* – ⏱ *Daily noon-1am.* Genuine Anglo-Saxon pub, with live sports on the big screen and nightly rock concerts. Tea time is from 4pm to 6pm, and cocktail time is from 6pm to 7pm.

SHOPPING

Most shops in Old Nice are closed on Mondays.

Shopping streets – The streets surrounding the Cathédrale Ste-Réparate have many shops selling typical Provençal articles: fabrics (*Rue Paradis and Rue du Marché*), arts and crafts (*Rue du Pont-Vieux and Rue de la Boucherie*), olive oil and santons (*Rue St-François-de-Paul*).

Alziari – *14 Rue St-François-de-Paule – ☎ 04 93 85 76 92 – www.alziari.com.fr –* ⏱ *Tue-Sat. 8.30am-12.30pm, 2.15-7pm*. One of the best addresses in town for olive oil and regional specialities.

La Maison de l'Olive – *18 Rue Pairolière – ☎ 04 93 80 01 61.* Marseille soaps made from pure olive oil, lotions and scents for the body and home, and regional products such as dried tomatos, lemon jam, marinated capers and olives, and Provençal herbs and spices.

À l'Olivier – *7 Rue St-François-de-Paule - ☎ 04 93 13 44 97 - nice@olivier-on-line. com.* Every brand of French olive oil with the AOC label is sold in this boutique, originally opened in 1822, in Nice since 2004. Also a fine selection of elegant glassware, dishes, tablecloths.

Confiserie Auer – *7 Rue St-François-de-Paule – ☎ 04 93 85 77 98 – www.maison-auer.com –* ⏱ *Tue-Sat. 9am-1.30pm, 2.30-6pm*. A gorgeous vintage boutique selling candied fruit and crystallised flowers from the Nice region, as well as chocolates, and calissons from Aix.

Confiserie Florian – *14 Quai Papacino, on the Port – ☎ 04 93 55 43 50 – www. confiserieflorian.com –* ⏱ *Guided tours of the factory 9am-noon, 2-6.30pm*. Candied fruit, lemon, orange and grapefruit preserve, chocolates and sweets, crystallised petals and delicious jams made with rose, violet and jasmine blossom.

Maison Poilpot - Aux Parfums de Grasse – *10 Rue St-Gaétan – ☎ 04 93 85 60 77 – Daily except Mon 9.30am-noon, 2.30-6pm*. This traditional perfumery produces more than 80 different fragrances, including popular Mediterranean scents such as mimosa, rose, violet and lemon.

L'Art Gourmand – *21 Rue du Marché – Old Town – ☎ 04 93 62 51 79 – www.nice-ville. com–* ⏱ *Open 10am-7pm (Jul-Aug 10am-11pm)*. This Old Nice boutique has many treats available to go or eat in: nougats, calisson, candied fruit, cookies, pastries, ice cream and northern France specialities. There's a tea room on the mezzanine decorated with murals.

Fenocchio – *2 Place Rossetti - Old Town – ☎ 04 93 80 72 52 – www.nice-ville.com–* ⏱ *Open Feb-Oct 10am-1am*. This famous ice cream and sorbet maker has some of the most amazing flavors, from avocado and sun-dried tomato to honey and pine nut. With almost 100 flavors to choose from, you'll have to go back more than once!

Domaine de la Source – *303 Chemin de Saquier – 10km/6mi from Nice on N 202 – St-Roman-de-Bellet – ☎ 04 93 29 81 60.* A family of horticulturists converted to wine growers run this tiny domain which produces the rare Bellet wines of Nice. There are reds and whites, aged in oak barrels before being bottled. Visitors get a tour of the winemaking process from the friendly owner.

MARKETS

Marché aux Poissons – The fish market is at the Place St-François daily except Monday, 6am to 1pm.

Marché aux Fleurs – The flower market is on the Cours Saleya Tuesday through Sunday morning, 6am to 5.30pm.

Marché aux Fruits et Légumes – The colorful food market on the Cour Saleya takes place Tuesday to Sunday, 6am-1.30pm.

Marché de la Liberation – locals' food market from the Avenue Malausséna to Place Charles-de-Gaulle.

Marché aux Puces – Flea market Tuesday to Saturday 10am-6pm, on Place Robilante.

Marché de la Brocante – Antique market Mondays on Cours Saleya, 7.30am-6pm.

LEISURE ACTIVITIES

Beaches – The Baie des Anges covers a 5km/3.1mi stretch of coastline with smooth pebbles (*galets*). There are many public beaches placed under close surveillance, and 15 private beaches providing a host of sporting activities.

Hiking – *14 Avenue Mirabeau – ☎ 04 93 62 59 99 – www.cafnice.org –* ⏱ *Office open Mon-Fri 4-8pm*. CAF (Club Alpin Français) organises one-day hiking tours across the Nice hinterland and Mercantour Park leaving from Nice.

Skiing – *www.guideriviera.com* – The nearby skiing resorts of Auron (☎ 04 93 23 02 66) and Valberg (☎ 04 93 02 52 27), which are only a two-hour drive away, are undoubtedly among the main attractions of the Nice area.

CALENDAR OF EVENTS

There are many traditional festivals throughout the year. Ask at the Tourism Office for a complete schedule.

Nice Carnival – This colorful, extravagant event invariably attracts large crowds every year. Festivities take place around Shrove Tuesday (Mardi Gras) and last for a fortnight. They include processions, floats, firework displays, costume balls and battles where showers of flowers and confetti are thrown!

Cougourdons Festival – Cougourdons are gourds that have been dried and painted. The city of Nice pays homage to these curious vegetables in early April.

Fête de la Mer et de la St-Pierre – A festival celebrating the sea and St-Peter on the port and Quai des Etats-Unis the last weekend in June.

Nice Jazz Festival – The former Roman amphitheatre is the prestigious backdrop for the jazz festival that is held in Nice the last two weeks of July, attended by leading performers from all over the world. ☎ 0 892 707 407.

Fête de la San Bertoumiéu – A festival of traditional arts and crafts, regional foods and entertainment in the Old Town the first weekend in September.

Crèche Vivante Lou Presèpi – A living nativity scene with people and animals, at Place Rossetti the week of Christmas.

Martial Raysse, Sosno, Verdet, Chacallis, Venet and Ben. Some of these artists' works are exhibited in the **Musée d'Art Moderne et d'Art Contemporain** in Nice, and modern works can also be seen in various public places around Nice.

Nice Today – Since 1860 the development of Nice, which then counted 40 000 inhabitants, has been remarkable. Thanks to the railway, Nice became the most popular resort town in France, and a prosperous commercial trade city. It's now the second largest town of Mediterranean France after Marseille and the fifth largest in France itself.

Nice is an administrative center as well as a university town, and its Centre Universitaire Méditerranéen, École Nationale des Arts Décoratifs, Conservatoire de Musique, Centre National d'Art Contemporain and major museums make for thriving cultural activity.

Walking Tours

The Seafront★★ *Allow 2hr*

▶ *Begin from the intersection of Boulevard Gambetta and Promenade des Anglais. See the map for nearby parking.*

Promenade des Anglais★★
Closed to traffic one Sunday per month.

This magnificent, wide promenade, facing due south and flanking the sea along its entire length, provides wonderful views of the Baie des Anges that extends from the Cap de Nice to the airport. Until 1820 access to the shore was difficult but the English colony, numerous since the 18C, undertook the construction of a coastal path, which gave way to the present promenade which still carries its name. Although taken over by six lanes of traffic, the legendary promenade has retained its mythical aura. The white stone and glass façades overlooking the sea still attract many a visitor. The Ruhl Casino and Hotel Méridien (1973), the 1930s Palais de la Méditerranée, the Baroque **Hôtel Negresco**, a striking Belle Époque structure (c1900) and the Musée Masséna. Visible on the façade of the Élysée Palace, overlooking Rue Honoré-Sauvan, is the monumental bronze *Venus* (1989) by the sculptor Sacha Sosno.

The young Russian princess Maria Bashkirtseff, nicknamed Moussia, who was noted for her eccentricity, spent ten winters in Nice, where she carried on a correspondence with Maupassant. She was dubbed *La Madone des Sleepings* (the sleeping-car madonna) by certain writers. A stone slab commemorates her stay at 63 Promenade des Anglais. Avenue de Verdun skirts the **Jardin Albert I,** a welcome oasis of greenery surrounding a fountain, *The Three Graces*, sculpted by Volti. It's also the starting point for sightseeing tours (👍 *see Address Book*).

Place Masséna

Started in 1815 in the Italian style, the buildings form an architectural unit in red ochre with arcades at street level. A fountain stands in the southern section: four bronze horses rise from a basin. The north side of the square opens into Avenue Jean-Médecin (once Avenue de la Victoire), which is the main shopping street, crowded with people and traffic. To the west extends what the 18C English called Newborough. Rue Masséna and Rue de France, its continuation, form the axis of a pedestrian area where you'll find smart shops, cinemas, cafés and restaurants.

To the east, beyond the bus station and Musée d'Art Moderne, there's an excellent view over the hills beyond Nice, with an almost Tuscan charm. At the corner of the Jardin Maréchal-Juin, surrounded by fountains, sits Tête Carrée (Square Head) by Sacha Sosno, which houses the Louis-Nucéra Library.

The Port

For 2 000 years ships simply tied up at the foot of the Château Hill. A deep-water port was excavated in 1750 under Charles-Emmanuel III, Duke of Savoy, in the marshy ground at Lympia. In the 19C it was extended and made deeper. Place Île de Beauté, a square facing the port whose houses are embellished with porticoes and pretty façades, was laid out around the same period. Today Nice harbor is a busy maritime center catering for a wide variety of needs: it is frequented by fishing boats, yachts, ferries heading for Corsica, luxury liners and merchant ships (exporting cement manufactured locally).

You can stroll through the flea markets at the Quai Lunel, before returning to the Promenade des Anglais.

Midday Cannon

Each day at noon a short cannon shot can be heard to remind people that it is lunchtime. This custom was introduced by a visiting Englishman, Sir Thomas Coventry, who grew tired of irregular meal times. He offered to buy and maintain a cannon for the town so that each day a shot could be fired at noon from the castle hill. The tradition has been maintained, although the cannon has now been replaced by an explosive device.

Old Nice★ *Allow 3hr*

After enjoying a whiff of the misty sea air, turn to the old quarter of town and set off for the Baroque district of Nice, hemmed in between the Château Hill and Rue des Ponchettes.

Cours Saleya

Once the elegant promenade of old Nice, it is now lined with shops and restaurants. The famous **flower and vegetable market** is held here in this picturesque quarter. Don't miss the mouthwatering sight of black and green olives, mesclun lettuce and fresh ingredients for a tasty ratatouille. You'll also see many carnations, the most widely grown flower in the Alpes-Maritimes, cultivated on the stepped terraces extending beyond Nice.

Note the the yellow front of the **Caïs de Pierla Palace,** where Picasso lived in a small room facing the sea between 1921 and 1938.

Chapelle de la Miséricorde★

🕐 *Open Tue 2.30-5.30pm.*

This fine example of Niçois Baroque belongs to the brotherhood of the Black Penitents. It was built in 1740 by Vittone according to the plans of the famous 17C Italian priest-architect, Guarini. The elegant symmetry of its façade is matched by a breathtaking interior, where angels circle the gilded beams and faux-marble columns. If the inordinately rich decoration is 19C (vault painted by Bistolfi), the full elliptic layout is characteristic of the Piedmontese Baroque style. In the sacristy are two primitive Niçois **retables**★ that represent the Virgin of Mercy: one by Jean Miralhet (1429) and the other by Louis Bréa (1515), which reveals perhaps the oldest image of Nice.

Left of the chapel, Place Pierre-Gautier leads to the former **Palais du Gouverneur et des Princes de Savoie** (17C).

Follow the Cours Saleya west to the Rue St-François-de-Paule, where you'll see the handsome, albeit forbidding, façade of the **Église St-François-de-Paule** (🕐 *Open weekdays 9am-noon, 3-6.30pm)* with its colorful bell-tower.

Socca

The day started early in those days in the Nice bar where my uncle and I enjoyed our *socca*. The ingredients include chick-pea flour, olive oil and salt beaten into a smooth mixture in a large copper pan. It is baked in a wood fire oven, a cooking time based on exact calculation or long experience and a speedy hand in cutting the cake into pieces when it is served. Socca will not wait; it must be eaten piping hot – seasoned with pepper.

The recipe has never changed. This is the same *socca* that used to be delivered all over the town. It was put in a box with a zinc lid and the trays in the delivery vans were kept warm with charcoal heaters. Nothing was more satisfying to labourers, office workers, women shopping or anyone else overcome by the desire for a little something in the morning. It is the same socca which the dockers, who had knocked back a laced coffee at 5 o'clock, used to consume in the bars of Nice at half past six. It was their breakfast.

Louis Nucera
Chemin de la Lanterne (1981)
Published by Éditions Grasset

Across the street is the **Nice Opéra** (1885), built according to plans drawn by Niçois architect François Aune, and approved by Charles Garnier.

▶ *Turn left onto Rue de la Poissonnerie.*

Chapelle de l'Annonciation
🕐 Open 9am-noon, 3.30-4pm, 5-6pm. ☎ 04 93 62 13 62.

Originally dedicated to St Giaume (St James the Apostle), the chapel is known locally as the **Chapelle Ste-Rita**, an Italian saint still venerated in Nice as the armfuls of flowers and pyramids of candles at her altar *(left on entering)* and in the sacristy clearly show.

The interior is a lavish illustration of local Baroque **decoration**★ with altars and rails inlaid with marble, sumptuous altarpieces, painted and coffered vaults, and fine paneling.

▶ *Continue straight ahead then take a right on the Rue de la Place-Vieille, which has a good view through the old town of the Château Hill. Then take a left.*

Église St-Jacques or Gésu★
🕐 Open on request by the reception of the cathedral, ☎ 04 93 62 34 40.

Built as a chapel in the 17C, this church is reminiscent of the Gesù Church in Rome. Twin fluted columns support a barrel vault opening into side chapels containing loggias for the noble families. The general effect is highly ornate: there are 164 painted and 48 carved cherubs. The ceiling is painted with scenes from the life of St James and there are several paintings presented by various brotherhoods. A 16C Pietà stands on the right.

NICE

Street Name Index

Galerie des Ponchettes
Galerie de la Marine

The **sacristy**, formerly the chapter-house, contains 14 huge walnut cupboards (1696), some of which display the church treasures.

▸ *The Rue du Jésus (across from the church when exiting) leads to the Rue Ste-Réparate and the cathedral of the same name.*

Cathédrale Ste-Réparate

The cathedral was built in 1650 by the Nice architect, J-A Guiberto, and dedicated to the patron of Nice, who was martyred in Asia Minor at the age of 15.

Colors enhance the well-proportioned façade in which the Baroque style is very evident between the ground level and the first cornice in the elegant arcading of the doorway and the decorative niches and medallions. The church is topped by an 18C bell-tower and a magnificent dome of 14 000 glazed tiles that stands out on the Nice skyline.

The **interior**★ is a riot of Baroque plasterwork and marble. The high altar and choir balustrade are of marble adorned with heraldic imagery. In the sacristy you'll find 17C panelling.

▸ *Proceed along Rue Rossetti opposite and take the third left turning into Rue Droite.*

Palais Lascaris

🕐 Open daily (except Tue) 10am-6pm. ⊚ Free entry (guided tours: Thur, Fri, Sun at 3pm, 3€). ☎ 04 93 62 72 40.

This Genoese-style palace, influenced by local tradition, was built in 1648 by J-B Lascaris, a descendant of the counts of Ventimiglia whose family was related to the Lascaris, emperors of Nicaea in Asia Minor in the 13C. The façade is decorated with balustraded balconies on consoles of carved marble and columns with flowered capitals. Delicate scrollwork ornaments the doorway.

On the ground floor a pharmacy from Besançon (1738) has been reconstructed to display a fine collection of flasks and tripods.

A grandiose balustraded **staircase**★, decorated with 17C paintings hanging in rock-work niches and 18C statues of Mars and Venus, leads to the second floor. The salon is hung with Flemish tapestries; the *trompe-l'œil* ceiling is the work of Italian artists from Genoa: the *Fall of Phaeton*, similar to one in Cagnes. In the next room hang two Flemish tapestries based on sketches by Rubens. On the other side of the staircase are the private apartments displaying 18C ceilings, painted medallions framed in stuccowork and Louis XV woodwork inlaid with silver.

On the **ground floor** the group of **salons** in Empire style, directly inspired by the Piedmontese château at Govone, has bay windows looking out on to the sea. The gallery contains statues and paintings (a marble bust of Marshal Masséna by Canova, a full-length portrait of Empress Joséphine by Baron Gros, a full-length marble statue of Napoleon as Roman Emperor by Chaudet) and Thomire vases. On the staircase, two remounted canvases by François Flameng are dedicated to the Masséna family. The **first floor** has a collection of Nice primitives by Jacques Durandi and Louis Bréa. There is also a Virgin in multi-colored stone, a 14C Burgundian piece and a 13C reliquary of St Commode from Limoges. Primitive Italian, Flemish and Spanish works hang on the walls, as well as a fine 16C French Crucifixion.

There are two rooms devoted to liturgical ornaments (15C-17C) and to church silver plate as well as Germanic sculpture (16C).

Among a fine collection of arms and armour (14C-18C) are a head guard belonging to Charles V, a *bourguignotte* (helmet) belonging to Philip II of Spain and a knight protected by German armour said to be "Maximilienne Cannelée" (16C).

Jewels from all over the world are displayed on the **second floor** as well as watercolors by Niçois painters (Trachel, Costa, A Mossa). There are also exhibitions of great Niçois citizens, the Revolution and the Empire (represented by a precious sketch of Bonaparte by David), and the history of Nice illustrated by watercolors, a fine model of the town in 1890 and an interesting collection of aristocratic and bourgeois costumes (19C).

Place St-François

This square with its pretty fountain is home to the local fish market every morning. To the right is the Classical façade of the former town hall that now serves as the Labour Exchange (Bourse du Travail).

Stuck to a house on the corner of Rue Droite and Rue de la Loge is a cannon ball which dates from the siege of Nice by the Turks, allies of François I (1543).

Continue along the lively Rue Pairolière, where several establishments serve *socca*, a local speciality that must be eaten while it is still hot.

Place Garibaldi

This attractive square with the yellow ochre arcades was laid out at the end of the 18C in typical Piedmont style. It marks the northern limit of the Old Town and the beginning of the new, and was the start of the royal route to Turin in the 1700s (which is where the Café de Turin, an excellent seafood restaurant on the corner, got its name). A statue of Garibaldi stands proudly among the fountains and greenery. The **Chapelle de Saint-Sépulcre** on the south side of the square belongs to the Brotherhood of Blue Penitents, built in the 18C with a Baroque interior decorated in different shades of blue.

▸ *From Place Garibaldi, take Rue Neuve past the Café de Turin until you reach the church of St-Martin-St-Augustin.*

Église St-Martin-St-Augustin

🕐 *Open daily (except Mon) 9am–noon, 2–5pm.* ☎ *04 93 92 60 45.*

This is the oldest parish in Nice, dating back to 1510. It's the site of Garibaldi's baptism as well as a mass performed by the Augustinian monk, Martin Luther, before the Protestant Reformation. The church has a fine Baroque **interior**★ with a Pietà. The central panel of an altarpiece by Louis Bréa lies on the left in the choir.
Outside, opposite the entrance, stands a low relief sculpted in 1923, a **memorial** that pays tribute to the local heroine Catherine Ségurane.

▸ *Follow the steep steps leading to the Château Hill along Rue St-Augustin (right when leaving the church) and Rue de la Providence.*

Château Hill

This is in fact the name given to the 92m/300ft high hill, arranged as a garden walk, on which Nice's fortress stood until it was destroyed in 1706 by Louis XIV's army.
From the wide platform on the summit there is a sweeping **panorama**★★ *(viewing table)*. Below the terrace is an artificial waterfall fed by water from the Vésubie. On the eastern side the **foundations of an 11C cathedral** (apse and apsidal chapels) have been uncovered. Below these ruins a Roman level and a Greek level have been excavated.
Walk around the ruins to the northwest corner of Château Hill *(follow the arrows to "Cimetière, Vieille Ville")* where there is a path affording **bird's-eye views** of the roofs of old Nice and the Baie des Anges.

▸ *Steps lead down from near a chapel on the left. Continue towards the Tour Bellanda.*

Tour Bellanda

Despite its appearance, this imposing circular bastion only dates from the 19C, when it was built as an identical replacement for one of the towers of the citadel which had been destroyed in 1706.
The composer Berlioz *(Roméo et Juliette, La Damnation de Faust)* lived here during the time he spent in Nice, which he wrote of with great enthusiasm: "Here I am in Nice, breathing the warm, balmy air... Here life and happiness come running swiftly to greet me, music folds me into her arms, and the future smiles on me... Here I am in Nice, strolling through orange groves..."

▸ *Continue down the steps to the Quai des Etats-Unis, where you can return to the Promenade des Anglais.*

Themed Visits

Modern and Contemporary Art

See the map for locations.

Musée des Beaux-Arts Jules-Chéret★★

33 Avenue des Baumettes, bus 38 (stop at Chéret). 🕐 *Open 10am–6pm.* 🕐 *Closed Mon and holidays.* ⊛ *4€ (free first and third Sun of each month).* ☎ *04 92 15 28 28.*

Since 1928 the Fine Arts Museum has been housed in an 1878 residence built in the Renaissance style of 17C Genoese palaces for the Russian princess Kotschoubey. The museum displays a rich collection of art of diverse inspiration, built up through donations and legacies around a nucleus of works sent to Nice by Napoleon III in 1860 for the creation of the very first Museum of Fine Arts.

Ground Floor

On the side of the façade there are three galleries. In the first vaulted gallery, taken up by the Italian Primitives, note *Death of Cleopatra* by Francesco Cozza and *David*

Conqueror of Goliath by Francesco Guarino. The second gallery displays 18C works such as *Portrait of an Old Man* by Fragonard, *Ollioules Gorges* by Hubert Robert and *Allegory of Human Life* by Donato Creti. The third gallery is given over to the important artistic dynasty, the **Van Loos**, whose most illustrious member, **Carle Van Loo,** was born in Nice in 1705. Works of his on display include *Theseus, Conqueror of the Bull at Marathon*. Jean-Baptiste Van Loo executed the famous portraits of Louis XV and Marie Leszczynska.

The great gallery branching off to the right of the entrance is decorated with large official paintings from the Third Republic, such as *Thamar* by Cabanel and some marvellous portraits of women. The patio which follows is home to *Bronze Age* by Rodin and *Triumph of Flora* by Carpeaux.

At the end of the gallery the small room on the right displays miniature 17C and 18C works.

First Floor

The main staircase leads to the hall on the first floor which was used originally by musicians because of its acoustics. It is now adorned with the works of **Jules Chéret**, who died in Nice in 1932.

The first floor is mainly devoted to the art of the second half of the 19C and the start of the 20C. The first of four large galleries, all used for temporary exhibitions, concentrates on the academic tradition (Boulanger, Trachel) and works by Oriental-ists such as *Rest during the Flight into Egypt* by Merson and the celebrated *Harem Servant* by Trouillebert. Among the sculptures on display is the original plaster cast of *The Kiss* by Rodin.

In the gallery, as well as a Carrière intimist, a fine series of works by the pre-Impres-sionist Félix Ziem evokes the romantic countryside.

The second gallery behind the façade displays paintings showing the evolution of the French countryside from the Classicism of Cordouan to Impressionism represented by Boudin *(Villefranche Anchorage)*, Monet, Sisley *(Avenue of Poplars near Moret)* and Bonnard *(Window Open on the Seine at Vernonnet)*. The third gallery is hung with pastels by Jules Chéret, the inventor of modern posters. The last room is reserved for collections by lesser-known 19C artists, grouped by subject: nudes, genre paintings, landscapes.

On the right, at the end of the gallery, two rooms display works linked to Maria Bashkirtseff, Bastien-Lepage, her spiritual mentor and to her rival Louise Breslau. The Van Dongen gallery houses the Fauvist artist's major works: *Pious Dream* and the celebrated *Dance of the Archangel*. In the display cases are ceramics by Picasso.

Musée Matisse★★

Villa des Arènes, Cimiez. Bus 15, 17, 20, 22 (stop at Arènes). 🚶 🕐 *Open daily (except Tue) 10am-5pm (Apr-Sep 6pm).* 🕐 *Closed 1 Jan, 1 May, 25 Dec* 🚌 *4€ (free the first and third Sun of each month).* ☎ *04 93 81 08 08. www.musee-matisse-nice.org.*

This museum on the top of the Cimiez hillside is housed in the splendid Villa des Arènes, a typical example of the development of urban architecture in Nice.

In 1670, on the site of a hut *(cabanoun)* buried in the ancient remains of Cimiez, a folly was built, with numerous symmetrical windows and façades decorated with colored pebble-dash and *trompe-l'œil* paintings and extended by balustraded terraces. The site of the villa, facing the sea, and the characteristic Genoese architecture are explained by the thriving trade linking together the rich families of Nice and Liguria. Its owner, the Consul of Nice, named it "Palais de Gubernatis". In the 19C successive additions were made by the new owners to adapt it to a large town house. In 1950, when it was *in extremis*, the town of Nice saved it from being divided up and rechristened it Villa des Arènes. Since its redevelopment in 1993, it has housed the collections and administrative offices of the Musée Matisse on its two levels.

A large composition of cut-out gouaches, *Flowers and Fruit,* which is Henri Matisse's last work (1953), greets visitors at the entrance.

About 30 canvases illustrate the progression of the artist from the timid attempts of his early works in 1890, *Still Life: Books*, to his blossoming in 1946, *Roccoco Armchair*. He went from a dark Realistic style to the discovery of the bright Mediterranean light, passing through the influence of Cézanne with *Still Life: A Harmonium* and Signac, *Young Woman with an Umbrella*, and building from *Portrait of Laurette* (1916) onwards, into an explosion of pure and brilliant color: *Odalisque with Red Case* (1926), *Window in Tahiti* (1935), *Nude in an Armchair* (1937), *Reader at the Yellow Table* (1944), *Still Life: Pomegranates* (1947) as well as the "pure blue" of *Blue Nude IV* (1952).

Drawings from his many different periods are also on display. Among the 235 works that make up the museum's collection, the most significant are 30 sketches for the mural *The Dance* (1933). There are also many examples of book illustrations.

Matisse's activity as a sculptor is also well represented by 54 of the total of 62 **bronze sculptures** he produced during his lifetime. Note in particular *The Serf* (c 1900) and *The Serpentine* (1909). The development of more abstract form shows in the series of *Jeannette* (1910-13), *The Nudes, Henriette* (1925-29) and culminates in the monumental work *Nudes from Behind*. Two rooms contain sketches and models for the chapel in Vence (👁 *see VENCE*), which Matisse worked on from 1948 to 1951. There are also the silkscreen prints: *The Sea, The Sky* (1947) and a huge **Beauvais tapestry**: *Polynesia*. Dotted around the museum are his personal belongings, his furniture and his private art collection, all of which are often depicted in his paintings. The museum is also equipped with an auditorium and an information centre on Matisse.

Musée Marc-Chagall★★

Avenue du Docteur-Ménard, Cimiez. Bus 15 (stop at Chagall). 👍 🕐 *Open daily (except Tue) 10am-5pm (Jul-Sep 6pm), last admission 30min before closing time.* 🕐 *Closed 1 Jan, 1 May, 25 Dec.* ⊜ *5.50€ (free first and third Sun of each month).* ☎ *04 93 53 87 20. www. musee-chagall.fr.*

The result of Chagall's donation to France, this museum built in 1972 by A Hermant houses the most important permanent collection of the painter's works. It is built partly in glass and hidden among the trees on a hilltop in Cimiez. The setting was designed especially bearing Chagall's "Biblical Message" in mind. The canvases are shown to their best advantage owing to the recessed walls and the large windows opening onto the bright Mediterranean light.

Welcoming the visitor into a world of lyrical, almost sacred fantasy is a multi-coloured tapestry (1971) showing Chagall's personal feeling for the Holy Scriptures brought from his past – born (1887) to a poor Jewish family in Vitebsk in Russia. He died in St-Paul in 1985.

This poetical lyricism is visible in all **17 canvases** which make up the "Biblical Message", an uninterrupted endeavour lasting 13 years (1954-67). In a large gallery are displayed 12 paintings evoking the Creation of Man, the Garden of Eden, the Story of Noah, Abraham, Jacob and Moses. Among Chagall's world of rich translucent colors lies a magic spell of poetic enchantment which yet does not detract from the seriousness of the subject matter. In a nearby gallery are five paintings illustrating the Song of Songs: dreamlike figures drift among glowing colors above the rooftops of sleepy villages.

There are also several sculptures by the artist. From the library door look outside and admire the large **mosaic** (1970), which is reflected in the pool: it represents the Prophet Elijah, transported to Heaven in a chariot of fire, surrounded by the signs of the Zodiac.

The circular gallery (used for concerts and conferences) is immersed in a bluish light emanating from the three large windows depicting the Creation of the World. The other rooms are used as a backdrop to temporary exhibitions or are devoted to the development of the "Biblical Message". Note the series of 39 gouaches painted by the artist in 1931 after his return from Palestine. Some of the themes were taken up again and appear in his larger canvases, 105 etchings and copperplate engravings for the Bible edited by Tériade in 1956.

Musée d'Art Moderne et d'Art Contemporain★★

Promenade des Arts. 🕐 *Open daily (except Tue) 10am-6pm.* 🕐 *Closed 1 Jan, 1 May, Easter, 25 Dec.* ⊜ *4€ (free first and third Sun of each month).* ☎ *04 93 62 61 62. www. mamac-nice.org.*

Designed by Yves Bayard and Henri Vidal, the Museum of Modern and Contemporary Art is made up of four square towers with roof-top terraces, linked by glass passage-ways. On the parvis, between the museum and the theatre, stands a monumental stabile by Alexander Calder.

The collections, exhibited in rotation on the two upper floors (first floor is devoted to temporary exhibits), presents French and American avant-garde art movements from the 1960s to the present. Both these countries were developing parallel art movements based on similar experiences. in France these ideas were often nurtured by artists living on the Riviera. In the 1960s the American **Pop Art** movement and the French **Nouveau Réalisme** (👁 *see Klein below*) attempted to express the reality of daily life in a modern society of consumerism and popular culture. Whereas Pop artists Andy Warhol, Roy Lichtenstein, Tom Wesselmann, James Rosenquist, George Segal,

Robert Rauschenberg and others appropriated objects belonging to mass culture, the New Realists, more derisive, sought inspiration from those same objects as symbols of modern life, by collecting or breaking them (Arman), compressing them (César), capturing them under glass (Spoerri), or wrapping them (Christo)...

A section of the museum is devoted to the French painter **Yves Klein** (1928-62), whose monumental work, *Wall of Fire,* is located on the roof-top terrace. Putting aside his association with the French movement (he was the founder of Nouveau Réalisme, a term that means "new realism" and was coined in 1960 by the art critic Pierre Restany), Klein attempted monochrome paintings, using gold and especially IKB (International Klein Blue) to capture and express space, energy or the universal essence of things.

The museum also holds works by artists belonging to the Nice School, who were closely in tune with the movements flourishing in the USA at that time but for the past 30 years have followed their own vision, such as Bernar Venet, Sacha Sosno, Gilli, Jean-Claude Fahri, Robert Malaval, Chubac...

Villa Arson

20 Avenue Stephen Liégeard. Bus 4, 7 (stop at Fanny). ⏲ *Open Jul-Sep 2-7pm, Oct-Jun 2-6pm.* 🚫 *Closed Tue and between expositions.* 🎟 *Free entry.* ☎ *04 92 07 73 73. www. villa-arson.org*

The Villa Arson is in the northern part of the city, set in a Mediterranean garden on the hill of St- Bartholomew with a panoramic view of the Baie des Anges. The 18C villa, influenced by the Bauhaus architectural movement, houses the École Nationale Supérieure d'Art, an artists' residence and a national center of contemporary art. The expositions (four per year) introduce artists of international fame, which you'll be able to discover in company of a guide, if you wish it.

Cimiez★ *Allow 3.5hr*

▷ *See the city map. Bus 15 also goes there (stop at Arènes).*

Cimiez hill is the sophisticated part of Nice, filled with elegant town houses and gardens. But long before it was settled by the French and visited by Queen Victoria (commemorated by a statue at the top of Boulevard de Cimiez), the Romans called this hilltop "Cemelenum". In 2C there were at least 20 000 Romans living here. Today there are still vestiges of their once flourishing city.

▷ *Starting from Place Jean-Moulin, behind the Acropolis, drive west along Boulevard Carabacel and follow the route marked on the plan.*

Arènes

The ellipse-shaped amphitheatre, which is only 67m/220ft by 56m/184ft, could hold 4 000 spectators.

Traces remain of the gangways and of the sockets on the external façade, which held the posts supporting a huge adjustable awning *(velum)* used to shelter spectators from the sun and rain. The amphitheatre was designed for spear contests and gladiatorial bouts but not for animal fights. Traditional festivals take place here all year round *(Fêtes des Mai, Fêtes des Cougourdons)* and there are live jazz performances during the summer season (🎵 *see Calendar of Events).*

Musée Archéologique

⏲ ♿ *Open 10am-6pm (last entrance 1hr before closure).* 🚫 *Closed Tue, holidays.* 🎟 *4€, including access to the archeological site (free entry first and third Sun of each month).* ☎ *04 93 81 59 57.*

Finds excavated at Cimiez and around Nice, as well as donations, make up the Archeological Museum's collections. There are ceramics and bronzes from the great Mediterranean civilisations (Greece, Etruria, Roman Africa), including some artefacts, such as the superb **mask of Silenus★**, salvaged from shipwrecks.

Another section concentrates on Ligurian and Roman civilizations from the region that became the Alpes-Maritimes in 14 BC, including the Bronze Age (statue of a warrior from Mont Bégo), Iron Age (items excavated from perched strongholds or *oppida*), and milestones (1C) from the Via Julia Augusta.

Roman civilization is represented by examples of daily life (pottery, glassware, statues, jewellery), and public life (inscriptions), a display of imperial coins in an interactive glass case, as well as models and maps of Cimiez, statues of the Imperial family (Antonia, Augustus's niece).

The ground floor presents the funerary customs found at Cimiez: incineration in the 1C and 2C *(stelae)* and inhumation beginning in the 3C *(sarcophagi).*

The tour ends with aspects of the paleo-Christian civilization (4C and 5C) such as pottery, coins and inscriptions.

Site Archéologique Gallo-Romain★

🕐 Same times and charges as for the Musée Archéologique.

Roman Baths

Steps lead down into the *decumanus maximus* (the main east-west street of a Roman town) with its central drain and shops. On the left are the **North Baths,** probably reserved for the Procurator and other important people. The summer bath consists of a marble basin surrounded by a peristyle embellished with Corinthian capitals. On the eastern side are the latrines. The northern building contains the **cold bath** (frigidarium); it was vaulted and its dimensions (10m/33ft high by 9m/30ft wide) give an idea of the huge scale of the northern baths (the warm room and the hot rooms built above the **underground stove** or *hypocaust*), and the public rooms, partially excavated.

On the other side of the main street are the less elaborate but fully equipped **East Baths** for the general public, which can be viewed from a walkway.

To the south of these baths runs a parallel street lined with houses and shops; some of the paving stones have survived.

The western end of this street opens into the *cardo maximus* (main street running north-south) which returns to the Matisse Museum. On the left-hand side are the **West Baths** for women only. The structure is quite well preserved, although it was used as a cathedral in the 5C. The choir, in the *frigidarium*, contains traces of an altar and a semicircular stone seat.

The neighboring room to the north was used as the **baptistery**.

▶ *Cross the public gardens planted with olive trees to the Place du Monastère.*

Place du Monastère

A twisted column of white marble, rising in the square in front of the church, bears a **Calvary** dating from 1477. On one side is the crucified seraph who appeared before St Francis and imprinted the stigmata of the Passion on his body.

Nearby in the Cimiez **cemetery** are buried the painters Raoul Dufy and Henri Matisse who were leading exponents of Fauvism. The latter's tomb lies in an olive grove to the north of the surrounding wall.

Monastère Franciscain★

The Franciscans, who in the 16C took over the buildings of a former Benedictine monastery founded in the 9C, have restored and considerably enlarged the abbey church.

Église Notre-Dame-de-l'Assomption

The church possesses three **masterpieces** ★★ by the local artist Louis Bréa, illustrating the Nice School.

To the right of the entrance stands a **Pietà** (1475), and although it is an early work, it is undoubtedly one of his most perfect creations. The arms of the cross and the stiff body of Christ emphasize the horizontal perspective, while the gold background reveals glimpses of a landscape. Weeping cherubs cluster round the Cross while the lonely figure of Mary holds her son on her knees. One of the two side panels represents St Martin sharing his scarlet cloak.

Quite different but of equal beauty is the **Crucifixion** by the same artist which is on the left in the choir. It is a later work (1512). The gold background has been replaced by an elaborate landscape showing perspective.

In the second chapel to the left lies a recumbent figure of Christ in wood (18C).

The **Deposition** in the third chapel, which is also attributed to Louis Bréa, complements the Cruxifixion and adheres to Renaissance principles: the figures obliquely aligned on the body of Christ are counterbalanced by the vertical lines of the landscape.

A huge half Renaissance-half Baroque altarpiece carved in wood and decorated with gold leaf screens off the monks' choir.

Musée Franciscain

🕐 Open daily (except Sun) 10am-noon, 3-6pm. 🕐 Closed public holidays. ⬤ Free entry. ☎ 04 93 81 00 04.

The **museum** recalls the work of the Franciscans in Nice from the 13C to the present day. The social and spiritual message of the Franciscans is proclaimed through documents and works of art (frescoes, engravings, sculptures) in a restored section of the old monastery. There are also a fine illuminated antiphonary (17C), the novices' chapel and a restored 17C cell.

Monastery Gardens★

On the south side of the monastery there are attractive terraced gardens with flower beds and lemon trees which look down on the Paillon Valley from a **viewpoint** over Nice, the castle and the sea, Mont Boron and the observatory to the east. A copse of cypress and holm oak marks the site of the former Ligurian *oppidum*.

Nice's Russian Heritage

Around the middle of the 19C, after Empress Alexandra Fedorovna, the widow of Tsar Nicolas I, had settled in Nice, many wealthy Russian aristocrats chose this city as their favorite place of residence. These "excentrics", as the locals would call them, applied themselves to re-creating the atmosphere of their native country on the Riviera, hiring the services of architects who combined the Slav spirit with Mediterranean influences. Baron Von Dewies, who designed the Russian railway system, commissioned the building of the Gothic **Château de Valrose** (Science Faculty of Nice University) and set up an isba from Kiev on his huge estate. At the west entrance to Nice, not far from the railway, the **Château des Ollières** (currently a hotel) features an impressive keep flanked by four turrets. The nearby **Palais Kotschoubey** houses the Musée des Beaux-Arts. Two other notable examples of Russian architecture are the **Palais Impérial** and the **Résidence Palladium** on Boulevard Tsarévitch, which was originally built for a Russian banker.

Cathédrale Orthodoxe Russe St-Nicolas★

🕐 *Open Mar-Oct 9am-noon, 2.30-6pm, Nov-15 Feb 9.30am-noon, 2.30-5pm* 🕐 *Closed 1 Jan and on the mornings of Russian Orthodox holidays.* 🌐 *2.50€.* ☎ *04 93 96 88 02.*

With its six gilded onion domes and its façade of ochre brick, the **Russian Orthodox cathedral** lends an exotic touch to the Nice skyline and symbolises the importance of the Russian colony on the Riviera. It is the largest Russian religious building outside Russia itself, built to accommodate the frequent visits to Nice of the Russian nobility, who were regularly joined by the Imperial Court. The Villa Bermond was donated by the dowager Empress in 1900 for the construction of the new cathedral. The Russian architect Préobrajensky drew the plans and oversaw the work. The choice of materials was enhanced by the generosity of Czar Nicolas II: the bricks came from England, the glazed tiles on the domes and the six crosses surmounting them from Italy, the domes are coated with fine gold leaf and the mosaic icons on the façades were handmade by Russian artists. The inauguration took place in December 1912 in the presence of the Imperial Russian family. Other icons and devotional articles found a home in the cathedral after 1917.

The interior, in the form of a Greek cross, is richly decorated with frescoes, panelling and icons. At the entrance to the choir is a sumptuous **iconostasis** ★ bringing together the finest examples of Russian religious art, taken from the church of Jaroslav and the church of St Basil the Blessed in Moscow. On the right of the choir is an icon of **Our Lady of Kazan**, painted on wood and decorated with silver and precious stones. At the end of the park on the left a **Byzantine chapel** is dedicated to Tsarevich Nicolas, the son of Czar Alexander II, who died of an illness here in 1866. His funeral was an imposing ceremony held locally at the Russian Church in Rue Longchamp.

Sights

Musée des Arts Asiatiques★★

Located in Parc Phœnix, near Nice-Côte-d'Azur airport. Underground car park (fee).
♿ 🕐 *Open10am-5pm; May to mid-Oct 10am-6pm.* 🕐 *Closed 1 Jan, 1 May, 25 Dec.* 🌐 *6€ (free for children under 18 and everyone the first and third Sun of each month).* ☎ *04 92 29 37 00. www.arts-asiatiques.com.*

Delicately poised on the lake in Phœnix Park, this dazzling construction in white marble presents sacred and traditional objects coming from several Asian countries. The building was designed by the Japanese architect **Kenzo Tange** in 1998, a faithful representation of the Far-East principles of cosmogony that associate the circle (sky) with the square (earth) and its four cardinal points. You can also discover these fascinating civilisations on your own with the help of audioguides.

On the first floor visitors are enlightened on the history of Buddhism thanks to an informative but also highly attractive exhibition featuring a series of stone Buddhas conducive to meditation, illustrating 4C Gandhara and 12C Khmer art.

On the ground floor, each gallery is devoted to a specific civilisation: China, Japan, Cambodia and India. Set against a sparsely decorated background that invites inner comtemplation, the various sculptures, ceramics and paintings are all of considerable beauty and they reflect the religious spirit of their country.

The basement has a more contemporary feel and is devoted to temporary art shows. Interactive terminals linked to the Asian continent present a wide selection of museums devoted to Oriental art throughout the world.

Parc Phœnix★

 ♿ 🕐 *Open Apr-Sep 9.30am-7.30pm; Oct-Mar 9.30am-5.30pm.* ☞ *2€ (child free with adult).* ☎ *04 93 18 03 33.*

This vast botanical garden (over 7ha/17 acres) inaugurated in 1991 is organised by theme and contains over 2 000 plant species from all over the world, grouped together with their corresponding animal life. Visitors can wander in this popular park around five large zones, each reflecting a particular period or climate.

The "Île des Temps Révolus" (Island of Bygone Times), in the middle of a big lake, takes visitors back into the past with a display of living plant fossils: cycads, ginkgo biloba, tree ferns etc. The crater of scents and colors next to it displays a selection of colours that blend in with the perfumes of each plant.

Throughout the park, discreetly positioned loudspeakers give out the calls and songs of the animals and birds that inhabit the particular zone of plant life the visitor is in.

In the second zone, an aviary houses a colorful collection of parrots and other tropical birds. The wadi-oasis reconstitutes part of an oasis in the Sahara.

The **giant greenhouse**★, known as the "Green Diamond", is a huge tropical hothouse covering 7 000m²/75 300sq ft beneath a 25m/82ft high roof in which seven climates of varying temperatures and hygrometry are housed: an orchid garden; a greenhouse containing plants from the southern hemisphere; an underground vivarium-insectarium; a lovely garden of ferns from various places; and in the center, a large tropical garden containing palm trees and Madasgascan traveler's trees as well as trees cultivated for food (banana, breadfruit, coffee, papaya). Carry on from the giant greenhouse to see the carnivorous plants and the butterfly house.

Nearby, the information center or **infothèque** provides visitors with databases to search for general and detailed information on tropical plants.

Outside, to the right, a garden of tropical plants and a beautiful rose garden flourish side by side.

The "Great Aztec Pyramid" is an original way of displaying what goes on beneath our feet, regarding both plants and animals that live underground.

A large circular fountain and various musical fountains add the finishing touches to the visitor's voyage of discovery.

Musée d'Art Naïf Jakovsky★

Avenue du Val-Marie. Leave the town center by Promenade des Anglais. 🕐 *Open daily (except Tue) 10am-noon, 2-6pm.* 🕐 *Closed 1 Jan, Easter, 1 May, 25 Dec.* ☞ *4€ (free the first and third Sun of each month).* ☎ *04 93 71 78 33.*

Housed in the elegant Château Ste-Hélène, the Anatole Jakovsky Bequest comprises 600 canvases (about half are on show) illustrating the amateur talents of many countries.

The Croatian artists *(mostly on the 1st floor)* include Generalic, Rabuzin, Kovacic and Petrovic. Among the French are Bauchant, Vivin, Vieillard, Restivo and Crociani *(Night Festival in Nice)* and more dreamlike paintings by Vercruyce and Lefranc *(Clock)*. There are also works by Italians, Swiss, Belgians and Americans, from both the north and the south (particularly Brazil).

One section has been set aside for a series of unusual portraits of Jakovsky.

Musée Masséna★

35 Promenade des Anglais. ⌕ *Closed for renovations through 2007.*

This museum surrounded by gardens was built in 1898, It was modelled on Italian residences of the First Empire and was made after plans by Georg Tersling and the Niçois A Messian for Victor Masséna, great-grandson of the Marshal. In 1919 his son André gave it to the town.

Japanese Tea Ceremony

Treat yourself to a Japanese **tea ceremony** in the museum's blissfully minimalist tea room set up next to the bookshop. Sundays *(except the first Sunday of the month and during August)* at 3pm and 4pm, reservations necessary. ☞ *10€.* ☎ *04 92 29 37 02.*

Acropolis-Palais des Congrès★
○ *Guided tours on request.* ☎ *04 93 92 82 35.*

This convention center resembles a majestic vessel anchored to the five robust vaults spanning the River Paillon. It was designed by a group of local architects and the names of its various parts were taken from Greek antiquity. Contemporary works of art meant to complement the architecture are displayed both inside and outside the building, and on the Esplanade Kennedy in front, including works by Volti *(Nikaia)*, Vasarely, Arman *(Music Power)*, César *(Thumb)*, Paul Belmondo, Moretti *(Louis Armstrong)*, and Cyril de la Patellière *(Mediterranean Tribute)*.

Théâtre de la Photographie et de l'Image
27 Boulevard Dubouchage ○ *Open 10am-6pm.* ○ *Closed Mon.* ⊷ *Free entry.* ☎ *04 97 13 42 20.*

Formerly known as the Théâtre de l'Artistique, this new exhibition space dedicated to photographic images benefits from the interesting architectural aspect of the building, worth a visit on its own. In addition to the temporary expositions is a documentation center which contains a collection of photographs of Nice and the region.

Muséum d'Histoire Naturelle
60 bis Boulevard Risso. ○ *Open 10am-6pm.* ○ *Closed Mon and holidays.* ⊷ *Free entry.* ☎ *04 97 13 46 80. www.mhnnice.org*

Nice's first museum, the Natural History Museum houses a curious collection of 7 000 casts of fungi, alongside an exhibition of minerals. There is also a stratigraphy section that explains fossils, geological phenomena and the formation of the earth's crust.

Musée de Terra Amata
25 Boulevard Carnot ○ *Open 10am-6pm.* ○ *Closed Mon and holidays.* ⊷ *4€ (free entry for children and everyone the first and third Sun of each month). Audiovisual tour with commentary in French, English, Italian and German.* ☎ *04 93 55 59 93.*

A model of a sand dune on a fossil beach, which has been uncovered 26m/85ft above the present sea-level on the western slopes of Mont Boron, is reproduced on the ground floor of the museum, built on the site of the excavation. An open hearth and a human footprint with a calcified surface were found in the hardened limestone. Bones, stone tools and traces of fire mark one of the earliest human settlements known in Europe. Articles, drawings, maps and a full-scale reconstruction of a shelter made of branches illustrate the life of the Achuelean hunters some 400 000 years ago (early Paleolithic).

Prieuré du Vieux-Logis
59 Avenue St-Barthélémy. ○ *Guided tours (1hr) 3-5pm.* ⊷ *Free entry.* ☎ *04 93 88 11 34.*

A medieval home has been reconstructed within a 16C farm and richly supplied with works of art, 14C to 17C furniture and items from everyday life (note the outstanding kitchen). There are numerous statues including a 15C Pietà from Franche-Comté.

Église Ste-Jeanne-d'Arc
11 Rue Gramond

This is a modern concrete church designed by Jacques Droz with three segmented cupolas and an ellipsoidal porch as its main doorway. The belfry wreathed in flames rises to a height of 65m/215ft. Inside, the soaring vaulting is striking. The Stations of the Cross are frescoes by Klementief (1934).

Driving Tours

1 Les Deux Monts★★ *Round trip of 11km/6mi – about 45min*

▶ *Leave Nice from Place Max-Barel on N 7, Moyenne Corniche, going east. After 2.5km/1.5mi turn sharp right onto a forest road. 1km/0.5mi further on turn sharp left onto a signposted path leading to the fort on Mont Alban.*

Mont Alban★★ *Alt 222m/728ft.*

A footpath circles the height from which there is a splendid **view** ★★ of the coastline: to the east lie Cap Ferrat, Cap d'Ail, the Bordighera Point and the limestone heights of Tête de Chien. To the west lie the Baie des Anges and the Garoupe Plateau. The fort, a massive 16C construction with bastions and watchtowers, can be explored on foot *(exterior only)*.

▶ *Return to the fork and proceed straight ahead to Mont Boron.*

Mont Boron★ *Alt 178m/584ft.*

From the mountains there are **views**★ extending over the Villefranche harbor and along the coast to Cap d'Antibes. On the horizon can be seen the mountains around Grasse and, further to the left, the Esterel range.

▶ *Return to Nice along the Corniche Inférieure (N 98).*

② **Plateau St-Michel**★★ *Round-trip of 19km/12mi – about 1hr.*

▶ *Leave Nice going east along Avenue des Diables-Bleus and the Grande Corniche (D 2564).*

Look back to enjoy views of Nice and the Baie des Anges and beyond Cap d'Antibes and the Paillon Basin. Ahead lie the fort of La Drète in the foreground and Mont Agel further back.

Observatoire du Mont-Gros

The private road to the Nice observatory leads off to the right of the Grande Corniche. ⏲ *Guided tours (1.5hr) Sat at 3pm.* ⊚ *4.5€.* ☎ *04 93 85 85 58. www.astrorama.net.*

This famous international center for astronomical research was founded in 1881 by the scientific patron Bischoffheim. Charles Garnier oversaw the construction of the buildings, while Gustave Eiffel built the metal frame supporting the great dome (26m/85ft in diameter). This houses an astronomical telescope called the "great equatorial". It is 18m/59ft long with an optical diameter of 76cm/30in and was for a long time the largest instrument of its kind in the world. Note the neo-Classical pediment at the entrance to the dome, typical of its period.

Beyond the Quatre-Chemins Pass, Cap Ferrat Peninsula and Villefranche-sur-Mer port come into view.

▶ *Bear right onto D 34 and after 500m/547yd leave the car in the car park.*

Plateau St-Michel Viewpoint★★

A viewing table points out all the main features of the coast from Cap d'Ail to the Esterel.

▶ *Continue along D 34 and then bear left onto the Moyenne Corniche (N 7).*

After a long tunnel there is a marvellous **view** ★ of Beaulieu, Cap Ferrat, Villefranche-sur-Mer, Nice and Cap d'Antibes. The road winds round above Villefranche harbor. After Col de Villefranche, Nice with its castle hill, the harbor and the Baie des Anges comes into sight. On the horizon is the outline of the Esterel and the limestone hills of Grasse.

▶ *Return to Nice via Place Max-Barel.*

③ **Tour of Mont Chauve**★ *Round-trip of 53km/33mi – allow a half-day.*

▶ *From Nice take Avenue du Ray north; turn sharp right on Avenue de Gairaut, D 14, towards Aspremont and after passing under the motorway (2km/1.2mi) bear right following D 14 and then turn left following the signs.*

Cascade de Gairaut

In two great steps the waters of the Vésubie Canal, which supplies the Nice area, tumble down into a basin. From the chapel terrace there is a beautiful **view** of the town.

▶ *Return to D 14.*

Soon afterwards there are fine views to the left of Nice, Mont Boron and Cap d'Antibes. As the road climbs towards Aspremont, the **view** extends to include the Baous, the Var Valley and the mountains.

Aspremont

The village, built to a concentric plan, perches prettily on its hilltop site. The **church** (⏲ *Closed between services)* has a Gothic nave decorated with frescoes and supported on solid cubic capitals. On the left there is a painted wooden Virgin and Child.

Above and behind the church once stood the castle, now destroyed. From the terrace that overlooks the town is a **panorama** ★ comprising several hill villages, Vence, Cap d'Antibes, the hills beyond Nice, Mont Chauve and Mont Cima.

▶ *On leaving the village, take D 719 over a little pass, Col d'Aspremont, between Mont Chauve and Mont Cima to the rich basin of Tourrette-Levens.*

Studios de la Victorine: the Story of Film-Making in Nice

With the dawning of cinema, Nice provided film-makers with the ideal ingredients for their future success: almost constant light and sunshine, the sea and the presence of magnificent hotels as natural backdrops.

Louis Feuillade, who made *Fantômas*, was one of the first to spot the potential of the area; the roofs of the Hôtel Négresco passed into cinematic posterity in the Fantô-mas-Judex chase.

The "azure cinema" really took off in 1920, however, when a large unoccupied estate west of the town centre, La Victorine, was acquired by the fabulously rich Hollywood producer Rex Ingram, who had launched Rudolf Valentino and Roman Navarro. He produced the epic *Mare Nostrum*, to promote his new studios.

From that time, La Victorine studios saw both French and European film-makers prosper for the following 10 years. Then changes in public tastes brought another decade of inactivity.

The Armistice of 1940 caused French cinema to seek refuge in Nice (Abel Gance, Prévert, Carné).

The filming of *Les Visiteurs du Soir* in 1943 revived the production of large-scale films.

In 1944 came *Les Enfants du Paradis,* co-produced by Marcel Carné and Jacques Pré-vert with Arletty and Jean-Louis Barrault, which was the greatest production at La Victorine.

The reconstruction of *Boulevard du Crime* in the middle of the war required more than 30t of scaffolding and nearly 3 500m² of fencing for the sets, as well as 2 000 extras who were recruited in Nice.

The worsening of the general situation and lack of money temporarily brought a halt to this creativity.

The 15 post-war years were good ones; they were followed by a lull.

Nowadays, after several abortive projects, a revival of filming seems to be under way.

Tourrette-Levens

Circled by mountains, this village on the Salt Route clings to a knife-edged rock. The 18C **church** (🕐 *Open on request,* ☎ *04 93 91 00 41*) presents a fine carved wooden altarpiece, also 18C, of the Virgin between St Sylvester and St Antony (behind the high altar).

A short walk through the village to the partially restored **château** (🕐 *Open May-Oct 2-6pm; Nov-Apr 2-5.30pm.* 🞉 *Free entry.* ☎ *04 93 91 03 20*) reveals **views** of the neighboring mountains, Chauve and Ferion, and the Gabre and Rio Sec Valleys. Your efforts will be rewarded by a charming **natural history exhibition** on tropical butterflies, including a diorama on creatures from all over the world.

▶ *Return to D 19 turning left down into the Gabre Valley.*

Gorges du Gabre

The gorges have been hollowed out of limestone walls.

▶ *Bear right onto D 114 towards Falicon.*

Falicon

This typical Niçois village huddles on a rocky outcrop among olive groves. The Bellevue inn *(panoramic view from the terrace)* displays mementoes belonging to the French author **Jules Romains** (1885-1972) who set one of his novels in Falicon.

Other illustrious guests, including Queen Victoria, were attracted to the village on account of its delightful surroundings.

The **church** (🕐 *open weekdays, visits on request at the town hall* ☎ *04 92 07 92 70*), which was founded by the Benedictines of St-Pons, has a square belfry and a façade in trompe-l'œil. In the nave is a beautiful 17C Nativity framed in gold.

Climb up the stairway to the left of the church and turn right onto a path leading to a terrace for a **view** ★ of Nice, the sea, the hills and Mont Agel.

▶ *Return to D 114 on the left. At the chapel of St-Sébastien turn right onto D 214, a narrow and dangerous road, to Mont Chauve. Leave the car at the end of the road.*

Mont Chauve d'Aspremont *Alt 854m/2 802ft.*

🚶 *30min on foot round-trip.*

"Chauve" means bald, and the mountain lives up to its name. A disused fort stands on the naked summit offering a magnificent **panorama** ★★: the snow-clad Alps and the Nice hills, and the coast from Menton to Cap Ferrat. On a very fine day Corsica is visible.

▸ *Return to D 114 turning left; 2km/1.2mi further on turn sharp right onto D 19. Go under the motorway; 1km/0.5mi later there is a right-hand turning up to St-Pons.*

Église St-Pons★

🕓 *Open 2.30–5pm.* ☎ *04 93 55 07 94.*

The Benedictine abbey of St Pontius was founded during Charlemagne's reign and played an important part in local affairs for 1 000 years. The church, which was rebuilt early in the 18C, stands on a headland above the Paillon Valley, its graceful silhouette and Genoese campanile visible from all sides. The elegant curves and counter-curves of the tall Baroque façade are echoed in the peristyle. The interior forms an ellipse, preceded by a vestibule and prolonged by a semicircular choir, ringed by side chapels opening out between powerful columns. The plasterwork is richly decorated.

④ **The Two Paillons★** *Round-trip of 90km/56mi – allow one day.*

The Paillon de l'Escarène, the main river, rises to the northeast of Col St-Roch, whereas the Paillon de Contes springs from the upper slopes of Rocca Seira to the northwest of the pass. They meet at Pont de Peille and flow into the sea at Nice. The suggested route goes up one valley and down the other with detours to La Turbie and Peille.

▸ *Leave Nice by Boulevard J.-B.-Verany and Route de Turin, D 2204 going north. In La Trinité bear right to Laghet.*

The road goes up the verdant Laghet Valley. The Roman road from La Turbie to Cimiez was on the opposite bank.

Sanctuaire Notre-Dame de Laghet

♿ 🕓 *Sanctuary open 7am–9.30pm. Museum open in summer 3.30–5.30pm; open in winter 3–5pm.* 👓 *Free entry.* ☎ *04 93 41 50 50. www.laghet.com.*

The sanctuary, founded in 1656, is a pilgrimage center, and its influence is felt on both sides of the border with Italy. Innumerable votive offerings, touching and amusing in their naivety, cover the church and cloisters. The best of them are displayed in the little **museum** on Place du Sanctuaire. The interior decor, in heavy Baroque, features a statue of Our Lady of Laghet carved in wood on the high altar.

▸ *The road winds steeply up through olive groves to the Grande Corniche; turn left.*

La Turbie★ *(see La TURBIE)*

▸ *Leave La Turbie on D 53 with its views of the sea and the Paillon Basin. On the left of the road is the Chapelle St-Martin.*

Église St-Martin-de-Peille

🔒 *Currently closed for restoration.* ☎ *04 93 91 71 71.*

The church stands in a secluded but beautiful setting of olive-tree clad mountains. It is a modern structure of very simple design, with plastic windows and the trunk of a giant olive tree used as the altar.

The road winds round the lower slopes of Mont Agel before descending to Peille. Near the last tunnel there is a fine **view** of Peille village.

Peille★ *(see PEILLE)*

▸ *Join Paillon Valley at La Grave. After 2.5km/1.5mi turn left onto D 121 which climbs to the eagle's nest of Peillon.*

Peillon★★ *(see PEILLON)*

▸ *Return to D 21 and turn right.*

The village of Peille comes into view on the slopes of Mont Castellet (right).

Gorges du Paillon★

The route crosses a beautifully lush and green wooded ravine.

L'Escarène

Built at the junction of the road to the resort of Peïra-Cava and the beginning of the hairpin bends leading up to Col de Braus, this large town stretches along the bottom of the Paillon Valley. It was an important staging post on the old road from Nice to Turin, called the Salt Route (*Route du Sel* – *see SOSPEL*). The old bridge with its single arch and Place de la Gabelle remain from that period.

From the Armée des Alpes bridge crossing the Paillon, there is a good view of the old village.

3045 △
MᵀCLAPIER

CUNEO

★ Cascade de
l'Estrech

Fontanalbe

Casterino

N 205

Roya

★ Tende

MᵀSACCARE
2200 △

la Brigue

D 143

Mᵗ du Grᵈ
Capelet △
2935

∨ Baisse de Valmasque
△ 2872
Mᵗ Bégo

D 43

Levense

N.-D. des-
Fontaines ★★

★★ Vallée des
Merveilles

St-Dalmas-
de-Tende

D.91

2685 △
CIME DU DIABLE

MERCANTOUR

Granile

HAUTE VALLÉE DE LA ROYA

N 204

Fontan

Gorges de Bergue ★

l'Authion ★★

Pᵗᵉ des.
3 Communes ★★
2082

1889

Mont
aux Morts

D 68

DU

N 204

Roya

★ Saorge ★★

★★ Gorges
de Saorge

10

1607
Col de Turini

7

Vallée

Cabanes Vieilles

la Giandola

Turini

D 2566

● Moulinet

Mᵗ Mangiabo
△ 1801

D 2204

● Breil-s-Roya

★ N.-D. de
la Menour

de

la

Cascade

879

Col de Brouis ★

Piene-Haute

★★ Gorges du
Piaon

Col du
Perus ∨

654

Mᵗ
Agaisen
△ 745

Col de
Vescavo

9

N 204

477

ITALIA

Nervia

Bévéra

Col
de Braus

St Roch

● Sospel ★

1002

Olivetta

204

Fort Suchet

847

D 2566

Bévéra

Braus

642

Col St-Jean

Col de Castillon

S 20

7

Meriansos

707

Clue de Braus

8

Castillon

du Caramel

es du Paillon
D 21

Forêt de Menton

▲ Viaduc du Caramel

Monti

Vallée
du Carei

Roya

Peille ★

Ste-Agnès

Castellar

A 10

GENOVA

S 1

la Grave

4

Gorbio

59

Ventimiglia

D 53

Mont Agel
1110 △

D 2566

● Peillon

Roquebrune-

St-Martin-de-Peille

Cap-Martin ★

MENTON ★★

N.-D.
Laghet

Cap Martin ★★

36

la Turbie

MONTE-CARLO ★★★

ze ★★

MONACO ★★★

Cap-d'Ail

MER   MÉDITERRANÉE

ARRIÈRE-PAYS NIÇOIS

0   5 km

Église St-Pierre★

This 17C church, flanked by two chapels of the Black and White Penitents, is the work of the Niçois architect Guibert, who designed Nice Cathedral. It has a very ornate Baroque façade, and the sizeable interior dates from the same period. The font on the right is hollowed out of an ancient Gallo-Roman altar topped by a gilded 17C statuette. The organ (1791) is by the Grinda brothers.

On the road to Col de Turini, the imposing mausoleum dedicated to the Ist Division France Libre, inaugurated in 1964 by General de Gaulle, commemorates the sacrifices and battles of the Liberation at the end of the Second World War.

▶ *Take D 2204 south to Col de Nice and turn right onto D 215.*

Glimpses of Berre-les-Alpes can be seen on the drive up.

Berre-les-Alpes

The village boasts a charming site at an elevation of 675m/2 215ft. From the cemetery there is a **panorama**★ of the Pre-Alps of Nice and the sea.

▶ *Return downhill on the same road bearing right onto D 615.*

The drive from Berre-les-Alpes to Contes is enchanting. The road winds its way through a typical inland Nice landscape of chestnut and olive groves interspersed with cypress and pine trees and clumps of mimosa on the terraced land.

Contes

Originally a Roman settlement, the village is built on a rocky promontory that dominates the River Paillon de Contes like a ship's prow. More modern constructions extend into the valley.

The south chapel of the church contains a remarkable altarpiece by an artist belonging to the Nice School (1525). The central panel representing Ste Madeleine has disappeared but the **predella**★ illustrates her life in five scenes. The

> ### Obedient Caterpillars
>
> According to legend, the village was invaded by a plague of caterpillars in the 16C. The intruders were solemnly tried and sentenced to exile. The villagers then organised a procession, and the caterpillars obediently left the village forever.

woodwork (doorway, gallery, pulpit) is 17C. An elegant Renaissance fountain plays in front of the church, where there is a fine view of the valley from the terrace.

Bordering Paillon *(on D 15, in the direction of Coaraze)* is a site with two mills: a 13C oil press still in use by the village *(Dec-Mar)*, and a 14C iron forge where large farming tools were made until 1958. You can visit the forge and, on the first floor, a reconstituted 19C country kitchen (🕐 *Open Sat 9.30am-12.30pm, 2-5pm;* 🕐 *Closed Nov;* 🎫 *1€;* ☎ *04 93 79 00 01).*

▶ *Take D 715 to La Grave; cross the Paillon and take D 815.*

The road winds uphill beneath the shade of pines and olives above the Paillon, until one can look down on the rocky outcrop of Contes and Berre-des-Alpes.

Châteauneuf-Villevieille

The village nestles against the hillside among olive groves on the site of a Ligurian settlement, later a Roman camp, overlooking the Paillon de Contes Valley. The 11C Romanesque church, **Madone de Villevieille,** (🕐 *Open 10am-6pm.* ☎ *04 93 79 23 76 or* ☎ *04 93 79 00 58.)* is decorated with festoons and Lombard bands. A Roman inscription has been incorporated into the façade. The east end with its massive buttresses has been cleared.

The interior was restored in the 17C and frescoes painted on the ceiling. Behind the high altar, a fine plaster altarpiece frames a 15C wooden statue of the Virgin and Child.

The deserted ruins of medieval walls and towers (🚶 *2km/1mi, 30min on foot there and back)* make a strange spectacle against the rocky landscape. The people of Châteauneuf-de-Contes retreated up here in the Middle Ages to be safe from attack. From the top of the bluff there is a sweeping **panorama** ★ taking in Mont Chauve, Mont Férion (west) and the Alps (northeast).

▶ *Go back to D 15, which leads to Nice via the Paillon Valley.*

⑤ Vallée du Var and Vallée de l'Esteron *66km/41mi – allow a half day.*

▶ *Leave Nice by Promenade des Anglais, which becomes Promenade Corniglion-Molinier, a pleasant drive along the Baie des Anges. Return to N 98, then turn right towards Plan-du-Var.*

The N 202, which hugs the east bank of the Var, allows quick access to the Nice hinterland. In a landscape composed of flower beds and vegetable plots, of vineyards and olive groves, the hill villages stand out one by one: on the west bank Gattières, Carros and Le Broc; on the east bank Aspremont and Castagniers at the foot of Mont Chauve, followed by St-Martin-du-Var and La Roquette-sur-Var. The **view** ★ includes the snow-capped Alps on the horizon.

▶ *Cross the river over Pont Charles-Albert and take D 17 to Gilette.*

The site of the village of Bonson, on an impressive rock spur high above the river on the west bank, comes into view followed by Gilette, in its unusual site nestling in a cleft.

Gilette

From Place de la Mairie follow the arrows up to the castle ruins for an impressive **view** ★ of the *corniche* roads, the Var Valley, its confluence with the Esteron and the Pre-Alps of Nice. There is a pleasant walk, bordered by acacias and plane trees, below the castle with fine views of the hill villages – Bonson and Tourette-du-Château – and of the Alps to the north.

▶ *From Gilette take D 17 north up the Esteron Valley; 2km/1mi beyond Vescous turn right onto a narrow road which climbs to Vieux-Pierrefeu.*

Vieux-Pierrefeu *Alt 618m/2 028ft.*

Austere and proud, Vieux-Pierrefeu is a handsome perched village with beautifully restored stonework throughout. The Esteron river attracts many water sport and canyoning fans to the area. High above the Esteron Valley, was a Roman signalling post (Petra Igniaria), this village was a link in the chain that ran from Hadrian's Wall on the border between England and Scotland to Rome and was used to transmit optical messages.

🚷 *The village is reserved for pedestrians.*

The church just down the road in Pierrefeu has been converted into a picture gallery called the **Musée "Hors du Temps"** (🕐 *Open daily (except Wed) Jul-Sep 3-7pm; and Sundays Oct-Jun 3-6.30pm.* 👓 *2€. Reserve in advance at the Town Hall,* ☎ *04 93 08 58 18).* This small museum houses a unique collection of paintings on the theme of Genesis, with the work of 40 contemporary artists including Brayer, Carzou, Folon, Erni, Vicari, Villemont and Moretti.

On the drive down D 17, you'll see views of the Var Valley, Bonson and La Roquette, perched on its rock.

Bonson

Built on a remarkable **site** ★ on a rocky spur high above the Var Valley, Bonson offers an exceptional **view**★★ from the church terrace of the Vésubie springing from its gorges and meeting with the waters of the Var, the Défilé de Chaudan (🕯 *see below*). This famous wooded area was razed by a terrible fire in 1994 which destroyed everything up to the edge of the village.

The **church** contains three beautiful Primitive paintings from the Nice School. On the back wall there is a **retable of St Antony**, where the figure of Ste Gertrude, who was invoked against the plague, is identified by the great rats climbing up her shoulders. In the south aisle is a **retable of John the Baptist**, attributed to Antoine Bréa (the center panel has been spoiled by overpainting). At the high altar, in a Renaissance frame, is a **retable of St Benedict**★, including the figure of Ste Agatha clutching her wounded breasts.

Mont Vial★ *20 km/12mi from Bonson.*

▶ *Take D 27 west towards Puget-Théniers.*

The picturesque road twists and turns along the flank of the hill with attractive glimpses of Gilette. After Tourette-du-Château take the road going sharply down to the right which winds to Le Vial ridge before reaching the summit (1 549m/5 082ft) *(U-turns possible).* An impressive **panorama** ★★ will reward those who have made the effort of climbing up. In fine weather the view extends over the course of the Var from Puget-Théniers to the mouth of the river.

▶ *Return to Bonson by the same route.*

The road loops down to Pont Charles-Albert, giving beautiful **views** ★ of the Var Valley. Cross the bridge and turn left onto N 202. North of Plan-du-Var cross the River Vésubie where it joins the Var. The road to the right climbs up the Gorges de la Vésubie (🕯 *see Vallée de la VÉSUBIE*).

Défilé du Chaudan★★

The defile, which is named after the little village of Chaudan at its southern end, has been created by the Var, which has worn a deep, narrow and winding channel through the rocks. The road follows the course of the river in and out of every bend and through four tunnels.

At the northern end, at **Pont de la Mescla,** the River Tinée flows into the Var.

▶ *Go back to Nice on N 202.*

6 **Vésubie Valley** – *see Vallée de la VÉSUBIE*
Plan-du-Var to the Madone d'Utelle
St-Jean-la-Rivière to St-Martin-Vésubie

7 **Turini Forest** – *see Forêt de TURINI*
The Authion★★
Vallon Ste-Élisabeth★
Col de Braus Route★★

8 **Col de Castillon Road** – *see MENTON: Pass Road*
Menton to Sospel

9 **Col de Brouis Road** – *see SOSPEL: Outings*
Sospel to La Giandola

10 **Saorge and Bergue Gorges** – *see SAORGE: Driving Tours*

11 **Route de Valdeblore** – *see SAINT-MARTIN-VÉSUBIE: Outings*

13 **Route des Crêtes** – *see VENCE*

PEILLE ★

POPULATION 2 045

MICHELIN MAP 341 F5

LOCAL MAP SEE NICE

The medieval village of Peille is perched in an exceptional setting of the Faquin ravine, surrounded by steep mountains and green olive trees. Looming nearby are the remains of a château that once belonged to the counts of Provence. This enchanting and wild place never fails to make an impression.

▶ **Orient Yourself:** Part of the Alpes-Maritimes region, Peille is located 11km/7mi inland from La Turbieon by D 53 (*see NICE: Driving Tour*). *Mairie (Town Hall),* ☎ *04 93 91 71 71.*

P Parking: You can park yor car on the north side of the village by the church, which is approached by a steep slope behind the hospice.

Walking Tour

The Town★

Peille is a typical perched village *(see The Region Today).* Descend the steps leading from D 53 to Rue de la Sauterie, a cobbled alleyway puctuated by covered passageways, sloping down towards Place A.-Laugier. Rue Centrale on the right takes you to a domed 13C building that used to be the chapel of St-Sébastien. It has been restored and now houses the town hall. Turn left and left again into Rue St-Sébastien: on the left of the crossroads stands the former salt tax office (Hôtel de la Gabelle).

The street opens out onto Place A.-Laugier, which borders what was once the consuls' residence. At the far end of the square, beyond the Gothic fountain, two arches beneath a house rest on a central Romanesque pillar. Pass beneath the right arch and turn right into Rue Lascaris, then left into Avenue Mary-Garden ending at the war memorial, where you'll find a superb view.

Address Book

TO KNOW MORE

The town has a small Musée du Terroir with displays on local ways and customs (🕐 *Open weekends and holidays 2pm.* ⊶ *Free entry.* ☎ *04 93 91 71 71).*

For coin ranges see Planning Your Trip, p.000.

WHERE TO EAT

⊜⊜ **Le Relais St-Martin "Chez Cotton"** – *St-Martin-de-Peille – 6km/3.6mi south of Peille towards La Turbie* – ☎ *04 93 41 16 03* – 🕐 *Closed Nov, evenings (except Jul-Aug)* – ⍾. If you are finding the beaches too hot, this perched village is a welcome pocket of coolness. The shaded terrace and large glassed-in dining room are the perfect setting for tasty regional cuisine and grilled meats. Pretty panorama of the nearby mountain and valley.

WHERE TO STAY

⊝ **Chambre d'Hôte Les Lavandes** – *247 Route de Peille – 2.5km/1.5mi south of Peille, towards La Turbie* – ☎ *04 92 10 86 23* – ⍾ – *5 rooms.* A former inn has been converted into a bed and breakfast with a strong Provençal touch. The rooms with a balcony offer lovely views of the surrounding mountains. Have breakfast on the terrace or inside the dining room decorated with flea-market finds.

*"Chez Nana" Restaurant Cauvin 04 93 79 90 41 open Th. -Mon. no credit/bank cards   ← Double Prix raisonnable   Smoking only outside   www.perso.wanadoo.fr/ alors.leo/

Church

🕐 *Open noon -7pm.* ☎ *04 93 91 71 71 (contact the town hall).*

This church with the elegant Romanesque belfry dates from the 12C and 13C, formed from two adjoining chapels. The one on the right features rounded vaulting, the one on the left crossed pointed arching. As you enter, an altar against the wall on the left is adorned with a fine altarpiece (16C), divided into 15 panels, by Honoré Bertone. The central panel depicting a Virgin of the Rosary has been removed and replaced by a statue. A picture on the right shows Peille as it was in the Middle Ages. A 14C mural represents Ste Anne and the Virgin and Child.

Viewpoint★

From the war memorial there is a view to the north of the gardens of Peille, the Faquin ravine, the church and Pic de Baudon in the distance. To the south is the Cime de Rastel and a glimpse of Nice and the Baie des Anges down the Paillon Valley.

Via Ferrata   *Allow 3.5hr.*

Park in the municipal car park at the entrance to the village and follow signs. ⊶ *3€. Equipment can be hired from the bar l'Absinthe,* ☎ *04 93 79 95 75. If you wish to be accompanied, request a mountain guide in Sospel or Tende.* ☎ *04 93 91 71 71.*

This challenging itinerary (total length 600m/1969ft) is a hair-raising experience that combines physical stamina and courage. Make your way along the narrow gangway (35m/115ft long, 50m/164ft above ground level), rope bridges and wire cables, with all the necessary safety measures!

PEILLON★★

POPULATION 1 227

MICHELIN MAP 341 F5

LOCAL MAP SEE NICE

Set back on a narrow spur overlooking the Paillon Valley, Peillon is undoubtedly one of the most spectacular villages on the Riviera. The strict architectural unity of the village was imposed by its site and the need for a highly strategic defensive system.

▶ **Orient Yourself:** A maze of vaulted passageways, the village of Peillon is easily reached from Nice (👙 *see Nice, Driving Tour* 4).

🅿 **Parking:** Park alongside the road going into the village. 🚹 *Mairie (Town Hall),* ☎ *04 93 79 91 04.*

Visit

Village★

Untouched since the Middle Ages, the village has few streets but many steep steps and covered alleys between the flower-decked houses huddled against each other. The 18C church with its octagonal lantern crowns the village. Inside are 17C and 18C paintings and an 18C wooden statue of Christ.

Chapelle des Pénitents-Blancs

🕐 *Guided tours Tue-Sat 1-7pm (Oct-May until 5pm). Reserve in advance with the Tourism Office.* ☎ *04 93 91 98 34. A timed lightswitch on the outside allows you to see the frescoes through the bars.*

The chapel's most interesting feature are the **frescoes**★ by Giovanni Canavesio. At the far end is the Crucifixion with St Antony and Ste Petronella. On the walls and ceiling are scenes from the Passion, in particular the Flagellation and Judas' Kiss, vividly portrayed.

The similarity of style with the chapel of Notre-Dame-des-Fontaines is striking. On the altar stands a Pietà in painted wood.

🚶 You can still walk along the old Roman road *(now a footpath, starting by the church)* that links Peillon to Peille – a 2hr walk from one town to the other.

Christ's Passion by Giovanni Canavesio, Peillon

E. Baret/ MICHELIN

A CHARMING INN

🍽 **Annexe Lou Pourtail** – ☎ *04 93 79 91 17* – 🕐 *Closed 20 Oct-20 Dec –* *6 rooms* – 🛏 – *Restaurant (*🍽🍽🍽*)*. At the foot of the village, an annex of the Auberge de la Madonne has become an old cottage inn bursting with charm: whitewashed walls, high vaulted ceilings and country furniture. Regional cooking served in the rustic dining room or on the garden terrace.

Le **PRADET** ☼

POPULATION 10 975

MICHELIN MAP 340 L7

LOCAL MAP SEE NICE

This charming resort nestling below the Massif de la Colle Noire has a good selection of small, easily accessible beaches tucked between the rocky outcrops. Its minerology museum and botanical trail make this a pleasant excursion from Toulon.

▶ **Orient Yourself:** Pradet sits on the eastern edge of Toulon, at the foot of the Colline de Paradis and Mont des Oiseaux, on route D 559 towards Hyères airport. 🅹 *Place du Général-de-Gaulle,* ☎ *04 94 21 71 69.*

Resort Life

Beaches

La Garonne Bay is punctuated by several attractive creeks. Some are accessible by car, but the best way to explore them is to take the coastal walking path which can be followed between each beach accessible by road.

Coastal Footpath★ *7km/4.2mi. Allow at least 3hr.*

🚶 *The winding path is very steep in places. Access to the beaches is often by steep steps cut out of the rock. The route signposted in yellow runs from the car park at the lovely Crique du Pin de Galle to Bau Rouge.*

The steep slope above **Pin de Galle** beach offers magnificent views over Toulon harbor. The numerous cabins in the pine wood add to the bucolic charm of the setting. The shaded path joins the road through the park before descending steeply to **Monaco**

Beach. At the end of this beach, part of which is used by nudists, the path begins beyond a low wall and climbs a cliff covered by superb *maquis* vegetation. After a headland, a little further on, there is a lovely view of the inlets along the coast. A well-marked path goes down to **Les**

Bonnettes Beach at the foot of a remarkable rocky inlet. In season there is a life-guards' post and an open-air café here. It was from this beach that Murat set out for Corsica.

The path then links **La Garonne Beach** with **Les Oursinières Beach.** Beyond Oursinières Port a footpath to the right leaves the road to Le Pradet. It leads past panoramic viewpoints on the cliffs to Bau Rouge with fine views over the coast eastwards towards Carqueiranne and of the Les Gardéens creek.

Sights

Musée de la Mine de Cap-Garonne★

In Le Pradet take D 86 south towards Plage de la Garonne. After the beach, take the road which climbs to the left, signposted "La Mine". 🚹 Kids ⏱ *Guided tours (1hr) during school holidays 2-5pm (Jul-Aug until 6pm); outside school holidays Wed, Sat-Sun and public holidays 2-5pm.* ⏱ *Closed 1-25 Jan and 25 Dec.* ✆ *6.20€ (child 3.80€).* ☎ *04 94 08 32 46. www.mine-capgaronne.fr.*

Wearing a hardhat, visitors get to explore the old copper ore mines used here for centuries. The first traces of workings go back to the 16C, but it was only with the concession granted in 1862 that commercial mining began. It went on until 1917, when the reduction in copper content of the ore meant that mining was no longer a profitable activity.

Musée de la Mine

The tour focuses on the redeveloped part of the galleries and, through several reconstructions and presentations, illustrates the long-standing evolution of working methods and the daily lives of miners at Cap Garonne as well as events during its lifetime such as loading ore for transport to England.

At the end of the tour, in a **great hall**★, there are tables equipped with magnifying glasses with which the many and various colours of copper ore extracted at Cap Garonne can be examined. Particularly notable are the magical blue needles of crystals of **cyanotrichite**, the principal ore of the mine.

🚹 A **botanical footpath** *(1.2km/0.7mi, explanatory panels, viewing table)* circles the mine area and affords fine views of the Massif de la Colle Noire and Giens peninsula.

Botanical Walking Trail

Situated at the heart of the town, the **Bois de Courbebaisse** (5ha/124 acres) is a pleasant way to discover local botanical species.

RAMATUELLE★

POPULATION 2 131

MICHELIN MAP 340 O6

LOCAL MAP UNDER MASSIF DES MAURES

Set among vineyards halfway up a slope, this pink-roofed village possesses all the features of an old Provençal town: narrow winding streets, vaulted arches and old houses, now restored, huddled against the old town wall near the church. Although quite isolated, Ramatuelle is a popular summer destination, with many festivals and the Pampelonne Beach just a short drive away.

▸ **Orient Yourself:** Ramatuelle lies 11km/7mi east of La Croix-Valmer (👆 *see Massif des MAURES*) and 11km/7mi south of St-Tropez (👆 *see St-TROPEZ*) on D 93. 🗐 *Place de l'Ormeau,* ☎ *04 94 12 64 00. www.golfe-infos.com.*

🅿 **Parking:** There are parking areas around the church, the cemetery and the Town Hall *(Mairie).*

S. Sauvignier/ MICHELIN

Visit

The Village

The narrow, winding roads passing beneath arches and flowery window boxes make for an enjoyable stroll through the village. The Romanesque **church** with its flat east end opens through a serpentine door (1620). Inside are two 17C Baroque altarpieces of magnificent gilded wood. Many door lintels, including that on the entrance to the church, mention the year in which the village was rebuilt: 1620.

At the bottom of the village, on Rue du Moulin Roux, you'll find prisons built under Napoléon III (late 1800s) that are often wrongly attributed to the Saracens because of their Arabic style.

Monument to the Resistance

Opposite the cemetery stands a memorial to the members of the Special Services who died in the Second World War. The submarines that stayed in contact with the members of the Resistance during the occupation used to wait offshore by the Roche-Escudelier.

An Unlucky Past

In spite of its isolated location, the village fell under the occupation of the Saracens who had otherwise made their lair in La Garde-Freinet. During the Wars of Religion in 1592, having opted to side with the Catholic League, Ramatuelle was destroyed after a siege.

Domaine du **RAYOL**★★

MICHELIN MAP 340 N7

The Domaine du Rayol is a reminder of the Riviera's period of luxury, created at the beginning of the 20th century when European industrial and banking families built holiday seaside resorts on the lush virgin landscape. Rayol itself enjoys an exceptional site★ on the Var coast, forming an amphitheatre on wooded slopes surrounded by cork oaks, mimosas and pines.

▶ **Orient Yourself:** Coming from St-Tropez, the road into the domaine branches off to the left at the entrance of the village Rayol-Canadel-sur-Mer (👣 *see Massif des MAURES*). ▯ *Place du Rayol, Rayol-Canadel-sur-Mer, ☎ 04 94 05 65 69.*

Magical Summer Nights

During the summer season, there are evening concerts of classical music in the Domaine du Rayol, with the opportunity to stroll through the illuminated gardens during the intervals.

Sights

The Domaine

🕐 *Open Apr-Sep 9.30am-12.30pm, 2.30-6.30pm; Oct-Mar 9.30am-12.30pm, 2-5.30pm.*
🕐 *Closed Mon, 15 Nov - 15 Jan. ☜ 6.50€ (child 3.50€). ☎ 04 98 04 44 00. www.domaine durayol.org*

In 1910 a Parisian banker, Courmes, after traveling extensively, had a house built here surrounded by exotic gardens. The stock market crash in 1929 put an abrupt end to the development of the estate.

The aeronautics engineer Potez, who was forced to take refuge on the coast in 1940, renovated the property and the returned the garden to its former glory. He had a belvedere built by Patek, with a circular pergola, linked to the coast by a magnificent flight of steps. In 1989 the Conservatoire du Littoral acquired the whole estate (20ha/49.5 acres) after several decades of neglect, in order to preserve some of the last wild shores of the Corniche des Maures.

The landscape gardener Gilles Clément has created a patchwork of gardens planted with vegetation found growing in Mediterranean climates all over the world. There are dragon trees; agaves from central America; extremely rare honey palms and Andean araucarias from Chile; eucalyptus, bottle brush and blue gum trees from Australia; strelitzia from South Africa; and bamboo from China. Between each continent, the winding paths offer glimpses of the turquoise sea and a headland carpeted with pines.

The Beach

The beach at Rayol-Canadel-sur-Mer *(2km/1mi west via D 599)*, a sheltered cove bordered by pines, is one of the nicest on the Maures coastline.

D. Pazery/ MICHELIN

Posidonia, the Lungs of the Mediterranean

This flowering plant, which looks like bunches of long green leaves, is an essential element of marine life in the Mediterranean. It grows on sandy seabeds on the narrow coastal fringes.

Posidonia plays the same role as forests: it provides a habitat for animal and plant species, a source of oxygen and stabilises the seabed.

It is threatened with damage and extinction by man's intervention: unpurified sewage discharge, uprooting by boats mooring, building on the coast and by the invasion of another species *(Caulerpa taxifolia)*.

Sentier Marin★

Open early Jul -Aug. Guided underwater tours of Mediterranean flora and fauna (1.5hr) Sun-Fri, advance reservation and payment required. 15€ (child 12€). All equipment is supplied on the premises (diver's suit, mask, fins and snorkel).

A trip from the little beach at Rayol offers an unusual view of underwater life in the Mediterranean. This tour, accompanied by wardens from the Conservatoire, is preceded by an introduction to the species most likely to be seen, their description and the best place to look for them among the posidonia. Discover the amazing lifestyle of the sea cucumber, the relentless activity of the gobies, whose inquisitive nature may surprise visitors, and the curious sexual habits of the rainbow wrasse. Other finds might include sea slugs (a local species), the distracting ballet of a shoal of bream, the sparkling colors of a solitary wrasse or a conger eel lying in wait in a crevice in the rocks which are scattered around the bay.

Corniches de la **RIVIERA**★★★

MICHELIN MAP 341 F/G5

Between Nice and Menton the mountains plunge sharply down to the sea. Running along these heights are three famous routes: the Grande Corniche, the Moyenne Corniche and the Basse Corniche Inférieure. The first, which climbs to 450m/1 476ft, affords the most spectacular views; the second, offers beautiful vistas along the shore; and the third provides access to all of the chic coastal resorts.

1 Grande Corniche★★★

MENTON TO NICE *31km/19mi. Allow 3hr (not including visits to Menton or Nice).*

The Grande Corniche, built by Napoléon along the route of the ancient Via Julia Augusta, is the highest of the three roads, passing through La Turbie from which it looks down from 450m/1 400ft onto the Principality of Monaco. It provides breathtaking views and access to the perched village of Roquebrune.

Menton★★ *see MENTON. Allow 3hr.*

▶ *From Menton take Avenue Carnot and Avenue de la Madone (N 7) going west. Either bear left onto D 52 to Cap Martin or continue uphill (N 7) bearing right onto D 2564 to Roquebrune.*

Roquebrune-Cap-Martin★

See ROQUEBRUNE-CAP-MARTIN.

▶ *From Roquebrune take D 2564 westwards.*

Le Vistaëro★★

From nearly 300m/1 000ft above the sea where the Vistaëro Hotel stands, there is a marvellous **view** ★★ extending out over Bordighera Point, Cap Mortola, Menton, Cap Martin, Roquebrune and, immediately below, Monte-Carlo Beach. To the right lie Monaco and Beausoleil, with Tête de Chien rising above them. Further inland, in a pass, can be seen La Turbie and the Alpine Trophy.

La Turbie★ *See La TURBIE.*

The Grande Corniche reveals distant **views** of Cap Ferrat and then of Èze village as the road reaches its highest point at 550m/1 804ft. In Pical a stone cross on the left commemorates Pope Pius VII's return from exile in 1814.

Col d'Èze *Alt 512m/1 680ft.*

Extended **view** to the north over the mountains and valleys of the upper Vésubie and Var. Owing to its strategic position, Mont Bastide, on the left, has been a Celto-Ligurian *oppidum* and a Roman camp.

▶ *On leaving Col d'Èze towards Nice, turn right on the road going up signed "Parc Départemental de la Grande Corniche-Astrorama".*

Astrorama

🕐 *Guided tours (3hr) Jul-Aug: Mon-Sat, 6-10.30pm; Sep-Jun: Fri-Sat 6-10.30pm.* 👓 *7€ (10€ with lecture).* ☎ *04 93 85 85 58. www.astrorama.net.*

After a series of hairpin bends, the road finally reaches a plateau which is home to an old gun battery belonging to the system of defence called the Batterie des Feuillerins. This now houses an astronomy research and observation center designed especially for members of the public with no previous knowledge of the subject.

Visitors can learn about the different theoretical and practical aspects of the discovery and observation of space. The site is relatively shielded from the interference of intense artificial light that reigns all along the densely populated coast, allowing for unimpeded views of the stars.

▶ *Drive up the road as far as the car park at Fort de la Revère (⚠ No access to the fort).*

Parc de la Revère

From the base of the fort there is a superb **panorama**★★ over the whole Var coast as far as Italy and, in winter, on very clear mornings it is possible to see the outline of Corsica to the southeast.

Belvédère d'Èze

1 200m/1 312yd beyond the pass, opposite a small café named the "Belvédère" in a right bend, there is a wide panoramic **view** ★★ in which one can distinguish Tête de Chien, Èze and the sea below, the Cap Ferrat Peninsula, Mont Boron, the Cap d'Antibes, the Lérins islands, the Esterel range with the summit of Cap Roux, and the French and Italian Alps.

Col des Quatre-Chemins

A short way beyond the pass (alt 327m/1 037ft) one can see the Alps through an opening made by the Paillon Valley.

Soon afterwards, the road descends steeply offering a wide **view** ★ of the Pre-Alps, and then of Nice and castle hill, the harbor, the Baie des Anges, Cap d'Antibes and the Esterel.

▶ *Enter Nice from the east by Avenue des Diables-Bleus.*

② Moyenne Corniche★★

NICE TO MENTON *31km/19mi. Allow 2hr.*

Shorter and less winding than the Grande Corniche, the Moyenne Corniche is a broad modern road built between 1910 and 1928. Well sited along the mountainside, it tunnels through the larger mountain chains and takes large sweeping curves into the delightful Mediterranean countryside. The route offers good views of the coast and the coastal resorts, and provides the only access by road to the amazing village of Èze.

▶ *Leave Nice by Place Max-Barel on N 7 heading east. A parapet along part of the road obscures the view of the sea and the coast; look for the small roadside parking areas provided at all the best viewpoints.*

Initially the view comprises the town, the old Château Hill, the port and the Baie des Anges. Soon you'll be able to see the Esterel chain and the chalky mountains of Grasse standing out on the horizon to the southwest.

Col de Villefranche *Alt 149m/489ft.*

From a bend in the road soon after the pass, Villefranche-sur-Mer harbor and Cap Ferrat come into sight.

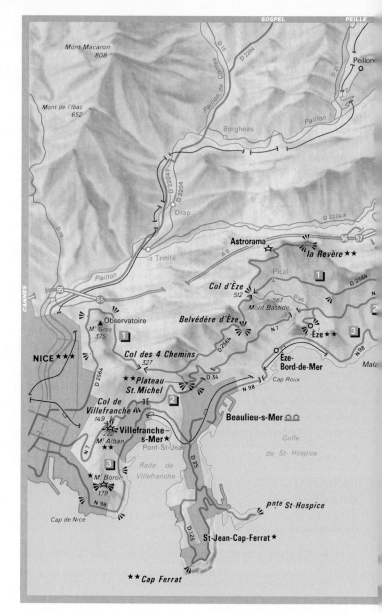

Just before entering a 180m/200yd-long tunnel, there is a very good **view**★★ of Beaulieu, Cap Ferrat, Villefranche-sur-Mer, Nice and Cap d'Antibes. After the tunnel, the old village of Èze comes into view, perched high on its rock against the backdrop of Tête de Chien (alt 556m/1 880ft), the mountain promontory dominating Cap d'Ail and Monaco.

Plateau St-Michel★★

▶ *2km/1.2mi from N 7. After the tunnel turn right onto the narrow D 34 which climbs back over the tunnel for 2km/1.2mi to a terrace car park.*

Walk up to the viewing table on the edge of the plateau (371m/1 217ft). The **panorama**★★ extends from the tip of Cap d'Ail to the Esterel.

Èze★★ ⏱ *See Èze.*

Beyond Èze the Moyenne Corniche circles the rocky escarpments of Tête de Chien and brings into sight new panoramic views overlooking Cap Martin and the long Bordighera headland in Italy. Below, in the foreground, lies the Principality of Monaco.

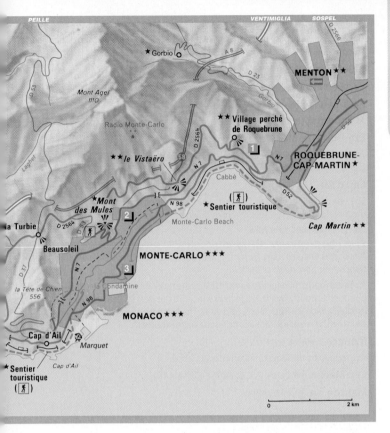

At the entrance to Monaco bear left onto N 7 which skirts the Principality and offers remarkable **views** ★ of Monte-Carlo, Cap Martin, the Italian coast and the coastal ranges.

Beausoleil★

This resort forms part of the Monte-Carlo conurbation although it is officially on French territory. Its houses, reached by stepped streets, project from the slopes of Mont des Mules like balconies over the sea.

▶ *Bear left onto D 53.*

Mont des Mules★

1km/0.6mi plus 30min there and back on foot along a marked path. From the top there is a fine **panorama** ★ *(viewing table).*

▶ *Return to N 7 which passes below the Vistaëro before joining the Basse Corniche at Cabbé.*

Cap Martin★★ ⓒ *See ROQUEBRUNE-CAP-MARTIN.*

Menton★★ ⓒ *See MENTON.*

③ Basse Corniche★★

NICE TO MENTON *33km/21mi – about 6hr.*

The Basse Corniche was conceived as long ago as the 18C by a prince of Monaco. Work was undertaken by the Empress of Russia in 1857 and completed in 1881. The road, running at the foot of the mountain slopes and following the contours of the coast, serves all the Riviera resorts.

▶ *From Nice take Boulevard Carnot, N 98, heading southeast.*

The road skirts the base of Mont Boron with **views** ★ of the Baie des Anges, Cap Ferrat, Villefranche-sur-Mer port, Èze and Tête de Chien in succession.

Villefranche-sur-Mer★ ⓒ *see VILLEFRANCHE-SUR-MER.*

Cap Ferrat★★ ⓒ *see CAP FERRAT.*

Beaulieu ⌂⌂ ⓒ *see BEAULIEU.*

As the road skirts Cap Roux, there is a view across the water to Cap d'Ail.

Èze-Bord-de-Mer

The resort lies beneath the cliffs below Èze-Village. As the road hugs the rocky coast, Cap d'Ail is in full view.

Cap d'Ail

Sheltered by pine, palm and cypress trees, the elegant properties of Cap d'Ail cover the lower slopes of the Tête de Chien down to the sea.

Coastal Path of Cap d'Ail★

▶ *1hr round-trip on foot. On the east side of the station, descend the steps into a tunnel that comes out on a road. Turn left and at Restaurant La Pinède, take another flight of steps on the right down to the sea.*

A coastal footpath running eastwards skirts the rocks at the foot of Cap d'Ail, which are pounded furiously by the sea in high winds. To the west lie Beaulieu and Cap Ferrat; gradually Monaco Rock looms into view. The footpath ends on Marquet beach. One can take the road into Monaco or return via the footpath.

Monaco ★★★ ⓒ *see MONACO.*

The road joins the Moyenne Corniche at Cabbé.

Cap Martin ★★ ⓒ *see ROQUEBRUNE-CAP-MARTIN.*

Menton ★★ ⓒ *see MENTON.*

ROQUEBRUNE-CAP-MARTIN★

POPULATION 11 692

MICHELIN MAP 341 F5

LOCAL MAPS SEE MENTON: EXCURSIONS AND CORNICHES DE LA RIVIERA

This pretty resort, covering the whole of Cap Martin, extends along the coast between Menton and Monte-Carlo. It is watched over by the perched medieval village of Roquebrune and its castle keep. This vestige of the Carolingian castle is the only one of its kind in France, a forerunner of the castles built 200 years later, when the feudal system was at its peak.

▶ **Orient Yourself:** Roquebrune village sits on the Grande Corniche above Menton and the resort of Roquebrune-Cap-Martin. 🏠 *214 Avenue Aristide-Briand,* ☎ *04 93 35 62 87. www.roquebrune-cap-martin.com.*

🅿 **Parking:** Parking is available at the village entrance.

🕐 **Organizing Your Time:** Allow at least an hour to tour the village on foot. To explore Cap Martin at a leisurely pace, both by car and on foot, allow a half day. And if you want to take the coastal path from Cap Martin to Monaco, a minimum of four hours is needed for this round-trip walk.

ⓒ **Also See:** *Corniches of the RIVIERA, MENTON*

A Bit of History

The castle was built at the end of the 10C by Conrad I, Count of Ventimiglia, to stop the Saracens from establishing themselves once again in the area. For several centuries it belonged to the Grimaldis (ⓒ *see MONACO*), who remodeled part of it and introduced artillery in its defences. Originally, the castle was a fortress enclosing the keep and

Traditional Processions

For the past 500 years a procession, representing the principal scenes of the Passion in six tableaux, is held on the afternoon of 5 August. Unchanged since it was first performed by those who made a vow in 1467 during an epidemic of the plague, the ceremony lasts for two hours.

The **Procession of the Entombment of Christ**★ is held at 9pm on Good Friday with a train of some 60 people walking through the village streets representing Roman centurions and legionaries, disciples carrying the statue of Christ and holy women. The town is decorated with lighted motifs recalling the symbols of the Passion and illuminated with hundreds of tiny lights formed by snail and sea shells filled with olive oil, in which a small cotton wick burns. This procession was instituted by the Brotherhood of the White Penitents, which has now been disbanded.

the village within its battlements, which were pierced by six fortified gateways. In the 15C, the keep became known as the castle and the rest of the fortress became the village, which up to the present has preserved its medieval character.

Walking Tour *1hr*

The Perched Village★★

The town's enviable situation and the medieval keep are not Roquebrune's sole attractions. To savor the charm of this delightful, stroll through the maze of steep covered alleys and quaint stairways that have preserved their ancient appearance despite the art galleries and craft and souvenir shops that have edged their way between the local tradesmen.

▶ *Start on Place de la République, once the barbican (the keep's advanced defence), then cross the Place des Deux-Frères to the Rue Grimaldi. Take the first street on the left.*

Rue Moncollet★

This street, long and narrow, has many covered and stepped passageways. Medieval houses with barred windows, where those invited to join the seigneurial court once lived, face the road in front, while at the back they lie against or are cut right into the rockface.

▶ *Rue Moncollet, bending slightly to the right, leads into Rue du Château. Go left to see the keep. After crossing the "flowered enclosure," you enter the ancient keep of the oldest feudal castle in France.*

Donjon★

🕐 *Open Apr-Sep: 10am-12.30pm, 2-6.30pm (Jul-Aug: 10am-12.30pm, 3-7.30pm); Feb-Mar and Oct: 10am-12.30pm, 2-6pm; Nov-Jan: 10am-12.30pm, 2-5pm.* 🎫 *3.50€.* ☎ *04 93 35 07 22.*

The keep overlooks by some 26m/80ft the façades of the houses opposite in Rue Moncollet. The 2-4m/6-12ft thick walls have been fitted with a great many defensive features: cannon embrasures, machicolations, battlements, loopholes etc.

A flight of 20 steps leads up to the first floor and the Hall of Feudal Ceremonies. Note particularly the cell recessed into the wall, a cube-shaped water tank in the center, and the 15C mullioned window, replacing the oblique slots 20cm/8in which once provided light. Below this hall is the storeroom, carved out of the rock. On the second floor is the small guard-room, on the right a comfortable prison and further on the archers' dormitory. On the third floor are the baronial apartments complete with furnishings, the dining room, a primitive kitchen with a bread oven and a bedroom containing ancient weapons.

The fourth floor includes the upper artillery platform, which affords a sweeping, circular **panorama**★★ of the picturesque roofs of the village, the sea, Cap Martin, the Principality of Monaco, and Mont Agel (military air base).

▶ *Return to Rue du Château and then turn left on Rue de la Fontaine .*

Olivier Millénaire

On the Chemin de Menton (200m/219yd beyond the end of the village) you'll find a 1 000-year-old **olive tree,** said to be one of the oldest trees in the world.

▶ *Return to Rue du Château (left), which leads to the church.*

Address Book

For coin ranges, see the Legend at the back of the guide.

EATING OUT

⊜⊜ **La Roquebrunoise** – *12 Avenue Raymond-Poincaré (in the old town) –* ☎ *04 93 35 02 19 –* ◷ *Closed Nov and Dec, Mon except Mon evening in Jul and Aug, and lunch Tue-Thu.* This pretty pink house on the edge of the village is a nice place to rest from your wanderings. The country-style dining room is hung with paintings. The food is unpretentious and tasty, and the tables on the terrace have a view of the sea and the château.

⊜⊜ **Au Grand Inquisiteur** – *18 Rue du Château (in the old town, access on foot only) –* ☎ *04 93 35 05 37 –* ◷ *Closed 28 Jun-5 Jul, 8 Nov-10 Dec, Tue except in Jul and Aug, and Mon. – Reservation required.* "The Great Inquisitor" is a strange name for a restaurant indeed! Nonetheless, the welcome is warm. In the heart of the village, in a pedestrian zone, this 14C building has a small dining room with a vaulted ceiling, furnished in a pleasing style. Traditional cooking.

WHERE TO STAY

⊜⊜ **Hôtel Westminster** – *14 Avenue Louis-Laurens, by N 98 Route de Monaco by the Basse Corniche road –* ☎ *04 92 41 41 40 – hotel@westminster06.com –* ◷ *Closed 22 Nov-6 Feb –* 🅿 *– 28 rooms –* ⊠. In a residential street, this pleasant little hotel has a terraced garden which rises above the sea. Enjoy your breakfast with a view on the balcony of your room. There is a train that runs behind the hotel, but it passes slowly.

⊜⊜ **Hôtel Victoria** – *7 Promenade Cap-Martin –* ☎ *04 93 35 65 90 –* ◷ *Closed 8 Jan-8 Feb –* 🅿 *– 32 rooms –* ⊠. This hotel is integrated into a residential building, with rooms decorated in wicker and bamboo furnishings. Some with balcony overlooking the sea. Colonial-style salon-bar.

Église Ste-Marguerite

◷ *Open 3-5pm. Guided tours available on request from the Tourism Office,* ☎ *04 93 35 62 87.*

The fairly plain Baroque façade masks the original 12C church, which has undergone many alterations over the years. Against the polychrome plasterwork of the interior hang two paintings by a local painter, Marc-Antoine Otto (17C): a Crucifixion (2nd altar) and a Pietà (above the door).

▶ *If you return to Rue de la Fontaine and take a right into the cemetery, you'll find the sarcophagus (square J, no.3), where Le Corbusier rests eternally, designed by the famous architect himself.*

Touring the Resort

Cap Martin★★

With its magnificent estates, Cap Martin is the wealthy residential suburb of Menton. It's served by roads that cut through olive groves and clumps of cypresses, perfumed by pine woods and banks of mimosa.

A massive tower of feudal appearance rises at the center, formerly the old beacon, now converted to a relay station for telecommunications. At its foot lie the ruins of the basilica of St-Martin, part of a priory built by the Lérins island monks in the 11C and destroyed by pirates about 1400.

East Coast of the Cap

From the road along the eastern shore there is a marvellous view ★★ of Menton in its mountain setting and of the Italian coast as far as Bordighera. There are several beaches below the old village: two at Cabbé facing southwest and one at Carnolès on the east side next to Menton.

Le Cabanon de Le Corbusier

◷ *Guided tours Tue and Fri at 10am by appointment at the Tourism Office.* ⊜ *8€.* ☎ *04 93 35 62 87, fax 04 93 28 57 00.*

This cabin, tucked in below promenade Le Corbusier which runs along the coast from Cabbé to Cap Martin, has a deceptively plain exterior. It is, in fact, a unique construction, whose dimensions were calculated by Le Corbusier using the **Modulor**, a measuring tool on a human scale invented by the architect for use in his projects.

Roquebrune-Cap-Martin

The Cabanon consists of a corridor decorated with a fresco painted by the architect and a room (10m2/108sq ft). Each piece of furniture has several functions. Even the windows, some of which are jointed, allow the passage of light and also ventilation from the sides. This building, where the architect lived on several occasions, and near where he ended his days, is still an object of curiosity for the uninitiated visitor and a point of reference for the study of architecture. "I have a château on the Riviera which measures 3.66m by 3.66m/12ft by 12ft. It is wonderfully comfortable and pleasant" confided Le Corbusier.

Coastal Path★
Park in Avenue Winston-Churchill car park at the seaward end of Cap Martin. A sign "Promenade Le Corbusier" near a restaurant indicates the beginning of the footpath.

4hr on foot round-trip. A coastal footpath runs from Cap Martin to Monte-Carlo beach, leading westwards round the headland over the rocks. After several minutes a series of steps and inclines skirts the grounds of private properties through wild and abundant vegetation. Gradually the view takes in Monaco in its natural amphitheatre, Cap Ferrat, Tête de Chien, La Turbie and Mont Agel behind Monaco, and the old village of Roquebrune with its castle. It's best seen in the afternoon light.

▶ *A flight of steps on the right crossing the railway line provides a shortcut back to Carnolès beach via the town hall.*

The coastal footpath continues beside the railway line to Cap Martin-Roquebrune Station above a sheer drop into the sea. Skirting the Cabbé beaches and the Bon Voyage rocks, the path goes on towards Monte-Carlo (rear view to Cap Martin), ending in a flight of steps near the Monte-Carlo Beach Hotel.

▶ *There are frequent trains to Carnolès from Monaco or Cap Martin-Roquebrune.*

ROQUEBRUNE-SUR-ARGENS

POPULATION 11 349

MICHELIN MAP 340 O5

The small town of Roquebrune, perched on a rocky peak at the foot of the Rocher de Roquebrune, was most likely founded in the early 11C, after the land had been reconquered from the Saracens (*See La GARDE-FREINET*)**. There still exist many traces of the town's past, including vestiges of the original ramparts and many 16C houses.**

▶ **Orient Yourself:** The town lies 12km/7.5mi west of Fréjus on the D 8, then the D 7. From the A 8, exit Puget-sur-Argens and take the N 7 west, then turn left on the D 7. *1 Rue Jean-Aicard, ☎ 04 94 19 89 89. www.ville-roquebrune-argens.fr.*

P **Parking:** There is parking at the foot of the village.

Sights

The Village

Originally a stronghold, the castrum located near the church was enlarged and surrounded by a curtain wall (destroyed in 1592 during the Wars of Religion). Traces of these ramparts are visible, particularly in Boulevard de la Liberté *(below the church)*, but most of them have been incorporated into the houses built on their foundations. At the foot of the clock tower stands the old fountain (known as the Fontaine Vieille), and opposite is the picturesque Rue des Portiques, lined with ancient houses, some of which date to the 16C. Inside the fortifications, the narrow, winding streets and two old doorways recall Roquebrune's medieval legacy.

Eglise St-Pierre-St-Paul

◷ *Open daily 8am-7pm. For a guided tour, contact the Tourism Office.* ☎ *04 94 45 72 70.*

The church was built in the 16C in the Gothic style and features an unusual façade, which was added in the 18C.

Inside, on the left, two chapels, remnants of the 11C building modified in the 14C, have thick quadripartite vaulting with rectangular-shaped diagonal and transverse arches. The first chapel contains a wooden altarpiece (1557) of John the Baptist in high relief flanked by St Claudius and St Bridget of Sweden, while the second chapel houses an altarpiece from the same period depicting the Last Judgement. In the nave, on the right on entering, is a 16C altarpiece composed of six carved panels depicting the Passion around a large crucifix. There are two other 16C painted panels in the gallery, while large canvases added in the 19C adorn the chancel and side chapels.

Musée du Patrimoine

Impasse Barbacane, the continuation of Rue des Portiques. ♿ ◷ *Open daily Jul-Aug 9am-12.30pm, 3-6.30pm; rest of the year Tue-Sun 9am-noon, 2-6pm.* ☞ *Free entry.* ☎ *04 94 19 89 89.*

Located in the old St-Jacques Chapel, the museum houses, for the most part, Prehistoric and Roman finds excavated in the Bouverie caves *(located not far from Roquebrune)* which were inhabited continuously from 30 000 to 8 000 BC. This settlement has been identified as **Bouverian** (c 15 000 to 10 000 BC), a culture unique to southeastern France, which corresponds to the Magdalenian culture elsewhere.

Also displayed are fine objects from the Neolithic Era, and remarkable Roman remains, in a reconstruction of a tomb under **tegulae**. In the sacristy there is a collection of ex-votos and historic documents.

Chapelle St-Pierre

⚊ *Closed to the public. From Roquebrune take D7 southeast.*

The chapel has preserved a Carolingian apse but was rebuilt in the Romanesque style in the 11C, after the Saracen invasion. A recessed tomb has been placed on the façade. The east end is surrounded by an ancient cemetery, the tombs of which were carved into the rock.

Driving Tour

Rocher de Roquebrune★ *14km/8.5mi round-trip – 1hr, excluding the climb.*

The proud silhouette of Roquebrune rock—partially covered with corkoaks, tree ferns and conifers—forms a small, solitary massif between the Maures and Esterel. Composed of red sandstone compacted and subsequently eroded, the rock forms a jagged silhouette that dominates the lower Argens Valley in a spectacular fashion.

▸ *From Roquebrune-sur-Argens, take the small road to the south opposite the cemetery.*

Chapelle Notre-Dame-de-Pitié

The chapel stands on rising ground amid pine and eucalyptus trees at the foot of a majestic red cliff, one of the first heights of the Maures Massif. Beyond the screen on the high altar stands a 17C retable framing a Pietà similar to a work by Annibale Carracci (in the Louvre in Paris). Next to the chapel, there is a **view** ★ of the Argens Plain, Fréjus, St-Raphaël and the Esterel heights.

▶ *Return to Roquebrune and turn left onto D 7. After 500m/547yd bear left; 1km/0.5mi farther on turn left again onto a forest road. After 2km/1.5mi leave the car where a path branches off to the right.*

Roquebrune Summit★

🚶 *2hr on foot round-trip; a difficult walk; keep to the path.* From the summit (alt 372m/1 073ft), there is an extended **view** ★ of the Maures, the lower Argens Plain, Fréjus Bay, the Esterel and the Alps on the horizon.

At the rock's summit stand three crosses of different shapes, which are the work of the sculptor Vernet. They were placed there in memory of three famous Crucifixions painted by Giotto, Grünewald and El Greco, using the summit of the rock to symbolise Golgotha.

▶ *Drive down the south face of Roquebrune rock and turn right onto D 25. After 1km/0.6mi (view of the River Argens), turn right along the north face. The road runs parallel to the motorway. Drive through the hamlet of La Roquette.*

Chapelle Notre-Dame-de-la-Roquette

🚶 *30min on foot round-trip. Leave the car in the car park beside the road and take the path on the right.* The ruined chapel, an ancient place of pilgrimage and meeting place for hikers is located in an attractive **setting** ★ of lotus, chestnut and holly trees beside a great rock chaos of red sandstone.

From the terrace (alt 143m/470ft) the **view** includes the lower Argens Valley and the Provençal tableland.

▶ *Return to the road; turn right to reach D 7 and Roquebrune-sur-Argens.*

SAINT-CYR-SUR-MER ≈≈

POPULATION 8 898

MICHELIN MAP 340 J6

This seaside resort lies in a sheltered harbor at the far end of a tranquil bay, with beaches of fine sand bordering fertile plains of grapevines and olive trees. Popular in both winter and summer for its mild climate, St-Cyr-sur-Mer is noteworthy for its history, as home to the only surviving Roman villa on the Mediterranean coast.

▶ **Orient Yourself:** There are three main districts in the town: to the north is the rail line running through the center of town; a long avenue of residential buildings leads to the coastline, with the Port de Lecques to the west, and Port de Madrague to the east. 🛈 *Place de l'Appel-du-18-Juin,* ☎ *04 94 26 73 73.*

Sights

Musée de Tauroentum

On the coast towards La Madrague, in the direction of Port de Lecques. ◷ *Open Jun-Sep daily (except Tue) 3-7pm; Oct-May weekends and school holidays 2-5pm.* ⊗ *3€.* ☎ *04 94 26 30 46.*

The museum is built on the foundations of a Roman villa. On display are some wreathed columns with Corinthian capitals from the villa's peristyle and a granite column from a pergola 80m/262ft long that adorned the seafront. The museum also contains three black and white 1C mosaics, fragments of frescoes and amphora. In the showcases are many Greek and Roman objects: coins, pottery, glass, jewelery and figurines.

Behind the museum a path leads to a pottery tile kiln and remains of houses (walls bearing traces of frescoes) and offers views of Les Lecques Bay.

Centre d'Art Sébastien

Boul. Jean-Jaurès. ◷ *Open Jun-Sep 9am-noon, 3-7pm; Oct-May 9am-noon, 2-6pm.* ◷ *Closed Tue and holidays.* ⊗ *1€.* ☎ *04 94 26 19 20.*

Set up in a former factory in 1993, this arts center hosts temporary exhibitions and houses a permanent collection of works painted by the artist Sébastien (1909-1990), who was friends with Picasso, Matisse, Jean Cocteau and André Gide.

Address Book

For coin ranges, see the Legend at the back of the guide.

EATING OUT

◯◯ **Restaurant La Calanque** – *Calanque du Port Alon – 5km/3mi south of St-Cyr, towards Bandol and Port Alon –* ☎ *04 94 26 20 08 – lacalanque83@aol. com – ◯ Closed 1 Nov-1 Feb, and Mon.* A rocky inlet is the heavenly backdrop to this restaurant serving grilled fish and other Mediterranean delicacies. Relax at the water's edge and have a paddle between courses.

WHERE TO STAY

◯◯ **Chanteplage** – *Les Lecques –* ☎ *04 94 26 16 55 – ◯ Closed Oct-Mar – ☐ – 18 rooms – ☐ – Restaurant (◯◯).* This homey establishment facing Les Lecques Bay is also within walking distance of the town. Its rooms enjoy balconies and pretty views all around. The two larger rooms on the third floor have a terrace.

◯◯◯ **Grand Hôtel des Lecques** – *Les Lecques – ☐ –* ☎ *04 94 26 23 01 – info@ lecques-hotel.com ◯ Closed 16 Nov-22 Mar – 58 rooms – ☐ – Restaurant (◯◯◯).* The paths cutting across the luxuriant park surrounding this hotel are bordered with palms, pine trees and morning glory. A most appealing setting for the formidable 19C mansion. Cheerful rooms appointed in Provençal tradition. Outdoor pool.

SHOPPING

Markets – Traditional market held on Sunday mornings; regional specialities at La Madrague Port (Monday and Thursday mornings), on Place Gabriel-Péri (Tuesday and Friday mornings) and at Les Lecques (Wednesday and Saturday mornings).

TAKING IT EASY

Beaches – 2 km/1.2mi of sandy beaches line the semi-circular bay running from Les Lecques to La Madrague. Initially narrow and dominated by the seafront promenade, the beach widens out on reaching La Madrague. Further west, *(10min by car),* the **Calanque de Port-d'Alon,** nestling in a pine forest, affords greater privacy.

Nouveau Port des Lecques – *Port authority –* ☎ *04 94 26 21 98. 431 moorings.*

Port de la Madrague – *Port authority –* ☎ *04 94 26 39 81.* 400 moorings including 37 set aside for tourist traffic.

Golf de Frégate – *D 559 , Route de Bandol –* ☎ *04 94 29 38 00 – www.fregate.dolce.com – ◯ Open Nov-Mar 8am-6pm, Aug-Oct 7.30am-7pm – ◯ 46-56€.* Beautiful 18-hole world class court and 9-hole model court offering pretty views of the sea.

Aqualand – ◯ – *ZAC des Pradeaux –* ☎ *08 92 68 66 13 – www.aqualand.fr – ◯ Jun-Sep 10am-7pm – ◯ 18.50€ (child 15.50€).* Water park with slides, wave pool, and swimming pools.

Lecques Aquanaut Center – *Nouveau Port des Lecques –* ☎ *04 94 26 42 18 – www. lecques-aquanaut.fr.* Diving club.

Excursion

The Coastal Path

Take D 87 from St-Cyr. Drive along the coast as far as la Madrague. The path begins at Pointe Grenier.

🚶 *4.5km/2.7mi to port d'Alon (yellow trail markers) or 6km/6.6mi to Bandol. The walk is not a difficult one, but do wear sturdy shoes and bring along drinking water.*

👁 *Be careful with children as there are some dangerous drop-offs.*

This path from la Madrague to Bandol offers hikers an opportunity to enjoy a view of the sea from far above. On the inland side, you can look out over vineyards and if you are a fan of flora, you may sight a local species of violet or mushroom. .

ST-MARTIN-VÉSUBIE ★

POPULATION 1 098

MICHELIN MAP 341 E3

LOCAL MAP SEE NICE

St-Martin-Vésubie stretches out along a rocky cliff between the Boréon and Madone-de-Fenestre streams. Encircled by tall summits and lush alpine greenery, the town is known as "Switzerland Niçoise." It has become an important summer **mountaineering centre** *(centre d'alpinisme)* for hiking, canyoning, horseback riding and hang-gliding.

🅿 **Parking:** Coming from the south on the D 2565, you'll arrive at the entrance to the old town. Parking can be found to the northwest.

Walking Tour

▷ *Start under the plane trees in the beautiful square Place Félix-Faure, half way along Allées de Verdun.*

Rue du Docteur-Cagnoli

A narrow street bordered by Gothic houses with handsome porches and lintels runs north-south through the town with a gutter down the middle.

Chapelle des Pénitents-Blancs

The chapel has a carved façade, a bulb-shaped bell-tower and, below the altar, a recumbent figure of Christ with cherubs at the four corners holds the instruments of the Passion.

▷ *Continue on the Rue Dr-Cagnoli.*

Maison des Gubernatis

At the bottom of the street at no 25 is a house built over an arcade that once belonged to the Count of Gubernatis.

Place de la Frairie

Turn left into Rue du Plan which leads to Place de la Frairie marked by a fountain. From the terrace overlooking the Madone de Fenestre Torrent, there is a **view** of the gushing river and the neighboring mountains, Cime de la Palu and Cime du Piagu. The church is behind the square.

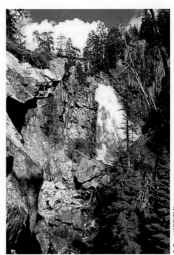

Le Boréon waterfall, St-Martin-Vésubie

E. Baret/ MICHELIN

Address Book

WHERE TO STAY

🍴 **La Châtaigneraie** – ☎ 04 93 03 21 22 – hotel-lachataigneraie@raiberti.com – 🕐 Closed Oct-May – 🅿 38 rooms – 🍽 – Restaurant (🍽). Pleasant accommodation nestling in a peaceful park, ideal for nature lovers who wish to go climbing or hiking in the Parc du Mercantour, or who simply need a taste of the countryside. Set menu for residents.

🍴 **Hostellerie de Rimplas** – 1 chemin des Cavaliers – Rimplas– ☎ 04 93 02 86 80 – 🍽 – 9 rooms – 🍽 – Restaurant 🍽. This large stone country house is set in a perched village built in 11C. Simple rooms with fresh linens, and a restaurant with set regional cuisine menus.

SHOPPING

Markets – Tuesday, Saturday and Sunday on the Place du Marché *(summer season)*.

SPORT

Ski – Le Boréon has 30km/18mi of cross-country ski trails.

A Mountaineering Pioneer on the Riviera

The Chevalier Victor de Cessole (1859-1940), a member of an old Nice family, took to climbing late in life and in an unusual manner. When his doctor recommended exercise and fresh air, he enrolled in the new Club Alpin Français when he was already in his thirties. His first contact with the high mountains at Madone de Fenestre awakened a passion for walking in the Alps.

He became a compulsive mountaineer, climbing successively the highest peaks in the Alpes-Maritimes (Mont Clapier, Mont Gélas) and setting several records in the Massif de l'Argentera. His recommended walks, described in illustrated brochures, are forerunners of the guide books of today. His activities earned him the presidency of the Club Alpin Français, a position which he held for 40 years, and enabled him to inaugurate and organise the chain of mountain refuges. In 1901 he opened the Nice refuge above Madone de Fenestre. He initiated the first skiing competitions and is considered to be the founder, in spirit at least, of Beuil, the oldest resort in the area. His interest in nature led him to establish the first measures for the protection of wildlife in the region – the banning of the picking of *Saxifraga florulenta*, now the emblem of the Parc du Mercantour. His extensive collection of books and papers, acquired during his research, and his interest in the local heritage are now contained in the De Cessole library, bequeathed to the Musée Masséna in Nice.

Church

This Roman building beautifully decorated in the 17C features a richly dressed statue of Our Lady of Fenestre: the Madone de Fenestre (see EXCURSIONS below), a 12C seated figure of polychrome wood. On the last Saturday in June, it's carried in procession to her mountain sanctuary where it remains until mid-September.

The second chapel's left-hand aisle houses two panels from an altarpiece attributed to Louis Bréa, and a third chapel houses a beautiful altar to the Rosary in carved and gilded wood (17C).

From the terrace you'll find a partial **view** of the Boréon Valley and Venanson village below the forested Tête du Siruol.

Excursions

Venanson★ 4.5km/3mi.

▶ Leave St-Martin-Vésubie via the bridge over the Boréon and take D 31 south.

The village square standing on a triangular rocky outcrop 1 164m/3 819ft high commands a good **view**★ of St-Martin, the Vésubie Valley and its mountain setting.

Chapelle St-Sébastien

 Open by appointment at the restaurant La Bella Vista. ☎ 04 93 03 25 11.

This 15C chapel is considered one of the most complete examples of Art Niçois, with the interior covered in **frescoes**★ by Baleison. At the far end beneath a Crucifixion, St Sebastian pierced by arrows; on the side walls and the ceiling, scenes from the saint's life inspired by the Golden Legend. Another panel takes prayer as its theme. The thoughts of the two figures are revealed by the direction of the lines from their faces; the one on the left sees only the wounds of Christ whom he adores, while the one on the right concentrates on his house and his wealth, which appear behind him.

Parish church

On the left of the entrance is a triptych of the Virgin and Child, flanked by St John and St Petronella. At the high altar a Baroque altarpiece (1645) of the Coronation of the Virgin features the donor. On the right stands an altarpiece of the Rosary.

Le Boréon★★ 8km/5mi

▶ From St-Martin-Vésubie take D 2565 north up the west bank of Le Boréon.

The resort stands on a superb site (1 500m/4 201ft) on the southern edge of the Parc National du Mercantour (see Introduction) by the **Cascade du Boréon**★ where the river drops 40m/130ft down a narrow gorge. Above the waterfall a small lake adds its calm beauty to the green landscape of pasture and woodland.

Le Boréon is the starting place for walks in the forest, up to the high peaks and mountain lakes. One can drive by car to the Vacherie du Boréon (2.5km/1.5mi to the east) beneath the distinctive silhouette of La Cougourde. There is also a road running west along the southern edge of the park for 4km/2.5mi up Salèse Valley.

Vallon de la Madone de Fenestre 12km/7.5mi east – about 30min.

▷ *From St-Martin take Avenue de Saravalle (northeast on the plan). Turn right onto D 94.*

The road climbs rapidly up the Madone Valley between Cime du Piagu and Cime de la Palu, crossing and re-crossing the river. A fine forest of pines and larches rises out of heavy undergrowth before giving way to high mountain pastures.

The road ends in a rugged rock **cirque**★★ that is much appreciated by mountaineers. Caïre de la Madone, huge and pointed, rises nearby, and the slopes of **Cime du Gélas** (3 143m/10 312ft), covered with frozen snow, dominate the northern horizon on the Italian border.

The **Madone de Fenestre** chapel is a place of pilgrimage that in summer houses the statue of Our Lady of Fenestre, which returns to St-Martin-Vésubie in solemn procession around mid-September.

Driving Tours of the Valleys

The Road to Valdeblore★★ *29km/18mi. Allow 2.5hr*

▷ *Leave St-Martin by the D 256 going north.*

The road linking the valleys of the Tinée and the upper Vésubie passes through the Valdeblore district, a region of green pastures and wooded slopes high in the mountains.

The road climbs north up the valley and overlooks the villages of St-Martin and Venanson. Just before the tunnel, there is a fine **view** ★ back down to the Vésubie Valley and St-Martin, up the Madone Valley and north to the Boréon.

La Colmiane

A ski resort in the Col St-Martin (alt 1 500m/4 921ft) consists of chalets and hotels dotted among the larches and pines.

▷ *At Col St-Martin turn left onto a narrow road which leads to the ski-lift.*

Pic de La Colmiane★★

⚡ *Ski-lift to the summit. Jul-Aug 10am-6pm (weekends only Sep-Jun).* ◉ *3.50€ (season ticket available).* ☎ *04 93 02 83 54*

From the top there is an immense **panorama**★★: south over Mont Tournairet, the Vésubie Valley and Turini Forest; east over the Mercantour chain; north and west over the Baus de la Frema to Mont Mounier with Valdeblore in the foreground.

Via Ferrata du Baus de la Frema★

At the pass turn right opposite the mini-golf (sign "Via Ferrata"). There is plenty of space to park on the way up the slope. The Via Ferrata begins at the end of the car park, after the information sign. 🕐 *Open May-Oct 8.30am-7pm.* ◉ *3€.* ☎ *04 93 23 25 90. www. colmiane.com.* 🗊 *A guide to the facilities is available from the tourist office in Valdeblore,* ☎ *04 93 23 25 90.*

This recent development, directly accessible by car, offers ideal facilities for learning rock-climbing and overcoming vertigo. There are three routes graded blue, red and black according to their difficulty. The first course takes at least 1.5hr. Those looking for big thrills will particularly enjoy crossing the footbridge (35m/115ft long; 50m/164ft above ground level) which links the two rocky peaks of the Aiguillettes.

Beyond the pass the road enters a green gulley, the highest part of the Valdeblore.

The Return of the Bearded Vulture

The bearded vulture, a magnificent bird with a huge wingspan (2.8m/9.6ft) is an example of a European endangered species. Its numbers were greatly reduced in the 19C in the Alps, although it survives in the Pyrenees and Corsica. The bearded vulture, which is the largest Alpine bird, has a curious way of life; alternating between soaring flight and perilous aerobatics, it flies over the steep, sloping pastures looking for the carcasses of chamois and sheep from which it takes the large bones (up to 3kg/6.6lb). It then drops the bones from a great height onto rocks in order to shatter them, hence their nickname of "bone-breaker" *(casseur d'os)*. It used to be looked on as the natural assistant of the shepherd.

The reintroduction of bearded vultures as chicks into the Parc du Mercantour (at Roubion) in 1993 was crowned with success. It takes eight years for the birds to reach maturity after which they can live for 40 years.

In 1996 five birds were released in the southern Alps and 60 throughout the Alps in an extensive international reintroduction programme, the only one of its kind.

St-Dalmas-de-Valdeblore

Have a stroll through the winding alleys of this village before visiting the Romanesque **Ste-Croix church** (🕐 *Open on request only, contact Mme Barbara Textoris,* ☎ *04 93 23 25 90*). Striking with its pyramidal Alpine-style bell-tower, stout buttresses and Lombard bands on the chevet, this church was built on the basilica plan over a pre-Romanesque groin-vaulted crypt. The interior was vaulted in the 17C to hide the original roof.

Above the high altar there is a polyptych by Guillaume Planeta of St Dalmas, St Roch and the Evangelists. In the north aisle is an altarpiece of St Francis attributed to André de Cella. Behind an altarpiece of the Rosary (17C) in the south apsidal chapel are the partial remains of some very old frescoes.

The road looks down on the Bramafan Valley and passes through La Roche at the foot of a grey rock spur.

La Bolline

The town, which is the administrative center of the Valdeblore district, makes a pleasant summer resort surrounded by chestnut woods which contrast with the Bois Noir (Black Forest) on the opposite slope.

▸ *West of La Bolline turn right onto D 66.*

Rimplas

The curious **site**★ of this village on the edge of the cliff (1 000m/3 281ft high) is very striking. From the chapel, dedicated to Mary Magdalene, at the edge of the ridge below the fort, there is an extensive **view**★ of the Tinée Valley, Bramafan Valley and the Valdeblore villages.

🚶 *2hr round-trip.* A nice and easy trail leads down into St-Sauveur-sur-Tinée by the GR 5 northwest of the village.

🚲 *By the road, follow the Valdeblore by the D 2565, then la Tinée by the D 2205, right for St-Saveur, left for Nice.*

ST-PAUL-DE-VENCE★★

POPULATION 2 847

MICHELIN MAP 341 D5

From afar, the first view of St-Paul-de-Vence looks so perfect, it looks unreal, like a bucolic film set. The rolling hills and rich valleys of the Vence countryside comprise its setting★. St-Paul-de-Vence is the epitome of the fortified towns that once guarded the Var frontier. Perched on a rocky spur behind ramparts that have remained more or less intact (it continued its defensive military activities until 1870), it has kept much of its medieval appearance, while becoming one of the most visited villages in France. Since 1967, the Fondation Maeght has also made St-Paul a prominent center for modern art.

▸ **Orient Yourself:** The village is 4km/2.5mi south of Vence on the D 2. the north gate. The protruding muzzle at the north gate belongs to a cannon captured at the Battle of Cérisoles (1544). A square machicolated tower houses the Tourist Office *(Syndicat d'Initiative)*, together with a permanent exhibition of modern paintings. In high season the narrow streets of the village are completely packed with pedestrian tourists. Try to visit off-season when you can get a better feel for the magical atmosphere of the place. 🛈 *Maison de la Tour, Rue Grande,* ☎ *04 93 32 86 95. www.saint-pauldevence.com.*

▸ **Parking:** Park the car in one of the car parks provided at the entrance to the village, before passing through the north gate.

Medieval Alleys

Rue Grande

Rue Grande is the main street *(closed to traffic)* running the full length of the village. Many of the arcaded 16C and 17C houses bearing coats of arms are now artists' studios, antique shops, and art and craft galleries. The urn-shaped **fountain** with its vaulted washing place in the square is of particular interest.

Illustrious Visitors

After a period of prosperity in the Middle Ages, the village declined in the last century to the benefit of Vence and Cagnes. It was "rediscovered" in the 1920s by painters such as Signac, Modigliani, Bonnard and Soutine who used to meet in a café which has since become the sumptuous Auberge de la Colombe d'Or, its walls covered with paintings as in a gallery. Other artists were to follow suit—sculptors, illustrators, writers and entertainers—making St-Paul a famous Riviera landmark. The village is also a great favorite among celebrities from the silver screen, such as the couple Simone Signoret and Yves Montand.

▶ *Climb up the stepped street above the fountain. Take the first right and then the first left to the church.*

Church

This Gothic building was constructed from the 12C to the 13C, with the vaulting rebuilt in the 17C and the bell-tower in the 18C. The nave and two aisles are divided by massive pillars and contain several works of art. At the end of the north aisle hangs a painting attributed to Tintoretto of Ste Catherine of Alexandria in a magnificent red cloak, sword in hand. The choir stalls are 17C carved walnut, and the south transept chapel is particularly noteworthy for its ornate stucco decoration. The other chapel is adorned with a Madonna of the Rosary (1588) with Catherine de' Medici featured among the crowd. The Stations of the Cross are modern although painted in tempera, a 16C technique.

The **treasury** in the side aisle is rich in 12C to 15C pieces: statuettes, ciborium, processional cross, reliquaries and in particular, a 13C enamel Virgin and Child, all of which testify to the skill of Provençal craftsmen. There is also a parchment signed by King Henri III.

Donjon

The **keep** opposite the church currently houses the town hall.

▶ *Return to Rue Grande and continue down to the south gate.*

Ramparts★

From the bastion of the south gate, overlooking the cemetery, there is a superb **view** of the Alps, the sea (Cap d'Antibes) and the Esterel.

The ramparts remain much as they were when built (1537-47) by François I in response to the challenge of the Citadel of Nice. Follow them around anti-clockwise using the parapet walk where possible; it commands good views both of the orange trees and flower fields in the valley and the hills and mountains inland.

Sights

Fondation Maeght★★

The permanent collection isn't open during the temporary expositions. ◷ *Open 10am-12.30pm, 2.30-6pm; Jul-Sep: 10am-7pm.* ⊚ *11€. No charge for children under 10 years of age.* ☎ *04 93 32 81 63.*

This modern art museum is located northwest of St-Paul in a pine wood on a hill, the Colline des Gardettes. Using white concrete and rose-coloured bricks, **José Luis Sert** has created an architectural complex in the true Mediterranean style.

Incorporated into the enclosure wall is a mosaic by Tal-Coat; in the park the visitor is greeted by a Calder stabile, as well as a bronze by Zadkine, Arp's *Giant Pip* and a fountain by Pol Bury, among other works. In another garden is a labyrinth with sculpture and ceramics by Miró. in the chapel of St-Bernard are stained-glass windows by Ubac and Braque; the

Fountain in Rue Grande, St Paul-de-Vence

S. Sauvignier/ MICHELIN

Address Book

For coin ranges, see the Legend at the back of the guide.

EATING OUT

⊖ **Chez Andréas** – *Western ramparts* – ☎ 04 93 32 98 32. Settle on the delightful terrace of this restaurant and sip a pastis as you admire the setting rays of the sun. A tastefully decorated dining room, with salads, the day's special and a choice of local wines.

⊖⊖ **La Cocarde de Saint Paul** – *23 Rue Grande* – ☎ 04 93 32 86 17. In the main street at the heart of St-Paul, this restaurant-tea shop will seduce you by its artful blend of Mediterranean colors. Excellent cuisine and homemade pastries.

⊖⊖ **La Ferme de St-Paul** – *1334 Route de la Colle* – ☎ 04 93 32 82 48 – ⊙ *Closed Nov- 20 Dec.* Tastefully restored old farmhouse boasting a superb decor: Provençal overtones, wooden beams, mahogany furniture, wrought-iron accessories and fine crockery. Quality cooking and interesting menu, where fish has pride of place. Charming terrace and antique shop set up in the outbuildings.

WHERE TO STAY

⊖ **Hostellerie Les Remparts** – *72 Rue Grande* – ☎ 04 93 32 09 88 – ⊙ *Closed mid-Jan to mid-Feb* – ▣ – *9 rooms* – ☕ – *Restaurant (*⊖⊖*)*. Handsome hostel restored with great taste, featuring stone walls, period furniture, hexagonal floor tiling and warm colours. Each room is named after a flower; the larger ones offers pretty views of the surrounding countryside.

⊖⊖ **Chambre d'Hôte La Bastide de St-Donat** – *Route du Pont de Pierre, Parc St-Donat – La Colle-sur-Loup – 2km/1.2mi south of St-Paul by D 6* – ☎ 04 93 32 93 41 – ☕ – *5 rooms.* The 1850 stone façade of this old sheep barn is deceptive. Step inside and you will be astonished by the lavish decoration. The handsomely restored rooms feature exposed beams, antique furniture and low-key colors. The charming terrace is a tranquil place, with the gentle babbling of the nearby stream.

⊖⊖⊖ **Hostellerie des Messugues** – *Quartier des Gardettes, by Route de la Fondation Maeght 2km/1.2mi* – ☎ 04 93 32 53 32 – ⊙ *Closed Oct-Mar* – ▣ – *15 rooms* – ☕. Just below the Maeght Foundation, in a lush and peaceful garden, lies this big Provençal villa surrounded by vines. The upstairs rooms are larger and slightly more comfortable. Do not miss the pool and its small island planted with banana trees.

CAFÉ LIFE

Café de la Place – *Place du Général-de-Gaulle* – ☎ 04 93 32 80 03 – *Jul-Aug daily 8am-1am; rest of the year daily 8am-8pm.* This café, set up on the main square where villagers like to congregate and play pétanque, is at the heart of life in St-Paul. It belongs to the legendary Colombe d'Or Hotel *(located opposite)*, once the property of the actor Yves Montand, and has welcomed many a celebrity in its time, notably Picasso and Prévert.

TENNIS

Tennis Club des Serres – *56 Chemin de Rome* – ☎ 04 93 32 85 09 – ⊙ *Daily.* Exclusive clay tennis court offering nice views of the nearby valley and sea. Highly reasonable rates.

MARKETS

Marché d'Yvette – Fruit and vegetable market beneath the wash house at the village entrance, every Tuesday, Thursday, and Saturday.

Flower Market – Fresh flowers beneath the wash house at the village entrance, every Saturday morning.

Regional Products – Country market on the Place de Gaulle every Wednesday morning 9.30am-1pm.

Stations of the Cross are the work of Ubac. A Braque mosaic forms the backdrop to a pond, while another by Chagall decorates the external wall of the bookshop.

The **museum** consists of two buildings divided by a court adorned with sculptures by Giacometti. The collection of modern art is exhibited in rotation in specially designed rooms: canvases, sculpture, ceramics and drawings by Braque, Chagall, Léger, Kandinsky, Miró, Giacometti, Bonnard, Bazaine, Hartung, Tapiès and Alechinsky, as well as works by several artists of a younger generation (Adami, Garache, Messagier, Viallat).

Musée d'Histoire Locale

Place de la Castre. ⊙ *Open 10am-12.30pm, 1.30-5.30pm.* ⊙ *Closed 15-30 Nov.* ⊖ *3€.* ☎ 04 93 32 41 13.

This museum offers an interesting account of the village's history. Eight illustrated scenes with life-size figures depict the stages marking its development, which often mirror those of Provence itself.

The tour begins with a scene illustrating the arrival of the Count of Provence, Raimond Bérenger V, in St-Paul in 1224. Subsequent scenes include the visit of Queen Jeanne, then that of François I during the "Truce of Nice" (☾ see VILLEFRANCHE). A visit by Vauban was instrumental in integrating the village into the defensive system guarding the border. Finally, there are local scenes of the war between the French republicans and the Austro-Sardinian alliance.

An exhibition of photographs of famous people who have stayed in St-Paul adds a contemporary note to this historical display.

ST-RAPHAËL

POPULATION 30 671

MICHELIN MAP 340 P5

LOCAL MAP SEE MASSIF DE L'ESTEREL

A fashionable summer and winter resort situated on Fréjus Bay, St-Raphaël has a well-sheltered beach at the foot of the Esterel. The railway brought prosperity to this town under the Second Empire, and a century later it has transformed into one of the great modern cities of the Riviera.

▶ **Orient Yourself:** St-Raphaël stretches along the coast of the Esterel for 35km/21mi, while the town is made up of several districts: the port, the old town, Valescure to the north, and the dependant resorts from Boulouris to Trayas. ▯ Rue Waldeck-Rousseau, ☎ 04 94 19 52 52. www.saint-raphael.com.

Kids **Especially for Kids:** A juggling or trapeze lesson at the École de Cirque (see Address Book).

A Bit of History

Origins – St-Raphaël, like Fréjus, is a daughter of Rome. A Gallo-Roman holiday resort stood on the site now occupied by the large Casino. It was built in terraces decorated with mosaics, and included thermal baths and a vivarium (fish reserve). At that period rich Romans came here to enjoy the sea air.

In the Middle Ages the villas were plundered by Saracen pirates. After their expulsion (end of the 10C), the Count of Provence left these deserted lands to the abbeys of Lérins and St-Victor in Marseille. The monks built a village around the church. In the 12C its defence was entrusted to the Templars. In the 18C the fishermen and peasants who lived in St-Raphaël occupied what are now the old quarters; marsh fever and anemia so weakened the inhabitants that they became known in the region as "pale faces".

After Corsica was united with France in 1768, the port of St-Raphaël became the terminus for a short-lived sea link with the island, also known as the Île de Beauté.

Bonaparte in St-Raphaël – On 9 October 1799 the small village was suddenly brought into the limelight when Bonaparte, returning from Egypt, landed there after a voyage of 48 days (a pyramid standing in Avenue Commandant-Guilbaud commemorates this event).

In 1814 St-Raphaël received Napoleon once again, this time as a defeated man leaving for Elba, his new and minute kingdom.

The Resort is Developed – **Alphonse Karr** (1808-90) was an extravagant personality who used his talents as journalist and pamphleteer to oppose Napoleon III from Nice, where he was in exile. His horticultural interests led him to settle in St-Raphaël in 1864 in a villa named "Maison Close." Writing to a Parisian friend, he said: "Leave Paris and plant your stick in my garden: the next morning, when you awake, you will see that it has grown roses." Writers and artists responded to his invitation: Alexandre Dumas, Maupassant, Berlioz and Gounod, among others.

Félix Martin, local mayor and civil engineer, followed Karr's lead and transformed the village into a smart resort, encouraging building, and linking St-Raphaël with Hyères (then an expanding resort) by means of a small railway along the coast. Martin engaged the architect Pierre Audlé, who left his mark on the design of the resort.

Illustrious guests marked their stay in St-Raphaël with works of art: Gounod composed *Roméo et Juliette* in 1869, Scott Fitzgerald wrote *Tender is the Night*, and Félix Ziem painted some of his pictures here.

Walking Tour

The original town center consists of an important and quite rare collection of seaside architecture dating from the beginning of the Third Republic (late 19th century).

Seafront

There is bustling activity on the waterfront by the old harbor, stimulated by the cafés and shops that line the broad sidewalks of Cours Jean-Bart and Quai Albert-Ier.
From beneath the palms and plane trees of Promenade René-Coty and Avenue du Général-de-Gaulle, there is a fine **view** of the sea and the twin rocks known as the Land Lion and the Sea Lion. The road follows the coast eastwards to the marina, with its terraces, shops and restaurants.

Villas

During the redevelopment of the residential area between Promenade René-Coty and Rue Alphonse-Karr, many of the exotically decorated villa façades were lost. Among those remaining in Promenade René-Coty is the Villa Roquerousse (1900) with its lavish ornamentation. There are also several characteristic façades still standing in Boulevard Félix-Martin: the charming oriental Villa Sémiramis, Villa Paquerettes decorated with ceramics, and a little farther on the shadow of Gounod still haunts *l'Oustelet dou Capelan* ("The Priest's House" in Provençal).

Both Plateau Notre-Dame and St-Sébastien hill are full of remarkable villas, and the Palladian inspiration of their designers is evident in the arrangement of the gardens and the flights of stairs.

Notre-Dame-de-la-Victoire-de-Lépante

This original **church**, in neo-Byzantine style, was built in 1883 by Pierre Aublé, the architect of many of the villas in St-Raphaël. The church was named by its creator who came from Greece.

Quartier de Valescure

This district, on the right bank of the Garonne, was once much patronised by foreign visitors. The director of the Paris Opera in 1880, Carvalho, laid out, with advice from Charles Garnier, a park decorated with vestiges from the Palais des Tuileries in Paris. At the crossroads of Rue Allongue and Rue Maréchal-Leclerc there is a fountain, a remnant of the extravagances of the period, which also came from the Tuileries.

Église St-Pierre-des-Templiers

This church, built in the 12C in the Romanesque-Provençal style, served as a fortress and a refuge for the population in the event of attack by pirates. The watchtower, which tops one of the apsidal chapels, brings to mind the military constructions of the Templars.

In one of the side chapels, a red sandstone monolith, once a pagan altar, now supports the altar table. The gilded wooden bust of St Peter is carried by the fishermen in procession to the Sea Lion in August.

Near the church are fragments of a Roman aqueduct that brought water to St-Raphaël.

Practical Information

TOURS

Guided Tours – Discover St-Raphaël's heritage, every Thursday 10am. 2.29€. For information contact the Tourism Office, ☎ 04 94 19 52 52.

Allovisit – 7 different routes in this self-guided audio-tour (through your portable telephone), available through the Tourism Office.

Nature Walks – The Tourism Office can also organize nature walks along the coastal footpaths or in the Esterel hills, in partnership with the ONF.

Sight

North of the railway station, the old town, once surrounded by ramparts, extends beyond the Hôtel de Ville. There are still ramparts to be seen in Rue Allongue and in the gardens of the Musée Archéologique. Rue des Remparts follows its original course.

Musée Archéologique

🕐 *Open Jul-Aug Wed-Sun 10am-5pm; rest of the year Wed 9am-noon, 2-5pm, Thu 9am-noon, Sat 2-5pm.* 🕐 *Closed public holidays.* 🚭 *Free entry.* ☎ *04 94 19 25 75.*

This archeology museum profits from the fact that St-Raphaël was situated at a crossroads for major land (*Via Aurelia*) and sea routes (between Massalia and the western Mediterranean) and is thus endowed with a rich heritage of archeological remains dating from Antiquity.

The rooms on the ground floor display a remarkable collection of **amphorae**★, dating from the 5C BC to the 5C AD. There is also an interesting reconstruction of the loading of a Roman galley. A gallery of technology contains a display on the evolution of scuba diving equipment and underwater photography, as well as on the process of preserving wood under water.

On the second floor, two rooms are reserved for the finds from the excavation of Prehistoric sites in the Esterel that date from the Paleolithic Era to the Bronze Age. In the garden, there is a milestone dating from 3 BC that was found on Cap Roux.

ST-TROPEZ★★

POPULATION 5 444

MICHELIN MAP 340 O6

LOCAL MAP SEE MASSIF DES MAURES

After almost a half-century of fame, St-Tropez, or St-Trop' as the locals say, is still in fashion. Its attraction lies in both its stunning location on the southern shore of one of the most beautiful bays of the Riviera, and its continuous stream of celebrities, artists, musicians, journalists and photographers who meet here every summer. The contrast of modern luxury yachts and the scruffy but color-ful Provençal facades of the little port of St-Tropez is what makes the Riviera so alluring to the throngs who visit here year after year.

▸ **Orient Yourself:** Unless you arrive by yacht, access to St-Tropez is famously slow and frustrating in the summer; traffic jams on the only road to the town (D 98a) are huge, starting at the La Foux intersection of D 559, N 98 and D 61. It's best to avoid the place altogether in July and August; otherwise try to get there as early as possible in the morning, or stay on the less crowded southern and eastern coasts of the St-Tropez peninsula. *Quai Jean-Jaurè*, ☎ *04 94 97 45 21. www.ot-saint-tropez.com.*

Ⓟ **Parking:** Parking in the village, even in parking garages, is difficult. The map designates free and paying parking areas on the peninsula, and whether they are covered or in the sun.

A Bit of History

The Legend of St Tropez – Tropez (Torpes), a Christian centurion beheaded in his native Pisa by order of Emperor Nero, was placed in a boat with his head beside him and cast adrift with a cock and a dog who were meant to devour his remains, which, however, they left intact. The boat is supposed to have drifted ashore where St-Tropez now stands.

Republic of St-Tropez (15C-17C) – In 1470 the Grand Seneschal of Provence accepted the offer of a Genoese gentleman, Raffaele de Garezzio, to settle with 60 Genoese families in St-Tropez, which had been destroyed by war at the end of the 14C. De Garezzio undertook to rebuild and defend the town, provided it was freed of all taxes. The town was quick to prosper.

St-Tropez became a sort of small republic administered by the heads of the families and later, by two consuls and 12 councillors who were elected.

Judge Suffren (18C) – Among the St-Tropézian navigators who contributed to the rise of the city and the defence of the kingdom in the 17C, the most famous is Pierre-Andre de Suffren (1729-1788), a judge with the Knights of Malta who became a captain of the royal navy *(you will see his statue on the quay)*. He was sent in reinforcement to the Indies, where he won several victories over the British in an extraordinary campaign. When the peace of Versailles was signed in 1783, he was promoted to vice-admiral. He died in 1788 at the age of 59 from an unfortunate blood-letting.

The "Bravades" – Two *bravades* or "acts of defiance" take place every year. The first of these acts, a simple religious procession in honour of St Tropez, has maintained its local importance since the end of the 15C. On 16 and 17 May the gilded wooden statue of St Tropez is car-ried through the town, escorted by the town captain, elected by the municipal council, and the corps of *bravadeurs*. Visi-tors come from all over to witness this boisterous festival, where red and white (the colors of the corsairs) prevail.

St-Tropez

S. Sauvignier/ MICHELIN

The second act celebrates the victory of the St-Tropez militia who, on 15 June 1637, fended off 22 Spanish galleys attempting to take the town by surprise and to make off with four of the king's ships anchored in the port.

A Popular Resort among Intellectuals – At the turn of the century, St-Tropez was a charming little village unknown to tourists and poorly served by a small rail line. In the harbor *tartans* (single-masted sailing vessels) laden with sand and wine were moored beside the fishing boats. It was then that Maupassant discovered it. The painters who followed Signac's example made it more widely known (& *see below*). Between the two World Wars, Colette, who used to spend the winter here, contributed to its fame. Other famous residents included politicians, the couturier Paul Poiret and later Jean Cocteau.

Starting with the 1950s, St-Tropez was fashionable with the literary set from St-Germain-des-Prés in Paris and then with the cinema stars, together with their fans, gaining the town an international reputation that hasn't faded over the decades.

Resort Life

The Port★★

The harbor is the hub of village life in St-Tropez. Fishing boats, commercial vessels and excursion craft share the mooring with a crowd of yachts, from the most humble to the most luxurious. On the waterfront and in the neighboring streets, the old pink and yellow houses have been converted into cafés and pastry shops, cabarets and restaurants, luxury boutiques, galleries and antique shops. In season a picturesque and cosmopolitan crowd strolls beneath the bronze statue of Admiral Suffren.

The Beaches ⌂⌂

The beaches around St-Tropez are truly heavenly, with their fine sand and charming rocky coves. The nearest is Bouillabaisse Beach (perfect for windsailing when the *mistral* is blowing). To the east of the town lies **Graniers Beach** *(access from Rue Cavaillon)*. Farther east round the headland stretches **Les Salins Beach** *(on Avenue Foch)*. But by far the most appealing and the most fashionable are the **Pampelonne**

Beaches☆☆, well sheltered from the *mistral* winds. Cannebiers Bay affords glimpses of the superb villas belonging to the rich and the famous: La Hune (Paul Signac), La Treille Muscate (Colette) and La Madrague (Brigitte Bardot).

Walking Tour

Môle Jean-Réveille★★

The attractive **panorama**★ from the top of the jetty includes all of St-Tropez: Portalet tower, the port, the town and its commanding citadel; the head of the bay, Grimaud and its castle ruins; Beauvallon; Ste-Maxime; Cap des Sardinaux; Issambres Point; Dramont headland; Cap Roux summit and, in the distance, the Esterel and in fine weather, the Alps.

La Ponche Quarter

Tucked between the port and the citadel, this is the oldest and most charming district of St-Tropez, where fishermen and artists used to live.

▶ *Turn right at the seaward end of Quai Jean-Jaurès onto Place de l'Hôtel-de-Ville.*

On the left stands a massive tower, all that remains of the 16C **Château de Suffren des Seigneurs de St-Tropez**.

▶ *Turn left beyond the Hôtel de Ville to reach the bay of La Glayel.*

Rue de la Ponche leads through the old gateway to a beach overlooked by the Vieille Tour *(old tower)* where fishing boats ride at anchor.

Address Book

For coin ranges, see the Legend at the back of the guide.

EATING OUT

💭💭 **Régis Restaurant** – *19 Rue de la Citadelle* – ☎ *04 94 97 15 53* – *info@regisrestaurant.com* – ⏱ *Closed 30 Oct-15 Mar*. Pasta in all shapes and sizes, cooked in various ways, as well as sushi and wok stir-frys, attract a regular clientele to this restaurant located on a steep, narrow street in St-Tropez. The food is served on the terrace or inside one of the small dining areas decked out in white.

💭💭 **La Cantina el Mexicano** – *16 Rue des Remparts* – ☎ *04 94 97 40 96* – *elmexicano@wanadoo.fr* – ⏱ *Closed Nov to Mar and for lunch*. After sipping your tequila, savour generous helpings of Mexican cuisine in this typical setting characterised by religious statues, painted wood furnishings and vases. Even the bathroom warrants a visit! Youngish clientele. Friendly, relaxed ambience.

💭💭 **Leï Salins** – *Plage des Salins* – ☎ *04 94 97 04 40* – ⏱ *Closed 15 Oct-31 Mar*. Open-air beach restaurant offering a tasty bill of fare consisting of salads and grilled, freshly caught fish. Charming seaside location coupled with attractive surroundings.

💭💭 **La Table du Marché** – *38 Rue Georges-Clemenceau* – ☎ *04 94 97 85 20*. Gourmets will love this temple of gastronomy located near Place des Lices, open at all hours of the day. In addition to the restaurant offering traditional French cuisine, La Table du Marché is also known for its homemade pastries that can be purchased on the premises: croissants, cakes and the legendary "gendarme de St-Tropez" – mouthwatering chocolate mousse in the shape of a policeman's cap filled with vanilla crème brûlée. Who can resist?

💭💭 **Au Vieux Gassin** – *Place deï Barri - Gassin* – ☎ *04 94 56 14 26* – ⏱ *Closed Jan, and dinner in winter*. A ravishing little hilltop village serves as the backdrop for this popular restaurant. A terrace with panoramic views is partially enclosed and heated in cooler weather, taking over a large section of the charming Place deï Barri. The regional menu had a few "exotic" specialities. Extraordinarily friendly service.

💭💭💭 **Leï Mouscardins** – *Port (Tour du Portalet)* – ☎ *04 94 97 29 00* – *info@lei-mouscardins.com* – ⏱ *Closed 9 Jan-4 Feb, 14 Nov-17 Dec, and Tue off-season*. Tucked away behind the harbor, near Tour du Portalet, this restaurant pays homage to Mediterranean tradition. It has a faithful following of food lovers, lured by its creative and lovingly prepared cuisine, presented to you in two dining rooms opening out onto St-Tropez Bay.

WHERE TO STAY

💭💭 **Hôtel Lou Cagnard** – *Avenue Paul-Roussel* – ☎ *04 94 97 04 24* – ⏱ *Closed 3 Nov-27 Dec* – 🅿 – *19 rooms* – 🛏. Enjoy breakfast seated in the shade of a mulberry tree in the tiny garden of this pretty Provençal house, just off Place des Lices. At night you'll be lulled to sleep by the chirping of cicadas... Highly reasonable prices for St-Tropez.

💭💭 **Bello Visto** – *Place deï-Barri – Gassin* – ☎ *04 94 56 17 30 or 04 94 56 47 33* – ⏱ *Closed Jan and Nov* – *9 rooms* – 🛏 – *Restaurant* (💭💭). There's truth in the name of this small family-run hotel and restaurant posted on the place of the ramparts (*barri*), at the top of Gassin. The majority of the rooms, like the terrace, profit from a "beautiful sight" over the Massif des Maures and the gulf of St-Tropez. Dining room with fireplace and Provençal cuisine.

◒◔◕ **Bastide des Salins** – *4km/ 2.4mi southeast of St-Tropez – ☎ 04 94 97 24 57 – info@labastidedessalins.com – ◔ Closed 6 Oct-31 Mar – ▱ – 14 rooms – ⌕.* You will be greeted like friends of the family at this old Provençal house surrounded by extensive leafy grounds. Barely 5 minutes from Place des Lices and yet totally isolated, this hotel offers large rooms decorated in the Provençal spirit, appointed with great simplicity.

◒◔◕ **Hôtel Ponche** – *Place Révelin – ☎ 04 94 97 02 53 – hotel@laponche.com – ◔ Closed 1 Nov-13 Feb – 18 rooms – ⌕ – Restaurant (◒◔◕).* The rooms of this cosy hotel occupy four village houses formerly belonging to fishermen; the blue one was a favourite of Romy Schneider's. You will be under the charm of the rooftop terraces nestling between the citadel and the bell-tower. The warm, bright hues and considerate service make the Hôtel Ponche an absolute must.

ON THE TOWN

St-Tropez has two facets. In summer, it is a town for the rich and wealthy and is given over to sailing, bathing, entertainment and nightlife. However, in winter, it looks more like a ghost town. Indeed, most businesses close down between November and April and the swinging bars, restaurants and hotels that have made the reputation of St-Tropez are completely deserted.

Bar du Château de la Messardière – *Route de Tahiti – ☎ 04 94 56 76 00 – www.messardiere.com – ◔ Mid-Mar to mid-Oct from 6pm.* This bar belongs to one of the Riviera's most prestigious hotels. Hushed, cosy ambience in the piano bar of this former 18C private residence. The terrace commands nice views of St-Tropez Bay.

Chez Nano – *2 Rue Sibille – ☎ 04 94 97 72 59 – ◔ Daily 7pm-3am – ◔ Closed Feb-Mar.* A must for any visitor to St-Tropez. Frequented by wealthy yacht owners and foreign patrons, Chez Nano exudes a cosy atmosphere and is often used as a venue for painting exhibitions.

Bar Sube – *15 quai de Suffren – ☎ 04 94 97 30 04 – ◔ Open 6-11pm, until 3am Jul-Aug – ◔ Closed 5-31 Jan.* This is one of the most beautiful bars of the city. Model boats decorate the interior, where the leather armchairs and fireplace make for a cordial and comfortable place. Small tables are installed on the balcony, with prime views of the old port.

WORKING OUT

Artemis – *Route des Plages – ☎ 04 94 97 86 69 – artemis-stkwanadoo.fr – ◔ Jul-Aug Mon-Sat 9am-9pm; Sep-Jun Mon-Fri 9am-*8pm, Sat 9am-2pm. This gym club features an unusual method unique in France, aimed at establishing a personalised programme for members: all the relevant information about their state of health is fed into a computer that decides on the number and nature of the fitness sessions. Artemis also has beauty treatments available.

FOR YOUR SWEET TOOTH

La Tarte Tropézienne – *Place des Lices – ☎ 04 94 97 71 42 – www.tarte-tropezienne.com – ◔ Daily 6.30am-10pm.* It was in this pâtisserie that the famous tarte tropézienne saw the light of day, invented in 1955 by Polish baker Alexandre Micka: a round delightfully moist, brioche cake flavored with orange blossom, filled with custard and sprinkled with crystallised suger.

Sénéquier – *Quai Jean-Jaurès – ☎ 04 94 97 00 90 – ◔ Daily 8am-7pm; Jul-Aug 7am-3am- ◔ Closed mid-Nov to mid-Dec.* The sidewalk terrace and crimson chairs of this tea room are famous throughout the world or so say the locals! Renowned personalities such as Jean Marais, Errol Flynn and Colette would come here for a cup of delicately fragrant tea, an iced coffee, a delicious ice cream or a few squares of homemade nougat.

SHOPPING

Markets – Tuesdays and Saturdays on Place des Lices.

Foire de la Ste-Anne – Fair on Place des Lices, every July 26.

Shopping streets – The most lively shopping streets are Rue Clemenceau, Rue Gambetta and Rue Allard, offering an impressive selection of local arts and crafts: pottery, glassware etc.

Les Sandales Tropéziennes – *16 Rue Georges Clemenceau – ☎ 04 94 97 19 55 – www.nova.fr – ◔ Oct-Mar Tue-Sat 9.30am-noon and 2.30-6.30pm; Apr-Sep daily until 8pm.* The Rondini house has been crafting St-Tropez sandals since 1927. The distinctive, namesake model in natural leather is the most popular, but the snakeskin version sells well, too!

Le Petit Village – *La Foux – near the commercial center just outside Gassin – Gassin – ☎ 04 94 56 32 04 – infos@petitvillage.com – ◔ Open Jun-15 Sep 8.30am-1pm, 2.30-7.30pm; rest of the year 8.30am-12.30pm, 2.30-6.30pm – ◔ Closed Sun.* This showroom brings together the wines from eight prestigious vineyards on the St-Tropez peninsula in a location just off the busy La Foux intersection. Includes the famous Château de Pampelonne vineyard. Free tastings and many regional products for sale.

TRANSPORT

MMG boat trips – *☎ 04 94 96 51 00.* Regular services to Ste-Maxime leaving from St-Tropez operate Apr to end of Oct, 10.40€ round-trip; to Les Issambres Jun-Sep, 11.20€ round-trip; to Port-Grimaud Apr-Oct, 9€ round-trip; to Les Cannebiers Bay at 3.30pm leaving from St-Tropez, 8€ round-trip and at 3pm leaving from Ste-Maxime, 11.80€round-trip.

LEISURE ACTIVITIES

Maison du Tourisme du Golfe de St-Tropez – *Gassin* – ☎ *04 94 55 22 00*. This tourist office issues a list of all the companies based in St-Tropez Bay that specialise in deep-sea diving.

▶ *Follow the street to the adorable Place des Remparts, then to Boulevard d'Aumale.*

Citadelle★

The citadel stands on a hillock at the east end of town. The hexagonal keep with three round towers was built in the 16C. In the 17C a fortified wall was added.

The ramparts command a fine **panorama**★ of St-Tropez, the bay, Ste-Maxime and the Maures.

▶ *Retrace your steps to the Rue d'Aumale and follow it to the Place de l'Ormeau.*

Church

The 19C church built tucked into the town was built in the Italian Baroque style with a bell-tower crowned with wrought-iron work. The interior contains some finely carved woodwork and to the left of the high altar, a bust of St Tropez, and, laid around it like a tribute of votive offerings, several old blunderbusses which exploded without hurting anyone during a bravade. At Christmas a beautiful 19C Provençal Nativity scene with figures in traditional costume adorns the church.

▶ *Go down Rue du Clocher, then take a left on the Rue des Commerçants, and left on the Rue du Marché.*

The charming **Place aux Herbes,** traditionally bathed in light and skillfully rendered by Marquet in his paintings, is the backdrop to a small market open in the mornings. Walk past the animated fish stalls, underneath Porte de la Poissonnerie and proceed to Quai Jean-Jaurès and the Tourism Office.

▶ *Leaving the port, take Rue Laugier, then Rue Gambetta.*

These two lively shopping streets are lined with boutiques of international renown.

▶ *Walk to Place des Lices.*

Place des Lices

This busy square is a popular meetingplace among locals and visitors alike. Its convivial cafés and restaurants, colorful market, venerable plane trees and sandy areas for playing *boules* attract huge crowds in both summer and winter.

Sights

L'Annonciade, Musée de St-Tropez★★

🕐 *Open Jul-Aug 10am-1pm, 3-10pm; Dec-Jun 10am-noon, 2-6pm.* 🕐 *Closed in Nov, 1 Jan, 1 May, Ascension, 25 Dec.* 👁 *4.50€ (5.50€ during expositions).* ☎ *04 94 97 04 01.*

The chapel of Our Lady of Annonciade, built in 1510 and deconsecrated during the Revolution, was split into two levels in the early 19C and set up as a museum in 1937. Georges Grammont (patron of the arts) donated some 10 sculptures and about 50 paintings covering 1890-1940. The collection confirms the important role St-Tropez played in the Post-Impressionist movement.

In 1892 **Paul Signac** (1863-1935) landed at St-Tropez. Enthralled by the site, he stopped to paint and ended up living there. Around him gathered other painters: Matisse, Bonnard, Marquet, Camoin, Dunoyer de Segonzac, some residing longer than others. Fascinated by the exceptional light in the region, these artists sought different methods of expressing color, contributing to, or instigating the great movements of the late 19C and 20C, such as Pointillism (👁 *see Introduction*), Fauvism, The Nabis and Expressionism.

Displayed amid the Pointillists, Signac is represented by his oils and watercolors (exhibited in rotation). He is surrounded by his followers H-E Cross *(St-Clair Beach)*, Théo van Rysselberghe, Maximilien Luce and several artists, like Derain (London scenes) and Picabia, who were momentarily part of the movement before taking a different direction.

La Nioulargue, a Sailing Festival

This great event at the end of the season in St-Tropez brings together real lovers of the sea and the most aristocratic traditional sailing boats (swans, ketches and schooners built during the 1920s for film stars or famous owners). Since its first meeting in 1981, more than 250 competitors (most of whom have previously taken part in the America's Cup) rush here every year in early October to take part in this race which has become the great European meeting of old boats.

The course starts at the Tour du Portalet, goes round the shallows marked by the Nioulargue (sea nest, in Provençal) buoy and returns to the harbour.

A spectator who has managed to find himself a good viewing point will be rewarded with the unforgettable sight of these large sailing boats in action. The skillful dances performed by ketches (recognisable by the small mast at the stern) and schooners (with the small mast in the bows) call for miraculous feats in anticipating manœuvres and great strength to move the enormous sails (the stress at the foot of the main mast can be as much as 500t!).

Ways to follow the race – Boarding a launch run by MMG, which operates a shuttle service in the gulf (see Address Book), or share the rental of a small boat so as to appreciate the skills of the skippers at close quarters. A more peaceful view of the scene is possible from the buttresses of the citadel; take a good pair of binoculars.

The Fauves, delighting in small touches of pure color, are represented by Matisse *(The Gypsy)*, Braque *(Estaque Landscape)*, Manguin, Vlaminck, Kees Van Dongen and Dufy. The Nabis group reacted against Impressionism, painting in primary colours on an essentially flat surface. They are represented by Bonnard, Vuillard *(Women Under a Lamp)*, Félix Vallotton *(Misia at Her Desk)*.

The Expressionists, who used painting as a means to convey the intensity of their emotions, via exaggerated facial expressions for example, are represented by Rouault, Chabaud *(Hôtel-Hôtel)*, Utrillo and his mother Suzanne Valadon.

The Rower, a Cubist work by Roger de La Fresnaye, landscapes and harbor scenes (Camoin, Bonnard, Marquet) complete this prestigious collection where the various artistic movements all tend to use the human figure as their central theme, regardless of how different their theories may be.

The sculpture, complementing the collection and of the same period, is by Maillol *(Nymph)* and Despiau; note also the sandstone vases by E Decœur.

Maison des Papillons (Musée Dany-Lartigue)

9 Rue Étienne-Berny. Kids   *Open May-Oct and mid-Dec to early Jan daily (except Sun) 2-6pm.*   *Closed Nov-Apr.*   *3€.*   *04 94 97 63 45. http://maisondespapillons.ifrance. com.*

This charming Provençal house, tucked into an alleyway away from the crowded port, is the former home of painter and entomologist Dany Lartigue, son of the photographer J.-H. Lartigue. It houses a collection of nearly 5 000 butterflies, comprising all the diurnal species existing in France, caught by the artist in person, as well as a donation of 20 000 exotic specimens. The staircase wall is hung with J.-H. Lartigue's photos and family souvenirs of the composer A Messager, the painter's grandfather. Artistic arrangements show the capacities for mimicry of insects in their natural environment. A pleasant patio with a fountain leads out from this room and contains two paintings illustrating local festivals. Upstairs rare and exotic species (such as the famous black Apollon of Mercantour and numerous Zerynthis and Parnassus) are grouped in display cases.

Musée Naval

  Open Apr-Sep daily (except Tue) 10am-12.30pm, 1.30-6.30pm (Oct-Mar until 5.30pm).   *Closed holidays.*   *4€ (child under 8 years free).*   *04 94 97 59 43.*

This Maritime Museum in the citadel keep is an annexe of the Musée de la Marine in the Palais de Chaillot in Paris. In the courtyard are two handsome 16C Spanish bronze cannons. Within the keep are displayed models of ships (including a reconstruction of a Greek galley), engravings and seascapes illustrating the history and local activities of St-Tropez with an explanation of the 1944 Allied landing. Note the full-scale cross-section of a torpedo from the local naval shipyard. The exhibition room illustrates a different theme each year.

There is a magnificent **view**★★ from the keep terrace overlooking the town, St-Tropez Bay, the Maures and the Esterel. On a clear day the Alps can be spotted in the far distance.

Driving Tour

Moulins de Paillas and Gassin ★ *Round-trip 28km/18mi*

This tour into the countryside around St-Tropez offers extensive views of the coast and the Maures hinterland and includes villages that have retained their original character.

Chapelle Ste-Anne

▶ *1km/0.7mi. From St-Tropez take Avenue Paul-Roussel and Route de Ste-Anne.*

Standing on a volcanic rock spike in the shelter of huge trees, this attractive Provençal chapel is a place of pilgrimage for seafarers and *"bravadeurs"* with a **view**★ of the sea in all directions, particularly of St-Tropez and the bay. The road passes through the vineyards above Pampelonne Bay.

▶ *Turn right onto D 61 towards Ramatuelle.*

Ramatuelle★ ⓒ *see RAMATUELLE.*

▶ *Turn right onto D 89 towards Col de Paillas.*

Moulins de Paillas★★

Beyond three ruined olive mills, there is a radio beacon on a circular platform.

▶ *Follow the signposted path.*

On walking round the enclosure, there are glimpses through the trees of a fine **panoramic view**★★ *(seawards from north to south)* over Cap Roux and the rough peaks of the Esterel, the coast of the Maures Massif, Ste-Maxime, St-Tropez Bay, the long stretch of Pampelonne beach, Cap Camarat lighthouse rising white above the pine woods, and, out to sea, the Île du Levant and Île de Port-Cros; *(inland)* Gassin *(below)*, the Pradels range *(southwest)* and the Sauvette chain *(northwest)*, as well as Cogolin and Grimaud in the valley *(north-northwest)*.

▶ *Return to the junction and turn right to Gassin.*

Gassin *Alt 201m/659ft.*

In contrast to modern resorts, this village has proudly retained its Provençal character, with its network of alleyways sometimes linked by flights of steps.

The **Terrasse des Barri,** planted with lotus trees and exuding delightful Mediterranean fragrances, provides a **view**★ of St-Tropez Bay, Cavalaire Bay and the Îles d'Hyères; when the mistral blows, the Alps are visible *(east)*.

Around the town, there are several vineyards producing local AOC Côtes de Provence wines. The festival of St Laurent, the patron saint of the village, is celebrated on the second Sunday in August with a special meal including generous helpings of garlic mayonnaise *(aïoli)*.

▶ *Take D 559, then D 98 to return to St-Tropez.*

Hiking Tours

St-Tropez Peninsula★★

This walk cannot be completed in a single day, as the time required exceeds 11hr.

Although in high season tourism takes over the town of St-Tropez, the surrounding country presents a traditional landscape of rectangular vineyards alternating with rows of cypress trees and immaculate farmhouses *(mas)* in the shade of rustling umbrella pines. The coastline consists of the rocky headlands of Cap Camarat, Cap Taillat and Cap Lardier and the long ribbon of fine sand in Pampelonne Bay, which has been preserved from concrete invasion by the active intervention of the Coastal Conservatory.

The Customs Officers' Footpath

This footpath, which follows the whole of the Var coastline, hugging the shore, dates from the First Empire (early 19C). It was commissioned by Fouché when he was Minister and was originally intended to facilitate the patrolling of armed customs officers, who enjoyed powers as wide-ranging as those granted to the police. They were ordered to crack down on smugglers of salt and, subsequently, of tobacco and arms. Since 1976 the path has been restored and all private properties adjoining the shore are obliged to allow a passage (at least 3m/10ft wide) across their land. Walls and solid fences erected prior to that date are, however, exempt. Nearly 200km/124mi of Varois coastline are subject to these provisions.

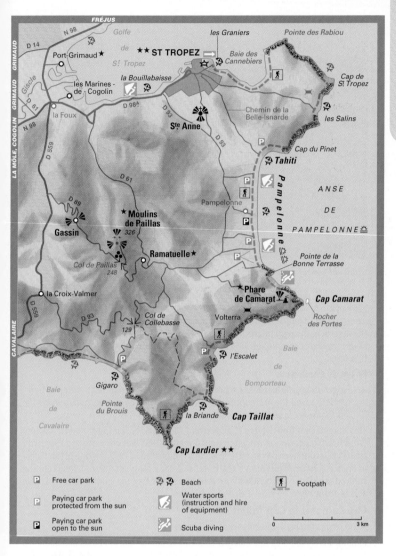

The Coastal Path *11hr.*

🚶 The path, signposted in yellow, links St-Tropez with Cavalaire beach via Cap Camarat and Cap Lardier *(about 40km/24mi):* a distance that requires more than one day of hiking.

St-Tropez to Tahiti Beach *Allow 3hr.*

🚶 The path leaves from Graniers Beach at the western edge of the harbor. It follows the contours of the coast and provides superb views of the foothills of the Maures and the overhanging red rocks of the Esterel. Via Rabiou Point and Cap de St-Tropez, the path reaches Les Salins beach, the first stopping point where refreshment is available in the open-air cafés *(guingettes)* during the summer season. The path then rounds Cap Pinet and comes out on Tahiti beach at the north end of Pampelonne Bay.

Tahiti Ceach to Cap Camarat
Allow 2hr.

> ### 😊 Tips for Ramblers 😊
>
> It is advisable to wear stout walking shoes to cross the steep rocky points where the path has collapsed and to bring plenty to drink. Avoid the hottest hours of the day when visibility is reduced by a heat haze. The sandy beaches are small at Gigaro, Briande and l'Escalet; however the path winds its way along many inlets that are an invitation to wander through unspoilt countryside.

La Briande beach, Ramatuelle

🚶 The path follows a track parallel with the long sandy stretch of Pampelonne Beach *(5km/3mi)* to Bonne-Terrasse Point. On reaching Bonne-Terrasse Bay, the path climbs the first rocks through thicker vegetation. Near Rocher des Portes there is a footpath *(right)* towards Camarat lighthouse which is visible through a forest of arbutus and tree ferns.

Phare de Camarat ★

▶ *From Ramatuelle take D93 east; turn right on the road signposted "Route du Phare" running along the promontory beyond Les Tournels camp site; park outside the lighthouse enclosure which is a pedestrian area.*

This magnificent **lighthouse** (🕐 *Open mid-Jun to end of Sep 10am-noon,2-4pm.* 🕐 *Closed during renovation works)* commissioned in 1831 was converted to electricity after the Second World War and completely automated in 1977. It is one of the tallest in France (129.8m/426ft above sea-level) and has a range of 60km/37mi. From the summit there are superb **views** ★★ over Pampelonne Bay, the whole of the peninsula and St-Tropez Bay.

Cap Camarat to Cap Taillat *Allow 2hr.*

🍴 *No refreshments available except in L'Escalet.*

🚶 After skirting Rocher des Portes, the path leads to the beach at L'Escalet passing a succession of coves which are easily accessible and isolated by great rock slabs ideal for sunbathing. This walk offers the unexpected sight of the imposing **Château de Volterra** (⌖ *closed to the public)* overlooking the bay. The path then reaches Cap Taillat.

▶ *It is possible to join the route from the customs cabin at the entrance to the car park at l'Escalet.*

The path cuts across the base of the headland and disappears into scrub vegetation dominated by ilex until l'Escalet Beach. The area boasts a wide range of forest species. Beyond these woods the countryside is carpeted with vineyards. **Cap Taillat** is in fact a growing sand bar connecting the rocky reef to the coast, turning it into a peninsula. At the very end stands a semaphore signal.

History of the Cap Lardier Estate

In Edwardian times a remarkable vineyard occupied the site of the present development and Mas de Gigaro; these date from the 1950s when the estate was sold and made into a camp site. At the beginning of the 1970s, a banking institution purchased the estate, together with a few plots of land around Brouis beach, with a view to building a marina. The residents rallied against this plan, and when the Conservatoire du Littoral bought the estate in 1976, the conservation of this unspoilt part of the coastline was guaranteed.

🚶 Cap Taillat to Gigaro via Cap Lardier *Allow 2hr.*

Most of the route falls within the **protected site**★★ of Cap Lardier run by the Conservatoire du Littoral, in charge of preserving France's coastal heritage. The path runs along an uninterrupted succession of steep cliffs from which there is a view of Briande Bay ending in the east in the characteristic silhouette of Cap Taillat.
It is possible to return to Gigaro from Briande Beach by the inland path (route DFCI) through dense pinewoods, ending at the information booth in Gigaro.

▶ *There is a car park on the sea front or on the left just before the pinewood. In season there is an information booth near the sign at the edge of the Gigaro pinewoods.*

ST-VALLIER-DE-THIEY

POPULATION 2 261

MICHELIN MAP 341 C5

This medieval village, once a Roman stronghold, is situated in the middle of a fertile plateau at the foot of the Pre-Alps and is a popular holiday destination for the inhabitants of Grasse, just 12km/7.5mi to the southeast. Its Romanesque church, old seigneurial château now housing the town hall, and line of houses along the old fortified wall attest to the rich historical heritage of this village.
🛈 *10 Place de la Tour,* ☎ *04 93 42 78 00.*

🅿 **Parking:** Park at the Place du Grand-Pré *(except on market day on Fridays in summer)* or Place St-Roch *(Friday market fall through spring).*

Sights

Church

The Romanesque church, which dates from the early 12C and was restored in the 17C, has a lovely 13C nave with pointed barrel vaulting and houses twoBaroque altarpieces. The bell-tower is decorated with arcading, a remnant from the original construction, and surmounted by an elegant 19C campanile.

Souterroscope de la Baume Obscure★

▶ *From St-Vallier-de-Thiey drive south towards St-Cézaire; turn right onto the road to the cemetery (signposted "Grotte Baume Obscure"). Continue beyond the cemetery (unsurfaced track) for 2km/1.2mi to a large car park opposite a shelter built over the ticket office.*

Kids ⏰ *Audio guide tour 1hr. Open May-Sep 10am-5pm, Sun and public holidays 10am-6pm; Jul-Aug 10am-6pm; Oct-Apr daily (except Mon) 10am-5pm.* ⏰ *Closed mid-Dec to mid-Feb.* 🎟 *7.65€ (child 3.80€).* ☎ *04 93 42 61 63. A warm sweater and shoes with non-slip soles advised. Narrow passages.*

The cave consists of an underground network of galleries. They were not brought to light until 1958 because of the long, narrow tunnels leading to them that tended to put off early explorers.
The detailed exploration of those galleries currently open to the public was eventually completed in 1980, as was the introduction of facilities suitable for guided tours.
Experts have mapped 1 200m/1 312yd of the underground network; the tour of the cave actually covers 500m/547yd and takes visitors down 50m/164ft to the **Galerie du Pas de Course**. There is a constant temperature of 14°C/57°F.
At the end of a long corridor, once filled in with clay, visitors will discover nine galleries containing features such

S. Sauvignier/ MICHELIN

Grotto de la Baume

as vast domes, natural dams forming cascades and a profusion of thread-like stalactites, resembling thin, straight spaghetti hanging down, an absolute forest of needle-shaped concretions scattered all over the ceilings. In the gallery with the gours, note the unusual color of the water brought out by the lighting, and the ground that is formed from an enormous petrified flow of calcite at the base of a stalagmite. This whole network of caves is also widely renowned for the variety of strange formations it has generated.

Grottes des Audides

▷ *Located 3.5km/2.7mi south on the N 85, then the D 4. See CABRIS.*

Excursions

Plateau de Caussols★

From St-Vallier-de-Thiey to Gourdon – 30km/19mi – allow 2hr.

▷ *On leaving the village, take N 85 towards the Pas de la Faye, then D 5 to the right, which twists and turns along the side of the mountain, affording lovely views of the St-Vallier Basin. After going through a pass, Col de Ferrier, the road overlooks the wooded valley of Nans. Leave the main road, which skirts the Audiberghe Mountain, taking D 12 leading off to the right (sign "Caussols").*

The **Plateau de Caussols,** sitting at an average altitude of 1 000m/3 281ft, is itself enclosed by higher land. It is one of the rare examples of karst relief in France. The north of the plateau features a landscape of cultivated land and meadows thanks to its fertile soil; the south, on the other hand, reflects a less orderly setting, with dolines, swallowholes and chasms forming a landscape typical of limestone relief eroded by rainwater. *Walkers should take care when near these pits and chasms, especially in rainy weather.* There is a particularly spectacular example of this feature to be seen by taking the small road to the right, leaving the centre of the sprawling village of **Caussols** to the east. The narrow road crosses the plateau diagonally to reach **Les Claps**★ (Provençal for "rocks"). These are in fact a remarkable rock chaos. The mineral nature of this feature is all the more striking for the absence of any plantlife nearby. Some stone dwellings *(bories)* indicate that man was once resident here. Turning around to face the plateau gives a view of the domes of the CERGA Observatory.

▷ *Return to D 12 and follow it for 2km/1.2mi towards Gourdon. 2km/1.2mi after Caussols on D 12, a road leads off to the left signposted "St-Maurice – Observatoire du CERGA". After passing the houses, continue past the sign "Route Privée," which indicates the entrance to the CERGA property.*

Observatoire du CERGA

🕐 *Guided tours (1.5hr) May-Sep Sun at 3.30pm.* 👁 *4.50€.* ☎ *04 93 85 85 58. www.astrorama.net.*

The **Plateau de Calern,** at an altitude of 1 300m/4265ft, is home to the various installations and equipment of the CERGA Observatory, specialised in geodynamic and astronomical research. The site is unique from a geological point of view. The observatory, inaugurated in 1974, is aimed at developing modern instrumentation for astronomy and monitoring the movements of the earth. It is associated with the Observatoire de la Côte d'Azur, which includes the observatory at Nice.

The tour of the observatory brings visitors into contact with the teams who work with interferometers (for measuring diameters of stars), the Schmidt telescope (for observing the sky), laser telemeters (for measuring the distance from the earth to the moon and to the satellites) and astrolabes (for calculating the position of the stars).

▷ *Return to D 12 and follow it towards Gourdon.*

The road continues straight to the eastern edge of the plateau and then begins its descent into Gourdon. There is a lovely **view**★ of the Loup Valley from the first big bend.

Gourdon★ *See GOURDON.*

The first major bend in the road on the way to Gourdon reveals a magnificent **view**★ of the Valée du Loup (*see Vallée du LOUP).*

WHERE TO STAY

🛏 **Villa Quercus** – *2 Chemin Blaqueirette – At the edge of the village, across from the pharmacist's shop –* ☎ *04 92 60 03 84 – claudine.henry@ wanadoo.fr –* 🕐 *Closed Nov to Feb –* 🚭 *– 4 rooms.* The main advantages of this villa are its big shaded garden, home to a swimming pool, and its pleasing covered terrace for summer breakfasts. The rooms display an interesting medley of decorative styles. Fully equipped kitchen at residents' disposal.

The Route Napoléon

In the town square, a column bearing a bust of Napoléon commemorates the Emperor's passage on 2 March 1814.

SAINTE-MAXIME ☼ ☼

POPULATION 11 785

MICHELIN MAP 340 O6

LOCAL MAP SEE MASSIF DES MAURES

The fashionable resort of Ste-Maxime lies along the north shore of St-Tropez Bay, facing south in a pretty setting protected from the *mistral* by wooded hills. Besides the fishing harbor, there's s a well-appointed marina and a beautiful beach of fine sand. In summer the town center becomes a pedestrian-only zone.

▶ **Orient Yourself:** Ste-Maxime sits on the edge of the Massif des Maures and 14km/9mi across the bay from St-Tropez on the N 98. ⓘ *Promenade Simon-Loriere,* ☏ *04 94 55 75 55. www.sainte-maxime.com.*

⛐ **Also See:** *Massif des MAURES, St-TROPEZ*

Visit

Seafront

Running along the beach, then the port, the pleasantly shaded Promenade Simon-Lorière commands fine views of St-Tropez. It is accessible to road traffic under the name Avenue Charles-de-Gaulle. Here stands the first marker on the route taken by the Allied forces in 1944 from Ste-Maxime to Langres in the north of France.

Tour Carrée des Dames

▶ *Opposite the church, facing the port.*

A square defensive tower, built in the 16C by the Lérins monks and later used as law courts, has been transformed into a **Museum of Local Tradition** (Musée des Traditions Locales – ⓞ *Open Wed-Sun 10am-noon, 3-6pm.* ⊛ *2.30€.* ☏ *04 94 96 70 30*). Ste-Maxime and its surrounding area are presented with exhibits on nature (sea), history and regional customs (arts and crafts, Provençal dress).

Church

The doorway of this church is decorated with modern ceramic tympanum. Inside is a fine Baroque (17C) green and ochre marble altar from the Chartreuse de la Verne. Note the 15C choir stalls.

Excursion

Parc St-Donat – *10km/6mi – allow 1hr.*

▶ *From Ste-Maxime take Boulevard Georges-Clemenceau, D 25 north.*

A leisure park has been laid out in the woods between Col de Gratteloup and St-Donat Chapel. The main attraction is the Museum of Mechanical Musical Instruments (**Musée**

D. Pazery/ MICHELIN

Address Book

For coin ranges, see the Legend at the back of the guide.

EATING OUT

Chez Sophie – *4 Place des Sarrasins – ☏ 04 94 96 71 00 – ⏱ Closed Nov-Dec.* Charming restaurant that epitomises the Provençal spirit: colorful decoration, wooden furnishings, terrace shaded by a plane tree, menu inspired by regional cuisine...The dishes and tasty homemade desserts are served by charming locals with a genuine Mediterranean drawl.

La Maison Bleue – *48 Rue Paul-Bert – ☏ 04 94 96 51 92 – la.maisonblue@ wanadoo.fr – ⏱ Closed 6 Nov-27 Dec.* A Provençal house entirely dedicated to pasta and its history: early advertising posters, enamelled plaques and old wrappers adorn the ochre walls of this restaurant, whose terrace is pleasantly shaded by plane trees. Naturally, the menu too pays tribute to pasta by offering a wide choice of spaghetti dishes.

WHERE TO STAY

L'Auberge Provençale – *19 Boulevard Aristide-Briand – ☏ 04 94 55 76 90 – ⏱ Closed 20 Dec-10 Jan – 15 rooms – Restaurant (☺☺☺).* Despite its unprepossessing façade, this inn offers charming accommodation in keeping with Provençal tradition. The renovated bedrooms and bathrooms have been given warm, earthy hues and the southern cuisine relies on fresh market produce.

Le Chardon Bleu – *29 Rue de Verdun – ☏ 04 94 55 52 22 – ⏱ Closed Jan – 25 rooms – ☐.* Conveniently situated at the heart of the resort, barely 150 yards from the sea, this hotel offers air-conditioned rooms with small balconies. Two rooms have a big terrace, ideal for late-morning breakfasts in the sun!

ON THE TOWN

Unlike those in St-Tropez, the cafés and pubs in Ste-Maxime are open all year round, making it a lively seaside resort both in summer and winter.

Big Pierrot's Café – *24 Rue d'Alsace – ☏ 04 94 49 16 65 – ⏱ Sun-Thu 5pm-1am, Fri-Sat 5pm-3am.* Small pub in a 300-year-old building, one of the oldest in town. The fireplace on the first floor is a recent acquisition, barely 150 years old! The house speciality here is, of course, beer.

Café de France – *Place Victor-Hugo – ☏ 04 94 96 18 16 – ⏱ Jul-Aug: daily 7am-2am Oct-Mar: 7am-8pm; Sep and Apr-Jun: 7am-midnight.* A whiff of the past permeates this brasserie, originally opened in 1852 when Ste-Maxime was a modest fishing village. Old-time photographs and an ancient mirror evoke this bygone era. The big terrace sheltered by plane trees faces the marina. Fresh oysters in season.

Bar de l'Amarante Golf Plaza – *Avenue Célestin – ☏ 04 94 56 66 66 – www.golf-plaza.fr – ⏱ Mar-Jan from 6.30pm.* Prestigious hotel bar set against a backdrop of cork oaks and Mediterranean scrubland, overlooking Sainte-Maxime and Saint-Tropez Bay. Additional facilities include a golf course, a fitness club and a large-scale game of chess.

OUTDOOR PERFORMANCES

Théâtre de la Mer – *Promenade Simon Lorière – ☏ 04 94 55 75 55/04 94 49 20 01 – www.ste-maxime.com – Jun-Sep: Check the programme (45 shows, mostly free of charge).* Every summer this open-air theatre stages concerts of classical music and contemporary pop, folk dance, and firework displays.

SPORTS AND LEISURE

Héli Sécurité – *Quartier Perrat - Z.A. Grimaud – ☏ 04 94 43 39 30 – airhelico@ aol.com – ⏱ Daily 9am-7pm.* This flying club organises recreational flights in helicopters but also ensures shuttle services between airports or resorts.

Club Nautique de Sainte Maxime – *Boulevard Jean-Moulin – ☏ 04 94 96 07 80 – www.cnsm83.fr.st – ⏱ Open school holidays: Mon-Sat 8.30am-6.30pm, Sun 1.30-6.30pm.* This water sports club organises sailing courses during the school holidays. Equipment available for rental in July and August.

Golf de Sainte-Maxime – *Route du Débarquement – ☏ 04 94 55 02 02 – ste.maxime@bluegreen.com – ⏱ Open summer 7am-8.30pm, winter 9am-5.30pm.* Superb, undulating golf course laid out over the heights of Sainte-Maxime, dominating St-Tropez Bay. Bar with terrace facing the sea.

Les Bateaux Verts – *14 Quai Léon-Condroyer – ☏ 04 94 49 29 39.* Coastall excursions from Easter to October: tours of the Gulf of St-Tropez, the inlets of the Esterel, îles d'Hyères.

SNACK TIME

La Tarte Tropézienne – *112 Avenue Charles-de-Gaulle – ☏ 04 94 96 01 65 – www.tarte-tropezienne.com – ⏱ Daily in summer 6am-8pm.* Bakery and pastry boutique overlooking the marnia, with savory snacks as well as the famously sweet Tarte Tropézienne.

MARKETS

Artisan Market – Daily on the pedestrian streets mid-June to mid-July.

Food Market – In a covered venue near Place du Marché every morning (except Monday in winter); open market Thursday morning at Place des Sarrasins.

Fair – Lively fair every Friday at the Place Jean Mermoz.

du Phonographe et de la Musique Mécanique) – ⛐ ⏰ *Open Easter to end of Sep daily except Mon and Tue, 10am-noon, 3.30-6pm; July-Aug 10am-noon, 4-6.30pm.* 🎟 *3€. ☏ 04 94 96 50 52).* The building, which recalls a turn-of-the-century barrel organ, houses an astonishing collection of 350 musical instruments and sound recording machines. Among the rare and bizarre exhibits are a melophone (1780, forerunner of the accordion), musical boxes from all periods, barrel organs and pianolas, phonographs from 1878 (Edison) to the present day, a 1903 dictaphone, a Pathegraphe for the study of foreign languages (first audiovisual machine) and even a singing bird (Bontemps, 1860).

SANARY-SUR-MER ⛱

POPULATION 16 995

MICHELIN MAP340 J7 - LOCAL MAP SEE EXCURSIONS

The charming resort, all pink and white, is lively all year round. It has a little fishing port bordered by palm trees and a bay with fine beaches well-protected from the Mistral winds by the wooded hills dominated to the north by the Gros Cerveau. The name Sanary derives from St Nazaire, who is venerated in the local church. ⓘ *2 quai du Général-de-Gaulle, Sanary-sur-Mer,* ☎ *04 94 74 01 04. www. sanarysurmer.com.*

Especially for Kids: Treat your children to a thrilling, underwater boat ride *(see Aquascope in the Address Book).*

Sights

Chapelle Notre-Dame-de-Pitié
Access via Boulevard Courbet.

The chapel was built in 1560 on a hillock west of the town and it is decorated with votive offerings, mostly naive paintings. From the stepped approach bordered by oratories there is **view**⋆ of Sanary Bay with the Toulon hills rising in the background, and the coast as far as the Embiez Archipelago beyond which loom the heights of Cap Sicié.

Tour Romane
On the port. ⏰ *Open Jul-Aug 10am-12.30pm, 4-7.30pm; off-season weekends and holidays 10am-12.30pm, 3-6.30pm.* 🎟 *Free entry.* ☏ *04 94 74 01 04.*

This 13C watchtower (21.5m/70.5ft tall), enclosed by a hotel, shelters a museum dedicated to F. Dumas, one of the pioneers, with Taillez and Cousteau, of deep-sea diving. The first floor is devoted to the old tools of underwater hunting. The second

Sanary port

focuses on diving equipment of the years 1940 to 1970. The third floor presents objects and amphoraes coming from the ancient wrecks of the bottom of bay of Sanary. Panoramic view of the city from here.

Excursions

1 **Gros Cerveau**★★ *13km/8mi – about 1.25hr.*

▶ *From Sanary take Avenue de l'Europe-Unie .*

The D 11 crosses a fertile plain culivated with fowers, vines and fruit trees.

▶ *At the entrance to Ollioules turn left onto D 20.*

At the start of the drive through terraced gardens and vineyards, the view extends both over the hillock on which the Six-Fours Fort stands and over the inner harbor of Toulon at the foot of Mont Faron. Gradually the panorama extends southeast over Toulon and Cap Sicié Peninsula from an impressive *corniche* road.

Farther on the **view**★ is magnificent: to the right, the Grès de Ste-Anne (enormous rocks riddled with caves), Beausset Plain, the Ste-Baume Massif, the Évenos hills and the Ollioules Gorges; on the left, a view of the coast.

▶ *8km/5mi after Ollioules (sign) make a U-turn to a platform.*

A short walk will reveal a marvellous **view**★★ of the coast stretching from the Giens Peninsula to Île Verte off La Ciotat.

2 **Mont Caume**★★ *23km/14.3mi northeast – allow 2hr.*

▶ *Leave Sanary on Avenue de l'Europe-Unie going east and follow D 11 to Ollioules.*

Ollioules

Old arcaded houses and a Provençal Romanesque church stand at the foot of the 13C castle. A Fête des Fleurs is held here every May, with parades, displays and sales of cut flowers (ℹ *information from the Tourism Office,* ☎ *04 94 63 11 74*).

▶ *Beyond Ollioules turn left onto N 8 which immediately enters the gorges.*

Gorges d'Ollioules★

The arid and sinuous gorges were formed by the Reppe which tumbles into the sea in Sanary Bay. As the road emerges at the northern end there is a view on the left of the Grès de Ste-Anne, a curious mass of sandstone rocks, hollowed and pitted by erosion.

▶ *In Ste-Anne-d'Évenos, turn right onto D 462.*

The road climbs a ravine dominated by the abrupt Barre des Aiguilles on the left.

▶ *Turn right towards Évenos and park the car near a cross set in a rock.*

Évenos★ *15min on foot there and back.*

Address Book

For coin ranges, see the Legend at the back of the guide.

EATING OUT

◯ **Chez Mico** – *18 Rue Barthélémy-de-Don* – ☎ *04 94 74 16 73* – ⏱ *Closed Mon-Tue off-season.* A local institution for over 35 years, this restaurant serves Meditarranean cuisine in an eclectic dining room decorated with old cooking utensils, travel souvenirs, carnival masks and witches. There's a seperate room for non-smokers.

◯ **L'Océan Jazz** – *74 Route de la Gare* - ☎ *04 94 07 36 11* – ⏱ *Closed Sat lunch and Sun.* As the name indicates, this little restaurant far from the bustle of the seafront is all about jazz. Concerts are organized Saturday nights from April through September. On sunny days the terrace is very pleasant. The cuisine focuses on Provençal dishes made from the freshest, local ingredients.

◯◯ **Restaurant du Théâtre** – *Impasse de l'Enclos – Near the theatre* – ☎ *04 94 88 04 16* – ⏱ *Closed Sun evening and Mon.* Take a few steps down and enter this U-shaped restaurant appointed with rustic furnishings. Your attention will soon be caught by the mouthwatering sight of salmon, meats, prawns and skewered game roasting in the open fireplace!

WHERE TO STAY

◯◯ **Chambre d'Hôte Villa Lou Gardian** – *646 Route de Bandol* – ☎ *04 94 88 05 73* – ⌂ – *4 rooms.* Despite its location near a main road, the colorful, minimalist decorated rooms of this recently renovated hotel are comparatively quiet. It is advisable to choose one nearer the pool. A large garden, a tennis court and a table d'hôte set up in the summer patio await your arrival.

ENTERTAINMENT

Centre National de Création et de Diffusion Culturelles – *Chateauvallon* – *info@chateauvallon.com* – ⏱ *Open Mon-Sat 9pm-noon, 2-7pm* – ⏱ *Closed Aug.* This location in Chateauvallon has in indoor theatre for 400 and an open-air amphitheatre for 1 200. The program is diverse, with theatre, music, dance, circus, and arts shows throughout the year.

SEEING THE SEA

Aquascope – 🖼 – *Quai d'Honneur (opposite the town hall)* – ♿ *Boat trips (30min)* ⏱ *Daily Jul-Aug 9am-6.30pm; Apr-Jun and Sep 2-5pm; Jan and Mar Sat-Sun and public holidays. 12€ (child 8€).* Try this unusual approach to the discovery of marine flora and fauna by boarding a semi-submersible boat affording close-up views of the sea depths.

SHOPPING

Market – Local markets are held in the port on Wednesday mornings.

CALENDAR

Les Floralies – Floral display festival in May (every 2 years).

St-Pierre et de la Lavande – Festival of the sea, every June.

Festival Brésilien – Brazilian festival in July (every 2 years).

Fête de la St-Nazaire – Patron saint festival every August, with Provençal games.

Les Voix du Gaou – Music festival of salsa, raggamuffin, soul, reggae, rock, Corsican, raï and variety music the last two weeks in July on the l'île du Gaou, pedestrian access only.

🔲 The village is a jumble of half-ruined and abandoned houses, built of grey basaltic stone, clinging to the steep rock slopes. The 13C church has a bell-tower with two bays. Over all brood the ruins of a 16C castle. Its keep, also made of basalt, stands on the edge of a volcano from which the lava slag is still visible. The platform commands a **view** of Destel Gorges, Croupatier hill, Ollioules Gorges and Gros Cerveau in the foreground, with Cap Sicié and the Ste-Baume Massif on the horizon.

▶ *Continue east along D 62 turning left at Col du Corps de Garde onto D 662.*

Mont Caume

Mont Caume rises to 801m/2 628ft, and its steep approach road offers fine viewpoints. From the top *(climb the mound)* there is a magnificent **panorama** ★★ of the coast, from Cap Bénat to La Ciotat Bay and inland towards the Ste-Baume Massif.

③ **Cap Sicié Peninsula★** *Round tour of 25km/15.5mi. Allow 2hr (not including Île des Embiez).*

▶ *From Sanary take Avenue d'Estienne-d'Orves.*

The road skirts Bonnegrâce Beach and Pointe Nègre: views of Sanary Bay and Bandol.

Le Brusc

Fishing village and resort; ferries to Île des Embiez leave from the port.

Ile des Embiez – *See Île des EMBIEZ.*

Petit Gaou

The rocky promontory pounded by the sea, once an island, resembles a Breton seascape. There is an extensive **view** of the coast and the neighboring islands.

> ### Ottoman Influence
>
> The former mayor and architect **Marius Michel** (1819-1907), nicknamed Michel Pacha on account of his love of Ottoman civilisation, added a whiff of Eastern promise by designing several houses in the Oriental style.

Grand Gaou

Accessible by a pedestrian bridge, this island was designated as a nature preserve in 2000 to keep its wild aspect. The botanical path crosses places where wooden barriers protect parcels of vegetation that are reestablishing their growth. There are special designated areas for picnics, and in summer a music and culture festival, Festival des Voix du Gaou (*see the Calendar in the Address Book*).

▶ *Return to Le Brusc and take D 16 towards Six-Fours; in Roche-Blanche bear right.*

The road runs parallel to the coast about 1km/0.6mi inland but gives glimpses of La Ciotat, Bandol and Sanary. At the crossroads there is a **view** ★★ of the Toulon harbor, Cap Cépet, the Giens Peninsula and the Îles d'Hyères.

▶ *Turn right and park next to the radio station.*

Chapelle Notre-Dame-du-Mai★★

Walk round the radio station to the chapel. ⏱ *Open first Sat of the month Oct-Apr. Call to reserve,* ☎ *04 94 25 50 39.*

The chapel is a place of pilgrimage (14 September) dedicated to Our Lady of the May Tree, also known as Our Lady of Good Protection, and contains many votive offerings. From the top of Cap Sicié there is a dizzying drop to the sea and a splendid **panorama**★★ of the coast from the Îles d'Hyères to the calanques lying east of Marseille.

▶ *Return to the crossroads continuing straight ahead.*

The narrow road cuts through **Forêt de Janas,** a fine plantation of conifers, before rejoining D 16 (turn left).

Six-Fours-les-Plages *see SIX-FOURS-LES-PLAGES.*

▶ *Return to Sanary on D 559.*

Capital of German Literature

The little port of Sanary, known to German painters in the 1920s, became a refuge for many intellectuals who had fled from Hitler's regime in the 1930s. A German refugee journalist christened Sanary "Capital of German Literature". Famous residents featured Thomas Mann and his brother Heinrich, who stayed at Villa "La Tranquille", the writer Feuchtwanger, as well as Alma Mahler and Franz Werfel. Zwieg visited the resort on his way to the United States.

After the armistice in 1940, many were able to seek refuge in the USA thanks to the intervention of President Roosevelt. However, some of the lesser-known figures were interned at Camp des Milles near Aix-en-Provence. In the port, above the bowling area, a plaque commemorates the names of these refugees and a leaflet detailing the villas that were used is available from the bookshop.

SAORGE★★

POPULATION 323

MICHELIN MAP 341 G4 - LOCAL MAP SEE NICE

In a rugged **setting**★★ the stone-covered houses and the proud belfries of the church and chapels cling to the steep slopes of a natural amphitheatre where the Roya Valley temporarily broadens out. Saorge was originally a Ligurian settlement and then a Roman colony. In the Middle Ages the town was said to be impregnable but it has yielded twice: in 1794, to the French under Masséna, and in April 1945. *Mairie (Town Hall), ☎ 04 93 04 51 23. Vallées Roya-Bévéra, ☎ 04 93 04 92 05. www.royabevera.com.*

Walking Tour

Old Town★

Park the car at the north entrance of the village.

The stepped and twisting streets, sometimes arched, make an interesting walk past 15C houses with decorative doorways and carved lintels. On the far side of the square, go straight, then right and right again to reach a terrace offering a beautiful **view**★ into the bottom of the Gorges de la Roya.

Église St-Sauveur

Built in the 16C and revaulted in the 18C, the church comprises three naves supported by columns with gilded Corinthian capitals and decorated with altarpieces. The **organ**, which was built in 1847 by the Lingiardi of Pavia, was shipped by sea from Genoa to Nice and thence to Saorge on muleback. The south nave presents an 18C canvas depicting Elijah with the Virgin and Child, a fine Renaissance tabernacle, a 15C font beneath a painting by a local artist (1532), and a Virgin in gilded wood beneath a canopy (1708). To the left is a 16C Primitive of the Annunciation over the altar.

▷ *Leave from the southern end of the village, bearing right at the road fork.*

Madonna del Poggio

⚬ᴈ *Private property.*

The early Romanesque building boasts a soaring **belfry** with six rows of Lombard bands and a fine chevet. The three naves rest on columns crowned by capitals decorated with a stylised leaf motif. This is the oldest religious building in the Roya Valley. The return to the village offers a fine **view** of Saorge and terraced olive groves.

▷ *Take a sharp right at the road fork towards the monastery.*

Saorge

Couvent des Franciscains

Open Apr-Oct daily (except Tue), guided visits (1hr) 10am-noon, 2-6pm; Nov-Mar 2-5pm. Free entry. ☎ 04 93 04 55 55.

Overlooking the village from the south, the 17C buildings of the Franciscan convent, to which the monks returned in 1969 after a long absence, are prettily set among olive trees. The church, which is in the Baroque style, has a porch surmounted by a balustrade. The bell-tower is capped by a bulbous roof of colored tiles. Small **cloisters** are decorated with unrefined but nonetheless pretty paintings on pious themes.

From the terrace, a splendid **view**★★ of Saorge, the Roya Valley and the gorges.

TABLE WITH A VIEW

Le Bellevue – 5 Rue L.-Périssol – ☎ 04 93 04 51 37 – Closed Mon night and Tue. Interrupt your tour of the covered alleys and settle in the cheerful yellow dining room with its ceiling enhanced by wainscoting. Panoramic views of the village and the Roya Gorges.

Driving Tour

Saorge Gorges and Bergue Gorges 10 39km/24mi. Allow 4hr.see Local Map for Nice.

Breil-sur-Roya – see BREIL-SUR-ROYA.

▶ Leave Breil-sur-Roya to the north by N 204.

The road to Col de Brouis (see SOSPEL) forks off to the left.

La Giandola – see SOSPEL.

Gorges de Saorge★★

The road follows the river's every curve in narrow *corniche* style beneath overhanging rocks. The Nice-Cuneo railway also passes through these gorges by way of tunnels and other engineering feats.

At the end of the gorges, there is a view between two rock cliffs of the extraordinary **setting**★★ of Saorge built in curved tiers, on a hillside clad in olive trees.

Gorges de Bergue★

Beyond Fontan, the road ascends gorges cut through red schist where the rock appears deeply colored and foliated. The valley widens out into the St-Dalmas-de-Tende Basin (see TENDE).

SEILLANS★

POPULATION 2 115

MICHELIN MAP 340 O4

Seillans is a surrealist village par excellence. First of all, it's the village that was often visited by Gounod and Alphonse Karr, and it's the place the Dadaist illustrator **Max Ernst** (1891-1976) chose to live towards the end of his life. Secondly, the ivory and pink houses cascade down the steep slope of the Canjuers Plateau at an even steeper angle than the average perched village. Quaint cobbled lanes lead up to the church and the old castle with its ramparts and fountain. Today the main activity in Seillans is the production of honey and aromatic herbs, exported to countries all over the world.

▶ **Orient Yourself:** Seillans is in the Var department, in the foothills of the Canjuers plain (see the FAYENCE Driving Tour: "Le col du Bel-Homme"). Rue du Valat, ☎ 04 94 76 85 91. www.seillans-var.com.

P **Parking:** Park at the top of the village, before the chateau and Tourism Office.

The Dada Master

Max Ernst settled in Seillans with his wife, the painter Dorothée Tanning, in 1964. A small **museum** (Dorothy Tanning Bequest: Museum – Open Jul-Aug Tues-Fri 10am-noon, 3-7pm; rest of the year 2-5.30pm. Closed holidays. 2€. ☎ 04 94 50 45 54) displays several of his lithographs, remarkable for their strong imaginative streak and sense of humour.

Walking Tour

Church

◷ *Open daily except Sunday.*

The rebuilding of the church in 1477 incorporated a few sections dating from the 11C. The interior is decorated (*right*) with two beautiful triptychs: a 15C Coronation of the Virgin painted on wood and a marble stoup (1491). From the church there is a fine view over Fayence in the plain to the Tanneron Massif.

Chapelle Notre-Dame-de-l'Ormeau

1km/0.6mi southeast on the Fayence road. ◷ *Open Jul-Aug Tue 5.30-6.30pm, Thu 11am-noon; Sep-Jun:Thu 11am-noon. Guided tours possible as part of a village tour; information at the Tourism Office,* ☎ *04 94 76 85 91.*

This Romanesque chapel, which is dedicated to Our Lady of the Elm Tree, is flanked by a bell-tower of dressed stone but marred by the subsequent addition of an open porch.

The interior contains a remarkable 16C **altarpiece**★★. In the center, a crowd of people climb the Tree of Jesse. The predella, beneath a wooden peristyle, illustrates (left to right) the life of Ste Anne, the birth and marriage of the Virgin and the Annunciation.

To the left of the altarpiece is a fine low-relief sculpture of the Assumption (17C); to the right, in a recess, an early statue of Our Lady of the Elm Tree.

To the left of the entrance there is a Roman tombstone with an inscription. The walls are adorned with numerous votive offerings dating from around 1800.

E. Baret/ MICHELIN

Shepherds' adoration in the chapel N.-D. de l'Ormeau

SIX-FOURS-LES-PLAGES ⚓

POPULATION 32 742

MICHELIN MAP 340 K7

LOCAL MAP SEE SANARY-SUR-MER: EXCURSIONS

The name comes from the Latin *sex furni,* a fortified post that was the first sign of settlement left by the Phocaeans from Massilia. During the Middle Ages the village was clustered around the summit of a hill and protected by three rows of ramparts. The Collégiale St-Pierre is all that remains from this highly fortified site. Since the 19C the villagers moved beyond these walls down to the Reynier plain, closer to the sandy beaches and wild coastline that now attract so many visitors in the summer.

▶ **Orient Yourself:** The *commune* of Six-Fours-les-Plages encompasses no fewer than 125 hamlets and districts around the central town of Reynier. There are many beaches, but nearest and largest *(2km/1.5mi of sand)* is Bonnegrâce near Sanary. Be sure to pick up a map from the Tourism Office, located along the seafront (route D 559). 🛈 *Promenade Charles-de-Gaulle,* ☎ *04 94 07 02 21. www. six-fours-les-plages.com.*

Walking Tour

Old Six-Fours

▶ *Access via Avenue du Maréchal-Juin; turn left onto a narrow road.*

The steep climb offers alternating views of Sanary Bay and the Toulon anchorage.

Fort de Six-Fours★ *Alt 210m/689ft.*

Address Book

For coin ranges, see the Legend at the back of the guide.

EATING OUT

🍽 **Le Ligure** – *60 Avenue John-Kennedy, Route de Playes –* ☎ *04 94 25 63 87 –* ⏰ *Closed 15 Nov-15 Dec, Sun evening and Mon off season.* Outstanding views can be had of Sanary Bay from the panoramic terrace of this restaurant painted in Provençal colours. The bill of fare concentrates on fish, seafood and freshly cooked pizzas.

🍽 **La Marmite** – *Quai St-Pierre,–Port du Brusc –* ☎ *04 94 34 04 81 – lamarmite@ infonie.fr –* ⏰ *Closed Jan, Sun evening and Mon except Jul-Aug.* Cosy setting with wide bay windows offering glimpses of the nearby harbor. The attractive prices and unfussy cooking are the other assets.

🍽🍽 **Saint-Pierre - Chez Marcel** – *47 Montée de la Citadelle - Le Brusc –* ☎ *04 94 34 02 52 – saintpierrebrusc@aol.com.* Located near the port, this former fishing house has a bright dining room where delicious regional specialities are served.

WHERE TO STAY

🛏 **L'Île Rose** – *242 Promenade du Général-de-Gaulle –* ☎ *04 94 07 10 56 – www.hilrose@club-internet.fr –* ⏰ *Closed Nov –* 🅿 *– 21 rooms –* 🍽 *– Restaurant (*🍽🍽*).* This small hotel is popular on account of its choice location barely 20 yards from Bonnegrâce Beach. Every morning. on opening your shutters, you will be rewarded by views of Sanary Bay and the Embiez Islands.

🛏🛏 **Hôtel du Parc** – *112 Rue Marius-Bondil – Le Brusc –* ☎ *04 94 34 00 15 –* ⏰ *Closed Nov-15 Mar – 17 rooms -* 🍽. Just 200m/650ft from the port of Brusc and its beaches, this hotel is also the ideal starting point for hikes and mountain biking in the forest of the Cap Sicié. The hotel is situated in a large house with a luminous dining room overlooking a back garden.

SPORTS AND LEISURE

Six-Fours/Embiez is one of France's designated "stations nautiques", with many water sports and activities available. 🛈 *Contact the Tourism Office for more information or visit www.france-nautisme. com.*

Hiking – In addition to the coastal walking trails (see Coastal Trails), the massif of the Cap Sicié has 5 hiking itineraries (*about 2hr each*) to explore on your own or with a guide. Contact the Tourism Office for more information.

Cycling – Six-Fours has 5 circular bike trails (with guide markings) from 10km/6.2mi to 25km/15mi. Map available from the Tourism Office.

From the platform at the entrance to the 19C fort (○–☞ closed to the public), a **panorama**★ extends from east to west over Toulon harbor, St-Mandrier Peninsula, Cap Sicié, Sanary Bay, Le Brusc and the Île des Embiez.

Collégiale St-Pierre

🕐 *Jun-Sep 10am-noon, 3-7pm; Oct-May 10am-noon, 2-6pm.* 🕐 *Closed Tue.* ☎ *04 94 34 24 75.*

At the foot of the fortress stands the church of the now abandoned village of old Six-Fours. Early Christians persecuted for their religious views fled and sought refuge in this collegiate church. Subsequently, it was occupied in the 5C, as evidenced by the altar, the baptistry and various sections of the apsidal chapel. The monks of Montmajour, then those of St-Victor, built a priory and a chapel in the 11C. The church features two naves set at right angles; in the 17C a Gothic-style nave was built. The Romanesque nave contains a polyptych attributed to Louis Bréa. In the Gothic chapels are a late-16C Flemish Descent from the Cross and a Virgin attributed to Pierre Puget.

Coastal Trails★

To follow this by the road see "Driving Tour ③ Cap Siciéa" in Sanary-sur-Mer. The first of the two hikes here is easy (6km/3.7mi), the second a bit more difficult (10km/6.2mi).

🥾 *1.5hr. Start from Bonnegrâce beach (on the edge of Sanary).* The path runs along the beaches through low thorny vegetation and over the Cap Négre to the little fishing port of Le Brusc with its busy small boats *(pointus)*.

🥾 *4hr. Start from Brusc.* From the roundabout go up the Chemin de Gardiole and, via the Chemin de Lèque, the Haute Lecques. You leave the pavement at the end of the Rue de Gargadoux *(yellow markings)*. This part of the coastal trail is called the "Corniche Merveilleuse". The schistous nature of the rock and the acidic soil, exceptional in the area, support the development of a mixed vegetation of Mediterranean coniferous trees, leafy trees (holm oak, kermes oak and cork oak), eucalyptus, and aromatic plants. Climb up to the **Chapel Notre-Dame-de-Mai** (🍃 *see Driving Tour ③ SANRAY-SUR-MER*). The trail continues until the Cap Sicié, skirting the eastern end of the massif until you reach the beach of Fabrégas.

Excursions

Notre-Dame-de-Pépiole – *3km/2mi. Allow 1hr.*

▷ *From Six-Fours drive north. After a short distance turn left at the roundabout onto a narrow road (signposted "Monuments Historiques"). Park on the terrace, 100m/110yd from the chapel.*

This chapel of yellow, rose and grey stone, surmounted by two charming campaniles, stands in a most attractive **setting**★ of pines, cypress trees, olive trees, vines and broom, against the mountainous backdrop of Toulon.

The **Chapelle Notre-Dame-de-Pépiole** (🕐 *Guided tours 3-6pm on request,* ☎ *04 94 63 23 03 or 04 94 63 38 29*) is one of the oldest early Christian buildings in France, constructed between 5C-6C. For centuries it was hidden under heavy layers of plaster which helped to preserve it. It originally consisted of three separate chapels. In the 12C great lateral arcades of blue stone were added to create a unique place of worship. The chapel on the left contains a 17C statue of Notre-Dame-de-Pépiole.

Mediterranean Caviar

Edible sea urchins, known as sea chestnuts, have been appreciated since ancient times for their fine "eggs"; they are therefore intensively harvested, leading to great scarcity on the shores of the Mediterranean. This echinoderm lives on algae, tiny animals and bacteria caught by its spines. It attaches itself to the sea by means of the suckered feet around its mouth. It moves very slowly (about 1cm/less than 0.5in a minute) by moving its spines. At certain times of the year bacterial infection can cause it to lose its spines. The edible part of the sea urchin consists of its sexual organs, divided into five branches, which are orange in the female and off-white in the male. Fishing for sea urchins is prohibited between May and August (when there is no 'r' in the month); during this period the creatures are empty. Professional fishermen, who use diving equipment, carry a gauge to check that the sea urchins are more than 5cm/2in in diameter and catch them in large nets which contain up to 20 dozen creatures.

Information campaigns designed to bring about more active conservation of sea urchins are led by the Institut Océanographique Paul-Ricard at Les Embiez and other similar institutes.

SOSPEL★

POPULATION 2 885

MICHELIN MAP 341 F4 - LOCAL MAP SEE NICE

This cool mountain village straddling the Bévéra was once the capital of the County of Ventimiglia in the 13C, then a bishopric during the Great Schism. Later it became one of the main stopping points along the **Salt Road** *(Route du Sel)* linking Turin, capital of the Kingdom of Sardinia, to the coast. Today its old houses and olive groves, surrounded by high mountains, create a picturesque backdrop for the many sports enthusiasts who come for hiking, canyoning and river rafting in the nearby Merlanson, Roya and Bévéra rivers.

▶ **Orient Yourself:** Sospel lies 19km/12mi north of Menton on narrow, winding roads. An old bridge, Pont-Vieux, connects the left bank and the right bank. ▯ *Le Pont-Vieux, Sospel,* ☎ *04 93 04 15 80. www.sospel-tourisme.com.* ▯ *Vallées Roya-Bévéra,* ☎ *04 93 04 92 05. www.royabevera.com.*

Walking Tour

The Old Town★

A map of the village is available at the Tourism Office.

Right Bank

The church and arcaded houses on Place St-Michel make a charming sight. The oldest house (Palais Ricci) to the right of the church bears a plaque recording Pope Pius VII's stay in 1809.

Église St-Michel

At the time of the Great Schism this church was a cathedral. The Romanesque bell-tower with Lombard bands flanks an imposing Baroque façade. The interior decor is pure Baroque: altar with baldaquin, huge altarpieces, *trompe-l'œil* frescoes, and gilding. A denticulated cornice runs the length of the nave walls.

In the north apsidal chapel the **Immaculate Virgin**★ is one of François Bréa's most accomplished works: a retable of the Virgin against a charming landscape thronged with angels.

Old Streets

To the right of the parvis, large stairways lead to the ruins of a Carmelite convent, now almost hidden by vegetation. Carry on to reach the remains of some fortifications, including a huge 15C corner tower and, further on, a semicircular arched gateway. Go through this gateway and follow a stairway to **Rue St-Pierre,** which runs on from the cathedral parvis. The road, which is lined by arcades, leads to the little square behind the *mairie* (town hall) in which there is a pretty wall fountain.

E. Baret/ MICHELIN

Old bridge, Sospel

In Rue St-Pierre note the emblazoned door lintels (nos 3, 20 and 29). Most of these carved stones are surmounted by a grill covering the semicircular archway and providing natural air-conditioning. There is an interesting façade (no 30) endowed with two Renaissance windows. The ground floor, in Gothic style, features a diagonal rib window and door.

Papal Revenge

When Napoléon had the pope driven out of the Papal States annexed to the Empire, Pius VII had him excommunicated from the Catholic Church.

Fountains

The economic supremacy of the town in past times is recalled by numerous sculpted fountains scattered around the village. On Place de la Cabraïa, the most imposing fountain has two levels and was used as a drinking trough. This place is in fact named after the flocks of goats that were once seen here. There are other fountains on Place St-Nicolas (the oldest), at the end of Rue de la République and on Place St-Pierre, behind the town hall.

Old Bridge★

The toll tower on the 11C bridge was destroyed during the Second World War. It has been rebuilt and now houses the *Syndicat d'Initiative* (Tourism Office) and, in season, an information center about the Parc National du Mercantour.

Left Bank

Cross the old bridge, paved with cobblestones, to visit Place St-Nicolas with its old houses and pretty paving. Beneath the arcades of the erstwhile community center, decorated with a paschal lamb in bas-relief, there is a lovely 15C fountain. Rue de la République to the right once housed a host of small businesses and enormous cellars used as warehouses by passing merchants before they settled their toll at the bridge. The houses along this road feature beautifully carved stone lintels (nos 14, 15, -23 and 51). In a recess (right, after no 51) there is an elegant Provençal fountain. The picturesque and narrow Rue des Tisserands leads to the 17C Ste-Croix Chapel.

Excursions

Fort St-Roch★

▶ *1km/0.6mi south of the village, on D 2204 to Nice. After the cemetery, take an old army road to the right (signed).*
🕐 *Guided tours (1.5hr) Apr to end of Oct Sat-Sun and public holidays 2-6pm; Jun-Sep daily (except Mon).* 🎫 *5€ (child 3€).* ☎ *04 93 04 00 70.*

This military construction was designed to block the Bévéra Valley and cover the Col de Brouis and the exit of the railway tunnel coming from Breil. Completed in 1932, it amounts essentially to an underground town, 50m/164ft deep, which was able to

---

Address Book

THE OLD BRIDGE INN

🍴 **L'Auberge du Pont Vieux** – *3 Avenue Jean-Médecin* – ☎ *04 93 04 00 73* – 🕐 *Closed for two weeks in Mar, June and Oct; and Sun evening off-season.* Comfortable inn set up on the premises of a former 14C monastery, providing generous meals that pay homage to Provençal cooking. The dining area is enhanced by wood paneling and brightly colored tablecloths. All the bedrooms have been renovated.

SHOPPING

The village is known for its production of honey and its handcrafted objects made with olive wood.

Markets – Place Gianotti on Thursdays and Place de la Cabraïa on Sunday mornings (especially honey and goat's cheese). There is a market selling regional produce on St Michel's festival day.

LEISURE ACTIVITIES

ABC d'Air – ☎ *04 93 21 11 39*. The summit of Mont Agaisen overlooking the village is a perfect starting-point for paragliding, affording fine views of the valley below. Maiden paragliding flights.

Azalpe – *2 Rue Collet* – ☎ *06 07 23 81 54* – 🕐 *Call 5-8pm.* Mountain guide available to accompany you on a canyoning excursion or to the Via Ferrata development (La Colmiane, Tende and Peille), including rental of suitable equipment.

Hiking – A list of all the signposted hiking paths starting from the village is available from the Tourism Office. There are also facilities for exploring the neighboring countryside on horseback.

survive for up to three months without contact with the outside world. The fort was part of the Alpine Maginot Line of fortifications built in the region during the 1930s. The tour covers over 2km/2.6mi of underground galleries, including the kitchens, an electricity generating station, an operations block, ventilation chambers, the firing stations – up a 45° slope served by a funicular which was used for ammunition, a small cinema and the artillery rooms (81mm mortar and 75mm gun), as well as the periscopes which enabled the inhabitants of the fort to view their surroundings. This interesting visit is completed by a museum containing a retrospective on the Alpine Army between 1939 and 1945.

Piène-Haute via Col de Vescavo★ *9km/5.6mi – allow half a day.*

▷ *From Sospel take D 2204 east. After 2km/1.2mi turn right onto a road signed "Piène-Olivetta". After 4km/2.5mi D 93 reaches Col de Vescavo (alt 478m/1 568ft) which overlooks the bank on the Italian side of the Bévéra. The road then meanders through pine trees and olive groves to the border checkpoint before the Italian village of Olivetta. Follow D 193 to the left.*

The road continues to climb up to the charming little village of **Piène-Haute**, in solitary splendor on an outcrop 613m/2 011ft in altitude. The best place to park is on the esplanade at the entrance to the village. Before setting off downhill on foot, admire the **view**★ of the old houses huddled side by side, overlooked by the castle ruins. Tiny streets crammed with flowers and bursting with color lead to the pretty square fronting the *mairie* (town hall). The church, on a rise, has a beautiful carved bell-tower and houses an unusual red marble altarpiece. Above the village, by the castle ruins, there are splendid views of the valley of the Roya and the hamlet of Piène-Basse on the border.

Hiking Tours

Botanical Trail

▷ *The path is below D 93 to the right towards the Olivetta frontier post. Go down the slope from the road towards the railway, then turn left under the bridge. A signpost near a ruin marks the start of the botanical footpath.*

⏱ *1.5hr on foot round-trip.* This delightful footpath, signposted and marked with boards detailing the plants to be seen, goes through a wood of young oak trees, alders growing in a damp area, and then scrubland which was once cultivated in terraces, and a holm oak wood.

Mont Agaisen

▷ *7km/4.3mi by car and then From Sospel take the road that runs alongside the post office and then climbs up the north bank of the Bévéra. After 1.5km/1mi, turn right and follow a road uphill towards Serres des Bérins.*

⏱ *1.5hr on foot round-trip.* The road winds its way up the hillside between orchards, offering pretty glimpses of the valley. On entering the Bérins district, take the surfaced road on the right, heading south. After a short stretch through some woods, the old army road reaches the first small forts of the fortified complex of Mont-Agaisen (⊶ *not open to the public).* Leave the car in any free space along the road to the climb. Follow the path that leads to the summit (alt 745m/2 444ft) on foot. Here and there you will come across a casemate or a firing turret. Heading due south will bring you to the edge of the summit, near a large metal cross. There is a good view of the

---

The Salt Road

Owing to its essential role in the preservation of meat and the tanning of hides, salt has always been of considerable interest to tradesmen. Provençal salt-works have supplied Piedmont since the Middle Ages. The salt was unloaded from sailing barges in Nice and transported by mule to Turin. Among the routes used at the time, the one favored by the princes of Savoy crossed Col de Braus, Col de Brouis and Col de Tende and passed through Sospel and Saorge. This strategic highway became known as the Salt Road (Route du Sel). The returning caravans carried rice from Piedmont, as well as hemp and cloth. The heavy traffic (more than 5 000t of salt a year), which by the end of the 18C was using close to 15 000 mules, obliged the authorities to improve the road and make it suitable for carts and carriages; they also drew up plans for a tunnel under Col de Tende but it was not completed until 1883.

The road, which is now embellished with works of modern art, is still the main highway between the Riviera and the cities of Piedmont.

village, the Bévéra Valley and Mont Barbonnet, recognisable by its fortified glacis. There are many other viewpoints on the summit, towards Col de Brouis, for example, or north towards the sunken valley dominated by the bare peak of Mont Mangiabo (alt 1 801m/5 909ft).

⬆ *3 hr.* The more experienced ramblers can opt for a variation on this excursion, leaving from the village and undertaking it entirely on foot. In this case, they should leave from the Groupe Scolaire overlooking the village and follow the path leading off to the right, marked "GR 52 – Mont Agaisen".

The track merges with that of GR 52. Follow the red and white blazes along this for about 1km/0.6mi. Turn left onto a surfaced road at the junction, and follow it uphill for another half a mile or so until you reach the first ruins of military buildings and rejoin the car itinerary described above.

Driving Tour

Col de Brouis Road ⑨ *21km/13mi – about 1hr.* 👣 *see local map NICE.*

This road is an extension of the Col de Braus Road (👣 *see Forêt de TURINI*) towards Turin, formerly known as the "Salt Road", linking the Bévéra Valley to the Roya Valley.

▶ *From Sospel take D 2204 east.*

There is a view to the rear over Sospel guarded by the Fort du Barbonnet.

Col du Pérus *Alt 654m/2 146ft.*

The road runs above the Bassera ravine.

Col de Brouis★ *Alt 879m/2 884ft.*

This pass takes its name from the particular type of heather-like shrub that thrives in the area, known locally as brouis. The monument above the car park on the right commemorates the last French attack of April 1945 against the German forces, who had been driven back into the valleys. A broad **view**★ opens up of the peaks on the far bank of the Roya.

The road descends two steep slopes before winding down to La Giandola.

La Giandola

Attractive mountain hamlet with a Renaissance church tower.

Beyond La Giandola the road climbs the Roya Valley which becomes ever more enclosed.

▶ *Return by the same itinerary; it's also possible to take a detour via Breil-sur-Roya (👣 see BREIL-SUR-ROYA) or go back through the Vallée de la Roya, to Saorge, 5km/3mi away. (👣 see SAORGE).*

Massif du **TANNERON**

MICHELIN MAP 341 C6

Far from the beaten path and yet easily accessible from Cannes, the Massif du Tanneron lies to the north of the Esterel, with the rounded contours and rock formations characteristic of the Maures. From mid-January through March, the countryside is covered in brilliant displays of yellow mimosas contrasting with the crisp winter sky. Situated halfway between the Lac de St-Cassien and La Siagne, the Massif du Tanneron is separated from the Esterel to the north by a valley through which the N 7 and Provençal motorway run.

The Tanneron is well known for its mimosa trees, introduced in the 19C. But this massif was once covered with sea pines and chestnut trees. The forest has been much reduced under the triple assault of man (cultivation rights have existed since the Middle Ages), the cochineal (a parasitic insect which kills pine trees), and fire. Even the mimosa trees have suffered, with two damaging hard frosts in the mid-1990s.

Driving Tour

From Cannes to Mandelieu *56km/35mi – allow half a day.*

▶ *From Cannes take N 7 west towards Fréjus. For a description of the route as far as the Logis-de-Paris crossroads ⓛ see Massif de l'ESTEREL ②.*

Then turn right onto D 237 which offers **fleeting views** of La Napoule Bay and Mont Vinaigre. Beyond Les Adrets de l'Esterel the view extends to the Pre-Alps of Grasse. The road crosses over the Provençal motorway on the edge of the Montauroux woods before skirting St-Cassien Lake.

Lac de St-Cassien

▶ *Before Pré-Claou bridge turn right onto D 38.*

The road rises through a pine wood with pleasant **glimpses** of the lake, the dam and the mountain peaks on the horizon. Near the hamlet of Les Marjoris the road winds over mimosa-clad slopes down to the River Verrerie.

▶ *Before reaching Tanneron village, turn right onto a steep narrow road.*

Chapelle Notre-Dame-de-Peygros★ *Alt 412m/1 352ft.*

From the terrace of the Romanesque chapel, there is a fine **panorama**★ of the Lac de St-Cassien, the Siagne Valley and Grasse. Mont Agel on the coast and the Alps on the Italian border stand out to the east, and the Esterel and the Maures Massifs dominate the southern horizon.

Follow signs to the small outlet where locally produced honey (*miel*) can be sampled and purchased.

▶ *Pass through Tanneron to the Val-Cros crossroads.*

The drive down reveals fine **views** of Auribeau, Grasse and the broad Siagne Valley.

Auribeau-sur-Siagne★

▶ *7km/4.3mi – leaving from the Val-Cros crossroads (alt 296m/971ft).*

A narrow twisting road sunk between banks of mimosa leads up to the charming village, which dates from the 12C, on a hill beside the Siagne. It was rebuilt in 1490 by settlers from Genoa. Pass under the 16C Porte Soubran, the Upper Gateway, and stroll through the stepped and, at times, narrow streets. The old houses (restored) huddle around the **church** (ⓛ *Open Sun 10am-4pm, call ☎ 04 93 42 25 46),* which contains a 15C silver-gilt and enameled reliquary and a 16C chalice.

From the church square the **view** encompasses the wooded hills of the Siagne Valley, Grasse and its ring of mountains, Pic de Courmettes and the Valbonne Plateau.

Starting from the church's west façade, take the stepped streets (Degrés de l'Église and Degrés Soubran) leading to Porte Soutran, a fortified gateway with a rounded arch set in a bend of a street.

▶ *Return to the D 9 (towards Pegomas), then take the D 109 towards Mandelieu-la-Napoule. Take the D 309 in the direction of Tanneron, and at the intersection make a left onto the D 138.*

Mellow Yellow

Mimosa was introduced into the Mediterranean region from Australia in 1839 and is first mentioned near Cannes in 1864. Since then it has invaded the slopes of the Tanneron Massif and brought financial success to the region. Mimosa belongs to the acacia family of plants. There are three main varieties of mimosa tree. Silver wattle (*mimosa argenté*), has bluish-green bushes that blossom in winter and can be seen thriving on the terraces west of Cannes. The small trees are cultivated and the bright yellow flowers sold both in France and abroad. Blue-leaved wattle (*mimosa glauque*) is characterised by its greyish pendant twigs and is used for decorative purposes. Thirdly, the most common variety in Provence is four-seasons wattle (*mimosa des quatre saisons*), which grows in huge swathes and flowers all year round. The leaves are light green and the delicately fragrant pale yellow balls are a familiar sight in many parks and gardens of the Riviera.

Flowering can be induced or improved by forcing techniques. Fronds are cut prematurely and shut up in a dark room for two or three days at a temperature of 22-25°C/71-77°F with very high humidity. Mimosa can also be cut when the flowers are still in bud; a special powder mixed with hot water will cause the flowers to open. Tonnes of cut flowers from the Tanneron are sold in France and abroad each year.

Address Book

COUNTRY INN

🍽🍽 **Auberge de Nossi-Bé** – *66 Route du Village – Auribeau-sur-Siagne* – ☎ *04 93 42 20 20* – *info@nossi-be.net* – ⏰ *Closed 1 Nov-15 Dec and Wed – 6 rooms – Restaurant (🍽🍽). Appealing stone house with a terrace commanding superbs views of the valley and wooded heights near La Siagne. Smallish but well-kept rooms in the rustic tradition. French cuisine.*

SHOPPING

Vial Bernard – *Les Carreiros – Tanneron –* ☎ *04 93 60 66 32 –* ⏰ *Open daily 9am-noon, 2-6pm. This honey producer's domaine, surrounded by 10ha/25acres of mimosa, eucalyptus, and citrus trees, is simply enchanting. The beehives on site, in the Mercantour and in the Alps, produce lightly scented honey that can be tasted and purchased on the premises. Other honey/wax products and greenhouse plants and flowers also for sale.*

HIKING

🥾 The Grand Duc forest has three hiking trails beginning at the picnic area. *Information available from the Tourism Office in Mandelieu.*

Road to Mandelieu★★

The slopes of the massif are covered by scrub. The drive through the mimosa down a steep hill to Mandelieu-la-Napoule is marvellous, with many **views**★★ of the Esterel, the town and its aerodrome, La Napoule Bay, Cannes and the Îles des Lérins, the Siagne Valley, Grasse and the Pre-Alps. On the horizon loom the majestic Alps.

▸ *Return to Cannes by D 92 and N 98 along the seafront.*

TENDE★

POPULATION 1 844

MICHELIN MAP 341 G3 - LOCAL MAP SEE NICE

Tende (alt 816m/2 677ft) has a breathtaking Alpine **setting**★ on the banks of the Roya, beneath the steep rockface of the Riba de Bernou. The tall austere houses beneath their shingled roofs seem to be stacked on top of one another. A jagged tooth of wall sticking 20m/65ft into the air is all that remains of the former splendor of the Lascaris family, whose castle was pulled down by the French during the War of the League of Augsburg in 1692. A curious terraced cemetery near the walls adds a bizarre touch. Tende commands access to the road over the pass into Italy and, together with St-Dalmas, it is the starting point for organised excursions to the Vallée des Merveilles.

▸ **Orient Yourself:** The old town huddles below the château ruins on the left bank of the Roya River. Tende, full of dizzying switchbacks all the way up to its peak, was once part of the Old Salt Route for Cuneo and Turin. 🏛 *Avenue du 16-Septembre-1947,* ☎ *04 93 04 73 71. www.tendemerveilles.com.* 🏛 *Vallées Roya-Bévéra,* ☎ *04 93 04 92 05. www.royabevera.com.*

Visit

Old Town★

Most of the houses, some dating from the 15C, are built with the local stone of green and purple schist. The maze of narrow streets features several carved lintels bearing escutcheons, huge overhanging eaves, and balconies on all floors. Note the Renaissance bell-towers on the chapels of the Black and White Penitents. From above the town on the site of the old castle, the **view**★ looks down onto the village, its shingled-roofed houses and bell-towers.

Collégiale Notre-Dame-de-l'Assomption

This collegiate church was built in the early 15C with green schist, except for the Lombard tower capped with a pretty little dome. The Renaissance-style **doorway** is flanked by two Doric columns resting on two lions, inspired by Romanesque art. The entablature is decorated with statues of Christ and the Apostles. The tympanum illustrates the Assumption. The inside is divided equally into three aisles by thick, green-schist (from the Roya) columns. The lords of Lascaris are buried here. The sacristy ceiling is decorated with 17C frescoes and stuccowork.

Sight

Musée des Merveilles★

Avenue du 16-Septembre-1947, opposite the Customs Office. ♿ 🧒 🕐 *Open May to mid-Oct daily (except Tue) 10am-6.30pm; mid-Oct to end of Apr daily (except Tue) 10am-5pm.* 🕐 *Closed mid-Mar to end of Mar and mid-Nov to end of Nov, 1 Jan, 25 Dec.* 🎟 *4.55€ (child 2.30€; no charge 1st Sun of each month).* ☎ *04 93 04 32 50. www.museedesmerveilles.com.*

A visit to this museum, with its modern façade consisting of 12 parallel piped columns and a square green stone from the Roya depicting rock art motifs, is recommended as the ideal complement to a walk around the sites of Mont Bégo. The history of the Vallée des Merveilles and its inhabitants is illustrated in the museum, centering on three themes: relief models and animations show the regional geology; archeology forms a major exhibit with dioramas reconstructing daily life in the Bronze Age, many casts of the carvings, the original stela known as *chef de tribu* (moved because of erosion damage) and objects discovered during excavations; modern popular and pastoral traditions are brought to life in an exhibition of objects and dioramas which show a continuity with Prehistoric life.

Changing Borders

When the county of Nice was attached to France, the Italian king Victor-Emmanuel II managed to keep the upper Roya Valley for his hunting excursions! At the end of WWII, the peace treaty with Italy, confirmed on 12 October, 1947 by a plebiscite, finally ended this situation, and the upper valleys of the Roya, Tinée and Vésubie were attached to France, thus aligning the border naturally along the waterways.

Excursion

St-Dalmas-de-Tende

Attractive resort surrounded by chestnut forests, St-Dalmas is a good jumping-off point for excursions into the Vallée des Merveilles, and offers numerous facilities for cycling, riding, skiing and hiking. The resort, with its vast and luxurious façades, reminds visitors that back in the 1930s it used to be the main frontier post on the road linking Nice to Cuneo.

La Brigue *6.5km/3.5mi southeast.* 👣 *See La BRIGUE.*

Granile

▶ *10km/6.2mi to the south. Go towards Casterino (D 91), turning left after 1km/0.6mi. The road twists for 5km/3mi through chestnut woods and Scots pine before finishing in a cul-de-sac at Granile (park the car before the first houses).*

B. Kaufmann/ MICHELIN

Old town, Tende

Address Book

EATING OUT

Auberge Tendasque – *65 Avenue du 16-Septembre-1947* – ☎ *04 93 04 62 26* – 🕐 *Closed Tue Jun-Oct and evenings Oct-Jun except Sat* – 🍴 *12.96/19.82€*. This modest restaurant sits within walking distance of the fascinating Musée des Merveilles, which presents the archeological and geological heritage of the region. Good provençal cuisine. Reasonable prices.

WHERE TO STAY

Prieuré – *06430 St-Dalmas-de-Tende* – *4km/2.4mi S of Tende by N 204* – ☎ *04 93 04 75 70* – 🕐 *Closed between Christmas and 1 Jan* – 🛏 *24 rooms: 40.40/57.17€* – 🍴 *5.64€* – *Restaurant 14/21€*. Tastefully restored former priory containing large, well-kept rooms with a modern decor and fine furniture. The vaulted dining hall opens out onto a pleasant patio. The menu offers Mediterranean cuisine. Sit down under the arbour on the terrace and admire the sight of Mont Bego in the distance.

SPORTS AND LEISURE

Lucien Bérenger – ☎ *04 93 04 77 85* – *www.berangeraventures.com.* Professional mountain guide.

Via Ferrata – Rope bridges and vertiginous canyon crossings using special mountain-climbing equipment, the course itself is quite demanding *(5hr)*, but you can also opt for the shorter version *(2.5hr). Map of the course and tickets available at the Tourism Office. 3.50€ (children 2-18 years 1€).*

Ski – Fans of the slopes can find the nearest ski resorts across the Italian border at Limone *(accessible by train)*. Cross-country skiing and snowshoeing can be found in Casterino. *For information contact the Tourism Office.*

This charming village, seemingly isolated on the side of a mountain, has an unusual appearance with its mountain houses decorated with wooden balconies and roofs covered with stone slabs. There is an impressive view of the Gorges de la Roya and *(east)* of the ridge of peaks on the frontier.

To the south of the village, a path leads either to N 204 at the foot of the valley or to the village of Bergue (or Berghe) further south.

▶ *Return to St-Dalmas-de-Tende and continue up the valley.*

The apple trees in the meadows contrast with the rock-strewn olive groves in the regions round Sospel and Breil. At a bend, Tende comes into view.

Abbaye du **THORONET**★★

MICHELIN MAP 340 M5 - LOCAL MAP SEE BRIGNOLES

Le Thoronet, the oldest of the three Cistercian abbeys in Provence (along with Sénanque and Silvacane) is surrounded by wooded hills in a tranquil, isolated spot, in keeping with the strict rules of the Cistercian Order. The abbey is situated between Lorgues (👣 *see LORGUES*) and the Lac de Carcès (👣 *see Driving Tour* 1 *in BRIGNOLES*). From the A 8, exit Le Cannet.

A Bit of History

From foundation to the present – In 1136 monks from the abbey of Mazan (Haut-Vivarais) settled in the valley of the River Florège near Tourtour, but later they moved to Le Thoronet near Lorgues and finally established themselves on land presented to them by Raymond Bérenger, Count of Barcelona and Marquis of Provence. The abbey soon became prosperous from the many donations it received, particularly from the lords of Castellane. The church, the cloisters and the monastic buildings were built between 1190 and 1190.

Like many other Cistercian abbeys in the 14C, Le Thoronet sank into decline. First internal dissension and later the Wars of Religion caused the monks to desert the premises. In 1787 it was attached to the See of Digne. During the Revolution it was sold and yet again abandoned. In 1854 it was bought by the State and saved from ruin at the instigation of Prosper Mérimée.

The restoration and consolidation work which has been carried out since then has been made even more necessary by the damage caused by the bauxite extraction site nearby and the subsidence caused by the weather.

The Poet Abbot

In the late 12C, the abbey's most famous abbot was appointed – **Folquet de Marseille.** His family came from Genoa but he gave up a career in trade to devote himself to poetry. He became a famous troubadour, quoted by Dante, and then in 1196 decided to become a Cistercian monk. In 1201 he was appointed Abbot of Le Thoronet and then Bishop of Toulouse in 1205.

Abbey Tour *1hr*

🕐 *Open Apr–Sep 10am–6.30pm, Sun 10am–noon, 2–6.30pm; Oct–Mar 10am–1pm, 2–5pm.*
🕐 *Closed 1 Jan, 1 May, 1 and 11 Nov, 25 Dec.* ⊗ *6.10€.* ☎ *04 94 60 43 90.*

Thanks to the quality of the surviving buildings (church and cloisters), and their simple but rigorous style, the abbey of Le Thoronet is widely considered one of the jewels of Cistercian architecture.

Church★

This was built in the style of the Provençal-Romanesque School.

Exterior

The building is squat, austere and rigorously geometric. It is extraordinarily similar in plan to the abbey church at Sénanque. The stonework is remarkable; the blocks have been accurately cut and assembled without mortar. The square bell-tower of stone is an exception to the architectural rules of the order, which allowed only simple wooden structures. It was permitted here because of the violent winds and the risk of fire.

In the west front there are four small windows and an oculus but no central door; instead there are two side doors opening into the aisles, both surmounted by a small window which is slightly off-center. The door on the left was for the lay brothers. In the south wall, on the opposite side to the cloisters, is a round-arched niche, one of the rare external funerary repositories in Provence.

Interior

The nave is covered with barrel vaulting, slightly pointed, supported on tranverse arches. It consists of three bays, prolonged by a fourth of the same height at right angles to the transept: only the raised arches indicate the presence of two arms of the transept which are vaulted like the nave. As at Sénanque, the eastern wall of each transept opens into two semicircular chapels which, on the outside, are rectangular in shape.

The chancel ends in an oven-vaulted apse, as at Sénanque, and is lit through three windows. It is preceded by a shallow bay, featuring a triumphal arch surmounted by an oculus. The aisles are lower than the nave and covered with rampant pointed vaulting resting on transverse arches.

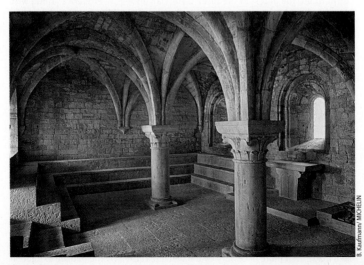

Chapterhouse

B. Kaufmann/ MICHELIN

Cloisters★

The cloisters on the north side of the church are austere and solidly built in the form of a trapezium. The south gallery is at about the same level as the church, but the west (exhibition of manuscripts and illuminated texts) and the north and east (which once supported another storey beneath a pitched roof) are lower because of the uneven ground; in all, seven steps were needed to compensate for the change of level. The galleries have transverse arches and barrel vaulting. The solid, round-headed arches which open onto the cloisters' garth (now a garden) are each divided in two by a stout column. Opposite the refectory door, projecting into the garth, is the **lavabo** where the monks washed their hands before meals. The hexagonal structure has been restored, and the water container is provided with holes and spouts through which the water ran into the basin below.

Address Book

EATING OUT

🍴 **Le Tournesol** – 9 Rue des Trois-Ormetox – Le Thoronet – 4km/2.4mi from the Abbey – ☎ 04 94 73 89 81 – ⏱ Closed Jan – 🍽. This tiny 17C house in a village alley will surprise you with its colorful walls and furniture, its homey cooking and its charming terrace giving onto the street.

CALENDAR

Rencontres de Musique Médiévale – A medieval music festival takes place in and around the abbey and church during the last two weeks of July.

Gregorian Chant – Every Sunday at noon the abbey is open to anyone who would like to attend the mass sung by the neighboring Sisters of Bethlehem.

Conventional buildings

These stand on the north side of the church near the cloisters. The door of the **library** (armarium), which is on the ground floor, is surmounted by a triangular lintel.

The **chapter-house**★ dates from the early Gothic period. The ogival vaulting, in which the ribs fan out like palm trees, is supported by two columns with roughly sculpted capitals, ornamented with leaves, pine cones, palm fronds and a hand gripping a staff. These are the only carvings in the abbey. The stone benches have been partially reconstructed. Next to the chapter-house is the **parlour** which also serves as a passage between the cloisters and the outer garden. The **dormitory** over the chapter-house is reached by a vaulted stairway and roofed with pointed vaulting supported on transverse arches. The 18 windows with double embrasures have been reglazed. At the southern end, jutting out above the cloisters, is the Abbot's chamber. The doors in the north gallery opened into the monks' room, the warming room, the refectory and the kitchen, which have all disappeared.

The **store room**, on the west side of the cloisters, has pointed vaulting and contains 18C vats for wine and olive oil as well as the remains of a press.

The lay-brother building, at the northwest corner of the store room, provided separate housing for the lay-brothers, who carried out manual labour for the monks and who lived a less restrained monastic life. It has been partially restored and comprises a refectory on the ground floor and a dormitory above.

Outbuildings

Beside the stream, the foundations of the **guesthouse** have been excavated. The tithe barn on the south side of the church was later converted into an oil mill and contains some mill stones and a mortar.

Monastic Austerity

There is hardly any sculpture or carved decoration in the church to detract from its majestic proportions and purity of line. There is, however, a gentle curve on the imposts on the pillars and the half-columns supporting the transverse arches rise to only 2.90m/9.5ft above the ground according to Cistercian tradition.

TOULON★★

POPULATION 519 640

MICHELIN MAP 340 K7

LOCAL MAP SEE EXCURSIONS

France's second largest naval port sits in one of the most secure and most beautiful harbors★★ of the Mediterranean, surrounded by pastel building façades and tall hills crowned by forts. Although cruise ships and military freighters have long since replaced the galleys of yesteryear, this modern town hasn't lost its nautical heritage, which can be found throughout the narrow streets of the old town and the qauys of the old port.

▶ **Orient Yourself:** The Old Town of Toulon is located on the Old Port, or Vieille Darse, bounded to the east by Cours Lafayette, to the west by Rue Anatole-France and to the north by Rue Landrin, which follows the line of the historic fortifications. The greater Toulon area includes the towns surrounding the harbors (Grande Rade and Petite Rade) as well as the Bay of Lazaret formed by the peninsula of the Presqu'île de St-Mandrier. Beyond are the mountain passes with Mont Faron at the summit. The Old Town is accessible to pedestrians only, and the rest of Toulon is served by buses and tour boats (see *Address Book*).

P **Parking:** The largest parking areas are located on the Place d'Armes, Place de la Liberté/Palais Liberté, and at the Centre Mayol.

Don't Miss: The most appealing areas of Toulon are the winding streets of the Old Town and the old port around the Arsenal and Quai Cronstadt. If you have access to a car, definitely do not miss the scenery and panoramic views from the top of Mont Faron.

Organizing Your Time: Plan on at least a half day for the walking tours, more if you plan to do some shopping along the Rues d'Alger, Jean-Jaurès, Hoche and Place Victor-Hugo. The afternoon can include a boat tour of the greater harbor and Presqu'ile de St-Mandrier, then one of the driving excursions up to Mont Faron or Le Coudon.

Especially for Kids: Children fascinated with ship building and model-making will find plenty to keep them interested in Toulon's arsenal and naval museums. There is also a zoo.

A Bit of History

The Age of the Galleys (17C and 18C) – One of the attractions for travelers of the 17C and 18C was to visit the galleys moored in the old port (Vieille Darse). The majestic vessels, whose triangular sails were decorated by the master sculptors and painters of the arsenal, seemed to fly across the surface of the water. The galley slaves had a different point of view. Four men were needed to pull each of the 25 or 26 oars. They were criminals of various ilk, Turkish slaves, politcial and religious prisoners, and "volunteers" driven by extreme poverty. They stayed with their oars at all times, even to eat and sleep.

In 1748, the system of galley slaves was abandoned, and the oarsmen became forced laborers, buiding ships and maintaining the harbor. This penal colony, the Bagne de Toulon, is described in detail by Victor Hugo in his novel *Les Misérables*. At its peak the colony held nearly 4 000 convicts. They formed a marginal but highly structured society, with a common feature – the chain weighing 7kg/15lb to which they were permanently attached. The woollen Phrygian caps that they wore indicated their status – a red cap for those convicted for a limited period, a green cap for those sentenced for life and a brown cap for a deserter. Many a novelist was inspired by the inhuman conditions. In 1854 the government introduced transportation to penal settlements in the French colonies, such as Guyana and New Caledonia. The Bagne de Toulon was finally closed on 1 January 1874, and all that remains, outside of literature, is a section of wall in the arsenal.

Bonaparte's First Feat of Arms – On 27 August 1793, Royalists handed Toulon over to an Anglo-Spanish fleet. A Republican army was sent to Toulon, with an artillery

Toulon Purple

In Roman times Toulon was celebrated for the manufacture of the imperial purple. The dye was obtained by steeping the color glands of the pointed conches (genus *Murex*) which proliferate along the coast in salt solution previously brought to boiling point for 10 days in lead vats. The purple obtained was used to dye silk and woollen materials. This sumptuous color was initially reserved for emperors but later its use spread, though the imperial treasury maintained a monopoly over its manufacture. The foundations of the old Toulon dye-works were uncovered during reconstruction work in the arsenal.

under the command of an obscure junior captain called Bonaparte. Between La Seyne and Tamaris, where Fort Carré or Fort Napoléon stands today, the British had built a fortification so strong that it was called "little Gibraltar."

A battery was installed facing the British fort, but was subjected to such terrible fire that the gunners faltered. The young Corsican made a sign inscribed "battery of fearless men". He soon had enough volunteers. Bonaparte set the example; he laid the guns and manned the sponge-rod. It was in this engagement that Sergeant Junot distinguished himself. As he was writing down an order dictated by Bonaparte, a shell burst nearby covering them both with flying earth: "Good!" said Junot, brushing himself down, "now I shall not need any sand to dry the ink". "Little Gibraltar" fell on 17 December. The foreign fleet withdrew after burning the French ships, the arsenal, and the provision depots, as well as taking part of the population with them. Afterwards, while Napoleon was being made a brigadier-general, Toulon came within a hair's breadth of being destroyed; 12 000 workers were requisitioned to raze "the infamous city", but at the last moment the Convention cancelled the order.

Second World War – In November 1942, in response to the Allied landings in North Africa, Hitler decided to invade the French free zone. The decision was therefore made to sink the French fleet (👆 *see below*).

On 19 August 1944, four days after the Allied landing on the Maures beaches, French troops attacked the Toulon defences, a plan of which had been smuggled out in 1942 by sailors in the Resistance. The city was liberated on 26 August. On 13 September the French fleet, which had taken part in the liberation, sailed into the harbor, where the sunken ships still lay on the bottom.

Post-war – Up to 1939 Toulon had been too dependent on the naval dockyard and very isolated by its geographic position. After the war efforts were made to diversify: the Arsenal broadened the scope of its production, commercial trade in the port was developed and new industries were introduced. The construction of holiday homes in the region sustained the building trade in the period after the post-war reconstruction boom, while improvements in the road network made the town more easily accessible.

Walking Tour

As you stroll through town, keep an eye out for the distinctive painted walls (Rue du Noyer, Rue Micholet, Ave Franklin Roosevelt) that illustrate the life and times of the town.

From the Station to the Arsenal 1

Place de la Liberté

This square is the heart of the modern town. The monumental fountain, Fontaine de la Fédération, erected in 1889 to celebrate the centenary of the Republic, is the work of André Allar. The superb Grand Hôtel (1870) in the background, with its charming old-fashioned façade, is the last remaining example of the buildings of the Edwardian era.

One of the Painted Walls of Toulon

D. Pazery/ MICHELIN

Address Book

PRACTICAL INFORMATION

Tourism Office –Place Raimu – ☎ 04 94 18 53 00 – www.toulontourisme.com.

Guided tours of the city – Guided tours *(1.5hr)* starting out from the Tourism Office are a great opportunity to discover the old town of Toulon: Jul-Aug Tue-Thu at 10am; Sep-Jun Wed and Fri at 2pm.

Train Touristique – ☎ 04 94 36 01 32. 5€ *(chiid 2.50€)*.

Departs from the Carré du Port for a tour with commentary *(50min)* of the Old Town to the beaches at Mourillon and the Tour Royale.

EATING OUT

For coin ranges, see the Legend at the back of the guide.

☺ **Al Dente** – *30 Rue Gimelli* – ☎ 04 94 93 02 50 – spaa.aldente@wanadoo.fr – ◷ *Closed Sun for lunch.* The main reason for coming here is the remarkable choice of pasta dishes and Italian specialities, with additional menus at highly affordable prices. Regular customers also appreciate the modern decor bursting with color.

☺☺ **La Chamade** – *25 Rue de la Comédie* – ☎ 04 94 92 25 58 – ◷ *Closed Aug and Sun.* This simple restaurant with the discreet façade is a local favorite for its bright and cheerful interior, carefully laid out tables with plenty of space between them for intimacy. The cuisine is fresh and modern, based on what the chef finds in season at the market that week.

☺☺ **L'Eau à la Bouche** – *54 Rue Muiron* - ☎ 04 94 46 33 09 ◷ *Closed Easter vacation, 1-6 Jun, Dec holidays, Mon (except Jul-Sep) Sat lunch and Sun.* Situated next to the Mourillon arsenal on the route to the Tour Royale, this restaurant is decorated with a naval theme. The menu is drawn up on a chalk board, with plenty of seafood specialities.

☺☺☺ **Chez Daniel "Restaurant du Rivage"** – *La Seyne-sur-Mer – 4km/2.4mi south of La Seyne by Route de St-Mandrier and country lane* – ☎ 04 94 94 85 13 – ◷ *Closed Nov, Sun evening and Mon Sep-Jun.* A small rocky inlet is the choice setting for this seafood restaurant that knows the true meaning of Provençal life. The freshly caught fish offered to diners may come from the sea or from the big fish tank set up on the premises. One of the dining rooms proudly displays a collection of old barouches and farming tools.

WHERE TO STAY

☺ **Les 3 Dauphins** – *9 Place des 3 Dauphins* – ☎ 04 94 92 65 79 – *14 rooms* – ☐. The windows of this recently renovated hotel give onto a tiny square dominated by a bust of Raimu. The smallish rooms have been tastefully appointed and decorated in cheerful shades. Charming welcome and service.

☺☺ **Grand Hôtel Dauphiné** – *10 Rue Berthelot* – ☎ 04 94 92 20 28 – contact@ grandhoteldauphine.com – ☐ *55 rooms* – ☐. This centrally located hotel is the perfect starting-point for a tour of the old city and its intricate maze of streets. The lively rooms hung with printed fabric are above all functional.

☺☺ **Val'Hôtel** – *Avenue René-Cassin, ZA Paul Madon – La Valette – Take exit 5 off the A 57, behind the Leroy-Merlin store, follow signs to ZI de Toulon-la-Valette* – ☎ 04 94 08 38 08 – www.val-hotel.com – ☐ – ☐ – ☐ *42 rooms* – ☐ – *Restaurant (☐).* This hotel offers several advantages: a lush garden setting; tlarge, colorful rooms with balcony or terrace; and inexpensive weekend rates. Hopefully, these features will soon make you forget the motorway exit nearby.

☺☺ **La Corniche Best Western** – *17 littoral Frédéric-Mistral across from the Port St-Louis and near the Mourillon beaches* - ☎ 04 94 41 35 12 - info@cornichehotel.com - ☐ *- 80 rooms* - ☐. This hotel just two steps from the beaches at Mourillon has views over the sea, perfect for those looking for a seaside holiday atmosphere.

☺☺☺ **New Hôtel de l'Amirauté** – *4 Rue Adolphe-Guiol* – ☎ 04 94 22 19 67 – *58 rooms* – ☐. In the center of town, this hotel is a good opportunity to combine a business trip with the delights of tourism. The decor is reminiscent of the large luxury liners of bygone times. Functional, efficiently soundproofed rooms.

ON THE TOWN

Like many big cities, Toulon swarms with people. The city is lively at night as well as by day, thanks to the many bars, cafés and restaurants. Request a list of bars and restaurants that feature nightly concerts, karaoke, dancing, piano bars, etc., from the Tourism Office.

Café-Théâtre de la Porte d'Italie – *Place Armand-Vallée* – ☎ 04 94 92 99 75 – *Check the programme of events.* This café-théâtre presents clarinet and jazz concerts, stand-up comedy and pantomime shows year round.

Opéra de Toulon – *Boulevard de Strasbourg* – ☎ 04 94 92 70 78 / 04 94 93 03 76 – operadetoulon@wanadoo.fr. Built in 1862, the Opéra de Toulon is ranked 2nd in France on account of its seating capacity and remarkable acoustics. The 2005-2006 season included *The Magic Flute, Pétrouchka, Aïda, Boléro*, and a Wagner festival.

Zénith-Oméga – *Place des Lices* – ☎ 08 36 68 06 86 – www.zenith-omega-toulon.com. This concert hall organises various events such as stage productions, classical concerts, pop music, alongside international fairs and exhibitions.

TRANSPORT

Pedestrian area – The district in the old part of town bordered by Rue Anatole-France, Avenue de la République, Avenue de Besagne and Boulevard de Strasbourg is closed to traffic.

Buses – The RMTT (☎ 04 94 03 87 03, www.rmtt.com) provides an efficient bus service covering Toulon and its outskirts. Plans, timetables and tickets can be obtained from the newsstand on Place de la Liberté.

Boat shuttle service – SITCAT/RMTT on Quai Cronstadt or 720 Avenue du Colonel-Picot – ☎ 04 94 03 87 03. There are several daily services to and from La Seyne-sur-Mer, Les Sablettes, Tamaris and St-Mandrier-sur-Mer.

These lines are part of the local transport system and they charge the same rates as the buses.

Pass Téléphérique – This day pass is good for the entire RMTT network (bus and boat) and allows RT access to the téléphérique on Mont Faron. 5€.

CULINARY SPECIALITIES

The café terraces on Quai Cronstadt provide a good view of the life of the old port – Bar du Soleil, La Gourmandise and Le France. The natives of Toulon (moccots) particularly enjoy l'escabèche de sardine, la cade (a flat cake made from chickpeas, similar to socca in Nice), la pompe à l'huile (a hard cake, oiled and flavoured with orange water) and the famous sweet doughnut (chichifregi) which can be bought from the stalls in the Lafayette market. Several restaurants specialise in fish dishes (Place du Théâtre and Rue Jean-Jaurès).

In Mourillon many restaurants have terraces which are ideal places to sit and try the seafood dishes (Corniche Henri-Fabre, Port St-Louis).

SHOPPING

The best place to go shopping is the area around Rue Jean-Jaurès, Rue Hoche, Place Victor-Hugo and Rue d'Alger. Rue Lamalgue (near the Port St-Louis) is a good market street for gourmet treats.

Provençal Market – Tuesday through Sunday mornings on the Cour Lafayette.

Côté Tissus – 8 Rue de la Fraternité – ☎ 04 94 46 37 92 – ◷ Tue-Sat 9am-noon, 2.30-7pm. Delightful boutique with stone walls that sells Provençal fabric. The arch on the right reminds visitors that a river flowed through the premises over 100 years ago.

Les Navires de la Royale – 30 Rue des Riaux – ☎ 06 14 45 19 38 – ◷ Mon-Sat 9am-noon, 2-6pm. Amateur sailors should make a point of visiting this shop, owned by Jean-Michel Delcourte, an enthusiastic lover of all things maritime! His days are spent making and restoring all sorts of boats, ranging from yachts to schooners to catamarans.

Palmer – 62 Cours Lafayette – ☎ 04 94 92 22 65 – ◷ Tue-Sat 8am-12.30pm, 3-7pm. Over 150 herbs and spices from all corners of the world are sold in this colorful little boutique. Also dried fruits, beans, nuts... the friendly owner is more than happy to give advice.

Puyricard – 10 Boulevard Berthelot – ☎ 04 94 91 64 10 – ◷ Mon afternoon to Sat 9am-7pm. This prestigious chocolate boutique sells delightful pralines, ganaches, pâtes d'amande, caramels, calissons, candied fruits, sugared chestnuts, and nougat de Sault, all direct from its kitchens in Aix-en-Provence.

Grosso – 9 Rue Lamalgue – ☎ 04 94 46 37 22. Monsieur Grosso has been making cheeses for over 25 years, and 70% of the cheeses in his boutique come from his own farms nearby. Known for his brebis and goats' cheeses, he also sells Iberian ham and Corsican dried sausages.

HAVING A DIP

Mourillon beach ◻ – To the east, along Littoral Frédéric-Mistral, between Fort St-Louis and the water sports center. First-aid posts, restaurants, bathroom facilities. To avoid paying the fee charged by the Mourillon car park, go there by bus ! Lines 3, 13 and 23 (Mourillon) or 7 and 23 (Magaud and Méjean coves) will drop you at the beach. The long Toulon beach, separated from the road by a large park, consists of four curved stretches of coastline covered with fine sand or gravel, or a combination of both, depending on their location. The lands descends into the sea on a gradual slope and bathers are sheltered by the piers.

Méjean and Magaud beaches – From Le Mourillon, follow directions to La Garde-Le Pradet. At the entrance to La Garde, Chemin de la Mer leads to two natural sandy beaches, the twin coves of Magaud (on the left) and Méjean (on the right).

SIT BACK AND RELAX

Le Tigre – Sommet du Mont Faron – ☎ 04 94 88 08 00 – ◷ Jun-Sep: daily 9.30am-10pm; Oct-May: daily 10am-6pm. This café-restaurant perched atop Mont Faron commands outstanding views of Toulon anchorage. The Souza family, who own the nearby zoo, settled here in April 2000 and will be delighted to explain the local sights to you (binoculars available). Warm welcome.

Bar à Thym – 32 Boulevard de Cunéo – ☎ 04 94 41 90 11 / 04 94 41 90 10 – www.barathym.com – ◷ Mon-Tue 6pm-1am; Wed-Sat 6pm-3am; May-Sep 6pm-5am. Popular watering hole for the younger generation. The impressive choice of beers (over 100, including 12 draught beers) is a definite asset. Choose between the live concerts (Tue-Wed-Thu) or the evenings run by a disc jockey. Special evenings on a particular theme are also organised (Fri-Sat).

On either side of the square, Boulevard Strasbourg and Avenue du Général-Leclerc (built on the site of the former fortifications) form the main axis of the town, separating the old town to the south from the new town to the north. The Opéra Municipal (1862), formerly the largest auditorium outside Paris, was the center of attraction in the evenings until just before the Second World War. The many local cafés and cabarets helped to give this district a festive atmosphere.

Place Victor-Hugo

Farther on you will discover one of the façades belonging to the Théâtre de Toulon, one of France's finest regional theatres. Go around the building to admire the principal façade, recently restored, and to enjoy Place Victor-Hugo and its lively sidewalk cafés.

▶ *Take Rue Jean-Jaurès and turn left on Rue-Anatole France.*

Place d'Armes

The building on this square was commissioned by Colbert as a venue for him to review his troops, originally called Champ de Bataille. It soon became a highly popular meetingplace among local nobility and officers leaving on overseas assignments, featuring many restaurants and cafés, bandstands, etc. It was also home to the headquarters of leading daily newspapers such as *Le Petit Marseillais.*

Corderie

To the south of Place d'Armes. ⚬— *Military property, not open to the public.*

This building (320m/1 050ft long), designed by Vauban to house the naval rope factory, now houses the navy's administrative offices. The fine **door**★ (1689) came from the former Jesuit college and was added to the façade in 1976. Magnificent allegories of Law (Loi) and Might (Force) frame the top floor.

▶ *Continue on Rue-Anatole France.*

Musée de la Marine★

♿ ⏱ *Open Apr-Sep 10am-6.30pm; Oct-Mar daily (except Tue) 10am-noon, 2-6pm.* ⏱ *Closed mid-Dec to mid-Jan, 1 May.* 👁 *4.60€ (children under 18 free).* ☎ *04 94 02 02 01. www.musee-marine.fr.*

Entrance to the Naval Museum is through an impressive 18C doorway of four marble columns supporting a pediment, flanked by statues of Mars (left) and Bellona (right). On entering, the visitor is transported straight into the Quai de l'Artillerie and the old arsenal – the subject of this large, likelife fresco was taken from a painting (18C) by Joseph Vernet. Note the sky painted in gold leaf. On the ground floor there are large-scale models of a frigate, La Sultane, and of an 18C vessel, the *Duquesne*. The room is decorated with statues of great 17C admirals carved in wood by Puget's pupils and an impressive figurehead of Neptune. Fine paintings by Vernet's pupils, drawings and other exhibits recall Toulon's seafaring history and its prison. Note in the stairwell another figurehead, Bellona in gilded and painted wood (1807). On the first floor there is an interesting collection of model ships and submarines from the 19C to the present.

Arsenal Maritime

The naval arsenal covers some 240ha/593 acres overall and employs in the region of 6 300 civilians. Its main activity is the maintenance of the French Mediterranean fleet: frigates, aircraft carriers, sloops, submarines and minesweepers. Some of the dry docks date from the 17C.

A Military Past ②

The Port★

Construction of the old port (Vieille Darse or Darse Henri-IV) began in 1589 on the orders of the Duke of Épernon, Governor of Provence. Expenses were borne by the town of Toulon which imposed a 25% tax on olive oil. The two breakwaters, closing the harbor on the south side, except for a 30m/100ft wide passage across which a chain was slung, were completed in 1610.

At that time there was no royal fleet; when the king required ships, he leased them from lords and captains who had them built, armed and equipped. It was Richelieu who created a military arsenal to build and repair warships. Under Louis XIV the port proved too small and Vauban had the new port (Darse Neuve) excavated between 1680 and 1700. This became the naval port while the old port was turned over entirely to merchant shipping. In the 19C the navy needed yet more space, and in 1836 an annexe, which is still in use, was built at Mourillon. In 1852 Napoleon III established the harbor at

Castigneau but 10 years later the port was again declared too small and the emperor created the Missiessy Harbor.

Quai Cronstadt

Attracted by the shops and cafés, an animated crowd throngs the waterfront. The tall modern buildings with their many-colored windows form a screen between the old port and the old town. The only reminders of the past are the famous **atlantes**★ by Pierre Puget, which support the main balcony of the old town hall.

The Port Today

While retaining its position as a naval port, Toulon is increasing its commercial role. Merchant shipping is directed to the new facilities in Brégaillon Bay on the west side of the inner harbor, while the east side is used by the passenger ferries going to the Îles d'Hyères, Corsica and Sardinia and by pleasure boats and cruise liners throughout the year.

Boat Tour: Petite Rade and Grande Rade★

🕐 *Tour with commentary (1hr) from landing-stage on Quai Cronstadt, beside the Préfecture Maritime, mid-Apr to end of Oct mornings and afternoons. ⮾ 8.50€. Reservations from SNRTM, 1247 Route du Faron, ☎ 04 94 93 07 56.*

The tour of the inner and outer harbors leaves from Quai Cronstadt in the old port. The Toulon Roads are home to the Force d'Action Navale, which includes two aircraft carriers, *Foch* and *Clemenceau*, the largest vessels in the French navy. They alternate between time in port and time on duty patrolling the Mediterranean. The military port is lined with naval vessels: minesweepers, anti-submarine or missile-launcher frigates and, sometimes, the slender, dark contours of a nuclear submarine.

The tour then passes the naval graveyard, where ships at the end of their useful life wait to be broken up, and approaches La Seyne Port, with its lifting bridge and the large area once occupied by the shipyards.

The Tamaris coast road leads to Balaguier Bay, where there are two forts, Balaguier and l'Ayguillette. The structures on piles in the centre of the bay mark the position of mussel beds. The tour returns via Lazaret Bay, along the St-Mandrier Peninsula and the long sea wall, which affords excellent **views**★ over Toulon, stretched out between the sea and mountains.

▶ *At the roundabout Général-Bonaparte, follow the Avenue de la Tour-Royale.*

Tour Royale

⛌ *Closed for renovations. ☎ 04 94 02 02 01.*

Known also as the Grosse Tour or Mitre Tower, this was built by Louis XII in the early 16C for defensive purposes (its walls are 7m/23ft thick at the base). It then served as a prison. From the watchpath there is a lovely **panorama** ★ of Toulon, with Mont Faron looming beyond it, the anchorages and the coast from the Gien Peninsula to Cap Sicié.

Atlantes by Puget on the old town hall, Toulon

J.-L. Gallo/ MICHELIN

Old Town★ ③

The ancient heart of Toulon, with its characteristic confusion of streets, is bounded to the east by Cours Lafayette, to the west by Rue Anatole-France and to the north by Rue Landrin, a perimeter which follows the line of the fortifications in the reign of Henri IV. A long-term renovation plan started in 1985 has already restored many of the charming façades and fountains of this picturesque old quarter.

▶ *Enter the Place de l'Amiral-Senès then turn right onto the Rue Notre-Dame.*

Église St-Louis

This church is a fine example of neo-Classical architecture, built in the late 18C in the form of a Greek temple. It comprises three naves separated by a double Doric colonnade supporting a coffered vault. Ten Corinthian columns in the choir support a windowed cupola decorated with a foliage frieze. The pulpit is elaborately carved.

▶ *Continue on the Rue Vezzani.*

The 18C reproduction of a ship's prow seems to sprout out of a wall, in homage to the shipbuilding of the town.

▶ *Take the Rue Pomet right.*

The curious fountain of the Place du Globe evokes the Bagne of Toulon.

Maison de la Photographie, Musée de la Figurine

🕐 *Tues-Sat 10am-12.30pm, 1.30-6pm.* ⊙ *Free entry.* ☎ *04 94 93 07 59.*

Two museums in the former public bath house include the Musée de la Photographie, which hosts regular temporary exhibitions, and the Musée de la Figurine, with 3 000 figurines on display in dioramas of historic scenes, such as Bonaparte's campaign in Egypt.

▶ *Take the Rue du Noyer, just off the Place Raimu. Have a peek on the right to see the mural painting on the Rue Micholet. Return to the Rue de la Glacière (with its vaulted passages) and turn left, then follow the Rue Andrieux.*

Fontaine des Trois-Dauphins

The character of Place Puget is embellished by this curious fountain sculpted in 1780 by two local artists with plants growing in its basins. The three intertwined dolphins are covered in moss and calcium deposits, on which grow ferns, a fig tree, a medlar and an oleander! Place Puget is pleasantly shaded and the cafés surrounding it are ideal places for sitting and enjoying the coolness.

Northwest of Place Puget is **Place des Trois-Dauphins** containing a bust of Raimu.

▶ *Return to Place Puget and go down the Rue Hoche.*

Rue d'Alger

This modernized pedestrian precinct is the main commercial street leading to the old port, Vieille Darse.

Toulon naval harbour

Félix Mayol

The Mayol Center and Stadium perpetuate the memory of the comedian who was the first of a long line of performers from Toulon. Félix Mayol (1872-1941) was 20 when he started the fashion for the quiff of hair that characterised his silhouette as well as for the sprig of lily of the valley that he always wore in his buttonhole. In 1910, when he was the comedian at a café-concert in Paris, he bought the hall where he was appearing and rechristened it *Concert Mayol*. From his home town he hired comedians whose fame had not yet spread beyond the Toulon district – including Raimu, Sardou, Tramel and the singer Turcy – who were ironically named *Des Comiques à l'Huile* by Parisians at their first performances. During his career Mayol produced more than 500 works and light comedies.

▶ *Turn left onto the Rue Seillon, then follow the Rue de la Fraternité.*

Église St-François-de-Paule
🕐 *Open Sun (during services), and the rest of the week on advance request.* ☎ *04 94 92 28 91.*

This small church was built in 1744 by the Recollects. Its double-arched façade and Genoan bell-tower identify it with the Nice Baroque style.

▶ *Backtrack to the square and turn right at the first street.*

Rue Méridienne and Place à l'Huile lead to Place de la Poissonnerie which for several centuries accommodated the covered Fish Market (Halles aux Poissons), one of the livelier spots in Toulon. The last market building was demolished in 1898.

▶ *Go up the Rues Pressensé, then Rue des Boucheries.*

Cathédrale Ste-Marie
The cathedral was constructed in the 11C and restored in the 12C. In the 17C it was enlarged and the classical façade was erected. The bell-tower dates from 1740. Inside is a fairly dark interior, mixing Romanesque and Gothic, since the 17C architects retained the plan of the earlier building.
There are several interesting works of art: in the north aisle, an Annunciation by Pierre Puget; in the south aisle, a canvas by J-B Van Loo, the *Triumph of the Eucharist,* and one by Pierre Puget, *The Vision of St Felix of Cantalice.* The elaborately carved pulpit dates from 1824, and the Baroque altar in marble and plasterwork was designed by a pupil of Puget.

▶ *Continue to the Cour Lafayette.*

Cours Lafayette
The vegetable and flower market held here every morning (except Monday) is a noisy, bustling, brightly colored occasion.

Musée du Vieux Toulon
🕐 *Open Mon-Sat 2-5.45pm.* 🕐 *Closed public holidays.* ✑ *Free entry.* ☎ *04 94 62 11 07.*

This museum, located in the headquarters of the old bishopric, has two galleries displaying maps, engravings and paintings recalling great moments in the history of the city since the Middle Ages. The display cases contain ceramics, statuettes, costumes and exhibits of Provençal traditions. In the second gallery, there is a lovely relief map of the city, made in 1880.

▶ *Leave the Old Town by the Rue Garibaldi.*

Porte d'Italie
This bastioned gate, built in 1790 on the site of ancient fortifications, is the only remnant of the defences which surrounded Toulon. Honoré de Balzac used it as a backdrop when Vidocq made use of a funeral cortège to help him escape from the town.

Sights

Musée de Toulon et du Var
🕐 *Open 9.30am-noon, 2-6pm; Sat-Sun 1-6pm.* 🕐 *Closed public holidays.* ✑ *Free entry.* ☎ *04 94 36 81 10.*

This museum occupies the right wing of a Renaissance-style building. The left wing is reserved for the Museum of Art *(see below)*. Two galleries on the ground floor house the stuffed zoological collection (birds, mammals, primates etc). Note the two large sperm whales' jaws.

TOULON

Musée d'Art

🕐 *Open 1-7pm (Sep-Jun until 6pm).* 🕐 *Closed Mon and public holidays.* ✏ *Free entry.* ☎ *04 94 36 81 01.*

The Flemish, Dutch, Italian and French Schools (16C-18C) are all represented in the museum's collections, which also feature works by 19C artists, including a large number of Provençal painters, such as the Toulon landscapist Vincent Courdouan. The museum also possesses a very eclectic collection of contemporary painting and sculpture, exhibited in rotation.

Jardin Alexandre-I

This garden is home to some attractive trees, including magnolias, palms and cedars. The bust of Puget is by Injalbert and the 1914-18 War Memorial is by Honoré Sausse. Look for the water fountain by Hercule called, appropriately, "Fontaine du Buveur" (Drinker's Fountain).

Excursions

Mont Faron★★★

This small limestone massif of Mont Faron (*alt 584m/1 916ft*), bordered by deep valleys, dominates the city of Toulon. It is a pleasant drive in summer over pine-clad slopes, providing good **views**★ of Toulon, the inner and outer harbors, the St-Mandrier and Cap Sicié Peninsulas and Bandol.

Téléphérique du Mont Faron★

▶ *Take Boulevard Ste-Anne and follow signs ("Téléphérique du Mont Faron") to the cable-car station in Avenue Perrichi. At busy periods it is possible to park below the station on the left.*

🕐 *Operates Feb-Nov 9.30am-noon, 2-6.30pm (5.30pm in winter)* 🕐 *Closed Dec-Jan, public holidays (except 14 Jul and 15 Aug), and Mon (except in summer).* ✏ *5.80€.* ☎ *04 94 92 68 25.*

The cable-car ride (*6min*) offers fine **views**★ over the town, the harbor and the limestone cliffs circling Toulon. To the left the remains of many small forts can be seen. The view from the terrace of the upper station is for customers only. A pleasant view can also be had by walking about 10m/33ft to the left along the access road to Mont Faron.

Musée-Mémorial du Débarquement en Provence★

♿ 🕐 *Open Jul-Sep 9.45am-12.45pm, 1.45-6.30pm (last admission 1hr before closing time); May-Jun daily (except Mon) 9.45am-12.45pm, 2-6pm; Oct-Apr daily (except Mon) 9.45-12.45am, 2-5.30pm.* ✏ *3.80€.* ☎ *04 94 88 08 09.*

Installed in the Beaumont Tower left of the road is the memorial to commemorate the liberation of the southeast of France by the Allies in August 1944. The first section is devoted to the memory of the English, American, Canadian and French who took part. In the second part there is a diorama of the liberation of Toulon and Marseille and a cinema (*15min documentaries, filmed during the landing*).

From the terrace (*accessible during a tour of the museum*) there is a magnificent sweeping **panorama**★★★ (*three viewing tables*) of Toulon, the harbors, the Mediterranean, and the islands and mountains all around Toulon.

Zoo

Kids ♿ 🕐 *Open May-Sep 10am-6.30pm; Oct-Apr 2-5.30pm. Closed when raining.* 📷 *7€ (child 5€).* ☎ *04 94 88 07 89.*

This zoo specializes in the reproduction of endangered animals, particularly snow panthers and ocelots. Other animals include lions, tigers, hyenas, bears and monkeys.

Solliès-Ville

▶ *15km/9.3mi northeast – 1hr 30min. From Toulon take A 97 motorway. At the La Farlède junction follow directions to La Farlède and then D 67 to Solliès-Ville.*

The old town of Solliès-Ville clings to the side of a hill overlooking the rich Gapeau Plain. Below lies Solliès-Pont, a busy market town in a region famous for its cherry orchards and its fig trees. Solliès-Ville markets more than three-quarters of the French production of figs.

The **church** *(Same hours as the Maison Jean-Aicard)* with two naves combines Romanesque traits with Gothic arches. The monolith at the high altar is thought to be a 15C ciborium, the walnut organ case from 1499, and the crucifix on the pillar from the 13C. There is a 17C altarpiece (left) and another from the 16C near the pulpit. The lords of Solliès are buried in the crypt.

Maison Jean-Aicard

🕐 *Guided tours (1.75hr) May-Oct (except Sun, Mon mornings and Tue) 10am, 2.30pm, and 4.30pm; Nov-Apr the 1st and 3rd week of each month at 10am, 2pm, and 4pm, Sun 2pm and 4pm; 2nd and 4th week of each month Wed-Fri 10am, 2pm and 4pm, Mon 2pm and 4pm.* 🕐 *Closed Pentecost, Easter, 1 Nov, 25 Dec, 1 Jan.* 📷 *Free entry.* ☎ *04 94 33 72 02.)*

This is the house of the poet, novelist and dramatist Jean Aicard (1848-1921) which has been converted into a small museum. He became a member of the Académie Française in 1909.

On **Esplanade de la Montjoie**, the ruined castle of the Forbins, lords of Solliès, commands a beautiful **view**★ of the Gapeau Valley and the Maures Massif.

Driving Tours

The roads used in these excursions, although serving military installations, are classified as part of the civilian network. Traffic is permitted up to the entrance of these installations without formality, but the military authorities categorically forbid anyone to enter certain places indicated by notices and signposts, particularly at the immediate approaches to the forts of Croix-Faron, Lieutenant-Girardon and Cap Brun.

1 **Tour of the Harbors**★★ *17km/10.5mi south. Allow 1hr.*

▶ *Leave Toulon by highway A 50, then D 559 and turn left towards La Seyne.*

La Seyne-sur-Mer

La Seyne, built beside the bay which bears its name, looks eastwards towards the inner harbor. It has a port for fishing boats and pleasure craft but is basically an industrial town that depended for its livelihood upon the naval shipyards. These were founded in 1856, when they built ships for the merchant navy, as well as producing some of the most outstanding vessels of the war fleets.

A small bay, bordered by the forts of Éguillette and Balaguier built in the 17C to enclose, with the Tour Royale, the entry of the Petite Rade, allows a good overview of Toulon, Le Faron and Le Coudon.

The Unusual Military Career of the St-Mandrier Peninsula

The hill of La Croix aux Signaux, a secret German naval base, was from September 1943 to August 1944 an assembly base for midget submarines which left via an access tunnel ending up on Cavalas beach. In 1929, however, the Marine Nationale Française had buried there (14m/46ft deep) two enormous gun turrets each holding two 340 guns, 17m/56ft long, covering a sector from Le Lavandou to La Ciotat! Shelling preparations for the landing in Provence in 1944 brought an end to development of this base.

It was from the rifle range at St-Mandrier that the first French liquid-powered rocket was launched in March 1945, inaugurating the European space race.

Fort Balaguier

🕐 *Open mid-Jun to mid-Sep daily (except Mon) 10am-noon, 3-7pm; mid-Sep to mid-Jun daily (except Mon) 10am-noon, 2-6pm.* 🕐 *Closed in Jan, 1 May, 25 Dec.* 🎫 *2€.* ☎ *04 94 94 84 72.*

The fort was recaptured from the English in 1793 by the young Napoleon. Set up in the fort's rooms, with walls 4m/13ft thick, is a naval museum containing an interesting collection of model ships and memorabilia from the Napoleonic era. On the walls hang seascapes and paintings of the Toulon region.

The 17C chapel contains objects relevant to the Toulon galleys and naval prisons: registers, chains and works of art made by the prisoners.

From the terrace overlooking the fort's garden and its aviary, there is a remarkable **view**★ of the coastline from Toulon to the Île du Levant.

Tamaris

George Sand wrote several of her novels in this shaded resort on the hillside. From here you'll discover a fine view of St-Mandrier Peninsula.

Villa Tamaris-Pacha

🕐 *Open daily (except Mon) 2-6.30pm.* 🕐 *Closed 1 Jan, 1 May and 25 Dec.* 🎫 *Free entry.* ☎ *04 94 06 84 00.*

The history of this magnificent residence, still unfinished, is worthy of the *Arabian Nights*. Towards the middle of the 19C, the Frenchman Marius Michel, a native of Sanary-sur-Mer, became, by a series of happy coincidences, the concessionnaire of the lighthouses, quays and warehouses of Constantinople. He was thus the creator

D. Pazery/ MICHELIN

Mont Faron cable-car

of the modern port of Istanbul and of reconnaissance of the coasts under the Ottoman administration. As the Var coast closely resembled the Golden Horn and the Bosphorus, he chose to build his wife a palace inspired by the Florentine villas in Tamaris. After three years of hard work, when his wife was stabbed and killed by a mentally ill person in 1893, Michel Pacha, as he was nicknamed, stopped all work on the villa and the palace remained unoccupied for a century. Now redeveloped, the villa houses a cultural institution and organises exhibitions.

Beside the bay, a luxurious house (private property), also the work of Michel Pacha, displays the ornately carved Mauresque style.

All along Le Lazaret Bay are small cabins perched on stilts above the mussel beds.

Les Sablettes

This long wide beach of fine sand looks out to the open sea. The houses were rebuilt after the last war in the neo-Provençal style, designed by the architect F Pouillon. Take the road along the narrow sandy isthmus, which links the peninsula to the land mass, where you'll find a fine view of Toulon surrounded by mountains.

Presqu'île de St-Mandrier★

The road round the peninsula offers a **view**★ of the whole harbor and of Toulon and its setting before skirting the bight of St-Georges, which houses an aeronaval base and training center for marine engineers as well as the fishing and leisure port of **St-Mandrier-sur-Mer**. A right-hand turning at the entrance to the town climbs steeply to a small cemetery with a **panorama**★★ of Toulon, Cap Sicié and the Îles d'Hyères.

② Corniche du Mont Faron★★ *30min.*

The Corniche du Mont Faron provides the best view of the whole of Toulon harbour. The best time is late afternoon, when the light is ideal.

▷ *To reach the Corniche du Mont Faron take Pont de Ste-Anne, Avenue de la Victoire and Boulevard Ste-Anne (left).*

The drive along the magnificent Corniche Marius-Escartefigue and the slopes of Mont Faron provides views of Toulon and its surroundings – the old town clustered around the port and the suburbs set against the surrounding mountains.

The **view**★ of the harbors is very fine: the Petite Rade between Le Mourillon and La Seyne backed by the cliffs of Cap Sicié; the Grande Rade, partially enclosed *(south)* by the St-Mandrier Peninsula and its low narrow isthmus and *(east)* by Cap Carqueiranne, Giens Bay and Giens Peninsula.

③ Baou de Quatre Oures★ *11km/6.8mi northwest – 1hr.*

▷ *From Toulon take Avenue St-Roch, Rue Dr-Fontan, Avenue Général-Gouraud and then turn left onto Avenue des Routes; on Place Macé turn right onto D 62 (Avenue Clovis). After 4km/2.5mi turn left onto D 262.*

About 3km/2mi further on is a platform offering a magnificent **view**★★ of Toulon, the harbors and the coast.

▶ *The narrow road to the top (4km/2.5mi) crosses a firing range (open to traffic).*

At the top there is a fine **panorama**★★ of the coast from Cap Bénat to La Ciotat and inland from Ste-Baume to the Maures.

④ Le Coudon★ *Round-trip 36km/22– about 1.5hr.*

▶ *From Toulon take Pont de Ste-Anne and Avenue de la Victoire; turn left onto Boulevard Ste-Anne and right onto Boulevard Escartefigue. Then turn left onto Avenue de la Canaillette, which leads to D 46. Turn right and right again onto D 446, a steep and narrow road.*

Le Coudon★ *Alt 702m/2 303ft.*

At the start of the climb you can see Mont Coudon in its entirety and also La Crau and the surrounding plain. The road, which narrows after going through pine woods and then olive groves, finally comes out onto a wasteland scattered with evergreen oaks. The **view**★ widens continuously until at the entrance to Fort Lieutenant-Girardon the entire coast from the Giens Peninsula to the former island of Gaou near Le Brusc is visible.

▶ *Return to D 46 and turn right. After 2.5km/1.5mi – D 846 crosses a dam to Le Revest-les-Eaux.*

Le Revest-les-Eaux

This is a delightful old village with a 17C church at the foot of Mont Caume overlooked by a "Saracen tower". Its 17C château, with two pepperpot towers, now houses a café-bar. The church is from the same era. In the Comoni Maison is a currency museum, one of only three in France. It's also possible to visit the suprising little **Musée Copte et Byzantine** (🕐 Apr-Sep Sat 4-6pm; Oct-Mar Sat 3-5pm. ☎ 04 94 98 94 78), with its collection of icons and liturgical objects from 4C through 19C.

▶ *Return to Toulon through the Las Valley (D 846) between the mountains of Faron and Croupatier.*

TOURRETTES-SUR-LOUP★

POPULATION 3 870

MICHELIN MAP 341 D5

This is violet country, where the pretty flowers are cultivated under the olive trees, but what strikes visitors the most is the village itself. Tourettes-sur-Loup is an unusual fortified town, standing on a rock plateau above a sheer drop, with its outer houses forming the rampart. Route des Quenières, the continuation of Route St-Jean, provides the best view★. The weavers, potters, sculptors, engravers and painters who have come to live in Tourettes have made it a lively arts and crafts center. 🏛 *5 Route de Vence, ☎ 04 93 24 18 93. www.tourrettessurloup.com.*

🅿 **Parking:** Coming from Vence on D 2210, leave your car at the parking area before the entrance to the village and follow the sidewalk to the central square. There's a nice view if you are arriving from the direction of Grasse (*20km/13mi southwest*).

Visit

Old Village★

To see this medieval village, pass under the belfry gate in the south corner of the main square and follow the Grande Rue in a semicircle through the village. This steep, paved street lined with shops where craftsmen can be seen plying their trade, will take you down to the old walls. There you'll enjoy a superb view of the surrounding landscape. Walk up the other side and re-enter the square through another gate.

Church

In the 15C nave *(south)* is a triptych by the Bréa School: St Antony flanked by St Pancras and St Claude. In the chapel *(south)* a handsome altarpiece in carved wood depicts

Address Book

For coin ranges, see the Legend at the back of the guide.

EATING OUT

Le Médiéval – ☎ *04 93 59 31 63 –* ○ *Closed 15 Dec-15 Jan, Wed, Thu and nights Nov-Mar.* While strolling the charming village streets you'll find this family-run restaurant with the rustic dining room. Traditional French cooking without surprises, and big servings without the big prices.

Auberge de Tourrettes – *11 Route de Grasse –* ☎ *04 93 59 30 05 – info@ aubergedetourrettes.fr –* ○ *Closed 10 Jan-10 Feb, Tue and Wed Oct-May.* A pink façade with green shutters, a fine dining room streaming with light and a terrace commanding pretty views of the valley are three good reasons to end up at this charming inn. Not to mention the tasty meals made with fresh local ingredients. Extend your stay by checking into one of the charming bedrooms.

WHERE TO STAY

Chambre d'Hôte Mas des Cigales – *1673 Route des Quenières – 2km/1.2mi from Tourrettes, Route de St-Jean –* ☎ *04 93 59 25 73 –* ✉ *– 6 rooms.* Handsome villa surrounded by a leafy garden. From the terrace running alongside the pool, you can look down onto a small waterfall, a tennis court and, in the far distance, the sea. The rooms are comfortable and tastefully appointed. Attentive welcome.

THE ART OF WEAVING

– 10 Grande Rue – ☎ *04 93 59 36 36 – Open 10am-1pm and 3-7pm.* ○ *Closed Nov and 2 weeks in Jan.* Among the distinguishing features of this shop are the fine hand-woven ties made with merino wool that have become collector's pieces over the years. In their charming boutique with stone walls, dominated by a huge loom, Hélène Chenard and her daughter Nathalie perpetuate the long-standing tradition of weaving, producing a wide range of garments, running from bright candy colors to more subtle shades of mauve, pink and almond green. The long stoles (*étoles*) are particularly elegant and the shawls, cloaks and three-quarter coats are perfect for a cool winter's night. The shop also stocks a fine collection of women's summer wear: diaphanous blouses, stylish dresses etc.

CALENDAR

Fête des Violettes – Every first or second week in March (according to the flowering season), a two-day festival with a Provençal market, tours of the flower fields, and a huge violet parade through the village.

scenes from the life of the Virgin. There are other altarpieces in the transepts as well as reliquaries and busts from the 15C, 16C and 17C. Behind the high altar stands a Gallo-Roman altar originally dedicated to Mercury.

Chapelle St-Jean

○ *Open by request, in season, through the Tourism Office.* ☎ *04 93 24 18 93.*

This chapel was decorated in 1959 with naive frescoes by Ralph Souplaut. On the far wall are John the Baptist and St John the Divine on either side of the cross, symbolising the link between the Old and New Testaments.

TOURTOUR★

POPULATION 472

MICHELIN MAP 340 M4

This village east of Aups (see AUPS), set in a cool and wooded region and flanked on each side by an old castle, occupies a dominant position (alt. 625m/2 050ft) on a ridge backing onto the last foothills of the Pre-Alps, facing the Varois Plain. Remains of the 12C Abbaye de Florielle, founded by the Cistercian monks before they moved to Thoronet, can still be seen. ⓘ *Avenue des Ormeaux, ☎ 04 94 70 54 36. www.tourisme-tourtour.com.*

🄿 **Parking:** There is parking at the entrance of the village behind the church.

Walking Tour

Old Village★

The village has retained its medieval character with the remains of fortifications, attractively restored houses and narrow, sloping streets, linked by vaulted passages, which converge on the central square.

The two large olive trees growing in this square replaced the elms planted at the time of the visit of Anne of Austria in 1638. A vaulted passageway leads from the square beside the **clock tower** *(tour de l'horloge)* to an old mill, which now houses the Fossil Museum (see Sights).

Beside the museum building *(left)* are the ruins of a 12C castle which has been restored and now houses an art and antiques gallery. Further up the road, you'll pass by a charming wash house on the way to a two-storey medieval tower, the **Tour Grimaldi.**

Église St-Denis

This 11C church, standing on its own at the southeastern edge of the ridge, was extensively modified in the last century.

Viewpoint★

From the grassy esplanade in front of the church there is a wide **panorama**★★ *(viewing table)* over the Argens and Nartuby valleys, extending *(east)* to the Maures and *(west)* to Ste-Baume, Mont Ste-Victoire and the Luberon. A few miles farther on *(east)* is the residential village of St-Pierre-de-Tourtour, in a lovely forest setting, designed in its entirety by Beaumont who was responsible for Les Issambres.

The church and its cemetery

D. Pazery/ MICHELIN

Address Book

WHERE TO STAY

⊖⊜⊜ **Auberge St-Pierre** – *3km/1.5mi east of Tourtour on the D 51 and secondary road* – ☎ *04 94 70 57 17 – aubergestpierre@ wanadoo.fr* – ⏲ *Closed 18 Oct-3 Apr* – ▣ – *16 rooms* – ☲ – *restaurant (⊖⊜)*. Nature lovers will enjoy this hotel hidden within the vast grounds of a Provençal estate. Not far from the village of Tourtour, the rooms are calm and bright, handsomely furnished. The estate has a pool, tennis, fitness room, and mountain biking trails.

SHOPPING

Markets – Wednesday and Saturday on Place des Ormeaux.

REGIONAL PRODUCE

Ferme de Tourtour – *Route de Villecroze* – ☎ *04 94 70 56 18 – claude.catrice@ wanadoo.fr*. Mouthwatering delicacies can be purchased here, such as pâtés, foie gras, tapenades (seasoning made of capers, olives, anchovies, olive oil, lemon and aromatics), anchoïades (mashed anchovies with crushed garlic), jams and preserves, fruit purée.

Sights

Musée des Fossiles

♿ ⏲ *Guided tours (30min) mid-Jun to mid-Sep daily (except Tue) 3-6pm.* ⊜ *Free entry.* ☎ *04 94 70 57 20 or* ☎ *04 94 70 56 06.*

This museum contains an interesting exhibition of local fossils, dinosaur eggs, large ammonites and fossil impressions.

▶ *Go down below the old castle to the oil mill.*

Moulin à Huile

♿ ⏲ *Guided tours (1hr) mid-Jun to mid-Sep; mid-Dec to mid-Jan, depending on temporary exhibitions; call in advance.* ⊜ *1.80€. For times contact the tourism office* ☎ *04 94 70 57 20 or* ☎ *04 94 70 56 06. www.tourisme-tourtour.com.*

This communal oil mill has been in service since the 17C and has three presses. During the autumn, when production takes place, 5 000l/1 100gal of oil are produced here, showing the continuing importance of the industry in this region. During the summer, the mill houses exhibitions of paintings. The town hall occupies the former Château des Raphelis, a solid 16C building with pepperpot towers.

La **TURBIE**★

POPULATION 3 021

MICHELIN MAP 341 F5

LOCAL MAPS SEE NICE AND CORNICHES DE LA RIVIERA

The hilltop village of La Turbie (alt. 480m/1 575ft), built in a pass on the Grande Corniche, is most famous for its Alpine Trophy, a masterpiece of Roman art and of major archeological importance. La Turbie also features splendid panoramas of the coast. At night, the lights of Monaco and its historic Monte-Carlo Casino are a magnificent spectacle.

▸ **Orient Yourself:** La Turbie is situated on Grande Corniche at the base of the massive Tête de Chien promontory above Monaco. It straddles the Roman Via Julia Augusta, the ancient main road from Genoa to Cimiez. The Trophy is visible from across the valleys.

🅿 **Parking:** Park at the foot of the village.

A Bit of History

When Caesar died, the greater part of the Alps was occupied by several unconquered tribes who posed a constant threat to communications between Rome and its possessions in Gaul and Spain.

Augustus decided to put an end to this situation and extend Roman rule into the Alps. Several campaigns were mounted between 25 BC and 14 BC and new provinces were established linking Italy, Gaul and Germania. One of them was the "Maritime Alps" with Cimiez as its capital. In 6 BC the Senate and the Roman people decreed that these important victories should be commemorated by the erection of a trophy. The position chosen was on the Via Julia Augusta, which had been built during the campaigns, at the foot of Mont Agel, where the Mediterranean coast is visible in both directions for several miles. There is only one other Roman trophy still standing (at Adam-Klissi in Romania, 150km/93mi from Bucharest). During the years of peace under the Romans a settlement grew up around the monument. Its Latin name, *Tropea Augusti*, gradually evolved into La Turbie.

Walking Tour

▸ *Start from Avenue Général-de-Gaulle.*

You'll see a 19C fountain, built at the end of a Roman aqueduct which was brought back into service at around the same time. Below, from the southwest corner of the Place Neuve, is a fine **view**★ of the coast as far as the Maures Massif.

Rue Comte-de-Cessole

This street, part of the former Via Julia Augusta, built by the Romans, now goes through the West Gate, climbing between medieval houses to the Trophy. A house on the right bears a plaque with the verses Dante dedicated to La Turbie. Another plaque shows that the town appeared in the Antonine Itinerary (a reference list of the staging posts on the main roads of the Roman Empire with the distances between them). Fine view of the Trophy at the top of the street.

Église St-Michel-Archange
Light switch in the first chapel on the right when entering.

The church, set back from the street, is a fine example of the Nice Baroque style. Built in the 18C on an ellipsoidal plan, it has a shallow concave façade (two storeys beneath a triangular pediment) and a bell-tower surmounted by a cupola of colored tiles.

Interior★ – *Walk around clockwise.* The decoration of the nave and chapels is Baroque, with the cradle vaulting, supported by tall pillars, adorned with frescoes and mouldings.

There are two paintings by J-B Van Loo: *St Charles Borromeo* and *Mary Magdalene* and a copy of Raphaël's *St Michael*, which is in the Louvre. The chapel on the left of the choir contains a Pietà from the Bréa School and *St Mark Writing his Gospel*, attributed to Veronese. The 17C communion table is in onyx and agate. The high altar in multicolored marble comes from the abbey of St-Pons in Nice and was used for the Cult of Reason during the Revolution. Above it is an 18C Christ in painted wood.

Trophée des Alpes

Also 18C are the two triptychs in the choir. In the first chapel on the right is a canvas attributed to Ribera and a 15C Virgin and Child. In the second chapel a painting of Mary by the Murillo School and a Flagellation in Rembrandt's style.

▶ *Return to the Rue de Cessole.*

At the top of the hill have a look at the Trophy. Then go down again towards the Rue Droite, which traces the old Via Julia towards Italy, before passing under the East Gate. Here you'll find terraces with **panoramic views**★★★ of the Principality of Monaco, the Italian Riviera, Cap Martin, Èze, Cap Ferrat, the Esterel, the heights of the Corniche, the Laghet Valley, and Mont Agel.

▶ *Return to the Avenue Charles-de-Gaulle.*

Sight

Trophée des Alpes★

 ♿ 🕐 *Open mid-May to mid-Sep 9.30am-6.30pm; mid-Sep to mid-May daily (except Mon) 10am-1.30pm and 2.30-5pm.* 🕐 *Closed 1 Jan, 1 May, 1 and 11 Nov, 25 Dec.* 🎟 *4.60€ Free the first Sun of the month Oct-May.* ☎ *04 93 41 20 84.*

The **Alpine Trophy** (originally 50m/164ft high and 38m/125ft wide) consisted of a square podium bearing a lengthy inscription to Augustus and a list of the 44 conquered peoples; a large circular Doric colonnade with niches containing statues of the leaders who took part in the campaigns; a stepped cone serving as a base for a huge statue of Augustus, flanked by two captives. Stairways gave access to all levels.

Most of the monument is built with beautiful white stone produced in local quarries. After the Romans left, it was damaged and despoiled. in the Middle Ages it was converted into a defensive structure (the blind arcading at the top dates from this period) and so was preserved from further deterioration. It survived Louis XIV's order for it to be blown up. Later it served as a source of building stone, particularly for the construction of the church of St-Michel-Archange. At the beginning of the modern era, all that remained was a ruined tower emerging from a cone of rubble.

Directed by Jules Formigé, skillful and patient restoration has been carried out through the generous help of Edward Tuck, an American. The trophy has been rebuilt up to about 35m/115ft high, but a large part of it has been left untouched. The inscription has been restored (Pliny had quoted it) and replaced in its original position; it is the longest left to us from Roman times. Its elevated position means that the Trophy is visible from a long way off.

Museum

Plans, drawings and photographs recount the story of the Trophy and its restoration *(model reconstruction)*. The display includes milestones, inscriptions, fragments of the Trophy, pieces of sculpture and documents on the other Roman monuments in Europe.

Forêt de **TURINI**★★

MICHELIN MAP 341 F4 - LOCAL MAP SEE NICE

For people living on the coast between Nice and Menton, the forest of Turini evokes another world of cool green shade. The huge forest, only 25km/15.5mi from the Mediterranean coast, is unusual, since its trees are generally found in more northerly latitudes. The lower slopes are covered with maritime sea pines and young oaks, but higher up there are maple, beech, chestnut, spruce, larch and superb pine trees, some of which reach 35m/115ft on the northern slopes. In winter the snowy slopes pose one of the most difficult challenges of the Monte-Carlo Rally.

▶ **Orient Yourself:** Situated in the Nice hinterland 15.5km/9.5mi from Menton, the forest covers a total of 3 500ha/1 350acres between the Vésubie and Bévéra valleys. Several roads meet at Col de Turini, which is a good starting point for visiting this beautiful district.

Driving Tours

The Authion★★ ⑦ *Round-trip 18km/11mi from Col de Turini – allow 45min.*

▶ *The roads are usually blocked by snow in winter and sometimes late into spring. A nature trail explains the flora and fauna of the forest.*

From Col de Turini the Authion road (D 68) passes through pine and larch woods. As the road climbs, the mountain scenery becomes more magnificent. 4km/2.5mi from the pass stands a war memorial to those who perished in 1793 and 1945.

Monument aux Morts

The Authion Massif has twice been a backdrop to military action. In 1793 the Convention's troops fought here against the Austrians and Sardinians, and in 1945 there was a bitter struggle before the Germans were driven out. Panoramic **view** ★ from the memorial.

Continue along D 68 bearing right at the fork to Cabanes Vieilles, an old military camp which was damaged in the fighting in 1945. The road runs through Alpine pastures and offers marvellous **views**★ of the Roya Valley.

▶ *Turn right by another monument onto a track which leads (500m/547yd) to a platform where it is possible to turn the car round.*

Pointe des Trois-Communes★★

At this altitude (2 082m/6 830ft) there is a marvellous **panorama**★★ of the peaks in the Mercantour National Park and the Pre-Alps of Nice.

▶ *Return to D 68; at the war memorial take the road back to Col de Turini.*

Monte-Carlo Rally

Vallon de Ste-Élisabeth★ 7 *Round-trip 15km/10mi from Col de Turini – 1hr.*

The road (D 70) winds northwest cutting its way between the mountain peaks (Cime de la Calmette and Tête du Scoubayoun) overlooking the small Vésubie tributary which flows down the Ste-Élisabeth Valley.

Gorges de Ste-Élisabeth

This rugged gorge cuts a savage gash between the deep, concertina-like folds in the rock strata.

▶ *Soon after the tunnel, at a bend in the road, stop by the Chapelle St-Honorat.*

St-Honorat Viewpoint★

The view extends from the terrace by the chapel over the perched village of Bollène, seen particularly clearly from this angle. You can also see up the Vésubie from Lantosque to Roquebillière, and north to the Mercantour peaks.

La Bollène-Vésubie

This pleasant village stands on a hill in a chestnut wood at the foot of a mountain peak, Cime des Vallières. The streets are laid out concentrically, climbing between the 18C houses to the church.

The road winds its serpentine course down into the Vésubie Valley on the D 2565 *(towards Nice)*, giving breathtaking views at it goes.

Col de Braus Road★★ 7 *Round-trip 76km/47mi leaving from Col de Turini – allow one day.*

The drive to Peïra-Cava passes through the thickest part of Turini Forest. There are fine **views** west into the valley of the Vésubie and the surrounding mountains.

Cime de Peïra-Cava★★ *1.5km/1mi – plus 30min on foot round-trip.*

▶ *On entering the village of Peïra-Cava turn left up a steep hill by the post office; bear right at the fork and leave the car in the car park.*

🚶 It is an easy climb to the top *(follow the lift)*, where you'll have a panoramic **view**★★ of the Vésubie Valley and mountains on one side and of the Bévéra Valley, Le Mercantour and the high peaks on the Franco-Italian frontier on the other. South beyond the Pre-Alps of Nice lies the sea and, in fine weather, a glimpse of Corsica.

Peïra-Cava★ *Alt 1 450m/4 757ft.*

The village is a winter sports center and a summer resort. It stands on a narrow ridge between the Vésubie and Bévéra valleys with an almost aerial view of the district.

▶ *Beyond the village a sharp right turn leads to a car park: a walk of 50m/55yd leads to some steps on the left.*

Hit the Slopes

In winter the Turini Camp-d'Argent ski resort (alt 1 700m/5 577ft) allows you to visit the forest on skis or snow shoes.

Pierre Plate★★

This peak provides a **panoramic view**★★ similar to the view from Cime de Peïra-Cava *(viewing table)*.

Return downhill to D 2566 and continue south through the forest. In La Cabanette turn left onto D 21 to Lucéram. The road descends through a succession of steep bends with magnificent **views**★ on all sides. On the edge of the forest a left-hand turn takes a picturesque route over Col de l'Orme to Col de Braus.

▶ *D 21 continues to Lucéram.*

Lucéram★ 👣 *See LUCÉRAM.*

▶ *South of Lucéram D 2566 descends the Paillon Valley to L'Escarène.*

L'Escarène – 👣 *See NICE* 4 *: Les Deux Paillons.*

From L'Escarène D 2204 climbs northeast up the Braus Valley to Sospel through a series of astonishing bends scaling the Pre-Alps of Nice. The road over Col de Braus, which links the Paillon and Bévéra valleys, is a section of the old Piedmont road from Nice to Turin.

Touët-de-l'Escarène

The route passes through this charming little village with a Baroque church. Olive groves soon give way to a landscape of Spanish broom.

Clue de Braus

This rift that opens up beyond Touët village is short but impressive. From St-Laurent (hamlet) one can reach the Braus waterfall (🚶 *15min there and back; leave the car by the restaurant).*

Over the next 3km/2mi, the D 2204 winds around 16 hairpin bends. As the road climbs the **view**★ extends from the white dome of the Nice observatory on top of Mont Gros to Cap d'Antibes and the Esterel Massif outlined against the sea.

Col de Braus *Alt 1 002m/3 287ft.*

It is interesting to look back down over the series of hairpin bends that carry the road up to the pass. Beyond the pass the road descends through 18 more bends offering extensive **views**★★ of the mountains of the Bévéra Valley, particularly the Authion and Cime du Diable ("Devil's Peak").

The road runs around Mont Barbonnet, which is crowned with the fortifications of Fort Suchet.

Col St-Jean

At Col St-Jean, between the dwellings on the left, an old army road leads off to the entrance porch of **Fort Suchet** (🕐 *Open Jul to end of Aug. Contact the Tourism Office in Sospel.* ☎ *04 93 04 15 80),* built 1883-86 and then modernised in the 1930s. Note in particular the two striking turrets on top.

After the Col St-Jean, the road draws near the Merlanson Valley, and then reaches Sospel. On a level with the casemates of Fort St-Roch (👣 *see SOSPEL),* there is a good view of the village.

Sospel★ 👣 *See SOSPEL.*

Olive groves reappear in the wide depression at Sospel. Then the D 2566 climbs northwest through the forest up the **Bévéra Valley**★. The river has created a very deep, narrow and winding channel lined by rocky and wooded heights. There is a beautiful waterfall on the right.

Gorges du Piaon★★

The *corniche* road runs beneath an overhang of rock high above the bed of the stream, which is strewn with huge boulders.

Chapelle Notre-Dame-de-la-Menour

An oratory marks the beginning of a path *(right)* that provides a good view of the valley and the gorge. A great flight of steps leads up to the chapel, which has a two-storey Renaissance façade.

The route passes through a fresh green gorge and the charming village of Moulinet before returning through the forest to the Col de Turini.

UTELLE ★

POPULATION 488

MICHELIN MAP 341 E4

LOCAL MAP SEE NICE

Sitting at an altitude of 800m/2 625ft, the village projects like a balcony over the Vésubie Valley facing Turini Forest and the Gordolasque Mountains to the north. The terraced olive groves and magnificent views form the backdrop to the winding, 9km/5mi drive full of hairpin turns leading up to the village. Once the most important town between Tinée and Vésubie, this somewhat isolated village has retained much of its original character, with a fountain in the square, old houses with sundials, and its ruined fortifications. ▯ *Mairie (Town Hall)* ☎ *04 93 03 17 01 or* ☎ *04 93 03 19 85. www.vesubian.com.*

🅿 **Parking:** You'll find places to park just outside the town perimeter.

Sights

Église St-Véran

🕓 *Open on advance request, call in advance* ☎ *04 93 03 15 22.*

Built in the 14C on the basilica plan and altered in the 17C, the church has an elegant Gothic porch with carved panels illustrating the legend of St Veranus in 12 tableaux.

The architecture of the interior, groin and barrel vaulting supported by archaistic Romanesque columns and capitals, contrasts surprisingly with the generous Classical decoration verging on Baroque. At the high altar a **carved wooden altarpiece**★ depicting scenes from the Passion is dominated by a statue of St Veranus. There is an altarpiece of the Annunciation (Nice School) above the first altar in the north aisle and a 13C recumbent Christ below the altar in the south aisle. Fine 17C woodwork (choir, pulpit) and 16C carved font. The sacristy contains some handsome vestments in silk and Genoan velvet.

> **WHERE TO STAY**
>
> 🍽🍽 **L'Aubergerie Del Campo** – *Route d'Utelle – St-Jean-la-Rivière – 5km/3mi east of Utelle by D 132 –* ☎ *04 93 03 13 12 –* 🚫 *–* 🕓 *Closed 1st week in Jul; reservation recommended for evenings.* Small inn built on the ruins of a former sheep barn offering Provençal cooking in a homey, slightly bohemian ambience. Unpretentious dining room lit by tiny windows and charming terrace overlooking the Vésubie Gorges.

Chapelle des Pénitents-Blancs

The chapel, which is near the church, contains a carved wooden altarpiece of the Descent from the Cross by Rubens and six large 18C paintings.

Excursion

Madone d'Utelle Panorama★★★

▶ *6km/4mi southwest.*

The sanctuary of the Madonna of Utelle, founded in 850 by Spanish sailors who had survived a storm, was rebuilt in 1806. It is a place of pilgrimage where faithful disciples can pay tribute to the Holy Virgin on 15 August and 8 September.

A short distance from the chapel stands a viewing table (alt 1 174m/3 852ft) covered by a dome. You'll enjoy a breathtaking **panorama**★★★ over a wide expanse of the Alpes-Maritimes *département* and the Mediterranean.

VALBONNE

POPULATION 10 746

MICHELIN MAP 341 D6

This hospitable spot (*vallis bona* in Latin, meaning "happy valley") has been occupied since Antiquity, the village growing from what was once an abbey. Today its tidy grid of picturesque streets, lovingly restored, is home to art galleries, chic gift boutiques and gourmet restaurants. A colorful Provençal market takes place throughout the village streets every Friday morning.

▶ **Orient Yourself:** Valbonne village is situated in the Brague river valley between Grasse (11.5km/7mi) and Biot (9km/6mi) on the D 4, surrounded by pines and holm oaks. Many of the residents work in the nearby Sophia-Antipolis technology and science park.

P **Parking:** The village itself is a pedestrian zone, with several large free-parking areas to the west and south of the town. ▯ *1 Place de l'Hôtel-de-Ville, Valbonne, ☎ 04 93 12 34 50. www.tourisme-valbonne.com.*

Walking Tour

Old Village
Map available at the Tourism Office.

Reconstructed by the Lérins monks in the 16C, the village is a curious example of checker-board development, with odd-looking rampart-houses. The **main square** with its 15C-17C arcading and old elm trees is an attractive backdrop to the lively cafés and restaurants. Every year around St Blaise's Day *(3 February)* the Feast of the "Servan grape" (which ripens late) is celebrated.

Not far away *(Rue de la Fountain, northeast of the square)*, you won't miss the **Museum of Ceramics and Barbotine** (⌖ ⏱ *Open Wed-Thu 2-6pm, Fri-Sat 10am-noon, 1-7pm, 1st Sun of the month 10am-5pm. Open on Tue by request.* ☞ *1.50€.* ☎ *04 93 42 02 15*), which displays in two tiny rooms artistic creations from Vallauris (1880-1950). Kitsch prevails in this plentiful private collection of practical and decorative ceramics.

Church
South of the village on the Brague River.

In 1199 the Chalais Order founded an abbey, which came under the control of Lérins before becoming the parish church. The building, in the form of a Latin cross with a square chevet, has been badly restored on several occasions but has retained the austere character typical of Chalais buildings.

Address Book

For coin ranges, see the Legend at the back of the guide.

EATING OUT

⊜ **Auberge Fleurie** – *Route de Cannes – 1.5km/0.5mi by the D 3 –* ☎ *04 93 12 02 80 –* ⏱ *Closed 6 Dec-12 Jan, Mon, Tue.* Choose between the dining room or the outdoor veranda to enjoy the generous helpings of imaginative and carefully prepared cuisine with dishes such as duck pâté with eggplant *(aubergines)*.

WHERE TO STAY

⊜⊜⊜ **Château de la Bégude** – *Opio – 2km/1.2mi northeast of Valbonne by Route de Biot –* ☎ *04 93 12 37 00 –* ⏱ *Closed 16 Nov-19 Dec –* begude@opengolfclub.com *– 33 rooms –* P *–* ⊠ *– Restaurant (*⊜⊜*).* If you wish to indulge in a luxurious stay, come to this 17C manor and dip into the pool or try your hand at golf. The château is set up on the site of the Opio-Valbonne golf course. It successfully combines the pleasures of old stone with the modern conveniences of the 21st century. The restaurant is also used as a club-house and bar available to golfers.

FOREST HIKES

▣ *9km/5.5mi.* A scenic, wooded path runs along the Brague River between Valbonne and Biot village, accessible from the bridge next to the church. The Parc Valmasque, accessible from the Sophia-Antipolis Science and Technology Park, has 20km/13mi of trails under the pines between Valbonne and Mougins.

The abbey houses an interesting **Musée du Patrimoine** (*Open May-Sep 3-7pm; Oct-May Open 2-6pm. Closed Mon. 2€. 04 93 12 96 54*) that enlightens visitors on the area's heritage with tools, costumes, a reconstituted kitchen and bedroom.

Excursion

Sophia-Antipolis (Parc international d'Activités)

Southeast of Valbonne.

A wooded plateau (2 300ha/5 683 acres) has been chosen to house the premises of an **International Science Park,** created in 1969. About two-thirds of the area has been carefully landscaped to provide a pleasant, natural setting for the third or so that is occupied by offices, housing and leisure facilities. The project completed so far has centered on four main sectors of activity: information technology, electronics and telecommunications; health and biotechnology; teaching and research; science and the environment.

East end and bell tower, Valbonne church

This complex is the latest stage in the **Route des Hautes-Technologies** linking together a number of centres involved in developing high technology between Aix-en-Provence and Valbonne.

VALLAURIS

POPULATION 25 773 WITH GOLFE-JUAN

MICHELIN MAP 341 D6

Vallauris lies close to the sea among rounded hills fragrant with orange blossom and mimosa. The center was laid out on a grid plan in the 16C after being razed to the ground in 1390. The town's traditional craft of pottery was in decline when Picasso gave it a new breath of life. A bronze statue he created still stands on the marketplace fronting the church, presented to the town where he became an honorary citizen. Vallauris is now an important ceramics center in France, and its Biennial International Festival of Ceramic Art *(July to mid-October)* enjoys a worldwide reputation.

▶ **Orient Yourself:** Attached to the same municipality as the seaside resort of Golfe-Juan *(2km/0.5mi on the D 135)*, the modern town of Vallauris stretches out eastwards of the Old Town and its château. *Square du 8-Mai-1945, 04 93 63 82 58. Office in Golfe-Juan: in the parking area of the Vieux-Port, 04 93 63 73 12. www.vallauris-golf-juan.com.*

P **Parking:** Parking can be found at the top of the town *(above the château)* or below *(next to the Tourism Office)*.

Sights

Château-Museum★

Open daily (except Tue) 10am-noon, 2-6pm (until 5pm in winter). Closed holidays. 3€ (free entry the 1st Sun of each month). 04 93 64 16 05. www.vallauris-golfe-juan.fr.

Originally a priory attached to Lérins, it was rebuilt in the 16C and is a rare example of Renaissance architecture in Provence. It is a rectangular two-storey building with a round pepper-pot tower at each corner. It houses three museums: **Musée National "La Guerre et la Paix"**, **Musée Magnelli,** and the **Musée de la Céramique**.

Address Book

EATING OUT

🍴🍴 **Gousse d'Ail** – *11 Avenue de Grasse* – ☎ *04 93 64 10 71* – 🕐 *Closed 1-15 Jul, 25 Oct-10 Nov, Tue, Sun evening and Mon.* Discreetly tucked away behind the church, this restaurant certainly deserves its name by serving typical, garlicky Provençal cooking in a rustic setting. Warm, friendly welcome. On Fridays, don't forget to order the speciality of the house, which, needless to say is... aïoli!

CERAMICS

Tour of traditional pottery workshops – *Rue du Plan.* 🕐 *Weekdays at 10.30am and 3.30pm.* 🎫 *Free entry. Information at the Tourism Office,* ☎ *04 93 63 82 58.*

Galerie Madoura – *Rue Suzanne-et-Georges-Ramié* – ☎ *04 93 64 66 39* - *www.madoura.com* – 🕐 *Closed lunch, weekends, and Nov.* Exhibition and sale of ceramics made on the premises as well as reproductions of pieces crafted by Picasso. **Pottery classes** – *Espace Grandjean – Boulevard des Deux-Vallons –* 🕐 *Summer weekdays –* 🎫 *170€ –* ☎ *04 93 63 07 61.*

CALENDAR

Fête de la Poterie – Pottery fesitval; second Sun in August.

Musée National "La Guerre et la Paix"

Only the Romanesque chapel of the priory has survived. Deconsecrated, it was decorated in 1952 by Picasso with a huge composition: *War and Peace.* This work evokes the horrors of war; black invaders, trampling the symbols of civilization underfoot, attack a knight in shining armour who is just (his spear forms the arm of a balance) and peaceful (his shield bears the device of a dove). The figures on the opposite wall are depicted indulging in honest labour and the innocent virtues of peace. The end panel symbolises fraternity between races.

Musée de la Céramique

This museum is one of the rare ones in France to display collections of contemporary cermics, including the ones which have won awards at the Biennial Festival *(in the vaulted rooms).*

A fine Renaissance staircase leads to two rooms on the second floor displaying ceramics by Picasso (plates, dishes, humorously decorated vases).

On the first floor are the traditional Vallauris ceramics, especially the Art Nouveau, but also Art Déco and 1950s creations.

Musée Magnelli

Six rooms are devoted to the **Magnelli bequest:** works in oil, collage and gouache together with a large mural. Alberto Magnelli (1888-1971) was born in Florence but spent the greater part of his life in France. The rooms are arranged from left to right to trace the evolution of the artist's style, from large washes of pure color he turned to Abstract art, which he temporarily abandoned in the 1920s.

Musée de la Poterie

Rue Sicard. ♿ 🕐 *Open May-Oct 9am-6pm, Sun and public holidays 2-6pm; Feb-Apr 2-6pm.* 🕐 *Closed Nov-Jan.* 🎫 *2€.* ☎ *04 93 64 66 51.*

Located in a pottery workshop that is still operational, the Pottery Museum shows how clay was worked in the first half of the 20C. Displays illustrate the techniques used for extracting clay from the earth, its preparation, shaping, glazing and baking in the wood-fired kiln. Old pottery is also on view.

A visit to the present workshop helps one to appreciate the evolution of the potter's techniques.

Here and in the neighboring streets are the pottery shops and workshops *(ateliers de céramique),* their displays of ceramics spilling out onto the pavement. High-quality work vies for attention with second-rate wares.

Espace Jean-Marais

♿ 🕐 *Open Jul-Aug 10am-12.30pm, 2-6.30pm; the rest of the year (except Sun-Mon) l0am-12.30pm, 2-5.30pm.* 🎫 *1.50€.* ☎ *04 93 63 46 11.*

In the old gallery of the artist, you'll discover another facet of Jean Marais through his sculptures, paintings and ceramics, which were inspired by the universe of Jean Cocteau films in which the actor played *(Beauty and the Beast, Orphée).*

Excursion

Golfe-Juan ☆☆

It was on the beach of Golfe-Juan that Napoleon and his army of 1 100 men landed from the island of Elba with their sailing ships on 1 March, 1815. Napoléon rested in an inn by the beach road before leaving for Cannes (see *Route NAPOLÉON*). This small fishing port developed in the second half of the 19C by exporting ceramics made in the area. With its 3km/1.8mi of fine sand and large choice of water sports, Golfe-Juan has become a popular summer resort. The beaches (public and private) extend on both sides of the Old Port.

VENCE★

POPULATION 16 982

MICHELIN MAP 341 D5 - LOCAL MAP SEE NICE

Vence sits on a hillside winter and summer resort 10km/6mi inland from the sea, between Nice and Antibes. Here, Mimosas, roses and carnations are cultivated, and olive and orange trees thrive. It's a picturesque old market town, favored by artists and art galleries, sheltered from the cold north winds by the foothills of the Alps. The wines from the surrounding stony hillsides (La Gaude, St-Jeannet) are highly regarded. *Place du Grand-Jardin, ☎ 04 93 58 06 38. www.ville-vence.com.*

Parking: The town extends well beyong the village ramparts to the west, where you'll find three parking garages.

A Bit of History

An Episcopal Town – Vence, founded by the Ligurians, was an important Roman town. With the coming of Christianity, it acquired greater influence, that of an episcopal seat. Among the bishops from 374 to 1790 were St Veranus (5C) and St Lambert (12C), Alessandro Farnese, an Italian prince who became Pope Paul II (16C), Antoine Godeau (see below) and Surian, a great preacher.

During the Wars of Religion, Vence was besieged by the Huguenot Lesdiguières in 1592, but held out. The victory is commemorated each year at Easter.

The Lords of Vence (13C) – The bishops of Vence were in continual conflict with the barons of Villeneuve, lords of the town. This family drew its fame from **Romée de Villeneuve**, an able Catalan who in the 13C reorganised the affairs of the Count of Provence, Bérenger V. The count had four marriageable daughters and an empty treasury. Romée induced Blanche of Castille to ask for the eldest, Marguerite, for the future St Louis. Eleanor married Henry II and became Queen of England and another became Empress of Austria. The last daughter, Beatrix, heiress of Provence, married Charles of Anjou, brother of St Louis in 1246, and became Queen of the Two Sicilies.

Bishop Godeau (17C) – The memory of Antoine Godeau has remained vivid throughout the region. His beginnings did not seem likely to lead him to a bishopric. He was the oracle of the House of Rambouillet. Small, skinny, swarthy, he was, nevertheless, in great demand among some cultured society ladies *(les précieuses)* because of his wit, his fluency and his rich and ready poetical vein: they called him Julie's dwarf (Julie d'Angennes was the daughter of the Marquise de Rambouillet) and also, tongue-in-cheek, the "Jewel of the Graces." His reputation was unprecedented. Richelieu made him

Chapelle du Rosaire (Chapelle Matisse)

S. Sauvignier/ MICHELIN

the first member of the French Academy. At the age of 30, Godeau, no doubt weary of verse-making, took holy orders and the following year, was made Bishop of Grasse and Vence. The towns would not accept a joint bishop and so for several years he remained between the two dioceses, finally opting for Vence. The former wit and ladies' confidant took his new role seriously. He repaired his cathedral, which was falling into ruins, introduced various industries (perfumery, tanning and pottery) and undertook a number of measures aimed at bringing prosperity to his poor and primitive diocese. He died in 1672 at the age of 67.

Walking Tour

▷ *Start from Place du Grand-Jardin.*

Before entering the old town, stop to look at Place du Frêne and the enormous ash tree that gives the square its name. According to legend, the tree was planted in memory of the visit of François I and Pope Paul III in 1538.

Old Town

The old town was enclosed within elliptical walls, parts of which can still be seen, pierced by five gateways.

Skirt the 15C square tower adjoining the château to reach and pass beneath the Peyra Gateway (1441). This part of town is bustling with artists, craftsmen and boutiques.

Place du Peyra★

The square is picturesque with a striking square tower and gushing fountain in the form of an urn (1822). It was the forum of the Roman town.

▷ *From the south side of the square take Rue du Marché and turn left to reach Place Clemenceau, site of the cathedral.*

Ramparts

Leave the cathedral (⌖ *see Sights*) through the east door which opens onto Place Godeau, overlooked by the square tower with its parapet and surrounded by old houses. At the center stands a Roman column erected to the god Mars. Take Rue St-Lambert and then Rue de l'Hôtel-de-Ville to reach the 13C Signadour Gateway and turn left.

The next gate on the left is the Orient *(east)* gateway, opened in the 18C. The date 1592 carved on a stone *(top left)* refers to the siege of the Protestant Duke François de Lesdiguières during the Wars of Religion. Boulevard Paul-André follows the line of the ramparts, where several narrow stepped streets branch off to fine **views** of the high peaks *(baous)* and the foothills of the Alps. Re-enter the old town through the Gothic Lévis Gateway (13C) and walk up Rue du Portail-Lévis between handsome old houses to Place du Peyra.

Address Book

For coin ranges see the Legend at the back of the guide.

EATING OUT

Crêperie Bretonne Hervé – *6 Place Surian* – ☎ *04 93 24 08 20* – ⏰ *Closed 6-31 Jan, Wed evening and Thu Sep-May.* In the heart of the old quarter, a spruce creperie combines Breton tradition with a touch of Provence. The big terrace giving onto the square is an invitation to sit down and sample one of the tasty pancakes on the menu.

Le Pêcheur de Soleil – *1 Place Godeau* – ☎ *04 93 58 32 56* – ⏰ *Closed Nov-Feb.* Fancy a pizza? This restaurant in the medieval quarter of Vence is definitely the right place to choose. An astounding choice of homemade pizzas, freshly baked in an open oven, are served in a rustic dining room whose beams are decorated with old-fashioned kitchen utensils. In summer, eat out on the terrace at the foot of the cathedral.

Chez Jordi – *8 Rue de Hôtel-de-Ville* – ☎ *04 93 58 83 45* – ⏰ *Closed 1 Jul-15 Aug, 15 Dec-31 Jan, Sun and Mon – Reservation required.* This modest restaurant in a secluded alley serves generous helpings and will prepare Spanish specialities at your request: paella, zarzuela.

Auberge des Seigneurs – *Place du Frêne* – *b 04 93 58 04 24* – ⏰ *Closed 2 Nov-14 Mar, Tue-Thu lunch, and Mon.* Handsome 17C mansion standing at the entrance to the old medieval district. The rustic setting with its thick wooden tables is alleviated by the refined silverware. A few rooms are available for weary travelers.

WHERE TO STAY

Hôtel La Victoire – *Place du Grand-Jardin* – ☎ *04 93 58 61 30* – *hotel.victoire@free.fr* – *15 rooms* – ☐. The main asset of this hotel located on Vence's main square is the excellent quality/price ratio. The well-kept rooms are pleasantly furnished in the 1970s style; the ones on the third floor are slightly darker. Homey welcome.

Parc Hôtel – *50 Avenue Foch* – ☎ *04 93 58 27 27* – *resa@le-parc-hotel.net* – ☐ – *13 rooms* – ☐. Turn-of-the-century residential mansion giving onto a courtyard lined with palm trees. The recently renovated, smallish rooms are brightly decorated.

Villa Roseraie – *Route de Courségoules* – ☎ *04 93 58 02 20* – ⏰ *Closed 16 Nov-14 Feb* – *14 rooms* – ☐ – ☐. A 1900 villa is the setting for this tastefully appointed hotel in which the small rooms are cool and attractive. Tempting outdoor pool. Pretty terrace adorned with sculptures.

La Bastide aux Oliviers – *1260 Chemin de la Sine – Route de Tourrettes-sur-Loup* – ☎ *04 93 24 20 33* – *bastidolivnetcourrier.com* – ☐ – *4 rooms.* Three beautiful bedrooms and a suite done up in Provençal tones await you in this country house built in light stone lost among pines and olive trees. The terrace affords a lovely view of the Loup Valley.

La Tour de Vence – *310 Chemin du Baou des Noirs – northeast of Vence towards St-Jeannet* – ☎ *04 93 24 59 00* – ⏰ *Closed Nov-Dec* – ☐ – *4 rooms– Restaurant* (☐). Who can resist the charm of this superb mansion built with stones taken from a former Burgundy monastery? Cosy, comfortable rooms decorated with great taste. Breathtaking views of the Mediterranean coastline and surrounding mountains.

MARKETS

Flowers and regional produce – daily (except Monday) on Place du Grand-Jardin and Place Surian.

Second-hand books and furniture – Wednesdays on Place du Grand-Jardin.

Other markets – Tuesdays and Fridays on Place Clemenceau, Place Godeau, Rue de l'Évêché, Impasse Cahours (morning only).

CALENDAR

Fête de Pâques – Coinciding with Easter (end of March to early April) celebrations, this festival commemorates the village victory over the Hugenot siege during the Wars of Religion, 1592, with parades, music and dancing.

"Les Nuits du Sud" – Music Festival, mid-July to early August.

Fête Ste-Elizabeth – Village patron saint festival, first weekend in August.

Moyen Pays Fête – Traditional Folk Festival, beginning of October.

Sights

Cathedral

⏰ *Guided tours of the choir stalls by appointment in summer.* ☎ *04 93 58 42 00.*

The Roman temple of Mars built on this site was replaced in the 5C by a Merovingian church incorporated into subsequent structures. The present church, the old cathedral, was begun in the Romanesque style but was later altered and enlarged several times.

Some Roman inscriptions have been included in the Baroque façade. Those on either side of the door are dedicated to the emperors Elagabalus and Gordian.

The interior consists of a nave and four aisles. The tomb of St Lambert and his epitaph are to be found in the second chapel on the right. A 5C Roman sarcophagus, said to be the tomb of St Veranus, is in the third chapel on the right. The north aisle contains a handsome carved doorway with Flamboyant Gothic rose windows and a 16C retable of angels. Some fine pieces of Carolingian carving have been incorporated in certain of the pillars. The baptistery contains a mosaic by Chagall, *Moses in the Bulrushes*. The most unusual feature is the **organ loft,** where the singing desk and the **choir stalls**★ have risers, elbow rests and misericords by Jacques Bellot, a sculptor from Grasse (15C) whose lively imagination sometimes bordered on the irreverent.

Chapelle du Rosaire or Chapelle Matisse★

🕐 *Open Mon, Wed and Sat 2-5.30pm; Tue and Thu 10-11.30am, 2-5.30pm, Sun 10am (mass). Also open Fri during school holidays 2-5.30pm.* 🕐 *Closed mid-Nov to mid-Dec.* 💶 *2.50€ (child 1€).* ☎ *04 93 58 03 26.*

"Despite its imperfections I think it is my masterpiece... the result of a lifetime devoted to the quest for truth." This was Henri Matisse's opinion of the chapel which he had designed and decorated between 1947 and 1951. The fame of this artist and the daring of his design, a contemporary echo of the genius of the medieval masters, aroused enormous interest in the building.

From the outside it resembles an ordinary Provençal house with a roof of colored tiles surmounted by a huge wrought-iron cross with gilt tips.

Inside, the community nave and the parish nave meet at the altar, which is set at an angle.

Everything is white—floor, ceiling, tiled walls—except for the small high stained-glass windows that make a floral pattern in lemon, bottle green and ultra-marine. The decoration, furnishings and vestments are strikingly plain and simple. The mural compositions, the Stations of the Cross and St Dominic have been reduced to a play of black lines on a white background. Although not in sequence, the Stations of the Cross provide a visual progression towards Calvary at the climax of the composition. The gallery, containing studies made by Matisse for his finished designs, is well worth a visit.

Château de Villeneuve – Fondation Émile Hugues

🕐 *Open daily (except Mon) 10am-12.30pm, 2-6pm; Jul-Sep daily (except Mon) 10am-6pm.* 🕐 *Closed 1 Jan, 1 May, 25 Dec.* 💶 *5€.* ☎ *04 93 24 24 23 or* ☎ *04 93 58 15 78.*

The old castle of the Barons of Villeneuve, built in the 17C, incorporates the 13C watchtower. The foundation was set up to forge a link between local heritage and artistic creativity inspired by the region. Note the lovely interior decoration on each floor. Thematic exhibitions show to full advantage works by the great masters of the 20C, such as Matisse, Dubuffet, Dufy and Chagall, inspired by the time they spent in Vence. Alternating with these are exhibitions on modern and contemporary art.

Excursion

Galerie Beaubourg-Château Notre-Dame-des-Fleurs

3km/2mi northwest along D 2210. 🕐 *Open on request.* 💶 *5€.* ☎ *04 93 24 52 00.*

The estate was built in the 19C on the site of an 11C Benedictine abbey, Notre-Dame-des-Crottons (Our Lady of the Caves), which housed the bishops of Vence from 1638 to 1728. Its name was changed to Notre-Dame-des-Fleurs (Our Lady of the Flowers) by its owner, a Grasse perfumer.

A gallery of contemporary art displays the works of many artists in the rooms and gardens including César, Schnabel, Tinguely, St-Phalle, Ben, Klein, etc.

From the terrace, decorated with aromatic plants, the **view**★ extends from Cap Ferrat to the Esterel. The pre-10C Romanesque chapel was restored in 1988; its chancel is adorned with a stained-glass window by Bernard Dhonneur.

Nearby, the bishop's private chapel contains a 6C Virgin.

Driving Tour

Routes des Crêtes★★ 🔟 *Round-trip 59km/37mi – half a day*

▶ *Leave Vence by D 2210, going northeast towards St-Jeannet.*

The road skirts three peaks – Baou des Blancs, Baou des Noirs and Baou de St-Jeannet – and provides a long leisurely view of the **site**★ of St-Jeannet.

Gattières

This perched village looks out over vineyards and olive groves to the Var Valley and the neighboring hamlets. The charming Romanesque-Gothic **church** (🕐 *Guided visits possible on request, contact Raymonde or Marie-Rose ☎ 04 93 08 67 07 or 04 93 08 66 35*) contains a naïve painted sculpture of St Nicholas and the three children he revived *(right of chancel)* and a beautiful modern Christ in the choir.

▷ *Leave Gattières by D 2209 going west and north.*

The *corniche* road skirts the edge of the Grasse Pre-Alps overlooking the Var and provides an attractive glimpse of Gattières to the south.

Carros

The old village occupies a remarkable **position**★ huddled around the castle (13C-16C). Just below the village a rock, which bears traces of an old mill, has been made into a terrace: **panorama**★★ *(viewing table)*.

The road from Carros to Le Broc provides magnificent **views**★ of numerous hill villages, of the Var, flowing in its several channels around the banks of flat white pebbles which lie in its broad bed, and of its confluence with the Esteron.

▷ *Follow the D 1.*

Le Broc

This hill village has a fountain (1812) in the square, which is surrounded by arcades. The 16C **church** (🕐 *Guided tours weekdays 9am-noon, 2-5pm*) was decorated by the modern painter Guillonet. From the village there is a fine view of the Var Valley.

The road overlooks the confluence of the Esteron and the Var before turning west into the Bouyon ravine.

Bouyon

Every part of the village offers a **view**★ of Mont Cheiron (alt 1 778m/5833ft), the Var and Esteron valleys and the Alps of the Franco-Italian border.

▷ *South of Bouyon the road (D 8) skirts the northern flank of Mont Chiers passing through Bézaudun-les-Alpes to Coursegoules.*

Coursegoules

Perched on a rocky spit at the foot of the south face of Mont Cheiron, the tall houses rise above the ravine of the nascent River Cagne.

The Jaboulet workshops established in this tiny village are famous for their santons, said to be the most beautifully crafted in the region.

▷ *Take D 2 southeast to Vence.*

The road runs through barren countryside beside the River Cagne which turns into a waterfall when it rains. There is always something interesting to look at along this stretch.

Col de Vence★★ *Alt 970m/3 182ft.*

Just south of the pass a fine **panorama**★★ opens up to the high peaks east of the Var as far as Mont Agel, along the coast from Cap Ferrat, past the Baie des Anges, Cap d'Antibes and the Lérins islands to the Esterel. To the north the white slopes of Mont Cheiron stand out dramatically against the sky.

The road descends through the barren limestone *garrigue* on the southern edge of the Pre-Alps of Grasse.

🚶 **Hike** *4hr from the pass to St-Jeannet.* ♿ *see local map.*

After you pass the Col de Vence, there is a trail to the left which leads to St-Jeannet via the GR 51 footpath, stretching alongside the Cagne. Beautiful views!

VALLÉE DE LA **VÉSUBIE**★★

MICHELIN MAP 341 E3/4

LOCAL MAP SEE NICE

Drawing its source amid mountains of 2 500m/8 000ft, the Vésubie is fed by the snows of the last high Alpine ranges. The valley, one of the most beautiful above Nice, presents a number of characteristics. The upper valley has Alpine green pastures, pine forests, cascades and peaks, while the middle valley, between Lantosque and St-Jean-la-Rivière, shows signs of Mediterranean climate —the slopes are less steep and terraced with vines and olive trees. In its lower reaches below St-Jean-la-Rivière, the torrent has created a gorge with vertical walls through which it passes to join the Var as it emerges from the Défilé du Chaudan.

The Vésubie, an eastern tributary of the Var, is formed by two torrents: the Madone de Fenestre and the Boréon, which rise near the Italian border.

🛈 *Place Félix-Faure, St-Martin-Vésubie,* ☎ *04 93 03 21 28. www.vesubian.com.*

Driving Tour

Plan-du-Var to St-Martin-Vésubie *110km/68mi – about 5hr.*

▶ *D 2565 follows the bed of the narrow, winding Gorges de la Vésubie★★★: the steep rock walls are layered in many colors. In St-Jean-la-Rivière turn left onto the road (D 32) which climbs towards Utelle, giving views of the Vésubie Gorges.*

La Madone d'Utelle★★★ 🕒 *See UTELLE.*

▶ *Make a U-turn at St-Jean-la-Rivière and turn left onto the D 2565.*

Beyond St-Jean-la-Rivière, the valley squeezes between bluffs of rock, widening slightly at Le Suquet to skirt the eastern foothills of the Brec d'Utelle.

Lantosque

This village is sited on a limestone ridge which crosses the valley. There is a canyoning via-ferrata course (*2hrs*) which crosses the Gorges of Lantosque (*Contact the Mairie for more information,* ☎ *04 93 03 00 02*).

Roquebillière

This little town has been rebuilt six times since the 6C owing to rock falls and floods. The last landslide in 1926 left some of the austere old houses, but it was necessary to rebuild on the west bank of the Vésubie where the 15C church already stood.

E. Baret/ MICHELIN

Vallon de Gordolasque

The Return of the Wolf

The presence of wolves *(canis lupus)* in the Parc du Mercantour, detected by tracks found in 1989, was verified during the winter of 1992. Observations made in spring 1995 confirmed the presence of a pack of eight wolves, and also probably an isolated couple.

Arriving in one of the successive migrations from the Abruzzi (Central Italy) where the wolf population is estimated at more than 500, the wolf is constantly seeking new territories where its capacity for adaptation is astounding. The pack is the basic family unit, consisting of the parents and their offspring from the last two years, about six to eight members.

The return of the wolf is a sign of ecological health in the area. The Parc du Mercantour conducts a campaign of awareness and education with shepherds who are directly involved in the new problems of living with wolves. Measures have been taken: penning of flocks at night and the introduction of a sheepdog (the Pyrenean Patou) with a great deterrent effect on the wolves' attacks. The creation of a Maison du Loup in the park has helped to inform the public.

Located in the new town, the **Église St-Michel-du-Gast** (🕐 *Guided tour on advance request.*   *Free entry.* 📞 *04 93 03 45 62 or 04 93 03 51 60)* is one of many examples in Provence of the Romanesque and Gothic styles combined. Sadly, the Romanesque spire is disfigured by a clock. Three Gothic naves are supported by squat Romanesque columns. An **altarpiece** from the Nice School is dedicated to St Antony; the predella represents scenes from his legend. The Maltese Cross carved on the volcanic stone of the font shows that the church was originally owned by the Knights of St John. Fine collection of 17C and 18C priestly vestments in the sacristy.

WHERE TO STAY

⊜⊜ **Auberge du Bon Puits** – *Le Suquet – 5.5km/3.4mi south of Lantosque towards Nice –* 📞 *04 93 03 17 65 –* 🕐 *Closed Dec to Easter and Tue except Jul-Aug –* 🍴. This roadside inn made with local stone stands on the banks of the Vésubie. The dining hall features visible beams and an open fireplace. There are a few rooms as well as an ornamental park with ponies and a playing area for children.

▶ *On leaving Roquebillière-Vieux turn right onto a narrow road to Belvédère (D 71).*

It is a picturesque road up the **Vallon de la Gordolasque**★★ between Cime du Diable (Devil's Peak) and Cime de la Valette.

Belvédère

The **site**★ of this charming village overlooks both the Gordolasque and the Vésubie. From the terrace behind the mairie (town hall) there is a fine **view**★ of Roquebillière-Vieux immediately below backed by Tournairet Mountain, of the Vésubie downstream to Mont Férion and Turini Forest.

The road (D 171) continues up the valley past massive rocks and tumbling waterfalls, including the **Cascade du Ray**★ where the river divides into two gushing waterfalls.

The road follows the valley due north divided from the eastern parallel valley, Vallée des Merveilles, by Cime du Diable. Further north are the indented rocks of the Grand Capelet.

Cascade de l'Estrech★

The road ends near a path (🚶1km/0.6mi of mountain track) that leads to the beautiful Estrech waterfall which flows down from a **cirque**★★ of snow-capped mountains dominated by Cime du Gélas and Mont Clapier, both of which reach 3 000m/4 828ft.

▶ *Return to D 2565, then turn right onto the D 72.*

Berthemont-les-Bains

This therapeutic spa, in a lovely, shaded setting, has naturally sulphrous waters of 30°C/86°F used as long ago as in Roman times. The ailments treated include respiratory diseases, rheumatism and diseases of the joints.

As the road climbs, the valley changes to a landscape of chestnuts, pines and green pastures which has earned the region round St-Martin-Vésubie the title of "Suisse Niçoise" (Nice's Switzerland). Venanson overlooks the valley from the west bank.

VILLECROZE

POPULATION 1 087

MICHELIN MAP 340 M4

Situated 8km/5mi south of Aups (see AUPS), Villecroze lies in the wooded foothills of the Provençal tableland surrounded by a landscape of vineyards, orchards and olive groves. The village has developed around a group of caves, partly converted into dwellings. *Rue Ambroise-Croizat, ☎ 04 94 67 50 00.*

P **Parking:** the village has adequate parking at its entrance, with everything easily accessible on foot.

Visit

The Village

The flavor of the Middle Ages lingers in the village's streets and structures such as the 15C clock tower, the surprising Rue des Arcades and the the 18C Romanesque church, Eglise Notre-Dame, with its wall belfry.

Parc Municipal

▸ *Entrance via Route d'Aups, then a right-hand turn leading to a car park.*

A beautiful waterfall cascades 40m/130ft down the cliff face and forms a stream in an oasis of greenery beside a lovely rose garden. A marked path leads to the caves *(grottes).*

> ## Address Book
>
> ### WHERE TO EAT
>
> ⊝⊝ **La Cascade** – *Chez Martine – Avenue Ambroise-Croizet – village center* – ☎ *04 94 67 57 10 –* Ⓛ *Closed Sun dinner and Mon.* Country-style cuisine with a Provençal touch is served in this family-run restaurant on the vilage's main road above Place du Général-de-Gaulle. The dinng room is simple, but always has a convivial atmosphere.
>
> ### SHOPPING
>
> **Market** – Thursday morning on Place du Général-de-Gaulle.

Sights

Caves

Ⓛ *Guided tours (15min) Jul to mid-Sep 10am-noon, 2.30-7pm; May-Jun 2-6pm; winter school holidays 2-6pm; Mar and mid-Sep to mid-Oct Sat-Sun 2-6pm.* Ⓛ *Closed mid-Oct to winter school holidays.* ⊛ *2€.* ☎ *04 94 70 63 06.*

In the 16C the caves were partially converted into dwellings by the lords of Villecroze. Some mullioned windows set into the rock remain. The tour includes several little chambers with attractive concretions.

Belvédère de Villecroze★

▸ *From Tourtour take D 51 towards Villecroze.*

The little road winds through woods which soon give way to strangely shaped rocks and caves. About 1km/0.6mi before Villecroze, a belvedere can be seen beside the road. The circular **panorama**★ from the viewing table takes in Tourtour, the Plans de Provence, Villecroze, Salernes, Gros Bessillon and *(farther east)* the Maures and Ste-Baume.

VILLEFRANCHE-SUR-MER★

POPULATION 6 833

MICHELIN MAP 341 E5

LOCAL MAP SEE CORNICHES DE LA RIVIERA

Located 6km/4mi east of Nice on the Basse Corniche, Villefranche is a fishing port and holiday resort built on the wooded slopes encircling one of the most beautiful harbors★★ in the Mediterranean. The deep bay of 25-60m/13-33 fathoms, where cruise liners and warships can lie at anchor, lies between the Cap Ferrat Peninsula and the Mont Boron heights. Three lighthouses and a semaphore dot the harbor. Villefranche has preserved its 17C character in its port, citadel and picturesque old streets lined with sorbet-colored houses.

▶ **Orient Yourself:** A row of brightly painted houses lines the waterfront of this delightful fishing harbor. Rue du Poilu is the main street in a network of narrow alleys, some of which are stepped or vaulted, such as the strange **Rue Obscure,** where the population took refuge during bombings.

▣ **Parking:** There is parking (absolutely packed in summer) around the citadel and the old port. ▯ *Jardin François-Binon,* ☎ *04 93 01 73 68. www.villefranche-sur-mer. com.*

A Bit of History

The Origins of Villefranche – The town owes its name to the Count of Provence, Charles II of Anjou, nephew of St Louis, who founded it at the start of the 14C and granted it commercial independence. Between its cession to Savoy in the late 17C and the excavation of the Lympia harbour in Nice in the mid-18C, Villefranche was the major port of the Savoyard and then the Sardinian states.

The Congress of Nice – In 1538, the Congress of Nice was convened by Pope Paul III, former Bishop of Vence, to bring peace between François I and Charles V. During the Congress, Charles V stayed in Villefranche, François I in Villeneuve-Loubet and the Pope, acting as mediator, in Nice.

The Queen of France, sister of Charles V, went to see her brother, whose ship was moored at Villefranche. Charles, giving his hand to the Queen and followed by the Duke of Savoy and lords and ladies of his suite, advanced majestically along the wooden gangway between the jetty and the ship. With a cracking noise the gangway collapsed, and the Emperor, the Queen and the Duke could only splash about helplessly in the water until, soaked and dishevelled, they were pulled ashore by onlookers. The peace of Nice lasted for barely five years.

Villefranche-sur-Mer Bay

Address Book

For coin ranges, see the Legend at the back of the guide.

EATING OUT

🍽 **La Caravelle** – *3 Rue de l'Église, in the old town* – ☎ *04 93 01 81 10* – ⏰ *Closed Nov-Dec, for lunch and Wed off- season.* Small restaurant with a terrace that pays homage to the sea, whose decor is painted in shaded tones of blue. Homey cooking, unpretentious service and a friendly welcome are the hallmarks of La Caravelle, whose owner offers invaluable advice about the Villefranche area.

🍽🍽 **La Grignotière** – *3 Rue du Poilu* – ☎ *04 93 76 79 83* – ⏰ *Closed for lunch except Sun, and Wed evening off season.* Nouvelle cuisine is an unknown expression in this restaurant, which makes a point of serving hearty meals made with fresh ingredients of excellent quality. Follow the example of the local population and tuck into a gargantuan dinner unashamedly!

WHERE TO STAY

🛏🛏 **Le Riviera** – *2 Avenue Albert-1* – ☎ *04 93 76 62 76* – ⏰ *Closed Jan* – *24 rooms* – 🍴. Unpretentious, prettily restored hotel lying on the Corniche Inférieure. The rooms, of different sizes, are gradually being refurbished. Some afford views of the sea. Agreeable rooftop terrace for summer breakfasts.

TOURS

Guided tours – Guided tours of the town *(1.75hr)* are organised by the tourist office on Wednesdays at 10am. 5€. Treat yourself to breakfast and a guided tour of the village (with commentary) on Fridays between April and September. *8€. Reserve at the Tourism Office.* ☎ *04 93 01 73 68.*

Tourist Train – *La Rafale* – 🚃 *6€ (child 3€)* – ⏰ *Operates 15 Apr-Oct* – ☎ *04 93 09 40 60.* Departures from Place Wilson for round-trip tour *(1hr)* of the village with commentary.

From Naval Base to Zoological Station – The Russian presence in Villefranche increased at the end of the 18C and has been remarkably consistent ever since. The strategic potential of the harbor did not escape the notice of the Russian naval authorities of the period. Each conflict between the Russian Empire and Turkey brought about the temporary anchorage of Russian naval units at Villefranche. It was, however, just after the Crimean War, in 1856, that Villefranche harbor became even more useful to the Russian military fleet deprived of access to the Mediterranean via the Bosphorus. In 1857 an agreement was reached with the King of Sardinia for the transfer of storehouses and the harbor at Villefranche to Russia, who would use it as a depot for fuel and provisions as well as a home base for the Imperial nobility on holiday on the coast. Uniting with the Comté de Nice maintained these arrangements, but interest in the site evolved at the end of the century.

In 1893 a team of Russian scientists and academics from Kiev replaced the soldiers to carry out oceanographic research, taking advantage of the upcurrent in the harbor. These studies, in spite of political ups and downs between the two nations, were continued until the 1930s, when the premises were reclaimed by the Université de Paris, who established a marine zoology station of international repute there.

Église St-Michel

This Italian Baroque church contains 18C altarpieces and several noteworthy statues: in the north transept is a crucifix carved with impressive realism from the trunk of a fig tree by an unknown convict in the 17C, and a 16C polychrome wood statue of St Roch and his dog stands against a pillar *(left)*. The typically French organ, dated 1790 and recently restored, was built by the well-known Grinda brothers of Nice.

Harbor (Darse)

Once a military port where galleys were built and manned, this is now a marina for yachts and pleasure boats.

Sights

Chapelle St-Pierre★

⏰ *Open mid-Jun to mid-Sep 10am-noon, 4-8.30pm; mid-Sep to mid-Dec 9.30am-noon, 2-6pm; mid-Dec to mid-Mar 9.30am-noon, 2-5pm; mid-Mar to mid-Jun open 9.30am-noon, 3-7pm.* ⏰ *Closed Mon, mid-Nov to mid-Dec, 25 Dec.* 🎫 *2€.* ☎ *04 93 76 90 70.*

This chapel was decorated in 1957 by **Jean Cocteau.** The staring eyes on either side of the door—the flames of the Apocalypse—were painted later to resemble ceramics.

The frescoes are typical of Cocteau's style of drawing, in precise but ample lines. His theme, the life of St Peter, is illustrated by simple realistic scenes. There are also some secular scenes celebrating the young women of Villefranche and gypsies. They are linked together by geometric motifs.

Citadelle

🕐 *Open Jul-Aug 10am-noon, 2.30-7pm; Jun and Sep 9am-noon, 2.30-6pm, Sun 2.30-6pm; Oct-May 9am-noon, 2-5.30pm, Sun 2-5.30pm.* 🕐 *Closed Tue, Nov.* 🎟 *Free entry.* ☎ *04 93 76 90 70.*

This stronghold was constructed in 1560 by the Duke of Savoy to guard the port. It was much admired by Vauban and spared by Louis XIV together with Fort du Mont Alban, when the defences of the County of Nice were destroyed.

The building was restored in 1981 and comprises the town hall, the former chapel of St Elmo used for temporary exhibitions, an auditorium and an open-air theatre. The casemates of the citadel house a collection of **submarine archeology.** The exhibits come from the wreck of a Genoese ship that sank in the Villefranche harbor in the 16C and was excavated in the 1980s.

The citadel is also home to three museums (*same hours as the citadel*).

Musée Volti★

The main courtyard of the citadel and the surrounding vaulted casemates provide an admirable setting for a collection of sculptures by Antoniucci Volti, a citizen of Villefranche of Italian origin.

His work is strictly representational. He concentrates exclusively on the human body, not without humor, as in the group in beaten copper exhibited in the courtyard. He excels in countless representations of the female figure: supremely elegant (*Parisiennes*), gracefully reclining (*Nikaïa*), seated with dignity (*Cachan Maternity*), crouching or curled up (*Lotus*). Some of his most recent works verge on the monumental (*Queen, Minerva*). The sculptures are complemented by several very fine drawings in red chalk.

Musée Goetz-Boumeester

The main collection was given to the town of Villefranche by the painter-engraver **Henri Goetz,** born in 1909, and his wife Christine Boumeester (1904-71). There are about 100 works, representing 50 years of pictorial research ranging from the figurative to the Abstract. There are also some souvenir works signed by Picasso, Miró, Hartung, Picabia and others.

Collection Roux

This is an exhibit of ceramic figurines displayed in small tableaux evoking everyday life in the Middle Ages and during the Renaissance. The scenes are based on treaties and other documents dating from these periods.

VILLENEUVE-LOUBET

POPULATION 13 104.

MICHELIN MAP 341 D6

Villeneuve-Loubet embodies all the contrasts of the Côte d'Azur: an old village coupled with a modern seaside resort. Sitting on the banks of the Loup River, the medieval castle and its surrounding village are bordered on the coast by a vast beach, which includes a modern marina. Villeneuve-Loubet's 4km/2mi of pebble beaches and "kid-friendly" resort activities make this an enjoyable place to visit.

The property of the Villeneuve family, the castle was restored in the 19C. The tall pentagonal keep was begun in the 9C. François I stayed in the castle during his negotiations with Charles V, leading to the Treaty of Nice, which was signed i the castle in 1538. *16 Avenue de la Mer, ☎ 04 92 02 66 16. www.ot-villeneuveloubet.org.*

Walking Tours

The Old Village

Follow the charming sloping alleys to the foot of the 13C **Villeneuve Château** *(◔ Guided tours ⊚ 5€, and map of the village with commentary, available through the Tourism Office.*
◔ See the Address Book for others tours that are offered by the Tourism Office.

The Riverbanks *2km/1.3mi*

▸ *Start from the village.*

▸ This hike leads you along the shady banks of the Loup River.

Sights

Musée Escoffier de l'Art Culinaire★

◔ *Open Jul-Aug 2-7pm Wed, Fri 10am-noon, 2-7pm; rest of the year daily (except Sat) 2-6pm.* ◔ *Closed Nov, holidays.* ⊚ *5€.* ☎ *04 93 20 80 51. www.fondation-escoffier.org.*

In the native house of Auguste Escoffier are his personal souvenirs, objects and indications of the international scope of this ambassador of French cuisine. Ustensils

---

Address Book

NATURE WALK

The Vaugrenier Natural Park *(access by the RN 7)* stretches over 100ha/247 acres with both prairie and forest areas. There are 6km/4mi of trails and a small wetland marsh for observing waterfowl.

TWO TOURS

The Balade Gourmande combines a tour of the village, a visit to the Musée Escoffier and a special surprise tasting. *By request through the Tourism Office, 6€.* ☎ *04 92 02 66 16.*

Called the Concrete Mountains by some, the Marina-Baie-des-Anges has been recognized by the Ministry of Culture as a 20C heritage site. It's up to you to decide. Take a guided tour (2€). *Contact the Tourism Office (above).*

The Birth of Peach Melba

Native of Villeneuve, the illustrious cook Auguste Escoffier (1846-1935) made his name in Nice, then Paris in the Petit Moulin-Rouge before forging a reputation in the deluxe hotel he created with César Ritz. "Cook of the Kings and King of the Cooks," he knew how to create personalized dishes that would delight (he created the Peach Melba in the honor of a professional singer of the same name). His trademarks were innovation, lightness, simplicity and quality.

Marina Baie des Anges, Villeneuve-Loubet

of his time, a Provençal kitchen reconstituted, a collection of miniature cars (used for dining room service) and1 500 menus from 1820 to today, illustrate the chef's art of cooking.

Musée d'Histoire et d'Art
Rue de l'Hôtel-de-Ville. ☺ *Open 9.30am-noon, 2-6pm, Sat 9.30am-noon, Sun 10.30am-12.30pm.* ☺ *Closed holidays.* ☺ *Free entry.* ☎ *04 92 02 60 39 or 04 93 20 16 49.*
The first floor is reserved for temporary art expositions. The second and third floors are devoted to the great conflicts that involved France in the 20C: two world wars, the wars of Indo-China (1945-1954) and Algeria (1954-1962), interventions in Chad and Zaire (1969-1984), Lebanon (1982-1987); and the Gulf War (1991).

MAPS AND PLANS

COMPANION PUBLICATIONS

Motorists who plan ahead will always have the appropriate maps at hand. Michelin products are complementary: for each of the sites listed in The Green Guide, map references are indicated which help you find your location on our range of maps. The image below shows the maps to use for each geographic area covered in this guide.

To travel the roads in this region, you may use any of the following:

• the regional map at a scale of 1:200 000 no 528, which covers the main roads and secondary roads, and includes useful indications for finding tourist attractions. This is a good map to choose for travelling in a wide area. At a quick glance, you can locate and identify the main sights to see. In addition to identifying the nature of the road ways, the map shows castles, churches and other religious edifices, scenic view points, megalithic monuments, swimming beaches on lakes and rivers, swimming pools, golf courses, race tracks, air fields, and more. You may also consult Michelin maps nos 340 and 341.

And remember to travel with the latest edition of the map of France no 721, which gives an overall view of the region of Provence, and the main access roads which connect it to the rest of France. The entire country is mapped at a 1:1 000 000 scale and clearly shows the main road network.

Michelin is pleased to offer a route-planning service on the Internet: www.ViaMichelin.com. Choose the shortest route, a route without tolls, or the Michelin recommended route to your destination; you can also access information about hotels and restaurants from The Michelin Guide, and tourist sites from The Green Guide.

There are a number of useful maps and plans in the guide, listed on the following page.

Bon voyage!

Little Red Riding Hood

But Little Red Riding Hood had her local map with her, and so she did not fall into the trap. She did not take the path through the wood and she did not meet the big bad wolf. Instead, she chose the picturesque touring route straight to Grandmother's house, and arrived safely with her cake and her little pot of butter.

The End

With Michelin maps, go your own way.

Key

Selected monuments and sights

◉ ⇨	Tour - Departure point
🏛 ⚲	Catholic church
🏛 ⚴	Protestant church, other temple
◩ ⬜ ⛩	Synagogue - Mosque
▰	Building
▪	Statue, small building
⚴	Calvary, wayside cross
◎	Fountain
●━━◗	Rampart - Tower - Gate
✕	Château, castle, historic house
∴	Ruins
∪	Dam
✿	Factory, power plant
☆	Fort
∩	Cave
▢	Troglodyte dwelling
⊤	Prehistoric site
▼	Viewing table
|/	Viewpoint
▲	Other place of interest

Special symbol

🏖	Beach

Sports and recreation

🏇	Racecourse
🤸	Skating rink
≈ ≈	Outdoor, indoor swimming pool
🎥	Multiplex Cinema
⚓	Marina, sailing centre
⌂	Trail refuge hut
▫━■━▫	Cable cars, gondolas
▫━┼┼┼━▫	Funicular, rack railway
🚂	Tourist train
◇	Recreation area, park
🐎	Theme, amusement park
⚱	Wildlife park, zoo
✺	Gardens, park, arboretum
◔	Bird sanctuary, aviary
🚶	Walking tour, footpath
😊	Of special interest to children

Abbreviations

A	Agricultural office (Chambre d'agriculture)
C	Chamber of Commerce (Chambre de commerce)
H	Town hall (Hôtel de ville)
J	Law courts (Palais de justice)
M	Museum (Musée)
P	Local authority offices (Préfecture, sous-préfecture)
POL.	Police station (Police)
⛨	Police station (Gendarmerie)
T	Theatre (Théâtre)
U	University (Université)

	Sight	Seaside resort	Winter sports resort	Spa
Highly recommended ★★★	★★★	🏖🏖🏖	❄❄❄	♨♨♨
Recommended ★★	★★	🏖🏖	❄❄	♨♨
Interesting	★	🏖	❄	♨

Additional symbols

🛈	Tourist information
═══ ═══	Motorway or other primary route
❶ ❶	Junction: complete, limited
⊨══⊨ ═══	Pedestrian street
ɪ═══ɪ	Unsuitable for traffic, street subject to restrictions
▥▥▥ ----	Steps – Footpath
🚂 🚆	Train station – Auto-train station
🚌 🚌 S.N.C.F.	Coach (bus) station
⋯•⋯	Tram
Ⓜ	Metro, underground
P R	Park-and-Ride
♿	Access for the disabled
✉	Post office
☎	Telephone
⌧	Covered market
⁖✕⁖	Barracks
△	Drawbridge
℧	Quarry
✗	Mine
B F	Car ferry (river or lake)
🛥	Ferry service: cars and passengers
⛴	Foot passengers only
③	Access route number common to Michelin maps and town plans
Bert (R.)...	Main shopping street
AZ B	Map co-ordinates

Hotels and restaurants

Hotels- price categories:

	Provinces	Large cities
🛏	<40 €	<60 €
🛏🛏	40 to 65 €	60 to 90 €
🛏🛏🛏	65 to 100 €	90 to 130 €
🛏🛏🛏🛏	>100 €	>130 €

Restaurants- price categories:

	Provinces	Large cities
🛏	<14 €	<16 €
🛏🛏	14 to 25 €	16 to 30 €
🛏🛏🛏	25 to 40 €	30 to 50 €
🛏🛏🛏🛏	>40 €	>50 €

20 rooms: Number of rooms:
38.57/57.17 € price for one person/ double room

🍽 *6.85 €* Price of breakfast; when not given, it is included in the price of the room (i.e., for bed-and-breakfast)

120 sites: Number of camp sites and cost
12.18 € for 2 people with a car

12.18 € lunch- Restaurant: fixed-price menus
16.74/38.05 € served at lunch only – mini/maxi price fixed menu (lunch and dinner) or à la carte

rest. Lodging where meals are served
16.74/38.05 € mini/maxi price fixed menu or à la carte

meal 15.22 € "Family style" meal

reserv Reservation recommended

🚫 No credit cards accepted

P Reserved parking for hotel patrons

🏊 Swimming Pool

▤ Air conditioning

🚭 Hotel: non-smoking rooms Restaurant: non-smoking section

♿ Rooms accessible to persons of reduced mobility

The prices correspond to the higher rates of the tourist season

NOTES

NOTES